WIT

Images of **Women**

in American
Ponul-- ---

Images
of Women

*in American
Popular Culture*

Second Edition

Angela G. Dorenkamp
Assumption College

John F. McClymer
Assumption College

Mary M. Moynihan
The University of New Hampshire

Arlene C. Vadum
Assumption College

Harcourt Brace College Publishers

*Fort Worth • Philadelphia • San Diego • New York • Orlando • Austin • San Antonio
Toronto • Montreal • London • Sydney • Tokyo*

Publisher	Ted Buchholz
Senior Acquisitions Editor	Drake Bush
Assistant Editor	Kristie Kelly
Project Editors	Louise Slominsky, Kristen Trompeter
Production Manager	Melinda Esco
Art Director	Peggy Young

Text and cover design by Diana Jean Parks.
Cover illustration by Gary Head, represented by Brooke & Company, Dallas, Texas.

Interior illustrations by courtesy of the Dover Pictorial Archive Series, Dover Publications Inc.

Photo credits: Page 1, (left) The Bettman Archive, (right) from the collection of the authors; Page 59, *Survey Graphic,* March 1925, portrait by Winold Reiss; Page 119, from the collection of the authors; Page 175, Charles Dana Gibson; Page 227, State Historical Society of Wisconsin; Page 271, National Archives; Page 325, (top) from the collection of the authors, (bottom) *Having Our Say,* by Sarah and A. Elizabeth Delany with Amy Hill Hearth. Published by Kodansha America Inc. © by Amy Hill Hearth, Sarah Louise Delany, and Annie Elizabeth Delany. Photo by Brian Douglas; Page 373, from the collection of the authors.

Requests for permission to make copies of any part of the work should be mailed to: Permissions Department, Harcourt Brace & Company, 6277 Sea Harbor Drive, Orlando, Florida 32887-6777

Address editorial correspondence to:
Harcourt Brace College Publishers
301 Commerce Street, Suite 3700
Fort Worth, TX 76102

Address orders to:
Harcourt Brace & Company
6277 Sea Harbor Drive
Orlando, FL 32887-6777
1-800-782-4479, or
1-800-433-0001 (in Florida)

ISBN 0-15-501013-1

Library of Congress Catalog Card Number: 94-79777

Printed in the United States of America

5 6 7 8 9 0 1 2 3 4   090   9 8 7 6 5 4 3 2 1

*To Our
Mothers
and
Foremothers*

Preface

Long before it first became a book in 1985, this anthology was a collection of stories, advertising copy, poetry, magazine articles, advice books, romance novels, marriage manuals, political manifestos, and editorials. Some items dated back to the beginning of the republic; others had been clipped from yesterday's newspapers. All dealt with images of women in popular culture or with reactions to those images. We had collected them for use in our interdisciplinary course in women's studies, which we were in the process of developing with the assistance of a grant from the National Endowment for the Humanities.

After several years of trying out different readings with our students, we culled about a hundred pieces for the first edition of *Images.* Some, like the 1848 Seneca Falls *Declaration of Rights and Sentiments,* were very well known. Others, like Fanny Fern's barbed social commentary on mid-nineteenth-century American mores, have since become celebrated. Still others, like the *Harper's Bazar* article from 1908 called "How to Get Plump," continue to rest in obscurity. Each, however, bears witness to the importance of images in the ongoing struggle in American culture to define—and often to delimit—women's rights and roles.

We knew, as we wrote in the preface to the first edition, that "no collection can include everything" that teachers of women's studies and history courses might wish. So we asked those who adopted the text to share their ideas for additions and deletions with us. Many have done just that with the result that this new edition differs markedly from the first. It includes much more material on issues of violence and abuse; it explores in much greater depth the experiences of women of color. The struggle over the equal rights amendment, so pressing in the early- to mid-1980s when we were preparing the first edition, no longer figures largely in either national debates or this book. Perhaps most importantly, we have increased the number of selections that explore the impact of popular culture on women's lives.

We have also attempted to build upon what readers saw as the strengths of the first edition. Primary among these is the focus upon popular culture. Using evidence from popular sources to illuminate basic themes in women's studies and women's history affords a number of benefits. One is the accessibility of the materials themselves. Because they were written to appeal to a wide and varied audience, they usually have a high level of readability; even the oldest selections engage the attention of contemporary students. Another benefit is that the mass media generally reflect the accepted wisdom of the day about women—their nature, place, and roles—so students come to recognize not only the power of such widely disseminated images in shaping social expectations, but also the difficulty dissenters like Elizabeth Cady Stanton faced in trying to change them.

We have continued to stress the contested nature of these images by assembling influential statements of dominant beliefs about women and linking them with the protests they inspired. Several anthologies include Charlotte Perkins Gilman's "The Yellow Wall-Paper," but we also excerpt relevant sections of *Fat and Blood: And How to Make Them* (1877) by S. Weir Mitchell, the celebrated physician whose "rest cure" for "nervous" women Gilman's story protested. This editorial practice is based upon our belief that we do students a disservice when we give them a feminist classic like "The Yellow Wall-Paper" without providing some context. Until students read Mitchell they cannot fully understand why the physician-husband in Gilman's story behaved as he did. We have selected readings that convey the struggles in which women have been engaged. In addition, we have included selections from diaries, letters, memoirs, poetry, and fiction to illustrate the effects of both images and struggles on private lives. Our choices reflect a wide range of viewpoints, from unregenerate male supremacy to radical feminism.

We have also continued to strive to make *Images* genuinely interdisciplinary. Rather than separate historical material from literary works or both from theory, as is common practice, we deliberately refrain from making those distinctions. Every text is literary; each exists in time; each was produced in a particular social context; each makes certain assumptions about the behavior of women and men. As a consequence, we have retained our thematic organization of materials, but we have reorganized the sequences within chapters to make them more chronological since readers suggested it would be helpful to hear echoes and reprises of these themes over time.

Because we want students to draw their own conclusions, we have kept the editorial matter to a minimum. Headnotes sketch the historical, literary, and social contexts of individual selections, identify their authors and describe the media in which they first appeared, but do not interpret or assess their significance. So too with the essays that introduce each chapter. They provide background information and suggest something about the rationale for the choice of materials, but they are not forums for our own version of feminism. Instead this text invites, even requires, students and teachers to construe and construct meanings, to make connections, to analyze and interpret. Women's studies and history courses are frequently empowering experiences for students. A central element of that empowerment should be the recognition that they can study their own lives on their own terms.

Part One considers popular notions of woman's "nature," ranging from claims that women are more nurturing or less analytical than men to critiques of such "essentialist" ideas. Part Two takes up the related notion of woman's "place." Is there—should there be—a woman's "sphere," a set of activities or roles for which women are especially suited? Who gets to define what that "sphere" will include? How have women struggled against the limitations any definition necessarily imposes? Woven through both sections is a theme that becomes explicit in Part Three, which collects materials on images of women as sexual objects and as victims of sexual and other forms of violence. Objectification is most blatant in pornography, but it also underlies the ideas on woman's nature of Charles D. Meigs, the nineteenth-century physician whose *Woman: Her Diseases and Remedies* was a standard text in medical schools for decades. His view that women's brains were too small for mathematics or other forms of abstract reasoning but "just big enough for love" epitomized what historian Barbara Welter called "the cult of true womanhood." Objectification also shaped the "double task" Elise Johnson McDougald faced, as an African American in the 1920s, in contesting stereotypes that worked to keep her in her "place."

Parts Four, Five, and Six deal with specific roles women play as "sweethearts and wives," mothers, and workers. Here our goal is both to illustrate some of the more significant images against which women have had to struggle and to show something of the enormous diversity of women's real lives. Part Seven deals with sisters—real and ideal—and Part Eight with visions, some dating back to the nineteenth century, of a future in which women could live lives of their own choosing.

The logic of this organization proceeds from popular perceptions about what women are like physically, morally, intellectually, and socially (Parts One through Three), to pronouncements about their "proper" roles and duties (Parts Four through Six), to women's prospects for gaining control over their own destinies (Parts Seven and Eight). Not everyone who adopts this book will want to follow this order. We have taken considerable care to make chapters, and even individual selections, independent of each other. As a result, instructors should be able to assign the readings in any sequence they wish. They should also be able to use *Images* with other readings, or with American history, literature, psychology, sociology, or women's studies texts.

Because we have benefited so much from the suggestions of those who used the first edition we request again that instructors share with us their experiences in using the book as well as their suggestions for additions and deletions. To the extent possible we want this to be your book as well as ours.

Acknowledgments

The first edition of this book grew out of our work together on an interdisciplinary course in women's studies. Both the book and the course were made possible by an institutional grant from the National Endowment for the Humanities (#ED-20030). Work on the first and second editions was also supported by the Assumption College Faculty Development Fund.

Many of our colleagues at Assumption College and the University of New Hampshire gave moral and scholarly support that lightened our task at critical points. Among these are Cathryn Adamsky and Barbara White of the UNH Women's Studies Program; Regina Edmonds, Richard Oehling, Neil Rankin, and Nancy Scott at Assumption College.

We particularly wish to thank the staffs of the Assumption College Library, the University of New Hampshire Library, the Worcester Historical Society, the Worcester Public Library, the American Antiquarian Society, and the Library of Congress. Lorett Treese, the Archivist at Bryn Mawr, and Caroline Rittenhouse, the former Bryn Mawr Archivist, were also very helpful.

We would also like to acknowledge the following reviewers for this edition of *Images of Women:* Jean Bryant, Florida State University; Alice Kemp, University of New Orleans; Maureen St. Laurent, Vanderbilt University; and Virginia Scharff, University of New Mexico.

Others who helped with the project merit our special thanks as well. They include Suzanne Allen, Robert Morris College; Susan Frankel, Diane Strong, and Kerrie Faia, University of New Hampshire; Don Fehrenbacher; Linda Frost; Wilma Garcia, Oakland University; Betty Hoskins and Susan Vogel. Among those who gave us good advice at Harcourt Brace are Drake Bush, Senior Acquisitions Editor; Kristie L. Kelly, Assistant Editor; Louise Slominsky, Project Editor; Melinda Esco, Production Manager; and Peggy Young, Art Director.

Finally, we wish to thank those family members who provided support and encouragement during the many months we worked on this anthology: Erica, John, Thomas, and Monica Dorenkamp; Joan Buscemi and Peter McClymer; Abby Kelley and Robert Moynihan; Jesse and Casey Rankin.

In revising this anthology, we have given serious consideration to the suggestions for change that students and reviewers have made. We want to thank the students who used the first edition of this text, especially those at Oakland University, who took the time to send us written reviews. We believe this edition is better than the first and want to share the credit for any improvement with our students and reviewers. To them, and to others who read all or parts of this book and tried to save us from various errors, we extend the traditional exoneration for whatever errors remain.

Contents

Preface   vii

One
Woman's Nature   1

Alexis de Tocqueville   *How the Americans Understand the Equality of the Sexes*   5
Charles D. Meigs, M.D.   *Sexual Peculiarities*   8
Sojourner Truth   *Speech at Akron Women's Rights Convention, 1851*   12
M. Carey Thomas   *Diary Excerpts (1870, 1871)*   13
Edward H. Clarke, M.D.   *Sex in Education*   16
Elizabeth Cady Stanton, et al.   *Comments on Genesis*   18
Elise Johnson McDougald   *The Double Task*   22
Ashley Montagu   *The Natural Superiority of Women*   27
John C. Ewers   *Deadlier Than the Male*   30
Maxine Hong Kingston   *The Woman Warrior: Memoirs of a Girlhood Among Ghosts*   34
Adrienne Rich   *Compulsory Heterosexuality and Lesbian Existence*   40
Carol Gilligan   *In a Different Voice*   43
Mark Davidson   *The Politics of Biology: A Conversation with Ruth Hubbard*   46
Emma Willard School   *Some Questions to Ask Your Daughter Before She Chooses Her High School*   48
Katha Pollitt   *Are Women Morally Superior to Men?*   50

Two
Woman's Place   59

Sarah Moore Grimké   *The Pastoral Letter of the General Association of Congregational Ministers of Massachusetts*   63
Letters on the Equality of the Sexes   64
Seneca Falls Convention   *Declaration of Sentiments*   67
James Gordon Bennett   *Woman's Rights Convention*   71
Julia A.J. Foote   *Public Effort—Excommunication*   73

S. Weir Mitchell   *Rest*   75

Charlotte Perkins Gilman   *The Yellow Wall-Paper*   78

Josephine St. Pierre Ruffin   *Address to the First National Conference of Colored Women*   89

Jane Addams   *Twenty Years at Hull House*   92

Kate L. Gregg   *One Way to Freedom*   94

Margaret Sanger   *The Turbid Ebb and Flow of Misery*   97

Betty Friedan   *The Problem That Has No Name*   100

U.S. Supreme Court Reports   *Roe v. Wade*   103

Meg Brodhead and Claire Schaeffer-Duffy   *Thoughts on Abortion for Our Sisters*   107

Anonymous   *A Young Man Writes*   108

Susan Faludi   *Blame It on Feminism*   111

Audre Lorde   *The Transformation of Silence into Language and Action*   116

Three
Woman As Object   119

Susan Sontag   *The Double Standard of Aging*   122

Godey's Lady's Book   *Health and Beauty*   131

Harper's Bazar   *How to Get Plump*   133

Anaïs Nin   *The Diary of Anaïs Nin (March 1937)*   138

Nora Ephron   *A Few Words About Breasts*   139

Marge Piercy   *Barbie Doll*   146

Lisa Jones   *A Doll Is Born*   147

Camille Paglia   *Madonna*   149

Suzanne Gordon   *Madonna the Feminist*   151

Gloria Steinem   *Erotica v. Pornography*   153

Ellen Willis   *Feminism, Moralism, and Pornography*   157

Harriet Jacobs   *Incidents in the Life of a Slave Girl*   162

Time Magazine   *The Trials of Convicting Rapists: An Interview with Linda Fairstein*   165

Gerald Caplan   *Battered Wives, Battered Justice*   169

Ntozake Shange   *With No Immediate Cause*   172

Four
Sweethearts and Wives 175

Bonnie Kreps *Annie Oakley* 179
T.H. Bayly *Why Don't the Men Propose?* 181
Fanny Fern *A Model Husband* 183
Sullivan Ballou *A Letter from the Battlefield* 184
Alice Cary *The Bridal Veil* 186
Louisa May Alcott *Happy Women* 187
Kate Chopin *The Dream of an Hour* 189
Alfred Henry Lewis *How to Choose a Wife* 191
Radclyffe Hall *The Well of Loneliness* 193
Betty Smith *A Tree Grows in Brooklyn* 197
Anne Moody *Coming of Age in Mississippi* 201
John F. DeYonker, D.O. and the Rev. Thomas E. Tobin, C.SS.R. *Your Marriage* 203
Marabel Morgan *The Total Woman* 206
John Krich *Here Come the Brides* 210
Abigail Van Buren *Women Are No Give-Aways* 216
Lucy Stone and Henry B. Blackwell *1855 Marriage Contract* 217
Caryl Rivers *Can a Woman Be Liberated and Married?* 219

Five
Mothers 227

Frances Ellen Watkins Harper *The Slave Mother* 231
Lucy Stone *Only a Mother—No Trivial Thing* 232
Zitkala-Ša *Impressions of an Indian Childhood* 234
Fanny Fern *A Word to Mothers* 238
Frank Crane, D.D. *Motherhood Today and Yesterday* 239
Crystal Eastman *Mother-Worship* 241
Philip Wylie *Mom* 245
Ferdinand Lundberg and Marynia F. Farnham, M.D. *Modern Woman: The Lost Sex* 247
Tillie Olsen *I Stand Here Ironing* 249
Del Martin and Phyllis Lyon *Lesbian Mothers* 254

Alice Walker   *Everyday Use*   259

Jane Adams   *My Daughter and Me: Déjà Vu Over and Over Again*   265

Anna Quindlen   *Separating Mom from the Concept Called Mother*   268

Six
Workers   271

Elinore Rupert Stewart   *Letters of a Woman Homesteader*   275

Florence Kelley   *I Go to Work*   277

G.E.D.   *Stenography in New York City*   281

Anzia Yezierska   *How I Found America*   283

Emma Goldman   *The Traffic in Women*   287

Connie Field   *The Life and Times of Rosie the Riveter*   291

Frances Levison   *American Woman's Dilemma*   300

Barbara Baer and Glenna Matthew   *Dolores Huerta: A Woman of the Boycott*   304

Maria Laurino   *I'm Nobody's Girl: New York's New Indentured Servants*   309

Karen Kenyon   *A Pink-Collar Worker's Blues*   315

Lynda Edwards   *Worldly Lessons*   317

Barbara Presley Noble   *The Debate Over la Différence*   322

Seven
Sisters   325

Emily Dickinson   *Letters of Emily Dickinson (1845, 1848, and 1854)*   328

Susan Glaspell   *Trifles: A Play in One Act*   332

Maimie Pinzer   *Letter to Fanny Quincy Howe*   347

Alice Childress   *In the Laundry Room*   352

Toni Morrison   *Maureen Peal*   354

Susan Lee   *Friendship, Feminism and Betrayal*   361

Boston Gay Collective   *In Amerika They Call Us Dykes*   366

Sarah Booth Conroy   *A Century of Being Sisters*   370

Eight
Visions 373

Sojourner Truth *Address on Woman's Rights* 376

Elizabeth Cady Stanton *The Solitude of Self* 377

Charlotte Perkins Gilman *A Unique History* 381

Rene Mansfield *Is the Civilized World Becoming Womanized?* 386

Adlai Stevenson *A Purpose for Modern Woman* 389

Adrienne Rich *Commencement Address at Smith College, 1979* 393

Gloria Steinem *What It Would Be Like If Women Win* 399

Shulamith Firestone *Alternatives* 402

Vivian Gornick *Lesbians and Women's Liberation: "In Any Terms She Shall Choose"* 407

Sister M. Theresa Kane, R.S.M. *Statement to Pope John Paul II* 411

Starhawk *Power, Authority, and Mystery: Ecofeminism and Earth-based Spirituality* 412

Wendy Kaminer *Feminism's Identity Crisis* 416

June Jordan *Where Is the Love?* 420

Images
of Women

*in American
Popular Culture*

Part One

Woman's Nature

"'MASCULINITY' IS IDENTIFIED WITH COMPETENCE, AUTONOMY, SELF-CONTROL. . . ."

"'FEMININITY' IS IDENTIFIED WITH INCOMPETENCE, HELPLESSNESS, PASSIVITY, NONCOMPETITIVENESS, BEING NICE."
—SUSAN SONTAG

In 1960 *Good Housekeeping* magazine published an article entitled "How to Know When You're Really Feminine." Its author, Leonard Robinson, wrote the article to correct popular misconceptions about femininity that he believed were causing needless confusion and self-doubts in women. He promised his readers "one clear, infallible formula" for judging their femininity, based on a single, "deep and permanent" trait possessed by every woman.

Robinson found specialists in agreement that woman's psychology is firmly anchored in her biology; more specifically, that her psychology stems from "the fact that nature has made her . . . womb-centered." Her "womb-centeredness" assures a woman's devotion to husband and family, they agreed, and "gives her the unique psychological trait which is the very core of femininity"—"essential feminine altruism." "For the true woman," that is, the woman with this trait, "children and husband come first, way before self, for that is how her altruism expresses itself." According to one expert, "If this basic altruism is undeveloped in a woman, it doesn't matter what else she has. A bust measurement of 40, fearlessness in childbirth, and all the perfumes of Arabia won't make her truly feminine." And conversely, when essential feminine altruism motivates her behavior, any woman can be certain that she is genuinely feminine.

This article, purporting to unlock the secret of femininity, is by no means unique. Throughout the past two centuries, the period covered by the readings, the question of woman's nature has sparked debate. And there has been no shortage of experts, most often male, to advise women on the criteria for "true femininity." Likewise, a large and responsive female audience, concerned about their femininity and eager to mea-sure up to accepted standards of womanliness, has sought their advice. Traditionally, the clergy, speaking with the authority of scripture, have been a potent force in defining "woman's nature." And because of their presumed special understanding of woman's biology, physicians also have acquired expert status in describing women. More recently, psychologists and other scientists have joined their ranks.

The *Good Housekeeping* article claimed that femininity springs from "womb-centeredness." But, depending on the historical epoch and the "trait" being considered, experts have used every conceivable physical distinction between the sexes to explain woman's "true" intellectual, emotional, or social qualities. They have focused on differences in the size and functioning of women's brains compared to men's, the greater sensitivity and complexity of their nervous systems, the appearance and functioning of their external genitals or internal reproductive organs, the passivity of ova compared to sperm, and the differences between the sex chromosomes, hormones, and muscular development of women and men as explanations of women's behavior.

Although woman's nature is presumably unchanging, being based in her biology, popular views of it show remarkable variability over time. Major shifts in imagery have occurred even from one decade to the next, and certain ideas have dropped out, only to recur later. During the colonial period, women and men worked together in the home, and women were represented in the major trades. But the early nineteenth-century movement of the workplace out of the home led, by midcentury, to a new concept of the home and of woman, its guardian. When "home" began to be thought of, not as a bustling center of familial livelihood, but instead as an island of tranquility in an increasingly urbanized and industrialized society, a narrow and restrictive view of woman developed along with it. Only toward the end of the nineteenth century did a new image of woman emerge, along with greater educational and work opportunities for many women and expanded demands by women for their rights. These developments culminated in the early twentieth-century "flapper," with her unparalleled, and heretofore "masculine," new freedoms.

While some of the reforming zeal of the 1920s was lost in the ensuing decades, the image of woman as capable and autonomous persisted. During World War II, women took over formerly male jobs in unprecedented numbers. They had done so during World War I as well. But, ironically, the end of World War II signaled the appearance of the most restrictive and exclusively domestic feminine ideal of the century, one Betty Friedan labeled the "feminine mystique." Indeed, a major goal of the current women's movement has been to undo the image of woman that developed during the 1950s.

During the 1960s and 1970s, feminists increasingly questioned the assumption of difference and called for an end to sex-role stereotyping. Attention focused more and more on examining and changing the arbitrary social arrangements that foster and maintain women's powerlessness. This trend continued during the 1980s, even as another trend emerged. Some feminists then reclaimed the idea that women differ from men in important ways; but, they argued, women's distinctive perceptions and concerns deserved appreciation, not the devaluation they usually received. Interest in possible biological determinants of women's behaviors continued throughout this period, as

did research on the social origins of sex differences in behavior.

Today all of these trends coexist with ideas very similar to those that Robinson reported decades ago. One magazine article published in 1993 argued that "femininity is unconditional love," that is, "love without ifs." Its author went on: "The ability to give love of that kind has its source in biology, in the system that enables women to reproduce, that gifts women with maternal feelings." But articles offering advice to women on their femininity are rarer now than in the past. Today, most of the self-help literature directed at women offers advice on how to get what they want out of life, not how to be truly feminine.

Despite variations in the popular imagery, the notion of a fixed feminine nature has persisted and has been used to draw conclusions about woman's "proper sphere." The experts quoted in the *Good Housekeeping* article concluded that woman's "womb-centeredness" ensures her commitment to husband and family, and her service to others. A century earlier, an editorial in *Harper's New Monthly Magazine* (1854), warning against women assuming public functions, argued: "Her flaccid muscles, tender skin, highly nervous organization, and aptitude for internal injury, decide the question of offices involving hard bodily labor; while the predominance of instinct over reason, and of feeling over intellect, as a rule, unfits her for judicial or legislative command. Her power is essentially a silent and unseen moral influence; her functions are those of wife and mother." Such cases illustrate how theories about woman's nature have been used to woman's disadvantage, to close off avenues of achievement and satisfaction to her.

Society has often devalued the characteristics attributed to women and given men title to the more respected traits. Sometimes the devaluation is subtle indeed. "Essential feminine altruism," the "deep and permanent" standard of femininity cited in *Good Housekeeping*, required the true woman always to place the needs of her husband and children before her own—"way before" her own. In this definition, husband and children are assumed to be worthy and important; the self-sacrificing woman is not. As this example illustrates, to strive to be "feminine" or "womanly" has meant to attempt to match impossible standards of perfection, and, at the same time, to be moved to accept decidedly negative self-images.

Though women are praised for enthusiastically conforming to popular ideals of femininity, to embrace these cultural definitions commonly has meant sacrificing the fulfillment of certain fundamental needs in order to avoid the loss of satisfaction of other, equally basic, needs. Not to live up to accepted standards means to court rejection, and even declassification, as unnatural or unwomanly. And for women, who have been indoctrinated from early childhood to believe that their identity rests in their relationships with others, this is a particularly dreadful prospect. In the readings, women speak of their efforts to live with idealized images of femininity and of their attempts to reconcile the fact of their womanhood with their seemingly incompatible desires for autonomy, self-respect, and creativity.

Despite the power of the cultural images in shaping women's experience, complete and unquestioning acceptance of the popular views has never existed. As the readings document, throughout the past two centuries, some women and men have been able to transcend cultural perceptions and prescriptions, and have risked the almost inevitable public censure, to experiment with change or to tamper with cherished beliefs. Some have spoken from personal pain or from witnessing the suffering of others, some from unrelenting pride, some from anger, some from seeing that they or others have been forgotten or misrepresented in the popular white, middle- and upper-class imagery. And because of their courage, women today have a different legacy—new understandings and new possibilities—and new power to transcend restrictive and untenable definitions of their nature. In the words of the early twentieth-century sociologist Elsie Clews Parsons:

> To be declassified is very painful to most persons and so the charge of unwomanliness has ever been a kind of whip against the would-be woman rebel. Not until she fully understands how arbitrary it is will she cease to feel its crack.

HOW THE AMERICANS UNDERSTAND THE EQUALITY OF THE SEXES

Alexis de Tocqueville

A lexis de Tocqueville is by far the most celebrated of the many foreign visitors who recorded their impressions of the new republic, and his *Democracy in America* (published in two volumes: 1835, 1840) became a best-seller in the United States as well as in France. Americans are still fond of quoting his largely laudatory opinions of their society and politics, even managing occasionally to ponder his famous warning about the potential tyranny of the majority.

De Tocqueville and his companion, Gustave Beaumont, spent nine months in 1831–32 touring the United States and preparing a report on America's new penitentiary system for the French government. His interest in things American went far beyond prisons, however, and he spent much of his time trying to gauge the success of America's experiment in self-government. His views of American women are less well known, but they were highly influential in the decades before the Civil War.

Near the conclusion of his second volume, de Tocqueville attributed the greatest share of the credit for the success of American democracy to the character of American women. And he praised Americans for resolving the apparent paradox of proclaiming equality as their highest ideal while restricting women to the home and hearth. His explanation of why the restricted roles of women did not contradict the nation's democratic ethos provided a ready rationale for many conservative social commentators. The logic of his argument, especially his premises, merits special attention since his conclusions proved so popular.

I have shown how democracy destroys or modifies the different inequalities which originate in society: but is this all? or does it not ultimately affect that great inequality of man and woman which has seemed, up to the present day, to be eternally based in human nature? I believe that the social changes which bring nearer to the same level the father and son, the master and servant, and superiors and inferiors generally speaking, will raise woman and make her more and more the equal of man. But here, more than ever, I feel the necessity of making myself clearly understood; for there is no subject on which the coarse and lawless fancies of our age have taken a freer range.

There are people in Europe who, confounding together the different characteristics of the sexes, would make of man and woman beings not only equal but alike. They would give to both the same functions, impose on both the same duties, and grant to both the same rights: they would mix them in all things—their occupations, their pleasures, their business. It may readily be conceived, that by thus attempting to make one sex equal to the other, both are degraded; and from so preposterous a medley of the works of nature, nothing could ever result but weak men and disorderly women.

It is not thus that the Americans understand that species of democratic equality which may be established between the sexes. They admit, that as nature has appointed such wide differences between the physical and moral constitutions of man and woman, her manifest design was to give a distinct employment to their

HOW THE AMERICANS UNDERSTAND . . .   From Alexis de Tocqueville, *Democracy in America: Part the Second, The Social Influence of Democracy,* trans. Henry Reeve. (New York: J. & H. G. Langley, 1840) 224–27.

various faculties; and they hold that improvement does not consist in making beings so dissimilar do pretty nearly the same things, but in getting each of them to fulfil their respective tasks in the best possible manner. The Americans have applied to the sexes the great principle of political economy which governs the manufactures of our age, by carefully dividing the duties of man from those of woman, in order that the great work of society may be the better carried on.

In no country has such constant care been taken as in America to trace two clearly distinct lines of action for the two sexes, and to make them keep pace one with the other, but in two pathways which are always different. American women never manage the outward concerns of the family, or conduct a business, or take a part in political life; nor are they, on the other hand, ever compelled to perform the rough labor of the fields, or to make any of those laborious exertions which demand the exertion of physical strength. No families are so poor as to form an exception to this rule. If on the one hand an American woman cannot escape from the quiet circle of domestic employments, on the other hand she is never forced to go beyond it. Hence it is that the women of America, who often exhibit a masculine strength of understanding and a manly energy, generally preserve great delicacy of personal appearance and always retain the manners of women, although they sometimes show that they have the hearts and minds of men.

Nor have the Americans ever supposed that one consequence of democratic principles is the subversion of marital power, or the confusion of the natural authorities in families. They hold that every association must have a head in order to accomplish its object, and that the natural head of the conjugal association is man. They do not therefore deny him the right of directing his partner; and they maintain, that in the smaller association of husband and wife, as well as in the great social community, the object of democracy is to regulate and legalize the powers which are necessary, not to subvert all power.

This opinion is not peculiar to one sex, and contested by the other: I never observed that the women of America consider conjugal authority as a fortunate usurpation of their rights, or that they thought themselves degraded by submitting to it. It appeared to me, on the contrary, that they attach a sort of pride to the voluntary surrender of their own will, and make it their boast to bend themselves to the yoke, not to shake it off. Such at least is the feeling expressed by the most virtuous of their sex; the others are silent; and in the United States it is not the practice for a guilty wife to clamour for the rights of woman, while she is trampling on her holiest duties.

It has often been remarked that in Europe a certain degree of contempt lurks even in the flattery which men lavish upon women: although a European frequently affects to be the slave of woman, it may be seen that he never sincerely thinks her his equal. In the United States men seldom compliment women, but they daily show how much they esteem them. They constantly display an entire confidence in the understanding of a wife, and a profound respect for her freedom; they have decided that her mind is just as fitted as that of a man to discover the plain truth, and her heart as firm to embrace it; and they have never sought to place her virtue, any more than his, under the shelter of prejudice, ignorance, and fear.

It would seem that in Europe, where man so easily submits to the despotic sway of women, they are nevertheless curtailed of some of the greatest qualities of the human species, and considered as seductive but imperfect beings; and (what may well provoke astonishment) women ultimately look upon themselves in the same light, and almost consider it as a privilege that they are entitled to show themselves futile, feeble, and timid. The women of America claim no such privileges.

Again, it may be said, that in our morals we have reserved strange immunities to man; so that there is, as it were, one virtue for his use, and another for the guidance of his partner; and that, according to the opinion of the public, the very same act may be punished alternately as a crime or only as a fault. The Americans know not this iniquitous division of duties and rights; among them the seducer is as much dishonoured as his victim.

It is true that the Americans rarely lavish upon women those eager attentions which are commonly paid them in Europe; but their conduct to women always implies that they suppose them to be virtuous and refined; and such is the respect entertained for the moral freedom of the sex, that in the presence of a woman the most guarded language is used, lest her ear should be offended by an expression. In America a young unmarried woman may, alone and without fear, undertake a long journey.

The legislators of the United States, who have mitigated almost all the penalties of criminal law, still make rape a capital offence, and no crime is visited with more inexorable severity by public opinion. This may be accounted for; as the Americans can conceive nothing more precious than a woman's honour, and nothing which ought so much to be respected as her independence, they hold that no punishment is too severe for the man who deprives her of them against her will. In France, where the same offence is visited with far milder penalties, it is frequently difficult to get a verdict from a jury against the prisoner. Is this a consequence of contempt of decency or contempt of woman? I cannot but believe that it is a contempt of one and of the other.

Thus the Americans do not think that man and woman have either the duty or the right to perform the same offices, but they show an equal regard for both their respective parts; and though their lot is different, they consider both of them as beings of equal value. They do not give to the courage of woman the same form or the same direction as to that of man; but they never doubt her courage: and if they hold that man and his partner ought not always to exercise their intellect and understanding in the same manner, they at least believe the understanding of the one to be as sound as that of the other, and her intellect to be as clear. Thus, then, while they have allowed the social inferiority of woman to subsist, they have done all they could to raise her morally and intellectually to the level of man; and in this respect they appear to me to have excellently understood the true principle of democratic improvement.

As for myself, I do not hesitate to avow, that, although the women of the United States are confined within the narrow circle of domestic life, and their situation is in some respects one of extreme dependence, I have nowhere seen women occupying a loftier position; and if I were asked, now that I am drawing to the close of this work, in which I have spoken of so many important things done by the Americans, to what the singular prosperity and growing strength of that people ought mainly to be attributed, I should reply—to the superiority of their women.

SEXUAL PECULIARITIES
Charles D. Meigs, M.D.

Charles D. Meigs, M.D. (1792–1869), was a professor of midwifery and the diseases of women and children at Jefferson Medical College in Philadelphia from 1841 to 1861, and he also maintained a large and lucrative private practice. This prestige helped produce a large audience for his book. Although ostensibly written for his medical students, Meigs' *Woman: Her Diseases and Remedies* became something of a best-seller and went through several editions.

At the heart of the book is Meigs' forceful summing up of what polite society of his day thought woman's nature was. So successfully did Meigs capture these beliefs that when historian Barbara Welter wrote her classic essay on "The Cult of True Womanhood," it was to Meigs' text that she turned again and again for evidence. "True womanhood," a phrase Meigs never used himself, consisted of a series of moral virtues and social characteristics—piety, purity, submissiveness, and domesticity—which Meigs and other spokespeople for "respectable" society imputed to woman's physical and moral natures. Thus, the chastity that men struggled to acquire supposedly came naturally to women. And woman's proper sphere of influence was reflected in her body structure. To Meigs, for example, woman's head appeared "almost too small for intellect, but just big enough for love."

Popular writers of the day favored the self-consciously literary style, filled with classical references, that Meigs used. Whatever difficulty this style may occasion is offset by the importance of Meigs' ideas.

The female is naturally prone to be religious. Hers is a pious mind. Her confiding nature leads her more readily than men to accept the proffered grace of the Gospel. If an undevout astronomer is mad, what shall we say of an irreligious woman? See how the temples of the Christian worship are filled with women. They flock thither with their young children, and endeavor to implant in their souls the seeds of virtue and piety, to be reared in that pure soil and by their watchful nurture, into plants that shall blossom like the immortal amaranth among the stars. See, then, what and how great is the influence that women exert on the morals of society, of whole nations, of the whole world! Wherever there is a true civilization, woman reigns in society. It is not until she comes to sit beside him, in view of all the people, that man ceases to be barbarous, or semi-barbarous, brutal, and ignorant.

She spreads abroad the light of civilization and improvement as soon as she issues from the prison of the Harem or Zenana, to live with him in the world. Who made us human? Whose were the hands that led us to kneel down, and whose the lips that taught our infant voices the earliest invocations to Heaven? Is it not so, that after the world and fortune have done their best, or their worst by us, we, in late years, and early, forget not those pious mothers, who so steadfastly strove to bias our young minds in favor of whatsoever is true, whatsoever is pure, whatsoever is of good report! How can we forget the rewards we received at her hands for all our good, and her gentle, and sometimes tearful reprovings of our evil inclinations and practices? She was not only our teacher and pattern, but our companion and playfellow, for, of a truth, she was of a childlike temper—and that was the secret of the bond that united us to her so long and so closely. . . .

SEXUAL PECULIARITIES   From Charles D. Meigs, *Woman: Her Diseases and Remedies, A Series of Lectures to His Class,* 4th ed., rev. and enl., abridged (Philadelphia: Blanchard & Lea, 1859) 62–67.

The male is less versatile than the woman. His mission is more adventurous and dangerous. *He* enters on the path of ambition, that dark and dangerous, or broad and shining road.

He pursues the devious track of politics with a resolute will; reaching ever onwards to the possession of fame and patronage, and rank and wealth, and power.

She sits at home to adorn the tent or the cottage with wreaths of flowers, or to guide the tendrils that give shade to his bower. She plies the busy loom—and the sweet sounds of her singing—how often have I listened as they accompany the hum and buzz of her wheel, as she gracefully advances and retires by turns, forming the threads about to be woven into garments for her husband or child! Her nimble fingers, all day long, ply the shining needle, to fashion the robe for her spouse—or to arrange the more elegant embellishments of her person, that they may engage his admiration, and augment the flame of his love. For woman, man's love is the moving spring of all her actions. This is at the foundation even of her vanity. Lais herself is said to have sacrificed even her rage for wealth, at times, to the gratification of her vanity; and though the lioness tearing a ram to pieces, which was sculptured upon her tomb, was the emblem of her insatiable avarice, yet Lais lived more for love than for gain.

What say you of the fortitude of woman? She bears the evils of life without repining or complaining against the providence of God. Is she evil entreated, prevented, injured? That which sets a man on fire with an insane rage, kindles in her bosom, perhaps, only a virtuous feeling of indignation. She bears the greatest crosses. How beautifully does Shakespeare say so in the words,

> She never told her love,
> But let Concealment, like a worm i' the bud,
> Feed on her damask cheek;
> And sate, like Patience on a monument,
> Smiling at grief.

She dies a willing martyr for religion, for country—for her children.

Who can number the Lucretias and Portias? How many are like unto the charming Roland? Think of the calm features of Charlotte Corday! Did you read of the deeds and the death of La Puçelle?

Women possess a peculiar trait—modesty, which is one of the most charming of their attributes; springing probably from their natural timidity and sense of dependence, of which it is the ideal in expression. All rude, boisterous, and immodest speech or action unsexes and disgraces woman. Hence, modesty is one of the strongest of her attractions; and she sometimes, perhaps, affects to possess it for the purpose of riveting her chains on the conqueror man. . . .

The attribute of modesty certainly lends the most powerful aid to the other charms of a woman. It is one of the qualities given to her in order to be a strong fence for her children, for it binds her to the domestic altar—her children could not but endure damage and loss, should she leave them at home to plunge into the torrent of public affairs, or mingle freely with the distracting world! Her modesty, gentleness, and timidity, assimilate her to the characters of children, whose best playfellow, nurse, and instructress she is. Come out from the world, and be separate from it, is peculiarly a command for her.

There is in the Museo Pio-Clementino, at Rome, an antique statue, which the learned Visconti asserts to be a statue of Modesty, and which, as I am informed, is among the most beautiful of the works of ancient art now remaining in the world. It is completely clothed from head to foot, and veiled. It seems to me that such a work is proof enough of the ancient admiration of the quality in question; for the artist who could produce, and the people who could appreciate, such an exquisite specimen of taste and right feeling, must have had a keen perception of the charm.

By her physical form and proportion, she is still more trenchantly divided from the male. Look at two statues, male and female. Take the Venus de Medici as the consummate exposition—the very eidolon of the female form, just as Praxiteles in the greatest verve, fervor, and enthusiasm of his genius, and he alone of all mankind, could conceive the idea of the Queen of the Loves.

Compare her with the Apollo of the Belvidere—she has a head almost too small for intellect, but just big enough for love. His magnificent forehead, calm as heaven, and almost as high as it, rises above those eyes that are following the shaft he has sped with his clanging silver bow.

> The front of Jove himself,
> An eye like Mars, to threaten and command;
> A station, like a feathered Mercury, new-lighted on
> Some heaven-kissing hill.

Her thorax seems built as the sanctuary of that beautiful bosom, whence is destined to flow the sweet nutriment of the winged boy.

Man's vast chest is for breathing, for eloquence and command. From its capacious stores of oxygen he draws the elements of the most strenuous, the most protracted exertions. He breathes deep, that he may ascend the highest hills and the sharpest crags in pursuit of his game or his prey, and that his loud harmonious voice may command his armies in the midst of the conflict, or sway the forum with its tones. Like Virgil's wild horse, he is equal to the longest career—nothing can stay him in his race.

See his loins how they are narrowed down, as they approach the hips, that he may balance himself, as it were, on the point of an inverted cone, prompt for the quickest motion. His pelvis contains no variable organs, requiring ample space for extraordinary developments; but its depth and solidity afford origin and insertion to the powerful muscles by whose immense strength he can act well in the wild, rude, and adventurous life to which he is ordained.

The cone, on the other hand, is reversed in the female. The apex is above, and the base at the hips. It is within that bony cell that are hidden those miraculous organs that out of nothing can evolve the wondrous work of reproduction. The pelvis is broad and shallow, light in substance, its excavation ample, and its pubic arch round or Roman; while his is Gothic or lanceolate. From under this arch a child could not go; the other gives it easy utterance. His organisms are permanent—hers are mutable. The uterus—no bigger than a thumb—comes in gestation to be twelve inches long and nine in width. Its invisible vessels and nerves come to be great cords and tubes, and its undiscoverable muscles acquire a force to rend itself in pieces in its rage, or, what seems still more miraculous, to expel a full-grown infant from its cavity, against the enormous resistance of flesh and bone. She is a germiparous and vitelliferous creature. She—the female—possesses that strange compound or concrete which you call stroma, ovarian *stroma*, of which I already have spoken, but must again speak. Now, that stroma lives by the common blood it receives out of a common endangium, and yet it has a nerve which enables it to convert that blood into vitellus or yelk. The perpetuation of races and germs depends on the elimination of that matter. There is no animal germ without it—so that an organ so small, so unobvious, is endowed with the vast responsibility of keeping up the living scheme of the world—with its moralities—its lives—its actions—its trial—which, were it to cease, there would be left no flowers to bloom, no insects to sport in the evening beam, no choral song of birds, no lowing of cattle, no bleating of flocks, nor voices of men to thank and praise and acknowledge the Author of every good and every perfect gift.

Think, gentlemen, of such great power—and ask your own judgments whether such an organ can be of little influence in the constitution of the woman; whether *she* was not made in order that *it* should be made, and whether it may not on occasion become a disturbing radiator in her economy, and how much so. You will answer yes, if you know that her ovary is her sex—and that she is peculiar because of, and in order that she might have this great, this dominant organ planted within the recesses of her body.

Men cannot suffer the same pains as women. *What* do you call the pain of parturition? There is no name for it but *Agony*.

Why does she love her child more than its father does? Why, he grew to her! He was perhaps an acinus cast out of her stroma, and after drawing his blood from her own blood, he drank life at the living well of her bosom, and character from her monitions and example. What were Cornelia's jewels! Who was Washington's mother!

A young lady after a very severe and dangerous labor, while still languid and pale, was asked this question: Mary, shall we have some verses from you, now that the baby is born? "Yes," and the impromptu was the following:

My Little Ida

> I've a wee thing to love—an infant new-born,
> With cheeks like a rose, and breath fresh as the morn,
> And methought when she first op'd her bright beaming eyes,
> That *twin* stars had fall'n in my bed from the skies.
>
> Her hands although idle, no mischief have done,
> Her feet are too tiny in sin's path to run,
> No word e'er escaped her of slander or guile,
> Her lips close as they open, *always* with a smile.
>
> At night, when she makes her soft pillow my breast,
> How calm, how unbroken, how peaceful my rest!
> For I know that pure angels whom no eye can see,
> To guard my sweet babe, then approach near to me.
>
> I have gaz'd with delight on the lovely and fair,
> On locks dark as midnight and bright golden hair,
> But beauty to me was a something unknown,
> Till I looked on my first-born and called her my own.

What do we owe her?—life, peace, liberty, social order. *She* built up this great frame of society in civilization. . . .

Christianity is propagated by her domestic influence. The loom is her work, and the tapestried walls are of her imagining. Were it not for her, we were this day clothed in sheep skins and goat skins, and should lie down in dens and caves. It is for her that the looms of Cashmere, the silks of China, the gauzes of Hindustan, the mousselines of Lyons, the laces of Belgium and England are formed; the carpets of Ispahan and Dresden, Cornelius's blazing chandelier, all the riches displayed by Levy and Bailey are for her. Everything that man is and hath, except his brute force and brutal inclinations, are of her and for her.

SPEECH AT AKRON WOMEN'S RIGHTS CONVENTION, 1851

Sojourner Truth

Sojourner Truth epitomized just about everything that an ideal antebellum woman was not supposed to be: She was African American; she was tall and gaunt; she was physically powerful; and she was illiterate. She was a speaker who never appeared demure, reserved, or submissive.

Because of her power some of her opponents could deny that she was indeed a woman. It was just too much of a challenge to their belief that women, regardless of color, ought to be domestic, submissive, and frail. A rumor started that Sojourner Truth was a "Negro man" who spoke on women's rights. The rumor was so widespread that at one of her appearances, it is said, Truth bared her breasts to prove she was a woman.

Born a slave around 1797, Truth received the name "Isabella" from her master. In 1827, when mandatory emancipation was proclaimed for slaves in New York, Isabella reunited with two of her children and moved to New York City. After early work as a missionary, she lived quietly doing domestic work and raising her children. In 1843, she rejected her slave name, took the name Sojourner Truth, and began to travel and preach again. Truth was a charismatic speaker, and her reputation as an abolitionist and preacher grew during the 1840s and 1850s.

In this famous speech to the Women's Rights Convention in Akron, Ohio, in 1851, Sojourner Truth's constant refrain "And a'n't I a woman?" questioned the many romanticized images of women that prevented them from gaining the right to vote.

The tumult subsided at once, and every eye was fixed on this almost Amazon form, which stood nearly six feet high, head erect, and eyes piercing the upper air like one in a dream. At her first word there was a profound hush. She spoke in deep tones, which, though not loud, reached every ear in the house, and away through the throng at the doors and windows.

"Wall, chilern, whar dar is so much racket dar must be somethin' out o' kilter. I tink dat 'twixt de niggers of de Souf and de womin at de Norf, all talkin' 'bout rights, de white men will be in a fix pretty soon. But what's all dis here talkin' 'bout?

"Dat man ober dar say dat womin needs to be helped into carriages, and lifted ober ditches, and to hab de best place everywhar. Nobody eber helps me into

SPEECH AT AKRON WOMEN'S RIGHTS CONVENTION, 1851   From Susan B. Anthony, Elizabeth Cady Stanton, and Matilda Joslyn Gage, eds., *History of Woman Suffrage,* vol. 1 (New York: Fowler & Wells, 1881) 116.

carriages, or ober mud-puddles, or gibs me any best place!" And raising herself to her full height, and her voice to a pitch like rolling thunder, she asked, "And a'n't I a woman? Look at me! Look at my arm! (and she bared her right arm to the shoulder, showing her tremendous muscular power). I have ploughed, and planted, and gathered into barns, and no man could head me! And a'n't I a woman? I could work as much and eat as much as a man—when I could get it—and bear de lash as well! And a'n't I a woman? I have borne thirteen chilern, and seen 'em mos' all sold off to slavery, and when I cried out with my mother's grief, none but Jesus heard me! And a'n't I a woman?

"Den dey talks 'bout dis ting in de head; what dis dey call it?" ("Intellect," whispered some one near.) "Dat's it, honey. What's dat got to do wid womin's rights or nigger's rights? If my cup won't hold but a pint, and yourn holds a quart, wouldn't ye be mean not to let me have my little half-measure full?" And she pointed her significant finger, and sent a keen glance at the minister who had made the argument. The cheering was long and loud.

"Den dat little man in black dar, he say women can't have as much rights as men, 'cause Christ wan't a woman! Whar did your Christ come from?" Rolling thunder couldn't have stilled that crowd, as did those deep, wonderful tones, as she stood there with outstretched arms and eyes of fire. Raising her voice still louder, she repeated, "Whar did your Christ come from? From God and a woman! Man had nothin' to do wid Him." Oh, what a rebuke that was to that little man.

Turning again to another objector, she took up the defense of Mother Eve. I can not follow her through it all. It was pointed, and witty, and solemn; eliciting at almost every sentence deafening applause; and she ended by asserting: "If de fust woman God ever made was strong enough to turn de world upside down all alone, dese women togedder (and she glanced her eye over the platform) ought to be able to turn it back, and get it right side up again! And now dey is asking to do it, de men better let 'em." Long-continued cheering greeted this. "'Bleeged to ye for hearin' on me, and now ole Sojourner han't got nothin' more to say."

DIARY EXCERPTS (1870, 1871)
M. Carey Thomas

When Bryn Mawr, a women's college under Quaker auspices, opened in 1885, M. Carey Thomas (1857–1935) was hired as its first dean, a post she held for several years. She was Bryn Mawr's president from 1894 to 1922, the first fourteen years serving also as dean. Under her direction the college came to be recognized as one of the country's leading academic institutions. In addition to her work at Bryn Mawr, Thomas was instrumental in getting Johns Hopkins Medical School to admit women at a time when less respected schools would not consider it. She earned a reputation as a distinguished leader in higher education and as an activist for women's rights.

Although her father believed that higher education was not necessary for women, given their future domestic lives, Thomas never accepted such views. Perhaps she was influenced more by the Quaker belief in the spiritual equality of the sexes, which was also a part of her background. Or perhaps her family's insistence that the girls have the same freedoms as the boys had a greater influence on her. At any rate, she never married but instead actively sought a career.

She persuaded her father, against his better judgment, to allow her to enter Cornell University, where she earned the AB degree in 1877. Then she attended graduate classes at the University of Leipzig. Later she transferred to the University of Zurich because, unlike Leipzig, it granted the Ph.D. degree to women. After obtaining her doctorate in English there in 1882, she was hired by Bryn Mawr College.

The first selection from M. Carey Thomas' journal was written when she was thirteen. She was called Minnie at that time. Her journal entry of November 25th read in part: "Have come across such a glorious book called 'Boys Play Book of Science' am going to read it through and see if whether ain't some experiments Bess and I can try." The second selection from the journal was written three months after the first. The spelling and punctuation here appear in the original.

 SEVENTH DAY 26th [NOVEMBER 26, 1870]   Set a mouse trap last night in case Bess & I might want to get his skeleton caught him but he was'nt dead   neither Julie nor Netty would kill him so I heroicly dropped the trap in to a pail of water & rushed out of the room. Then took my slippers into mothers room who is lots better & is sitting up & *sewed sewed sewed*   Oh the monotony of worstered! Laurie aint worth half this bother. "But there are moments when the gush of feeling hath its sway" & in one of those moments I escaped to refresh myself by looking over my cabnet. Pretty soon I heard some one calling "Min" & knew it must be Bess 'cause no one else ever calls me Min Well first we roasted some chestnuts And proceeded to the more important duty of getting to skeleton of a mouse. The poor little fellow being drowned by this time we took our victim out in the yard   bared our glittering knives & commenced operations but the horrid little mouse's fur was so soft that we couldn't make a hole in [it] & besides it made us sick & our hands trembled so we could'nt do a thing but concluding that it was *feminine* nonsense we made a hole & squeezed his insides out it was the most disgusting thing I ever did. We then took off his skin   it came of[f] elegantly just like a glove & then holding it by the tail we chased poor Julie all around   she was so afraid of it. Just as if it was any worse than a chicken & finaly put it on the fire to boil to Julie's great disgust   when it had boiled some we took it again and picked all the meat of[f] it & saved its tongue & eyes to look through the microscope & then the mouse looked like a real skeleton   we then put it out the window to bleach & then as Bess had to go I walked down with her   Was'nt it funny she had been thinking about experiments too & so we planned together & are going to spend our money in instruments instead of candy & then we will invite our friends to see our experiments. I think I'd almost rather be a chemical fellow than a doctor. When I got [home] I found that Netty had thrown away our tongue & eyes & worst of all woe woe is me that our skeleton that had taken us 3 mortal hours to get had fallen out of the window & smashed   oh my we are unfortunate Oh Science!   why wilt thou not protect thy votaries? In the afternoon lolled around learnt Greek & sewed everlasting slippers. Bess said when she told her father about our getting the mouse he looked grave and said "Bessie Bessie thee is loosing all thy *feminine* traits" I [am] afraid that I have'nt got any to loose for I greatly prefer cutting up mice to sewing worsted.

DIARY EXCERPTS (1870, 1871)   From M. Carey Thomas, Reel #1, microfilm ed. of Thomas papers, Bryn Mawr College Archives. Used with permission of the Bryn Mawr College Archives.

FIRST DAY FEB. 26th [1871] I have at length come to the conclusion that it will be more interesting to me when, as an old dried up woman with aid of spectacles I descipher these scrawls to read what I thought than what I did & accordingly I am going to commit my reflections to paper trusting to kind fortune to keep them from careless eyes.

An english man Joseph Beck was here to dinner the other day & he dont blieve in the Education of women. Neither does Cousin Frank King & my such a disgusson as they had. Mother of course was for. They said that they did'nt see any good of a womans learning Latin or Greek it did'n't make them any more entertaining to their *husbands*. A woman had plenty of other things to do sewing cooking taking care of children dressing & flirting. "What noble elevating things for a whole life time to be occupied with", In fact they talked as if the whole end & aim of a womans life was to get *married* & when she attained that *greatest state* of *earthly bliss* it was her duty to amuse her husband & to learn nothing   never to execise the powers of her mind so that he might have the *exquisite* pleasure of knowing more than his wife   of course they talked the usual cant of woman being to *high* to *exalted* to do anything & sit up in perfect ignorance with folded hands & let men worship at her shrine meaning in other words like all the rest of such high faluting stuff that woman ought to be *mere dolls* for men to be amused with to kiss fondle pet &, love maybe, but as for associating with them on terms of equality, they would'nt think of such a thing. Now I don't mean to say [that] these two men believed this but these were the principles they upheld. I got perfectly enraged how *unjust*—how *narrow minded*—how *utterly uncomprehensible* to deny that women ought to be educated & worse than all to deny that they have equal powers of mind. If I ever live & grow up my *one* aim & consentrated purpose *shall* be & is to show that a woman *can learn can reason can compete* with men in the grand fields of literature & science & conjecture that opens before the 19 century that a woman can be a woman & a *true* one with out having all her time engrossed by dress & society—that the woman who has fought all the battles of olden time over again whilesst reading the spirited pages of Homer Vergil Herroditus who has sympathised in the longings after something beyond mere daily exhistance found in the works of Socrates, Plato & Eschelus, who has reasoned out all the great laws which govern the universe with Newton, Cirago, Gallileo who has mourned with Dante reasoned & speculated with Shiller Goethe & Jean Paul been carried away by Carlyle "mildly enchanted by Emerson" who has idealised with Milton & emerged with strengthen intelect from the intricate labyrinth of Geometry Trigonometry & Calculous is not any less like what God really intended a woman to be than the trifling ballroom butterfly than the ignorant [rag] doll baby which *they* admire. My firm fixed purpose (for Puncheon, I heard him lecture on Eliga yesterday says that unless you have one you will never *do* or *be* anything) is to have a througher knowledge of French Latin Greek & German & then to read & study carefully all the principle authors especially the old german metaphyseans & to go high in mathamatics for even if they aint any "practical" use they stregnth the mind & I think I would like to take some science for my espesiallity & then my greatest hope & ambition is too be an author an essayist an historian to write hearty earnest true books that may do their part towards elevating the human race towards inducing some at least to let the money bags on which they are wasting such a wealth of hope & desire & intellect drop from their hands & aim at something higher than merely providing for our miserable earthly exhistance to look higher then the miserable [silly] disappointments of every day life & not to live on in utter forgetfulness of God & their duty to their fellow men. In the words of Longfellow I would like. . . .

> 'When departing leave behind me
> Footprints on the sands of time
> Footprints that perhaps another sailing on lifes dreary main
> A folorn a shiprecked brother seeing may take heart again'
> It seems to me that that is a purpose worth striving after. Oh may it
> not be *only* a purpose.
> 'I wait for the *future* the birds cannot sing it.
> Not one as he sits on the tree
> The bells cannot ring it. But long years
> On bring it. Such as *I wish it*'

SEX IN EDUCATION
Edward H. Clarke, M.D.

In the 1860s, women were demanding entry into the already crowded medical profession and there was a growing feminist sentiment that female practitioners exclusively should treat women's unique physical problems. In response to such pressures, medical experts were claiming that women should not train as doctors, first, because they did not have the intellectual aptitude and, second, because they could not perform their medical duties responsibly at certain points in their menstrual cycles. Yet when male peers bodily removed female medical students from classes in Philadelphia, Dr. Edward Clarke, one-time professor and member of the board of Harvard Medical School, deplored the incident, arguing that women had every right to enter medicine, provided that they could demonstrate their fitness for it.

Because of his liberal views, Clarke was invited in 1872 to address the New England Women's Club in Boston on the subject of the relation of sex to education. Club members expected a defense of women in higher education. Instead, Clarke stunned his audience by concluding that higher education was destroying the health and reproductive capacities of young women. Just when energy was most needed to develop their reproductive systems, he asserted, women were depleting their energy supplies by building up their brains.

A year later Clarke expanded his ideas into a book, *Sex in Education: or, A Fair Chance for the Girls*, from which this excerpt is taken. The first edition was sold out in a week, and the book went through seventeen editions in thirteen years. Despite widespread criticism of his work, Clarke's ideas continued to shape popular views and educational practices for years to come.

Miss D—— entered Vassar College at the age of fourteen. Up to that age, she had been a healthy girl, judged by the standard of American girls. Her parents were apparently strong enough to yield her a fair dower of force. The catamenial function first showed signs of activity in her Sophomore Year, when she was fifteen years old. Its appearance at this age* is confirmatory evidence of the normal state of her health

---

*It appears, from the researches of Mr. Whitehead on this point, that an examination of four thousand cases gave fifteen years six and three-quarter months as the average age in England for the appearance of the catamenia—Whitehead, *On Abortion, & c.*

SEX IN EDUCATION   From Edward H. Clarke, *Sex in Education: or, A Fair Chance for the Girls* (Boston: James R. Osgood, 1873) 79–85.

at that period of her college career. Its commencement was normal, without pain or excess. She performed all her college duties regularly and steadily. She studied, recited, stood at the blackboard, walked, and went through her gymnastic exercises, from the beginning to the end of the term, just as boys do. Her account of her regimen there was so nearly that of a boy's regimen, that it would puzzle a physiologist to determine, from the account alone, whether the subject of it was male or female. She was an average scholar, who maintained a fair position in her class, not one of the anxious sort, that are ambitious of leading all the rest. Her first warning was fainting away, while exercising in the gymnasium, at a time when she should have been comparatively quiet, both mentally and physically. This warning was repeated several times, under the same circumstances. Finally she was compelled to renounce gymnastic exercises altogether. In her Junior Year, the organism's periodical function began to be performed with pain, moderate at first, but more and more severe with each returning month. When between seventeen and eighteen years old, dysmenorrhœa was established as the order of that function. Coincident with the appearance of pain, there was diminution of excretion; and, as the former increased, the latter became more marked. In other respects she was well; and, in all respects, she appeared to be well to her companions and to the faculty of the college. She graduated before nineteen, with fair honors and a poor physique. The year succeeding her graduation was one of steadily-advancing invalidism. She was tortured for two or three days out of every month; and, for two or three days after each season of torture, was weak and miserable, so that about one sixth or fifth of her time was consumed in this way. The excretion from the blood, which had been gradually lessening, after a time substantially stopped, though a periodical effort to keep it up was made. She now suffered from what is called amenorrhœa. At the same time she became pale, hysterical, nervous in the ordinary sense, and almost constantly complained of headache. Physicians were applied to for aid: drugs were administered; travelling, with consequent change of air and scene, was undertaken; and all with little apparent avail. After this experience, she was brought to Boston for advice, when the writer first saw her, and learned all these details. She presented no evidence of local uterine congestion, inflammation, ulceration, or displacement. The evidence was altogether in favor of an arrest of the development of the reproductive apparatus, at a stage when the development was nearly complete. Confirmatory proof of such an arrest was found in examining her breast, where the milliner had supplied the organs Nature should have grown. It is unnecessary for our present purpose to detail what treatment was advised. It is sufficient to say, that she probably never will become physically what she would have been had her education been physiologically guided.

This case needs very little comment: its teachings are obvious. Miss D——went to college in good physical condition. During the four years of her college life, her parents and the college faculty required her to get what is popularly called an education. Nature required her, during the same period, to build and put in working-order a large and complicated reproductive mechanism, a matter that is popularly ignored,—shoved out of sight like a disgrace. She naturally obeyed the requirements of the faculty, which she could see, rather than the requirements of the mechanism within her, that she could not see. Subjected to the college regimen, she worked four years in getting a liberal education. Her way of work was sustained and continuous, and out of harmony with the rhythmical periodicity of the female organization. The stream of vital and constructive force evolved within her was turned steadily to the brain, and away from the ovaries and their accessories. The result of this sort of education was, that these last-mentioned organs, deprived of sufficient opportunity and nutriment, first began to perform their functions with pain, a warning of error that was unheeded; then, to cease to grow;* next, to set up once a month a grumbling torture that made life miserable; and, lastly, the brain and the whole nervous system, disturbed, in obedience to the law, that, if one member suffers, all the members suffer, became neuralgic and hysterical. And so Miss D—— spent the few years next succeeding her graduation in conflict with dysmenorrhœa, headache, neuralgia, and hysteria. Her parents marvelled at her ill-health; and she furnished another text for the often-repeated sermon on the delicacy of American girls.

COMMENTS ON GENESIS

Elizabeth Cady Stanton and the Revising Committee

Elizabeth Cady Stanton (1815–1902) helped to organize the first women's rights convention at Seneca Falls, New York, in 1848, and she helped to draft its famous Declaration of Sentiments. From 1868 to 1872, Stanton edited *The Revolution*, a radical weekly paper devoted to issues related to the woman question. She was also instrumental in getting the woman suffrage amendment introduced into Congress for the first time in 1878. It was reintroduced at every succeeding Congress until the vote was attained in 1920. In addition to these projects and her other writing and lecturing, Stanton was the mother of seven children. She began work on *The Woman's Bible* just before her eightieth birthday in 1895, and Part I was published later that year.

"The Old Testament," she wrote, "makes woman a mere after-thought in creation; the author of evil; cursed in her maternity; a subject in marriage; and all female life, animal and human, unclean. The Church in all ages has taught these doctrines and acted on them, claiming divine authority therefor." *The Woman's Bible* challenged "the injustices to women contained in the Scriptures or their interpretations." To this end, a Revising Committee of eight women organized to comment on the Old and New Testament passages referring to women and on those passages where women were conspicuous by their absence. Some women agreed to serve but withdrew their names later fearing to associate themselves with such a radical project.

According to Stanton, when Part I of *The Woman's Bible* was published, some New York newspapers devoted an entire page to it, including pictures of members of the Revising Committee and their critics. And newspapers all over the country and abroad quoted and reviewed it. The clergy called it "the work of women, and the devil." Several editions were published and an expanded Revising Committee worked on Part II, published in 1898.

The comments on Genesis below were written by Stanton; by Ellen Battelle Dietrick, a like-minded Bostonian who had herself published articles on dress reform and woman suffrage; and by Lillie Devereux Blake, author of a feminist novel and short stories and a leader in the woman suffrage movement.

---

*The arrest of development of the uterus, in connection with amenorrhœa, is sometimes very marked. In the New York Medical Journal for June, 1873, three such cases are recorded, that came under the eye of those excellent observers, Dr. E. R. Peaslee and Dr. T. G. Thomas. In one of these cases, the uterine cavity measured one and a half inches; in another, one and seven-eighths inches; and, in a third, one and a quarter inches. Recollecting that the normal measurement is from two and a half to three inches, it appears that the arrest of development in these cases occurred when the uterus was half or less than half grown. Liberal education should avoid such errors.

Genesis i: 26, 27, 28.

26 And God said, Let us make man in our image, after our likeness: and let them have dominion over the fish of the sea, and over the fowl of the air, and over the cattle, and over all the earth, and over every creeping thing that creepeth upon the earth.

27 So God created man in his *own* image, in the image of God created he him; male and female created he them.

28 And God blessed them, and God said unto them, Be fruitful, and multiply, and replenish the earth, and subdue it; and have dominion over the fish of the sea, and over the fowl of the air, and over every living thing that moveth upon the earth.

Here is the sacred historian's first account of the advent of woman; a simultaneous creation of both sexes, in the image of God. It is evident from the language that there was consultation in the Godhead, and that the masculine and feminine elements were equally represented. Scott in his commentaries says, "this consultation of the Gods is the origin of the doctrine of the trinity." But instead of three male personages, as generally represented, a Heavenly Father, Mother, and Son would seem more rational.

The first step in the elevation of woman to her true position, as an equal factor in human progress, is the cultivation of the religious sentiment in regard to her dignity and equality, the recognition by the rising generation of an ideal Heavenly Mother, to whom their prayers should be addressed, as well as to a Father.

If language has any meaning, we have in these texts a plain declaration of the existence of the feminine element in the Godhead, equal in power and glory with the masculine. The Heavenly Mother and Father! "God created man in his *own image, male and female.*" Thus Scripture, as well as science and philosophy, declares the eternity and equality of sex—the philosophical fact, without which there could have been no perpetuation of creation, no growth or development in the animal, vegetable, or mineral kingdoms, no awakening nor progressing in the world of thought. The masculine and feminine elements, exactly equal and balancing each other, are as essential to the maintenance of the equilibrium of the universe as positive and negative electricity, the centripetal and centrifugal forces, the laws of attraction which bind together all we know of this planet whereon we dwell and of the system in which we revolve.

In the great work of creation the crowning glory was realized, when man and woman were evolved on the sixth day, the masculine and feminine forces in the image of God, that must have existed eternally, in all forms of matter and mind. All the persons in the Godhead are represented in the Elohim the divine plurality taking counsel in regard to this last and highest form of life. Who were the members of this high council, and were they a duality or a trinity? Verse 27 declares the image of God male and female. How then is it possible to make woman an afterthought? We find in verses 5–16 the pronoun "he" used. Should it not in harmony with verse 26 be "they," a dual pronoun? We may attribute this to the same cause as the use of "his" in verse 11 instead of "it." The fruit tree yielding fruit after "his" kind instead of after "its" kind. The paucity of a language may give rise to many misunderstandings.

COMMENTS ON GENESIS   From Elizabeth Cady Stanton et al., *The Woman's Bible, Part I* (New York: European, 1895) 14–19.

The above texts plainly show the simultaneous creation of man and woman, and their equal importance in the development of the race. All those theories based on the assumption that man was prior in the creation, have no foundation in Scripture.

As to woman's subjection, on which both the canon and the civil law delight to dwell, it is important to note that equal dominion is given to woman over every living thing, but not one word is said giving man dominion over woman.

Here is the first title deed to this green earth giving alike to the sons and daughters of God. No lesson of woman's subjection can be fairly drawn from the first chapter of the Old Testament.

E. C. S.

The most important thing for a woman to note, in reading Genesis, is that that portion which is now divided into "the first three chapters" (there was no such division until about five centuries ago), contains two entirely separate, and very contradictory, stories of creation, written by two different, but equally anonymous, authors. No Christian theologian of to-day, with any pretensions to scholarship, claims that Genesis was written by Moses. As was long ago pointed out, the Bible itself declares that all the books the Jews originally possessed were burned in the destruction of Jerusalem, about 588 B.C., at the time the people were taken to Babylonia as slaves to the Assyrians (see II Esdras, ch. xiv, v. 21, Apocrypha). Not until about 247 B.C. (some theologians say 226 and others 169 B.C.) is there any record of a collection of literature in the re-built Jerusalem, and, then, the anonymous writer of II Maccabees briefly mentions that some Nehemiah "gathered together the acts of the kings and the prophets and those of David" when "founding a library" for use in Jerusalem. But the earliest mention anywhere in the Bible of a book that might have corresponded to Genesis is made by an apocryphal writer, who says that *Ezra* wrote "all that hath been done in the world since the beginning," after the Jews returned from Babylon, under his leadership, about 450 B.C. (see II Esdras, ch. xiv, v. 22, of the Apocrypha).

When it is remembered that the Jewish books were written on rolls of leather, without much attention to vowel points and with no division into verses or chapters, by uncritical copyists, who altered passages greatly, and did not always even pretend to understand what they were copying, then the reader of Genesis begins to put herself in position to understand how it can be contradictory. Great as were the liberties which the Jews took with Genesis, those of the English translators, however, greatly surpassed them.

The first chapter of Genesis, for instance, in Hebrew, tells us, in verses one and two, "As to origin, created the gods (Elohim) these skies (or air or clouds) and this earth. . . . And a wind moved upon the face of the waters." Here we have the opening of a polytheistic fable of creation, but, so strongly convinced were the English translators that the ancient Hebrews must have been originally monotheistic that they rendered the above, as follows: "In the beginning God created the heaven and the earth. . . . And the spirit of God [!] moved upon the face of the waters."

It is now generally conceded that some one (nobody pretends to know who) at some time (nobody pretends to know exactly when), copied two creation myths on the same leather roll, one immediately following the other. About one hundred years ago, it was discovered by Dr. Astruc, of France, that from Genesis ch. i, v. 1 to Genesis ch. ii, v. 4, is given one complete account of creation, by an author who always used the term "the gods" (*Elohim*), in speaking of the fashioning of the universe, mentioning it altogether thirty-four times, while, in Genesis ch. ii, v. 4, to the end of chapter iii, we have a totally different narrative, by an author of unmistakably different style, who uses the term "Iahveh of the gods" twenty times, but "Elohim" only three times. The first author, evidently, attributes creation to a council of gods, acting in concert, and seems never to have heard of Iahveh. The second attributes creation to Iahveh, a tribal god of ancient Israel, but represents Iahveh as one of two or more gods, conferring with them (in Genesis ch. xiii, v. 22) as to the danger of man's acquiring immortality.

Modern theologians have, for convenience sake, entitled these two fables, respectively, the Elohistic and the Iahoistic stories. They differ, not only in the point I have mentioned above, but in the order of the "creative acts"; in regard to the mutual attitude of man and woman, and in regard to human freedom from prohibitions imposed by deity. In order to exhibit their striking contradictions, I will place them in parallel columns:

Elohistic

Order of Creation:
First—Water.
Second—Land.
Third—Vegetation.
Fourth—Animals.
Fifth—Mankind; male and female.

In this story male and female man are created simultaneously, both alike, in the image of the gods, *after* all animals have been called into existence.

Here, joint dominion over the earth is given to woman and man, without limit or prohibition.

Everything, without exception, is pronounced "very good."

Man and woman are told that "every plant bearing seed upon the face of the earth and *every tree*. . . . "To you it shall be for meat." They are thus given perfect freedom.

Man and woman are given special dominion over all the animals—"every creeping thing that creepeth upon the earth."

Iahoistic

Order of Creation:
First—Land.
Second—Water.
Third—Male Man, only.
Fourth—Vegetation.
Fifth—Animals.
Sixth—Woman.

In this story male man is sculptured out of clay, *before* any animals are created, and *before* female man has been constructed.

Here, woman is punished with subjection to man for breaking a prohibitory law.

There is a tree of evil, whose fruit, is said by Iahveh to cause sudden death, but which does not do so, as Adam lived 930 years after eating it.

Man is told there is *one tree* of which he must not eat, "for in the day thou eatest thereof, thou shalt surely die."

An animal, a "creeping thing," is given dominion over man and woman, and proves himself more truthful than Iahveh Elohim. (Compare Genesis chapter ii, verse 17, with chapter iii, verses 4 and 22.)

Now as it is manifest that both of these stories cannot be true; intelligent women, who feel bound to give the preference to either, may decide according to their own judgment of which is more worthy of an intelligent woman's acceptance. Paul's rule is a good one in this dilemma, "Prove all things: hold fast to that which is good." My own opinion is that the second story was manipulated by some Jew, in an endeavor to give "heavenly authority" for requiring a woman to obey the man she married. In a work which I am now completing, I give some facts concerning ancient Israelitish history, which will be of peculiar interest to those who wish to understand the origin of woman's subjection.

E.B.D.

Many orientalists and students of theology have maintained that the consultation of the Gods here described is proof that the Hebrews were in early days polytheists—Scott's supposition that this is the origin of the Trinity has no foundation in fact, as the beginning of that conception is to be found in the earliest of all known religious nature worship. The acknowledgment of the dual principal, masculine and feminine, is much more probably the explanation of the expressions here used.

In the detailed description of creation we find a gradually ascending series. Creeping things, "great sea monsters," (ch. i, v. 21, literal translation). "Every bird of wing," cattle and living things of the earth, the fish of the sea and the "birds of the heavens," then man, and last and crowning glory of the whole, woman.

It cannot be maintained that woman was inferior to man even if, as asserted in chapter ii, she was created after him without at once admitting that man is inferior to the creeping things, because created after them.

L.D.B.

THE DOUBLE TASK
Elise Johnson McDougald

The 1920s witnessed the "Harlem Renaissance" in which black poets, musicians, and other artists turned a Jewish and Italian neighborhood into the cultural capital of black America. The attractions of Harlem for ambitious young African Americans were many. Here they could find newspapers and magazines devoted to their lives. Here was a black theater which, under the leadership of Noble Sissle and Eubie Blake, was starting to crack into the previously all-white world of Broadway. Here were nightclubs, such as the famous Cotton Club, where Duke Ellington and other young musicians were developing a new American music, jazz. Here also were some opportunities, however limited, to achieve economic success. Harlem, in short, became a true mecca.

The following essay, written by a black social worker, appeared in a special issue of the *Survey Graphic* devoted to social questions on Harlem. McDougald sought to explain what it was like to be a black woman in the 1920s, facing the "double task" of overcoming racism and sexism.

Throughout the long years of history, woman has been the weather-vane, the indicator, showing in which direction the wind of destiny blows. Her status and development have augured now calm and stability, now swift currents of progress. What then is to be said of the Negro woman today?

In Harlem, more than anywhere else, the Negro woman is free from the cruder handicaps of primitive household hardships and the grosser forms of sex and race subjugation. Here she has considerable opportunity to measure her powers in the intellectual and industrial fields of the great city. Here the questions naturally arise: "What are her problems?" and "How is she solving them?"

To answer these questions, one must have in mind not any one Negro woman, but rather a colorful pageant of individuals, each differently endowed. Like the red and yellow of the tiger-lily, the skin of one is brilliant against the star-lit darkness of a racial sister. From grace to strength, they vary in infinite degree, with traces of the race's history left in physical and mental outline on each. With a discerning mind, one catches the multiform charm, beauty and character of Negro women; and grasps the fact that their problem cannot be thought of in mass.

Because only a few have caught this vision, the attitude of mind of most New Yorkers causes the Negro woman serious difficulty. She is conscious that what is left of chivalry is not directed toward her. She realizes that the ideals of beauty, built up in the fine arts, exclude her almost entirely. Instead, the grotesque Aunt Jemimas of the street-car advertisements proclaim only an ability to serve, without grace or loveliness. Nor does the drama catch her finest spirit. She is most often used to provoke the mirthless laugh of ridicule; or to portray feminine viciousness or vulgarity not peculiar to Negroes. This is the shadow over her. To a race naturally sunny comes the twilight of self-doubt and a sense of personal inferiority. It cannot be denied that these are potent and detrimental influences, though not generally recognized because they are in the realm of the mental and spiritual. More apparent are the economic handicaps which follow her recent entrance into industry. It is conceded that she has special difficulties because of the poor working conditions and low wages of her men. It is not surprising that only the determined women forge ahead to results other than mere survival. The few who do prove their mettle stimulate one to a closer study of how this achievement is won in Harlem.

Better to visualize the Negro woman at her job, our vision of a host of individuals must once more resolve itself into groups on the basis of activity. First, comes a very small leisure group—the wives and daughters of men who are in business, in the professions and in a few well-paid personal service occupations. Second, a most active and progressive group, the women in business and the professions. Third, the many women in the trades and industry. Fourth, a group weighty in numbers struggling on in domestic service, with an even less fortunate fringe of casual workers, fluctuating with the economic temper of the times.

The first is a pleasing group to see. It is picked for outward beauty by Negro men with much the same feeling as other Americans of the same economic class. Keeping

THE DOUBLE TASK   From Elise Johnson McDougald, "The Double Task," *Survey Graphic* Mar. 1925: 689–91.

their women free to preside over the family, these women are affected by the problems of every wife and mother, but touched only faintly by their race's hardships. They do share acutely in the prevailing difficulty of finding competent household help. Negro wives find Negro maids unwilling generally to work in their own neighborhoods, for various reasons. They do not wish to work where there is a possibility of acquaintances coming into contact with them while they serve and they still harbor the misconception that Negroes of any station are unable to pay as much as persons of the other race. It is in these homes of comparative ease that we find the polite activities of social exclusiveness. The luxuries of well-appointed homes, modest motors, tennis, golf and country clubs, trips to Europe and California, make for social standing. The problem confronting the refined Negro family is to know others of the same achievement. The search for kindred spirits gradually grows less difficult; in the past it led to the custom of visiting all the large cities in order to know similar groups of cultured Negro people.

A spirit of stress and struggle characterizes the second two groups. These women of business, profession and trade are the hub of the wheel of progress. Their burden is twofold. Many are wives and mothers whose husbands are insufficiently paid, or who have succumbed to social maladjustment and have abandoned their families. An appalling number are widows. They face the great problem of leaving home each day and at the same time trying to rear children in their spare time—this too in neighborhoods where rents are large, standards of dress and recreation high and costly, and social danger on the increase.

The great commercial life of New York City is only slightly touched by the Negro woman of our second group. Negro business men offer her most of their work, but their number is limited. Outside of this field, custom is once more against her and competition is keen for all. However, Negro girls are training and some are holding exceptional jobs. One of the professors in a New York college has had a young colored woman as secretary for the past three years. Another holds the head clerical position in an organization where reliable handling of detail and a sense of business ethics are essential. For four years she has steadily advanced. Quietly these women prove their worth, so that when a vacancy exists and there is a call, it is difficult to find even one competent colored secretary who is not employed. As a result of opportunity in clerical work in the educational system of New York City a number have qualified for such positions, one being appointed within the year to the office work of a high school. In other departments the civil service in New York City is no longer free from discrimination. The casual personal interview, that tenacious and retrogressive practice introduced in the Federal administration during the World War has spread and often nullifies the Negro woman's success in written tests. The successful young woman just cited above was three times "turned down" as undesirable on the basis of the personal interview. In the great mercantile houses, the many young Negro girls who might well be suited to salesmanship are barred from all but the menial positions. Even so, one Negro woman, beginning as a uniformed maid, has pulled herself up to the position of "head of stock."

Again, the telephone and insurance companies which receive considerable patronage from Negroes deny them proportionate employment. Fortunately, this is an era of changing customs. There is hope that a less selfish racial attitude will prevail. It is a heartening fact that there is an increasing number of Americans who will lend a hand in the game fight of the worthy.

In the less crowded professional vocations, the outlook is more cheerful. In these fields, the Negro woman is dependent largely upon herself and her own race for work. In the legal, dental, medical and nursing professions, successful women practitioners have usually worked their way through college and are "managing" on the small fees that can be received from an underpaid public. Social conditions in America are hardest upon the Negro because he is lowest in the economic scale. This gives rise to a demand for trained college women in the profession of social work. It has met with a response from young college women, anxious to devote their education and lives to the needs of the submerged classes. In New York City, some fifty-odd women are engaged in social work, other than nursing. In the latter profession there are over two hundred and fifty. Much of the social work has been pioneer in nature: the pay has been small with little possibility of advancement. For even in work among Negroes, the better paying positions are reserved for whites. The Negro college woman is doing her bit in this field at a sacrifice, along such lines as these: in the correctional departments of the city, as probation officers, investigators, and police women; as Big Sisters attached to the Childrens' Court; as field workers and visitors for relief organizations and missions; as secretaries for travelers-aid and mission societies; as visiting teachers and vocational guides for the schools of the city; and, in the many branches of public health nursing, in schools, organizations devoted to preventive and educational medicine, in hospitals and in private nursing.

In New York City, nearly three hundred Negro women share the good conditions in the teaching profession. They measure up to the high pedagogical requirements of the city and state law and are increasingly, leaders in the community. Here too the Negro woman finds evidence of the white workers' fear of competition. The need for teachers is still so strong that little friction exists. When it does seem to be imminent, it is smoothed away, as it recently was at a meeting of school principals. From the floor, a discussion began with: "What are we going to do about this problem of the increasing number of Negro teachers coming into our schools?" It ended promptly through the suggestion of another principal: "Send all you get and don't want over to my school. I have two now and I'll match their work to any two of your best whom you name." One might go on to such interesting and more unusual professions as journalism, chiropody, bacteriology, pharmacy, etc., and find that, though the number in any one may be small, the Negro woman is creditably represented in practically every one. According to individual ability she is meeting with success.

Closing the door on the home anxieties, the woman engaged in trades and in industry faces equally serious difficulty in competition in the open working field. Custom is against her in all but a few trade and industrial occupations. She has, however been established long in the dressmaking trade among the helpers and finishers, and more recently among the drapers and fitters in some of the best establishments. Several Negro women are themselves proprietors of shops in the country's greatest fashion district. Each of them has, against great odds, convinced skeptical employers of her business value; and, at the same time, has educated fellow workers of other races, doing much to show the oneness of interest of all workers. In millinery, power sewing-machine operating on cloth, straw and leather, there are few Negro women. The laissez-faire attitude of practically all trade unions makes the Negro woman an unwilling menace to the cause of labor.

In trade cookery, the Negro woman's talent and past experience is recognized. Her problem here is to find employers who will let her work her way to managerial positions, in tea-rooms, candy shops and institutions. One such employer became convinced that the managing cook, a young colored graduate of Pratt Institute, would continue to build up a business that had been failing. She offered her a partnership. As in the cases of a number of such women, her barrier was lack of capital. No matter how highly trained, nor how much speed and business acumen has been acquired, the Negro's credit is held in doubt. An exception in this matter of capital will serve to prove the rule. Thirty years ago, a young Negro girl began learning all branches of the fur trade. She is now in business for herself, employing three women of her race and one Jewish man. She has made fur experts of still another half-dozen colored girls. Such instances as these justify the prediction that the foothold gained in the trade world will, year by year, become more secure.

Because of the limited fields for workers in this group, many of the unsuccessful drift into the fourth social grade, the domestic and casual workers. These drifters increase the difficulties of the Negro woman suited to housework. New standards of household management are forming and the problem of the Negro woman is to meet these new business-like ideals. The constant influx of workers unfamiliar with household conditions in New York keeps the situation one of turmoil. The Negro woman, moreover, is revolting against residential domestic service. It is a last stand in her fight to maintain a semblance of family life. For this reason, principally, the number of day or casual workers is on the increase. Happiness is almost impossible under the strain of these conditions. Health and morale suffer, but how else can her children, loose all afternoon, be gathered together at night-fall? Through it all she manages to give satisfactory service and the Negro woman is sought after for this unpopular work largely because her honesty, loyalty and cleanliness have stood the test of time. Through her drudgery, the women of other groups find leisure time for progress. This is one of her contributions to America.

It is apparent from what has been said, that even in New York City, Negro women are of a race which is free neither economically, socially nor spiritually. Like women in general, but more particularly like those of other oppressed minorities, the Negro woman has been forced to submit to over-powering conditions. Pressure has been exerted upon her, both from without and within her group. Her emotional and sex life is a reflex of her economic station. The women of the working class will react, emotionally and sexually, similarly to the working-class women of other races. The Negro woman does not maintain any moral standard which may be assigned chiefly to qualities of race, any more than a white woman does. Yet she has been singled out and advertised as having lower sex standards. Superficial critics who have had contact only with the lower grades of Negro women, claim that they are more immoral than other groups of women. This I deny. This is the sort of criticism which predicates of one race, to its detriment, that which is common to all races. Sex irregularities are not a matter of race, but of socio-economic conditions. Research shows that most of the African tribes from which the Negro sprang have strict codes for sex relations. There is no proof of inherent weakness in the ethnic group.

Gradually overcoming the habitual limits imposed upon her by slave masters, she increasingly seeks legal sanction for the consummation and dissolution of sex contracts. Contrary to popular belief, illegitimacy among Negroes is cause for shame and grief. When economic, social and biological forces combined bring about unwed motherhood, the reaction is much the same as in families of other racial groups. Secrecy is maintained if possible. Generally the married aunt, or even the mother, claims that the illegitimate child is her own. The foundling asylum is seldom sought. Schooled in this kind of suffering in the days of slavery, Negro women often temper scorn with sympathy for weakness. Stigma does fall upon the unmarried mother, but perhaps in this matter the Negroes' attitude is nearer the modern enlightened ideal for the social treatment of the unfortunate. May this not be considered another contribution to America?

With all these forces at work, true sex equality has not been approximated. The ratio of opportunity in the sex, social, economic and political spheres is about that which exists between white men and women. In the large, I would say that the Negro woman is the cultural equal of her man because she is generally kept in school longer. Negro boys, like white boys, are usually put to work to subsidize the family income. The growing economic independence of Negro working women is causing her to rebel against the domineering family attitude of the cruder working-class Negro man. The masses of Negro men are engaged in menial occupations throughout the working day. Their baffled and suppressed desires to determine their economic life are manifested in overbearing domination at home. Working mothers are unable to instill different ideals in their sons. Conditions change slowly. Nevertheless, education and opportunity are modifying the spirit of the younger Negro men. Trained in modern schools of thought, they begin to show a wholesome attitude of fellowship and freedom for their women. The challenge to young Negro womanhood is to see clearly this trend and grasp the proferred comradeship with sincerity. In this matter of sex equality, Negro women have contributed few outstanding militants. Their feminist efforts are directed chiefly toward the realization of the equality of the races, the sex struggle assuming a subordinate place. . . .

We find the Negro woman, figuratively, struck in the face daily by contempt from the world about her. Within her soul, she knows little of peace and happiness. Through it all, she is courageously standing erect, developing within herself the moral strength to rise above and conquer false attitudes. She is maintaining her natural beauty and charm and improving her mind and opportunity. She is measuring up to the needs and demands of her family, community and race, and radiating from Harlem a hope that is cherished by her sisters in less propitious circumstances throughout the land. The wind of the race's destiny stirs more briskly because of her striving.

THE NATURAL SUPERIORITY OF WOMEN

Ashley Montagu

A physical anthropologist by training, Ashley Montagu is a prolific writer, popularizer of science, and a student of human behavior. Much of his writing is designed to debunk various "highly popular and erroneous ideas and practices."

In a 1952 magazine article, which attracted widespread public attention, Montagu questioned "the myth of female inferiority." Contrary to the Freudian premise that women are incomplete men, Montagu argued that, chromosomally, men are incomplete women. In place of female "penis envy," he saw unconscious male "womb and breast envy." And, rather than seeing woman as delicate and vulnerable, he offered evidence of her superior resistance to physical and psychological stress.

Mixed with Montagu's highly provocative ideas were some conventional notions about woman's nature and proper roles. He concluded, for example, that it is women's function "to teach men how to be human" and to raise their "children to be, like themselves, loving and cooperative."

The stir caused by the publication of this article encouraged Montagu to express his ideas in book form. With the book's publication in 1953, he became a celebrity who appeared frequently on television. The excerpts below are from Montagu's book, *The Natural Superiority of Women.*

The myth of female inferiority is so old, and has been for so long a part of the ideas and institutions of men, that it has been generalized for almost every aspect of the female being. Is there a trait in which women have not been considered inferior to men? It would be difficult to think of one. . . .

The female is shorter, slighter, and weaker than the male; these facts are obvious to everyone. The male, it is asserted, is clearly superior in these respects to the female. Let us here recall our definition of superiority in terms of the conferring of survival benefits upon the possessors of the particular traits under discussion. Do the greater size and muscular power of the male, from the biological standpoint, confer greater survival benefits upon him? . . . Do the lesser size and muscular power of the female confer lesser survival benefits upon her? The answer to these questions, on the basis of the scientifically established and verifiable facts, is a resounding "No!" On the contrary, the facts prove that the biological advantages are with the female. . . .

It should be clear that in societies which sanction a certain amount of violent behavior, men, owing to their greater muscular power, consider themselves "superior" to women in this respect, and that women readily grant them this "superiority." But it must be understood that such "superiority" is a social superiority, *not* a biological one, because the male's greater muscular power enables him to obtain certain social advantages, and maintain them, over the female. If the adequate functioning and survival of the male depended upon violent conflict with the female, then there would be no question concerning the biological superiority of the male's greater muscular power; but the efficient functioning and survival of the male does *not* depend upon violent conflict with the female—any more than it depends upon violent conflict with anyone else.

The greater muscular power of the male has, to a large extent, been a socially valuable trait, especially during the long period of man's history when so much of the labor expended in human societies was in the form of muscle power. Today, when machines do over 90 per cent of the work formerly done mainly by masculine muscle, muscular power is ceasing to be as great a social advantage as it once was.

Let us apply another test. What is the answer to the question: Which sex survives the rigors of life, whether normal or extreme, better than the other? The answer is: The female sex.

THE NATURAL SUPERIORITY OF WOMEN   From Ashley Montagu, *The Natural Superiority of Women* (New York: Macmillan, 1953) 49–66, 72–79, 129–131. Reprinted with the permission of Simon & Schuster from THE NATURAL SUPERIORITY OF WOMEN, New and Revised Edition, by Ashley Montagu. Copyright © 1953, renewed 1981 by Ashley Montagu.

Women endure all sorts of divitalizing conditions better than men: starvation, exposure, fatigue, shock, illness, and the like. This immediately raises the question of the supposed "weakness" of the female. Is not the female supposed to be "the weaker vessel"? "Weakness" is a misleading word which has, in this connection, confused most people. "Feminine weakness" has generally meant that the female is more fragile and in general less strong than the male. But the fact is that the female is constitutionally stronger than the male and only muscularly less powerful; she has greater stamina and lives longer. The male pays heavily for his greater body build and muscular power. Because his expenditure of energy is greater than that of the female, he burns himself out more rapidly, and hence dies at an earlier age. . . .

Does there exist some biological differentiating factor which may serve to explain or possibly throw some light upon the origin and meaning of these differences? The answer is "Yes." And I should like this "Yes" to resound all over the world, for I do not know that anyone has made anything of a key fact which lies at the base of practically all the differences between the sexes and the biological superiority of the female to the male. I refer to the chromosomal structure of the sexes, the chromosomes being the small cellular bodies which contain the hereditary particles, or genes, which so substantially influence one's development and fate as an organism.

In the sex cells there are twenty-four chromosomes, but only one of these is a sex chromosome. There are two kinds of sex chromosomes, X and Y. Half the sperm cells carry X- and half carry Y-chromosomes. All the female ova in the female ovaries contain only X-chromosomes. When an X-bearing sperm fertilizes an ovum, the offspring is always female. When a Y-bearing chromosome fertilizes an ovum, the offspring is always male. It is the initial difference in chromosome composition which determines the differences between the sexes in a constitutionally decisive manner. . . .

What the origin of the X- and Y-chromosomes may have been no one knows, but I find it amusing and helpful to think of the Y-chromosome as an undeveloped X-chromosome, or perhaps as a remnant of an X-chromosome. It is as if in the evolution of sex a fragment at one time broke away from an X-chromosome, carrying with it some rather unfortunate genes, and thereafter in relation to the other chromosomes was helpless to prevent them from expressing themselves in the form of an incomplete female, the creature we call the male! This "just-so" story makes the male a sort of crippled female, a creature who by virtue of the fact that he has only one X-chromosome is not so well equipped biologically as the female.

❧ ❧ ❧

The function of the myth that women are emotionally weaker than men has been to maintain the prejudice that while man is the supremely rational and intelligent creature, woman is the creature of her emotions. The strong, silent man stands by with a stiff upper lip and a face rendered immobile by a trained incapacity for emotional expression, and thus marmoreally ministers to the supposed need for sympathy and support of his frail, emotional, nervous "little woman." Is it any wonder, then, that there are so many more men than women in our mental institutions, that all over the world they commit suicide so much more frequently than women, succumb to so many more nervous breakdowns than women, have four times as many stomach ulcers, and show the physical and functional disorders of emotional distur-bances, in general, so much more frequently than women?

Though women *are* more emotional than men, men are emotionally weaker than women; that is, men break more easily under emotional strain than women do. Women are emotionally stronger than men because they bend more easily, and are more resilient. . . .

"Emotionally unstable" woman has been the support of "emotionally stable" man, I suspect, from the beginning of human history. Women have had to be equipped not only to withstand the stresses and strains which in the course of a life-time assault the mind and body of one person, but at least of two. For one of the principal functions of a wife has been to serve not only as a recipient of her hus-band's emotional responses to life's situations but also as a scapegoat upon which her husband's unexpended aggressiveness could exhaust itself, thus offering him the psychological relief from tension in the only place in which he could find it—the home. Were it not for this blessed arrangement, who knows to what new heights the frequency of mental breakdown in males might not have soared?

DEADLIER THAN THE MALE
John C. Ewers

John C. Ewers' portraits of nineteenth-century Native American women of the Plains stand in stark contrast to the "true woman" image of the encroaching white society of the time. Although the lot of many Native American women was "women's work" around the camp or village, the tribes about which Ewers writes appear to have accepted individual differences among women. Although most women in these tribes filled traditional roles, some women, Ewers learned, found places for themselves as warriors and hunters.

Ewers, an ethnologist, was Museum Director of the Smithsonian Institution in 1965 when he wrote this article for *American Heritage, The Magazine of History*. Ewers has written several books, including *Images of a Vanished Life* (1985) and *Blackfeet: Their Art and Culture* (1987).

When I first met Elk Hollering in the Water on the Blackfeet Reservation in Mon-tana in 1941, she was a frail little old lady in her middle seventies. She was short and she was spare. I doubt if she ever weighed as many as one hundred pounds. Nothing about her appearance would remind one of artists' conceptions of the legendary Amazons. Nevertheless, Elk Hollering in the Water was a combat veteran in her own right, a fighting member of the most aggressive tribe of the upper Missouri. As a lively teen-ager she had accompanied her stalwart husband, Bear Chief, on raids against enemy tribes. And she had won honors by "taking things from the enemy."

Aged men of her tribe, men who had journeyed on many war excursions against the Crows, Crees, Assiniboins, Flatheads, and Sioux, readily acknowledged Elk Hol-lering in the Water's claim. Furthermore, they assured me that womanly participa-tion in what we commonly regard as the man's game of war was not considered

DEADLIER THAN THE MALE   From John C. Ewers, "Deadlier Than the Male," *American Heritage* June/July 1965: 10–13. Reprinted by permission of American Heritage magazine, a division of Forbes Inc. Copyright © Forbes Inc., 1965.

abnormal conduct in the days of intertribal conflict on the upper Missouri prior to the middle 1880s. Young childless women sometimes joined their husbands on fatiguing and dangerous horse-stealing raids upon distant enemy villages in preference to remaining at home praying and worrying about the safety of their mates. Sometimes small war parties travelled two or three hundred miles before their scouts located an enemy camp. Usually the women cooked for the entire party and performed other menial tasks during the outward journey. But they also took active parts in the dawn attacks on enemy camps and helped to drive the stolen horses homeward. Sometimes the fleeing raiders were overtaken by angry enemy warriors bent upon recapturing their pilfered livestock. Then the horse thieves, female and male, had to fight for their lives as well as for their newly acquired property.

Women warriors also appeared among the Crows, south of the Yellowstone. The Crows were a small tribe, but they were wealthier in horses than any other Indians on the upper Missouri. They fought valiantly to protect their herds from frequent raids by the Blackfeet from the north and the mighty Sioux from the east. To protect themselves from extermination by those more powerful tribes, the Crows made alliances with the white men.

Some thirty years ago or more an aged Crow woman, Pretty Shield, told Frank Bird Linderman of a brave Crow girl who aided General Crook against the Sioux and Cheyenne under Crazy Horse in the historic Battle of the Rosebud on June 17, 1876, only a week prior to the Custer debacle on the Little Big Horn. The Other Magpie was her name. She was wild and she was pretty. But she had no man of her own. When some 175 Crow warriors rode off to join Three Stars (General Crook) in his campaign against the hostile Sioux and Cheyenne, The Other Magpie went along. She had recently lost a brother at the hands of the Sioux, and she was eager for revenge. In the Battle of the Rosebud, the Crow scouts bore the brunt of the hostile Indian attack. Many of these scouts carried improved .50 caliber breech-loading rifles. But The Other Magpie's only weapons were her belt knife and a long, thin willow coup stick. Yet she counted coup on a live Sioux warrior and later took his scalp—one of only eleven scalps taken by the Crows in the day's bitter fighting.

Pretty Shield remembered the return of the Crows from that battle. She saw The Other Magpie proudly carrying a bright feather tied to the end of her coup stick to symbolize her recent achievement. And she saw her cut the Sioux scalp she had taken into several pieces and give them to the men so that they would have more scalps to dance with.

The greatest of all the women warriors among the upper Missouri tribes lived among the Crows in the middle of the nineteenth century. Rudolph Kurz, a romantic young Swiss artist who had journeyed into the wilderness to draw primitive Indians, met her at Fort Union near the mouth of the Yellowstone on October 27, 1851. He confided to his journal for that day, "In the afternoon the famous Absaroka amazon arrived. Mr. Denig [the factor in charge of the trading post] called me to his office that I might have an opportunity to see her. She looked neither savage nor warlike. On the contrary, as I entered the room, she sat with her hands in her lap, folded, as when one prays. She is about 46 years old; appears modest in manner and good natured rather than quick to quarrel." Kurz was so awed by this woman and so delighted to receive as a present a scalp she had taken in battle that he neglected to draw her portrait. Unfortunately, no likeness of this remarkable woman has been preserved. But Edwin T. Denig wrote a short biographical sketch of Woman Chief, as she was known to the Indians. He had known her for twelve years prior to her untimely death in 1854.

Woman Chief was not a Crow Indian by birth. She was a Gros Ventre girl who, at the age of about ten, was captured by the Crows. The Crow family that adopted her soon found that she showed little interest in helping the women with their domestic tasks. She preferred to shoot birds with a bow and arrow, to guard the family horses, and to ride horseback fast and fearlessly. Later she learned to shoot a gun accurately, and she became the equal if not the superior of any of the young men in hunting on foot or on horseback.

She grew taller and stronger than most women. She could carry a deer or bighorn home from the hunt on her back. She could kill four or five buffalo in a single chase, butcher them, and load them on pack horses without assistance. Yet, despite her prowess in men's activities, she always dressed like a woman. Although she was rather good-looking, she didn't attract the fancy of young men. After her foster father died she took charge of his lodge and family, acting as both father and mother to his children.

Her first war experience was gained in a defensive action outside the white-men's trading post in the Crow country. A Blackfoot war party approached the post and called upon the traders and Crows to come out and parley. This young woman alone had the nerve to answer their invitation. And when the treacherous enemy charged upon her, she killed one and wounded two others before running to safety in the traders' fort. This deed of daring marked her as a woman of unusual courage in the eyes of the Crows. They composed songs in her honor telling of her bravery, and sang them in their camps.

A year later she led her first war party against the Blackfeet; seventy horses were stolen. She succeeded in killing and scalping one Blackfoot and in capturing the gun of another. Her continued success as a war leader won her greater and greater honors among the Crows until she gained a place in the council of chiefs of the tribe, ranking third in a band of 160 lodges. Thereafter she was known as Woman Chief. This was a station and a title never before known among Crow women.

In the summer of 1854, twenty years after Woman Chief had begun to acquire a reputation as a warrior, she sought to try her skill as a peacemaker. She proposed a visit to the Gros Ventres, the tribe of her birth, to negotiate a peace between them and her adopted tribe, the Crows. Her friends, both Indian and white, sought to dissuade her from this bold undertaking. They well knew that the Gros Ventres looked upon her as a leader of their enemies. But Woman Chief persisted. In company with four Crows she travelled north of the Missouri, where she met a large party of Gros Ventres en route home from a visit to the trading post of Fort Union. She approached them boldly, talked to them in their own language, and smoked with them. While she journeyed with them to the main Gros Ventre camp, some of the party turned upon her and her four Crow comrades and coldly shot them down.

Weasel Tail, a Blood Indian who was over eighty years of age when I met him some twenty-odd years ago, told me that he was the son of very poor parents. In his late teens and early twenties he repeatedly joined horse-raiding expeditions in the hope of bettering both his economic status and his social prestige in his tribe. His wife, Throwing Down, used to go along with him during the early years of their marriage and before their first child was born. Weasel Tail explained, "She told me she loved me, and if I was to be killed she wanted to be killed with me. My wife was in five battles with me. She carried a six-shooter and knew how to use it. Once she stole a horse, a saddlebag filled with ammunition, and a war club from the enemy."

Weasel Tail told me the story of Running Eagle, most famous of all Blackfoot women warriors, who was killed in action about the time of Weasel Tail's birth in 1860. He had known several older men who had been members of war parties under Running Eagle's leadership, and they often had talked about her. One of these men was White Grass, who later became a prominent band chief among the Piegans, a Blackfoot tribe.

Running Eagle was a large, strong woman. When she was still young, her husband was killed in a fight with the Crows. Seeking some way to avenge his death, Running Eagle prayed to the sun, and thought she heard the sun answer, "I will give you great power in war. But if you give yourself to any other man you will be killed."

In a short time Running Eagle became a successful leader of sizable war parties. When on the warpath, she wore men's leggings, a peculiar loin cloth doubled over like a diaper, and a woman's dress. Although men who went to war under her leadership respected her highly, she was never proud. She insisted upon cooking for the men of her party, and she also mended their worn moccasins. When one young brave complained that it was not proper for a Blackfoot war leader to have to mend moccasins, she replied, "I am a woman. You men don't know how to sew."

One winter White Grass joined an expedition of about thirty men under Running Eagle's leadership, bound southward to the Crow country beyond the Yellowstone. They had not gone far before one of the younger men began to grumble because the leader was a woman. Running Eagle heard him and said, "You are right. I am only a woman." Then she sang her sacred war song, "All of you bachelors, try your best." The dissenter was so impressed by her manner that he decided to stay with the party to observe how this woman behaved.

When they reached the Yellowstone River, Running Eagle sang another song, "I should like to marry a buffalo bull, to have a two-year-old heifer for a sister, and to have a fall calf." Then she told her companions, "My brothers, I shall leave camp tonight. Tomorrow morning you must follow my footsteps in the snow."

So saying, she picked up her gun and walked off alone into the darkness. At daybreak she sighted a buffalo herd. She crawled toward it and shot first a large fat bull, then a two-year-old heifer, and then a fall calf. When the others overtook her they found her sitting down, quietly cleaning her gun. As they approached she told them calmly, "See, I have killed my husband, my two-year-old sister, and my baby."

After she had helped the men cut up the buffalo, Running Eagle ordered four men to scout ahead, saying, "I'm afraid the Nez Percés may be near here." Two days later the scouts returned and reported that they had seen no enemy signs. But not long after the party resumed its journey they discovered a Nez Percé encampment in the Yellowstone River bottom. Unfortunately, a Nez Percé horseman saw them at the same time. While he summoned the men of his camp, the Piegans hastily retreated and dug foxholes for protection against a Nez Percé attack. Running Eagle dug her hole a little in advance of her companions. From her pouch she took her war medicine—two feathers attached to a flat disk of brass—and tied it in her hair. Then she sang her war song.

When the Nez Percés charged, Running Eagle killed the first man to come within range. Then she cried out, "Brothers, I got the first one. You lie still. I shall keep killing them." Inspired by their leader's courage and calmness under fire, the doughty Piegans repulsed the Nez Percé attack, killing a number of the enemy. As the Nez Percés withdrew to care for their dead and wounded, Running Eagle howled like a wolf and shouted, "Now we are going to quit fighting." She led her happy warriors home without a casualty.

Toward spring of the following year, young White Grass again joined a war party led by Running Eagle. On the Sun River they sighted a camp of Flatheads who had crossed the Rockies to hunt buffalo on the plains. Running Eagle confided to her followers, "Last night I dreamed that some horses were given to me. Tonight we shall find them in the Flathead camp."

Shortly before daybreak the Piegans silently approached the tepees of the sleeping Flatheads. Running Eagle swiftly gave her orders: "Brothers, catch the horses you can rope outside the camp. I am no good with a rope. I'll go into the camp and see what's there." She sang her war song and prayed to the sun. "Sun, I am not a man. But you gave me this power to do what I desired." Then she walked quietly into the enemy camp, quickly cut loose five prize horses picketed near their owners' tepees, and led them away. Meanwhile, the men of her party roped a goodly number of the loose horses. When Running Eagle returned, the party was ready to make a fast getaway. She then told her comrades, "I'll take the lead. I am only a woman. I'm not as strong as you men. Keep any of those who may fall asleep on their horses from falling behind." For two days and two nights they rode without stopping to sleep. After the party reached their home camp, Running Eagle gave a bay and a roan to her eldest brother and a horse to each of her other relatives.

Running Eagle led several successful raids upon the Flatheads before those Indians learned that a woman had been a principal cause of their misfortunes. Then they set a trap for her by posting night guards to look out for any strange woman in their camp. The next time Running Eagle walked into the enemy village, the guard accosted her and asked her name. Running Eagle could not understand the Flathead tongue. As she hastily backed away, the Flathead sentry lifted his gun and shot and killed her. Some of the old Blackfoot Indians claimed that Running Eagle lost her life because she had broken her promise to the sun. She had fallen in love with a handsome young member of her war party, and she had not resisted his advances.

THE WOMAN WARRIOR: MEMOIRS OF A GIRLHOOD AMONG GHOSTS

Maxine Hong Kingston

Maxine Hong Kingston's autobiographies recall what it was like to grow up the daughter of Chinese immigrant parents in the American world of Stockton, California, in the 1940s and 1950s. In *The Woman Warrior*, Kingston wrote about her struggles to reconcile two images of women that were part of her Chinese heritage, one the warrior woman, Fa Mu Lan, the heroine of her mother's "talk-stories," and the other the silent slave and wife she was told she would grow up to be. In the following excerpt from that book, Kingston describes an encounter she had with a silent Chinese-American classmate who reminded her of parts of herself she could not accept.

Kingston also wrote *China Men* (1980), *Hawaii: One Summer* (1987), *Through the Black Curtain* (1988), and *Tripmaster Monkey: His Fake Book* (1989). *The Woman Warrior* was selected as one of *Time* magazine's top ten nonfiction books of the decade in 1979.

Normal Chinese women's voices are strong and bossy. We American-Chinese girls had to whisper to make ourselves American-feminine. Apparently we whispered even more softly than the Americans. Once a year the teachers referred my sister and me to speech therapy, but our voices would straighten out, unpredictably normal, for the therapists. Some of us gave up, shook our heads, and said nothing, not one word. Some of us could not even shake our heads. At times shaking my head no is more self-assertion than I can manage. Most of us eventually found some voice, however faltering. We invented an American-feminine speaking personality, except for that one girl who could not speak up even in Chinese school.

She was a year older than I and was in my class for twelve years. During all those years she read aloud but would not talk. Her older sister was usually beside her; their parents kept the older daughter back to protect the younger one. They were six and seven years old when they began school. Although I had flunked kindergarten, I was the same age as most other students in our class; my parents had probably lied about my age, so I had had a head start and came out even. My younger sister was in the class below me; we were normal ages and normally separated. The parents of the quiet girl, on the other hand, protected both daughters. When it sprinkled, they kept them home from school. The girls did not work for a living the way we did. But in other ways we were the same. . . .

I hated the younger sister, the quiet one. I hated her when she was the last chosen for her team and I, the last chosen for my team. I hated her for her China doll hair cut. I hated her at music time for the wheezes that came out of her plastic flute.

One afternoon in the sixth grade (that year I was arrogant with talk, not knowing there were going to be high school dances and college seminars to set me back), I and my little sister and the quiet girl and her big sister stayed late after school for some reason. The cement was cooling, and the tetherball poles made shadows across the gravel. The hooks at the rope end were clinking against the poles. We shouldn't have been there so late; there was laundry work to do and Chinese school to get to by 5:00. The last time we had stayed late, my mother had phoned the police and told them we had been kidnapped by bandits. The radio stations broadcast our descriptions. I had to get home before she did that again. But sometimes if you loitered long enough in the schoolyard, the other children would have gone home and you could play with the equipment before the office took it away. . . .

I did a flip off the fire escape and ran across the schoolyard. The day was a great eye, and it was not paying much attention to me now. I could disappear with the sun; I could turn quickly sideways and slip into a different world. It seemed I could run faster at this time, and by evening I would be able to fly. As the afternoon wore

THE WOMAN WARRIOR   From Maxine Hong Kingston, "A Song for a Barbarian Reed Pipe," *The Woman Warrior* (New York: Knopf, 1975) 200–12. Copyright © 1975, 1976 by Maxine Hong Kingston. Reprinted by permission of Alfred A. Knopf, Inc.

on we could run into the forbidden places—the boys' big yard, the boys' playroom. We could go into the boys' lavatory and look at the urinals. The only time during school hours I had crossed the boys' yard was when a flatbed truck with a giant thing covered with canvas and tied down with ropes had parked across the street. The children had told one another that it was a gorilla in captivity; we couldn't decide whether the sign said "Trail of the Gorilla" or "Trial of the Gorilla." The thing was as big as a house. The teachers couldn't stop us from hysterically rushing to the fence and clinging to the wire mesh. Now I ran across the boys' yard clear to the Cyclone fence and thought about the hair that I had seen sticking out of the canvas. It was going to be summer soon, so you could feel that freedom coming on too.

I ran back into the girls' yard, and there was the quiet sister all by herself. I ran past her, and she followed me into the girls' lavatory. My footsteps rang hard against cement and tile because of the taps I had nailed into my shoes. Her footsteps were soft, padding after me. There was no one in the lavatory but the two of us. I ran all around the rows of twenty-five open stalls to make sure of that. No sisters. I think we must have been playing hide-and-go-seek. She was not good at hiding by herself and usually followed her sister; they'd hide in the same place. They must have gotten separated. In this growing twilight, a child could hide and never be found.

I stopped abruptly in front of the sinks, and she came running toward me before she could stop herself, so that she almost collided with me. I walked closer. She backed away, puzzlement, then alarm in her eyes.

"You're going to talk," I said, my voice steady and normal, as it is when talking to the familiar, the weak, and the small. "I am going to make you talk, you sissy-girl." She stopped backing away and stood fixed.

I looked into her face so I could hate it close up. She wore black bangs, and her cheeks were pink and white. She was baby-soft. I thought that I could put my thumb on her nose and push it bonelessly in, indent her face. I could poke dimples into her cheeks. I could work her face around like dough. She stood still, and I did not want to look at her face anymore; I hated fragility. I walked around her, looked her up and down the way the Mexican and Negro girls did when they fought, so tough. I hated her weak neck, the way it did not support her head but let it droop; her head would fall backward. I stared at the curve of her nape. I wished I was able to see what my own neck looked like from the back and sides. I hoped it did not look like hers; I wanted a stout neck. I grew my hair long to hide it in case it was a flower-stem neck. I walked around to the front of her to hate her face some more.

I reached up and took the fatty part of her cheek, not dough, but meat, between my thumb and finger. This close, and I saw no pores. "Talk," I said. "Are you going to talk?" Her skin was fleshy, like squid out of which the glassy blades of bones had been pulled. I wanted tough skin, hard brown skin. I had callused my hands; I had scratched dirt to blacken the nails, which I cut straight across to make stubby fingers. I gave her face a squeeze. "Talk." When I let go, the pink rushed back into my white thumbprint on her skin. I walked around to her side. "Talk!" I shouted into the side of her head. Her straight hair hung, the same all these years, no ringlets or braids or permanents. I squeezed her other cheek. "Are you? Huh? Are you going to talk?" She tried to shake her head, but I had hold of her face. She had no muscles to jerk away. Her skin seemed to stretch. I let go in horror. What if it came away in my hand? "No, huh?" I said, rubbing the touch of her off my fingers. "Say 'No,' then,"

I said. I gave her another pinch and a twist. "Say 'No.'" She shook her head, her straight hair turning with her head, not swinging side to side like the pretty girls'. She was so neat. Her neatness bothered me. I hated the way she folded the wax paper from her lunch; she did not wad her brown paper bag and her school papers. I hated her clothes—the blue pastel cardigan, the white blouse with the collar that lay flat over the cardigan, the homemade flat, cotton skirt she wore when everybody else was wearing flared skirts. I hated pastels; I would wear black always. I squeezed again, harder, even though her cheek had a weak rubbery feeling I did not like. I squeezed one cheek, then the other, back and forth until the tears ran out of her eyes as if I had pulled them out. "Stop crying," I said, but although she habitually followed me around, she did not obey. Her eyes dripped; her nose dripped. She wiped her eyes with her papery fingers. The skin on her hands and arms seemed powdery-dry, like tracing paper, onion paper. I hated her fingers. I could snap them like breadsticks. I pushed her hands down. "Say 'Hi,'" I said. "'Hi.' Like that. Say your name. Go ahead. Say it. Or are you stupid? You're so stupid, you don't know your own name, is that it? When I say, 'What's your name?' you just blurt it out, O.K.? What's your name?" Last year the whole class had laughed at a boy who couldn't fill out a form because he didn't know his father's name. The teacher sighed, exasperated and was very sarcastic, "Don't you notice things? What does your mother call him?" she said. The class laughed at how dumb he was not to notice things. "She calls him father of me," he said. Even we laughed although we knew that his mother did not call his father by name, and a son does not know his father's name. We laughed and were relieved that our parents had had the foresight to tell us some names we could give the teachers. "If you're not stupid," I said to the quiet girl, "what's your name?" She shook her head, and some hair caught in the tears; wet black hair stuck to the side of the pink and white face. I reached up (she was taller than I) and took a strand of hair. I pulled it. "Well, then, let's honk your hair," I said. "Honk. Honk." Then I pulled the other side—"ho-o-n-nk"—a long pull; "ho-o-n-n-nk"—a longer pull. I could see her little white ears, like white cutworms curled underneath the hair. "Talk!" I yelled into each cutworm.

I looked right at her. "I know you talk," I said. "I've heard you." Her eyebrows flew up. Something in those black eyes was startled, and I pursued it. "I was walking past your house when you didn't know I was there. I heard you yell in English and in Chinese. You weren't just talking. You were shouting. I heard you shout. You were saying, 'Where are you?' Say that again. Go ahead, just the way you did at home." I yanked harder on the hair, but steadily, not jerking. I did not want to pull it out. "Go ahead. Say, 'Where are you?' Say it loud enough for your sister to come. Call her. Make her come help you. Call her name. I'll stop if she comes. So call. Go ahead."

She shook her head, her mouth curved down, crying. I could see her tiny white teeth, baby teeth. I wanted to grow big strong yellow teeth. "You do have a tongue," I said. "So use it." I pulled the hair at her temples, pulled the tears out of her eyes. "Say, 'Ow'" I said. "Just 'Ow.' Say, 'Let go.' Go ahead. Say it. I'll honk you again if you don't say, 'Let me alone.' Say, 'Leave me alone,' and I'll let you go. I will. I'll let go if you say it. You can stop this anytime you want to, you know. All you have to do is tell me to stop. Just say, 'Stop.' You're just asking for it, aren't you? You're just asking for another honk. Well then, I'll have to give you another honk. Say, 'Stop.'" But she didn't. I had to pull again and again.

Sounds did come out of her mouth, sobs, chokes, noises that were almost words. Snot ran out of her nose. She tried to wipe it on her hands, but there was too much of it. She used her sleeve. "You're disgusting," I told her. "Look at you, snot streaming down your nose, and you won't say a word to stop it. You're such a nothing." I moved behind her and pulled the hair growing out of her weak neck. I let go. I stood silent for a long time. Then I screamed, "Talk!" I would scare the words out of her. If she had had little bound feet, the toes twisted under the balls, I would have jumped up and landed on them—crunch!—stomped on them with my iron shoes. She cried hard, sobbing aloud. "Cry, 'Mama,'" I said. "Come on. Cry, 'Mama.' Say, 'Stop it.'"

I put my finger on her pointed chin. "I don't like you. I don't like the weak little toots you make on your flute. Wheeze. Wheeze. I don't like the way you don't swing at the ball. I don't like the way you're the last one chosen. I don't like the way you can't make a fist for tetherball. Why don't you make a fist? Come on. Get tough. Come on. Throw fists." I pushed at her long hands; they swung limply at her sides. Her fingers were so long, I thought maybe they had an extra joint. They couldn't possibly make fists like other people's. "Make a fist," I said. "Come on. Just fold those fingers up; fingers on the inside, thumbs on the outside. Say something. Honk me back. You're so tall, and you let me pick on you.

"Would you like a hanky? I can't get you one with embroidery on it or crocheting along the edges, but I'll get you some toilet paper if you tell me to. Go ahead. Ask me. I'll get it for you if you ask." She did not stop crying. "Why don't you scream, 'Help?'" I suggested. "Say, 'Help.' Go ahead." She cried on. "O.K. O.K. Don't talk. Just scream, and I'll let you go. Won't that feel good? Go ahead. Like this." I screamed not too loudly. My voice hit the tile and rang it as if I had thrown a rock at it. The stalls opened wider and the toilets wider and darker. Shadows leaned at angles I had not seen before. I was very late. Maybe a janitor had locked me in with this girl for the night. Her black eyes blinked and stared, blinked and stared. I felt dizzy from hunger. We had been in this lavatory together forever. My mother would call the police again if I didn't bring my sister home soon. "I'll let you go if you say just one word," I said. "You can even say 'a' or 'the,' and I'll let you go. Come on. Please." She didn't shake her head anymore, only cried steadily, so much water coming out of her. I could see the two duct holes where the tears welled out. Quarts of tears but no words. I grabbed her by the shoulder. I could feel bones. The light was coming in queerly through the frosted glass with the chicken wire embedded in it. Her crying was like an animal's—a seal's—and it echoed around the basement. "Do you want to stay here all night?" I asked. "Your mother is wondering what happened to her baby. You wouldn't want to have her mad at you. You'd better say something." I shook her shoulder. I pulled her hair again. I squeezed her face. "Come on! Talk! Talk! Talk!" She didn't seem to feel it anymore when I pulled her hair. "There's nobody here but you and me. This isn't a classroom or a playground or a crowd. I'm just one person. You can talk in front of one person. Don't make me pull harder and harder until you talk." But her hair seemed to stretch; she did not say a word. "I'm going to pull harder. Don't make me pull anymore, or your hair will come out and you're going to be bald. Do you want to be bald? You don't want to be bald, do you?"

Far away, coming from the edge of town, I heard whistles blow. The cannery was changing shifts, letting out the afternoon people, and still we were here at school. It was a sad sound—work done. The air was lonelier after the sound died.

"Why won't you talk?" I started to cry. What if I couldn't stop, and everyone would want to know what happened? "Now look what you've done," I scolded. "You're going to pay for this. I want to know why. And you're going to tell me why. You don't see I'm trying to help you out, do you? Do you want to be like this, dumb (do you know what dumb means?), your whole life? Don't you ever want to be a cheerleader? Or a pompom girl? What are you going to do for a living? Yeah, you're going to have to work because you can't be a housewife. Somebody has to marry you before you can be a housewife. And you, you are a plant. Do you know that? That's all you are if you don't talk. If you don't talk, you can't have a personality. You'll have no personality and no hair. You've got to let people know you have a personality and a brain. You think somebody is going to take care of you all your stupid life? You think you'll always have your big sister? You think somebody's going to marry you, is that it? Well, you're not the type that gets dates, let alone gets married. Nobody's going to notice you. And you have to talk for interviews, speak right up in front of the boss. Don't you know that? You're so dumb. Why do I waste my time on you?" Sniffling and snorting, I couldn't stop crying and talking at the same time. I kept wiping my nose on my arm, my sweater lost somewhere (probably not worn because my mother said to wear a sweater). It seemed as if I had spent my life in that basement, doing the worst thing I had yet done to another person. "I'm doing this for your own good," I said. "Don't you dare tell anyone I've been bad to you. Talk. Please talk."

I was getting dizzy from the air I was gulping. Her sobs and my sobs were bouncing wildly off the tile, sometimes together, sometimes alternating. "I don't understand why you won't say just one word," I cried, clenching my teeth. My knees were shaking, and I hung on to her hair to stand up. Another time I'd stayed too late, I had had to walk around two Negro kids who were bonking each other's head on the concrete. I went back later to see if the concrete had cracks in it. "Look. I'll give you something if you talk. I'll give you my pencil box. I'll buy you some candy. O.K.? What do you want? Tell me. Just say it, and I'll give it to you. Just say, 'yes,' or, 'O.K.,' or, 'Baby Ruth.'" But she didn't want anything.

I had stopped pinching her cheek because I did not like the feel of her skin. I would go crazy if it came away in my hands. "I skinned her," I would have to confess.

Suddenly I heard footsteps hurrying through the basement, and her sister ran into the lavatory calling her name. "Oh, there you are," I said. "We've been waiting for you. I was only trying to teach her to talk. She wouldn't cooperate, though." Her sister went into one of the stalls and got handfuls of toilet paper and wiped her off. Then we found my sister, and we walked home together. "Your family really ought to force her to speak," I advised all the way home. "You mustn't pamper her."

The world is sometimes just, and I spent the next eighteen months sick in bed with a mysterious illness. There was no pain and no symptoms, though the middle line in my left palm broke in two. Instead of starting junior high school, I lived like the Victorian recluses I read about. I had a rented hospital bed in the living room, where I watched soap operas on TV, and my family cranked me up and down. I saw no one but my family, who took good care of me. I could have no visitors, no other relatives, no villagers. My bed was against the west window, and I watched the seasons change the peach tree. I had a bell to ring for help. I used a bedpan. It was the best year and a half of my life. Nothing happened.

But one day my mother, the doctor, said, "You're ready to get up today. It's time to get up and go to school." I walked about outside to get my legs working, leaning on a staff I cut from the peach tree. The sky and trees, the sun were immense—no longer framed by a window, no longer grayed with a fly screen. I sat down on the sidewalk in amazement—the night, the stars. But at school I had to figure out again how to talk. I met again the poor girl I had tormented. She had not changed. She wore the same clothes, hair cut, and manner as when we were in elementary school, no make-up on the pink and white face, while the other Asian girls were starting to tape their eyelids. She continued to be able to read aloud. But there was hardly any reading aloud anymore, less and less as we got into high school.

I was wrong about nobody taking care of her. Her sister became a clerk-typist and stayed unmarried. They lived with their mother and father. She did not have to leave the house except to go to the movies. She was supported. She was protected by her family, as they would normally have done in China if they could have afforded it, not sent off to school with strangers, ghosts, boys.

COMPULSORY HETEROSEXUALITY AND LESBIAN EXISTENCE

Adrienne Rich

The essay from which the following excerpt is taken provoked a great deal of discussion when it appeared originally in the feminist journal *Signs* in 1980. In a foreword to a 1982 reprinting, its author Adrienne Rich explained that the essay was written "to challenge the erasure of lesbian existence from so much of scholarly feminist literature," "to encourage heterosexual feminists to examine heterosexuality as a political institution which disempowers women—and to change it," and "to sketch, at least, some bridge over the gap between *lesbian* and *feminist.*"

Rich is a prize-winning poet and essayist whose work appeals to a wide audience. The essay excerpted here was reprinted in *Blood, Bread, and Poetry: Selected Prose 1979–1985* (1986). Rich's *Commencement Address at Smith College, 1979* appears later in this book.

The assumption that "most women are innately heterosexual" stands as a theoretical and political stumbling block for feminism. It remains a tenable assumption partly because lesbian existence has been written out of history or catalogued under disease, partly because it has been treated as exceptional rather than intrinsic, partly because to acknowledge that for women heterosexuality may not be a "preference" at all but something that has had to be imposed, managed, organized, propagandized, and maintained by force is an immense step to take if you consider yourself freely and "innately" heterosexual. Yet the failure to examine heterosexuality as an

COMPULSORY HETEROSEXUALITY AND LESBIAN EXISTENCE   From Adrienne Rich, *Blood, Bread, and Poetry: Selected Prose 1979–1985* (New York: W. W. Norton, 1986) 15–57. Reprinted by permission of the author and W. W. Norton & Company, Inc. Copyright © 1986 by Adrienne Rich.

institution is like failing to admit that the economic system called capitalism or the caste system of racism is maintained by a variety of forces, including both physical violence and false consciousness. To take the step of questioning heterosexuality as a "preference" or "choice" for women—and to do the intellectual and emotional work that follows—will call for a special quality of courage in heterosexually identified feminists, but I think the rewards will be great: a freeing-up of thinking, the exploring of new paths, the shattering of another great silence, new clarity in personal relationships.

I have chosen to use the terms *lesbian existence* and *lesbian continuum* because the word *lesbianism* has a clinical and limiting ring. *Lesbian existence* suggests both the fact of the historical presence of lesbians and our continuing creation of the meaning of that existence. I mean the term *lesbian continuum* to include a range—through each woman's life and throughout history—of woman-identified experience, not simply the fact that a woman has had or consciously desired genital sexual experience with another woman. If we expand it to embrace many more forms of primary intensity between and among women, including the sharing of a rich inner life, the bonding against male tyranny, the giving and receiving of practical and political support, if we can also hear it in such associations as *marriage resistance* and the "haggard" behavior identified by Mary Daly (obsolete meanings: "intractable," "willful," "wanton," and "unchaste," "a woman reluctant to yield to wooing"), we begin to grasp breadths of female history and psychology which have lain out of reach as a consequence of limited, mostly clinical, definitions of *lesbianism*.

Lesbian existence comprises both the breaking of a taboo and the rejection of a compulsory way of life. It is also a direct or indirect attack on male right of access to women. But it is more than these, although we may first begin to perceive it as a form of naysaying to patriarchy, an act of resistance. It has, of course, included isolation, self-hatred, breakdown, alcoholism, suicide, and intrawoman violence; we romanticize at our peril what it means to love and act against the grain, and under heavy penalties; and lesbian existence has been lived (unlike, say, Jewish or Catholic existence) without access to any knowledge of a tradition, a continuity, a social underpinning. The destruction of records and memorabilia and letters documenting the realities of lesbian existence must be taken very seriously as a means of keeping heterosexuality compulsory for women, since what has been kept from our knowledge is joy, sensuality, courage, and community, as well as guilt, self-betrayal, and pain.

Lesbians have historically been deprived of a political existence through "inclusion" as female versions of male homosexuality. To equate lesbian existence with male homosexuality because each is stigmatized is to erase female reality once again. Part of the history of lesbian existence is, obviously, to be found where lesbians, lacking a coherent female community, have shared a kind of social life and common cause with homosexual men. But there are differences: women's lack of economic and cultural privilege relative to men; qualitative differences in female and male relationships—for example, the patterns of anonymous sex among male homosexuals, and the pronounced ageism in male homosexual standards of sexual attractiveness. I perceive the lesbian experience as being, like motherhood, a profoundly *female* experience, with particular oppressions, meanings, and potentialities we cannot comprehend as long as we simply bracket it with other sexually stigmatized existences. Just as the term *parenting* serves to conceal the particular and significant reality of being a parent who is actually a mother, the term *gay* may serve the purpose of blurring the very outlines we need to discern, which are of crucial value for feminism and for the freedom of women as a group.

As the term *lesbian* has been held to limiting, clinical associations in its patriarchal definition, female friendship and comradeship have been set apart from the erotic, thus limiting the erotic itself. But as we deepen and broaden the range of what we define as lesbian existence, as we delineate a lesbian continuum, we begin to discover the erotic in female terms: as that which is unconfined to any single part of the body or solely to the body itself; as an energy not only diffuse but, as Audre Lorde has described it, omnipresent in "the sharing of joy, whether physical, emotional, psychic," and in the sharing of work; as the empowering joy which "makes us less willing to accept powerlessness, or those other supplied states of being which are not native to me, such as resignation, despair, self-effacement, depression, self-denial." In another context, writing of women and work, I quoted the autobiographical passage in which the poet H. D. described how her friend Bryher supported her in persisting with the visionary experience which was to shape her mature work:

> I knew that this experience, this writing-on-the-wall before me, could not be shared
> with anyone except the girl who stood so bravely there beside me. This girl said
> without hesitation, "Go on." It was she really who had the detachment and integrity of
> the Pythoness of Delphi. But it was I, battered and dissociated . . . who was seeing the
> pictures, and who was reading the writing or granted the inner vision. Or perhaps, in
> some sense, we were "seeing" it together, for without her, admittedly, I could not have
> gone on.

If we consider the possibility that all women—from the infant suckling at her mother's breast, to the grown woman experiencing orgasmic sensations while suckling her own child, perhaps recalling her mother's milk smell in her own, to two women, like Virginia Woolf's Chloe and Olivia, who share a laboratory, to the woman dying at ninety, touched and handled by women—exist on a lesbian continuum, we can see ourselves as moving in and out of this continuum, whether we identify ourselves as lesbian or not.

We can then connect aspects of woman identification as diverse as the impudent, intimate girl friendships of eight or nine year olds and the banding together of those women of the twelfth and fifteenth centuries known as Beguines who "shared houses, rented to one another, bequeathed houses to their room-mates . . . in cheap subdivided houses in the artisans' area of town," who "practiced Christian virtue on their own, dressing and living simply and not associating with men," who earned their livings as spinsters, bakers, nurses, or ran schools for young girls, and who managed—until the Church forced them to disperse—to live independent both of marriage and of conventual restrictions. It allows us to connect these women with the more celebrated "Lesbians" of the women's school around Sappho of the seventh century B.C., with the secret sororities and economic networks reported among African women, and with the Chinese marriage-resistance sisterhoods—communities of women who refused marriage or who, if married, often refused to consummate their marriages and soon left their husbands, the only women in China who were not footbound and who, Agnes Smedley tells us, welcomed the births of daughters and organized successful women's strikes in the silk mills. It allows us to connect and compare disparate individual instances of marriage resistance: for example, the strategies available to Emily Dickinson, a nineteenth-century white woman genius, with the strategies available to Zora Neale Hurston, a twentieth-century Black woman genius. Dickinson never married, had tenuous intellectual friendships with men, lived self-convented in her genteel father's house in Amherst, and wrote a lifetime of passionate letters to her sister-in-law Sue Gilbert and a smaller group of such letters to her friend Kate Scott Anthon. Hurston married twice but soon left each husband, scrambled her way from Florida to Harlem to Columbia University to Haiti and finally back to Florida, moved in and out of white patronage and poverty, professional success, and failure; her survival relationships were all with women, beginning with her mother. Both of these women in their vastly different circumstances were marriage resisters, committed to their own work and selfhood, and were later characterized as "apolitical." Both were drawn to men of intellectual quality; for both of them women provided the ongoing fascination and sustenance of life.

If we think of heterosexuality as *the* natural emotional and sensual inclination for women, lives such as these are seen as deviant, as pathological, or as emotionally and sensually deprived. Or, in more recent and permissive jargon, they are banalized as "life styles." And the work of such women, whether merely the daily work of individual or collective survival and resistance or the work of the writer, the activist, the reformer, the anthropologist, or the artist—the work of self-creation—is undervalued, or seen as the bitter fruit of "penis envy" or the sublimation of repressed eroticism or the meaningless rant of a "man-hater." But when we turn the lens of vision and consider the degree to which and the methods whereby heterosexual "preference" has actually been imposed on women, not only can we understand differently the meaning of individual lives and work, but we can begin to recognize a central fact of women's history: that women have always resisted male tyranny. A feminism of action, often though not always without a theory, has constantly re-emerged in every culture and in every period. We can then begin to study women's struggle against powerlessness, women's radical rebellion, not just in male-defined "concrete revolutionary situations" but in all the situations male ideologies have not perceived as revolutionary—for example, the refusal of some women to produce children, aided at great risk by other women; the refusal to produce a higher standard of living and leisure for men. . . . We can no longer have patience with Dinnerstein's view that women have simply collaborated with men in the "sexual arrangements" of history. We begin to observe behavior, both in history and in individual biography, that has hitherto been invisible or misnamed, behavior which often constitutes, given the limits of the counterforce exerted in a given time and place, radical rebellion. And we can connect these rebellions and the necessity for them with the physical passion of woman for woman which is central to lesbian existence: the erotic sensuality which has been, precisely, the most violently erased fact of female experience.

IN A DIFFERENT VOICE

Carol Gilligan

Carol Gilligan, a Professor of Education at Harvard University, was troubled by the fact that women rarely scored at the highest stages on traditional tests of moral development. The conclusion frequently drawn from such findings was that women lacked moral maturity, but in Gilligan's view, an equally likely explanation for women's lower scores was the failure of the prevailing theories to incorporate the full range of human experience. Gilligan decided to study women's moral reasoning herself by interviewing women about their real-life moral decision making. The results of her research, reported in her book *In a Different Voice* (1982), excerpted here, suggested a distinctive morality based on the importance of relationships and an ethic of care.

Ms. magazine named Carol Gilligan "Woman of the Year" for 1983. The editors' citation read: "Gilligan's work has created a new appreciation for a previously uncatalogued female sensibility, as well as possibilities for new understanding between the genders. But her contributions go beyond these. Because we live in a world where our survival may depend on our sense of connection, Gilligan's work has implications for a rather different kind of future—one in which humanity takes its cues not from Big Brother, but from sisters, mothers and daughters."

"It is obvious," Virginia Woolf says, "that the values of women differ very often from the values which have been made by the other sex." Yet, she adds, "it is the masculine values that prevail." As a result, women come to question the normality of their feelings and to alter their judgments in deference to the opinion of others. In the nineteenth century novels written by women, Woolf sees at work "a mind which was slightly pulled from the straight and made to alter its clear vision in deference to external authority." The same deference to the values and opinions of others can be seen in the judgments of twentieth century women. The difficulty women experience in finding or speaking publicly in their own voices emerges repeatedly in the form of qualification and self-doubt, but also in intimations of a divided judgment, a public assessment and private assessment which are fundamentally at odds.

Yet the deference and confusion that Woolf criticizes in women derive from the values she sees as their strength. Women's deference is rooted not only in their social subordination but also in the substance of their moral concern. Sensitivity to the needs of others and the assumption of responsibility for taking care lead women to attend to voices other than their own and to include in their judgment other points of view. Women's moral weakness, manifest in an apparent diffusion and confusion of judgment, is thus inseparable from women's moral strength, an overriding concern with relationships and responsibilities. The reluctance to judge may itself be indicative of the care and concern for others that infuse the psychology of women's development and are responsible for what is generally seen as problematic in its nature.

Thus women not only define themselves in a context of human relationship but also judge themselves in terms of their ability to care. Women's place in man's life cycle has been that of nurturer, caretaker, and helpmate, the weaver of those networks of relationships on which she in turn relies. But while women have thus taken care of men, men have, in their theories of psychological development, as in their economic arrangements, tended to assume or devalue that care. When the focus on individuation and individual achievement extends into adulthood and maturity is equated with personal autonomy, concern with relationships appears as a weakness of women rather than as a human strength.

The discrepancy between womanhood and adulthood is nowhere more evident than in the studies on sex-role stereotypes reported by Broverman, Vogel,

Broverman, Clarkson, and Rosenkrantz. The repeated finding of these studies is that the qualities deemed necessary for adulthood—the capacity for autonomous thinking, clear decision-making, and responsible action—are those associated with masculinity and considered undesirable as attributes of the feminine self. The stereotypes suggest a splitting of love and work that relegates expressive capacities to women while placing instrumental abilities in the masculine domain. Yet looked at from a different perspective, these stereotypes reflect a conception of adulthood that is itself out of balance, favoring the separateness of the individual self over connection to others, and leaning more toward an autonomous life of work than toward the interdependence of love and care.

The discovery now being celebrated by men in mid-life of the importance of intimacy, relationships, and care is something that women have known from the beginning. However, because that knowledge in women has been considered "intuitive" or "instinctive," a function of anatomy coupled with destiny, psychologists have neglected to describe its development. In my research, I have found that women's moral development centers on the elaboration of that knowledge and thus delineates a critical line of psychological development in the lives of both of the sexes. The subject of moral development not only provides the final illustration of the reiterative pattern in the observation and assessment of sex differences in the literature on human development, but also indicates more particularly why the nature and significance of women's development has been for so long obscured and shrouded in mystery.

The criticism that Freud makes of women's sense of justice, seeing it as compromised in its refusal of blind impartiality, reappears not only in the work of Piaget but also in that of Kohlberg. While in Piaget's account of the moral judgment of the child, girls are an aside, a curiosity to whom he devotes four brief entries in an index that omits "boys" altogether because "the child" is assumed to be male, in the research from which Kohlberg derives his theory, females simply do not exist. Kohlberg's six stages that describe the development of moral judgment from childhood to adulthood are based empirically on a study of eighty-four boys whose development Kohlberg has followed for a period of over twenty years. Although Kohlberg claims universality for his stage sequence, those groups not included in his original sample rarely reach his higher stages. Prominent among those who thus appear to be deficient in moral development when measured by Kohlberg's scale are women, whose judgments seem to exemplify the third stage of his six-stage sequence. At this stage morality is conceived in interpersonal terms and goodness is equated with helping and pleasing others. This conception of goodness is considered by Kohlberg and Kramer to be functional in the lives of mature women insofar as their lives take place in the home. Kohlberg and Kramer imply that only if women enter the traditional arena of male activity will they recognize the inadequacy of this moral perspective and progress like men toward higher stages where relationships are subordinated to rules (stage four) and rules to universal principles of justice (stages five and six).

Yet herein lies a paradox, for the very traits that traditionally have defined the "goodness" of women, their care for and sensitivity to the needs of others, are those that mark them as deficient in moral development. In this version of moral development, however, the conception of maturity is derived from the study of men's lives and reflects the importance of individuation in their development. Piaget, challenging the common impression that a developmental theory is built like a pyramid from its base in infancy, points out that a conception of development instead hangs from its vertex of maturity, the point toward which progress is traced. Thus, a change in the definition of maturity does not simply alter the description of the highest stage but recasts the understanding of development, changing the entire account.

When one begins with the study of women and derives developmental constructs from their lives, the outline of a moral conception different from that described by Freud, Piaget, or Kohlberg begins to emerge and informs a different description of development. In this conception, the moral problem arises from conflicting responsibilities rather than from competing rights and requires for its resolution a mode of thinking that is contextual and narrative rather than formal and abstract. This conception of morality as concerned with the activity of care centers moral development around the understanding of responsibility and relationships, just as the conception of morality as fairness ties moral development to the understanding of rights and rules.

THE POLITICS OF BIOLOGY: A CONVERSATION WITH RUTH HUBBARD

Mark Davidson

Ruth Hubbard, a prize-winning biologist, is a leader in the current feminist critique of science. She challenges the objectivity of scientific theories and research claiming biologically-based behavioral differences between the sexes. According to Hubbard, most assumptions of difference have been constructed by male scientists to keep women in their current roles. And "It is well to be suspicious when 'objective science' confirms long-standing prejudices," she cautions.

Ruth Hubbard is the author or coauthor of many books, most recently *The Politics of Women's Biology* (1990) and *Exploding the Gene Myth* (with Elijah Wald, 1993). She is currently an Emeritus Professor of Biology at Harvard University.

In October, 1986, at an "Images of Women" conference at Scripps College in Claremont, Calif., you lectured on "The Politics of Women's Biology." In what sense do you regard women's biology as political?

Women's biology for the most part has been described by physicians and scientists who have been mostly economically privileged white males with personal and political interests in describing women in ways that make it appear natural for women to fulfill roles essential to the well-being of those privileged men.

Hence, the role of "the little woman"?

Exactly. Women commonly are assigned social roles that become self-fulfilling prophecies. If the social establishment wills it, we are frail. But we are physically robust in societies that demand *that* quality of us in the field, factory, or home. By describing us, society's norms actually prescribe for us.

THE POLITICS OF BIOLOGY: A CONVERSATION WITH RUTH HUBBARD   From Mark Davidson, "'You've Got a Long Way to Go, Baby': A Conversation About the Women's Movement with Ruth Hubbard," *USA Today* Sept. 1987: 94–95. Copyright © by the Society for the Advancement of Education.

A good example is the average gender differences in height. The female hormone estrogen has the effect of slowing the growth of the long bones, and therefore girls do not grow as fast or as many years after the onset of puberty as boys. But social factors such as diet and the way of life can delay the onset of puberty and produce taller women—a phenomenon confirmed by recent data showing that many tall female athletes began menstruating later than is common in our society.

Physical differences between male and female athletes have been biologically misinterpreted by researchers who ignored the fact that boys in our society are traditionally encouraged to be more active than girls. When women were first allowed to run marathons, about 20 years ago, the difference between the male and female top records was almost an hour and a half. Now, after two decades of similar opportunity as runners, the women have reduced the difference to 15 minutes. So, in this realm and others, there's no telling what a woman's biological limits are—or if she indeed has any biological limits as compared with men.

And, of course, this same principle applies to women in all sorts of activity, both physical and mental. Women have been conditioned so long and so profoundly to think of themselves as inferior to men and have been given so much less chance to develop their abilities—from construction work to theoretical physics—that we have yet to see what women can do.

Back in 1952, anthropologist Ashley Montagu, in his The Natural Superiority of Women, *argued that men are biologically inferior to women because men are really incomplete females. Are you familiar with that viewpoint?*

Yes. And more recently, physician-author Mary Jane Sherfey and others have advanced the notion that the basic development pattern is female and that males are just variants on the female pattern. But that's really no more scientific than the old notion that the basic pattern is male. I don't see anything useful in responding to discrimination against women by attempting to prove that women are biologically superior. The biological differences between men and women do not support the idea that either sex is superior.

Given your opposition to any implication of gender superiority, how do you feel about the idea of "women's intuition"?

I think the effect of that idea may be sexist. Intuition is nice, but it's something you learn to have if you don't have power. It's something you acquire when you have to figure out what people who have more power than you do *want*—without being able to *ask* them.

The "typically women's traits" have a lot to do with women having learned certain skills which we begin to learn as little children. Little girls act like women in many ways because they know that's what they'll grow up to be. And little boys quite early get to act like men in the same manner.

So this early training in stereotypical behavior is another way that women in our society are shortchanged?

Women are shortchanged in terms of sheer power. But men in this system of sex stereotyping are also shortchanged, with results I regard as tragic. Men in our society are not generally permitted to express emotion other than through anger, aggression, and sex. And that limits the male repertory of interacting with each other and with women and with children.

Coming to understand that made it possible for me to understand the extreme discomfort I have felt when I have watched fathers and other men play with kids. A man who is clearly fond of a kid feels compelled to engage in roughhousing, such as boxing, because that's the only way he feels permitted to express his love for that kid. He can't just pick up the child and hug it and stroke it. As far as the emotional vocabulary is concerned, men are brought up to be practically mute. And I think that causes a great deal of suffering for men, women, and children.

What are the biological differences between men and women that you feel are beyond dispute?

I'd say the obvious reproductive differences. . . .

Including the hormones?

With the hormones, the answer is not that simple. Women and men have all the same hormones. The differences involve the proportions of the hormones, and those can change over time and under varying circumstances.

The biological differences between men and women consist of the basic reproductive structure and functions that lead to men producing sperm, women producing eggs, women gestating embryos inside their body, and women being able to lactate those babies once they come out—though Margaret Mead and other anthropologists have cited anthropological evidence that men can lactate.

Apart from the basic reproductive differences, are there any innate behavioral differences between men and women?

There are probably biologically innate differences between all of us as individuals. And there are many more differences *among* women and *among* men than there are *between* women and men. Even for the supposedly innate female dedication to child-nurturing, you're just as likely to find men with that dedication and women who lack it.

So whatever the social role or job is, society should look for the individual who can do it best regardless of gender. The only exceptions I can think of are sperm donor and surrogate mother.

SOME QUESTIONS TO ASK YOUR DAUGHTER BEFORE SHE CHOOSES HER HIGH SCHOOL

Emma Willard School

When Emma Willard founded her school in 1814, she envisioned a different type of education for girls than that which was then available. Her school offered girls a curriculum comparable, though not identical, to that which their brothers received—the higher subjects, including mathematics, biology, history, literature, geography, philosophy, and modern languages, as well as traditional subjects suited to her particular nature and roles. The school still provides an alternative to the regular coeducational experience.

In 1981, Emma Willard School launched a four-year longitudinal study of the psychological development of adolescent girls, under the direction of Carol Gilligan. The study was published as a set of essays entitled *Making Connections: Essays on the Relational Worlds of Adolescent Girls at Emma Willard School* (1990), which Gilligan coedited with Nona Lyons and Trudy Hanmer, Associate Principal at Emma Willard School.

The following is an advertisement for Emma Willard School that appeared in *The New York Times* in 1994.

EMMA WILLARD SCHOOL

EXTRAORDINARY EDUCATION FOR GIRLS SINCE 1814.

What does photosynthesis have to do with the "Greenhouse Effect"? • What do these words mean: hypotenuse, serf, protagonist, ulna, onomatopoeia, declension, suffrage? • Why are some twins fraternal and others identical? • What do The Rolling Stones have to do with Shakespeare? • Should a good essay always begin with its conclusion? • What's the difference between a character in a book and a person's character? • How does a camera separate us from reality? • Are any of your classes ever taught together . . . say, English and history? • Among the high schools you are considering, which of these student honors are held by girls: class president, student council president, editor of the yearbook or newspaper, president of the debate club? • How much time do you spend on homework? • How much time do you spend getting dressed for school? • How often do you try to answer questions in class and not get called on? • Can you balance being feminine with success?

Your daughter's answers will give you an update on her junior high achievement in "The Three R's," and a sense of her critical thinking and problem-solving abilities.

As you and your daughter consider her choice of high schools, remember: Not all schools are created equal for girls.

Front-page articles in this newspaper and other national media have reported on research by psychologists and educators at such universities as Harvard, American, and Michigan whose studies reveal that coeducation perpetuates sexual stereotyping and an academic environment in which boys prevail at girls' expense:

Boys are called on four times more often and are interrupted far less • boys dominate discussions • boys are questioned more and challenged to take intellectual risks • reports of girls' sexual harassment by male classmates are increasing • juniors and seniors at girls' schools have much higher self-esteem and more confidence about life and leadership than similar girls at coed schools • girls at single-gender schools are more serious about academics than their coed counterparts and significantly outperform them on SATs and Achievement tests • in public schools, single-gender classrooms for girls in math and science yield higher results.

Clearly, some girls do manage to make themselves heard. However, research shows that even when girls *do* achieve, they feel their achievement is an anomaly.

Schools such as Emma Willard, the first boarding and day school in America to offer girls an education equal to that of their brothers, are uniquely qualified to prepare girls to excel and to believe in themselves as achievers; to recognize that success need not be at odds with their femininity.

We believe girls should read brilliant literature *and* write and speak brilliantly; study history *and* possess the ideals and self-confidence to take their places on the world's stage; learn that mathematics describes the music of the spheres *and* the balance sheets of corporations they may, as women, lead.

Reprinted with the permission of Emma Willard School.

There is a critical connection between self-confidence and success—in academics, in relationships, in careers. A girl's high school years are the time for academic rigor—and getting the right answers at home and at school—as she prepares for a life of promise and responsibility.

ARE WOMEN MORALLY SUPERIOR TO MEN?
Katha Pollitt

Research claiming that relationships are central to women's sense of self has inspired a shift in social scientists' theories about women. In the following essay, Katha Pollitt offers a critique of the new "difference" theories and examines their implications for women. Pollitt, an award-winning poet and essayist, has been applauded for the clarity and intelligence of her writing.

 Some years ago I was invited by the wife of a well-known writer to sign a women's peace petition. It made the points such documents usually make: that women, as mothers, caregivers and nurturers, have a special awareness of the precariousness of human life, see through jingoism and cold war rhetoric and would prefer nations to work out their difficulties peacefully so that the military budget could be diverted to schools and hospitals and housing. It had the literary tone such documents usually have, as well—at once superior and plaintive, as if the authors didn't know whether they were bragging or begging. We are wiser than you poor deluded menfolk, was the subtext, so will you please-please-please listen to your moms?

To sign or not to sign? Of course, I was all for peace. But was I for peace *as a woman?* I wasn't a mother then—I wasn't even an aunt. Did my lack of nurturing credentials make my grasp of the horrors of war and the folly of the arms race only theoretical, like a white person's understanding of racism? Were mothers the natural leaders of the peace movement, to whose judgment nonmothers, male and female, must defer, because after all we couldn't *know,* couldn't *feel* that tenderness toward fragile human life that a woman who had borne and raised children had experienced? On the other hand, I was indeed a woman. Was motherhood with its special wisdom somehow deep inside me, to be called upon when needed, like my uterus?

Complicating matters in a way relevant to this essay was my response to the famous writer's wife herself. Here was a woman in her 50s, her child-raising long behind her. Was motherhood the only banner under which she could gain a foothold on civic life? Perhaps so. Her only other public identity was that of a wife, and wifehood, even to a famous man, isn't much to claim credit for these days. ("To think I spent all those years ironing his underpants!" she once burst out to a mutual friend.) Motherhood was what she had in the work-and-accomplishment department, so it was understandable that she try to maximize its moral status. But I was not in her

ARE WOMEN MORALLY SUPERIOR TO MEN?   From Katha Pollitt, "Are Women Morally Superior to Men?" *The Nation* 28 Dec. 1992: 799–807. Copyright © 1992 The Nation Company, Inc. Reprinted from The Nation magazine.

situation: I was a writer, a single woman, a jobholder. By sending me a petition from which I was excluded even as I was invited to add my name, perhaps she was telling me that, by leading a nondomestic life, I had abandoned the moral high ground, was "acting like a man," but could redeem myself by acknowledging the moral pre-eminence of the class of women I refused to join.

The ascription of particular virtues—compassion, patience, common sense, non-violence—to mothers, and the tendency to conflate "mothers" with "women," has a long history in the peace movement but goes way beyond issues of war and peace. At present it permeates discussions of just about every field, from management training to theology. Indeed, although the media like to caricature feminism as denying the existence of sexual differences, for the women's movement and its opponents alike "difference" is where the action is. Thus, business writers wonder if women's nurturing, intuitive qualities will make them better executives. Educators suggest that female students suffer in classrooms that emphasize competition over coopera-tion. Women politicians tout their playground-honed negotiating skills, their egoless devotion to public service, their gender-based commitment to fairness and caring. A variety of political causes—environmentalism, animal rights, even vegetarianism—are promoted as logical extensions of women's putative peacefulness, closeness to nature, horror of aggression and concern for others' health. (Indeed, to some extent these causes are arenas in which women fight one another over definitions of femininity, which is why debates over disposable diapers and over the wearing of fur—both rather minor sources of harm, even if their opponents are right—loom so large and are so acrimonious.) In the arts, we hear a lot about what women's "real" subjects, methods and materials ought to be. Painting is male. Rhyme is male. Plot is male. Perhaps, say the Lacanian feminists, even logic and language are male. What is female? Nature. Blood. Milk. Communal gatherings. The moon. Quilts.

Haven't we been here before? Indeed we have. Woman as a sharer and carer, woman as earth mother, woman as guardian of all the small rituals that knit together a family and a community, woman as beneath, above, or beyond such manly concerns as law, reason, abstract ideas—these images are as old as time. Open defenders of male supremacy have always used them to declare women flatly inferior to men; covert ones use them to place women on a pedestal as too good for this naughty world. Thus, in the *Eumenides*, Aeschylus celebrated law as the defeat by males of primitive female principles of bloodguilt and vengeance, while the Ayatollah Kho-meini thought women should be barred from judgeships because they were too ten-derhearted. Different rationale, same outcome: Women, because of their indifference to an impersonal moral order, cannot be full participants in civic life.

There exists an equally ancient line of thought, however, that uses femininity to posit a subversive challenge to the social order: Think of Sophocles' Antigone, who resists tyranny out of love and piety, or Aristophanes' Lysistrata, the original women's strike for peace-nik, or Shakespeare's Portia, who champions mercy against the savage letter of the law. For reasons of power, money and persistent social structures, the vision of the morally superior woman can never overcome the dominant ethos in reality but exists alongside it as a kind of permanent wish or hope: If only powerful and powerless could change places, and the meek inherit the earth! Thus, it is perpetually being rediscovered, dressed in fashionable clothes and presented, despite its antiquity, as a radical new idea.

In the 1950s, which we think of as the glory days of traditional sex roles, the anthropologist Ashley Montagu argued in "The Natural Superiority of Women" that females had it all over males in every way that counted, including the possession of two X chromosomes that made them stabler, saner and healthier than men, with their X and Y. Montagu's essay, published in *The Saturday Review* and later expanded to a book, is witty and high-spirited and, interestingly, anticipates the current feminist challenge to male-defined categories. (He notes, for example, that while men are stronger than women in the furniture-moving sense, women are stronger than men when faced with extreme physical hardship and tests of endurance; so when we say that men are stronger than women, we are equating strength with what men have.) But the fundamental thrust of Montagu's essay was to confirm traditional gender roles while revising the way we value them: Having proved to his own satisfaction that women could scale the artistic and intellectual heights, he argued that most would (that is, should) refrain, because women's true genius was "humanness," and their real mission was to "humanize" men before men blew up the world. And that, he left no doubt, was a full-time job.

Contemporary proponents of "difference feminism" advance a variation on the same argument, without Montagu's puckish humor. Instead of his whimsical chromosomal explanation, we get the psychoanalytic one proposed by Nancy Chodorow in *The Reproduction of Mothering*: Daughters define themselves by relating to their mothers, the primary love object of all children, and are therefore empathic, relationship-oriented, nonhierarchical and interested in forging consensus; sons must separate from their mothers, and are therefore individualistic, competitive, resistant to connection with others and focused on abstract rules and rights. Chodorow's theory has become a kind of mantra of difference feminism, endlessly cited as if it explained phenomena we all agree are universal, though this is far from the case. The central question Chodorow poses—Why are women the primary caregivers of children?—could not even be asked before the advent of modern birth control, and can be answered without resorting to psychology. Historically, women have taken care of children because high fertility and lack of other options left most of them no choice. Those rich enough to avoid personally raising their children often did, as Rousseau observed to his horror.

Popularizers of Chodorow water down and sentimentalize her thesis. They embrace her proposition that traditional mothering produces "relational" women and "autonomous" men but forget her less congenial argument that it also results in sexual inequality, misogyny and hostility between mothers and daughters, who, like sons, desire independence but have a much harder time achieving it. Unlike her followers, Chodorow does not romanticize mothering: "Exclusive single parenting is bad for mother and child alike," she concludes; in a tragic paradox, female "caring," "intimacy" and "nurturance" do not soften but *produce* aggressive, competitive, hypermasculine men.

Thus, in her immensely influential book *In a Different Voice*, Carol Gilligan uses Chodorow to argue that the sexes make moral decisions according to separate criteria: women according to an "ethic of care," men according to an "ethic of rights." Deborah Tannen, in the best-selling *You Just Don't Understand*, claims that men and women grow up with "different cultural backgrounds"—the single-sex world of children's play in which girls cooperate and boys compete—"so talk between men and women is cross-cultural communication." While these two writers differ in important ways—Tannen, writing at a more popular level, is by far the clearer thinker and the one more interested in analyzing actual human interactions in daily life—they share important liabilities, too. Both largely confine their observations to the white middle class—especially Gilligan, much of whose elaborate theory of gendered ethics rests on interviews with a handful of Harvard–Radcliffe undergraduates—and seem unaware that this limits the applicability of their data. (In her new book, *Meeting at the Crossroads*, Gilligan makes a similar mistake. Her whole theory of "loss of relationship" as the central trauma of female adolescence rests on interviews with students at one posh single-sex private school.) Both massage their findings to fit their theories: Gilligan's male and female responses are actually quite similar to each other, as experimenters have subsequently shown by removing the names and asking subjects to try to sort the test answers by gender; Tannen is quick to attribute blatant rudeness or sexism in male speech to anxiety, helplessness, fear of loss of face—anything, indeed, but rudeness and sexism. Both look only at what people say, not what they do. For Tannen this isn't a decisive objection because verbal behavior is her subject, although it limits the applicability of her findings to other areas of behavior; for Gilligan, it is a major obstacle, unless you believe, as she apparently does, that the way people say they would resolve farfetched hypothetical dilemmas—Should a poor man steal drugs to save his dying wife?—tells us how they reason in real-life situations or, more important, what they do.

But the biggest problem with Chodorovian accounts of gender difference is that they credit the differences they find to essential, universal features of male and female psychosexual development rather than to the economic and social positions men and women hold, or to the actual power differences between individual men and women. In *The Mismeasure of Woman,* her trenchant and witty attack on contemporary theories of gender differences, Carol Tavris points out that much of what can be said about women applies as well to poor people, who also tend to focus more on family and relationships and less on work and self-advancement; to behave deferentially with those more socially powerful; and to appear to others more emotional and "intuitive" than rational and logical in their thinking. Then, too, there is the question of whether the difference theorists are measuring anything beyond their own willingness to think in stereotypes. If Chodorow is right, relational women and autonomous men should be the norm, but are they? Or is it just that women and men use different language, have different social styles, different explanations for similar behavior? Certainly, it is easy to find in one's own acquaintance, as well as in the world at large, men and women who don't fit the models. Difference feminists like to attribute ruthlessness, coldness, and hyperrationality in successful women— Margaret Thatcher is the standard example—to the fact that men control the networks of power and permit only women like themselves to rise. But I've met plenty of loudmouthed, insensitive, aggressive women who are stay-at-home mothers and secretaries and nurses. And I know plenty of sweet, unambitious men whose main satisfactions lie in their social, domestic and romantic lives, although not all of them would admit this to an inquiring social scientist. We tend to tell strangers what we think will make us sound good. I myself, to my utter amazement, informed a

telephone pollster that I exercised regularly, a baldfaced lie. How much more difficult to describe truthfully one's moral and ethical values—even if one knew what
they were, which, as Socrates demonstrated at length, almost no one does. . . .

While Chodorow's analysis of psychosexual development is the point of departure for most of the difference feminists, it is possible to construct a theory of gendered ethics on other grounds. The most interesting attempt I've seen is by the
pacifist philosopher Sara Ruddick. Although not widely known outside academic
circles, her *Maternal Thinking* makes an argument that can be found in such mainstream sources as the columns of Anna Quindlen in *The New York Times*. For Ruddick it is not psychosexual development that produces the Gilliganian virtues but
intimate involvement in child-raising, the hands-on work of mothering. Men too can
be mothers if they do the work that women do. (And women can be Fathers—a
word Ruddick uses, complete with arrogant capital letter, for distant, uninvolved
authority-figure parents.) Mothers are patient, peace-loving, attentive to emotional
context and so on, because those are the qualities you need to get the job done, the
way accountants are precise, lawyers are argumentative, writers self-centered. Thus
mothers constitute a logical constituency for pacifist and antiwar politics, and, by
extension, a "caring" domestic agenda. . . .

Ruddick claims to be describing what mothers do, but all too often she is really
prescribing what she thinks they ought to do. . . .

As Gilligan does with all women, Ruddick scrutinizes mothers for what she
expects to find, and sure enough, there it is. But why look to mothers for her peaceful constituency in the first place? Why not health professionals, who spend their
lives saving lives? Or historians, who know how rarely war yields a benefit remotely
commensurate with its cost in human misery? Or I don't know, gardeners, blame-
lessly tending their innocent flowers? You can read almost any kind of work as
affirming life and conferring wisdom. Ruddick chooses mothering because she's
already decided that women possess the Gilliganian virtues and she wants a non-
essentialist peg to hang them on, so that men can acquire them too. A disinterested
observer scouring the world for labor that encourages humane values would never
pick child-raising: It's too quirky, too embedded in repellent cultural norms, too hot.

Despite its intellectual flabbiness, difference feminism is deeply appealing to
many women. Why? For one thing, it seems to explain some important phenomena:
that women—and this is a cross-cultural truth—commit very little criminal violence
compared with men; that women fill the ranks of the so-called caring professions;
that women are much less likely than men to abandon their children. Difference
feminists want to give women credit for these good behaviors by raising them from
the level of instinct or passivity . . . to the level of moral choice and principled decision. Who can blame women for embracing theories that tell them the sacrifices they
make on behalf of domesticity and children are legitimate, moral, even noble? By
stressing the mentality of nurturance—the *ethic* of caring, maternal *thinking*—Gilligan and Ruddick challenge the ancient division of humanity into rational males and
irrational females. They offer women a way to argue that their views have equal status with those of men and to resist the customary marginalization of their voices in
public debate. Doubtless many women have felt emboldened by Gilliganian
accounts of moral difference: Speaking in a different voice is, after all, a big step up
from silence.

The vision of women as sharers and carers is tempting in another way too. Despite much media blather about the popularity of the victim position, most people want to believe they act out of free will and choice. The uncomfortable truth that women have all too little of either is a difficult hurdle for feminists. Acknowledging the systematic oppression of women seems to deprive them of existential freedom, to turn them into puppets, slaves and Stepford wives. Deny it, and you can't make change. By arguing that the traditional qualities, tasks and ways of life of women are as important, valuable and serious as those of men (if not more so), Gilligan and others let women feel that nothing needs to change except the social valuation accorded to what they are already doing. It's a rationale for the status quo, which is why men like it, and a burst of grateful applause, which is why women like it. Men keep the power, but since power is bad, so much the worse for them.

Another rather curious appeal of difference feminism is that it offers a way for women to define themselves as independent of men. In a culture that sees women almost entirely in relation to men, this is no small achievement. Sex, for example— the enormous amount of female energy, money and time spent on beauty and fashion and romance, on attracting men and keeping them, on placating male power, strategizing ways around it or making it serve one's own ends—plays a minute role in these theories. You would never guess from Gilligan or Ruddick that men, individually and collectively, are signal beneficiaries of female nurturance, much less that this goes far to explain why society encourages nurturance in women. No, it is always children whom women are described as fostering and sacrificing for, or the community, or even other women—not husbands or lovers. It's as though wives cook dinner only for their kids, leaving the husband to raid the fridge on his own. And no doubt many women, quietly smoldering at their mate's refusal to share domestic labor, persuade themselves that they are serving only their children, or their own preferences, rather than confront the inequality of their marriage.

The peaceful mother and the "relational" woman are a kinder, gentler, leftish version of "family values," and both are modern versions of the separate-spheres ideology of the Victorians. In the nineteenth century, too, some women tried to turn the ideology of sexual difference on its head and expand the moral claims of motherhood to include the public realm. Middle-class women became social reformers, abolitionists, temperance advocates, settlement workers and even took paying jobs in the "helping professions"—nursing, social work, teaching—which were perceived as extensions of women's domestic role although practiced mostly by single women. These women did not deny that their sex fitted them for the home, but argued that domesticity did not end at the front door of the house, or confine itself to dusting (or telling the housemaid to dust). Even the vote could be cast as an extension of domesticity: Women, being more moral than men, would purify the government of vice and corruption, end war and make America safe for family life. . . .

Accepting the separate-spheres ideology had obvious advantages in an era when women were formally barred from higher education, political power and many jobs. But its defects are equally obvious. It defined all women by a single standard, and one developed by a sexist society. It offered women no way to enter professions that could not be defined as extensions of domestic roles—you could be a math teacher but not a mathematician, a secretary but not a sea captain—and no way to challenge any but the grossest abuses of male privilege. Difference feminists are making a similar bid for power on behalf of women today, and are caught in similar contradictions. Once again, women are defined by their family roles. Child-raising is seen as women's glory and joy and opportunity for self-transcendence, while Dad naps on the couch. Women who do not fit the stereotype are castigated as unfeminine— nurses nurture, doctors do not—and domestic labor is romanticized and sold to women as a badge of moral worth. . . .

Difference theorists would like to separate out the aspects of traditional womanhood that they approve of and speak only of those. But the parts they like (caring, nurturing, intimacy) are inseparable from the parts they don't like (economic dependence and the subordination of women within the family). The difference theorists try to get around this by positing a world that contains two cultures—a female world of love and ritual and a male world of getting and spending and killing—which mysteriously share a single planet. That vision is expressed neatly in a recent pop-psychology title, *Men Are from Mars, Women Are from Venus.* It would be truer to say men are from Illinois and women are from Indiana—different, sure, but not in ways that have much ethical consequence.

The truth is, there is only one culture, and it shapes each sex in distinct but mutually dependent ways in order to reproduce itself. To the extent that the stereotypes are true, women have the "relational" domestic qualities *because* men have the "autonomous" qualities required to survive and prosper in modern capitalism. She needs a wage earner (even if she has a job, thanks to job discrimination), and he needs someone to mind his children, hold his hand and have his emotions for him. This—not . . . some treason to her sex—explains why women who move into male sectors act very much like men: If they didn't, they'd find themselves back home in a jiffy. The same necessities and pressures affect them as affect the men who hold those jobs. Because we are in a transition period, in which many women were raised with modest expectations and much emphasis on the need to please others, social scientists who look for it can find traces of empathy, caring and so on in some women who have risen in the world of work and power, but when they tell us that women doctors will transform American medicine, or women executives will transform the corporate world, they are looking backward, not forward. If women really do enter the work force on equal terms with men—if they become 50 percent of all lawyers, politicians, car dealers and prison guards—they may be less sexist (although the example of Russian doctors, a majority of them female, is not inspiring to those who know about the brutal gynecological customs prevailing in the former U.S.S.R.). And they may bring with them a distinct set of manners, a separate social style. But they won't be, in some general way, more honest, kind, egalitarian, empathic or indifferent to profit. To argue otherwise is to believe that the reason factory owners bust unions, doctors refuse Medicaid patients and New York City school custodians don't mop the floors is because they are men.

The ultimate paradox of difference feminism is that it has come to the fore at a moment when the lives of the sexes are becoming less distinct than they ever have been in the West. Look at the decline of single-sex education (researchers may tout the benefits of all-female schools and colleges, but girls overwhelmingly choose coeducation); the growth of female athletics; the virtual abolition of virginity as a requirement for girls; the equalization of college-attendance rates of males and females; the explosion of employment for married women and mothers even of small children; the crossing of workplace gender lines by both females and males; the cultural pressure on men to be warm and nurturant fathers, to do at least some housework, to choose mates who are their equals in education and income potential.

It's fashionable these days to talk about the backlash against equality feminism—I talk this way myself when I'm feeling blue—but equality feminism has scored amazing successes. It has transformed women's expectations in every area of their lives. However, it has not yet transformed society to meet those expectations. The workplace still discriminates. On the home front few men practice egalitarianism, although many preach it; single mothers—and given the high divorce rate, every mother is potentially a single mother—lead incredibly difficult lives.

In this social context, difference feminism is essentially a way for women both to take advantage of equality feminism's success and to accommodate themselves to its limits. It appeals to particular kinds of women—those in the "helping professions" or the home, for example, rather than those who want to be bomber pilots or neurosurgeons or electricians. At the popular level, it encourages women who feel disadvantaged or demeaned by equality to direct their anger against women who have benefited from it by thinking of them as gender traitors and of themselves as suffering for their virtue—thus the hostility of nurses toward female doctors, and of stay-at-home mothers toward employed mothers. . . .

Although it is couched in the language of praise, difference feminism is demeaning to women. It asks that women be admitted into public life and public discourse not because they have a right to be there but because they will improve them. Even if this were true, and not the wishful thinking I believe it to be, why should the task of moral and social transformation be laid on women's doorstep and not on everyone's—or, for that matter, on men's, by the you-broke-it-you-fix-it principle. Peace, the environment, a more humane workplace, economic justice, social support for children—these are issues that affect us all and are everyone's responsibility. By promising to assume that responsibility, difference feminists lay the groundwork for excluding women again, as soon as it becomes clear that the promise cannot be kept.

No one asks that other oppressed groups win their freedom by claiming to be extra-good. And no other oppressed group thinks it must make such a claim in order to be accommodated fully and across the board by society. For blacks and other racial minorities, it is enough to want to earn a living, exercise one's talents, get a fair hearing in the public forum. Only for women is simple justice an insufficient argument. It is as though women don't really believe they are entitled to full citizenship unless they can make a special claim to virtue. Why isn't being human enough?

In the end, I didn't sign that peace petition, although I was sorry to disappoint a woman I liked, and although I am very much for peace. I decided to wait for a petition that welcomed my signature as a person, an American, a citizen implicated, against my will, in war and the war economy. I still think I did the right thing.

Part Two

Woman's Place

"Let Mary be brought up to her trade," wrote Charles Meigs in his popular medical treatise of 1859, *Woman: Her Diseases and Remedies.* "What is that?" he went on. "It is taking care of a family—wisely, happily, elegantly, with good temper; . . . Mr. Clay, Mr. Webster, Colonel Benton, and Mr. Calhoun will take care of politics; General Scott and General Taylor will take care of the soldiers; let the daughters take care of the children, and learn to be bright at the breakfast table, elegant at dinner, enchanting as pourers of tea, and the ornaments and grace of the salon."

Meigs' statement sums up the popular nineteenth-century "separate spheres" doctrine. For Meigs, and other like-minded men of his day, there was but one true calling for women—as wife and mother—which they defended on the grounds that only in filling this role could a woman fulfill herself. According to this view, a woman's life should center on the family, and her rewards should come from nurturing and supporting others, cheerfully and lovingly; and

"THROUGH IT ALL, SHE IS COURAGEOUSLY STANDING ERECT, DEVELOPING WITHIN HERSELF THE MORAL STRENGTH TO RISE ABOVE AND CONQUER FALSE ATTITUDES."
—ELISE JOHNSON McDOUGALD

they, rather than she, should be the achievers in the world outside the home. Even women whose economic or social circumstances prevented them from following the letter of this law were to follow it in spirit.

Although many proponents of separate spheres rested the case on woman's nature, some were willing to concede that women are not naturally domestic or deferential. In fact, some traditionalists openly acknowledged how difficult it is for women to conform to these roles. Such people defended woman's confinement to the home by arguing that preservation of the social order, domestic harmony, and the well-being of children required this sacrifice on her part.

Women who were not middle-class or white were rendered invisible in the separate spheres doctrine. Slave women laboring alongside men in the cotton fields could hardly be included in Meigs' image of women as "ornaments" of the home. Nor could countless other women working on farms, in factories, or in businesses. Nor, for that matter, could women who worked exclusively within the home. The work of housewives, burdened with many children and few labor-saving products or devices, was never-ending and exhausting.

Even the more privileged women that Meigs had in mind looked for ways to find relief from the restrictions of their domestic roles. They worked in reform societies to abolish slavery and to end the evils of alcohol abuse. They found their own niches outside the home—as midwives, nurses, and teachers. They also found ways to share their ideas and to be heard in a society that defined woman's role as a "silent" and "moral" one. Women gave public lectures in spite of the ridicule they received for it ("She is a man all but the pantaloons"). They wrote newspaper columns, travel books, poetry, novels, and letters directed at female audiences.

In their writing, women could criticize the status quo and the theories that supported it. They poked fun at men's inflated sense of their own importance,

at their self-serving beliefs, and at their near-sightedness. Newspaper editor Jane Swisshelm, for example, wrote in 1853 that "thousands of women toil in avocations which public opinion pretends to assign to men." She added that men talk about separate spheres only when women try to take up "honorable professions requiring talent," not when women do menial work that men don't want to do themselves.

By the time the first Woman's Rights Convention was held in Seneca Falls, New York, in 1848, a woman-defined assessment of woman's status and of her rightful place in society had begun to emerge. The women at the convention envisioned a future for woman different from the one that man had marked out for her, within a new status fully equal to man's—a future in which women would choose their own destinies.

The women at Seneca Falls thought that woman suffrage and legal recognition of women as full citizens would go far toward accomplishing these ends. But women, before and since, have focused on other routes to freedom as well—self-expression, economic independence, education, control over reproduction, egalitarian marriages, to name a few. The particular goals that women have sought to bring about their liberation are as varied as the circumstances of women's lives and as diverse as women themselves.

The readings illustrate some of women's struggles to resist and change the status quo. Many of these struggles have been solitary ones. But developing a feminist perspective and fighting the system are difficult on one's own. Proponents of tradition often explain a woman's dissatisfactions with her life as a psychological problem, born of a failure to adjust. They label women who reject their prescribed roles, or claim roles reserved for men, as "unfeminine" and "unnatural."

Resisting societal norms becomes easier when women find others who share their perspectives and seek similar goals. The nineteenth-century woman's movement began when women, treated as second-class citizens in male-dominated reform societies, joined together to form their own societies. They organized their own woman's rights conventions, publishing feminist tracts, letters, and newspapers. Their experiences together helped to forge a feminist consciousness.

Thereafter women continued to work together in organizations and clubs for legal and social reforms affecting women. When facing insurmountable barriers, women have been inventive, forming their own schools and colleges, and even their own professions. But, as the readings illustrate, it would be a mistake to conclude that women always have agreed on goals, or strategies, or whether or not problems exist. Even today, women with diverse backgrounds and interests continue to be challenged to become sensitive to one another's perspectives and concerns.

Women's biggest steps into public life occurred during the two world wars and the depression between them. In those years, working in jobs formerly reserved for men, women's success seemed to call for an end to separate spheres thinking. Nevertheless, at the end of World War II, a modern version of nineteenth-century separate spheres ideology emerged, isolating middle-class women in their homes. Betty Friedan's 1963 book, *The Feminine Mystique*, acknowledged women's unhappiness under this regime and called for a change in women's roles. Her book helped to initiate the modern women's movement.

Another spur to the present women's movement came from women working in the civil rights and student movements of the 1960s. These women became painfully aware of their low status, even in the eyes of "liberal" men, when they found that they were asked to make coffee and duplicate leaflets, but were not allowed to speak at meetings or to assume roles as equals with men. Like their nineteenth-century counterparts, these women separated from the male-dominated organizations to form their own groups. They developed consciousness-raising groups to share their experiences as women and to support one another in fighting oppression. And so, the modern women's movement began.

But advances for women have not come easily, no matter how well organized women are. The same battles are fought repeatedly, sometimes generation after generation, before change eventually comes. And although the nineteenth-century ideas we began with may seem antique, Americans have cherished them over the years. Like antiques that are stored away and forgotten for a time, sooner or later they are rediscovered, dusted off, polished, and once more made the focus of attention. The events of the past two centuries reveal that society abandons the idea of home life as the preferred vocation for women only out of necessity, reactivating it whenever the particular military or economic crisis that weakened its influence is resolved.

Even today, many women are encouraged to get an education only so they will have "something to fall back on." Many people still see the career woman as merely "marking time" until the right man comes along. The childless woman continues to be an object of pity. Housework and child care are still, for the most part, female responsibilities. Even in the most liberated of modern households, women typically must reconcile jobs and domestic responsibilities in ways that men do not have to.

Nevertheless, the years of struggle have made a difference. Discriminatory laws of the past have been wiped off the books, and laws benefitting women have been passed. Women now have educational and occupational options unheard of in Meigs' day. And, perhaps for the first time, a considerable portion of the population currently believes that women's ideal roles are not exclusively domestic ones and that women legitimately belong in positions of influence.

With the 1992 congressional election, the new House of Representatives and the new Senate included record numbers of women—47 out of the 434 representatives, and 6 out of the 100 senators. As women continue to expand the definition of their proper place, even into the highest positions in government, the idea that a woman's place is in the home has lost much of its power to control women's aspirations. For a record number of women, a 1980s T-shirt defying tradition and calling for women's empowerment has come true. The T-shirt reads:

A WOMAN'S PLACE IS IN THE
HOUSE . . . AND THE SENATE.

WOMAN'S PLACE IN RELIGION: TWO VIEWS

Sarah Moore Grimké's *Letters on the Equality of the Sexes and the Condition of Woman* is perhaps the earliest full statement of the feminist critique of woman's "sphere" by an American. It predates the famous Seneca Falls Declaration of Sentiments (1848), for example, by a full decade.

Grimké (1792–1873), along with her equally celebrated sister Angelina, first achieved renown as an advocate of the abolition of slavery. Their fame in this regard came, in the first instance, because they had been raised as part of the slaveholding class on a South Carolina plantation. They could thus claim to be speaking from personal knowledge when detailing the evils of the South's "peculiar institution." Their prominence in the antislavery crusades of the 1830s soon catapulted the sisters into a second, equally stormy, controversy. This was over the propriety of women taking an active role in public affairs of any kind. It is, as a result, no coincidence that Sarah Grimké wrote her letters on the equality of the sexes to Mary S. Parker, president of the Boston Female Anti-Slavery Society. The Pastoral Letter of the General Association of Congregational Ministers, which Grimké subjected to such withering analysis in her *Letters,* follows here in excerpted form.

THE PASTORAL LETTER OF THE GENERAL ASSOCIATION OF CONGREGATIONAL MINISTERS OF MASSACHUSETTS

We invite your attention to the dangers which at present seem to threaten the female character with wide spread and permanent injury.

The appropriate duties and influence of women, are clearly stated in the New Testament. Those duties and that influence are unobtrusive and private, but the sources of mighty power. When the mild, dependent, softening influence of woman upon the sternness of man's opinions is fully exercised, society feels the effects of it in a thousand forms. The power of woman is in her dependence, flowing from the consciousness of that weakness which God has given her for her protection and which keeps her in those departments of life that form the character of individuals and of the nation. There are social influences which females use in promoting piety and the great objects of christian benevolence, which we cannot too highly commend. We appreciate the unostentatious prayers and efforts of woman, in advancing the cause of religion at home and abroad:—in Sabbath schools, in leading religious inquirers to their pastor for instruction, and in all such associated effort as becomes the modesty of her sex; and earnestly hope that she may abound more and more in these labours of piety and love. But when she assumes the place and tone of a man as a public reformer, our care and protection of her seem unnecessary, we put ourselves in self defence against her, she yields the power which God has given her for protection, and her character becomes unnatural. If the vine, whose strength and beauty is

THE PASTORAL LETTER . . .   From *Minutes of the General Association of Congregational Ministers of Massachusetts at Their Meeting at North Brookfield, June 28, 1837, with the Narrative of the State of Religion and the Pastoral Letter* (Boston: Crocker & Brewer, 1837) 20–21.

to lean upon the trellis work and half conceal its clusters, thinks to assume the independence and the overshadowing nature of the elm, it will not only cease to bear fruit, but fall in shame and dishonour into the dust.

We cannot, therefore, but regret the mistaken conduct of those who encourage females to bear an obtrusive and ostentatious part in measures of reform, and countenance any of that sex who so far forget themselves as to itinerate in the character of public lecturers and teachers.

We especially deplore the intimate acquaintance and promiscuous conversation of females with regard to things "which ought not to be named"; by which that modesty and delicacy which is the charm of domestic life, and which constitute the true influence of women in society are consumed, and the way opened, as we apprehend, for degeneracy and ruin. We say these things, not to discourage proper influences against sin, but to secure such reformation as we believe is scriptural and will be permanent.

LETTERS ON THE EQUALITY OF THE SEXES
Sarah Moore Grimké

Haverhill, 7th Mo. 1837

DEAR FRIEND,

When I last addressed thee, I had not seen the Pastoral Letter of the General Association. It has since fallen into my hands, and I must digress from my intention of exhibiting the condition of women in different parts of the world, in order to make some remarks on this extraordinary document. I am persuaded that when the minds of men and women become emancipated from the thraldom of superstition and "traditions of men," the sentiments contained in the Pastoral Letter will be recurred to with as much astonishment as the opinions of Cotton Mather and other distinguished men of his day, on the subject of witchcraft; nor will it be deemed less wonderful, that a body of divines should gravely assemble and endeavor to prove that woman has no right to "open her mouth for the dumb," than it now is that judges should have sat on the trials of witches, and solemnly condemned nineteen persons and one dog to death for witchcraft.

But to the letter. It says, "We invite your attention to the dangers which at present seem to threaten the FEMALE CHARACTER with wide-spread and permanent injury." I rejoice that they have called the attention of my sex to this subject, because I believe if woman investigates it, she will soon discover that danger is impending, though from a totally different source from that which the Association apprehends,—danger from those who, having long held the reins of *usurped* authority, are unwilling to permit us to fill that sphere which God created us to move in, and who have entered into league to crush the immortal mind of woman. I rejoice, because I

LETTERS ON THE EQUALITY OF THE SEXES   From Sarah Moore Grimké, *Letters on the Equality of the Sexes and the Condition of Woman* (Boston: Isaac Knapp, 1838) 14–21.

am persuaded that the rights of woman, like the rights of slaves, need only be examined to be understood and asserted, even by some of those, who are now endeavoring to smother the irrepressible desire for mental and spiritual freedom which glows in the breast of many, who hardly dare to speak their sentiments.

"The appropriate duties and influence of women are clearly stated in the New Testament. Those duties are unobtrusive and private, but the sources of *mighty power*. When the mild, *dependent*, softening influence of woman upon the sternness of man's opinions is fully exercised, society feels the effects of it in a thousand ways." No one can desire more earnestly than I do, that women may move exactly in the sphere which her Creator has assigned her; and I believe her having been displaced from that sphere has introduced confusion into the world. It is, therefore, of vast importance to herself and to all the rational creation, that she should ascertain what are her duties and her privileges as a responsible and immortal being. The New Testament has been referred to, and I am willing to abide by its decisions, but must enter my protest against the false translation of some passages by the MEN who did that work, and against the perverted interpretation by the MEN who undertook to write commentaries thereon. I am inclined to think, when we are admitted to the honor of studying Greek and Hebrew, we shall produce some various readings of the Bible a little different from those we now have.

The Lord Jesus defines the duties of his followers in his Sermon on the Mount. He lays down grand principles by which they should be governed, without any reference to sex or condition:—"Ye are the light of the world. A city that is set on a hill cannot be hid. Neither do men light a candle and put it under a bushel, but on a candlestick, and it giveth light unto all that are in the house. Let your light so shine before men, that they may see your good works, and glorify your Father which is in Heaven." I follow him through all his precepts, and find him giving the same directions to women as to men, never even referring to the distinction now so strenuously insisted upon between masculine and feminine virtues: this is one of the anti-christian "traditions of men" which are taught instead of the "commandments of God." Men and women were CREATED EQUAL; they are both moral and accountable beings, and whatever is *right* for man to do, is *right* for woman.

But the influence of woman, says the Association, is to be private and unobtrusive; her light is not to shine before man like that of her brethren; but she is passively to let the lords of the creation, as they call themselves, put the bushel over it, lest peradventure it might appear that the world has been benefitted by the rays of *her* candle. So that her quenched light, according to their judgment, will be of more use than if it were set on the candlestick. "Her influence is the source of mighty power." This has ever been the flattering language of man since he laid aside the whip as a means to keep woman in subjection. He spares her body; but the war he has waged against her mind, her heart, and her soul, has been no less destructive to her as a moral being. How monstrous, how anti-christian, is the doctrine that woman is to be dependent on man! Where, in all the sacred Scriptures, is this taught? Alas! she has too well learned the lesson which MAN has labored to teach her. She has surrendered her dearest RIGHTS, and been satisfied with the privileges which man has assumed to grant her; she has been amused with the show of power, whilst man has absorbed all the reality into himself. He has adorned the creature whom God gave him as a companion, with baubles and gewgaws, turned her attention to personal attractions, offered incense to her vanity, and made her the instrument of his selfish gratification, a plaything to please his eye and amuse his hours of leisure. "Rule by obedience and by submission sway," or in other words, study to be a hypocrite, pretend to submit, but gain your point, has been the code of household morality which woman has been taught. The poet has sung, in sickly strains, the loveliness of woman's dependence upon man, and now we find it re-echoed by those who profess to teach the religion of the Bible. God says, "Cease ye from man whose breath is in his nostrils, for wherein is he to be accounted of?" Man says, depend upon me. God says, "HE will teach us of his ways." Man says, believe it not, I am to be your teacher. This doctrine of dependence upon man is utterly at variance with the doctrine of the Bible. In that book I find nothing like the softness of woman, nor the sternness of man: both are equally commanded to bring forth the fruits of the Spirit, love, meekness, gentleness, &c.

But we are told, "the power of woman is in her dependence, flowing from a consciousness of that weakness which God has given her for her protection." If physical weakness is alluded to, I cheerfully concede the superiority; if brute force is what my brethren are claiming, I am willing to let them have all the honor they desire; but if they mean to intimate, that mental or moral weakness belongs to woman, more than to man, I utterly disclaim the charge. Our powers of mind have been crushed, as far as man could do it, our sense of morality has been impaired by his interpretation of our duties; but no where does God say that he made any distinction between us, as moral and intelligent beings.

"We appreciate," says the Association, "the *unostentatious* prayers and efforts of woman in advancing the cause of religion at home and abroad, in leading religious inquirers TO THE PASTOR for instruction." Several points here demand attention. If public prayers and public efforts are necessarily ostentatious, then "Anna the prophetess, (or preacher) who departed not from the temple, but served God with fastings and prayers night and day," "and spake of Christ to all them that looked for redemption in Israel," was ostentatious in her efforts. Then, the apostle Paul encourages women to be ostentatious in their efforts to spread the gospel, when he gives them directions how they should appear, when engaged in praying, or preaching in the public assemblies. Then, the whole association of Congregational ministers are ostentatious, in the efforts they are making in preaching and praying to convert souls.

But woman may be permitted to lead religious inquirers to the PASTORS for instruction. Now this is assuming that all pastors are better qualified to give instruction than woman. This I utterly deny. I have suffered too keenly from the teaching of man, to lead any one to him for instruction. The Lord Jesus says,—"Come unto me and learn of me." He points his followers to no man; and when woman is made the favored instrument of rousing a sinner to his lost and helpless condition, she has no right to substitute any teacher for Christ; all she has to do is, to turn the contrite inquirer to the "Lamb of God which taketh away the sins of the world." More souls have probably been lost by going down to Egypt for help, and by trusting in man in the early stages of religious experience, than by any other error. Instead of the petition being offered to God,—"Lead me in thy truth, and TEACH me, for thou art the God of my salvation,"—instead of relying on the precious promises—"What man is he that feareth the Lord? him shall HE TEACH in the way that he shall choose"—

"I will instruct thee and TEACH thee in the way which thou shalt go—I will guide thee with mine eye"—the young convert is directed to go to man, as if he were in the place of God, and his instructions essential to an advancement in the path of righteousness. That woman can have but a poor conception of the privilege of being taught of God, what he alone can teach, who would turn the "religious inquirer aside" from the fountain of living waters, where he might slake his thirst for spiritual instructions, to those broken cisterns which can hold no water, and therefore cannot satisfy the panting spirit. The business of men and women, who are ORDAINED OF GOD to preach the unsearchable riches of Christ to a lost and perishing world, is to lead souls to Christ, and not to Pastors for instruction.

The General Association says, that "when woman assumes the place and tone of man as a public reformer, our care and protection of her seem unnecessary; we put ourselves in self-defence against her, and her character becomes unnatural." Here again the unscriptural notion is held up, that there is a distinction between the duties of men and women as moral beings; that what is virtue in man, is vice in woman; and women who dare to obey the command of Jehovah, "Cry aloud, spare not, lift up thy voice like a trumpet, and show my people their transgression," are threatened with having the protection of the brethren withdrawn. If this is all they do, we shall not even know the time when our chastisement is inflicted; our trust is in the Lord Jehovah, and in Him is everlasting strength. The motto of woman, when she is engaged in the great work of public reformation should be,—"The Lord is my light and my salvation; whom shall I fear? The Lord is the strength of my life; of whom shall I be afraid?" She must feel, if she feels rightly, that she is fulfilling one of the important duties laid upon her as an accountable being, and that her character, instead of being "unnatural," is in exact accordance with the will of Him to whom, and to no other, she is responsible for the talents and the gifts confided to her. As to the pretty simile, introduced into the "Pastoral letter," "If the vine whose strength and beauty is to lean upon the trellis work, and half conceal its clusters, thinks to assume the independence and the overshadowing nature of the elm," &c. I shall only remark that it might well suit the poet's fancy, who sings of sparkling eyes and coral lips, and knights in armor clad; but it seems to me utterly inconsistent with the dignity of a Christian body, to endeavor to draw such an anti-scriptural distinction between men and women. Ah! how many of my sex feel in the dominion, thus unrighteously exercised over them, under the gentle appellation of *protection,* that what they have leaned upon has proved a broken reed at best, and oft a spear.

Thine in the bonds of womanhood,
SARAH M. GRIMKÉ.

DECLARATION OF SENTIMENTS
SENECA FALLS CONVENTION

The 1848 Seneca Falls "Declaration" is, without doubt and quite properly, the most famous document produced by the woman's movement in the United States. Elizabeth Cady Stanton, Lucretia Mott, Martha C. Wright, and Mary Ann McClintock wrote it in "Mrs. McClintock's parlor." The Declaration of Independence served as their model.

The secrets of its power are several. One is, as Stanton and her coeditors of the *History of Woman Suffrage* put it almost forty years later, "the Declaration and resolutions . . . demanded all [that] the most radical friends of the movement have since claimed. . . ." A second source of its continuing hold over the imagination is its faithful echoing of Jefferson's Declaration. This simple literary device enabled Stanton and her coauthors to claim, as their birthright, the same republican political creed male Americans professed to live by. It allowed them to claim too the revolutionary tradition which, by the mid-nineteenth century, the almost godlike Founding Fathers had invoked to justify the overthrow of established but unjust conditions.

Finally, the Seneca Falls "Declaration" marked the birth, not of feminist thinking, but of the feminist movement in the United States. So it stood as the model for the countless subsequent declarations women's rights conventions would adopt.

When, in the course of human events, it becomes necessary for one portion of the family of man to assume among the people of the earth a position different from that which they have hitherto occupied, but one to which the laws of nature and of nature's God entitle them, a decent respect to the opinions of mankind requires that they should declare the causes that impel them to such a course.

We hold these truths to be self-evident: that all men and women are created equal; that they are endowed by their Creator with certain inalienable rights; that among these are life, liberty, and the pursuit of happiness; that to secure these rights governments are instituted, deriving their just powers from the consent of the governed. Whenever any form of government becomes destructive of these ends, it is the right of those who suffer from it to refuse allegiance to it, and to insist upon the institution of a new government, laying its foundation on such principles, and organizing its powers in such form, as to them shall seem most likely to effect their safety and happiness. Prudence, indeed, will dictate that governments long established should not be changed for light and transient causes; and accordingly all experience hath shown that mankind are more disposed to suffer, while evils are sufferable, than to right themselves by abolishing the forms to which they were accustomed. But when a long train of abuses and usurpations, pursuing invariably the same object evinces a design to reduce them under absolute despotism, it is their duty to throw off such government, and to provide new guards for their future security. Such has been the patient sufferance of the women under this government, and such is now the necessity which constrains them to demand the equal station to which they are entitled.

The history of mankind is a history of repeated injuries and usurpations on the part of man toward woman, having in direct object the establishment of an absolute tyranny over her. To prove this, let facts be submitted to a candid world.

He has never permitted her to exercise her inalienable right to the elective franchise.

He has compelled her to submit to laws, in the formation of which she had no voice.

He has withheld from her rights which are given to the most ignorant and degraded men—both natives and foreigners.

DECLARATION OF SENTIMENTS . . .   From Elizabeth Cady Stanton et al., eds., *History of Woman Suffrage,* 2nd ed., vol. 1 (Rochester: Charles Mann, 1889) 70–73.

Having deprived her of this first right of a citizen, the elective franchise, thereby leaving her without representation in the halls of legislation, he has oppressed her on all sides.

He has made her, if married, in the eye of the law, civilly dead.

He has taken from her all right in property, even to the wages she earns.

He has made her morally, an irresponsible being, as she can commit many crimes with impunity, provided they be done in the presence of her husband. In the covenant of marriage, she is compelled to promise obedience to her husband, he becoming, to all intents and purposes, her master—the law giving him power to deprive her of her liberty, and to administer chastisement.

He has so framed the laws of divorce, as to what shall be the proper causes, and in case of separation, to whom the guardianship of the children shall be given, as to be wholly regardless of the happiness of women—the law, in all cases, going upon a false supposition of the supremacy of man, and giving all power into his hands.

After depriving her of all rights as a married woman, if single, and the owner of property, he has taxed her to support a government which recognizes her only when her property can be made profitable to it.

He has monopolized nearly all the profitable employments, and from those she is permitted to follow, she receives but a scanty remuneration. He closes against her all the avenues to wealth and distinction which he considers most honorable to himself. As a teacher of theology, medicine, or law, she is not known.

He has denied her the facilities for obtaining a thorough education, all colleges being closed against her.

He allows her in Church, as well as State, but a subordinate position, claiming Apostolic authority for her exclusion from the ministry, and, with some exceptions, from any public participation in the affairs of the Church.

He has created a false public sentiment by giving to the world a different code of morals for men and women, by which moral delinquencies which exclude women from society, are not only tolerated, but deemed of little account in man.

He has usurped the prerogative of Jehovah himself, claiming it as his right to assign for her a sphere of action, when that belongs to her conscience and to her God.

He has endeavored, in every way that he could, to destroy her confidence in her own powers, to lessen her self-respect, and to make her willing to lead a dependent and abject life.

Now, in view of this entire disenfranchisement of one-half the people of this country, their social and religious degradation—in view of the unjust laws above mentioned, and because women do feel themselves aggrieved, oppressed, and fraudulently deprived of their most sacred rights, we insist that they have immediate admission to all the rights and privileges which belong to them as citizens of the United States.

In entering upon the great work before us, we anticipate no small amount of misconception, misrepresentation, and ridicule; but we shall use every instrumentality within our power to effect our object. We shall employ agents, circulate tracts, petition the State and National legislatures, and endeavor to enlist the pulpit and the press in our behalf. We hope this Convention will be followed by a series of Conventions embracing every part of the country.

The following resolutions were discussed by Lucretia Mott, Thomas and Mary Ann McClintock, Amy Post, Catharine A. F. Stebbins, and others, and were adopted:

WHEREAS, The great precept of nature is conceded to be, that "man shall pursue his own true and substantial happiness." Blackstone in his Commentaries remarks, that this law of Nature being coeval with mankind, and dictated by God himself, is of course superior in obligation to any other. It is binding over all the globe, in all countries and at all times; no human laws are of any validity if contrary to this, and such of them as are valid, derive all their force, and all their validity, and all their authority, mediately and immediately, from this original; therefore,

Resolved, That such laws as conflict, in any way, with the true and substantial happiness of woman, are contrary to the great precept of nature and of no validity, for this is "superior in obligation to any other."

Resolved, That all laws which prevent woman from occupying such a station in society as her conscience shall dictate, or which place her in a position inferior to that of man, are contrary to the great precept of nature, and therefore of no force or authority.

Resolved, That woman is man's equal—was intended to be so by the Creator, and the highest good of the race demands that she should be recognized as such.

Resolved, That the women of this country ought to be enlightened in regard to the laws under which they live, that they may no longer publish their degradation by declaring themselves satisfied with their present position, nor their ignorance, by asserting that they have all the rights they want.

Resolved, That inasmuch as man, while claiming for himself intellectual superiority, does accord to woman moral superiority, it is pre-eminently his duty to encourage her to speak and teach, as she has an opportunity, in all religious assemblies.

Resolved, That the same amount of virtue, delicacy, and refinement of behavior that is required of woman in the social state, should also be required of man, and the same transgressions should be visited with equal severity on both man and woman.

Resolved, That the objection of indelicacy and impropriety, which is so often brought against woman when she addresses a public audience, comes with a very ill-grace from those who encourage, by their attendance, her appearance on the stage, in the concert, or in feats of the circus.

Resolved, That woman has too long rested satisfied in the circumscribed limits which corrupt customs and a perverted application of the Scriptures have marked out for her, and that it is time she should move in the enlarged sphere which her great Creator has assigned her.

Resolved, That it is the duty of the women of this country to secure to themselves their sacred right to the elective franchise.

Resolved, That the equality of human rights results necessarily from the fact of the identity of the race in capabilities and responsibilities.

Resolved, therefore, That, being invested by the Creator with the same capabilities, and the same consciousness of responsibility for their exercise, it is demonstrably the right and duty of woman, equally with man, to promote every righteous cause by every righteous means; and especially in regard to the great subjects of morals and religion, it is self-evidently her right to participate with her brother in teaching them, both in private and in public, by writing and by speaking, by any instrumentalities proper to be used, and in any assemblies proper to be held; and this being a self-evident truth growing out of the divinely implanted principles of human nature, any custom or authority adverse to it, whether modern or wearing the hoary sanction of antiquity, is to be regarded as a self-evident falsehood, and at war with mankind.

At the last session Lucretia Mott offered and spoke to the following resolution:

Resolved, That the speedy success of our cause depends upon the zealous and untiring efforts of both men and women, for the overthrow of the monopoly of the pulpit, and for the securing to woman an equal participation with men in the various trades, professions, and commerce.

The only resolution that was not unanimously adopted was the ninth, urging the women of the country to secure to themselves the elective franchise. Those who took part in the debate feared a demand for the right to vote would defeat others they deemed more rational, and make the whole movement ridiculous.

But Mrs. Stanton and Frederick Douglass seeing that the power to choose rulers and make laws, was the right by which all others could be secured, persistently advocated the resolution, and at last carried it by a small majority.

Thus it will be seen that the Declaration and resolutions in the very first Convention, demanded all the most radical friends of the movement have since claimed—such as equal rights in the universities, in the trades and professions; the right to vote; to share in all political offices, honors, and emoluments; to complete equality in marriage, to personal freedom, property, wages, children; to make contracts; to sue, and be sued; and to testify in courts of justice. At this time the condition of married women under the Common Law, was nearly as degraded as that of the slave on the Southern plantation. The Convention continued through two entire days, and late into the evenings. The deepest interest was manifested to its close.

WOMAN'S RIGHTS CONVENTION
James Gordon Bennett

The Seneca Falls "Declaration" was widely publicized, and—as Stanton and her coeditors of *History of Woman Suffrage* later said—"unsparingly ridiculed by the press, and denounced by the pulpit, much to the surprise and chagrin of the leaders." Whether or not they were "wholly unprepared to find themselves the target for the jibes and jeers of the nation," as they claimed forty years afterwards, become such a target they did.

One leading critic was James Gordon Bennett, probably the most famous newspaper publisher of the day. In the editorial reprinted here he struck a note of amused condescension much favored by early opponents of feminism.

This is the age of revolutions. To whatever part of the world the attention is directed, the political and social fabric is crumbling to pieces; and changes which far exceed the wildest dreams of the enthusiastic Utopians of the last generation, are now pursued with ardor and perseverance. The principal agent, however, that has

WOMAN'S RIGHTS CONVENTION   From Elizabeth Cady Stanton et al., eds., *History of Woman Suffrage,* 2nd ed., vol. 1 (Rochester: Charles Mann, 1889) 805.

hitherto taken part in these movements has been the rougher sex. It was by man the flame of liberty, now burning with such fury on the continent of Europe, was first kindled; and though it is asserted that no inconsiderable assistance was contributed by the gentler sex to the late sanguinary carnage at Paris, we are disposed to believe that such a revolting imputation proceeds from base calumniators, and is a libel upon woman.

By the intelligence, however, which we have lately received, the work of revolution is no longer confined to the Old World, nor to the masculine gender. The flag of independence has been hoisted, for the second time, on this side of the Atlantic; and a solemn league and covenant has just been entered into by a Convention of women at Seneca Falls, to "throw off the despotism under which they are groaning, and provide new guards for their future security." Little did we expect this new element to be thrown into the cauldron of agitation which is now bubbling around us with such fury. We have had one Baltimore Convention, one Philadelphia Convention, one Utica convention, and we shall also have, in a few days, the Buffalo Convention. But we never dreamed that Lucretia Mott had convened a fifth Convention, which, if it be ratified by those whom it purposes to represent, will exercise an influence that will not only control our own Presidential elections, but the whole governmental system throughout the world. . . . The declaration is a most interesting document. We published it in *extenso* the other day. The amusing part is the preamble, where they assert their equality, and that they have certain inalienable rights, to secure which governments, deriving their just powers from the consent of the governed, are instituted; and that after the long train of abuses and usurpations to which they have been subjected, evincing a design to reduce them under absolute despotism, it is their right, it is their duty, to throw off such government.

The declaration is, in some respects, defective. It complains of the want of the elective franchise, and that ladies are not recognized as teachers of theology, medicine, and law. . . . These departments, however, do not comprise the whole of the many avenues to wealth, distinction, and honor. We do not see by what principle of right the angelic creatures should claim to compete with the preacher, and refuse to enter the lists with the merchant. A lawyer's brief would not, we admit, sully the hands so much as the tarry ropes of a man-of-war; and a box of Brandreth's pills are more safely and easily prepared than the sheets of a boiler, or the flukes of an anchor; but if they must have competition in one branch, why not in another? There must be no monopoly or exclusiveness. If they will put on the inexpressibles, it will not do to select those employments only which require the least exertion and are exempt from danger. The laborious employments, however, are not the only ones which the ladies, in right of their admission to all rights and privileges, would have to undertake. It might happen that the citizen would have to doff the apron and buckle on the sword. Now, though we have the most perfect confidence in the courage and daring of Miss Lucretia Mott and several others of our lady acquaintances, we confess it would go to our hearts to see them putting on the panoply of war, and mixing in scenes like those at which, it is said, the fair sex in Paris lately took prominent part.

It is not the business, however, of the despot to decide upon the rights of his victims; nor do we undertake to define the duties of women. Their standard is now unfurled by their own hands. The Convention of Seneca Falls has appealed to the country. Miss Lucretia Mott has propounded the principles of the party. Ratification meetings will no doubt shortly be held, and if it be the general impression that this lady is a more eligible candidate for the Presidential chair than McLean or Cass, Van Buren or old "Rough and Ready," then let the Salic laws be abolished forthwith from this great Republic. We are much mistaken if Lucretia would not make a better President than some of those who have lately tenanted the White House.—*New York Herald,* James Gordon Bennett, Proprietor.

PUBLIC EFFORT—EXCOMMUNICATION
Julia A. J. Foote

Julia Foote was born in 1823 in Schenectady, New York, the child of former slaves who had bought their freedom. As an adult, Foote, a Methodist preacher, traveled through many of the eastern states and Canada attracting large and receptive audiences wherever she spoke.

The reading below is from Foote's autobiography, one of a handful of recently rediscovered African-American spiritual narratives. Like the others, it was written as a prayer and as a dialogue with its readers to inspire them to the same special relationship with God that its author enjoyed.

The excerpt begins as Foote awakens from a spiritual vision in which she receives the call to preach and a letter authorizing her to do so, which she had tucked into her bosom.

When I came to myself, I found that several friends had been with me all night, and my husband had called a physician, but he had not been able to do anything for me. He ordered those around me to keep very quiet, or to go home. He returned in the morning, when I told him, in part, my story. He seemed amazed, but made no answer, and left me.

Several friends were in, during the day. While talking to them, I would, without thinking, put my hand into my bosom, to show them my letter of authority. But I soon found, as my friends told me, it was in my heart, and was to be shown in my life, instead of in my hand. Among others, my minister, Jehial C. Beman, came to see me. He looked very coldly upon me and said: "I guess you will find out your mistake before you are many months older." He was a scholar, and a fine speaker; and the sneering, indifferent way in which he addressed me, said most plainly: "You don't know anything." I replied: "My gifts are very small, I know, but I can no longer be shaken by what you or any one else may think or say."

From this time the opposition to my life-work commenced, instigated by the minister, Mr. Beman. Many in the church were anxious to have me preach in the hall, where our meetings were held at that time, and were not a little astonished at the minister's cool treatment of me. At length two of the trustees got some of the elder sisters to call on the minister and ask him to let me preach. His answer was: "No; she can't preach her holiness stuff here, and I am astonished that you should ask it of me." The sisters said he seemed to be in quite a rage, although he said he was not angry.

PUBLIC EFFORT—EXCOMMUNICATION   From Julia A. J. Foote, *A Brand Plucked from the Fire* (Cleveland: Lauer & Yost, 1879) 71–76.

There being no meeting of the society on Monday evening, a brother in the church opened his house to me, that I might preach, which displeased Mr. Beman very much. He appointed a committee to wait upon the brother and sister who had opened their doors to me, to tell them they must not allow any more meetings of that kind, and that they must abide by the rules of the church, making them believe they would be excommunicated if they disobeyed him. I happened to be present at this interview, and the committee remonstrated with me for the course I had taken. I told them my business was with the Lord, and wherever I found a door opened I intended to go in and work for my Master.

There was another meeting appointed at the same place, which I, of course, attended; after which the meetings were stopped for that time, though I held many more there after these people had withdrawn from Mr. Beman's church.

I then held meetings in my own house; whereat the minister told the members that if they attended them he would deal with them, for they were breaking the rules of the church. When he found that I continued the meetings, and that the Lord was blessing my feeble efforts, he sent a committee of two to ask me if I considered myself a member of his church. I told them I did, and should continue to do so until I had done something worthy of dismembership.

At this, Mr. Beman sent another committee with a note, asking me to meet him with the committee, which I did. He asked me a number of questions, nearly all of which I have forgotten. One, however, I do remember: he asked if I was willing to comply with the rules of the discipline. To this I answered: "Not if the discipline prohibits me from doing what God has bidden me to do; I fear God more than man." Similar questions were asked and answered in the same manner. The committee said what they wished to say, and then told me I could go home. When I reached the door, I turned and said: "I now shake off the dust of my feet as a witness against you. See to it that this meeting does not rise in judgment against you."

The next evening, one of the committee came to me and told me that I was no longer a member of the church, because I had violated the rules of the discipline by preaching.

When this action became known, the people wondered how any one could be excommunicated for trying to do good. I did not say much, and my friends simply said I had done nothing but hold meetings. Others, anxious to know the particulars, asked the minister what the trouble was. He told them he had given me the privilege of speaking or preaching as long as I chose, but that he could not give me the right to use the pulpit, and that I was not satisfied with any other place. Also, that I had appointed meeting on the evening of his meetings, which was a thing no member had a right to do. For these reasons he said he had turned me out of the church.

Now, if the people who repeated this to me told the truth—and I have no doubt but they did—Mr. Beman told an actual falsehood. I had never asked for his pulpit, but had told him and others, repeatedly, that I did not care where I stood—any corner of the hall would do. To which Mr. Beman had answered: "You cannot have any place in the hall." Then I said, "I'll preach in a private house." He answered me: "No, not in this place; I am stationed over all Boston." He was determined I should not preach in the city of Boston. To cover up his deceptive, unrighteous course toward me, he told the above falsehoods.

From his statements, many erroneous stories concerning me gained credence with a large number of people. At that time, I thought it my duty as well as privilege to address a letter to the Conference, which I took to them in person, stating all the facts. At the same time I told them it was not in the power of Mr. Beman, or any one else, to truthfully bring anything against my moral or religious character—that my only offence was in trying to preach the Gospel of Christ—and that I cherished no ill feelings toward Mr. Beman or any one else, but that I desired the Conference to give the case an impartial hearing, and then give me a written statement expressive of their opinion. I also said I considered myself a member of the Conference, and should do so until they said I was not, and gave me their reasons, that I might let the world know what my offence had been.

My letter was slightingly noticed, and then thrown under the table. Why should they notice it? It was only the grievance of a woman, and there was no justice meted out to women in those days. Even ministers of Christ did not feel that women had any rights which they were bound to respect.

REST

S. Weir Mitchell

S. Weir Mitchell (1829–1914), novelist and poet, medical researcher and distinguished physician, was a specialist in the nervous disorders of women. Some of his patients suffered from nervous exhaustion; others were diagnosed as hysteric. Most had been treated by many doctors before him, for gastric, spinal, or uterine troubles; his work with such difficult cases had earned him an international reputation. The most fashionable women sought Mitchell's services, and he was the toast of Philadelphia society.

His treatment, known as the "rest cure," consisted of isolation and rest; excessive feeding with dietary supplements; and "passive exercise," that is, massage and electrical stimulation of the body. Mitchell had discovered during the Civil War that rest could cure battle fatigue. He believed that running a household, caring for children, nursing sick relatives, or getting a college education could produce similar fatigue in women, which also could be helped with rest. Because his patients frequently had digestive problems, were underweight and anemic, and sometimes were addicted to drugs and opiates, he put them on the special diet. The massage and electrical stimulation were needed to prevent the debilitating effects of total bed rest.

The rest cure also had a "moral," or psychological, aspect. Mitchell believed that the treatment would not be successful unless the patient cooperated in fighting the disease. And such cooperation was sometimes difficult to acquire. "For the most entire capacity to make a household wretched," wrote Mitchell, "there is no more complete human receipt [recipe] than a silly woman who is to a high degree nervous and feeble, and who craves pity and power." In his view, to get such women to obey his behavioral prescriptions, the doctor had to inspire complete confidence even to the point of promoting childlike acquiescence.

 Whether we shall ask a patient to walk or take rest is a question which turns up for answer almost every day in practice. Most often we incline to insist on exercise, and are led to do so from a belief that women walk too little, and that to move about a good deal every day is good for everybody. I think we are as often wrong as right. A good brisk daily walk is for well folks a tonic, breaks down old tissues, and creates a wholesome demand for food. The same is true for some sick

REST   From S. Weir Mitchell, *Fat and Blood: And How to Make Them* (Philadelphia: Lippincott, 1877) 37–44.

people. The habit of horse exercise or a long walk every day is needed to cure or to aid in the cure of disordered stomach and costive bowels, but if all exertion gives rise only to increase of trouble, to extreme sense of fatigue, to nausea, what shall we do? And suppose that tonics do not help to make exertion easy, and that the great tonic of change of air fails us, shall we still persist? And here lies the trouble: there are women who mimic fatigue, who indulge themselves in rest on the least pretence, who have no symptoms so truly honest that we need care to regard them. These are they who spoil their own nervous systems as they spoil their children, when they have them, by yielding to the least desire and teaching them to dwell on little pains. For such people there is no help but to insist on self-control and on daily use of the limbs. They must be told to exert themselves, and made to do so if that can be. If they are young this is easy enough. If they have grown to middle life, and made long habits of self-indulgence, the struggle is always useless. But few, however, among these women are free from some defect of blood or tissue, either original or having come on as a result of years of indolence and attention to aches and ailments which should never have had given to them more than a passing thought, and which certainly should not have been made an excuse for the sofa or the bed.

Sometimes the question is easy to settle. If you find a woman who is in good state as to color and flesh, and who is always able to do what it pleases her to do, and who is tired by what does not please her, that is a woman to order out of bed and to control with a firm and steady will. That is a woman who is to be made to walk, with no regard to her aches, and to be made to persist until exertion ceases to give rise to the mimicry of fatigue. In such cases the man who can insure belief in his opinions and obedience to his decrees secures very often most brilliant and sometimes easy success; and it is in such cases that women who are in all other ways capable doctors fail, because they do not obtain the needed control over those of their own sex. There are still other cases in which the same mischievous tendencies to repose, to endless tire, to hysterical symptoms, and to emotional displays have grown out of defects of nutrition so distinct that no man ought to think for them of mere exertion as a sole means of cure. The time comes for that, but it should not come until entire rest has been used, with other means, to fit them for making use of their muscles. Nothing upsets these cases like overexertion, and the attempt to make them walk usually ends in some mischievous emotional display, and in creating a new reason for thinking that they cannot walk. As to the two sets of cases just sketched, no one need hesitate; the one must walk, the other should not until we have bettered her nutritive state. She may be able to drag herself about, but no good will be done by making her do so. But between these two classes lies the larger number of such cases, giving us every kind of real and imagined symptom, and dreadfully well fitted to puzzle the most competent physician. As a rule, no harm is done by rest, even in such people as give us doubts about whether it is or is not well for them to exert themselves. There are plenty of these women who are just well enough to make it likely that if they had motive enough for exertion to cause them to forget themselves they would find it useful. In the doubt I am rather given to insisting on rest, but the rest I like for them is not at all their notion of rest. To lie abed half the day, and sew a little and read a little, and be interesting and excite sympathy, is all very well, but when they are bidden to stay in bed a month, and neither to read, write, nor sew, and to have one nurse,—who is not a relative,—then rest becomes for some women a rather bitter medicine, and they are glad enough to accept the order to rise and go about when the doctor issues a mandate which has become pleasantly welcome and eagerly looked for. I do not think it easy to make a mistake in this matter unless the woman takes with morbid delight to the system of enforced rest, and unless the doctor is a person of feeble will. I have never met myself with any serious trouble about getting out of bed any woman for whom I thought rest needful, but it has happened to others, and the man who resolves to send any nervous woman to bed must be quite sure that she will obey him when the time comes for her to get up.

I have, of course, made use of every grade of rest for my patients, from insisting upon repose on a lounge for some hours a day up to entire rest in bed. In carrying out my general plan of treatment it is my habit to ask the patient to remain in bed from six weeks to two months. At first, and in some cases for four or five weeks, I do not permit the patient to sit up or to sew or write or read. The only action allowed is that needed to clean the teeth. In some instances I have not permitted the patient to turn over without aid, and this I have done because sometimes I think no motion desirable, and because sometimes the moral influence of absolute repose is of use. In such cases I arrange to have the bowels and water passed while lying down, and the patient is lifted on to a lounge at bedtime and sponged, and then lifted back again into the newly-made bed. In all cases of weakness, treated by rest, I insist on the patient being fed by the nurse, and, when well enough to sit up in bed, I insist that the meats shall be cut up, so as to make it easier for the patient to feed herself.

In many cases I allow the patient to sit up in order to obey the calls of nature, but I am always careful to have the bowels kept reasonably free from costiveness, knowing well how such a state and the efforts it gives rise to enfeeble a sick person.

Usually, after a fortnight I permit the patient to be read to,—one to three hours a day,—but I am daily amazed to see how kindly nervous and anæmic women take to this absolute rest, and how little they complain of its monotony. In fact, the use of massage and the battery, with the frequent comings of the nurse with food and the doctor's visits, seem so to fill up the day as to make the treatment less tiresome than might be supposed. And, besides this, the sense of comfort which is apt to come about the fifth or sixth day,—the feeling of ease, and the ready capacity to digest food, and the growing hope of final cure, fed as it is by present relief,—all conspire to make most patients contented and tractable.

The moral uses of enforced rest are readily estimated. From a restless life of irregular hours, and probably endless drugging, from hurtful sympathy and over-zealous care, the patient passes to an atmosphere of quiet, to order and control, to the system and care of a thorough nurse, to an absence of drugs, and to simple diet. The result is always at first, whatever it may be afterwards, a sense of relief, and a remarkable and often a quite abrupt disappearance of many of the nervous symptoms with which we are all of us only too sadly familiar.

All the moral uses of rest and isolation and change of habits are not obtained by merely insisting on the physical conditions needed to effect these ends. If the physician has the force of character required to secure the confidence and respect of his patients he has also much more in his power, and should have the tact to seize the proper occasions to direct the thoughts of his patients to the lapse from duties to others, and to the selfishness which a life of invalidism is apt to bring about. Such moral medication belongs to the higher sphere of the doctor's duties, and if he means to cure his patient permanently, he cannot afford to neglect them. Above all, let him be careful that the masseuse and the nurse do not talk of the patient's ills, and let him by degrees teach the sick person how very essential it is to speak of her aches and pains to no one but himself.

THE YELLOW WALL-PAPER
Charlotte Perkins Gilman

For much of her adult life, Charlotte Perkins Gilman (1860–1935) earned her living by lecturing all over the country. She wrote poetry and short stories, and for seven years she was sole writer and editor of *The Forerunner*, a magazine devoted to women and social change. Her famous novel, *Herland*, about a utopian society of women, was published in installments in the magazine. Gilman's most famous nonfiction book, *Women and Economics* (1898), analyzed the damage done to women by confining them to the domestic sphere.

In her personal life, Gilman also fought the confinements of domesticity. She married Charles Stetson at the age of twenty-four. But with the birth of her daughter a year later, Gilman lapsed into a deep depression. Unable to cope with domestic and maternal duties, she set out to visit friends in California. She felt better almost immediately, and her symptoms came back only as she approached home.

Upon her return, she was treated by S. Weir Mitchell. He diagnosed her problem as hysteria and administered "the rest cure." After a month, she was sent home with the prescription: "Live as domestic a life as possible. Have your child with you all the time. Lie down an hour after each meal. Have but two hours' intellectual life a day. And never touch pen, brush or pencil as long as you live."

Gilman later reported that this prescription almost drove her mad. Realizing that her choice was between staying with her husband and going mad, or leaving and staying sane, she left, taking her daughter with her. Later she divorced Stetson, and when he married her best friend, she gave up her daughter to the care of Stetson and his new wife. Gilman was criticized as unnatural for these decisions.

In 1900, Gilman married George Houghton Gilman, her cousin. In 1935 she committed suicide rather than face a slow and painful death from breast cancer.

It is very seldom that mere ordinary people like John and myself secure ancestral halls for the summer.

A colonial mansion, a hereditary estate, I would say a haunted house, and reach the height of romantic felicity—but that would be asking too much of fate!

Still I will proudly declare that there is something queer about it.

Else, why should it be let so cheaply? And why have stood so long untenanted?

John laughs at me, of course, but one expects that in marriage.

John is practical in the extreme. He has no patience with faith, an intense horror of superstition, and he scoffs openly at any talk of things not to be felt and seen and put down in figures.

John is a physician, and *perhaps*—(I would not say it to a living soul, of course, but this is dead paper and a great relief to my mind)—*perhaps* that is one reason I do not get well faster.

You see he does not believe I am sick!

THE YELLOW WALL-PAPER   From Charlotte Perkins Gilman, "The Yellow Wall-Paper," *The New England Magazine* Jan. 1892: 647–56.

Then he took me in his arms and called me a blessed little goose, and said he would go down cellar, if I wished, and have it whitewashed into the bargain.

But he is right enough about the beds and windows and things.

It is an airy and comfortable room as any one need wish, and, of course, I would not be so silly as to make him uncomfortable just for a whim.

I'm really getting quite fond of the big room, all but that horrid paper.

Out of one window I can see the garden, those mysterious deep-shaded arbors, the riotous old-fashioned flowers, and bushes and gnarly trees.

Out of another I get a lovely view of the bay and a little private wharf belonging to the estate. There is a beautiful shaded lane that runs down there from the house. I always fancy I see people walking in these numerous paths and arbors, but John has cautioned me not to give way to fancy in the least. He says that with my imaginative power and habit of story-making, a nervous weakness like mine is sure to lead to all manner of excited fancies, and that I ought to use my will and good sense to check the tendency. So I try.

I think sometimes that if I were only well enough to write a little it would relieve the press of ideas and rest me.

But I find I get pretty tired when I try.

It is so discouraging not to have any advice and companionship about my work. When I get really well, John says we will ask Cousin Henry and Julia down for a long visit; but he says he would as soon put fireworks in my pillow-case as to let me have those stimulating people about now.

I wish I could get well faster.

But I must not think about that. This paper looks to me as if it *knew* what a vicious influence it had!

There is a recurrent spot where the pattern lolls like a broken neck and two bulbous eyes stare at you upside down.

I get positively angry with the impertinence of it and the everlastingness. Up and down and sideways they crawl, and those absurd, unblinking eyes are everywhere. There is one place where two breadths didn't match, and the eyes go all up and down the line, one a little higher than the other.

I never saw so much expression in an inanimate thing before, and we all know how much expression they have! I used to lie awake as a child and get more entertainment and terror out of blank walls and plain furniture than most children could find in a toy-store.

I remember what a kindly wink the knobs of our big, old bureau used to have, and there was one chair that always seemed like a strong friend.

I used to feel that if any of the other things looked too fierce I could always hop into that chair and be safe.

The furniture in this room is no worse than inharmonious, however, for we had to bring it all from downstairs. I suppose when this was used as a playroom they had to take the nursery things out, and no wonder! I never saw such ravages as the children have made here.

The wall-paper, as I said before, is torn off in spots, and it sticketh closer than a brother—they must have had perseverance as well as hatred.

Then the floor is scratched and gouged and splintered, the plaster itself is dug out here and there, and this great heavy bed which is all we found in the room, looks as if it had been through the wars.

"But I don't mind it a bit—only the paper."

There comes John's sister. Such a dear girl as she is, and so careful of me! I must not let her find me writing.

She is a perfect and enthusiastic housekeeper, and hopes for no better profession. I verily believe she thinks it is the writing which made me sick!

But I can write when she is out, and see her a long way off from these windows.

There is one that commands the road, a lovely shaded winding road, and one that just looks off over the country. A lovely country, too, full of great elms and velvet meadows.

This wall-paper has a kind of subpattern in a different shade, a particularly irritating one, for you can only see it in certain lights, and not clearly then.

But in the places where it isn't faded and where the sun is just so—I can see a strange, provoking, formless sort of figure, that seems to skulk about behind that silly and conspicuous front design.

There's sister on the stairs!

🌿 🌿 🌿

Well, the Fourth of July is over! The people are all gone and I am tired out. John thought it might do me good to see a little company, so we just had mother and Nellie and the children down for a week.

Of course I didn't do a thing. Jennie sees to everything now.

But it tired me all the same.

John says if I don't pick up faster he shall send me to Weir Mitchell in the fall.

But I don't want to go there at all. I had a friend who was in his hands once, and she says he is just like John and my brother, only more so!

Besides, it is such an undertaking to go so far.

I don't feel as if it was worth while to turn my hand over for anything, and I'm getting dreadfully fretful and querulous.

I cry at nothing, and cry most of the time.

Of course I don't when John is here, or anybody else, but when I am alone.

And I am alone a good deal just now. John is kept in town very often by serious cases, and Jennie is good and lets me alone when I want her to.

So I walk a little in the garden or down that lovely lane, sit on the porch under the roses, and lie down up here a good deal.

I'm getting really fond of the room in spite of the wall-paper. Perhaps *because* of the wall-paper.

It dwells in my mind so!

I lie here on this great immovable bed—it is nailed down, I believe—and follow that pattern about by the hour. It is as good as gymnastics, I assure you. I start, we'll say, at the bottom, down in the corner over there where it has not been touched, and I determine for the thousandth time that I *will* follow that pointless pattern to some sort of a conclusion.

I know a little of the principle of design, and I know this thing was not arranged on any laws of radiation, or alternation, or repetition, or symmetry, or anything else that I ever heard of.

It is repeated, of course, by the breadths, but not otherwise.

Looked at in one way each breadth stands alone, the bloated curves and flourishes—a kind of "debased Romanesque" with *delirium tremens*—go waddling up and down in isolated columns of fatuity.

But, on the other hand, they connect diagonally, and the sprawling outlines run off in great slanting waves of optic horror, like a lot of wallowing seaweeds in full chase.

The whole thing goes horizontally, too, at least it seems so, and I exhaust myself in trying to distinguish the order of its going in that direction.

They have used a horizontal breadth for a frieze, and that adds wonderfully to the confusion.

There is one end of the room where it is almost intact, and there, when the crosslights fade and the low sun shines directly upon it, I can almost fancy radiation after all,—the interminable grotesque seems to form around a common centre and rush off in headlong plunges of equal distraction.

It makes me tired to follow it. I will take a nap I guess.

🙰 🙰 🙰

I don't know why I should write this.

I don't want to.

I don't feel able.

And I know John would think it absurd. But I *must* say what I feel and think in some way—it is such a relief!

But the effort is getting to be greater than the relief.

Half the time now I am awfully lazy, and lie down ever so much.

John says I mustn't lose my strength, and has me take cod liver oil and lots of tonics and things, to say nothing of ale and wine and rare meat.

Dear John! He loves me very dearly, and hates to have me sick. I tried to have a real earnest reasonable talk with him the other day, and tell him how I wish he would let me go and make a visit to Cousin Henry and Julia.

But he said I wasn't able to go, nor able to stand it after I got there; and I did not make out a very good case for myself, for I was crying before I had finished.

It is getting to be a great effort for me to think straight. Just this nervous weakness I suppose.

And dear John gathered me up in his arms, and just carried me upstairs and laid me on the bed, and sat by me and read to me till it tired my head.

He said I was his darling and his comfort and all he had, and that I must take care of myself for his sake, and keep well.

He says no one but myself can help me out of it, that I must use my will and self-control and not let any silly fancies run away with me.

There's one comfort, the baby is well and happy, and does not have to occupy this nursery with the horrid wall-paper.

If we had not used it, that blessed child would have! What a fortunate escape! Why, I wouldn't have a child of mine, an impressionable little thing, live in such a room for worlds.

I never thought of it before, but it is lucky that John kept me here after all, I can stand it so much easier than a baby, you see.

Of course I never mention it to them any more—I am too wise,—but I keep watch of it all the same.

There are things in that paper that nobody knows but me, or ever will.

Behind that outside pattern the dim shapes get clearer every day.

It is always the same shape, only very numerous.

And it is like a woman stooping down and creeping about behind that pattern. I don't like it a bit. I wonder—I begin to think—I wish John would take me away from here!

❦ ❦ ❦

It is so hard to talk with John about my case because he is so wise, and because he loves me so.

But I tried it last night.

It was moonlight. The moon shines in all around just as the sun does.

I hate to see it sometimes, it creeps so slowly, and always comes in by one window or another.

John was asleep and I hated to waken him, so I kept still and watched the moonlight on that undulating wall-paper till I felt creepy.

The faint figure behind seemed to shake the pattern, just as if she wanted to get out.

I got up softly and went to feel and see if the paper *did* move, and when I came back John was awake.

"What is it, little girl?" he said. "Don't go walking about like that—you'll get cold."

I thought it was a good time to talk, so I told him that I really was not gaining here, and that I wished he would take me away.

"Why, darling!" said he, "our lease will be up in three weeks, and I can't see how to leave before.

"The repairs are not done at home, and I cannot possibly leave town just now. Of course if you were in any danger, I could and would, but you really are better, dear, whether you can see it or not. I am a doctor, dear, and I know. You are gaining flesh and color, your appetite is better, I feel really much easier about you."

"I don't weigh a bit more," said I, "nor as much; and my appetite may be better in the evening when you are here, but it is worse in the morning when you are away!"

"Bless her little heart!" said he with a big hug, "she shall be as sick as she pleases! But now let's improve the shining hours by going to sleep, and talk about it in the morning!"

"And you won't go away?" I asked gloomily.

"Why, how can I, dear? It is only three weeks more and then we will take a nice little trip of a few days while Jennie is getting the house ready. Really dear you are better!"

"Better in body perhaps—" I began, and stopped short, for he sat up straight and looked at me with such a stern, reproachful look that I could not say another word.

"My darling," said he, "I beg of you, for my sake and for our child's sake, as well as for your own, that you will never for one instant let that idea enter your mind! There is nothing so dangerous, so fascinating, to a temperament like yours. It is a false and foolish fancy. Can you not trust me as a physician when I tell you so?"

So of course I said no more on that score, and we went to sleep before long. He thought I was asleep first, but I wasn't, and lay there for hours trying to decide whether that front pattern and the back pattern really did move together or separately.

❧ ❧ ❧

On a pattern like this, by daylight, there is a lack of sequence, a defiance of law, that is a constant irritant to a normal mind.

The color is hideous enough, and unreliable enough, and infuriating enough, but the pattern is torturing.

You think you have mastered it, but just as you get well underway in following, it turns a back-somersault and there you are. It slaps you in the face, knocks you down, and tramples upon you. It is like a bad dream.

The outside pattern is a florid arabesque, reminding one of a fungus. If you can imagine a toadstool in joints, an interminable string of toadstools, budding and sprouting in endless convolutions—why, that is something like it.

That is, sometimes!

There is one marked peculiarity about this paper, a thing nobody seems to notice but myself, and that is that it changes as the light changes.

When the sun shoots in through the east window—I always watch for that first long, straight ray—it changes so quickly that I never can quite believe it.

That is why I watch it always.

By moonlight—the moon shines in all night when there is a moon—I wouldn't know it was the same paper.

At night in any kind of light, in twilight, candlelight, lamplight, and worst of all by moonlight, it becomes bars! The outside pattern I mean, and the woman behind it is as plain as can be.

I didn't realize for a long time what the thing was that showed behind, that dim sub-pattern, but now I am quite sure it is a woman.

By daylight she is subdued, quiet. I fancy it is the pattern that keeps her so still. It is so puzzling. It keeps me quiet by the hour.

I lie down ever so much now. John says it is good for me, and to sleep all I can.

Indeed he started the habit by making me lie down for an hour after each meal.

It is a very bad habit I am convinced, for you see I don't sleep.

And that cultivates deceit, for I don't tell them I'm awake—O no!

The fact is I am getting a little afraid of John.

He seems very queer sometimes, and even Jennie has an inexplicable look.

It strikes me occasionally, just as a scientific hypothesis,—that perhaps it is the paper!

I have watched John when he did not know I was looking, and come into the room suddenly on the most innocent excuses, and I've caught him several times *looking at the paper!* And Jennie too. I caught Jennie with her hand on it once.

She didn't know I was in the room, and when I asked her in a quiet, a very quiet voice, with the most restrained manner possible, what she was doing with the paper—she turned around as if she had been caught stealing, and looked quite angry—asked me why I should frighten her so!

Then she said that the paper stained everything it touched, that she had found yellow smooches on all my clothes and John's, and she wished we would be more careful!

Did not that sound innocent? But I know she was studying that pattern, and I am determined that nobody shall find it out but myself!

☙ ☙ ☙

Life is very much more exciting now than it used to be. You see I have something more to expect, to look forward to, to watch. I really do eat better, and am more quiet than I was.

John is so pleased to see me improve! He laughed a little the other day, and said I seemed to be flourishing in spite of my wall-paper.

I turned it off with a laugh. I had no intention of telling him it was *because* of the wall-paper—he would make fun of me. He might even want to take me away.

I don't want to leave now until I have found it out. There is a week more, and I think that will be enough.

☙ ☙ ☙

I'm feeling ever so much better! I don't sleep much at night, for it is so interesting to watch developments; but I sleep a good deal in the daytime.

In the daytime it is tiresome and perplexing.

There are always new shoots on the fungus, and new shades of yellow all over it. I cannot keep count of them, though I have tried conscientiously.

It is the strangest yellow, that wall-paper! It makes me think of all the yellow things I ever saw—not beautiful ones like buttercups, but old foul, bad yellow things.

But there is something else about that paper—the smell! I noticed it the moment we came into the room, but with so much air and sun it was not bad. Now we have had a week of fog and rain, and whether the windows are open or not, the smell is here.

It creeps all over the house.

I find it hovering in the dining-room, skulking in the parlor, hiding in the hall, lying in wait for me on the stairs.

It gets into my hair.

Even when I go to ride, if I turn my head suddenly and surprise it—there is that smell!

Such a peculiar odor, too! I have spent hours in trying to analyze it, to find what it smelled like.

It is not bad—at first, and very gentle, but quite the subtlest, most enduring odor I ever met.

In this damp weather it is awful, I wake up in the night and find it hanging over me.

It used to disturb me at first. I thought seriously of burning the house—to reach the smell.

But now I am used to it. The only thing I can think of that it is like is the *color* of the paper! A yellow smell.

There is a very funny mark on this wall, low down, near the mopboard. A streak that runs round the room. It goes behind every piece of furniture, except the bed, a long, straight, even *smooch*, as if it had been rubbed over and over.

I wonder how it was done and who did it, and what they did it for. Round and round and round—round and round and round—it makes me dizzy!

I really have discovered something at last.

Through watching so much at night, when it changes so, I have finally found out. The front pattern *does* move—and no wonder! The woman behind shakes it!

Sometimes I think there are a great many women behind, and sometimes only one, and she crawls around fast, and her crawling shakes it all over.

Then in the very bright spots she keeps still, and in the very shady spots she just takes hold of the bars and shakes them hard.

And she is all the time trying to climb through. But nobody could climb through that pattern—it strangles so; I think that is why it has so many heads.

They get through, and then the pattern strangles them off and turns them upside down, and makes their eyes white!

If those heads were covered or taken off it would not be half so bad.

❦ ❦ ❦

I think that woman gets out in the daytime!

And I'll tell you why—privately—I've seen her!

I can see her out of every one of my windows!

It is the same woman, I know, for she is always creeping, and most women do not creep by daylight.

I see her in that long shaded lane, creeping up and down. I see her in those dark grape arbors, creeping all around the garden.

I see her on that long road under the trees, creeping along, and when a carriage comes she hides under the blackberry vines.

I don't blame her a bit. It must be very humiliating to be caught creeping by daylight!

I always lock the door when I creep by daylight. I can't do it at night, for I know John would suspect something at once.

And John is so queer now, that I don't want to irritate him. I wish he would take another room! Besides, I don't want anybody to get that woman out at night but myself.

I often wonder if I could see her out of all the windows at once.

But, turn as fast as I can, I can only see out of one at one time.

And though I always see her, she *may* be able to creep faster that I can turn!

I have watched her sometimes away off in the open country, creeping as fast as a cloud shadow in a high wind.

If only that top pattern could be gotten off from the under one! I mean to try it, little by little.

I have found out another funny thing, but I shan't tell it this time! It does not do to trust people too much.

There are only two more days to get this paper off, and I believe John is beginning to notice. I don't like the look in his eyes.

And I heard him ask Jennie a lot of professional questions about me. She had a very good report to give.

She said I slept a good deal in the daytime.

John knows I don't sleep very well at night, for all I'm so quiet!

He asked me all sorts of questions, too, and pretended to be very loving and kind. As if I couldn't see through him!

Still, I don't wonder he acts so, sleeping under this paper for three months.

It only interests me, but I feel sure John and Jennie are secretly affected by it.

❧ ❧ ❧

Hurrah! This is the last day, but it is enough. John to stay in town over night, and won't be out until this evening.

Jennie wanted to sleep with me—the sly thing! but I told her I should undoubtedly rest better for a night all alone.

That was clever, for really I wasn't alone a bit! As soon as it was moonlight and that poor thing began to crawl and shake the pattern, I got up and ran to help her.

I pulled and she shook, I shook and she pulled, and before morning we had peeled off yards of that paper.

A strip about as high as my head and half around the room.

And then when the sun came and that awful pattern began to laugh at me, I declared I would finish it to-day!

We go away to-morrow, and they are moving all my furniture down again to leave things as they were before.

Jennie looked at the wall in amazement, but I told her merrily that I did it out of pure spite at the vicious thing.

She laughed and said she wouldn't mind doing it herself, but I must not get tired.

How she betrayed herself that time!

But I am here, and no person touches this paper but me,—not *alive!*

She tried to get me out of the room—it was too patent! But I said it was so quiet and empty and clean now that I believed I would lie down again and sleep all I could; and not to wake me even for dinner—I would call when I woke.

So now she is gone, and the servants are gone, and the things are gone, and there is nothing left but that great bedstead nailed down, with the canvas mattress we found on it.

We shall sleep downstairs to-night, and take the boat home to-morrow.

I quite enjoy the room, now it is bare again.

How those children did tear about here!

This bedstead is fairly gnawed!

But I must get to work.

I have locked the door and thrown the key down into the front path.

I don't want to go out, and I don't want to have anybody come in, till John comes.

I want to astonish him.

I've got a rope up here that even Jennie did not find. If that woman does get out, and tries to get away, I can tie her!

But I forgot I could not reach far without anything to stand on!

This bed will *not* move!

I tried to lift and push it until I was lame, and then I got so angry I bit off a little piece at one corner—but it hurt my teeth.

Then I peeled off all the paper I could reach standing on the floor. It sticks horribly and the pattern just enjoys it! All those strangled heads and bulbous eyes and waddling fungus growths just shriek with derision!

I am getting angry enough to do something desperate. To jump out of the window would be admirable exercise, but the bars are too strong even to try.

Besides I wouldn't do it. Of course not. I know well enough that a step like that is improper and might be misconstrued.

I don't like to *look* out of the windows even—there are so many of those creeping women, and they creep so fast.

I wonder if they all came out of that wall-paper as I did?

But I am securely fastened now by my well-hidden rope—you don't get *me* out in the road there!

I suppose I shall have to get back behind the pattern when it comes night, and that is hard!

It is so pleasant to be out in this great room and creep around as I please!

I don't want to go outside. I won't, even if Jennie asks me to.

For outside you have to creep on the ground, and everything is green instead of yellow.

But here I can creep smoothly on the floor, and my shoulder just fits in that long smooch around the wall, so I cannot lose my way.

Why there's John at the door!

It is no use, young man, you can't open it!

How he does call and pound!

Now he's crying for an axe.

It would be a shame to break down that beautiful door!

"John dear," said I in the gentlest voice, "the key is down by the front steps, under a plantain leaf!"

That silenced him for a few moments.

Then he said—very quietly indeed, "Open the door, my darling!"

"I can't," said I. "The key is down by the front door under a plantain leaf!"

And then I said it again, several times, very gently and slowly, and said it so often that he had to go and see, and he got it of course, and came in. He stopped short by the door.

"What is the matter?" he cried. "For God's sake, what are you doing!"

I kept on creeping just the same, but I looked at him over my shoulder.

"I've got out at last," said I, "in spite of you and Jane. And I've pulled off most of the paper, so you can't put me back!"

Now why should that man have fainted? But he did, and right across my path by the wall, so that I had to creep over him every time!

ADDRESS TO THE FIRST NATIONAL CONFERENCE OF COLORED WOMEN

Josephine St. Pierre Ruffin

Josephine St. Pierre Ruffin (1842–1924) grew up in Boston and attended public schools there after they were desegregated in 1855. She married George Lewis Ruffin, who became the first African-American municipal judge in Massachusetts, and raised five children. In addition to working in the war relief effort, Ruffin founded and served a number of social welfare associations in Boston. She remained a tireless community leader all her life.

Ruffin's talents for organizing led her into the reform society movement. In 1894, she organized the Woman's Era Club, one of many local clubs for African-American women. These clubs provided companionship, helped women find employment, set up day nurseries and kindergartens, and established homes to protect young women when they first arrived in the cities. They also fought for equality for African Americans (who were excluded from most white women's clubs).

In 1900, Ruffin sought to attend the General Federation of Women's Clubs (GFWC) convention as a delegate of the Woman's Era Club and the Massachusetts State Federation of Women's Clubs. The GFWC refused to seat her because she represented a "colored club."

Ruffin served as the president of the Woman's Era Club for a decade and edited its newspaper, *The Woman's Era*, for many years. Recognizing the need to consolidate efforts, Ruffin called for the federation of clubs into the National Association of Colored Women. She delivered the following speech in 1895 at the Federation's first national conference.

It is with especial joy and pride that I welcome you all to this, our first conference. It is only recently that women have waked up to the importance of meeting in council, and great as has been the advantage to women *generally*, and important as it is and has been that they should confer, the necessity has not been nearly so great, matters at stake not nearly so vital, as that *we*, bearing peculiar blunders, suffering under especial hardships, enduring peculiar privations, should meet for a "good talk" among ourselves. Although rather hastily called, you as well as I can testify how long and how earnestly a conference has been thought of and hoped for and even prepared for. These women's clubs, which have sprung up all over the country, built and run upon broad and strong lines, have all been a preparation, small conferences in themselves, and their spontaneous birth and enthusiastic support have been little less than inspirational on the part of our women and a general preparation for a large union such as it is hoped this conference will lead to. Five years ago we had no colored women's clubs outside of those formed for special work; to-day, with little over a month's notice, we are able to call representatives from more than twenty clubs. It is a good showing, it stands for much, it shows that we are truly American women, with all the adaptability, readiness to seize and possess our opportunities, willingness to do our part for good as other American women.

The reasons why we should confer are so apparent that it would seem hardly necessary to enumerate them, and yet there is none of them but demand our serious consideration. In the first place we need to feel the cheer and inspiration of meeting each other, we need to gain the courage and fresh life that comes from the mingling of congenial souls, of those working for the same ends. Next, we need to talk over not only those things which are of vital importance to us as women, but also the things that are of especial interest to us as *colored* women, the training of our children, openings for our boys and girls, how they can be prepared for occupations and occupations may be found or opened for them, what *we* especially can do in the moral education of the race with which we are identified, our mental elevation and physical development, the home training it is necessary to give our children in order to prepare them to meet the peculiar conditions in which they shall find themselves, how to make the most of our own, to some extent, limited opportunities, these are some of our own peculiar questions to be discussed. Besides these are the general

ADDRESS TO THE FIRST NATIONAL CONFERENCE   From Josephine St. Pierre Ruffin, *The Woman's Era* Sept. 1895: 12–15.

questions of the day, which we cannot afford to be indifferent to: temperance, morality, the higher education, hygienic and domestic questions. If these things need the serious consideration of women more advantageously placed by reason of all the aid to right thinking and living with which they are surrounded, surely we, with everything to pull us back, to hinder us in developing, need to take every opportunity and means for the thoughtful consideration which shall lead to wise action.

I have left the strongest reason for our conferring together until the last. All over America there is to be found a large and growing class of earnest, intelligent, progressive colored women, women who, if not leading full useful lives, are only waiting for the opportunity to do so, many of them warped and cramped for lack of opportunity, not only to do more but to *be* more; and yet, if an estimate of the colored women of America is called for, the inevitable reply, glibly given, is, "For the most part ignorant and immoral, some exceptions, of course, but these don't count."

Now for the sake of the thousands of self-sacrificing young women teaching and preaching in lonely southern backwoods, for the noble army of mothers who have given birth to these girls, mothers whose intelligence is only limited by their opportunity to get at books, for the sake of the fine cultured women who have carried off the honors in school here and often abroad, for the sake of our own dignity, the dignity of our race and the future good name of our children, it is "mete, right and our bounden duty" to stand forth and declare ourselves and principles, to teach an ignorant and suspicious world that our aims and interests are identical with those of all good aspiring women. Too long have we been silent under unjust and unholy charges; we cannot expect to have them removed until we disprove them through *ourselves*. It is not enough to try to disprove unjust charges through individual effort, that never goes any further. Year after year southern women have protested against the admission of colored women into any national organization on the ground of the immorality of these women, and because all refutation has only been tried by individual work the charge has never been crushed, as it could and should have been at the first. Now with an army of organized women standing for purity and mental worth, we in ourselves deny the charge and open the eyes of the world to a state of affairs to which they have been blind, often willfully so, and the very fact that the charges, audaciously and flippantly made, as they often are, are of so humiliating and delicate a nature, serves to protect the accuser by driving the helpless accused into mortified silence. It is to break this silence, not by noisy protestations of what we are not, but by a dignified showing of what we are and hope to become that we are impelled to take this step, to make of this gathering an object lesson to the world. For many and apparent reasons it is especially fitting that the *women* of the race take the lead in this movement, but for all this we recognize the necessity of the sympathy for our husbands, brothers and fathers.

Our woman's movement is woman's movement in that it is led and directed by women for the good of women and men, for the benefit of *all* humanity, which is more than any one branch or section of it. We want, we ask the active interest of our men, and, too, we are not drawing the color line; we are women, American women, as intensely interested in all that pertains to us as such as all other American women; we are not alienating or withdrawing, we are only coming to the front, willing to join any others in the same work and cordially inviting and welcoming any others to join us.

If there is any one thing I would especially enjoin upon this conference it is union and earnestness. The questions that are to come before us are of too much import to be weakened by any trivialities or personalities. If any differences arise let them be quickly settled, with the feeling that we are all workers to the same end, to elevate and dignify colored American womanhood. This conference will not be what I expect if it does not show the wisdom, indeed the absolute necessity of a national organization of our women. Every year new questions coming up will prove it to us. This hurried, almost informal convention does not begin to meet our needs, it is only a beginning, made here in dear old Boston, where the scales of justice and generosity hang evenly balanced, and where the people "dare be true" to their best instincts and stand ready to lend aid and sympathy to worthy strugglers. It is hoped and believed that from this will spring an organization that will in truth bring in a new era to the colored women of America.

TWENTY YEARS AT HULL HOUSE
Jane Addams

Jane Addams (1860–1935), winner of the Nobel Peace Prize in 1931, was the most famous and most admired woman in the United States during the first third of this century. She was also, in the opinion of contemporaries like philosopher John Dewey, one of the most gifted members, male or female, of her generation. *Twenty Years at Hull House*, the first volume of her autobiography, recounts her struggles to find appropriate outlets for her great talent.

Addams discovered that the America of the 1880s had no place for intelligent, ambitious women other than missionary work. And she virtually invented a whole new type of career, a secularized mission to the urban poor called settlement work. The dedicated young women (and young men) who flocked to the settlements in turn invented a whole series of new career opportunities for themselves ranging from factory and housing inspection to social casework.

This excerpt from *Twenty Years at Hull House* candidly confronts the feelings of frustration and inadequacy the women of Addams' generation experienced when they sought to find a way, outside of marriage and motherhood, of engaging in meaningful work.

"It is true that there is nothing after disease, indigence and a sense of guilt, so fatal to health and to life itself as the want of a proper outlet for active faculties." I have seen young girls suffer and grow sensibly lowered in vitality in the first years after they leave school. In our attempt then to give a girl pleasure and freedom from care we succeed, for the most part, in making her pitifully miserable. She finds "life" so different from what she expected it to be. She is besotted with innocent little ambitions, and does not understand this apparent waste of herself, this elaborate preparation, if no work is provided for her. There is a heritage of noble obligation which young people accept and long to perpetuate. The desire for action, the wish to right wrong and alleviate suffering haunts them daily. Society smiles at it indulgently instead of making it of value to itself. The wrong to them begins even farther back, when we restrain the first childish desires for "doing good" and tell them that they must wait until they are older and better fitted. We intimate that social obligation begins at a fixed date, forgetting that it begins with birth itself. We treat them as children who, with strong-growing limbs, are allowed to use their legs but not their arms, or whose legs are daily carefully exercised that after a while their arms may be put to high use. We do this in spite of the protest of the best educators, Locke and Pestalozzi. We are fortunate in the meantime if their unused members do not weaken and disappear. They do sometimes. There are a few girls who, by the time they are "educated," forget their old childish desires to help the world and to play with poor little girls "who haven't play things." Parents are often inconsistent: they deliberately expose their daughters to knowledge of the distress in the world; they send them to hear missionary addresses on famines in India and China; they accompany them to lectures on the suffering in Siberia; they agitate together over the forgotten region of East London. In addition to this, from babyhood the altruistic tendencies of these daughters are persistently cultivated. They are taught to be self-forgetting and self-sacrificing, to consider the good of the whole before the good of the ego. But when all this information and culture show results, when the daughter comes back from college and begins to recognize her social claim to the "submerged tenth," and to evince a disposition to fulfill it, the family claim is strenuously asserted; she is told that she is unjustified, ill-advised in her efforts. If she persists, the family too often are injured and unhappy unless the efforts are called missionary and the religious zeal of the family carry them over their sense of abuse. When this zeal does not exist, the result is perplexing. It is a curious violation of what we would fain believe a fundamental law—that the final return of the deed is upon the head of the doer. The deed is that of exclusiveness and caution, but the return, instead of falling upon the head of the exclusive and cautious, falls upon a young head full of generous and unselfish plans. The girl loses something vital out of her life to which she is entitled. She is restricted and unhappy; her elders, meanwhile, are unconscious of the situation and we have all the elements of a tragedy.

We have in America a fast-growing number of cultivated young people who have no recognized outlet for their active faculties. They hear constantly of the great social maladjustment, but no way is provided for them to change it, and their uselessness hangs about them heavily. Huxley declares that the sense of uselessness is the severest shock which the human system can sustain, and that if persistently sustained, it results in atrophy of function. These young people have had advantages of college, of European travel, and of economic study, but they are sustaining this shock of inaction. They have pet phrases, and they tell you that the things that make us all alike are stronger than the things that make us different. They say that all men are united by needs and sympathies far more permanent and radical than anything that temporarily divides them and sets them in opposition to each other. If they affect art, they say that the decay in artistic expression is due to the decay in ethics, that art when shut away from the human interests and from the great mass of humanity is self-destructive. They tell their elders with all the bitterness of youth that if they expect success from them in business or politics or in whatever lines their ambition for them has run, they must let them consult all of humanity; that they must let them find out what the people want and how they want it. It is only the stronger young people, however, who formulate this. Many of them dissipate their energies in so-called enjoyment. Others not content with that, go on studying and go back to college for their second degrees; not that they are especially fond of study, but because they want something definite to do, and their powers have been trained in the direction of mental accumulation. Many are buried beneath this mental accumulation with lowered vitality and discontent. Walter Besant says they have had the vision that Peter had when he saw the great sheet let down from heaven, wherein was neither clean nor unclean. He calls it the sense of humanity. It is not philanthropy nor benevolence, but a thing fuller and wider than either of these.

This young life, so sincere in its emotion and good phrase and yet so undirected, seems to me as pitiful as the other great mass of destitute lives. One is supplementary to the other, and some method of communication can surely be devised. Mr. Barnett, who urged the first Settlement—Toynbee Hall, in East London—recognized this need of outlet for the young men of Oxford and Cambridge, and hoped that the Settlement would supply the communication. It is easy to see why the Settlement movement originated in England, where the years of education are more constrained and definite than they are here, where class distinctions are more rigid. The necessity of it was greater there, but we are fast feeling the pressure of the need and meeting the necessity for Settlements in America. Our young people feel nervously the need of putting theory into action, and respond quickly to the Settlement form of activity.

ONE WAY TO FREEDOM

Kate L. Gregg

In the 1920s, the vote had been won and many new opportunities opened up for women. Women looked forward to getting an education and finding work that would offer personal fulfillment. Unlike feminists of a previous era, they did not feel that they had to choose between satisfying personal lives and careers. Nor did they feel compelled to marry or become mothers.

It was to satisfy such readers that the editors of *The Nation*, a popular liberal magazine, decided to publish a series of autobiographies solicited from "These Modern Women." At the conclusion of the series, originally published anonymously, it was promised that a psychoanalyst and a behaviorist, new breeds of experts on women, would "analyze through these articles the underlying causes of the modern woman's rebellion."

After high school, Kate L. Gregg, the author of the autobiography reprinted below, attended normal school to earn her teaching certificate. She received a Ph.D. in English from the University of Wisconsin in 1916.

A little girl of six or seven, clinging to a rickety picket fence and listening, still and intent as if she listened with her whole body instead of with ears alone. Coming? Yes, of course, he was coming. Mama was too anxious. There—a little hint of sound again. The murmur of wagon wheels maybe on the hill beyond the second slough. Hope shot through her young heart. The wagon would rumble loudly and certainly when it came to the corduroy at the foot of the hill. Breathless she waited as if all life

---

ONE WAY TO FREEDOM   From Kate L. Gregg, "These Modern Women," *The Nation* 16 Feb. 1927: 165–67.

depended on her hearing. Her young mother came silently from the kitchen door and joined her.

"Yes, I thought I heard something, mama. Listen. Maybe now he will pass over the bridge at the slough." But even hope could hear nothing more definite than the wind in the fir trees at the edge of the little prairie. So they listened, mother and daughter both, in the spring, summer, autumn, winter twilight. Listened every time he went to town, and heartsick knew they hoped in vain.

It was always the same story. Oats to be ground into chop, hogs to be marketed, grain to be hauled to the warehouse, winter supplies to be bought, taxes to be paid, interest to be met—each time there was the sickening uncertainty as to whether he would come home cheery and happy when he ought to come or whether mother would have to do the farm chores, four little children left in the house alone with the fires, or trailing her skirts as she milked cows, fed horses, cleaned stables; and he, the father, would come a week later, hang-dog and ashamed because he had suc-cumbed to another periodical spree, and had spent not only himself but all the fam-ily income as well, derived from hogs, grain, hay, and dedicated to winter groceries, taxes, or interest.

Always there were children, four then, and more as the years went by until mother had given birth to eight. To the despair that grew in her in consequence of the repeated sprees was added the deadly certainty of another child inevitably near. When the fourth child was born, father disappeared the day after to be gone a week or ten days, and I can remember yet mother's explanation to hired girl and mid-wife—it was always both in one for us—that Mr.—— had been called away on busi-ness. Would he be home for dinner today? Day after day she could not say, she did not know. When we had moved for the third time, far away this time from anybody who had ever known us before, her hour for a sixth deliverance close at hand, and he, the father, gone again to exercise his individual liberty, I saw her one night get out the family revolver, oil it, load it, and place it under her pillow. When, white and sick from foreboding, I ventured to ask, "Why that?" she answered, "If it comes upon me when he is gone and nobody here to take care of me, I am through, that's all." Child of thirteen that I was then, I argued the silliness of that, and urged my own capacity to do as much as he could do.

This was the man I then knew best. Good natured, easy-going, loving my mother and his children in his own way, but selfish and irresponsible, *wicked* it seemed to me then, in his capacity for inflicting suffering and humiliation. Now after thirty years, and he ten years gone forever, I cannot find much easier words. As the oldest of the children and the nearest to my mother, I experienced her anxieties as if they had been my own, and because I loved her I hated the poverty, shame, and endless child-bearing forced upon her. I cannot remember a time when I did not look upon my father with reproach and often with feelings not to be described by so mild a term.

My mother's dominant passion for me, through these years, and for the five other daughters who came in the course of time, was a desire for our education, that we might fit ourselves for work and for salaries that would make us independent of marriage, or if we did elect it, able to leave it if it were unsatisfactory. She herself had been tied and fettered once for all because she had married at seventeen. An old-fashioned father had refused her the privilege of either going to school or learning a trade, and in marriage which had seemed to offer a way out she had found herself more helpless than ever on account of the never-ending succession of babies. I realize now that mother in her insistence on our schooling was preaching the economic independence of woman, though of that as such I am sure she had never heard. She preached it day after day with a singleness of aim and an earnestness that brought to pass what she desired even though the handicaps were well-nigh insurmountable. Education of her daughters every day in the school term, every school term through the years was not to be achieved without domestic battles won only by intensity of purpose and a desire to protect her own. Mother was proud that I never missed school on wash-days, cleaning days, or even when another new baby incapacitated her for a week or two. School for her children was a religion to this mother, and to one end—that we might be free.

She had, of course, educational ideals for her sons, but these were early frustrated by my father's insistence that no mere woman could ever know as much about the desirable education of a male child as a man, with the result that the boys left school in the eighth grade to learn the trade of their father. The younger had a flair for drawing, painting, mathematics, and might have turned into a creditable architect, but he had learned to handle the hock and trowel instead. As I look back I realize that a part of father's reluctance to have the boys remain at school was fear lest they be educated into disapproval of himself and his ideal of a man's life.

A great part of the subjection of woman in our family resulted from mother's complete separation from purse-strings. When we lived on the farm, she would earn eight or ten dollars in the course of a year through meals and beds furnished to farmers from the upper country who made our house their stopping-place as they came and went getting in their winter supplies. Yet even getting this much depended on two contingencies. If father was in town engaged in the usual preoccupation, she got the money; or if, he being on the farm, the lodger paid the reckoning into her own hand. Otherwise she lost it entirely. Mother never asked for money for herself, probably because she felt too much humiliated in the asking, but as her girls grew up and needed cash upon occasion, she did it for them. When I had reached high-school and later normal-school age and I needed a dollar a month to pay for my toll ticket across the interstate bridge, she and I alike dreaded the monthly ordeal of getting that dollar. As the time drew near we watched closely for the auspicious occasion that would make reproach least likely. The best time of all was on Saturday night just after supper, when father would be handing out ten dollar bills to the boys "to have a good time."

"Give Cora a dollar, too, daddy. She needs it for toll."

"What? Again?" and the smile of Jove benevolent faded into narrow-eyed suspicion.

As soon as I could attain to the educational distinction of a two years' certificate from the normal school, mother's dream for her eldest was realized, the toll battles were forgotten—one woman at last was free. Eighteen and free. Free to do as I wished with my own.

There were differences between my father and me as to what constituted my own. Through a good many years he suffered from my inability to see that I ought to turn my monthly pay checks over to him; and my silly way of hoarding money for more education gave him acute distress. I remember that when I left for the university, $750 cash in hand—the result of three years' teaching—he sulked in the barn-yard and refused to say goodby. He was indignant to see me throwing away my money.

But three years later when I returned I was astonished to know that he was proud that I had graduated and indeed was giving himself some credit for this higher education in the family.

Once the two-year certificate had freed me, not even love's young dream could rob me of wariness. The most desirable youth in the world, in a boy and girl affair, pleaded the blessedness that would ensue if we would but take the reins in our hands and the bits in our teeth (two separate arguments), but realist that I had to be I argued the necessity for his finishing college and getting himself established before we took any fatal steps. And the worst pitfall of all was safely avoided. The most desirable youth in the world was a no-account college student and a philanderer as well, and that was the end of him as an argument. Years afterward I met him again. He had become a second-rate bookkeeper, his wife had had seven children in as many years, of whom only two survived, and every pay-day he handed his salary over to a broker to be gambled on the stock exchange or he lost it in backroom crap games. The home was mortgaged and the wife was sticking it out until the children should be up from under her feet. He was still philandering.

Other men have come my way. One planned a house for me and insisted on a nice big kitchen. That was the end of him. Another dear kind soul with whom I thought I could live rapturously could not build a fire on a camping trip and fancied always when he was lost that the Pacific Ocean must be in the east. The psychoanalyst will say—but who cares what the psychoanalyst will say? I know myself that if I had done otherwise in any one of these three marriage opportunities I would have been a fool.

Having learned my lesson complete and being a creature with a sense of responsibility to womanhood, I have passed on the lesson as best I could. A good many years of my life have gone into helping mother pass it on to my father's other daughters, and being engaged in rearing his family I have felt less the lack of one of my own. All of my sisters have achieved something more than the usual education; some are teachers, some are business women, and any of the three who being married may find in marriage too many fetters has power and ability to strike the irons away. They have, in other words, freedom in their souls.

To confirm the fear of the good souls who tremble for the human race and see it tottering to total extinction as female educationists ply their guile upon the artless young, I might as well now confess that the thirties found me with a doctor's degree, and the forties with a full professorship, in which I enjoy unlimited scope for preaching to men and women alike the need for economic independence of women as an honorable and self-respecting basis for love and marriage. One can hardly hope that any lesson is ever learned complete. Perhaps the tranquil, peaceful, rich life I live is more of an argument than any words I shall ever say.

THE TURBID EBB AND FLOW OF MISERY

Margaret Sanger

Margaret Sanger (1879–1966) spent most of her life working for the legalization of birth control. Selling or providing information about contraceptives was prohibited in 1916, when she opened the first birth control clinic in the United States. By allying herself with health professionals, Sanger gradually gained support for her cause, and in 1936 the courts upheld the right of the medical professions to dispense birth control information. The endorsement of the American Medical Association followed within the year. Sanger's American Birth Control League later became the Planned Parenthood Federation of America.

Sanger maintained that she was most concerned with freeing working-class women from "involuntary motherhood" by permitting them control over their own bodies. The availability of birth control information would also allow women to express their sexuality more fully, since the fear of pregnancy, according to Sanger, explained in some part the myth of female passivity.

Sanger worked as an obstetrical nurse among the poor of New York's Lower East Side. In the following excerpt from her autobiography, she writes about one of the families whose "desperation linked to excessive childbearing" pushed her to campaign for birth control.

 One stifling mid-July day of 1912 I was summoned to a Grand Street tenement. My patient was a small, slight Russian Jewess, about twenty-eight years old, of the special cast of feature to which suffering lends a madonna-like expression. The cramped three-room apartment was in a sorry state of turmoil. Jake Sachs, a truck driver scarcely older than his wife, had come home to find the three children crying and her unconscious from the effects of a self-induced abortion. He had called the nearest doctor, who in turn had sent for me. Jake's earnings were trifling, and most of them had gone to keep the none-too-strong children clean and properly fed. But his wife's ingenuity had helped them to save a little, and this he was glad to spend on a nurse rather than have her go to a hospital.

The doctor and I settled ourselves to the task of fighting the septicemia. Never had I worked so fast, never so concentratedly. The sultry days and nights were melted into a torpid inferno. It did not seem possible there could be such heat, and every bit of food, ice, and drugs had to be carried up three flights of stairs.

Jake was more kind and thoughtful than many of the husbands I had encountered. He loved his children, and had always helped his wife wash and dress them. He had brought water up and carried garbage down before he left in the morning, and did as much as he could for me while he anxiously watched her progress.

After a fortnight Mrs. Sachs' recovery was in sight. Neighbors, ordinarily fatalistic as to the results of abortion, were genuinely pleased that she had survived. She smiled wanly at all who came to see her and thanked them gently, but she could not respond to their hearty congratulations. She appeared to be more despondent and anxious than she should have been, and spent too much time in meditation.

At the end of three weeks, as I was preparing to leave the fragile patient to take up her difficult life once more, she finally voiced her fears, "Another baby will finish me, I suppose?"

"It's too early to talk about that," I temporized.

But when the doctor came to make his last call, I drew him aside. "Mrs. Sachs is terribly worried about having another baby."

"She well may be," replied the doctor, and then he stood before her and said, "Any more such capers, young woman, and there'll be no need to send for me."

"I know, doctor," she replied timidly, "but," and she hesitated as though it took all her courage to say it, "what can I do to prevent it?"

THE TURBID EBB AND FLOW OF MISERY   From Margaret Sanger, *Margaret Sanger: An Autobiography* (New York: Dover, 1971) 89–92. From W. W. Norton, 1938; reprinted by Dover Publications, 1971. Reprinted with permission of Dover Publications, Inc., New York.

The doctor was a kindly man, and he had worked hard to save her, but such incidents had become so familiar to him that he had long since lost whatever delicacy he might once have had. He laughed good-naturedly. "You want to have your cake and eat it too, do you? Well, it can't be done."

Then picking up his hat and bag to depart he said, "Tell Jake to sleep on the roof."

I glanced quickly at Mrs. Sachs. Even through my sudden tears I could see stamped on her face an expression of absolute despair. We simply looked at each other, saying no word until the door had closed behind the doctor. Then she lifted her thin, blue-veined hands and clasped them beseechingly. "He can't understand. He's only a man. But you do, don't you? Please tell me the secret, and I'll never breathe it to a soul. *Please!*"

What was I to do? I could not speak the conventionally comforting phrases which would be of no comfort. Instead, I made her as physically easy as I could and promised to come back in a few days to talk with her again. A little later, when she slept, I tiptoed away.

Night after night the wistful image of Mrs. Sachs appeared before me. I made all sorts of excuses to myself for not going back. I was busy on other cases; I really did not know what to say to her or how to convince her of my own ignorance; I was helpless to avert such monstrous atrocities. Time rolled by and I did nothing.

The telephone rang one evening three months later, and Jake Sachs' agitated voice begged me to come at once; his wife was sick again and from the same cause. For a wild moment I thought of sending someone else, but actually, of course, I hurried into my uniform, caught up my bag, and started out. All the way I longed for a subway wreck, an explosion, anything to keep me from having to enter that home again. But nothing happened, even to delay me. I turned into the dingy doorway and climbed the familiar stairs once more. The children were there, young little things.

Mrs. Sachs was in a coma and died within ten minutes. I folded her still hands across her breast, remembering how they had pleaded with me, begging so humbly for the knowledge which was her right. I drew a sheet over her pallid face. Jake was sobbing, running his hands through his hair and pulling it out like an insane person. Over and over again he wailed, "My God! My God! My God!"

I left him pacing desperately back and forth, and for hours I myself walked and walked and walked through the hushed streets. When I finally arrived home and let myself quietly in, all the household was sleeping. I looked out my window and down upon the dimly lighted city. Its pains and griefs crowded in upon me, a moving picture rolled before my eyes with photographic clearness: women writhing in travail to bring forth little babies; the babies themselves naked and hungry, wrapped in newspapers to keep them from the cold; six-year-old children with pinched, pale, wrinkled faces, old in concentrated wretchedness, pushed into gray and fetid cellars, crouching on stone floors, their small scrawny hands scuttling through rags, making lamp shades, artificial flowers; white coffins, black coffins, coffins, coffins interminably passing in never-ending succession. The scenes piled one upon another on another. I could bear it no longer.

As I stood there the darkness faded. The sun came up and threw its reflection over the house tops. It was the dawn of a new day in my life also. The doubt and questioning, the experimenting and trying, were now to be put behind me. I knew I could not go back merely to keeping people alive.

I went to bed, knowing that no matter what it might cost, I was finished with palliatives and superficial cures; I was resolved to seek out the root of evil, to do something to change the destiny of mothers whose miseries were vast as the sky.

THE PROBLEM THAT HAS NO NAME
Betty Friedan

Betty Friedan's book, *The Feminine Mystique*, which became an instant best-seller in 1963, is now considered a classic of the modern feminist movement. It launched Friedan's career as indefatigable spokesperson for equal rights and the women's movement.

Friedan graduated from Smith College in 1942, studied psychology at the University of California–Berkeley, and married Carl Friedan in 1947. In 1957 she sent a questionnaire to her Smith College classmates and the answers they gave led her to write *The Feminine Mystique.*

Friedan's book questioned the myth of natural domesticity, or the feminine mystique. Friedan found too many suburban housewives suffering from "the problem that has no name," the "strange dissatisfied voice" repeating "Is this all there is?" Women's unhappiness under the feminine mystique, she argued, indicated the need for change—in the social role rather than in the woman herself.

In 1966, Friedan along with several other women founded the National Organization for Women (NOW). Friedan's most recent books are *The Second Stage* (1981) and *The Fountain of Age* (1993).

The problem lay buried, unspoken, for many years in the minds of American women. It was a strange stirring, a sense of dissatisfaction, a yearning that women suffered in the middle of the twentieth century in the United States. Each suburban wife struggled with it alone. As she made the beds, shopped for groceries, matched slipcover material, ate peanut butter sandwiches with her children, chauffeured Cub Scouts and Brownies, lay beside her husband at night—she was afraid to ask even of herself the silent question—"Is this all?"

For over fifteen years there was no word of this yearning in the millions of words written about women, for women, in all the columns, books and articles by experts telling women their role was to seek fulfillment as wives and mothers. Over and over women heard in voices of tradition and of Freudian sophistication that they could desire no greater destiny than to glory in their own femininity. Experts told them how to catch a man and keep him, how to breastfeed children and handle their toilet training, how to cope with sibling rivalry and adolescent rebellion; how to buy a dishwasher, bake bread, cook gourmet snails, and build a swimming pool with their own hands; how to dress, look, and act more feminine and make marriage more exciting; how to keep their husbands from dying young and their sons from growing into delinquents. They were taught to pity the neurotic, unfeminine, unhappy women who wanted to be poets or physicists or presidents. They learned that truly feminine women do not want careers, higher education, political rights—the independence and the opportunities that the old-fashioned feminists fought for.

Some women, in their forties and fifties, still remembered painfully giving up those dreams, but most of the younger women no longer even thought about them. A thousand expert voices applauded their femininity, their adjustment, their new maturity. All they had to do was devote their lives from earliest girlhood to finding a husband and bearing children.

By the end of the nineteen-fifties, the average marriage age of women in America dropped to 20, and was still dropping, into the teens. Fourteen million girls were engaged by 17. The proportion of women attending college in comparison with men dropping from 47 per cent in 1920 to 35 per cent in 1958. A century earlier, women had fought for higher education; now girls went to college to get a husband. By the mid-fifties, 60 per cent dropped out of college to marry, or because they were afraid too much education would be a marriage bar. Colleges built dormitories for "married students," but the students were almost always the husbands. A new degree was instituted for the wives—"Ph.T." (Putting Husband Through).

Then American girls began getting married in high school. And the women's magazines, deploring the unhappy statistics about these young marriages, urged that courses on marriage, and marriage counselors, be installed in the high schools. Girls started going steady at twelve and thirteen, in junior high. Manufacturers put out brassieres with false bosoms of foam rubber for little girls of ten. And an advertisement for a child's dress, sizes 3–6x, in the *New York Times* in the fall of 1960, said: "She Too Can Join the Man-Trap Set."

By the end of the fifties, the United States birthrate was overtaking India's. The birth-control movement, renamed Planned Parenthood, was asked to find a method whereby women who had been advised that a third or fourth baby would be born dead or defective might have it anyhow. Statisticians were especially astounded at the fantastic increase in the number of babies among college women. Where once they had two children, now they had four, five, six. Women who had once wanted careers were now making careers out of having babies. So rejoiced *Life* magazine in a 1956 paean to the movement of American women back to the home.

In a New York hospital, a woman had a nervous breakdown when she found she could not breastfeed her baby. In other hospitals, women dying of cancer refused a drug which research had proved might save their lives: its side effects were said to be unfeminine. "If I have only one life, let me live it as a blonde," a larger-than-life-sized picture of a pretty, vacuous woman proclaimed from newspaper, magazine, and drugstore ads. And across America, three out of every ten women dyed their hair blonde. They ate a chalk called Metrecal, instead of food, to shrink to the size of the thin young models. Department-store buyers reported that American women, since 1939, had become three and four sizes smaller. "Women are out to fit the clothes, instead of vice-versa," one buyer said.

Interior decorators were designing kitchens with mosaic murals and original paintings, for kitchens were once again the center of women's lives. Home sewing became a million-dollar industry. Many women no longer left their homes, except to shop, chauffeur their children, or attend a social engagement with their husbands. Girls were growing up in America without ever having jobs outside the home. In the late fifties, a sociological phenomenon was suddenly remarked: a third of American women now worked, but most were no longer young and very few were pursuing careers. They were married women who held part-time jobs, selling or secretarial, to put their husbands through school, their sons through college, or to help pay the mortgage. Or they were widows supporting families. Fewer and fewer women were entering professional work. The shortages in the nursing, social work, and teaching professions caused crises in almost every American city. Concerned over the Soviet Union's lead in the space race, scientists noted that America's greatest source of unused brain-power was women. But girls would not study physics: it was "unfeminine." A girl refused a science fellowship at Johns Hopkins to take a job in a real-estate office. All she wanted, she said, was what every other American girl wanted—to get married, have four children and live in a nice house in a nice suburb.

The suburban housewife—she was the dream image of young American women and the envy, it was said, of women all over the world. The American housewife—freed by science and labor-saving appliances from the drudgery, the dangers of childbirth and the illnesses of her grandmother. She was healthy, beautiful, educated, concerned only about her husband, her children, her home. She had found true feminine fulfillment. As a housewife and mother, she was respected as a full and equal partner to man in his world. She was free to choose automobiles, clothes, appliances, supermarkets; she had everything that women ever dreamed of.

In the fifteen years after World War II, this mystique of feminine fulfillment became the cherished and self-perpetuating core of contemporary American culture. Millions of women lived their lives in the image of those pretty pictures of the American suburban housewife, kissing their husbands goodbye in front of the picture window, depositing their stationwagonsful of children at school, and smiling as they ran the new electric waxer over the spotless kitchen floor. They baked their own bread, sewed their own and their children's clothes, kept their new washing machines and dryers running all day. They changed the sheets on the beds twice a week instead of once, took the rug-hooking class in adult education, and pitied their poor frustrated mothers, who had dreamed of having a career. Their only dream was to be perfect wives and mothers; their highest ambition to have five children and a beautiful house, their only fight to get and keep their husbands. They had no thought for the unfeminine problems of the world outside the home; they wanted the men to make the major decisions. They gloried in their role as women, and wrote proudly on the census blank: "Occupation: housewife."

For over fifteen years, the words written for women, and the words women used when they talked to each other, while their husbands sat on the other side of the room and talked shop or politics or septic tanks, were about problems with their children, or how to keep their husbands happy, or improve their children's school, or cook chicken or make slipcovers. Nobody argued whether women were inferior or superior to men; they were simply different. Words like "emancipation" and "career" sounded strange and embarrassing; no one had used them for years. When a Frenchwoman named Simone de Beauvoir wrote a book called *The Second Sex*, an American critic commented that she obviously "didn't know what life was all about," and besides, she was talking about French women. The "woman problem" in America no longer existed.

If a woman had a problem in the 1950's and 1960's, she knew that something must be wrong with her marriage, or with herself. Other women were satisfied with their lives, she thought. What kind of a woman was she if she did not feel this mysterious fulfillment waxing the kitchen floor? She was so ashamed to admit her dissatisfaction that she never knew how many other women shared it. If she tried to tell her husband, he didn't understand what she was talking about. She did not really understand it herself. For over fifteen years women in America found it harder to talk about this problem than about sex. Even the psychoanalysts had no name for it. When a woman went to a psychiatrist for help, as many women did, she would say, "I'm so ashamed," or "I must be hopelessly neurotic." "I don't know what's wrong with women today," a suburban psychiatrist said uneasily. "I only know something is wrong because most of my patients happen to be women. And their problem isn't sexual." Most women with this problem did not go to see a psychoanalyst, however. "There's nothing wrong really," they kept telling themselves. "There isn't any problem."

But on an April morning in 1959, I heard a mother of four, having coffee with four other mothers in a suburban development fifteen miles from New York, say in a tone of quiet desperation, "the problem." And the others knew, without words, that she was not talking about a problem with her husband, or her children, or her home. Suddenly they realized they all shared the same problem, the problem that has no name. They began, hesitantly, to talk about it. Later, after they had picked up their children at nursery school and taken them home to nap, two of the women cried, in sheer relief, just to know they were not alone.

ROE v. WADE
U.S. Supreme Court Reports

Using the precedent of British common law, United States courts permitted abortion until 1873 when Congress passed the Comstock Law, which prohibited the dissemination of abortion devices; thereafter most states passed their own laws making abortion a criminal offense. These laws were still in effect in the late 1960s when women began to rally publicly for the right to legal abortions. In 1970, New York liberalized its abortion laws, and other states soon followed; but anti-abortion laws were still in effect in most states as late as 1972.

That year two companion cases, *Roe v. Wade* and *Doe v. Bolton*, were heard by the U.S. Supreme Court. *Roe v. Wade* was a test of the Texas statute making abortion a felony except on "medical advice for the purpose of saving the mother's life." *Doe v. Bolton* tested a Georgia law that permitted abortion if the woman's life was endangered, if the child would be born severely defective, or if the pregnancy resulted from rape.

The Supreme Court invalidated both state statutes in a 7–2 decision in 1973. The arguments for its decision revolved around the issue of whether and when the state should interfere in a woman's decision to terminate a pregnancy.

An excerpt from the Court's decision in *Roe v. Wade*, written by Justice Harry Blackmun, follows. The appellant in this case is Roe; the appellee is the District Attorney of Dallas County, Texas. *Amici* are "friends of the court," people not directly involved in the case who give the Court advice pertinent to it. Citations of legal precedents have been omitted.

Jane Roe, a single woman who was residing in Dallas County, Texas, instituted this federal action in March 1970 against the District Attorney of the county. She sought a declaratory judgment that the Texas criminal abortion statutes were unconstitutional on their face, and an injunction restraining the defendant from enforcing the statutes.

ROE V. WADE   From U.S. Supreme Court Reports, *Roe v. Wade,* Opinion of the Court, October Term, 1972, 120, 147–152, 157–164.

Roe alleged that she was unmarried and pregnant; that she wished to terminate her pregnancy by an abortion "performed by a competent, licensed physician, under safe, clinical conditions"; that she was unable to get a "legal" abortion in Texas because her life did not appear to be threatened by the continuation of her pregnancy; and that she could not afford to travel to another jurisdiction in order to secure a legal abortion under safe conditions. She claimed that the Texas statutes were unconstitutionally vague and that they abridged her right of personal privacy, protected by the First, Fourth, Fifth, Ninth, and Fourteenth Amendments. By an amendment to her complaint Roe purported to sue "on behalf of herself and all other women" similarly situated. . . .

❧ ❧ ❧

Three reasons have been advanced to explain historically the enactment of criminal abortion laws in the 19th century and to justify their continued existence.

It has been argued occasionally that these laws were the product of a Victorian social concern to discourage illicit sexual conduct. Texas, however, does not advance this justification in the present case, and it appears that no court or commentator has taken the argument seriously. The appellants and *amici* contend, moreover, that this is not a proper state purpose at all and suggest that, if it were, the Texas statutes are overbroad in protecting it since the law fails to distinguish between married and unwed mothers.

A second reason is concerned with abortion as a medical procedure. When most criminal abortion laws were first enacted, the procedure was a hazardous one for the woman. This was particularly true prior to the development of antisepsis. Antiseptic techniques, of course, were based on discoveries by Lister, Pasteur, and others first announced in 1867, but were not generally accepted and employed until about the turn of the century. Abortion mortality was high. Even after 1900, and perhaps until as late as the development of antibiotics in the 1940's, standard modern techniques such as dilation and curettage were not nearly so safe as they are today. Thus, it has been argued that a State's real concern in enacting a criminal abortion law was to protect the pregnant woman, that is, to restrain her from submitting to a procedure that placed her life in serious jeopardy.

Modern medical techniques have altered this situation. Appellants and various *amici* refer to medical data indicating that abortion in early pregnancy, that is, prior to the end of the first trimester, although not without its risk, is now relatively safe. Mortality rates for women undergoing early abortions, where the procedure is legal, appear to be as low as or lower than the rates for normal childbirth. Consequently, any interest of the State in protecting the woman from an inherently hazardous procedure, except when it would be equally dangerous for her to forgo it, has largely disappeared. Of course, important state interests in the areas of health and medical standards do remain. The State has a legitimate interest in seeing to it that abortion, like any other medical procedure, is performed under circumstances that insure maximum safety for the patient. This interest obviously extends at least to the performing physician and his staff, to the facilities involved, to the availability of aftercare, and to adequate provision for any complication or emergency that might arise. The prevalence of high mortality rates at illegal "abortion mills" strengthens, rather than weakens, the State's interest in regulating the conditions under which abortions are performed. Moreover, the risk to the woman increases as her pregnancy continues. Thus, the State retains a definite interest in protecting the woman's own health and safety when an abortion is proposed at a late stage of pregnancy.

The third reason is the State's interest—some phrase it in terms of duty—in protecting prenatal life. Some of the argument for this justification rests on the theory that a new human life is present from the moment of conception. The State's interest and general obligation to protect life then extends, it is argued, to prenatal life. Only when the life of the pregnant mother herself is at stake, balanced against the life she carries within her, should the interest of the embryo or fetus not prevail. Logically, of course, a legitimate state interest in this area need not stand or fall on acceptance of the belief that life begins at conception or at some other point prior to live birth. In assessing the State's interest, recognition may be given to the less rigid claim that as long as at least *potential* life is involved, the State may assert interests beyond the protection of the pregnant woman alone. . . .

It is with these interests, and the weight to be attached to them, that this case is concerned.

ﾂ ﾂ ﾂ

The Constitution does not explicitly mention any right of privacy. In a line of decisions, however, going back perhaps as far as *Union Pacific R. Co. v. Botsford* (1891), the Court has recognized that a right of personal privacy, or a guarantee of certain areas or zones of privacy, does exist under the Constitution. In varying contexts, the Court or individual Justices have, indeed, found at least the roots of that right in the First Amendment; in the Fourth and Fifth Amendments; in the penumbras of the Bill of Rights; in the Ninth Amendment; or in the concept of liberty guaranteed by the first section of the Fourteenth Amendment. These decisions make it clear that only personal rights that can be deemed "fundamental" or "implicit in the concept of ordered liberty," are included in this guarantee of personal privacy. They also make it clear that the right has some extension to activities relating to marriage; procreation; contraception; family relationships; and child rearing and education.

This right of privacy, whether it be founded in the Fourteenth Amendment's concept of personal liberty and restrictions upon state action, as we feel it is, or, as the District Court determined, in the Ninth Amendment's reservation of rights to the people, is broad enough to encompass a woman's decision whether or not to terminate her pregnancy. The detriment that the State would impose upon the pregnant woman by denying this choice altogether is apparent. Specific and direct harm medically diagnosable even in early pregnancy may be involved. Maternity, or additional offspring, may force upon the woman a distressful life and future. Psychological harm may be imminent. Mental and physical health may be taxed by child care. There is also the distress, for all concerned, associated with the unwanted child, and there is the problem of bringing a child into a family already unable, psychologically and otherwise, to care for it. In other cases, as in this one, the additional difficulties and continuing stigma of unwed motherhood may be involved. All these are factors the woman and her responsible physician necessarily will consider in consultation.

On the basis of elements such as these, appellant and some *amici* argue that the woman's right is absolute and that she is entitled to terminate her pregnancy at whatever time, in whatever way, and for whatever reason she alone chooses. With this we do not agree. Appellant's arguments that Texas either has no valid interest at all in regulating the abortion decision, or no interest strong enough to support any limitation upon the woman's sole determination, are unpersuasive. The Court's decisions recognizing a right of privacy also acknowledge that some state regulation in areas protected by that right is appropriate. As noted above, a State may properly assert important interests in safeguarding health, in maintaining medical standards, and in protecting potential life. At some point in pregnancy, these respective interests become sufficiently compelling to sustain regulation of the factors that govern the abortion decision. The privacy right involved, therefore, cannot be said to be absolute. . . .

We, therefore, conclude that the right of personal privacy includes the abortion decision, but that this right is not unqualified and must be considered against important state interests in regulation. . . .

The State does have an important and legitimate interest in preserving and protecting the health of the pregnant woman, whether she be a resident of the State or a nonresident who seeks medical consultation and treatment there, and that it has still *another* important and legitimate interest in protecting the potentiality of human life. These interests are separate and distinct. Each grows in substantiality as the woman approaches term and, at a point during pregnancy, each becomes "compelling."

With respect to the State's important and legitimate interest in the health of the mother, the "compelling" point, in the light of present medical knowledge, is at approximately the end of the first trimester. This is so because of the now-established medical fact . . . that until the end of the first trimester mortality in abortion may be less than mortality in normal childbirth. It follows that, from and after this point, a State may regulate the abortion procedure to the extent that the regulation reasonably relates to the preservation and protection of maternal health. Examples of permissible state regulation in this area are requirements as to the qualifications of the person who is to perform the abortion; as to the licensure of that person; as to the facility in which the procedure is to be performed, that is, whether it must be a hospital or may be a clinic or some other place of less-than-hospital status; as to the licensing of the facility; and the like.

This means, on the other hand, that, for the period of pregnancy prior to this "compelling" point, the attending physician, in consultation with his patient, is free to determine, without regulation by the State, that, in his medical judgment, the patient's pregnancy should be terminated. If that decision is reached, the judgment may be effectuated by an abortion free of interference by the State.

With respect to the State's important and legitimate interest in potential life, the "compelling" point is at viability. This is so because the fetus then presumably has the capability of meaningful life outside the mother's womb. State regulation protective of fetal life after viability thus has both logical and biological justifications. If the State is interested in protecting fetal life after viability, it may go so far as to proscribe abortion during that period, except when it is necessary to preserve the life or health of the mother.

Measured against these standards, Art. 1196 of the Texas Penal Code, in restricting legal abortions to those "procured or attempted by medical advice for the purpose of saving the life of the mother," sweeps too broadly. The statute makes no distinction between abortions performed early in pregnancy and those performed later, and it limits to a single reason, "saving" the mother's life, the legal justification for the procedure. The statute, therefore, cannot survive the constitutional attack made upon it here.

THOUGHTS ON ABORTION FOR OUR SISTERS
Meg Brodhead and Claire Schaeffer-Duffy

The statement below, written in 1989 by Meg Brodhead and Claire Schaeffer-Duffy, and co-signed by thirteen other women, articulates the concerns of its authors over the *Roe v. Wade* decision. It was published in *Sojourner,* a monthly feminist news journal that was established to offer its readers a forum for expressing "their concerns as women."

We are women who believe abortion is the taking of human life. We are also pacifists. Our pacifism leads us to believe that the deliberate taking of human life is always violent, always wrong, even in circumstances in which one's own life is threatened. We proclaim this belief with the intention of defending the powerless and the oppressed.

Most of the world's powerless and oppressed are women. Unwanted pregnancies very often result from, and may seem to perpetuate, women's powerlessness and oppression. Abortion is one way women attempt to take control of their lives. It is understood as a necessary kind of self-defense against the sexual violence women experience, an affirmative rejection of forces that would define women as storehouses for the unborn. We are in sympathy—even solidarity—with women who have chosen abortion, just as we feel sympathy and solidarity with participants in Nicaragua's Sandinista revolution who have chosen the gun. But in both cases, we believe the cost in lives is terrible, and we must speak for a different way. Abortion, often chosen because of a woman's awareness of her own victimization, creates yet another victim, and the cycle of violence continues.

We believe true liberation begins when we renounce means that kill. The taking of human life as a solution to human problems stems from some of the worst masculine delusions that afflict society. We question the morals of a society that contends that an unborn, unwanted child would be a serious and everlasting impediment to a fulfilling life for a woman. What does such an attitude say about the value of children? What does it say about the value of human life in general? We lament the fact that the women's movement, noted for its compassion and openness to those marginalized by society, should draw the line of acceptability with the unborn.

Abortion perpetuates and reflects our own alienation from our bodies. The women's movement has encouraged us to make peace with our bodies, but as long as the movement feels the need to advocate abortion unconditionally, we have not done enough. The odds are still against us. We are raped, victimized by incest, demeaned and objectified by the media, told to have children, told not to have children. None of these possibilities grant control to the woman. Rarely is the space

THOUGHTS ON ABORTION FOR OUR SISTERS   From Meg Brodhead and Claire Schaeffer-Duffy, "Thoughts on Abortion for Our Sisters," *Sojourner* May 1989: 7. Reprinted by permission of the authors.

provided for a woman to fully realize that her body has or does not have the capacity to carry a human life. Our sexual choices need to be made in the context of our biological realities. We rally behind the claim "our bodies, ourselves," but we believe that if more women could claim this truth in a spirit of self-awareness and self-acceptance, there would be far fewer unwanted pregnancies. Women have always borne the burden of unwanted pregnancies. Abortion still treats pregnancy as "our burden" when, in reality, it is the responsibility of a woman and a man.

While we hold our beliefs passionately, we do not seek to have them realized through legislative means. We recognize that abortion is a political, social, religious but, also, extremely personal issue, and that the law is inadequate for this problem. Moreover, we are extremely skeptical that any policies of the U.S. government, which guards its power with more potential violence than any other nation on earth, could really have the good of women at heart. Laws about women's reproductive rights (as about most other issues) usually reflect the interests of male elites. This is equally true whether abortion is legal or illegal; and so, in a sense, the law is beside the point, and the fierce debate over the law may obscure deeper questions of how our liberation can be realized and in what kind of society.

We are women who have benefited from the women's movement in varying degrees. Feminism's courageous call for women to love and trust other women has engendered in us a new respect for ourselves and a desire for true freedom from sexism. We submit this statement in a spirit of gratitude for these gifts. We also submit this statement in a spirit of deep concern over the direction in which an unquestioning acceptance of abortion is taking the women's movement. We are women who not only desire our own liberation, but the liberation of all people. We seek to be liberated from fear, ignorance, and hatred. We do not believe abortion will help us reach this goal. We passionately urge all women and men to examine the underlying causes that would lead a woman to choose an abortion.

A YOUNG MAN WRITES

Anonymous

In the fall of 1991, a large television audience watched the Senate Judiciary Committee hearings on Judge Clarence Thomas, President George Bush's conservative nominee for the U.S. Supreme Court. Thomas was indeed confirmed, but the hearings sparked considerable controversy.

Anita Hill, a University of Oklahoma law professor, testified that Thomas had sexually harassed her ten years earlier when she worked for him at the Equal Employment Opportunity Commission. Thomas and Hill, both African Americans, underwent intensive questioning, and supporting witnesses were called for both sides.

Thomas claimed that he was the victim of racism and that the hearings were nothing less than a public lynching. Hill's credibility was impugned; the suggestion was made that her allegations were based on fantasy. Hill supporters distributed bumper stickers reading "Honk if you believe Anita." As a response to the hearings, women from all over the country organized their own political action committee, Emily's List, to provide financial backing so that more women would be elected to Congress in the next election.

Simone de Beauvoir, the French feminist writer, once observed that "even the most sensitive of men fail to understand the concrete situation of women"; and many women watching the Senate hearings also decided that "Men just don't get it." But the following letter, published in *New Yorker* magazine's "Talk of the Town" section, reveals that some men who watched the hearing did "get it" for the first time.

I am one of that generation of men who grew up and were educated at a time when the central tenets of feminism were more or less dogma among right-thinking people, and I have spent my whole life among women who identify themselves as feminists. I have four sisters, each of whom is, in one way or another, engaged in living out a feminist life. My wife is a feminist filmmaker. My mother is a feminist professor—one of the first women of her generation to a get Ph.D. in formal logic. And yet, proud as I am of all these women, I had always felt, as almost every man surely does to one degree or another, that to be ardently or uncritically feminist was to become, in a sense, feminized, and I maintained a certain ironic distance from what struck me as the more metaphysical reaches of feminist "theory"—all those claims about women and power, women and language, and women and the male definition of reality which fill feminist texts and papers. But in the last three days, watching the Senate Judiciary Committee hearings on Judge Clarence Thomas, and watching the Senate's (and the press's) treatment of Professor Anita Hill, I have had something like a conversion experience. I have begun to realize that in the past the more "abstract" and the more categorical reaches of the feminist catechism—not to mention its now familiar nuts and bolts—seemed a little unreal to me not because they weren't true but because I had never seen them made concrete and particular.

Women, I have long been told, live within a set of double binds. If a woman makes a charge against a man, the issue will always become not the man's behavior but the woman's character. And a corollary is that if a woman can be shown to have lied in the past about anything at all, the lie will be taken as compelling evidence that she may be lying now. On a Saturday-night news program, two male journalists invoked the names of Tawana Brawley and Janet Cooke while discussing the hearings, and then they had a long debate about which woman, Brawley or Cooke, Professor Hill more closely resembled—although no connection could be found between either the frightened teen-ager or the dishonest reporter and the college professor, whose integrity had not yet been impeached. *Of course* the comparison was apt, the two men seemed to assume: they're black, they're women, they lie.

Women, my sisters explain, talk to other women not just to solve problems but to share pain, and this is not a difference of "conversational style" but is rooted in women's understanding of the realities of power. "Why didn't you give her advice? Why didn't you counsel her to come forward?" the incredulous senators demanded as the professor's friends tried to explain that after they heard her complaints of sexual harassment they had felt powerless to offer any solution. They had just tried to offer understanding and an ear, they said—that was what she *wanted* them to do, knowing that any "solution" would do at least as much damage to her as it could do to him. I will never forget the looks on the faces of Professor Hill's women friends—a judge and a welfare administrator—as they tried to explain why their friend hadn't come forward; they were the looks of pained and compassionate grownups trying to explain something to children.

A YOUNG MAN WRITES   From "Notes and Comment," *The New Yorker* 28 Oct. 1991: 32–33. Copyright © 1991, The New Yorker Magazine, Inc. Reprinted by permission.

Women must always be seen as powerless and passive, my sisters have pointed out, and any action they take will always be reinterpreted by men in this light. Grown men, including Judge Thomas himself, put forward in all seriousness the notion that Professor Hill was merely mouthing a "concocted" story that had been skillfully assembled from disparate sources by "special-interest groups" and then taught to her. In the minds of her accusers, Professor Hill could not even be granted the dignity of strategies of her own, however malicious; in order to be dismissed, she first had to be made a "pawn."

A woman's attractiveness will always be held against her, I now understand, and a woman's unattractiveness will always be held against her, too. Professor Hill was good-looking, and therefore it was fair to speculate that she was out to snare Judge Thomas, and that her accusation was the product of her failure to do so. But she wasn't *that* good-looking, and so it was also fair to conclude that the whole thing must be "fantasy." "Quite frankly, Anita Hill is not worth that type of risk," one of the Judge's supporters said—not good-looking enough to throw a career away on.

A man's career is assumed—by the man, and by other men—to be the equivalent of a woman's life; a setback to his ambition will be taken as a threat to his very existence. A woman's career, on the other hand, is just a job. Many of the senators couldn't understand why Anita Hill didn't simply give up her career if she didn't like the way she was treated. Clarence Thomas is a judge: what he does for a living is to review the cases of men and women, many of whom believe themselves to be as innocent as he claims to be. Yet when he was asked to bear for a moment a version of the same kind of scrutiny, he saw himself as a martyr—a lynching victim. His rage was thought to be impressive. Had Professor Hill shown the slightest sign of anger, of course, it would have been further proof of her "unstable" and "vindictive" nature.

As my sisters long ago explained, in the seemingly distant context of discussions of late-nineteenth-century psychiatry, any woman who is difficult will eventually be called mad. On Saturday afternoon, Senator Arlen Specter blandly accused Professor Hill of perjury. By Sunday night, he had refined this conjecture: it was not that Professor Hill was lying but that she was simply unable to distinguish truth from fantasy. His tone suggested that this change in accusation had been made for her benefit—that she ought to be grateful for the superior male wisdom that recognized her as helpless in the grip of her delusions rather than as a deliberate liar.

Men define reality, and women seek refuge within the interstices of those definitions, my sisters have told me; the feminist theorists have written similar things, grandly and abstractly. I now see what this means in terms of practical conduct. Judge Thomas offered nothing except a blanket denial and a raft of wild accusations. Nonetheless, his anger was apparently judged by many other men, and by some women, to be admirable, as a kind of expression of masculinity: so admirable that it enabled him to redefine the hearings in terms of *his* suffering, *his* struggle, *his* martyrdom, *his* career—*his* reality. He turned the discussion to the historical generalities of racial oppression—of which his accuser had certainly had at least as much experience as he had—and was allowed to escape the responsibility of meeting the particular accusations of sexual oppression. The committee had treated Professor Hill in "a very polite and professional way," Senator Specter said on Tuesday, and this time he went on to accuse her of both perjury *and* delusional lying. Since she had been treated "politely," her claims could be dismissed, instead of refuted, and she could once again be rendered negligible.

Talking to my wife and mother and sisters about the hearings, I heard in their voices not so much anger as resignation and familiarity. "This comes to you as a *surprise?*" they said, in so many words. Watching these women over a lifetime, I realize, I had often been a little surprised when they would burst into rage and indignation about what seemed to me "petty" injustices and slights at the hands of men. They had on tap a vein of anger that bewildered me, rising, as it did, from lives that were so obviously successful and happy. I owe them an apology. They had experienced things that I had not, and had tried to tell me truths that I had chosen not to hear.

BLAME IT ON FEMINISM
Susan Faludi

Susan Faludi is a prize-winning journalist who has written for several major newspapers, including the *New York Times* and *The Wall Street Journal*. In 1991, while working for *The Wall Street Journal*, Faludi won both the John Hancock Award for Excellence in Business and Financial Journalism and the Pulitzer Prize for investigative journalism.

Faludi's interest in writing about feminism was sparked by reading some highly publicized reports of research claiming a "man-shortage" and an "infertility epidemic" plaguing single, well-educated women. Faludi decided to look more closely at this research. The result was *Backlash*, Faludi's best-selling book debunking these and other myths.

Labeled "feminism's new manifesto," *Backlash* received the National Book Critics Circle Award for general nonfiction. It is one of the most widely read feminist books since Friedan's *The Feminine Mystique.*

By the end of the decade, women were starting to tell pollsters that they feared their sex's social status was once again beginning to slip. They believed they were facing an "erosion of respect," as the 1990 Virginia Slims poll summed up the sentiment. After years in which an increasing percentage of women had said their status had improved from a decade earlier, the proportion suddenly shrunk by 5 percent in the last half of the '80s, the Roper Organization reported. And it fell most sharply among women in their thirties—the age group most targeted by the media and advertisers—dropping about ten percentage points between 1985 and 1990.

Some women began to piece the picture together. In the 1989 *New York Times* poll, more than half of black women and one-fourth of white women put it into words. They told pollsters they believed men were now trying to retract the gains women had made in the last twenty years. "I wanted more autonomy," was how one woman, a thirty-seven-year-old nurse, put it. And her estranged husband "wanted to take it away."

BLAME IT ON FEMINISM   From Susan Faludi, *Backlash: The Undeclared War Against American Women* (New York: Crown, 1991) xvii–xxiii. Copyright © 1991 by Susan Faludi. Reprinted by permission of the publisher.

The truth is that the last decade has seen a powerful counterassault on women's rights, a backlash, an attempt to retract the handful of small and hard-won victories that the feminist movement did manage to win for women. This counterassault is largely insidious: in a kind of pop-culture version of the Big Lie, it stands the truth boldly on its head and proclaims that the very steps that have elevated women's position have actually led to their downfall.

The backlash is at once sophisticated and banal, deceptively "progressive" and proudly backward. It deploys both the "new" findings of "scientific research" and the dime-store moralism of yesteryear; it turns into media sound bites both the glib pronouncements of pop-psych trend-watchers and the frenzied rhetoric of New Right preachers. The backlash has succeeded in framing virtually the whole issue of women's rights in its own language. Just as Reaganism shifted political discourse far to the right and demonized liberalism, so the backlash convinced the public that women's "liberation" was the true contemporary American scourge—the source of an endless laundry list of personal, social, and economic problems.

But what has made women unhappy in the last decade is not their "equality"—which they don't yet have—but the rising pressure to halt, and even reverse, women's quest for that equality. The "man shortage" and the "infertility epidemic" are not the price of liberation; in fact, they do not even exist. But these chimeras are the chisels of a society-wide backlash. They are part of a relentless whittling-down process—much of it amounting to outright propaganda—that has served to stir women's private anxieties and break their political wills. Identifying feminism as women's enemy only furthers the ends of a backlash against women's equality, simultaneously deflecting attention from the backlash's central role and recruiting women to attack their own cause.

Some social observers may well ask whether the current pressures on women actually constitute a backlash—or just a continuation of American society's long-standing resistance to women's rights. Certainly hostility to female independence has always been with us. But if fear and loathing of feminism is a sort of perpetual viral condition in our culture, it is not always in an acute stage; its symptoms subside and resurface periodically. And it is these episodes of resurgence, such as the one we face now, that can accurately be termed "backlashes" to women's advancement. If we trace these occurrences in American history . . . we find such flare-ups are hardly random; they have always been triggered by the perception—accurate or not—that women are making great strides. These outbreaks are backlashes because they have always arisen in reaction to women's "progress," caused not simply by a bedrock of misogyny but by the specific efforts of contemporary women to improve their status, efforts that have been interpreted time and again by men—especially men grappling with real threats to their economic and social well-being on other fronts—as spelling their own masculine doom.

The most recent round of backlash first surfaced in the late '70s on the fringes, among the evangelical right. By the early '80s, the fundamentalist ideology had shouldered its way into the White House. By the mid-'80s, as resistance to women's rights acquired political and social acceptability, it passed into the popular culture. And in every case, the timing coincided with signs that women were believed to be on the verge of breakthrough.

Just when women's quest for equal rights seemed closest to achieving its objectives, the backlash struck it down. Just when a "gender gap" at the voting booth surfaced in 1980, and women in politics began to talk of capitalizing on it, the Republican party elevated Ronald Reagan and both political parties began to shunt women's rights off their platforms. Just when support for feminism and the Equal Rights Amendment reached a record high in 1981, the amendment was defeated the following year. Just when women were starting to mobilize against battering and sexual assaults, the federal government stalled funding for battered-women's programs, defeated bills to fund shelters, and shut down its Office of Domestic Violence—only two years after opening it in 1979. Just when record numbers of younger women were supporting feminist goals in the mid-'80s (more of them, in fact, than older women) and a majority of all women were calling themselves feminists, the media declared the advent of a younger "postfeminist generation" that supposedly reviled the women's movement. Just when women racked up their largest percentage ever supporting the right to abortion, the U.S. Supreme Court moved toward reconsidering it.

In other words, the antifeminist backlash has been set off not by women's achievement of full equality but by the increased possibility that they might win it. It is a preemptive strike that stops women long before they reach the finish line. "A backlash may be an indication that women really have had an effect," feminist psychiatrist Dr. Jean Baker Miller has written, "but backlashes occur when advances have been small, before changes are sufficient to help many people. . . . It is almost as if the leaders of backlashes use the fear of change as a threat before major change has occurred." In the last decade, some women did make substantial advances before the backlash hit, but millions of others were left behind, stranded. Some women now enjoy the right to legal abortion—but not the 44 million women, from the indigent to the military work force, who depend on the federal government for their medical care. Some women can now walk into high-paying professional careers—but not the more than 19 million still in the typing pools or behind the department store sales counters. (Contrary to popular myth about the "have-it-all" baby-boom women, the largest percentage of women in this generation remain typists and clerks.)

As the backlash has gathered force, it has cut off the few from the many—and the few women who have advanced seek to prove, as a social survival tactic, that they aren't so interested in advancement after all. Some of them parade their defection from the women's movement, while their working-class peers founder and cling to the splintered remains of the feminist cause. While a very few affluent and celebrity women who are showcased in news articles boast about having "found my niche as Mrs. Andy Mill" and going home to "bake bread," the many working-class women appeal for their economic rights—flocking to unions in record numbers, striking on their own for pay equity and establishing their own fledgling groups for working women's rights. In 1986, while 41 percent of upper-income women were claiming in the Gallup poll that they were not feminists, only 26 percent of low-income women were making the same claim.

※ ※ ※

Women's advances and retreats are generally described in military terms: battles won, battles lost, points and territory gained and surrendered. The metaphor of combat is not without its merits in this context and, clearly, the same sort of martial accounting and vocabulary is already surfacing here. But by imagining the conflict as two battalions neatly arrayed on either side of the line, we miss the entangled nature, the locked embrace, of a "war" between women and the male culture they inhabit. We miss the reactive nature of a backlash, which, by definition, can exist only in response to another force.

In times when feminism is at a low ebb, women assume the reactive role—privately and most often covertly struggling to assert themselves against the dominant cultural tide. But when feminism itself becomes the tide, the opposition doesn't simply go along with the reversal: it digs in its heels, brandishes its fists, builds walls and dams. And its resistance creates countercurrents and treacherous undertows.

The force and furor of the backlash churn beneath the surface, largely invisible to the public eye. On occasion in the last decade, they have burst into view. We have seen New Right politicians condemn women's independence, antiabortion protesters fire-bomb women's clinics, fundamentalist preachers damn feminists as "whores" and "witches." Other signs of the backlash's wrath, by their sheer brutality, can push their way into public consciousness for a time—the sharp increase in rape, for example, or the rise in pornography that depicts extreme violence against women.

More subtle indicators in popular culture may receive momentary, and often bemused, media notice, then quickly slip from social awareness: A report, for instance, that the image of women on prime-time TV shows has suddenly degenerated. A survey of mystery fiction finding the numbers of female characters tortured and mutilated mysteriously multiplying. The puzzling news that, as one commentator put it, "So many hit songs have the B-word [bitch] to refer to women that some rap music seems to be veering toward rape music." The ascendancy of virulently misogynist comics like Andrew Dice Clay—who called women "pigs" and "sluts" and strutted in films in which women were beaten, tortured, and blown up—or radio hosts like Rush Limbaugh, whose broadsides against "femi-Nazi" feminists made his syndicated program the most popular radio talk show in the nation. Or word that in 1987, the American Women in Radio & Television couldn't award its annual prize for ads that feature women positively: it could find no ad that qualified.

These phenomena are all related, but that doesn't mean they are somehow coordinated. The backlash is not a conspiracy, with a council dispatching agents from some central control room, nor are the people who serve its ends often aware of their role; some even consider themselves feminists. For the most part, its workings are encoded and internalized, diffuse and chameleonic. Not all of the manifestations of the backlash are of equal weight or significance either; some are mere ephemera, generated by a culture machine that is always scrounging for a "fresh" angle. Taken as a whole, however, these codes and cajolings, these whispers and threats and myths, move overwhelmingly in one direction: they try to push women back into their "acceptable" roles—whether as Daddy's girl or fluttery romantic, active nester or passive love object.

Although the backlash is not an organized movement, that doesn't make it any less destructive. In fact, the lack of orchestration, the absence of a single string-puller, only makes it harder to see—and perhaps more effective. A backlash against women's rights succeeds to the degree that it appears *not* to be political, that it appears not to be a struggle at all. It is most powerful when it goes private, when it lodges inside a woman's mind and turns her vision inward, until she imagines the pressure is all in her head, until she begins to enforce the backlash, too—on herself.

In the last decade, the backlash has moved through the culture's secret chambers, traveling through passageways of flattery and fear. Along the way, it has adopted disguises: a mask of mild derision or the painted face of deep "concern." Its lips profess pity for any woman who won't fit the mold, while it tries to clamp the mold around her ears. It pursues a divide-and-conquer strategy: single versus married women, working women versus homemakers, middle- versus working-class. It manipulates a system of rewards and punishments, elevating women who follow its rules, isolating those who don't. The backlash remarkets old myths about women as new facts and ignores all appeals to reason. Cornered, it denies its own existence, points an accusatory finger at feminism, and burrows deeper underground.

Backlash happens to be the title of a 1947 Hollywood movie in which a man frames his wife for a murder he's committed. The backlash against women's rights works in much the same way: its rhetoric charges feminists with all the crimes it perpetrates. The backlash line blames the women's movement for the "feminization of poverty"—while the backlash's own instigators in Washington pushed through the budget cuts that helped impoverish millions of women, fought pay equity proposals, and undermined equal opportunity laws. The backlash line claims the women's movement cares nothing for children's rights—while its own representatives in the capital and state legislatures have blocked one bill after another to improve child care, slashed billions of dollars in federal aid for children, and relaxed state licensing standards for day care centers. The backlash line accuses the women's movement of creating a generation of unhappy single and childless women—but its purveyors in the media are the ones guilty of making single and childless women feel like circus freaks.

To blame feminism for women's "lesser life" is to miss entirely the point of feminism, which is to win women a wider range of experience. Feminism remains a pretty simple concept, despite repeated—and enormously effective—efforts to dress it up in greasepaint and turn its proponents into gargoyles. As Rebecca West wrote sardonically in 1913, "I myself have never been able to find out precisely what feminism is: I only know that people call me a feminist whenever I express sentiments that differentiate me from a doormat."

The meaning of the word "feminist" has not really changed since it first appeared in a book review in the *Athenaeum* of April 27, 1895, describing a woman who "has in her the capacity of fighting her way back to independence." It is the basic proposition that, as Nora put it in Ibsen's *A Doll's House* a century ago, "Before everything else I'm a human being." It is the simply worded sign hoisted by a little girl in the 1970 Women's Strike for Equality: I AM NOT A BARBIE DOLL. Feminism asks the world to recognize at long last that women aren't decorative ornaments, worthy vessels, members of a "special-interest group." They are half (in fact, now more than half) of the national population, and just as deserving of rights and opportunities, just as capable of participating in the world's events, as the other half. Feminism's agenda is basic: It asks that women not be forced to "choose" between public justice and private happiness. It asks that women be free to define themselves—instead of having their identity defined for them, time and again, by their culture and their men.

The fact that these are still such incendiary notions should tell us that American women have a way to go before they enter the promised land of equality.

THE TRANSFORMATION OF SILENCE INTO LANGUAGE AND ACTION

Audre Lorde

Audre Lorde (1934–1992) was a powerful and prolific writer, the recipient of numerous grants and awards. She published many books of poetry and essays, as well as a fictionalized biography entitled *Zami: A New Spelling of My Name* (1982). Her most recently published work, published posthumously, is *The Marvelous Arithmetics of Distance* (1993). Audre Lorde died of breast cancer in November 1992.

The essay below was presented to an audience of seven hundred at the Modern Language Association Convention in December 1977. It was reprinted in *Sister, Outsider* (1984), a book of Lorde's essays and speeches, which has become a classic of feminist literature.

I have come to believe over and over again that what is most important to me must be spoken, made verbal and shared, even at the risk of having it bruised or misunderstood. That the speaking profits me, beyond any other effect. I am standing here as a Black lesbian poet, and the meaning of all that waits upon the fact that I am still alive, and might not have been. Less than two months ago I was told by two doctors, one female and one male, that I would have to have breast surgery, and that there was a 60 to 80 percent chance that the tumor was malignant. Between that telling and the actual surgery, there was a three-week period of the agony of an involuntary reorganization of my entire life. The surgery was completed, and the growth was benign.

But within those three weeks, I was forced to look upon myself and my living with a harsh and urgent clarity that has left me still shaken but much stronger. This is a situation faced by many women, by some of you here today. Some of what I experienced during that time has helped elucidate for me much of what I feel concerning the transformation of silence into language and action.

In becoming forcibly and essentially aware of my mortality, and of what I wished and wanted for my life, however short it might be, priorities and omissions became strongly etched in a merciless light, and what I most regretted were my silences. Of what had I *ever* been afraid? To question or to speak as I believed could have meant pain, or death. But we all hurt in so many different ways, all the time, and pain will either change or end. Death, on the other hand, is the final silence. And that might be coming quickly, now, without regard for whether I had ever spoken what needed to be said, or had only betrayed myself into small silences, while I planned someday to speak, or waited for someone else's words. And I began to recognize a source of power within myself that comes from the knowledge that while it is most desirable not to be afraid, learning to put fear into a perspective gave me great strength.

I was going to die, if not sooner then later, whether or not I had ever spoken myself. My silences had not protected me. Your silence will not protect you. But for every real word spoken, for every attempt I had ever made to speak those truths for which I am still seeking, I had made contact with other women while we examined the words to fit a world in which we all believed, bridging our differences. And it was the concern and caring of all those women which gave me strength and enabled me to scrutinize the essentials of my living.

The women who sustained me through that period were Black and white, old and young, lesbian, bisexual, and heterosexual, and we all shared a war against the tyrannies of silence. They all gave me a strength and concern without which I could not have survived intact. Within those weeks of acute fear came the knowledge—within the war we are all waging with the forces of death, subtle and otherwise, conscious or not—I am not only a casualty, I am also a warrior.

What are the words you do not yet have? What do you need to say? What are the tyrannies you swallow day by day and attempt to make your own, until you will sicken and die of them, still in silence? Perhaps for some of you here today, I am the face of one of your fears. Because I am woman, because I am Black, because I am lesbian, because I am myself—a Black woman warrior poet doing my work—come to ask you, are you doing yours?

And of course I am afraid, because the transformation of silence into language and action is an act of self-revelation, and that always seems fraught with danger. But my daughter, when I told her of our topic and my difficulty with it, said, "Tell them about how you're never really a whole person if you remain silent, because there's always that one little piece inside you that wants to be spoken out, and if you keep ignoring it, it gets madder and madder and hotter and hotter, and if you don't speak it out one day it will just up and punch you in the mouth from the inside."

In the cause of silence, each of us draws the face of her own fear—fear of contempt, of censure, or some judgment, or recognition, of challenge, of annihilation. But most of all, I think, we fear the visibility without which we cannot truly live. Within this country where racial difference creates a constant, if unspoken, distortion of vision, Black women have on one hand always been highly visible, and so, on the other hand, have been rendered invisible through the depersonalization of racism. Even within the women's movement, we have had to fight, and still do, for that very visibility which also renders us most vulnerable, our Blackness. For to survive in the mouth of this dragon we call america, we have had to learn this first and most vital lesson—that we were never meant to survive. Not as human beings. And neither were most of you here today, Black or not. And that visibility which makes us most vulnerable is that which also is the source of our greatest strength. Because the machine will try to grind you into dust anyway, whether or not we speak. We can sit in our corners mute forever while our sisters and our selves are wasted, while our children are distorted and destroyed, while our earth is poisoned; we can sit in our safe corners mute as bottles, and we will still be no less afraid.

In my house this year we are celebrating the feast of Kwanza, the African-american festival of harvest which begins the day after Christmas and lasts for seven days. There are seven principles of Kwanza, one for each day. The first principle is Umoja, which means unity, the decision to strive for and maintain unity in self and community. The principle for yesterday, the second day, was Kujichagulia—self-determination—the decision to define ourselves, name ourselves, and speak for ourselves, instead of being defined and spoken for by others. Today is the third day of Kwanza, and the principle for today is Ujima—collective work and responsibility—the decision to build and maintain ourselves and our communities together and to recognize and solve our problems together.

Each of us is here now because in one way or another we share a commitment to language and to the power of language, and to the reclaiming of that language which has been made to work against us. In the transformation of silence into language and action, it is vitally necessary for each one of us to establish or examine her function in that transformation and to recognize her role as vital within that transformation.

For those of us who write, it is necessary to scrutinize not only the truth of what we speak, but the truth of that language by which we speak it. For others, it is to share and spread also those words that are meaningful to us. But primarily for us all, it is necessary to teach by living and speaking those truths which we believe and know beyond understanding. Because in this way alone we can survive, by taking part in a process of life that is creative and continuing, that is growth.

And it is never without fear—of visibility, of the harsh light of scrutiny and perhaps judgment, of pain, of death. But we have lived through all of those already, in silence, except death. And I remind myself all the time now that if I were to have been born mute, or had maintained an oath of silence my whole life long for safety, I would still have suffered, and I would still die. It is very good for establishing perspective.

And where the words of women are crying to be heard, we must each of us recognize our responsibility to seek those words out, to read them and share them and examine them in their pertinence to our lives. That we not hide behind the mockeries of separations that have been imposed upon us and which so often we accept as our own. For instance, "I can't possibly teach Black women's writing—their experience is so different from mine." Yet how many years have you spent teaching Plato and Shakespeare and Proust? Or another, "She's a white woman and what could she possibly have to say to me?" Or, "She's a lesbian, what would my husband say, or my chairman?" Or again, "This woman writes of her sons and I have no children." And all the other endless ways in which we rob ourselves of ourselves and each other.

We can learn to work and speak when we are afraid in the same way we have learned to work and speak when we are tired. For we have been socialized to respect fear more than our own needs for language and definition, and while we wait in silence for that final luxury of fearlessness, the weight of that silence will choke us.

The fact that we are here and that I speak these words is an attempt to break that silence and bridge some of those differences between us, for it is not difference which immobilizes us, but silence. And there are so many silences to be broken.

Part Three

Woman As Object

"Today's standard of womanhood is contained in three words, health, youth, and daintiness." So ran a 1925 advertisement which warned that "the charm of feminine immaculacy is continually threatened by the results of fatigue and listlessness, a general letdown of physical tone." Happily, women could stave off this threat by regular douching with "Lysol." They would particularly prize, according to the ad copy, its "gentle, deodorant qualities," as well as its "soothing" and "lubricating" effects.

The more things change, runs an old adage, the more they remain the same. Notions of the ideal woman shift, but, even as products promising perfection proliferate, and mall shelves groan under their combined weight, the basic cultural message endures. Ads, music videos, fashion and entertainment magazines, the "Style" sections of newspapers, all emphasize various attributes of the current ideal of female perfection. The reader (or listener, or viewer) is

"SHE WAS ADVISED TO PLAY COY,
EXHORTED TO COME ON HEARTY,
EXERCISE, DIET, SMILE AND WHEEDLE."
—MARGE PIERCY

invited to compare herself with these images. Any woman who falls short, these messages say repeatedly, is a failure. She must take immediate steps to correct, or at least disguise, any and every shortcoming. Advertisers, of course, are only too happy to tell her what she has to do; so are fitness and diet gurus, fashion editors, and designers. All are self-appointed experts who have made careers out of telling women how to lose or gain weight, how to dress for success (whether success means a promotion or a proposal), how—in a phrase—to please men.

We live in a culture in which women are, to a considerable extent, defined as physical objects rather than as persons. Men are not immune to the same social pressures, but, as Susan Sontag points out in her classic essay on "The Double Standard of Aging," men have traditionally had less at stake when it comes to measuring up to cultural ideals. The ideals for them, in addition, are more attainable. Little boys are urged to become "big and strong" even as little girls are enjoined to be "pretty." Boys grow up thinking of their bodies primarily in terms of what they enable them to do. Girls, in contrast, learn to think of theirs largely in terms of how boys will regard them. As Anaïs Nin noted in her *Diary,* she would, at sixteen, decode how pretty she was not from her mirror but from the eyes of the boy with whom she would dance. The boy who is not handsome is hardly a tragic figure; the girl who is not beautiful is.

Being beautiful means being able to attract men. And tastes in female beauty vary not only from individual to individual but also over time. In the years before World War I, the classic American beauty, the "Gibson Girl," was plump. Her arms were well rounded as were her other less visible charms. The fashions of the day emphasized wide hips and buttocks combined with an anatomically improbable "wasp waist." Today the ideal woman is slender, and even those women whose weights are below the standards for their height suggested by the Metropolitan Life Insurance Company in 1959 describe themselves as overweight. And these standard weights have been criticized by nutritionists and other health experts for being too low. Many of the women so desperately trying to lose weight, it turns out, are already too thin.

Women on diets can be comic figures. Cathy Guisewite's popular "Cathy" comic strip, for example, routinely pokes fun at her protagonist's hopeless quest for cellulite-free thighs and "buns of steel." But the health risks associated with obsessive dieting are no laughing matter. Nor are such severe eating disorders as anorexia nervosa and bulimia.

The slender woman born into an age that glorified plumpness, no less than the plump woman born into a world that worships slenderness, faced the injunction that she remake herself to conform to the dominant cultural norm. Fashions in beauty change, but the individual woman's obligation to improve upon nature remains constant. Women continue to be urged to regard themselves as a sort of sculpture. They are to chip away at their imperfections until they achieve the ideal, which is necessarily a frustrating process. Even those who come close to embodying the ideals of the day gain only the most fleeting surcease from self-doubt, for perfection, as the "Lysol" ad reminded the women of 1925, includes a quality—youth—that disappears all too soon, no matter how heroic the steps taken to combat the visible evidence of aging. Men, however, are allowed to age, Sontag contends. Lines in their faces can connote character; the gray at their temples can suggest the coming of wisdom. Not so for women. Lines, gray hair, a spreading waistline simply mean, for women, that they are growing old.

Age means the end of allure. It does not, however, mean the end of sexuality. Women's sexual drives, unlike men's, do not diminish as they reach middle or old age. This dissonance between culture and biology signifies what little influence women have historically had in determining the sexual rules of the game. Because rule number one has been that women exist to satisfy male needs and desires, a dominant motif in our culture's images of female sexuality is subservience. It is an image which, like slenderness, endangers as well as deforms. The articles, essays, and poems in this chapter address some of the forms these dangers take, including rape and sexual battering.

One of the most controversial aspects of the career of pop idol Madonna involves her use of such stereotypical elements of pornography as bondage and exhibitionism. Does this represent a cynical catering to misogynistic fantasies or a serious artistic effort to deconstruct the images previously used to degrade women? Images do have consequences, but it is difficult to link specific images to specific behavior. This conundrum is at the heart of the debate over pornography, a debate which has moved to the center of contemporary feminist discourse. It largely defines the terms of the current discussion of violence against women and threatens to divide the feminist movement.

The question of sexual violence is not new. In *Incidents in the Life of a Slave Girl*, Harriet Jacobs recounts her master's attempts to extort sexual favors. Jacobs hid from her master in an attic for years before finally escaping to the North. Other victims of harassment and rape have sometimes had to take equally desperate steps. What can victims do to protect themselves? Although they have more alternatives than their sisters had in earlier generations, Manhattan prosecutor Linda Fairstein maintains, many remain desperate indeed.

THE DOUBLE STANDARD OF AGING

Susan Sontag

Susan Sontag is a noted philosopher, literary critic, novelist, filmmaker, and social commentator. She is the author of books such as *On Photography, Against Interpretation, Styles of Radical Will*, and, her most recent novel, the best-selling *The Volcano Lover: A Romance*. Perhaps no other American intellectual has achieved such prominence in so many fields or exerted so much influence on the public understanding of so many issues. "The Double Standard of Aging," which appeared in the premier issue (1972) of the *Saturday Review of The Society*, is vintage Sontag. In it she takes an old idea, the double standard of morality that required women to be chaste but excused the sexual adventures of men—an idea which, according to conventional wisdom, was rapidly disappearing in the wake of the so-called sexual revolution of the 1960s—and examines whether an analogous double standard of aging is alive and flourishing.

 To be a woman is to be an actress. Being feminine is a kind of theater, with its appropriate costumes, *décor,* lighting, and stylized gestures. From early childhood on, girls are trained to care in a pathologically exaggerated way about their appearance and are profoundly mutilated (to the extent of being unfitted for first-class adulthood) by the extent of the stress put on presenting themselves as physically attractive objects. Women look in the mirror more frequently than men do. It is, virtually, their duty to look at themselves—to look often. Indeed, a woman who is not narcissistic is considered unfeminine. And a woman who spends literally *most* of her time caring for, and making purchases to flatter, her physical appearance is not regarded in this society as what she is: a kind of moral idiot. She is thought to be quite normal and is envied by other women whose time is mostly used up at jobs or caring for large families. The display of narcissism goes on all the time. It is expected that women will disappear several times in an evening—at a restaurant, at a party, during a theater intermission, in the course of a social visit—simply to check their appearance, to see that nothing has gone wrong with their make-up and hairstyling, to make sure that their clothes are not spotted or too wrinkled or not hanging properly. It is even acceptable to perform this activity in public. At the table in a restaurant, over coffee, a woman opens a compact mirror and touches up her make-up and hair without embarrassment in front of her husband or her friends.

All this behavior, which is written off as normal "vanity" in women, would seem ludicrous in a man. Women are more vain than men because of the relentless pressure on women to maintain their appearance at a certain high standard. What makes the pressure even more burdensome is that there are actually several standards. Men present themselves as face-and-body, a physical whole. Women are split, as men are not, into a body and a face—each judged by somewhat different standards. What is important for a face is that it be beautiful. What is important for a body is two things, which may even be (depending on fashion and taste) somewhat incompatible: first, that it be desirable and, second, that it be beautiful. Men usually feel sexually attracted to women much more because of their bodies than their faces. The traits that arouse desire—such as fleshiness—don't always match those that fashion decrees as beautiful. (For instance, the ideal woman's body promoted in advertising in recent years is extremely thin: the kind of body that looks more desirable clothed than naked.) But women's concern with their appearance is not simply geared to arousing desire in men. It also aims at fabricating a certain image by which, as a more indirect way of arousing desire, women state their value. A woman's value lies in the way she *represents* herself, which is much more by her face than her body. In defiance of the laws of simple sexual attraction, women do not devote most of their attention to their bodies. The well-known "normal" narcissism that women display—the amount of time they spend before the mirror—is used primarily in caring for the face and hair.

Women do not simply have faces, as men do; they are identified with their faces. Men have a naturalistic relation to their faces. Certainly they care whether they are good-looking or not. They suffer over acne, protruding ears, tiny eyes; they hate getting bald. But there is a much wider latitude in what is esthetically acceptable in a man's face than what is in a woman's. A man's face is defined as something he basically doesn't need to tamper with; all he has to do is keep it clean. He can avail himself of the options for ornament supplied by nature: a beard, a mustache, longer or shorter hair. But he is not supposed to disguise himself. What he is "really" like is supposed to show. A man lives through his face; it records the progressive stages of his life. And since he doesn't tamper with his face, it is not separate from but is completed by his body—which is judged attractive by the impression it gives of virility and energy. By contrast, a woman's face is potentially separate from her body. She does not treat it naturalistically. A woman's face is the canvas upon which she paints a revised, corrected portrait of herself. One of the rules of this creation is that the face *not* show what she doesn't want it to show. Her face is an emblem, an icon, a flag. How she arranges her hair, the type of make-up she uses, the quality of her complexion—all these are signs, not of what she is "really" like, but of how she asks to be treated by others, especially men. They establish her status as an "object."

For the normal changes that age inscribes on every human face, women are much more heavily penalized than men. Even in early adolescence, girls are cautioned to protect their faces against wear and tear. Mothers tell their daughters (but never their sons): You look ugly when you cry. Stop worrying. Don't read too much. Crying, frowning, squinting, even laughing—all these human activities make "lines." The same usage of the face in men is judged quite positively. In a man's face lines are taken to be signs of "character." They indicate emotional strength, maturity—qualities far more esteemed in men than in women. (They show he has "lived.") Even scars are often not felt to be unattractive; they too can add "character" to a man's face. But lines of aging, any scar, even a small birthmark on a woman's face, are always regarded as unfortunate blemishes. In effect, people take character in men to be different from what constitutes character in women. A woman's character is thought to be innate, static—not the product of her experience, her years, her actions. A woman's face is prized so far as it remains unchanged by (or conceals the traces of) her emotions, her physical risk-taking. Ideally, it is supposed to be a mask—immutable, unmarked. The model woman's face is Garbo's. Because women are identified with their faces much more than men are, and the ideal woman's face is one that is "perfect," it seems a calamity when a woman has a disfiguring accident. A broken nose or scar or a burn mark, no more than regrettable for a man, is a terrible psychological wound to a woman; objectively, it diminishes her value. (As is well known, most clients for plastic surgery are women.)

Both sexes aspire to a physical ideal, but what is expected of boys and what is expected of girls involves a very different moral relation to the self. Boys are encouraged to *develop* their bodies, to regard the body as an instrument to be improved. They invent their masculine selves largely through exercise and sport, which harden the body and strengthen competitive feelings; clothes are of only secondary help in making their bodies attractive. Girls are not particularly encouraged to develop their bodies through any activity, strenuous or not; and physical strength and endurance are hardly valued at all. The invention of the feminine self proceeds mainly through clothes and other signs that testify to the very effort of girls to look attractive, to their commitment to please. When boys become men, they may go on (especially if they have sedentary jobs) practicing a sport or doing exercises for a while. Mostly they leave their appearance alone, having been trained to accept more or less what nature has handed out to them. (Men may start doing exercises again in their forties to lose weight, but for reasons of health—there is an epidemic fear of heart attacks among the middle-aged in rich countries—not for cosmetic reasons.) As one of the norms of "femininity" in this society is being preoccupied with one's physical appearance, so "masculinity" means *not* caring very much about one's looks.

This society allows men to have a much more affirmative relation to their bodies than women have. Men are more "at home" in their bodies, whether they treat them casually or use them aggressively. A man's body is defined as a strong body. It contains no contradiction between what is felt to be attractive and what is practical. A woman's body, so far as it is considered attractive, is defined as a fragile, light body. (Thus, women worry more than men do about being overweight.) When they do exercises, women avoid the ones that develop the muscles, particularly those in the upper arms. Being "feminine" means looking physically weak, frail. Thus, the ideal woman's body is one that is not of much practical use in the hard work of this world, and one that must continually be "defended." Women do not develop their bodies, as men do. After a woman's body has reached its sexually acceptable form by late adolescence, most further development is viewed as negative. And it is thought irresponsible for women to do what is normal for men: simply leave their appearance alone. During early youth they are likely to come as close as they ever will to the ideal image—slim figure, smooth firm skin, light musculature, graceful movements. Their task is to try to maintain that image, unchanged, as long as possible. Improvement as such is not the task. Women care for their bodies—against toughening, coarsening, getting fat. They *conserve* them. (Perhaps the fact that women in modern societies tend to have a more conservative political outlook than men originates in their profoundly conservative relation to their bodies.)

In the life of women in this society the period of pride, of natural honesty, of unself-conscious flourishing is brief. Once past youth women are condemned to inventing (and maintaining) themselves against the inroads of age. Most of the physical qualities regarded as attractive in women deteriorate much earlier in life than those defined as "male." Indeed, they perish fairly soon in the normal sequence of body transformation. The "feminine" is smooth, rounded, hairless, unlined, soft, unmuscled—the look of the very young; characteristics of the weak, of the vulnerable; eunuch traits, as Germaine Greer has pointed out. Actually, there are only a few years—late adolescence, early twenties—in which this look is physiologically natural, in which it can be had without touching-up and covering-up. After that, women enlist in a quixotic enterprise, trying to close the gap between the imagery put forth by society (concerning what is attractive in a woman) and the evolving facts of nature.

Women have a more intimate relation to aging than men do, simply because one of the accepted "women's" occupations is taking pains to keep one's face and body from showing the signs of growing older. Women's sexual validity depends, up to a certain point, on how well they stand off these natural changes. After late adolescence women become the caretakers of their bodies and faces, pursuing an essentially defensive strategy, a holding operation. A vast array of products in jars and tubes, a branch of surgery, and armies of hairdressers, masseuses, diet counselors, and other professionals exist to stave off, or mask, developments that are entirely normal biologically. Large amounts of women's energies are diverted into this passionate, corrupting effort to defeat nature: to maintain an ideal, static appearance against the progress of age. The collapse of the project is only a matter of time. Inevitably, a woman's physical appearance develops beyond its youthful form. No matter how exotic the creams or how strict the diets, one cannot indefinitely keep the face unlined, the waist slim. Bearing children takes its toll: the torso becomes thicker; the skin is stretched. There is no way to keep certain lines from appearing, in one's mid-twenties, around the eyes and mouth. From about thirty on, the skin gradually loses its tonus. In women this perfectly natural process is regarded as a humiliating defeat, while nobody finds anything remarkably unattractive in the equivalent physical changes in men. Men are "allowed" to look older without sexual penalty.

Thus, the reason that women experience aging with more pain than men is not simply that they care more than men about how they look. Men also care about their looks and want to be attractive, but since the business of men is mainly being and doing, rather than appearing, the standards for appearance are much less exacting. The standards for what is attractive in a man are permissive; they conform to what is possible or "natural" to most men throughout most of their lives. The standards for women's appearance go against nature, and to come anywhere near approximating them takes considerable effort and time. Women must try to be beautiful. At the least, they are under heavy social pressure not to be ugly. A woman's fortunes depend, far more than a man's, on being at least "acceptable" looking. Men are not subject to this pressure. Good looks in a man is a bonus, not a psychological necessity for maintaining normal self-esteem.

Behind the fact that women are more severely penalized than men are for aging is the fact that people, in this culture at least, are simply less tolerant of ugliness in women than in men. An ugly woman is never merely repulsive. Ugliness in a woman is felt by everyone, men as well as women, to be faintly embarrassing. And many features or blemishes that count as ugly in a woman's face would be quite tolerable on the face of a man. This is not, I would insist, just because the esthetic standards for men and women are different. It is rather because the esthetic standards for women are much higher, and narrower, than those proposed for men.

Beauty, women's business in this society, is the theater of their enslavement. Only one standard of female beauty is sanctioned: the *girl*. The great advantage men have is that our culture allows two standards of male beauty: the *boy* and the *man*. The beauty of a boy resembles the beauty of a girl. In both sexes it is a fragile kind of beauty and flourishes naturally only in the early part of the life-cycle. Happily, men are able to accept themselves under another standard of good looks—heavier, rougher, more thickly built. A man does not grieve when he loses the smooth, unlined, hairless skin of a boy. For he has only exchanged one form of attractiveness for another: the darker skin of a man's face, roughened by daily shaving, showing the marks of emotion and the normal lines of age. There is no equivalent of this second standard for women. The single standard of beauty for women dictates that they must go on having clear skin. Every wrinkle, every line, every grey hair, is a defeat. No wonder that no boy minds becoming a man, while even the passage from girl-hood to early womanhood is experienced by many women as their downfall, for all women are trained to want to continue looking like girls.

This is not to say there are no beautiful older women. But the standard of beauty in a woman of any age is how far she retains, or how she manages to simulate, the appearance of youth. The exceptional woman in her sixties who is beautiful certainly owes a large debt to her genes. Delayed aging, like good looks, tends to run in fami-lies. But nature rarely offers enough to meet this culture's standards. Most of the women who successfully delay the appearance of age are rich, with unlimited leisure to devote to nurturing along nature's gifts. Often they are actresses. (That is, highly paid professionals at doing what all women are taught to practice as amateurs.) Such women as Mae West, Dietrich, Stella Adler, Dolores Del Rio, do not challenge the rule about the relation between beauty and age in women. They are admired pre-cisely because they *are* exceptions, because they have managed (at least so it seems in photographs) to outwit nature. Such miracles, exceptions made by nature (with the help of art and social privilege), only confirm the rule, because what makes these women seem beautiful to us is precisely that they do not look their real age. Society allows no place in our imagination for a beautiful old woman who does look like an old woman—a woman who might be like Picasso at the age of ninety, being photographed outdoors on his estate in the south of France, wearing only shorts and sandals. No one imagines such a woman exists. Even the special exceptions—Mae West & Co.—are always photographed indoors, cleverly lit, from the most flat-tering angle and fully, artfully clothed. The implication is they would not stand a closer scrutiny. The idea of an old woman in a bathing suit being attractive, or even just acceptable looking, is inconceivable. An older woman is, by definition, sexually repulsive—unless, in fact, she doesn't look old at all. The body of an old woman, unlike that of an old man, is always understood as a body that can no longer be shown, offered, unveiled. At best, it may appear in costume. People still feel uneasy, thinking about what they might see if her mask dropped, if she took off her clothes.

Thus, the point for women of dressing up, applying make-up, dyeing their hair, going on crash diets, and getting face-lifts is not just to be attractive. They are ways of defending themselves against a profound level of disapproval directed toward women, a disapproval that can take the form of aversion. The double standard about aging converts the life of women into an inexorable march toward a condition in which they are not just unattractive, but disgusting. The profoundest terror of a woman's life is the moment represented in a statue by Rodin called *Old Age*: a naked old woman, seated, pathetically contemplates her flat, pendulous, ruined body. Aging in women is a process of becoming obscene sexually, for the flabby bosom, wrinkled neck, spotted hands, thinning white hair, waistless torso, and veined legs of an old woman are felt to be obscene. In our direst moments of the imagination, this transformation can take place with dismaying speed—as in the end of *Lost Horizon,* when the beautiful young girl is carried by her lover out of Shangri-La and, within minutes, turns into a withered, repulsive crone. There is no equivalent nightmare about men. This is why, however much a man may care about his appearance, that caring can never acquire the same desperateness it often does for women. When men dress according to fashion or now even use cosmetics, they do not expect from clothes and make-up what women do. A face-lotion or perfume or deodorant or hairspray, used by a man, is not part of a disguise. Men, as men, do not feel the need to disguise themselves to fend off morally disapproved signs of aging, to outwit premature sexual obsolescence, to cover up aging as obscenity. Men are not subject to the barely concealed revulsion expressed in this culture against the female body—except in its smooth, youthful, firm, odorless, blemish-free form.

One of the attitudes that punish women most severely is the most visceral horror felt at aging female flesh. It reveals a radical fear of women installed deep in this culture, a demonology of women that has crystallized in such mythic caricatures as the vixen, the virago, the vamp, and the witch. Several centuries of witch-phobia, during which one of the cruelest extermination programs in Western history was carried out, suggest something of the extremity of this fear. That old women are repulsive is one of the most profound esthetic and erotic feelings in our culture. Women share it as much as men do. (Oppressors, as a rule, deny oppressed people their own "native" standards of beauty. And the oppressed end up being convinced that they *are* ugly.) How women are psychologically damaged by this misogynistic idea of what is beautiful parallels the way in which blacks have been deformed in a society that has up to now defined beautiful as white. Psychological tests made on young black children in the United States some years ago showed how early and how thoroughly they incorporate the white standard of good looks. Virtually all the children expressed fantasies that indicated they considered black people to be ugly, funny looking, dirty, brutish. A similar kind of self-hatred infects most women. Like men, they find old age in women "uglier" than old age in men.

This esthetic taboo functions, in sexual attitudes, as a racial taboo. In this society most people feel an involuntary recoil of the flesh when imagining a middle-aged woman making love with a young man—exactly as many whites flinch viscerally at the thought of a white woman in bed with a black man. The banal drama of a man of fifty who leaves a wife of forty-five for a girlfriend of twenty-eight contains no strictly sexual outrage, whatever sympathy people may have for the abandoned wife. On the contrary. Everyone "understands." Everyone knows that men like girls, that young women often want middle-aged men. But no one "understands" the reverse situation. A woman of forty-five who leaves a husband of fifty for a lover of twenty-eight is the makings of a social and sexual scandal at a deep level of feeling. No one takes exception to a romantic couple in which the man is twenty years or more the woman's senior. The movies pair Joanne Dru and John Wayne, Marilyn Monroe and Joseph Cotten, Audrey Hepburn and Cary Grant, Jane Fonda and Yves Montand,

Catherine Deneuve and Marcello Mastroianni; as in actual life, these are perfectly plausible, appealing couples. When the age difference runs the other way, people are puzzled and embarrassed and simply shocked. (Remember Joan Crawford and Cliff Robertson in *Autumn Leaves?* But so troubling is this kind of love story that it rarely figures in the movies, and then only as the melancholy history of a failure.) The usual view of why a woman of forty and a boy of twenty, or a woman of fifty and a man of thirty, marry is that the man is seeking a mother, not a wife; no one believes the marriage will last. For a woman to respond erotically and romantically to a man who, in terms of his age, could be her father is considered normal. A man who falls in love with a woman who, however attractive she may be, is old enough to be his mother is thought to be extremely neurotic (victim of an "Oedipal fixation" is the fashionable tag), if not mildly contemptible.

The wider the gap in age between partners in a couple, the more obvious is the prejudice against women. When old men, such as Justice Douglas, Picasso, Strom Thurmond, Onassis, Chaplin, and Pablo Casals, take brides thirty, forty, fifty years younger than themselves, it strikes people as remarkable, perhaps an exaggeration— but still plausible. To explain such a match, people enviously attribute some special virility and charm to the man. Though he can't be handsome, he is famous; and his fame is understood as having boosted his attractiveness to women. People imagine that his young wife, respectful of her elderly husband's attainments, is happy to become his helper. For the man a late marriage is always good public relations. It adds to the impression that, despite his advanced age, he is still to be reckoned with; it is the sign of a continuing vitality presumed to be available as well to his art, business activity, or political career. But an elderly woman who married a young man would be greeted quite differently. She would have broken a fierce taboo, and she would get no credit for her courage. Far from being admired for her vitality, she would probably be condemned as predatory, willful, selfish, exhibitionistic. At the same time she would be pitied, since such a marriage would be taken as evidence that she was in her dotage. If she had a conventional career or were in business or held public office, she would quickly suffer from the current of disapproval. Her very credibility as a professional would decline, since people would suspect that her young husband might have an undue influence on her. Her "respectability" would certainly be compromised. Indeed, the well-known old women I can think of who dared such unions, if only at the end of their lives—George Eliot, Colette, Edith Piaf—have all belonged to that category of people, creative artists and entertainers, who have special license from society to behave scandalously. It is thought to be a scandal for a woman to ignore that she is old and therefore too ugly for a young man. Her looks and a certain physical condition determine a woman's desirability, not her talents or her needs. Women are not supposed to be "potent." A marriage between an old woman and a young man subverts the very ground rule of relations between the two sexes, that is: whatever the variety of appearances, men remain dominant. Their claims come first. Women are supposed to be the associates and companions of men, not their full equals—and never their superiors. Women are to remain in the state of a permanent "minority."

The convention that wives should be younger than their husbands powerfully enforces the "minority" status of women, since being senior in age always carries with it, in any relationship, a certain amount of power and authority. There are no laws on the matter, of course. The convention is obeyed because to do otherwise makes one feel as if one is doing something ugly or in bad taste. Everyone feels intuitively the esthetic rightness of a marriage in which the man is older than the woman, which means that any marriage in which the woman is older creates a dubious or less gratifying mental picture. Everyone is addicted to the visual pleasure that women give by meeting certain esthetic requirements from which men are exempted, which keeps women working at staying youthful-looking while men are left free to age. On a deeper level everyone finds the signs of old age in women esthetically offensive, which conditions one to feel automatically repelled by the prospect of an elderly woman marrying a much younger man. The situation in which women are kept minors for life is largely organized by such conformist, unreflective preferences. But taste is not free, and its judgments are never merely "natural." Rules of taste enforce structures of power. The revulsion against aging in women is the cutting edge of a whole set of oppressive structures (often masked as gallantries) that keep women in their place.

The ideal state proposed for women is docility, which means not being fully grown up. Most of what is cherished as typically "feminine" is simply behavior that is childish, immature, weak. To offer so low and demeaning a standard of fulfillment in itself constitutes oppression in an acute form—a sort of moral neo-colonialism. But women are not simply condescended to by the values that secure the dominance of men. They are repudiated. Perhaps because of having been their oppressors for so long, few men really *like* women (though they love individual women), and few men ever feel really comfortable or at ease in women's company. This malaise arises because relations between the two sexes are rife with hypocrisy, as men manage to love those they dominate and therefore don't respect. Oppressors always try to justify their privileges and brutalities by imagining that those they oppress belong to a lower order of civilization or are less than fully "human." Deprived of part of their ordinary human dignity, the oppressed take on certain "demonic" traits. The oppressions of large groups have to be anchored deep in the psyche, continually renewed by partly unconscious fears and taboos, by a sense of the obscene. Thus, women arouse not only desire and affection in men but aversion as well. Women are thoroughly domesticated familiars. But, at certain times and in certain situations, they become alien, untouchable. The aversion men feel, so much of which is covered over, is felt most frankly, with least inhibition, toward the type of woman who is most taboo "esthetically," a woman who has become—with the natural changes brought about by aging—obscene.

Nothing more clearly demonstrates the vulnerability of women than the special pain, confusion, and bad faith with which they experience getting older. And in the struggle that some women are waging on behalf of all women to be treated (and treat themselves) as full human beings—not "only" as women—one of the earliest results to be hoped for is that women become aware, indignantly aware, of the double standard about aging from which they suffer so harshly.

It is understandable that women often succumb to the temptation to lie about their age. Given society's double standard, to question a woman about her age is indeed often an aggressive act, a trap. Lying is an elementary means of self-defense, a way of scrambling out of the trap, at least temporarily. To expect a woman, after "a certain age," to tell exactly how old she is—when she has a chance, either through the generosity of nature or the cleverness of art, to pass for being somewhat younger than she actually is—is like expecting a landowner to admit that the estate he has put up for sale is actually worth less than the buyer is prepared to pay. The double standard about aging sets women up as property, as objects whose value depreciates rapidly with the march of the calendar.

The prejudices that mount against women as they grow older are an important arm of male privilege. It is the present unequal distribution of adult roles between the two sexes that gives men a freedom to age denied to women. Men actively administer the double standard about aging because the "masculine" role awards them the initiative in courtship. Men choose; women are chosen. So men choose younger women. But although this system of inequality is operated by men, it could not work if women themselves did not acquiesce in it. Women reinforce it powerfully with their complacency, with their anguish, with their lies.

Not only do women lie more than men do about their age but men forgive them for it, thereby confirming their own superiority. A man who lies about his age is thought to be weak, "unmanly." A woman who lies about her age is behaving in a quite acceptable, "feminine" way. Petty lying is viewed by men with indulgence, one of a number of patronizing allowances made for women. It has the same moral unimportance as the fact that women are often late for appointments. Women are not expected to be truthful, or punctual, or expert in handling and repairing machines, or frugal, or physically brave. They are expected to be second-class adults, whose natural state is that of a grateful dependence on men. And so they often are, since that is what they are brought up to be. So far as women heed the stereotypes of "feminine" behavior, they *cannot* behave as fully responsible, independent adults.

Most women share the contempt for women expressed in the double standard about aging—to such a degree that they take their lack of self-respect for granted. Women have been accustomed so long to the protection of their masks, their smiles, their endearing lies. Without this protection, they know, they would be more vulnerable. But in protecting themselves as women, they betray themselves as adults. The model corruption in a woman's life is denying her age. She symbolically accedes to all those myths that furnish women with their imprisoning securities and privileges, that create their genuine oppression, that inspire their real discontent. Each time a woman lies about her age she becomes an accomplice in her own underdevelopment as a human being.

Women have another option. They can aspire to be wise, not merely nice; to be competent, not merely helpful; to be strong, not merely graceful; to be ambitious for themselves, not merely for themselves in relation to men and children. They can let themselves age naturally and without embarrassment, actively protesting and disobeying the conventions that stem from this society's double standard about aging. Instead of being girls, girls as long as possible, who then age humiliatingly into middle-aged women and then obscenely into old women, they can become women much earlier—and remain active adults, enjoying the long, erotic career of which women are capable, far longer. Women should allow their faces to show the lives they have lived. Women should tell the truth.

HEALTH AND BEAUTY
Godey's Lady's Book

"The first and greatest sign of health in woman is beauty," wrote William J. Cromie in 1914. Cromie was a physical education instructor at the University of Pennsylvania and author of the "Eight Minutes Common-Sense Exercise for the Nervous Woman" plan which, he claimed, would prevent fat from accumulating "upon the neck, abdomen, and hips." A woman could thus preserve "the symmetrical contour" of those parts of her body. Fashions in exercise, like fashions in female beauty, have changed over the years. But similarities over time are just as striking. Primary among these is the equation of health and beauty.

Godey's Lady's Book, source of this 1848 exercise advice, was the first major women's magazine. Previously, as the name *Lady's Book* suggests, collections of fashionable dress patterns, recipes, homemaking tips, and decorous fiction—the staples of women's magazines in the nineteenth century—had been published as books, which were often given as Christmas or birthday presents. *Godey's* brought these elements together in magazine form and wrought a publishing revolution.

I have stated that the effect of exercise is, by frequent contraction of the fibres, to brace the muscles and render them stronger, and generally to give more strength to the organs.

Nothing evidently can be more suitable to the organization of woman. Her tissues are soft and flexible; exercise renders them more firm and resisting: her fibres are thin and weak; exercise increases their size and strength: they are moistened with oils and juices; exercise diminishes the superabundant humidity.

In regard to strength in general, it may be observed that, in the present state of society, we have less need of it than the people of ancient times. Muscular strength is a kind of superiority no longer in such favor, and the aim of gymnastics is consequently nothing more than to endow the body with all the strength, vigor, and activity, compatible with health, without injury to the development of the intellectual faculties.

Moreover, the education which is suited to the male, is not calculated to render the female amiable and useful in society.

The constitution of women, indeed, bears only moderate exercise. Their feeble arms cannot support severe and long-continued labor. It renders them meagre, and deforms the organs, by compressing and destroying the cellular substance which contributes to the beauty of their outlines, and of their complexion. The graces accommodate themselves little to labor, perspiration, and sun-burning.

We must not, however, conclude from this, that females should be kept in a state of continual repose, or that the delicacy of their organization prevents their taking exercise.

It is a fact that labor, even the most excessive, is not so much to be feared as absolute idleness. The state of want which forces some women of the lowest class to perform labors that seem reserved for men, deprives them only of some attractions. Excessive indolence, on the contrary, destroys at once health, and that which women value more than health, though it never can subsist without it, namely, beauty.

HEALTH AND BEAUTY   From *Godey's Lady's Book* Aug. 1848: 111–12.

The more robust state of health in females brought up in the country, is attributable to the exercise they enjoy. Their movements are active and firm; their appetite is good, and their complexion florid; they are alert and gay; they know neither pain nor lassitude, although they are in action without cessation under all kinds of weather. It is exercise which gives them vigor, health, and happiness—exercise to which they are so frequently subjected, even in infancy and youth.

We observe, also, that in a family where there are several sisters of similar constitution, the one who from circumstances has been accustomed to regular and daily exercise, almost always possesses more strength and vigor.

Mothers and teachers, therefore, instead of fearing that their children should fatigue themselves by exertion in active sports, should subject them early to it. They will thus give them more than merely life and instruction; they will confer on them health and strength.

We now proceed to give illustrations of these exercises, or *extension motions.* These three figures are intended to show one variety of these exercises.

One. The forearms are bent upon the arms upward and toward the body, having the elbows depressed, the shut hands touching on the little finger sides, and the knuckles upward, the latter being raised as high as the chin, and at the distance of about a foot before it.

Two. While the arms are thrown forcibly backward, the forearms are as much as possible bent upon the arms, and the palmar sides of the wrists are turned forward and outward.

These two motions are to be repeatedly and rather quickly performed.

A modification of the same movements is performed as a separate extension motion, but may be given in continuation, with the numbers following these as words of command.

Three. The arms are extended at full length in front, on a level with the shoulders, the palms of the hands in contact.

Four. Thus extended, and the palms retaining their vertical position, the arms are thrown forcibly backward, so that the backs of the hands may approach each other as nearly as possible.

We now come to what is termed *"Exercise with the Rod."* Here are three illustrations.

The rod for this purpose should be light, smooth, inflexible, and need not be more than three or four feet in length.

First Exercises. The rod is first grasped near the extremities by the two hands, the thumbs being inward.

Without changing the position of the hands on the rod, it is then brought to a vertical position: the right hand being uppermost holds its above the head, the left is against the lower part of the body.

By an opposite movement, the right is lowered and the left raised.

This change is executed repeatedly and quickly.

Second Exercise. From the first position of the rod, it is raised over the head; and, in doing so, the closer the hands are, the better will be the effect upon the shoulder.

It is afterwards carried behind the back, holding so firmly that no change takes place in the position of the hands.

This movement is then reversed, to bring it back over the head to the first position.

HOW TO GET PLUMP

Harper's Bazar

We live in a culture which exalts the slender. Diet books invariably claim a substantial share of the best-seller listings; diet products and supplements crowd supermarket shelves; and much of the current interest in fitness and exercise arises from our desire to control our weight. We are, to a considerable extent, a nation of calorie counters and weight watchers.

This fascination with the slender is a recent phenomenon, one dating back to the second decade of the twentieth century but not further. The previous ideal of the beautiful is aptly captured in the title of the following article, "How to Get Plump." *Harper's Bazar*, then as now, was a magazine devoted to high fashion. Its editors were arbiters of style, and thin was anything but stylish in 1908. Those beyond the call of fashion, "those who do not consider beauty of sufficient importance to warrant an expenditure of time and effort," learned that slenderness was also unhealthy.

Of special interest are the "normal" weights listed in the article. The "normal" woman of 1908 would be considered overweight today, and the models who grace the pages of fashion magazines today would have had to gain thirty or forty pounds to model back then.

Those who are too thin do not take the same interest in trying to reach the ideal proportion between height and weight as do those who are too fat, although there is every reason why they should. The woman of five feet seven whose scale balances at ninety-seven, or even one hundred and seven, should be as anxious to increase her weight as her friend of the same height who weighs one hundred and eighty is to decrease hers. One is travelling as rapidly away from her own highest standard of good looks as the other, and both should take an equally vital interest in its restoration. The ways and means to attain this should appeal as much to one as to the other, and both should look upon the result as well worth the self-sacrifice and petty warfare against inclination entailed in its accomplishment. They must approach their objective point from opposite directions, but the point is the same, standing for increased beauty and health as well.

She who has lost weight rapidly from some acute disease can usually gain it back just as rapidly, and she who is suffering from some chronic illness and on that account cannot eat or digest the food which she has eaten, must necessarily take treatment for the fundamental cause of her illness from her physician before she considers the resulting thinness. It is those who are well and yet thin, who look upon themselves as the victims of an unhappy fate and refer with bitter resentment to their supposedly responsible parents or grandparents, who must be won away from their habit of looking upon their fate as inevitable. They must be taught that their condition is curable and that it must be struggled against instead of being accepted and made the best of. If their ancestors have persevered in using up too much force and taking in too little force-making fuel, they do not need to do the same. Inherited conditions are all too frequently the result of inherited bad habits, and this is one of them. One who thinks twice about the life of tireless energy forced upon the farmer's wife does not need an explanation for the characteristic "wiry thinness" inherited from generation to generation in the farm towns. A life of steady hard work upon one's feet is certainly not fat-producing, but it is generally possible to take life a little more easily and to select foods that will make it less exhausting. Moreover, the intensely active person, especially in town, is generally indulging herself in unnecessary nervous activity, throwing her valuable strength away recklessly, and living on her nerves, which were not intended for that purpose.

Even those who do not consider beauty of sufficient importance to warrant an expenditure of time and effort in its cultivation must realize that their thinness

---

HOW TO GET PLUMP   From "How to Get Plump," *Harper's Bazar* Aug. 1908: 786–89. Copyright © 1908. The Hearst Corporation. Courtesy of Harper's Bazaar.

indicates very plainly that they are using up in some way all the fuel that they are taking into their bodies and that, consequently, no reserve is being laid aside for an emergency. If the time comes, and it surely will, when they are forced to endure an unusual strain, either nervous or physical, they will find themselves sadly in need of this reserve force; for *fat is force* and *stored-up fat is stored-up force*. They may even be drawing daily upon the foods intended for the renewal of tissues after using up those intended for the production of energy. In that case the crisis will arrive more quickly. When it comes they call it nervous exhaustion or something similar, and do not appreciate the fact that extreme thinness should have warned them of the approaching danger, and that a normal amount of surplus fat might have carried them through the crisis. An abnormal amount of fat makes its possessor uncomfortable, and its pressure upon the vital organs is felt in time to give the danger signal, so that the fact that it is bad for the health as well as the looks is brought home to its possessor much more quickly than the dangers of a lack of necessary fat are brought home to those who are too thin. Those who are too thin are *dangerously* comfortable until the nervous tension snaps.

On the side of looks there is much to be said, a great deal, in fact, that is so apparent that there is no necessity of putting it into words. Thinness, up to a certain point, is now the fashion, but it is a thinness that does not include angles and hollows. The possibilities of ruffles and pads make those with troubles of this kind feel infinitely superior to their sisters who cannot resort to artificial helps so easily, but, after all, the consciousness of these concealed helps is humiliating at the best. Moreover, the face cannot be doctored in this way, and as age creeps on the wrinkles increase much more easily and rapidly when one is thin; the skin loses its flexibility when deprived of the needed fat and oil. Those who allow this to happen are soon numbered among those who look ten years older than they really are, a most unhappy point for any woman to reach.

Physicians, moreover, say that ninety-five per cent of these supposedly hopeless cases can be cured, and those who are struggling with the difficulties of reducing flesh laugh scornfully at the comparative difficulties which their friends must undergo to accomplish it. To the unprejudiced observer the path of the would-be fat person lies along much pleasanter ways than that of her unfortunate sister, although it is probably true that temperance in expenditure of energy is a difficult habit to form after a lifetime of reckless waste of that highly valuable commodity. Certainly little sympathy will be forthcoming for those living on the attractive diet recommended.

Both those who are too thin and those who are too fat have the same objective point in view—a perfect balance between the revenues of the body, consisting of food and air, and its expenditure, consisting of heat and energy. Those who are too fat must decrease the food and increase the energy, and those who are too thin must increase the food and decrease the energy; it is important that as much attention should be given to the decreasing quality as to the increasing.

Food is taken into the body for two purposes: first, to renew the tissues of the body, and second, to be used as fuel to form heat and energy for the activities of the body. Certain foods are primarily for one function and certain others are primarily for the other functions. Every normal person must have both, but the proportions may be varied according to special needs. The person who is too thin must, as a usual thing, have more of all kinds, but since her object is to increase fat she must take foods that do that, primarily, in large quantities. Fats, oils, sugars, and starches are the foods that contribute most largely to the production of fat, and it will usually be found that these are not the favorite articles of the person who is too thin. In most cases her reformation will consist more in kind than in quantity. These foods produce fat, and fat in its combination produces heat and energy, so that fat in reserve means force in reserve. The tissue-making foods will assist in making energy if there are not enough pure fats, but that is dangerous capital to borrow from. The conclusion is that fats must be taken into the system in excess of the supply needed for making energy, and that the thin person who wishes to maintain this excess must also economize on its expenditure.

The normal weights to be maintained are as follows:

Five feet 1 inch, 120 pounds; 5 feet 2 inches, 126 pounds; 5 feet 3 inches, 133 pounds; 5 feet 4 inches, 136 pounds; 5 feet 5 inches, 142 pounds; 5 feet 6 inches, 145 pounds; 5 feet 7 inches, 149 pounds; 5 feet 8 inches, 155 pounds; 5 feet 9 inches, 162 pounds.

In order to economize on the expenditure of energy it is necessary to learn how to take things easily. Even from the standpoint of accomplishment it is not always the person who rushes about his duties nervously, putting fully as much nervous activity into his work as calm, cool thought, who accomplishes the most in the end. Even when the energy is well directed it may be recklessly wasted in consideration of the time required for rest later on. One should learn how to move quietly and moderately about duties or pleasures without rush or hurry. When we are children we are constantly being restrained by our parents and told to stop and walk instead of running from place to place. Some people are never broken of the habit, and they are usually thin. If possible, one should sleep at least eight hours or nine hours out of the twenty-four, with as many naps between as possible. One should cultivate the habit of laziness, stopping at any and all times to relax the tensely drawn nerves and doing everything leisurely and without worry. Moderate exercise should be taken in the open air so that the appetite will be increased, the muscles hardened, the circulation increased, and the nerves relaxed, but this exercise should not be violent and should never reach the point of exhaustion. No nervous energy should be expended during it.

With our activities carefully economized we must study the subject of the foods required to form the needed fat. The thin person must indulge herself in exactly the foods forbidden the friend who is rigorously following a diet for flesh reduction. In her case we call it indulgence because it includes the foods usually looked upon as luxuries. If she does not enjoy the sweets recommended for her diet she will receive little sympathy from the majority of mankind.

The fat-producing foods are principally milk, cream, eggs, butter, olive oil; the sweets—sugar, honey, sweet desserts, jams, sweet fruits; the starchy vegetables—potatoes, pease, beans, corn, beets; wheat bread, rye, cereals of all kinds, rice, sago, etc. Of the fruits, peaches, grapes, bananas, prunes, and figs are especially recommended. The only foods cut out of a thin person's diet are the condiments—pickles, pepper, mustard, curry, salt, etc.; the acids, including acid fruits, the vinegar in salad dressing, etc.; and the stimulants, tea and coffee. It must not be forgotten that although the tissue-making foods, such as meats, fish, etc., are not fat-producing, they are required for their own especial functions. Some of the green vegetables and fruits are not fat-producing, but they are needed for other purposes. The fat-producing foods should be indulged in principally, but not to the exclusion of others.

The thin person should eat frequently and heartily. It is a good thing to take milk and eggs between meals as well as at meals. Milk made up partly of rich cream is, of course, much more fattening than thin milk. When heated very hot, but not to the boiling point, it is more effective than when taken cold. One can beat up an egg in it when taking it between meals or take the egg raw. A glass of hot milk is very good taken just before going to bed and also just after waking in the morning. The glass taken in the morning is especially good for a nervous stomach. It will frequently start the day right for those who find the morning a trying part of the day. Two quarts of milk and six eggs are not too much taken during the day. Cream should be poured generously over cereals and puddings and coffee, if the coffee is a necessity. Chocolate or milk is better for one who is thin than coffee, but if coffee is taken it should be made in the French way, largely of hot milk with some additional cream. Chocolate is both nourishing and fattening. Cream sauces will make vegetables and meats fattening when they would not be otherwise.

A quarter of a pound of butter should be consumed during the day. It is almost the best fattener there is. It should be spread thickly on bread. Olive oil is very pure and very effective. A salad dressing for a thin person should be made almost entirely of oil. A tablespoonful of pure oil taken after meals will help the good work along. Cod-liver oil is effective, but harder to take.

Cereals, rice, and potatoes are very good, indeed, and the cereals and rice are also very nourishing. Eggs are the very essence of food and the yolks contain a large percentage of fat. A box of pure candy or sweet chocolate for consumption at odd moments should be looked upon as a pleasant duty under these circumstances instead of a forbidden luxury. Sugar is pure energy.

When meat is eaten it should be both rare and fat. Salmon is the most fattening of all the fish.

Beer, ale, stout, and port are warranted to produce fat for those who do not want it, and may be relied upon to assist those who are thin if taken regularly.

A characteristic day's menu appropriate for one who is trying to gain weight is as follows:

At rising.—One glass hot milk.

Breakfast, at eight o'clock.—Sweet fruit, cereal with cream and sugar; two soft-boiled eggs; bread with thick layer of butter, jam, or honey; cup of chocolate or glass of milk.

At eleven.—Glass of milk; bread and butter.

Luncheon, at one o'clock.—Creamed fish; baked potatoes with butter; pease; pudding made of sago and eggs; glass of milk.

At four o'clock.—Glass of milk with egg beaten up in it; cake.

Dinner, at seven o'clock.—Cream soup; fat rare beefsteak; mashed potatoes; beans; creamed asparagus; beet salad, French dressing; rice pudding.

Bedtime.—Glass of hot milk; raw egg.

She who wishes to get fat should drink water or milk or both with her meals. Drinking water is said to make one eat more.

THE DIARY OF ANAÏS NIN (MARCH 1937)
Anaïs Nin

There is perhaps no more evocative description of a young woman's dawning awareness of herself as an object than this entry in Anaïs Nin's diary. Here we encounter first the young girl, oblivious to her own image, who, when she looks into a mirror, sees only the historical characters her imagination has conjured up or the blue bow her godmother has so meticulously tied for her. This Anaïs, aged six or ten, has not yet learned to wonder how she appears to others, especially to males. But, within a few years, she will.

Nin (1903–1977) achieved considerable acclaim as a writer. Most of her initial celebrity in the United States derived from her erotica, particularly *Delta of Venus* (1969). She also wrote a number of other novels, such as *A Spy in the House of Love* (1954), short stories, essays, and poetry. She also published her *Diary*. The film *Henry and June* is based upon her diary and explores her love affairs with American novelist Henry Miller and his wife.

I cannot remember what I saw in the mirror as a child. Perhaps a child never looks at a mirror. Perhaps a child, like a cat, is so much inside of himself that he does not see himself in the mirror. He sees a child. The child does not remember what he looks like. Later I remembered what I looked like. But when I look at photographs of myself one, two, three, four, five years old, I do not recognize myself. The child is *one*. At one with himself. Never outside of himself. I can remember what I did but not the reflection of what I did. No reflections. Six years old. Seven years old. Eight years old. Nine. Ten. Eleven. No images. No Reflections. Feelings. I can feel what I felt about my father's white mice, the horror they inspired in me, the revolting odor, the taste of a burnt omelette my father made for us while my mother was sick and expecting Joaquin in Berlin. The feel of the beach in Barcelona, the feel of the balcony there, the fear of death and the writing of a testament, the feelings in church, in the street. Sounds in the Spanish courtyard, singing, a memory of a gaiety which was to haunt me all my life, totally absent from America. The face of the maid Ramona, the music in the streets, children dancing on the sidewalks. Voices. The appearance of others, the long black mustache of Granados, the embrace of the nuns, drowning me in veils as they leaned over. No picture in the mind's eye of what I wore. The long black stockings of Spanish children I saw in a photograph. I do remember my passion for penny "surprise" packages, the passion for surprise. Yet at the age of six the perfection of the blue bow on my hair, shaped like a butterfly, preoccupied me, since I insisted that my godmother tie it because she tied it better than anyone else. I must have seen this bow in the mirror then. I do not remember whether I saw this bow, the little girl in the very short white-lace-edged dress, or again a photograph taken in Havana where all my cousins and I stood in a row according to our heights, all wearing enormous ribbons and short white dresses. In the mirror there never was a child. The first mirror had a frame of white wood. In it there is no Anaïs Nin, but Marie Antoinette with a white lace cap, a long black dress, standing on a pile of chairs, the chariot, riding to her beheading. No Anaïs Nin. An actress playing all the parts of characters in French history. I am Charlotte Corday plunging a knife into the tyrant Marat. I am, of course, Joan of Arc. At fourteen, the portrayal of a Joan burning at the stake was my brother's favorite horror story.

The first mirror in which the self appears is very large, it is inlaid inside of a brown wood wall in the room of a brownstone house. Next to it the window pours down so strong a light that the rest of the room is not reflected in the mirror. The image of the girl who approaches it is brought into luminous relief. Against a foggy darkness, the girl of fifteen stands with frightened eyes. She is looking at her dress, a dress of shiny worn blue serge, which was fixed up for her out of an old one belonging to a cousin. It does not fit her. It is meager. It looks poor. The girl is looking at the worn shiny dark-blue serge dress with shame. It is the day she has been told in school that she is gifted for writing. They had come purposely into the class to tell her. In spite of being a foreigner, in spite of having to use the dictionary, she had written the best essay in the class. She who was always quiet and who did not wish to be noticed, was told to come up the aisle and speak to the English teacher before everyone, to hear the compliment. And the joy, the dazzling joy which had first struck her was instantly killed by the awareness of the dress. I did not want to get up, to be noticed. I was ashamed of this meager dress with a shine on it, its worn air, its orphan air, its hand-me-down air.

There is another mirror framed in brown wood. The girl is looking at the new dress which transfigures her. What an extraordinary change. She leans over very close to look at the humid eyes, the humid mouth, the moisture and luminousness brought about by the change of dress. She walks up very slowly to the mirror, very slowly, as if she did not want to frighten reflections away. Several times, at fifteen, she walks very slowly towards the mirror. Every girl of fifteen has put the same question to a mirror: "Am I beautiful?" The face is masklike. It does not smile. It does not want to charm the mirror, or deceive the mirror, or flirt with it and gain a false answer. The girl is in a trance. She does not want to frighten the reflection away herself. Someone has said she is very pale. She approaches the mirror and stands very still like a statue. Immobile. Waxy. She never makes a gesture. Surprised. Somnambulistic? She only moves to become someone else, impersonating Sarah Bernhardt, Mélisande, *La Dame aux Camélias,* Madame Bovary, Thaïs. She is never Anaïs Nin who goes to school, and grows vegetables and flowers in her backyard. She is immobile, haunting, like a figure moving in a dream. She is decomposed before the mirror into a hundred personages, recomposed into paleness and immobility. Silence. She is watching for an expression which will betray the spirit. You can never catch the face alive, laughing, or loving. At sixteen she is looking at the mirror with her hair up for the first time. There is always the question. The mirror is not going to answer it. She will have to look for the answer in the eyes and faces of the boys who dance with her, men later, and above all the painters.

A FEW WORDS ABOUT BREASTS

Nora Ephron

" I suppose that for most girls, breasts, brassieres, that entire thing, has more trauma, more to do with the coming of adolescence, with becoming a woman, than anything else." So writes Nora Ephron, the well-known essayist, novelist, screenwriter, and film director. The reason, she continued, is "you could see breasts." The "you" in that sentence includes everyone, most especially boys. *They* were particularly likely to define sexual allure in terms of cup sizes, Ephron noted. And they were particularly likely to do so in the 1950s, she argued, for that was the decade of Jane Russell, cashmere sweaters, *Playboy*, and its first playmate, Marilyn Monroe.

There is some irony in the fact that this essay first appeared in *Esquire*, a "magazine for men." In the years before *Playboy*, it was the most successful of the many magazines that featured "cheesecake" photos of scantily clad models. So *Esquire* did much to diffuse the stereotype of the buxom starlet as the epitome of female beauty that caused Ephron such anguish as a teenager.

 I have to begin with a few words about androgyny. In grammar school, in the fifth and sixth grades, we were all tyrannized by a rigid set of rules that supposedly determined whether we were boys or girls. The episode in *Huckleberry Finn* where Huck is disguised as a girl and gives himself away by the way he threads a needle and catches a ball—that kind of thing. We learned that the way you sat, crossed your legs, held a cigarette, and looked at your nails—the way you did these things instinctively was absolute proof of your sex. Now obviously most children did not take this literally, but I did. I thought that just one slip, just one incorrect cross of my legs or flick of an imaginary cigarette ash would turn me from whatever I was into the other thing; that would be all it took, really. Even though I was outwardly a girl and had many of the trappings generally associated with girldom—a girl's name, for example, and dresses, my own telephone, an autograph book—I spent the early years of my adolescence absolutely certain that I might at any point gum it up. I did not feel at all like a girl. I was boyish. I was athletic, ambitious, outspoken, competitive, noisy, rambunctious. I had scabs on my knees and my socks slid into my loafers and I could throw a football. I wanted desperately not to be that way, not to be a mixture of both things, but instead just one, a girl, a definite indisputable girl. As soft and as pink as a nursery. And nothing would do that for me, I felt, but breasts.

I was about six months younger than everyone else in my class, and so for about six months after it began, for six months after my friends had begun to develop (that was the word we used, develop), I was not particularly worried. I would sit in the bathtub and look down at my breasts and know that any day now, they would start growing like everyone else's. They didn't. "I want to buy a bra," I said to my mother one night. "What for?" she said. My mother was really hateful about bras, and by the time my third sister had gotten to the point where she was ready to want one, my mother had worked the whole business into a comedy routine. "Why not use a Band-Aid instead?" she would say. It was a source of great pride to my mother that she had never even had to wear a brassiere until she had her fourth child, and then only because her gynecologist made her. It was incomprehensible to me that anyone could ever be proud of something like that. It was the 1950s, for God's sake. Jane Russell. Cashmere sweaters. Couldn't my mother see that? *"I am too old to wear an undershirt."* Screaming. Weeping. Shouting. "Then don't wear an undershirt," said my mother. "But I want to buy a bra." "What for?"

A Few Words About Breasts   From Nora Ephron, *Crazy Salad: Some Things About Women* (New York: Knopf, 1972) 3–12. Copyright © 1972 by Nora Ephron. Reprinted by permission of International Creative Management, Inc.

I suppose that for most girls, breasts, brassieres, that entire thing, has more trauma, more to do with the coming of adolescence, with becoming a woman, than anything else. Certainly more than getting your period, although that, too, was traumatic, symbolic. But you could see breasts; they were there; they were visible. Whereas a girl could claim to have her period for months before she actually got it and nobody would ever know the difference. Which is exactly what I did. All you had to do was make a great fuss over having enough nickels for the Kotex machine and walk around clutching your stomach and moaning for three to five days a month about The Curse and you could convince anybody. There is a school of thought somewhere in the women's lib/women's mag/gynecology establishment that claims that menstrual cramps are purely psychological, and I lean toward it. Not that I didn't have them finally. Agonizing cramps, heating-pad cramps, go-down-to-the-school-nurse-and-lie-on-the-cot cramps. But, unlike any pain I had ever suffered, I adored the pain of cramps, welcomed it, wallowed in it, bragged about it. "I can't go. I have cramps." "I can't do that. I have cramps." And most of all, gigglingly, blushingly: "I can't swim. I have cramps." Nobody ever used the hard-core word. Menstruation. God, what an awful word. Never that. "I have cramps."

The morning I first got my period, I went into my mother's bedroom to tell her. And my mother, my utterly-hateful-about-bras mother, burst into tears. It was really a lovely moment, and I remember it so clearly not just because it was one of the two times I ever saw my mother cry on my account (the other was when I was caught being a six-year-old kleptomaniac), but also because the incident did not mean to me what it meant to her. Her little girl, her firstborn, had finally become a woman. That was what she was crying about. My reaction to the event, however, was that I might well be a woman in some scientific, textbook sense (and could at least stop faking every month and stop wasting all those nickels). But in another sense—in a visible sense—I was as androgynous and as liable to tip over into boyhood as ever.

I started with a 28AA bra. I don't think they made them any smaller in those days, although I gather that now you can buy bras for five-year-olds that don't have any cups whatsoever in them; trainer bras they are called. My first brassiere came from Robinson's Department Store in Beverly Hills. I went there alone, shaking, positive they would look me over and smile and tell me to come back next year. An actual fitter took me into the dressing room and stood over me while I took off my blouse and tried the first one on. The little puffs stood out on my chest. "Lean over," said the fitter. (To this day, I am not sure what fitters in bra departments do except to tell you to lean over.) I leaned over, with the fleeting hope that my breasts would miraculously fall out of my body and into the puffs. Nothing.

"Don't worry about it," said my friend Libby some months later, when things had not improved. "You'll get them after you're married."

"What are you talking about?" I said.

"When you get married," Libby explained, "your husband will touch your breasts and rub them and kiss them and they'll grow."

That was the killer. Necking I could deal with. Intercourse I could deal with. But it had never crossed my mind that a man was going to touch my breasts, that breasts had something to do with all that, petting, my God, they never mentioned petting in my little sex manual about the fertilization of the ovum. I became dizzy. For I knew instantly—as naïve as I had been only a moment before—that only part of what she was saying was true: the touching, rubbing, kissing part, not the growing part. And I knew that no one would ever want to marry me. I had no breasts. I would never have breasts.

My best friend in school was Diana Raskob. She lived a block from me in a house full of wonders. English muffins, for instance. The Raskobs were the first people in Beverly Hills to have English muffins for breakfast. They also had an apricot tree in the back, and a badminton court, and a subscription to *Seventeen* magazine, and hundreds of games, like Sorry and Parcheesi and Treasure Hunt and Anagrams. Diana and I spent three or four afternoons a week in their den reading and playing and eating. Diana's mother's kitchen was full of the most colossal assortment of junk food I have ever been exposed to. My house was full of apples and peaches and milk and homemade chocolate-chip cookies—which were nice, and good for you, but-not-right-before-dinner-or-you'll-spoil-your-appetite. Diana's house had nothing in it that was good for you, and what's more, you could stuff it in right up until dinner and nobody cared. Bar-B-Q potato chips (they were the first in them, too), giant bottles of ginger ale, fresh popcorn with melted butter, hot fudge sauce on Baskin-Robbins jamocha ice cream, powdered-sugar doughnuts from Van de Kamp's. Diana and I had been best friends since we were seven; we were about equally popular in school (which is to say, not particularly), we had about the same success with boys (extremely intermittent), and we looked much the same. Dark. Tall. Gangly.

It is September, just before school begins. I am eleven years old, about to enter the seventh grade, and Diana and I have not seen each other all summer. I have been to camp and she has been somewhere like Banff with her parents. We are meeting, as we often do, on the street midway between our two houses, and we will walk back to Diana's and eat junk and talk about what has happened to each of us that summer. I am walking down Walden Drive in my jeans and my father's shirt hanging out and my old red loafers with the socks falling into them and coming toward me is . . . I take a deep breath . . . a young woman. Diana. Her hair is curled and she has a waist and hips and a bust and she is wearing a straight skirt, an article of clothing I have been repeatedly told I will be unable to wear until I have the hips to hold it up. My jaw drops, and suddenly I am crying hysterically, can't catch my breath sobbing. My best friend has betrayed me. She has gone ahead without me and done it. She has shaped up.

Here are some things I did to help:

Bought a Mark Eden Bust Developer.

Slept on my back for four years.

Splashed cold water on them every night because some French actress said in *Life* magazine that that was what *she* did for her perfect bustline.

Ultimately, I resigned myself to a bad toss and began to wear padded bras. I think about them now, think about all those years in high school I went around in them, my three padded bras, every single one of them with different-sized breasts. Each time I changed bras I changed sizes: one week nice perky but not too obtrusive breasts, the next medium-sized slightly pointy ones, the next week knockers, true knockers; all the time, whatever size I was, carrying around this rubberized appendage on my chest that occasionally crashed into a wall and was poked inward and had to be poked outward—I think about all that and wonder how anyone kept a straight face through it. My parents, who normally had no restraints about needling me—why did they say nothing as they watched my chest go up and down? My friends, who would periodically inspect my breasts for signs of growth and reassure me—why didn't they at least counsel consistency?

And the bathing suits. I die when I think about the bathing suits. That was the era when you could lay an uninhabited bathing suit on the beach and someone would make a pass at it. I would put one on, an absurd swimsuit with its enormous bust built into it, the bones from the suit stabbing me in the rib cage and leaving little red welts on my body, and there I would be, my chest plunging straight downward absolutely vertically from my collarbone to the top of my suit and then suddenly, wham, out came all that padding and material and wiring absolutely horizontally.

Buster Klepper was the first boy who ever touched them. He was my boyfriend my senior year of high school. There is a picture of him in my high-school yearbook that makes him look quite attractive in a Jewish, hornrimmed-glasses sort of way, but the picture does not show the pimples, which were air-brushed out, or the dumbness. Well, that isn't really fair. He wasn't dumb. He just wasn't terribly bright. His mother refused to accept it, refused to accept the relentlessly average report cards, refused to deal with her son's inevitable destiny in some junior college or other. "He was tested," she would say to me, apropos of nothing, "and it came out a hundred and forty-five. That's near-genius." Had the word "underachiever" been coined, she probably would have lobbed that one at me, too. Anyway, Buster was really very sweet—which is, I know, damning with faint praise, but there it is. I was the editor of the front page of the high-school newspaper and he was editor of the back page; we had to work together, side by side, in the print shop, and that was how it started. On our first date, we went to see *April Love*, starring Pat Boone. Then we started going together. Buster had a green coupe, a 1950 Ford with an engine he had hand-chromed until it shone, dazzled, reflected the image of anyone who looked into it, anyone usually being Buster polishing it or the gas-station attendants he constantly asked to check the oil in order for them to be overwhelmed by the sparkle on the valves. The car also had a boot stretched over the back seat for reasons I never understood; hanging from the rearview mirror, as was the custom, was a pair of angora dice. A previous girl friend named Solange, who was famous throughout Beverly Hills High School for having no pigment in her right eyebrow, had knitted them for him. Buster and I would ride around town, the two of us seated to the left of the steering wheel. I would shift gears. It was nice.

There was necking. Terrific necking. First in the car, overlooking Los Angeles from what is now the Trousdale Estates. Then on the bed of his parents' cabana at Ocean House. Incredibly wonderful, frustrating necking, I loved it, really, but no further than necking, please don't, please, because there I was absolutely terrified of the general implications of going-a-step-further with a near-dummy and also terrified of his finding out there was next to nothing there (which he knew, of course; he wasn't that dumb).

I broke up with him at one point. I think we were apart for about two weeks. At the end of that time, I drove down to see a friend at a boarding school in Palos Verdes Estates and a disc jockey played "April Love" on the radio four times during the trip. I took it as a sign. I drove straight back to Griffith Park to a golf tournament Buster was playing in (he was the sixth-seeded teen-age golf player in Southern

California) and presented myself back to him on the green of the 18th hole. It was all very dramatic. That night we went to a drive-in and I let him get his hand under my protuberances and onto my breasts. He really didn't seem to mind at all.

"Do you want to marry my son?" the woman asked me.

"Yes," I said.

I was nineteen years old, a virgin, going with this woman's son, this big strange woman who was married to a Lutheran minister in New Hampshire and pretended she was gentile and had this son, by her first husband, this total fool of a son who ran the hero-sandwich concession at Harvard Business School and whom for one moment one December in New Hampshire I said—as much out of politeness as anything else—that I wanted to marry.

"Fine," she said. "Now, here's what you do. Always make sure you're on top of him so you won't seem so small. My bust is very large, you see, so I always lie on my back to make it look smaller, but you'll have to be on top most of the time."

I nodded. "Thank you," I said.

"I have a book for you to read," she went on. "Take it with you when you leave. Keep it." She went to the bookshelf, found it, and gave it to me. It was a book on frigidity.

"Thank you," I said.

That is a true story. Everything in this article is a true story, but I feel I have to point out that that story in particular is true. It happened on December 30, 1960. I think about it often. When it first happened, I naturally assumed that the woman's son, my boyfriend, was responsible. I invented a scenario where he had had a little heart-to-heart with his mother and had confessed that his only objection to me was that my breasts were small; his mother then took it upon herself to help out. Now I think I was wrong about the incident. The mother was acting on her own, I think: that was her way of being cruel and competitive under the guise of being helpful and maternal. You have small breasts, she was saying; therefore you will never make him as happy as I have. Or you have small breasts; therefore you will doubtless have sexual problems. Or you have small breasts; therefore you are less woman than I am. She was, as it happens, only the first of what seems to me to be a never-ending string of women who have made competitive remarks to me about breast size. "I would love to wear a dress like that," my friend Emily says to me, "but my bust is too big." Like that. Why do women say these things to me? Do I attract these remarks the way other women attract married men or alcoholics or homosexuals? This summer, for example. I am at a party in East Hampton and I am introduced to a woman from Washington. She is a minor celebrity, very pretty and Southern and blond and outspoken, and I am flattered because she has read something I have written. We are talking animatedly, we have been talking no more than five minutes, when a man comes up to join us. "Look at the two of us," the woman says to the man, indicating me and her. "The two of us together couldn't fill an A cup." Why does she say that? It isn't even true, dammit, so why? Is she even more addled than I am on this subject? Does she honestly believe there is something wrong with her size breasts, which, it seems to me, now that I look hard at them, are just right? Do I unconsciously bring out competitiveness in women? In what form? What did I do to deserve it?

As for men.

There were men who minded and let me know that they minded. There were men who did not mind. In any case, *I* always minded.

And even now, now that I have been countlessly reassured that my figure is a good one, now that I am grown-up enough to understand that most of my feelings have very little to do with the reality of my shape, I am nonetheless obsessed by breasts. I cannot help it. I grew up in the terrible fifties—with rigid stereotypical sex roles, the insistence that men be men and dress like men and women be women and dress like women, the intolerance of androgyny—and I cannot shake it, cannot shake my feelings of inadequacy. Well, that time is gone, right? All those exaggerated examples of breast worship are gone, right? Those women were freaks, right? I know all that. And yet here I am, stuck with the psychological remains of it all, stuck with my own peculiar version of breast worship. You probably think I am crazy to go on like this: here I have set out to write a confession that is meant to hit you with the shock of recognition, and instead you are sitting there thinking I am thoroughly warped. Well, what can I tell you? If I had had them, I would have been a completely different person. I honestly believe that.

After I went into therapy, a process that made it possible for me to tell total strangers at cocktail parties that breasts were the hang-up of my life, I was often told that I was insane to have been bothered by my condition. I was also frequently told, by close friends, that I was extremely boring on the subject. And my girl friends, the ones with nice big breasts, would go on endlessly about how their lives had been far more miserable than mine. Their bra straps were snapped in class. They couldn't sleep on their stomachs. They were stared at whenever the word "mountain" cropped up in geography. And *Evangeline*, good God what they went through every time someone had to stand up and recite the Prologue to Longfellow's *Evangeline*: " . . . stand like druids of eld . . . / With beards that rest on their bosoms." It was much worse for them, they tell me. They had a terrible time of it, they assure me. I don't know how lucky I was, they say.

I have thought about their remarks, tried to put myself in their place, considered their point of view. I think they are full of shit.

BARBIE: TWO VIEWS

Uncounted millions of young women have grown up with Barbie since the doll was first introduced in 1959. Ruth Handler, cofounder of Mattel, the toy company that continues to make and market the dolls, designed the first Barbie. She based her creation on a cartoon character named Lilli, a sexy blond who safeguarded the Deutschmark in the German newspaper *Bild Zeitung* in the 1950s. Lilli dolls, marketed for businessmen, had become popular in Europe, and Handler decided to create an American version for little girls. She kept the blond hair and curvaceous body of the original and added the element of dress up. Girls could change Barbie's clothes and hair style and, in the process, imagine themselves as college students, business executives, doctors, astronauts, and in 1992, presidential candidates. Most often, however, they imagined themselves getting ready to go out on a date with Ken, Barbie's companion doll.

Barbie's hold on the imagination is the subject of the following two readings. One, by noted poet Marge Piercy, explores the fact that many young women grow up comparing themselves to Barbie. Yet, according to a report in the *Tufts University Diet & Nutrition Letter*

(January 1994), researchers calculate that, if Barbie were a real woman, she would be so underweight she would be unable to menstruate. Barbie's thin thighs, narrow hips, tiny buttocks, and concave stomach would be signs of anorexia nervosa in a real woman; and, she would have required implants to get those full breasts.

African Americans have long bemoaned another way in which Barbie can wreak psychological havoc. Young children of color can come to associate beauty with Barbie's northern European features and regard themselves as ugly. Mattel finally responded with an African-American version of Barbie, "Shani," the subject of Lisa Jones' essay. Mattel claimed, as Jones reported, that Shani would have thicker thighs and higher buttocks than Barbie, in keeping with the company's professed eagerness to provide little girls of color with dolls with whom they could identify. In fact, according to University of Massachusetts–Amherst anthropologists Jacqueline Urla and Alan Swedlund, Shani's buttocks are no higher than Barbie's. Nor are her thighs notably bigger. After all, they point out, Mattel markets the same wardrobe for both dolls.

BARBIE DOLL
Marge Piercy

This girlchild was born as usual
and presented dolls that did pee-pee
and miniature GE stoves and irons
and wee lipsticks the color of cherry candy.
Then in the magic of puberty, a classmate said:
You have a great big nose and fat legs.

She was healthy, tested intelligent,
possessed strong arms and back,
abundant sexual drive and manual dexterity.
She went to and fro apologizing.
Everyone saw a fat nose on thick legs.

She was advised to play coy,
exhorted to come on hearty,
exercise, diet, smile and wheedle.
Her good nature wore out
like a fan belt.
So she cut off her nose and her legs
and offered them up.

In the casket displayed on satin she lay
with the undertaker's cosmetics painted on,
a turned-up putty nose,
dressed in a pink and white nightie.
Doesn't she look pretty? everyone said.
Consummation at last.
To every woman a happy ending.

BARBIE DOLL   From Marge Piercy, "Barbie Doll," *Circles on the Water* (New York: Knopf, 1973) 92. Copyright © 1982 by Marge Piercy. Reprinted by permission of Alfred A. Knopf, Inc.

A DOLL IS BORN

Lisa Jones

This is my doll story (because every black journalist who writes about race gets around to it sometime). Back when I started playing with Barbies, there were no Christies (Barbie's black friend, born in 1968) or black Barbies (born in 1980, brown plastic poured into blond Barbie's mold). I had two blonds, which I bought with Christmas money from girls at school.

I cut off their hair and dressed them in African-print fabric. They lived together (polygamy, I guess) with a black G.I. Joe bartered from the Shepp boys, my downstairs neighbors. After an "incident" at school (where all of the girls looked like Barbie and none of them looked like me), I galloped down our stairs with one Barbie, her blond head hitting each spoke of the banister, thud, thud, thud. And galloped up the stairs, thud, thud, thud, until her head popped off, lost to the graveyard behind the stairwell. Then I tore off each limb, and sat on the stairs for a long time twirling the torso like a baton.

Do little black girls still grow up slaughtering or idolizing pink-fleshed, blue-eyed doll babies? Even after two cultural nationalist movements, four black Miss Americas, and integrated shelves at Kiddie City and Toys 'Я' Us? In 1987, Dr. Darlene Powell-Hopson, a clinical psychologist, replicated a landmark study done by a team of black therapists in the '40s (later used to argue *Brown v. Board of Education*). When asked which doll is the good doll, which doll is the right color, a large percentage of children, black and white, still chose the white doll. Powell-Hopson's twist was intervention. Before kids were asked to choose, they were told stories about the black dolls, stories that presented them as great beauties, as heroines. The percentages reversed.

Powell-Hopson got a call last summer. Some folks at Mattel toys had read her book, *Different and Wonderful: Raising Black Children in a Race Conscious Society.* Would she be interested in consulting them on a new product, a line of African-American fashion dolls to be introduced in fall of 1991? A number of black women were involved: There was Mattel product manager Deborah Mitchell and principal designer for Mattel's fashion doll group, Kitty Black-Perkins (who outfitted the first black Barbie). And Alberta Rhodes and her partners at Morgan Orchid Rhodes, who specialize in targeted PR. Powell-Hopson signed on.

These women midwifed "Shani," whose name according to Mattel means "marvelous" in Swahili (my Oxford University Press Swahili-English dictionary says "startling, a wonder, a novelty"). Touted as the first "realistically sculpted" black fashion doll to be manufactured by the mainstream, she made her debut at the American International Toy fair last month. Mattel threw a party for her, complete with a tribute to black designers and En Vogue singing the Negro National Anthem.

Mattel calls her "tomorrow's African American woman" (one-upping *Essence's* Today's Black Woman). She has a new body. ("Rounder, more athletic," says Mitchell, giggling into the phone, "her hips are broader. But she still can fit Barbie's clothes.") She has a new face (fuller lips and broader nose), new clothes ("spice tones, ethnic fabrics," says Black-Perkins, "not fantasy colors like pink or lavender"). And her new skin alludes to the range among African Americans. (Shani, the lead doll, is berry-brown. She has two friends: Nichelle, deep mahogany, and Asha, honey.)

I carry around a picture of Shani and her playmates to show the girlfriends, who are single, not mothers. And who don't know much about the hard time black parents have tracking down culturally affirming toys, as do Powell-Hopson and Black-Perkins, who are mothers.

Not so fast, they snap. "Why can't they make one with dreads?" says Susan, who wears extensions and works for the U.S. Attorney's office. "They must be from D.C." says honorary girlfriend Alejandro, eyeing their loud costumes and sculpted hair. "That light one, Asha, is gonna sell out and leave poor Shani and Nichelle on the shelf," says the ever color-struck Tamu. Deandra is the most upset: "It's the hair."

All three dolls have hair past shoulder length. Powell-Hopson had hopes that one of the dolls would have shorter hair, "an Afro, an asymmetrical cut, something." To be honest, says Mitchell, Mattel heard similar concerns in the focus groups: "To be truly realistic, one should have shorter hair. But little girls of all races love hair play. We added more texture. But we can't change the fact that long, combable hair is still a key seller." (When I relay this to Deandra, she grumbles, "More chicken-before-the-egg theories.") Fantasy hair or not, Powell-Hopson holds that the Shani doll shows "social consciousness on Mattel's part."

Social consciousness, marketing savvy, or, in '90s style, the right combination of both? Mattel knows that African Americans will make up nearly 20 per cent of the population by the next century. Sales of black Barbie doubled last year, following an ad campaign in black print media. Mattel decided to advertise after research showed most black consumers didn't know the doll existed. Black Barbie's been around for 10 years (21 years after what Mattel calls the "traditional, blond, blue-eyed Barbie"), but Mattel had never given her a major marketing push. (The doll had only appeared, as part of a group of other Barbies, in a few adult-directed TV spots: kids had never seen her on the tube on Saturday mornings.)

Fashion dolls aren't born everyday. At least not at Mattel. There's Barbie, her friends, boyfriend Ken, and a few celebrity dolls now and then. Shani is Mattel's first "non-Barbie fashion doll." The women behind Shani, like Mitchell and Powell-Hopson, want her to be more than just a Barbie in blackface. Shani's "character sketch" (the doll's publicity fact sheet) matches her, dare we say, ethnically correct physique. ("She's not just a pretty face . . . she's very conscious of her culture.") In '92, Shani gets a boyfriend. What about a play set? How about "Community Center," where Shani can teach black history to inner-city youth? Or "Corporate America," where Nichelle can argue with her boss about whether or not her braided hair is really appropriate in the board room?

MADONNA: TWO VIEWS

By the early 1990s, pop singer, actress, and sometime author Madonna had reached such staggering celebrity that scholarly and popular assessments of the meaning of her work for the future of feminism, for the sexual values of the young, for increased or diminished tolerance for so-called deviant sexual practices, indeed for virtually any issue one might imagine, had become a growth industry. College courses, like "Studies in Gender & Performance: Madonna Undressed" offered at the University of Colorado, analyzed her music and videos. So did scholarly anthologies, like *The Madonna Connection* (1992), which asserted Madonna's "usefulness as a paradigm case to advance . . . developments in cultural theory." Meanwhile, conservative critics like Daniel Harris, writing in *The Nation*, saw the academic interest in Madonna's work as evidence of the intellectual poverty of so-called postmodern criticism. Traditional moralists saw Madonna as unscrupulously merchandising herself.

Feminists also sought to come to terms with what Madonna's immense popularity might bode for their movement. Several, especially before the publication of the photographs of Madonna in her book *Sex* (1993), hailed her as a "true feminist." Others were deeply troubled by what they saw as her willingness to cater to stereotypical male fantasies about women. And still others claimed that Madonna was actually engaged in subverting those same stereotypes.

Many of these issues emerge in the following op-ed pieces from December 1990. Camille Paglia, author of the first, achieved notoriety with her *Sexual Personae*, an iconoclastic analysis of images of sexuality and gender in Western culture. Paglia is an outspoken critic of feminist thinking, although she insists that she is herself a feminist. Suzanne Gordon, a journalist and essayist, is a feminist theorist of long-standing.

MADONNA
Camille Paglia

Madonna, don't preach.

Defending her controversial new video, "Justify My Love," on *Nightline* last week, Madonna stumbled, rambled, and ended up seeming far less intelligent than she really is.

Madonna, 'fess up.

The video is pornographic. It's decadent. And it's fabulous. MTV was right to ban it, a corporate resolve long overdue. Parents cannot possibly control television, with its titanic omnipresence.

Prodded by correspondent Forrest Sawyer for evidence of her responsibility as an artist, Madonna hotly proclaimed her love of children, her social activism, and her condom endorsements. Wrong answer. As Baudelaire and Oscar Wilde knew, neither art nor the artist has a moral responsibility to liberal social causes.

"Justify My Love" is truly avant-garde, at a time when that word has lost its meaning in the flabby art world. It represents a sophisticated European sexuality of a kind we have not seen since the great foreign films of the 1950s and 1960s. But it does not belong on a mainstream music channel watched around the clock by children.

MADONNA   From Camille Paglia, "Madonna," *The New York Times* 14 Dec. 1990, rpt. in *Sex, Art, and American Culture* (New York: Vintage, 1993) 3–5. Copyright © 1995 by The New York Times Company. Reprinted by permission.

On *Nightline*, Madonna bizarrely called the video a "celebration of sex." She imagined happy educational scenes where curious children would ask their parents about the video. Oh, sure! Picture it: "Mommy, please tell me about the tired, tied-up man in the leather harness and the mean, bare-chested lady in the Nazi cap." Okay, dear, right after the milk and cookies.

Sawyer asked for Madonna's reaction to feminist charges that, in the neck manacle and floor-crawling of an earlier video, "Express Yourself," she condoned the "degradation" and "humiliation" of women. Madonna waffled: "But I chained myself! I'm in charge." Well, no. Madonna the producer may have chosen the chain, but Madonna the sexual persona in the video is alternately a cross-dressing dominatrix and a slave of male desire.

But who cares what the feminists say anyhow? They have been outrageously negative about Madonna from the start. In 1985, *Ms.* magazine pointedly feted quirky, cuddly singer Cyndi Lauper as its woman of the year. Great judgment: gimmicky Lauper went nowhere, while Madonna grew, flourished, metamorphosed, and became an international star of staggering dimensions. She is also a shrewd business tycoon, a modern new woman of all-around talent.

Madonna is the true feminist. She exposes the puritanism and suffocating ideology of American feminism, which is stuck in an adolescent whining mode. Madonna has taught young women to be fully female and sexual while still exercising control over their lives. She shows girls how to be attractive, sensual, energetic, ambitious, aggressive, and funny—all at the same time.

American feminism has a man problem. The beaming Betty Crockers, hangdog dowdies, and parochial prudes who call themselves feminists want men to be like women. They fear and despise the masculine. The academic feminists think their nerdy bookworm husbands are the ideal model of human manhood.

But Madonna loves real men. She sees the beauty of masculinity, in all its rough vigor and sweaty athletic perfection. She also admires the men who are actually like women: transsexuals and flamboyant drag queens, the heroes of the 1969 Stonewall rebellion, which started the gay liberation movement.

"Justify My Love" is an eerie, sultry tableau of jaded androgynous creatures, trapped in a decadent sexual underground. Its hypnotic images are drawn from such sadomasochistic films as Liliana Cavani's *The Night Porter* and Luchino Visconti's *The Damned*. It's the perverse and knowing world of the photographers Helmut Newton and Robert Mapplethorpe.

Contemporary American feminism, which began by rejecting Freud because of his alleged sexism, has shut itself off from his ideas of ambiguity, contradiction, conflict, ambivalence. Its simplistic psychology is illustrated by the new cliché of the date-rape furor: "'No' always means 'no.'" Will we ever graduate from the Girl Scouts? "No" has always been, and always will be, part of the dangerous, alluring courtship ritual of sex and seduction, observable even in the animal kingdom.

Madonna has a far profounder vision of sex than do the feminists. She sees both the animality and the artifice. Changing her costume style and hair color virtually every month, Madonna embodies the eternal values of beauty and pleasure. Feminism says, "No more masks." Madonna says we are nothing but masks.

Through her enormous impact on young women around the world, Madonna is the future of feminism.

MADONNA THE FEMINIST

Suzanne Gordon

Is she or is she not? That is the question. At least it was one that preoccupied a number of feminists when they heard about the banning of Madonna's latest video. Many came up with a novel interpretation of Madonna and her work: She is a feminist heroine, and her video a vivid preview of the feminism of the future.

But the interesting questions involved have less to do with the rock star than with prevailing definitions of feminism and women's progress.

What, after all, is feminism? What makes a truly liberated woman? Is feminism—as a social movement—no more than a collection of individual women who want to be equal to men in *a man's* world? Is the real liberated woman one who does little more than say yes to careerism, safe sex and "making it" in America's overhyped, sensationalistic, commercial culture?

Or is feminism about attaining equality *and* making a difference? Is it about helping the majority of women improve their lives by transforming that culture?

According to some of Madonna's feminist defenders, feminism apparently is more about adaptation than transformation. In her *New York Times* ode, Caryn James insisted that Madonna is redefining feminism. "Her desire for sexual control is defiant and blatant. If she is a throwback, it is to someone like Mae West—a playful, ironic, sexually confident woman who always got her man but never let him get her.

"That honesty about using sexuality to gain control and power separates Madonna from generations of femme fatales."

Lynn Layton, in the *Globe,* claimed Madonna should garner feminist support because she opposes violence against women and censorship (at least of her videos) and is a "woman who runs her own show."

Madonna's most passionate defender, Camille Paglia, declared Madonna "the true feminist."

Madonna, she reports, "has taught young women to be fully female and sexual while still exercising total control over their lives." She is liberated because she constantly remakes herself on stage and off, "changing her costume, style and hair color virtually every month. . . . Feminism says 'no more masks.' Madonna says we are nothing but masks."

The last word goes to Madonna. On "Nightline," she declared, "I may be dressing like a traditional bimbo, whatever, but I'm in charge. . . . And isn't that what feminism is all about; you know, equality for men and women? And aren't I in charge of my life, doing the things I want to do?"

Of course, it would be hard not to come to Madonna's defense after MTV banned a video that is no more offensive than most. It is refreshing to know that she will speak out against television's degradation of women. But does this a new feminist heroine and redefinition of feminism make?

MADONNA THE FEMINIST   From Suzanne Gordon, "Madonna the Feminist," *The Boston Globe* 26 Dec. 1990. Reprinted by permission of the author.

Madonna's champions define feminism as the right to do whatever you want to do, and whenever you want to do it. To them, feminism seems to have no collective content. It's little more than an individual woman's ability to be dominant and to remake herself moment by moment. But this "redefinition of feminism" sounds suspiciously like a feminine reworking of the traditional American self-made man, whose individual efforts land him the girl, the job and the power.

Many of us hoped that feminism was more than that. Many of us still insist it is far more than that. But perhaps we middle-aged feminists have failed where Madonna succeeds. Perhaps we have been unable to articulate and assertively promote a definition of feminism that will attract those younger women to whom Madonna so clearly appeals.

Madonna and her defenders have offered a serious challenge. Somehow feminists who want to transform our culture, not just adapt to it, have to convince young women that embracing feminism does not mean embracing victimhood, that you can be for others and still be for yourself, that you can "make it" in bed and in the marketplace, that women can, indeed, be visible without subjugating their souls behind traditional female—or male—masks.

PORNOGRAPHY DEBATE

The question of pornography and what, if anything, to do about it divides feminists like no other. At the heart of the debate is the question of harm. Advocates of suppressing pornography argue:

1. Men who consume pornography learn to view women as the pliant objects of their sexual desires;

2. Regular consumption of pornography reduces men's inhibitions and makes them more likely to act out these sexual desires;

3. Pornography portrays rape as something women secretly desire ("She was asking for it") or as something women come to enjoy as the attack proceeds ("Just lie back and enjoy it"); and

4. Pornography serves as a how-to manual for potential rapists by showing graphically and in step-by-step fashion how to overpower a struggling woman.

Those unwilling to support the suppression of pornography argue that so-called hard-core pornography differs from mainstream literature, film, and music largely in degree of explicitness. They see no difference in terms of their impact on tolerance for rape, to cite the most important case in point, between hard-core depictions in triple X-rated videos and less explicit but nonetheless violent portrayals in R-rated movies or PG-13-rated rap music videos. So-called hard-core pornography, they claim, cannot be distinguished in its effects from mainstream cultural materials. It is a point anti-pornography activists themselves make when they protest against "femicide" or slasher films such as the *Nightmare on Elm Street* series.

The two essays that follow largely began the contemporary debate over pornography. Gloria Steinem's "Erotica vs. Pornography" and Ellen Willis' "Feminism, Moralism, and Pornography" anticipated many of the later arguments because they focused so clearly on the issues of if—and how—we might distinguish between the pornographic and the erotic and if—and how—we might suppress pornography without putting free speech at risk. Steinem is the founding editor of *Ms.* magazine. Willis formerly wrote a regular column for *The Village Voice.*

EROTICA VS. PORNOGRAPHY
Gloria Steinem

If Nazi propaganda that justified the torture and killing of Jews were the theme of half of our most popular movies and magazines, would we not be outraged? If Ku Klux Klan propaganda that preached and even glamorized the enslavement of blacks were the subject of much-praised "classic" novels, would we not protest? We know that such racist propaganda precedes and justifies the racist acts of pogroms and lynchings. We know that watching a violent film causes test subjects to both condone more violence afterward and to be willing to perpetuate it themselves. Why is the propaganda of sexual aggression against women of all races the one form in which the "conventional wisdom" sees no danger? Why is pornography the only media violence that is supposed to be a "safety valve" to satisfy men's "natural" aggressiveness somewhere short of acting it out?

The first reason is the confusion of *all* nonprocreative sex with pornography. Any description of sexual behavior, or even nudity, may be called pornographic or obscene (a word whose Latin derivative means *dirty* or *containing filth*) by those who insist that the only moral purpose of sex is procreative, or even that any portrayal of sexuality or nudity is against the will of God.

In fact, human beings seem to be the only animals that experience the same sex drive and pleasure at times when we can and cannot conceive. Other animals experience periods of heat or estrus. Humans do not.

Just as we developed uniquely human capacities for language, planning, memory, and invention along our evolutionary path, we also developed sexuality as a form of expression, a way of communicating that is separable from our reproductive need. For human beings, sexuality can be and often is a way of bonding, of giving and receiving pleasure, bridging differentness, discovering sameness, and communicating emotion.

We developed this and other human gifts through our ability to change our environment, adapt to it physically, and so in the very long run to affect our own evolution. But as an emotional result of this spiraling path away from other animals, we seem to alternate between periods of exploring our unique abilities and feelings of loneliness in the unknown that we ourselves have created, a fear that sometimes sends us back to the comfort of the animal world by encouraging us to look for a sameness that is not there.

For instance, the separation of "play" from "work" is a feature of the human world. So is the difference between art and nature, or an intellectual accomplishment and a physical one. As a result, we celebrate play, art, and invention as pleasurable and important leaps into the unknown; yet any temporary trouble can send us back to a nostalgia for our primate past and a conviction that the basics of survival, nature, and physical labor are somehow more worthwhile or even more moral.

EROTICA VS. PORNOGRAPHY   From Gloria Steinem, *Outrageous Acts and Everyday Rebellions* (New York: Holt, 1983) 224–30. Copyright © 1983 by Gloria Steinem. Copyright © 1984 by East Toledo Productions, Inc. Reprinted by permission of Henry Holt and Co., Inc.

In the same way, we have explored our sexuality as separable from conception: a pleasurable, empathetic, important bridge to others of our species. We have even invented contraception, a skill that has probably existed in some form since our ancestors figured out the process of conception and birth, in order to extend and protect this uniquely human gift. Yet we also have times of atavistic suspicion that sex is not complete, or even legal or intended by God, if it does not or could not end in conception.

No wonder the very different concepts of "erotica" and "pornography" can be so confused. Both assume that sex can be separated from conception; that human sexuality has additional uses and goals. This is the major reason why, even in our current culture, both may still be condemned as equally obscene and immoral. Such gross condemnation of all sexuality that isn't harnessed to childbirth (and to patriarchal marriage so that children are properly "owned" by men) has been increased by the current backlash against women's independence. Out of fear that the whole patriarchal structure will be eventually upset if we as women really have the autonomous power to decide our sexual and reproductive futures (that is, if we can control our own bodies, and thus the means of reproduction), anti-equality groups are not only denouncing sex education and family planning as "pornographic," but are trying to use obscenity laws to stop the sending of all contraceptive information through the mails. Any sex or nudity outside the context of patriarchal marriage and forced childbirth is their target. In fact, Phyllis Schlafly has denounced the entire women's movement as "obscene."

Not surprisingly, this religious, visceral backlash has a secular, intellectual counterpart that relies heavily on applying the "natural" behavior of some selected part of the animal world to humans. This is questionable in itself, but such Lionel Tiger-ish studies make their political purpose even more clear by the animals they choose and the habits they emphasize. For example, some male primates carry and generally "mother" their infants, male lions care for their young, female elephants often lead the clan, and male penguins literally do everything except give birth, from hatching the eggs to sacrificing their own membranes to feed the new arrivals. Perhaps that's why many male supremacists prefer to discuss chimps and baboons (many of whom are studied in atypical conditions of captivity) whose behavior is suitably male-dominant. The message is that human females should accept their animal "destiny" of being sexually dependent and devote themselves to bearing and rearing their young.

Defending against such repression and reaction leads to the temptation to merely reverse the terms and declare that *all* nonprocreative sex is good. In fact, however, this human activity can be as constructive or destructive, moral or immoral, as any other. Sex as communication can send messages as different as mutual pleasure and dominance, life and death, "erotica" and "pornography."

The second kind of problem comes not from those who oppose women's equality in nonsexual areas, whether on grounds of God or nature, but from men (and some women, too) who present themselves as friends of civil liberties and progress. Their opposition may take the form of a concern about privacy, on the grounds that a challenge to pornography invades private sexual behavior and the philosophy of "whatever turns you on." It may be a concern about class bias, on the premise that pornography is just "workingmen's erotica." Sometimes, it's the simple argument that they themselves like pornography and therefore it must be okay. Most often, however, this resistance attaches itself to or hides behind an expressed concern about censorship, freedom of the press, and the First Amendment.

In each case, such liberal objections are more easily countered than the anti-equality ones because they are less based on fact. It's true, for instance, that women's independence and autonomy would upset the whole patriarchal apple cart: the conservatives are right to be worried. It's not true, however, that pornography is a private concern. If it were just a matter of men making male-supremacist literature in their own basements to assuage their own sexual hang-ups, there would be sorrow and avoidance among women, but not the anger, outrage, and fear produced by being confronted with the preaching of sexual fascism on our newsstands, movie screens, television sets, and public streets. It is a multi-billion-dollar industry, which involves the making of public policy, if only to decide whether, as is now the case, crimes committed in the manufacture and sale of pornography will continue to go largely unprosecuted. Zoning regulations on the public display of pornography are not enforced, the sexual slavery and exploitation of children goes unpunished, the forcible use of teenage runaways is ignored by police, and even the torture and murder of prostitutes for men's sexual titillation is obscured by some mitigating notion that the women asked for it.

In all other areas of privacy, the limitation is infringement on the rights and lives and safety of others. That must become true for pornography. Right now, it is exempt: almost "below the law."

As for class bias, it's simply not accurate to say that pornography is erotica with less education. From the origins of the words, as well as the careful way that feminists working against pornography are trying to use them, it's clear there is a substantive difference, not an artistic or economic one. Pornography is about dominance. Erotica is about mutuality. (Any man able to empathize with women can easily tell the difference by looking at a photograph or film and putting himself in the woman's skin. There is some evidence that poor or discriminated-against men are better able to do this than rich ones.) Perhaps the most revealing thing is that this argument is generally made *on behalf* of the working class by pro-pornography liberals, but not *by* working-class spokespeople themselves.

Of course, the idea that enjoying pornography makes it okay is an overwhelmingly male one. From Kinsey forward, research has confirmed that men are the purchasers of pornography, and that the majority of men are turned on by it, while the majority of women find it angering, humiliating, and not a turn-on at all. This was true even though women were shown sexually explicit material that may have included erotica, since Kinsey and others did not make that distinction. If such rare examples of equal sex were entirely deleted, pornography itself could probably serve as sex aversion-therapy for most women; yet many men and some psychologists continue to call women prudish, frigid, or generally unhealthy if they are not turned on by their own domination. The same men might be less likely to argue that anti-Semitic and racist literature was equally okay because it gave them pleasure, or that they wanted their children to grow up with the same feelings about people of other races, other classes, that had been inflicted on them. The problem is that the degradation of women of all races is still thought to be normal.

Nonetheless, there are a few well-meaning women who are both turned on by pornography and angered that other women are not. Some of their anger is misunderstanding: objections to pornography are not condemnations of women who have been raised to believe sex and domination are synonymous, but objections to the idea that such domination is the only form that normal sexuality can take. Sometimes, this anger results from an underestimation of themselves: being turned on by a rape fantasy is not the same thing as wanting to be raped. As Robin Morgan has pointed out, the distinguishing feature of a fantasy is that the fantasizer herself is in control. Both men and women have "ravishment" fantasies in which we are passive while others act out our unspoken wishes—but they are still *our* wishes. And some anger, especially when it comes from women who consider themselves feminists, is a refusal to differentiate between what may be true for them now and what might be improved for all women in the future. To use a small but related example, a woman may now be attracted only to men who are taller, heavier, and older than she, but still understand that such superficial restrictions on the men she loves and enjoys going to bed with won't exist in a more free and less-stereotyped future. Similarly, some lesbians may find themselves following the masculine–feminine patterns that were our only model for intimate relationships, heterosexual or not, but still see these old patterns clearly and try to equalize them. It isn't that women attracted to pornography cannot also be feminists, but that pornography itself must be recognized as an adversary of women's safety and equality, and therefore, in the long run, of feminism.

Finally, there is the First Amendment argument against feminist anti-pornography campaigns: the most respectable and public opposition, but also the one with the least basis in fact.

Feminist groups are not arguing for censorship of pornography, or for censorship of Nazi literature or racist propaganda of the Ku Klux Klan. For one thing, any societal definition of pornography in a male-dominant society (or of racist literature in a racist society) probably would punish the wrong people. Freely chosen homosexual expression might be considered more "pornographic" than snuff movies, or contraceptive courses for teenagers more "obscene" than bondage. Furthermore, censorship in itself, even with the proper definitions, would only drive pornography into more underground activity and, were it to follow the pattern of drug traffic, into even more profitability. Most important, the First Amendment is part of a statement of individual rights against government intervention that feminism seeks to expand, not contract: for instance, a woman's right to decide whether and when to have children. When we protest against pornography and educate others about it, as I am doing now, we are strengthening the First Amendment by exercising it.

The only legal steps suggested by feminists thus far have been the prosecution of those pornography makers who are accused of murder or assault and battery, prosecution of those who use children under the age of consent, enforcement of existing zoning and other codes that are breached because of payoffs to law-enforcement officials and enormous rents paid to pornography's landlords, and use of public-nuisance statutes to require that pornography not be displayed in public places where its sight cannot reasonably be avoided. All of those measures involve enforcement of existing law, and none has been interpreted as a danger to the First Amendment.

Perhaps the reason for this controversy is less substance than smokescreen. Just as earlier feminist campaigns to combat rape were condemned by some civil libertarians as efforts that would end by putting only men of color or poor men in jail, or in perpetuating the death penalty, anti-pornography campaigns are now similarly opposed. In fact, the greater publicity given to rape exposed the fact that white psychiatrists, educators, and other professionals were just as likely to be rapists, and changes in the law reduced penalties to ones that were more appropriate and thus more likely to be administered. Feminist efforts also changed the definition to sexual assault so that men were protected, too.

Though there are no statistics on the purchasers of pornography, clerks, movie-house owners, video-cassette dealers, mail-order houses, and others who serve this clientele usually remark on their respectability, their professional standing, suits, brief-cases, white skins, and middle-class zip codes. For instance, the last screening of a snuff movie showing a real murder was traced to the monthly pornographic film showings of a senior partner in a respected law firm; an event regularly held by him for a group of friends including other lawyers and judges. One who was present reported that many were "embarrassed" and "didn't know what to say." But not one man was willing to object, much less offer this evidence of murder to the police. Though some concern about censorship is sincere—the result of false reports that feminist anti-pornography campaigns were really calling for censorship, or of confusion with right-wing groups who both misdefine pornography and want to censor it—much of it seems to be a cover for the preservation of the pornographic status quo.

In fact, the obstacles to taking on pornography seem suspiciously like the virgin–whore divisions that have been women's only choices in the past. The right wing says all that is not virginal or motherly is pornographic, and thus they campaign against sexuality and nudity in general. The left wing says all sex is good as long as it's male-defined, and thus pornography must be protected. Women who feel endangered by being the victim, and men who feel demeaned by being the victimizer, have a long struggle ahead. In fact, pornography will continue as long as boys are raised to believe they must control or conquer women as a measure of manhood, as long as society rewards men who believe that success or even functioning—in sex as in other areas of life—depends on women's subservience.

But we now have words to describe our outrage and separate sex from violence. We now have the courage to demonstrate publicly against pornography, to keep its magazines and films out of our houses, to boycott its purveyors, to treat even friends and family members who support it as seriously as we would treat someone who supported and enjoyed Nazi literature or the teachings of the Klan.

But until we finally untangle sexuality and aggression, there will be more pornography and less erotica. There will be little murders in our beds—and very little love.

FEMINISM, MORALISM, AND PORNOGRAPHY
Ellen Willis

For women, life is an ongoing good cop–bad cop routine. The good cops are marriage, motherhood, and that courtly old gentleman, chivalry. Just cooperate, they say (crossing their fingers), and we'll go easy on you. You'll never have to earn a living or

FEMINISM, MORALISM, AND PORNOGRAPHY   From Ellen Willis, *Beginning to See the Light: Sex, Hope, and Rock-and-Roll* (Hanover and London: Wesleyan UP, 1992) 219–26. Copyright © 1992 by Ellen Willis, Wesleyan University Press. By permission of University Press of New England.

open a door. We'll even get you some romantic love. But you'd better not get stubborn, or you'll have to deal with our friend rape, and he's a real terror; we just can't control him.

Pornography often functions as a bad cop. If rape warns that without the protection of one man we are fair game for all, the hard-core pornographic image suggests that the alternative to being a wife is being a whore. As women become more "criminal," the cops call for nastier reinforcements; the proliferation of lurid, violent porn (symbolic rape) is a form of backlash. But one can be a solid citizen and still be shocked (naively or hypocritically) by police brutality. However widely condoned, rape is illegal. However loudly people proclaim that porn is as wholesome as granola, the essence of its appeal is that emotionally it remains taboo. It is from their very contempt for the rules that bad cops derive their power to terrorize (and the covert approbation of solid citizens who would love to break the rules themselves). The line between bad cop and outlaw is tenuous. Both rape and pornography reflect a male outlaw mentality that rejects the conventions of romance and insists, bluntly, that women are cunts. The crucial difference between the conservative's moral indignation at rape, or at *Hustler*, and the feminist's political outrage is the latter's understanding that the problem is not bad cops or outlaws but cops and the law.

Unfortunately, the current women's campaign against pornography seems determined to blur this difference. Feminist criticism of sexist and misogynist pornography is nothing new; porn is an obvious target insofar as it contributes to larger patterns of oppression—the reduction of the female body to a commodity (the paradigm being prostitution), the sexual intimidation that makes women regard the public streets as enemy territory (the paradigm being rape), sexist images and propaganda in general. But what is happening now is different. By playing games with the English language, antiporn activists are managing to rationalize as feminism a single-issue movement divorced from any larger political context and rooted in conservative moral assumptions that are all the more dangerous for being unacknowledged.

When I first heard there was a group called Women Against Pornography, I twitched. Could I define myself as Against Pornography? Not really. In itself, pornography—which, my dictionary and I agree, means any image or description intended or used to arouse sexual desire—does not strike me as the proper object of a political crusade. As the most cursory observation suggests, there are many varieties of porn, some pernicious, some more or less benign. About the only generalization one can make is that pornography is the return of the repressed, of feelings and fantasies driven underground by a culture that atomizes sexuality, defining love as a noble affair of the heart and mind, lust as a base animal urge centered in unmentionable organs. Prurience—the state of mind I associate with pornography—implies a sense of sex as forbidden, secretive pleasure, isolated from any emotional or social context. I imagine that in utopia, porn would wither away along with the state, heroin, and Coca-Cola. At present, however, the sexual impulses that pornography appeals to are part of virtually everyone's psychology. For obvious political and cultural reasons nearly all porn is sexist in that it is the product of a male imagination and aimed at a male market; women are less likely to be consciously interested in pornography, or to indulge that interest, or to find porn that turns them on. But anyone who thinks women are simply indifferent to pornography has never watched a bunch of adolescent girls pass around a trashy novel. Over the years I've enjoyed various pieces of pornography—some of them of the sleazy Forty-second Street paperback sort—and so have most women I know. Fantasy, after all, is more flexible than reality, and women have learned, as a matter of survival, to be adept at shaping male fantasies to their own purposes. If feminists define pornography, per se, as the enemy, the result will be to make a lot of women ashamed of their sexual feelings and afraid to be honest about them. And the last thing women need is more sexual shame, guilt, and hypocrisy—this time served up as feminism.

So why ignore qualitative distinctions and in effect condemn all pornography as equally bad? WAP organizers answer—or finesse—this question by redefining pornography. They maintain that pornography is not really about sex but about violence against women. Or, in a more colorful formulation, "Pornography is the theory, rape is the practice." Part of the argument is that pornography causes violence; much is made of the fact that Charles Manson and David Berkowitz had porn collections. This is the sort of inverted logic that presumes marijuana to be dangerous because most heroin addicts started with it. It is men's hostility toward women—combined with their power to express that hostility and for the most part get away with it—that causes sexual violence. Pornography that gives sadistic fantasies concrete shape—and, in today's atmosphere, social legitimacy—may well encourage suggestible men to act them out. But if *Hustler* were to vanish from the shelves tomorrow, I doubt that rape or wife-beating statistics would decline.

Even more problematic is the idea that pornography depicts violence rather than sex. Since porn is by definition overtly sexual, while most of it is not overtly violent, this equation requires some fancy explaining. The conference WAP held in September was in part devoted to this task. Robin Morgan and Gloria Steinem addressed it by attempting to distinguish pornography from erotica. According to this argument, erotica (whose etymological root is "eros," or sexual love) expresses an integrated sexuality based on mutual affection and desire between equals; pornography (which comes from another Greek root—"porne," meaning prostitute) reflects a dehumanized sexuality based on male domination and exploitation of women. The distinction sounds promising, but it doesn't hold up. The accepted meaning of erotica is literature or pictures with sexual themes; it may or may not serve the essentially utilitarian function of pornography. Because it is less specific, less suggestive of actual sexual activity, "erotica" is regularly used as a euphemism for "classy porn." Pornography expressed in literary language or expensive photography and consumed by the upper middle class is "erotica"; the cheap stuff, which can't pretend to any purpose but getting people off, is smut. The erotica-versus-porn approach evades the (embarrassing?) question of how porn is *used*. It endorses the portrayal of sex as we might like it to be and condemns the portrayal of sex as it too often is, whether in action or only in fantasy. But if pornography is to arouse, it must appeal to the feelings we have, not those that by some utopian standard we ought to have. Sex in this culture has been so deeply politicized that it is impossible to make clear-cut distinctions between "authentic" sexual impulses and those conditioned by patriarchy. Between, say, *Ulysses* at one end and *Snuff* at the other, erotica/pornography conveys all sorts of mixed messages that elicit complicated and private responses. In practice, attempts to sort out good erotica from bad porn inevitably come down to "What turns me on is erotic; what turns you on is pornographic."

It would be clearer and more logical simply to acknowledge that some sexual images are offensive and some are not. But logic and clarity are irrelevant—or rather, inimical—to the underlying aim of the antiporners, which is to vent the emotions traditionally associated with the word "pornography." As I've suggested, there is a social and psychic link between pornography and rape. In terms of patriarchal morality both are expressions of male lust, which is presumed to be innately vicious, and offenses to the putative sexual innocence of "good" women. But feminists supposedly begin with different assumptions—that men's confusion of sexual desire with predatory aggression reflects a sexist system, not male biology; that there are no good (chaste) or bad (lustful) women, just women who are, like men, sexual beings. From this standpoint, to lump pornography with rape is dangerously simplistic. Rape is a violent physical assault. Pornography can be a psychic assault, both in its content and in its public intrusions on our attention, but for women as for men it can also be a source of erotic pleasure. A woman who is raped is a victim; a woman who enjoys pornography (even if that means enjoying a rape fantasy) is in a sense a rebel, insisting on an aspect of her sexuality that has been defined as a male preserve. Insofar as pornography glorifies male supremacy and sexual alienation, it is deeply reactionary. But in rejecting sexual repression and hypocrisy—which have inflicted even more damage on women than on men—it expresses a radical impulse.

That this impulse still needs defending, even among feminists, is evident from the sexual attitudes that have surfaced in the antiporn movement. In the movement's rhetoric pornography is a code word for vicious male lust. To the objection that some women get off on porn, the standard reply is that this only shows how thoroughly women have been brainwashed by male values—though a WAP leaflet goes so far as to suggest that women who claim to like pornography are lying to avoid male opprobrium. (Note the good-girl-versus-bad-girl theme, reappearing as healthy-versus-sick, or honest-versus-devious; for "brainwashed" read "seduced.") And the view of sex that most often emerges from talk about "erotica" is as sentimental and euphemistic as the word itself: lovemaking should be beautiful, romantic, soft, nice, and devoid of messiness, vulgarity, impulses to power, or indeed aggression of any sort. Above all, the emphasis should be on *relationships*, not (yuck) *organs.* This goody-goody concept of eroticism is not feminist but feminine. It is precisely sex as an aggressive, unladylike activity, an expression of violent and unpretty emotion, an exercise of erotic power, and a specifically genital experience that has been taboo for women. Nor are we supposed to admit that we, too, have sadistic impulses, that our sexual fantasies may reflect forbidden urges to turn the tables and get revenge on men. (When a woman is aroused by a rape fantasy, is she perhaps identifying with the rapist as well as the victim?)

At the WAP conference lesbian separatists argued that pornography reflects patriarchal sexual relations; patriarchal sexual relations are based on male power backed by force; ergo, pornography is violent. This dubious syllogism, which could as easily be applied to romantic novels, reduces the whole issue to hopeless mush. If all manifestations of patriarchal sexuality are violent, then opposition to violence cannot explain why pornography (rather than romantic novels) should be singled out as a target. Besides, such reductionism allows women no basis for distinguishing between consensual heterosexuality and rape. But this is precisely its point; as a number of women at the conference put it, "In a patriarchy, all sex with men is pornographic." Of course, to attack pornography, and at the same time equate it with heterosexual sex, is implicitly to condemn not only women who like pornography, but women who sleep with men. This is familiar ground. The argument that straight women collaborate with the enemy has often been, among other things, a relatively polite way of saying that they consort with the beast. At the conference I couldn't help feeling that proponents of the separatist line were talking like the modern equivalents of women who, in an era when straightforward prudery was socially acceptable, joined convents to escape men's rude sexual demands. It seemed to me that their revulsion against heterosexuality was serving as the thinnest of covers for disgust with sex itself. In any case, sanitized feminine sexuality, whether straight or gay, is as limited as the predatory masculine kind and as central to women's oppression; a major function of misogynist pornography is to scare us into embracing it. As a further incentive, the good cops stand ready to assure us that we are indeed morally superior to men, that in our sweetness and nonviolence (read passivity and powerlessness) is our strength.

Women are understandably tempted to believe this comforting myth. Self-righteousness has always been a feminine weapon, a permissible way to make men feel bad. Ironically, it is socially acceptable for women to display fierce aggression in their crusades against male vice, which serve as an outlet for female anger without threatening male power. The temperance movement, which made alcohol the symbol of male violence, did not improve the position of women; substituting porn for demon rum won't work either. One reason it won't is that it bolsters the good girl–bad girl split. Overtly or by implication it isolates women who like porn or "pornographic" sex or who work in the sex industry. WAP has refused to take a position on prostitution, yet its activities—particularly its support for cleaning up Times Square—will affect prostitutes' lives. Prostitution raises its own set of complicated questions. But it is clearly not in women's interest to pit "good" feminists against "bad" whores (or topless dancers, or models for skin magazines).

So far, the issue that has dominated public debate on the anti-porn campaign is its potential threat to free speech. Here too the movement's arguments have been full of contradictions. Susan Brownmiller and other WAP organizers claim not to advocate censorship and dismiss the civil liberties issue as a red herring dragged in by men who don't want to face the fact that pornography oppresses women. Yet at the same time, WAP endorses the Supreme Court's contention that obscenity is not protected speech, a doctrine I—and most civil libertarians—regard as a clear infringement of First Amendment rights. Brownmiller insists that the First Amendment was designed to protect political dissent, not expressions of woman-hating violence. But to make such a distinction is to defeat the amendment's purpose, since it implicitly cedes to the government the right to define "political." (Has there ever been a government willing to admit that its opponents are anything more than antisocial troublemakers?) Anyway, it makes no sense to oppose pornography on the grounds that it's sexist propaganda, then turn around and argue that it's not political. Nor will libertarians be reassured by WAP's statement that "We want to change the definition of obscenity so that it focuses on violence, not sex." Whatever their focus, obscenity laws deny the right of free expression to those who transgress official standards of propriety—and personally, I don't find WAP's standards significantly less oppressive than Warren Burger's. Not that it matters, since WAP's fantasies about influencing the definition of obscenity are appallingly naive. The basic purpose of obscenity laws is and always has been to reinforce cultural taboos on sexuality and suppress feminism, homosexuality, and other forms of sexual dissidence. No pornographer has ever been punished for being a woman hater, but not too long ago information about female sexuality, contraception, and abortion was assumed to be obscene. In a male supremacist society the only obscenity law that will not be used against women is no law at all.

INCIDENTS IN THE LIFE OF A SLAVE GIRL
Harriet Jacobs

Historians and other scholars of American slavery long ignored the memoirs and autobiographies written by the men and women who had experienced the South's "peculiar institution" firsthand. Instead they poured over plantation and census records, travel accounts by European and northern visitors to the antebellum South, polemics decrying slavery and others defending it, newspaper editorials pro and con, and political speeches. They examined records produced by white people, and it was not until John Blassingame, a young African-American historian at Yale, published *The Slave Community* (1972) that historians began to mine slave accounts of plantation life.

Of the many remarkable books rediscovered in this process, none is more extraordinary than Harriet Jacobs' *Incidents in the Life of a Slave Girl.* The book was written by a woman although most slave narratives are by men. It dealt in detail with the author's heroic attempts to resist her master's sexual advances, a subject most other accounts of the slave experience only allude to. It recounted her years of hiding from her master when most slaves who attempted to hide were discovered in a matter of days. So unusual is *Incidents* that historians and literary scholars have devoted years of research simply to authenticating such elementary matters as the name of the author and the fact that the book is a memoir and not a novel.

Among its many other virtues, *Incidents* provides one of the earliest and fullest accounts of sexual harassment in American literature. Slavery would end; harassment is still with us.

 I would ten thousand times rather that my children should be the half-starved paupers of Ireland than to be the most pampered among the slaves of America. I would rather drudge out my life on a cotton plantation, till the grave opened to give me rest, than to live with an unprincipled master and a jealous mistress. The felon's home in a penitentiary is preferable. He may repent, and turn from the error of his ways, and so find peace; but it is not so with a favorite slave. She is not allowed to have any pride of character. It is deemed a crime in her to wish to be virtuous.

Mrs. Flint possessed the key to her husband's character before I was born. She might have used this knowledge to counsel and to screen the young and the innocent among her slaves; but for them she had no sympathy. They were the objects of her constant suspicion and malevolence. She watched her husband with unceasing vigilance; but he was well practised in means to evade it. What he could not find

INCIDENTS IN THE LIFE OF A SLAVE GIRL   From Harriet Jacobs (pseud. Linda Brent), L. Maria Child ed., *Incidents in the Life of a Slave Girl* (Boston: Published for the author, 1861) 29–34.

opportunity to say in words he manifested in signs. He invented more than were ever thought of in a deaf and dumb asylum. I let them pass, as if I did not understand what he meant; and many were the curses and threats bestowed on me for my stupidity. One day he caught me teaching myself to write. He frowned, as if he was not well pleased; but I suppose he came to the conclusion that such an accomplishment might help to advance his favorite scheme. Before long, notes were often slipped into my hand. I would return them, saying, "I can't read them, sir." "Can't you?" he replied; "then I must read them to you." He always finished the reading by asking, "Do you understand?" Sometimes he would complain of the heat of the tea room, and order his supper to be placed on a small table in the piazza. He would seat himself there with a well-satisfied smile, and tell me to stand by and brush away the flies. He would eat very slowly, pausing between the mouthfuls. These intervals were employed in describing the happiness I was so foolishly throwing away, and in threatening me with the penalty that finally awaited my stubborn disobedience. He boasted much of the forbearance he had exercised towards me, and reminded me that there was a limit to his patience. When I succeeded in avoiding opportunities for him to talk to me at home, I was ordered to come to his office, to do some errand. When there, I was obliged to stand and listen to such language as he saw fit to address to me. Sometimes I so openly expressed my contempt for him that he would become violently enraged, and I wondered why he did not strike me. Circumstanced as he was, he probably thought it was better policy to be forbearing. But the state of things grew worse and worse daily. In desperation I told him that I must and would apply to my grandmother for protection. He threatened me with death, and worse than death, if I made any complaint to her. Strange to say, I did not despair. I was naturally of a buoyant disposition, and always I had a hope of somehow getting out of his clutches. Like many a poor, simple slave before me, I trusted that some threads of joy would yet be woven into my dark destiny.

I had entered my sixteenth year, and every day it became more apparent that my presence was intolerable to Mrs. Flint. Angry words frequently passed between her and her husband. He had never punished me himself, and he would not allow any body else to punish me. In that respect, she was never satisfied; but, in her angry moods, no terms were too vile for her to bestow upon me. Yet I, whom she detested so bitterly, had far more pity for her than he had, whose duty it was to make her life happy. I never wronged her, or wished to wrong her; and one word of kindness from her would have brought me to her feet.

After repeated quarrels between the doctor and his wife, he announced his intention to take his youngest daughter, then four years old, to sleep in his apartment. It was necessary that a servant should sleep in the same room, to be on hand if the child stirred. I was selected for that office, and informed for what purpose that arrangement had been made. By managing to keep within sight of people, as much as possible, during the day time, I had hitherto succeeded in eluding my master, though a razor was often held to my throat to force me to change this line of policy. At night I slept by the side of my great aunt, where I felt safe. He was too prudent to come into her room. She was an old woman, and had been in the family many years. Moreover, as a married man, and a professional man, he deemed it necessary to save appearances in some degree. But he resolved to remove the obstacle in the way of his scheme; and he thought he had planned it so that he should evade suspicion. He was well aware how much I prized my refuge by the side of my old aunt, and he determined to dispossess me of it. The first night the doctor had the little child in his room alone. The next morning, I was ordered to take my station as nurse the following night. A kind Providence interposed in my favor. During the day Mrs. Flint heard of this new arrangement, and a storm followed. I rejoiced to hear it rage.

After a while my mistress sent for me to come to her room. Her first question was, "Did you know you were to sleep in the doctor's room?"

"Yes, ma'am."

"Who told you?"

"My master."

"Will you answer truly all the questions I ask?"

"Yes, ma'am."

"Tell me, then, as you hope to be forgiven, are you innocent of what I have accused you?"

"I am."

She handed me a Bible, and said, "Lay your hand on your heart, kiss this holy book, and swear before God that you tell me the truth."

I took the oath she required, and I did it with a clear conscience.

"You have taken God's holy word to testify your innocence," said she. "If you have deceived me, beware! Now take this stool, sit down, look me directly in the face, and tell me all that has passed between your master and you."

I did as she ordered. As I went on with my account her color changed frequently, she wept, and sometimes groaned. She spoke in tones so sad, that I was touched by her grief. The tears came to my eyes; but I was soon convinced that her emotions arose from anger and wounded pride. She felt that her marriage vows were desecrated, her dignity insulted; but she had no compassion for the poor victim of her husband's perfidy. She pitied herself as a martyr; but she was incapable of feeling for the condition of shame and misery in which her unfortunate, helpless slave was placed.

Yet perhaps she had some touch of feeling for me; for when the conference was ended, she spoke kindly, and promised to protect me. I should have been much comforted by this assurance if I could have had confidence in it; but my experiences in slavery had filled me with distrust. She was not a very refined woman, and had not much control over her passions. I was an object of her jealousy, and, consequently, of her hatred; and I knew I could not expect kindness or confidence from her under the circumstances in which I was placed. I could not blame her. Slaveholders' wives feel as other women would under similar circumstances. The fire of her temper kindled from small sparks, and now the flame became so intense that the doctor was obliged to give up his intended arrangement.

I knew I had ignited the torch, and I expected to suffer for it afterwards; but I felt too thankful to my mistress for the timely aid she rendered me to care much about that. She now took me to sleep in a room adjoining her own. There I was an object of her especial care, though not of her especial comfort, for she spent many a sleepless night to watch over me. Sometimes I woke up, and found her bending over me. At other times she whispered in my ear, as though it was her husband who was speaking to me, and listened to hear what I would answer. If she startled me, on such occasions, she would glide stealthily away; and the next morning she would tell me I had been talking in my sleep, and ask who I was talking to. At last, I began to be fearful for my life. It had been often threatened; and you can imagine, better than I can describe, what an unpleasant sensation it must produce to wake up in the dead of night and find a jealous woman bending over you. Terrible as this experience was, I had fears that it would give place to one more terrible.

My mistress grew weary of her vigils; they did not prove satisfactory. She changed her tactics. She now tried the trick of accusing my master of crime, in my presence, and gave my name as the author of the accusation. To my utter astonishment, he replied, "I don't believe it; but if she did acknowledge it, you tortured her into exposing me." Tortured into exposing him! Truly, Satan had no difficulty in distinguishing the color of his soul! I understood his object in making this false representation. It was to show me that I gained nothing by seeking the protection of my mistress; that the power was still all in his own hands. I pitied Mrs. Flint. She was a second wife, many years the junior of her husband; and the hoary-headed miscreant was enough to try the patience of a wiser and better woman. She was completely foiled, and knew not how to proceed. She would gladly have had me flogged for my supposed false oath; but, as I have already stated, the doctor never allowed any one to whip me. The old sinner was politic. The application of the lash might have led to remarks that would have exposed him in the eyes of his children and grandchildren. How often did I rejoice that I lived in a town where all the inhabitants knew each other! If I had been on a remote plantation, or lost among the multitude of a crowded city, I should not be a living woman at this day.

The secrets of slavery are concealed like those of the Inquisition. My master was, to my knowledge, the father of eleven slaves. But did the mothers dare to tell who was the father of their children? Did the other slaves dare to allude to it, except in whispers among themselves? No, indeed! They knew too well the terrible consequences.

THE TRIALS OF CONVICTING RAPISTS: AN INTERVIEW WITH LINDA FAIRSTEIN

Margaret Carlson

Until very recently, rape victims found the legal deck stacked against them if they attempted to bring charges against their attackers. Police were usually unsympathetic, often expressing in word or attitude the view that they had "probably been asking for it." District attorneys were uninterested in prosecuting such cases, even when they were sympathetic, because convictions were notoriously difficult to win. Worse yet, if the case did go to court, the victim often found that it was she—and her entire sexual history—and not the perpetrator who was on trial.

All of this has started to change, although slowly and unevenly, as state legislators, many of them women, have revised laws concerning victims' rights. Prosecutors, like New York Assistant District Attorney Linda Fairstein, have set up special units to handle rape cases. In this *Time* magazine interview Fairstein discusses the progress made as well as the distance yet to go before rape victims receive full justice.

Q. In acquaintance rape, there is an impression that a woman had better have led a sterling life or else she will suffer when the case comes to trial. For instance, a woman goes to a party, meets someone and goes to his house afterward. They have a drink. If the situation turns ugly and she is raped, she should be above reproach and have some broken bones, especially if her assailant is some clean-cut college guy.

A. Sadly, many people believe there are people who, because of their social class, appearance, whatever, can't commit these kinds of crimes. That's ridiculous, since rapists come in every size, shape and background. Part of what we do is shatter these preconceived notions. For example, acquaintances where there hasn't been a sexual relationship before the event is not a difficult case to try. Legislative changes and specialized police and prosecutorial units like ours have made it a lot easier.

Q. No one in her right mind would consent to group rape, to sodomy, to being force-fed alcohol to the point of stupefaction. Yet defense attorneys have successfully argued consent in outrageous circumstances, especially if the victim slips up on a detail—saying it was vodka, for example, when the defense proves it was gin.

A. If a jury finds enough inconsistencies in a story, they may reject the story. And if some acts are consensual and others aren't, you have to separate these for a jury. We've had a lot of experience where victims have used alcohol leading up to what becomes a sexual assault. A prosecutor should be able to present a picture that says yes, she did *x, y* and *z*, and that's what made her more vulnerable, that's what made her less able to repel an attacker. You have to get the jury to see that you may not want to take this woman home to dinner because she was doing cocaine all night or shooting heroin and then drinking beer chasers, but that doesn't mean she asked for it.

Q. If her story isn't coherent, that's a problem. But if her story is too coherent, that's a problem too. How can she remember something so traumatic so clearly?

A. I've heard that kind of excuse too, that she was not upset enough. There are some survivors who relive each part of the episode like a single camera frame and others who repress it. But each telling is different. With a serial rapist, for example, you know exactly what he says when he approaches each woman, what the language is, what the sexual acts are, how long it took. And yet it's fascinating to see five women at trial testify about a very similar event very differently, depending on each woman's emotional strength, at what point this happened in her life, how she's recovered.

Q. The rape victim is often the only witness. Isn't that a problem, especially if she kept her eyes shut the whole time?

A. Many crimes have only one witness. Most muggings are one witness against the person he identifies in a lineup three months later. A mugging, it's 90 seconds—don't scream, don't look at my face, give me your money—often from behind. A sex offense rarely lasts less than 15 or 20 minutes, and if the assailant has the victim in her apartment, on a rooftop, it can last an hour. So the information is there through every one of her senses, unlike other kinds of crime. No one forgets really. It's getting her to trust what you're doing, knowing that remembering can convict her assailant. And the conviction rate is very high. I take pleasure in being able to tell people about that high conviction rate because that's not what made-for-TV movies present.

THE TRIALS OF CONVICTING RAPISTS   From Margaret Carlson, "The Trials of Convicting Rapists," *Time* 14 Oct. 1991: 11–C8. Copyright © 1991 by Time Inc. Reprinted by permission.

Q. Your most famous case involved Robert Chambers, who was tried and convicted in 1988 for the murder of Jennifer Levin in Central Park. The episode quickly became known as the preppie murder case, attracting headlines around the world, producing a book and a movie. While the jury was out, you accepted a plea of manslaughter. Weren't you disappointed?

A. The trial lasted 11 weeks. The jury worked on the case for nine days, the longest deliberation of a single-defendant case in New York County history. We took the plea realizing there was not going to be a verdict. Of course I was disappointed.

Q. Jennifer Levin's parents were in the courtroom every day of the trial, being reminded that their daughter died a horrible death. Why do families put themselves through that?

A. It's part of the healing process, although no one ever heals from a loss like that. Since then, the Levins have thrown themselves into victims work and are active in Parents of Murdered Children. I remain very close to the family. They entrusted me with their daughter's memory. It's the survivors who give the work its purpose. I'm godmother to Jennifer's sister's child.

Q. What do you think about the recent naming of a rape victim by newspapers and a network without her permission?

A. I think it's very courageous for a survivor to let her name and face be attached to this crime, and doing so makes it easier for other survivors. But it's still too difficult for a lot of survivors, still too much of a stigma attached, especially in acquaintance rapes, where they are so often blamed unfairly for participating in what happened.

Q. Are women jurors harder on women than men are?

A. I've had women who are intelligent and have a lot of common sense who make terrific jurors, but too often women tend to be very critical of the conduct of other women, and they are often not good jurors in acquaintance-rape cases.

Q. Do you deal with male-on-male rape?

A. Yes, it's a serious problem. But again, its underreported because so many people stigmatize the victims.

Q. Do you have regrets about anyone who got away?

A. I had an acquittal in a case with a 13-year-old victim who was destroyed on cross-examination. The defendant was acquitted and then went out and raped and killed a woman in the same elevator in the same building about three weeks later. It was terribly painful. I knew the weight of that case was in my hands, and it was predictable to the detectives and all of us who worked on the case that this was the right guy—whether or not the victim could articulate the reasons why—and that he was a very, very dangerous man. I've taken plea bargains from defendants, settling for eight-year sentences rather than lose the cases altogether. Then the guy does his eight years and gets out and attacks somebody else. And you think to yourself, maybe if I had got 20 years . . .

Q. Rape is not sex, it's violence. Doesn't spending the better part of your professional life seeing sex mixed up with violence affect your attitude?

A. The professional has a very dark side, but I'm blessed with a life outside this job that's very bright, a wonderful marriage, a great family and great friends.

Q. When you leave the courthouse at night, do you look around every corner? Do you expect someone to jump out of the bushes?

A. You can't get paranoid, but this business has given me a healthier awareness. I tend to protect myself a little better. Not every corner, but I'm fairly cautious.

Q. After seeing thousands of rape cases, what would you tell a woman to do—talk back, be quiet, knee him in the groin?

A. It depends. Screaming, if you're in the lower tunnel in the bowels of Grand Central station and there's nobody around to hear you, does nothing more than aggravate the offender, and he uses more force. I've had women who have seen someone close enough—perhaps within earshot—and a scream and a kick in the groin worked to send the offender packing. I've never had self-defense training, but I've heard from many women that it gives them confidence about confronting the situation. Some have successfully talked people down from rape.

Q. Has sex in movies and TV programs, in sitcoms where teenage boys get laughs for seducing teenage girls, increased the number of rape incidents?

A. I haven't seen rapes that have occurred because of someone seeing a movie or TV show, but I certainly think the attitude that pervades those images takes its toll on some men's thinking.

Q. A pamphlet on date rape published by Swarthmore College says acquaintance rape "spans the spectrum of incidents and behavior ranging from crime legally defined as rape to verbal harassment and inappropriate innuendo." Isn't that going too far?

A. Terrible. It minimizes the traumatic nature of a forced act of intercourse by equating it to something that may upset the person, but it's not nearly on the level with acquaintance rape. I've been on campuses lecturing when people called kisses that are forced on you rape, but it is not, and it does a terrible disservice to rape survivors.

Q. Do you have more women in the sex-crimes unit? Do you find that women dealing with women is better?

A. We've had a very good mix traditionally over the years, but at the moment we have 14 women and two men. There are a lot of women now in the D.A.'s office. When I first came, there were only six women out of 200 in the D.A.'s office.

Q. Have you ever thought about private practice? You could be sitting in some mahogany-paneled office, Oriental rugs on the floor, a silver tea service instead of warm diet Coke from the vending machine and leftover plastic cups half-filled with day-old Slim Fast.

A. If I ever get up and don't want to come to work, maybe. But that's never happened in 19 years. And I'm lucky to have a very generous husband. The office has come such a long way. In 1972 there were 18 convictions in sexual-assault cases in New York City's five counties, and now, I think, the five counties combined have several hundred successful convictions every year. Women can recover from rape, from the hopelessness and from the feeling that the guy will never be punished. Recovery is helped immensely by a conviction.

BATTERED WOMAN SYNDROME: TWO VIEWS

As legal rules have changed to offer greater protection to female victims of violence, some experts have begun to charge that the rights of men may now be at risk. No change in legal practice raises these concerns more than the growing willingness of courts to allow women accused of assaulting or killing their husbands or boyfriends to claim that their previous battering at the hands of their victim lessened their responsibility for their actions. This is the so-called battered woman syndrome defense, and it holds that women who have suffered continuous physical and/or emotional abuse act in self-defense when they strike out at their batterers.

The legal point at issue is that of "immediate cause." When battered women do strike back, they often choose a moment when their batterer is asleep or otherwise unable to use force against them. As a result, when they plead self-defense, they must show that, even though they were in no *immediate* danger, they were nonetheless trying to protect themselves. This is where the "battered woman syndrome" comes in as a key part of the defense strategy. Critics of its admissability in court, such as Gerard Caplan, a law professor at George Washington University, believe that the defense gives women a virtual license to kill, since all a woman need do is claim that her victim had physically or emotionally harmed her at some point in the past. Poet Ntozake Shange, on the contrary, sees the "immediate cause" standard upheld by Caplan as depriving women of any chance to protect themselves.

BATTERED WIVES, BATTERED JUSTICE
Gerald Caplan

The rules of self-defense, so long a settled part of our law, may be changing for "battered" women who have killed their husbands. Some courts, relying on expert-witness testimony from feminist psychologists, have enlarged the defense to allow acquittals in cases which otherwise would have ended in manslaughter or murder convictions. In Ohio, outgoing Governor Richard Celeste commuted the sentences of 25 battered women who had finally attacked their husbands, and other governors are thinking of following suit.

The prosecution of Janice Leidholm is illustrative. Janice was charged with murdering her husband, Chester, in the early morning hours of August 7, 1981, at their farmhouse near Washburn, North Dakota. The Leidholms had, in the words of the North Dakota Supreme Court, a volatile marriage, "filled with a mixture of alcohol abuse, moments of kindness toward one another, and moments of violence." The homicide itself followed a rather tepid alcoholic argument—"Chester was shouting and Janice was crying"—during which Chester prevented Janice from calling the police by "shoving her away and pushing her down." Eventually the quarrel subsided and they went to bed; once Chester was asleep, Janice arose, secured a butcher knife, and in a few minutes, "from shock and loss of blood," Chester was dead.

An inventive lawyer might have tried to jiggle these facts into a temporary-insanity defense, a suspect diagnosis often employed to camouflage ordinary rage in appealing forensic garb. (It was used successfully in the famous "burning bed" case, where the defendant poured gasoline around her husband's bed and set fire to him as he slept in alcoholic stupor.) Instead, defense counsel advanced a theory that should have been curtly dismissed by the court. He argued self-defense "in reaction

BATTERED WIVES, BATTERED JUSTICE   From Gerald Caplan, "Battered Wives, Battered Justice," *The National Review* 25 Feb. 1991: 39–43. Copyright © by National Review Inc., 150 East 35th Street, New York, NY 10016. Reprinted by permission.

to severe mistreatment" by Chester over the years. Under longstanding legal principles, this was no defense. For one thing, evidence of Chester's past brutality would
be inadmissible—Chester was not on trial—unless it illuminated the events immediately preceding the killing. If Janice could show that as a result of past beatings, she
had learned to see signs of impending attacks that would not be apparent to an
untutored observer, only then could she detail her victimization for the jury. But
since even the most imaginative attorney could not argue that Chester, asleep, was
mounting an attack, Janice was not entitled to argue self-defense.

Inexplicably, the trial judge ruled otherwise. He both admitted the evidence of
prior abuse and instructed the jury on self-defense. More surprising, on appeal the
North Dakota Supreme Court not only agreed but, in reversing Janice Leidholm's
manslaughter conviction, held that on retrial she was entitled to a far more favorable
instruction on the law of self-defense. As the instruction had been given at her trial,
the jury was to decide whether Janice had behaved reasonably, like a person of
ordinary prudence and circumspection. That was wrong, the North Dakota
Supreme Court held. The true test was whether she had acted reasonably according
to *her* standards.

REASONABLE VIOLENCE?

This is no minor distinction. Since Janice depicted herself as having little self-esteem,
and being so dependent upon Chester that she was unable to leave him, the test—
what might be called "the reasonable battered wife" standard—is a contradiction in
terms. It makes no sense to define "the reasonable person" in terms that themselves
evidence unreasonableness—e.g., "hot-blooded," "impulsive," "helpless." What is
the reasonable violent person, or the reasonable helpless person? More important,
defining the legal standard subjectively deprives it of its value for making moral
judgments, for deciding whether Janice Leidholm is blameworthy.

In any case, under any definition of reasonableness, the reasonable thing for Janice to have done was to leave Chester, not kill him.

Why Janice didn't do so is unclear. One possibility—perhaps the most obvious
one—is that things were not as bad as she said. Another, offered by some feminist
psychologists, is that Janice suffered from "battered-woman syndrome."

Dr. Lenore Walker, the inventor of this concept, claims that victims of battered-
woman syndrome are unable to leave their abusers even when circumstances permit.
According to Dr. Walker, over time a battered wife despairs of being able to control
her husband's violence. "Repeated batterings, like electrical shocks, diminish . . .
[her] motivation to respond." The victim gives up and settles into a languid state of
"learned helplessness," a concept Dr. Walker borrowed from laboratory experiments
which showed that dogs subjected to repeated shocks eventually become too dispir-
ited to accept opportunities to escape.

Dr. Walker has written three books, most recently, *Terrifying Love: Why Battered
Women Kill and How Society Responds.* More troublingly, she has been a witness in
over 150 criminal cases.

As a witness, Dr. Walker's approach is to depict the battered woman as "just like
you and me" and to denounce as prejudice or ignorance any hint that battered wives
are other than victims of circumstance. There is, she asserts, "nothing special about
their personalities." Experience, of course, suggests the opposite: that most women
have enough sense to leave a man before he lands the first blow—or, at least,

immediately thereafter. Dr. Walker disagrees. "Any woman" who meets up with the wrong man "is in danger of becoming a battered woman."

This is either poor social science or empathy caricatured; and may explain why Dr. Walker has been able to find self-defense in cases that the layman would recognize as first-degree murder. In one, a wife, though separated from her husband, hired a hit man, lured her husband back into the house, and, after the hired killer had fired two shots, yelled to him, "He's not dying fast enough—hit him again." Fortunately, in that case, the court excluded Dr. Walker's testimony as irrelevant.

But common sense is often left outside the courtroom door. In another case, involving a woman who shot her sleeping husband twice, following his threat to kill their baby, the expert witness, Julie Blackman, argued that the wife "exhibited characteristics of . . . [battered-woman] syndrome. . . . I emphasized . . . [her] unsuccessful attempts to leave the relationship . . . [and] although the [husband's] threat did not closely precede . . . [the killing] . . . she reported that she had relived her fear as she stood at the foot of the bed and fired the gun into her husband's sleeping body." It worked. The wife, incredibly, was acquitted on grounds of self-defense.

Although Dr. Walker acknowledges that battered women do exhibit "bizarre" behavior, she attributes this to their victimization. Once free of their husbands, "most . . . cease to manifest any so-called behavioral disturbances or personality disorders, [proving] that . . . their previously abnormal behavior was directly caused by their victimization." A homicide by a battered woman is "simply a terrified human being's *normal* response to an abnormal and dangerous situation."

All this sounds more like tract than treatise (and Dr. Walker, in her professional success, reminds one of the missionaries who went to Hawaii to do good and wound up doing well). Reduced to its essence, battered-woman syndrome is not a physician's diagnosis but an advocate's invention. It means: Blame the deceased.

Unfortunately, the term has received judicial recognition. The early decisions did exclude expert testimony on battered-woman syndrome as unscientific. The District of Columbia Court of Appeals, for example, cited Dr. Walker's remark—"I tend to place all men in an especially negative light"— as evidence of bias; and the Wyoming Supreme Court accused her of reaching her conclusions before "engag[ing] in research . . . to substantiate those theories." But as Dr. Walker and others continued to publish, judicial resistance wilted. Most courts now allow expert testimony on battered-woman syndrome (just this year, the Ohio Supreme Court reversed a decade-old precedent to admit it), and a few have swallowed Dr. Walker's "learned helplessness" adaptation in one gulp. The New Jersey Supreme Court, for example, mimicked Dr. Walker by finding that battered women "become so demoralized and degraded by the fact that they cannot predict or control the violence that they sink into a state of psychological paralysis and become unable to take any action at all to improve or alter the situation."

Of course, such reasoning doesn't explain how women who are that helpless manage to stab their husbands repeatedly in the chest with butcher knives, shoot them at close range, or hire hit men to do the job. Nor does it explain why, if battered women are capable of such violent actions, they are incapable of non-homicidal responses such as leaving the house.

Far-fetched as Dr. Walker's theories are, however, one can't read many accounts of abused women without wanting to say something on their behalf. The small number of battered women who kill should not be grouped with the premeditated murderer or hired killer. Many acted only after years of cruelty. The killing was an outburst, the accumulation of years of rage. Even when the victim was, like Chester, asleep, his death may not have been the product of calculation. A woman just abused may be unable to calm herself (as the law requires) once the moment of danger has passed. Nor is flight always possible. Some women don't flee their homes because no safe port exists where an enraged husband can't find them or their children; they are cornered, and, so cornered, they are explosive.

But this is learned violence, not helplessness. Lenore Walker's insistence that killing "out of anger would be a male's response" is wrong; the impulse to retaliate is universal. "If one allows that the accumulated irritation of a working day can be . . . [discharged] by kicking the dog," writes psychiatrist Anthony Storr, there is no reason why more serious grievances "should not be stored for much longer, perhaps even a lifetime"; and, at times, produce outbursts like Janice Leidholm's, disproportionately savage to the immediate provocation, but revenging a history of victimization.

Under modern law, however, such acts are forbidden. The law holds a monopoly on punishment, requiring the victim to seek its protection. Janice was expected to give evidence to convict Chester. But if Janice was like most, she didn't want Chester put away, only better behaved, and refused to cooperate once an arrest rendered him contrite. And if the North Dakota police were like most, they quickly tired of responding to domestic-violence calls from the same household. Even if indefatigable, they had no legal way of preventing a determined man from attacking his wife.

Victims like Janice don't often appreciate this. Probably Janice thought the legal system incapable of effectively taking her side. Perhaps, like Bernhard Goetz, she had become unhinged by its failure to protect her in the past. Perhaps she believed that her status as one who has been repeatedly victimized accorded her greater rights to look after herself. But regardless of what Janice believed, she was not entitled to acquittal; death is not the penalty the law assigned for Chester's offenses.

Judges who allow expert testimony on battered-woman syndrome don't fully understand this. They install, perhaps unwittingly, an escape route lacking a scientific predicate and appealing to popular prejudice. And judges who allow a jury to find self-defense where the victim was asleep, or eating or bathing, or otherwise unoffending when slain ignore long-settled, dearly won legal principles evincing respect for life.

WITH NO IMMEDIATE CAUSE

Ntozake Shange

every 3 minutes a woman is beaten
every five minutes a
woman is raped/every ten minutes
a lil girl is molested

WITH NO IMMEDIATE CAUSE   From Ntozake Shange, "With No Immediate Cause," *Nappy Edges* (New York: St. Martins, 1991) 114–17. Copyright © 1972, 1974, 1975, 1976, 1977, 1978 by Ntozake Shange.

yet i rode the subway today
i sat next to an old man who
may have beaten his old wife
3 minutes ago or 3 days/30 years ago
he might have sodomized his
daughter but i sat there
cuz the young men on the train
might beat some young women
later in the day or tomorrow
i might not shut my door fast
enuf/push hard enuf
every 3 minutes it happens
some woman's innocence
rushes to her cheeks pours from her mouth
like the betsy wetsy dolls have been torn
apart/their mouths
menses red & split/every
three minutes a shoulder
is jammed through plaster and the oven door
chairs push thru the rib cage hot water or
boiling sperm decorate her body
i rode the subway today
& bought a paper from a
man who might
have held his old lady onto
a hot pressing iron/i dont know
maybe he catches lil girls in the
park & rips open their behinds
with steel rods/i can't decide
what he might have done i only
know every 3 minutes
every 5 minutes every 10 minutes/so
i bought the paper
looking for the announcement
the discovery/of the dismembered
woman's body/the
victims have not all been
identified/today they are
naked and dead/refuse to
testify/one girl out of 10's not
coherent/i took the coffee
& spit it up/i found an
announcement/not the woman's
bloated body in the river/floating
not the child bleeding in the
59th street corridor/not the baby
broken on the floor/

"there is some concern
that alleged battered women
might start to murder their
husbands & lovers with no
immediate cause"
i spit up i vomit i am screaming
we all have immediate cause
every 3 minutes
every 5 minutes
every 10 minutes
every day
women's bodies are found
in alleys & bedrooms/at the top of the stairs
before i ride the subway/buy a paper/drink
coffee/i must know/
have you hurt a woman today
did you beat a woman today
throw a child across a room
     are the lil girl's panties
     in yr pocket
did you hurt a woman today

i have to ask these obscene questions
the authorities require me to
establish
immediate cause

every three minutes
every five minutes
every ten minutes
every day.

Part Four

Sweethearts and Wives

"I AM OPTIMISTIC . . . FOR THE FUTURE OF LIBERATED MARRIAGE . . . BECAUSE IT ALLOWS BOTH PARTIES MORE OPTIONS."

—CARYL RIVERS

Love and marriage may go together like a horse and carriage, as the popular song asserts, but the ride has not always been smooth, especially for women. "In America," Alexis de Tocqueville wrote in the widely read *Democracy in America* (1835), "the independence of woman is irrecoverably lost in the bonds of matrimony." The French observer viewed this loss as necessary, but the American women and men who issued the *Declaration of Sentiments* (1848) at Seneca Falls just a few years later thought otherwise.

The *Declaration* inveighed against the fact that a married woman had no right to property, not even to her own wages; that she was required to promise obedience to her husband, who became her master; that she was forced into dependence; and that in cases of separation or divorce, the husband was given custody of children as well as property. In other words, when she married, a woman exchanged the rule and name of her father for the rule and name of her husband. (It is still common for the father of the bride to "give her away" to her prospective husband.) "He has made her, if married," one article of the *Declaration* stated, "in the eye of the law, civilly dead."

Work site and home site were the same in the rural economy of the early Republic, but the development of the market economy in the nineteenth century changed the family from a unit of production to one of consumption. Husbands went off to factories and offices, leaving wives behind to do the work of the house. For a great number of women, marriage and motherhood became the only vocation open to them, the only way to achieve economic security.

Magazines and advice books assured women that they would find total fulfill-ment in housework and child care. As "angels in the house," they maintained a refuge from the public world for their husbands. By reinforcing ideals of female domesticity, piety, submissiveness, conformity, and sexual purity, popular publications attempted to hold the line against changing values. Courtship became the main activity of the marriage market, and women learned to alter their own preferences and even their personalities in order to shape themselves to potential suitors.

Scarlett O'Hara, for instance, the spirited and independent heroine of Margaret Mitchell's best-seller of 1936, *Gone with the Wind*, got tired of "being unnatural" in order to find a husband. "I'm tired of saying, 'How wonderful you are!' to fool men who haven't got one-half the sense I've got, and I'm tired of pretending I don't know anything, so men can tell me things and feel important while they're doing it," she complained. Until recently, even the entrance of women into higher education had not substantially affected this charade: Hollywood films of the 1930s and 1940s often presented the college campus as a place where women went to pursue the M.R.S. degree rather than the B.A. The hit Broadway musical of 1946, *Annie Get Your Gun,* in which Annie Oakley sang "You Can't Get a Man with a Gun," echoes the perceived need for women to downplay their own abilities in order to be unthreatening and therefore attractive to men.

As the practical aims of marriage combined with the growing ideal of romantic love, weddings became formal public events. By the twentieth century, businesses specializing in wedding products and services had been established. Brides' magazines proliferated, offering guidance on everything from the most fashionable patterns of china and silverware to the kinds of canapés to serve at the reception. The trappings of the event were matters for comparison and often overshadowed the seriousness of the commitment.

These middle-class wedding customs reflected the influence of "romantic love," which was itself in part an expression of the increasing freedom to choose one's mate. But love did not quite conquer all. It did not, for example, conquer differences in social and economic class. Alliances with the poor, especially with those who were immigrants or non-white, were discouraged on the grounds that they might weaken the race and lead to lower moral standards. It was by playing into this perception that the heroine of *Stella Dallas*, a best-seller and subsequently a long-running radio serial, persuades her daughter to live with her father and his second wife in their mansion. The question the popular radio soap opera of the 1940s, *Our Gal Sunday*, posed—Could a girl from a small mining town in the West find happiness married to a titled Englishman?—also reflected this class bias.

Married women who took work into their homes or who worked outside did so out of economic necessity, but they remained responsible for domestic tasks as well. The current paradigm of the "superwoman," who holds a full-time job in addition to performing all domestic chores, is by no means a contemporary phenomenon. But the "ideal" wife did not work outside the home. At the turn of the century, economist Thorstein Veblen described such women of the leisure class as displayers of wealth and idleness, both of which served to verify their husbands' social and economic status. Charlotte Perkins Gilman viewed all dependent wives as combinations of housemaids and prostitutes. "The transient trade we think evil," she wrote in

Women and Economics (1898), "the bargain for life we think good."

The experiences of African-American women differed markedly from those of their white middle-class sisters, not only because they suffered the effects of racism, but also because, as slaves, they had been perceived primarily as workers. In spite of the popular stereotypes of the domestic Mammy and Aunt Jemima, most women slaves were field-workers; their domestic lives in the slave quarters were in many ways a respite from the oppression of owners and overseers. After Emancipation, African-American women entered domestic service in great numbers, making it possible for white women of leisure to avoid such chores.

The social pressure to marry was so intense that women who chose not to commit themselves to men were considered unfortunate or deviant. Unmarried women—called spinsters or old maids—were allowed into the domestic hierarchy to do women's work in the homes of relatives in order to "earn their keep." Others entered teaching, a profession which did not allow females to marry, or religious orders. At the turn of the century, approximately four times as many women as men were in religious orders in the Boston area.

Extant marriage contracts from the nineteenth century indicate that egalitarian marriages were possible, although rare, since such agreements violated the social norm. The marriage contract of Lucy Stone and Henry Blackwell is perhaps the best known, although Stone did give up her career for five years after the birth of their daughter. The more recent popularity of such prenuptial agreements is based more on economics, on the recognition that marriage is not always permanent, and on the growing acceptance of serial marriage. As life spans have lengthened, married people have found it more difficult to maintain certain commitments, and divorce, once a scandal of no small proportion, has become common.

Of course, divorce was not unknown in the nineteenth century, and its effects on women often were devastating: Fanny Fern, for instance, was left penniless after her divorce from her second husband. Lucy Stone, Elizabeth Cady Stanton, and Susan B. Anthony, among other leaders of the suffrage movement, strongly favored the liberalization of divorce laws because of their negative economic effects on women. "While in most states the divorce laws are the same for men and women," wrote Susan B. Anthony in 1897, "they never can bear equally upon both while all the property earned during marriage belongs wholly to the husband."

During the sixty years from 1867 to 1927, the rate of divorce increased 2000 percent. At the same time, as women outlived men, the number of widows also increased; these divorced and widowed women often found themselves limited by the dependent roles that they had accepted in their marriages. Today they are called "displaced homemakers," women who, without husbands and without marketable skills, have been left with little or no means of support.

But even within the constraints of marriage, many women led active and productive lives as members of female networks, providing volunteer services to their communities and mutual support in times of need. In light of the circumscribed roles they were expected to play, the achievements of married women such as Elizabeth Cady Stanton, Angelina Grimké, Harriet Beecher Stowe, Edith Wharton, and Eleanor Roosevelt were extraordinary indeed, even when their class advantages are considered.

Still, historically, marriage has meant the acceptance of a double standard for women. Women were destined for one occupation; men for many. Women were bred to dependence; men to independence. Wives were expected to be pure and faithful; husbands were expected to have "sown their wild oats" and to have minor—or major—dalliances.

The popular image of the happy housewife may not be as pervasive now as it has been in the past, but it seems to hover below the surface of events, ready to be resurrected in times of social or economic necessity. "Marriage is a great institution," said Mae West, "but I'm not ready for an institution yet." And neither are many women and men who see marriage as a partnership of equals, a partnership in which the independence of women is *not* "irrecoverably lost in the bonds of matrimony." Love and marriage still go together like a horse and carriage, perhaps, but more and more women are learning to drive.

ANNIE OAKLEY
Bonnie Kreps

Annie Moses (1860–1926) stood less than five feet tall and weighed under one hundred pounds. As a teenager, the story goes, she earned enough by selling the game she shot (the birds were always shot through the head) to pay off the mortgage on her widowed mother's farm.

When she was fifteen she won a sharpshooting competition against Frank Butler and, about a year later, she married him. Together they put on shooting demonstrations, and Butler, who was ten years older than Annie, taught her to read. It was at this time that she changed her last name to Oakley, the name of a Cincinnati suburb.

In 1885, Butler and Oakley joined Buffalo Bill's Wild West Show, and for the next seventeen years, they toured the United States and Europe. Oakley became famous, and Butler became her manager. Graceful and soft-spoken offstage, Oakley often did needlework in her tent between performances. Sitting Bull thought of her as an adopted daughter and gave her a Native American name meaning "Little Miss Sure Shot."

The following account, which appeared in a popular "self-help" book, compares the lives of Annie Oakley and Frank Butler with the depiction of their lives in the Irving Berlin musical *Annie Get Your Gun*. The musical opened on Broadway with Ethel Merman in the title role on May 16, 1946, ran for 1,147 performances, and was made into a movie with Betty Hutton and Howard Keel in 1950. The lyrics to some of the most popular songs from the musical give some indication of how Oakley's life was reinterpreted for the benefit of this entertainment. Berlin's Annie learns to suppress her talents to please a man, a process Kreps labels the "Annie Oakley Complex."

It is not a fact that "You Can't Get a Man with a Gun," for instance, since that is exactly what the historical Annie Oakley did. The musical appeared soon after the end of World War II, however, when women were encouraged to return home, leaving the work they had done while the men were gone. Thus, "The Girl That I Marry Will Have to Be As Soft and As Sweet As a Nursery"—not as strong and capable as a welder, for instance—was again the popular image. In any case, Annie Oakley was an internationally known sharpshooter and Frank Butler her capable manager; together they lived happily ever after. They died in 1926, eighteen days apart, and are both buried in the Moses plot in Ohio.

To be an autonomous woman is to live on the horns of the dilemma created by men's fear of a woman who is both competent and sexual, and that is indeed to be all mixed up. Which is why those of us who most want to achieve and who are most capable of doing so are prone to develop the Annie Oakley Complex.

But wait . . . a closer look reveals that there are *two* Annie Oakleys. There's the Annie of the boisterous musical *Annie Get Your Gun* and there's the Annie Oakley on whose life that musical purports to be based. Never was fiction more opposed to reality than in this complete falsification of her life. The artificial contrast created between fiction and fact is useful, however, because it tells us much about the Annie Oakley Complex and even more about romantic love.

Fiction: According to the musical, Annie is a rough country bumpkin whose skill with guns is so phenomenal that she can outshoot any man. She's discovered by Buffalo Bill, who makes her a star of his Wild West Show. The ace shooter of that show is Frank Butler, with whom Annie falls in love on sight. Hopelessly, as it turns out,

ANNIE OAKLEY   From Bonnie Kreps, *Loving Without Losing Your Self* (Los Angeles: RGA, 1992) 77–81. Copyright © 1992 by The RGA Publishing Group, Inc. Reprinted by permission.

because he despises her for not being the kind of woman he would want to marry. . . . They become a shooting team, but not for long, because Butler is so disturbed by Annie's superior prowess that he leaves to join rival Pawnee Bill's show. Annie goes on to become a solo sensation with the Buffalo Bill Show in Europe. On her triumphant return a contest is arranged between her and Butler to determine once and for all who is the champion. Realizing that "You Can't Get a Man with a Gun," Annie deliberately loses. Whereupon Butler, now able to see her as a woman, joins her in the romantic union that is the musical's rousing finale.

Fact: The true story of Annie Oakley is that she actually *did* "get" her man with a gun. She was fifteen in 1875 when she first met Frank Butler, then twenty-five and a ranking sharpshooter of the time. They met in order to compete against each other in a specially arranged match. Here is Butler's own account of this match and its outcome:

> I was shooting with a show and meeting all comers on the outside with my shotgun. . . .
> On reaching Cincinnati we put up at a hotel where farmers stopped. Some of the guests
> heard we could shoot and soon I was tackled by one who wanted to know what I could
> do. I told him I could beat anything then living, save Carver and Bogardus. He said he
> had an unknown who would shoot me . . . ten days from that time for $100 a side. I
> laughed and took the bet, barring only the two men mentioned. . . . From the day this
> match was made until I went I had heard nothing more. . . . I almost dropped dead
> when a little slim girl in short dresses stepped out to the mark with me. . . . I never shot
> better in my life. Never were the birds so hard for two shooters as they flew from us,
> but never did a person make more impossible shots than did that little girl. She killed
> twenty-three and I killed twenty-one. It was her first big match—my first defeat.
> The next day I came back to see the little girl who had beaten me, and it was not long
> until we were married.

Although Butler is said to have quipped that he married Annie because, "It was the only way I could get my money back," they came as close to living happily ever after as real life allows. Their marriage was often described as idyllic during the fifty years they worked and traveled together, Annie as a famous shot and Frank as her manager. She did join the Buffalo Bill Show, in 1885, but Frank never performed there during the more than seventeen years when she was the show's sensation in America and Europe, earning a reputed weekly salary of $1,000. Frank's devotion to Annie is apparent in the many poems he wrote to her, as it is in the many interviews printed in the press. They had no children but gave a lot of money to the children of relatives; they also made large donations to charities caring for poor children. In the spring of 1926 they moved back to Ohio. This was where Will Rogers visited them. He told his public:

> I went out to see Annie Oakley the other day as I was playing in Dayton, Ohio. She
> lives there with her husband, Frank Butler, and her sister. Her hair is snow white. She is
> bedridden from an auto accident a few years ago. I have talked with Buffalo Bill
> cowboys who were with the show for years, and they worshipped her. . . . I want you to
> write to her, all of you who remember her, and those that can go see her. Her address is
> 706 Lexington Avenue, Dayton, Ohio. She will be a lesson to you. She is a greater
> character than she was a rifle shot.

Rogers might well have said the same of Frank Butler. These two remarkable people, who died within eighteen days of each other in 1926, are a far greater lesson in love than Tristan and Iseult. Unfortunately, rather than learning from their example, we have instead seen fit to bury them in history while character-assassinating them in the legends of Americana.

Why was the true love story of Annie Oakley and Frank Butler discarded as the basis for the musical? Because that story is not romantic. The true story does not contain the proper elements of a script that defines the situation, names the actors, and plots their behavior so that something romantic happens. *Annie Get Your Gun*, on the other hand, contains all of these elements. It's practically a textbook case of how autonomous people, be they female or male, must adjust the picture of themselves in order for romance to blossom. In fact, *all three* major elements of the true story between Annie and Frank had to be changed in order to create . . . romance. . . .

Thus the extraordinary whole human being who was Annie Oakley is bolted to the commonplace that is the feminine stereotype: a woman who assumes a mask of inferiority by deliberately lying about her competence. The equally extraordinary human being who was Frank Butler is likewise bolted to the commonplace that is the masculine stereotype: a strutting man, whose "masculine pride" requires him at all times to maintain the exhausting fiction that "Anything You Can Do I Can Do Better." And the mutually enhancing partnership of equals that was their love relationship is degraded into the sly politics of the ego that we call romance.

How does the Annie Oakley Complex work? The contrast between the Annie of fact and the Annie of fiction says it all. Here we have the real-life Annie, a many-sided woman who was described by the contemporary press in glowing terms: the "brilliant conversationalist" who also was "blithesome" and "vivacious"; the toast of European royalty who yet delighted people with her "unassuming manners and rare modesty"; the person of slight physical stature with "the low sweet voice" who also was "frank and genial" and possessed an "unusual force of character." In short, a full-fledged woman who never adjusted the picture of herself and nevertheless found love with a man who actively treasured her unstifled self until the day he died.

This woman's fictional counterpart . . . commits *faux pas* after grammatical blunder . . . [and] denigrates her phenomenal prowess. . . . In short, she is the gauche misfit who "proves" herself by diminishing that self; who affirms that the great quest of a woman's life is not to use her given talents to have a direct relationship with life but to stifle and dishonor those talents in order to find fulfillment with Mr. Right. The romantic lesson she learns is to graduate from the cheap but straightforward skirmish of "Anything You Can Do I Can Do Better" to the careful deceit of conquest and surrender.

WHY DON'T THE MEN PROPOSE?

T. H. Bayly

From its beginning in the 1830s, *Godey's Lady's Book* was the arbiter of taste and fashion for white middle-class women. Its famous editor, Sarah Josepha Hale, wielded the power of her office with care and discretion. Although she never fully supported the movement for women's rights, she did campaign for higher education for women, against tight corsets, and for the admission of women to the health professions. She also succeeded in keeping the Civil War out of the magazine.

Along with the moral tales, the articles of advice covering everything from food to furbelows, and the fashion plates, Hale included some poetry, usually uplifting or inspirational. The following poem, however, pokes gentle fun at the lengths to which some young women would go in order to elicit a proposal of marriage. The persona of the poem addresses her complaint to her mother, whom she considers her chief advisor in this campaign.

Why don't the men propose, mamma?
  Why don't the men propose?
Each seems coming to a point,
  And then away he goes!
It is no fault of yours, mamma,
  That every body knows;
You fete the finest men in town,
  Yet, oh! they won't propose!

I'm sure I've done my best, mamma,
  To make a proper match;
For coronets and eldest sons
  I'm ever on the watch;
I've hopes when some distingue beau
  A glance upon me throws:
And though he'll dance, and smile, and flirt,
  Alas! he won't propose!

I've tried to win by languishing
  And dressing like a blue;
I've bought big books, and talk'd of them
  As if I'd read them through!
With hair cropp'd like a man, I've felt
  The heads of all the beaux;
But Spurzheim could not touch their hearts,
  And oh! they won't propose.

I threw aside the books, and thought
  That ignorance was bliss;
I felt convinced that men preferred
  A simple sort of Miss;
And so I lisp'd out naught beyond
  Plain "yeses" or plain "noes,"
And wore a sweet unmeaning smile;
  Yet, oh, they won't propose!

Why Don't the Men Propose?   From T. H. Bayly, "Why Don't the Men Propose?" *Godey's Lady's Book* Feb. 1835: 85.

Last night, at Lady Ramble's rout,
   I heard Sir Harry Gale
Exclaim, "Now I propose again;"
   I started, turning pale;
I really thought my time was come,
   I blush'd like any rose;
But oh! I found 'twas only at
   Escarte he'd propose!

And what is to be done, mamma?
   Oh, what is to be done?
I really have no time to lose,
   For I am thirty-one;
At balls I am too often left
   Where spinsters sit in rows;
Why won't the men propose, mamma?
Why *won't* the men propose?

A MODEL HUSBAND

Fanny Fern

Sara Willis Payson Parton, or Fanny Fern (1811–1872), was a nationally known columnist and best-selling author of the mid-nineteenth century. The first collection of her periodical pieces, *Fern Leaves from Fanny's Port-Folio* (1853), sold 80,000 copies in the first year after its publication, a number comparable to a sale of 800,000 today. A *Second Series,* from which the following selection is taken, was published the next year.

Fanny Fern's work, which included novels as well as children's books, combines the sentimental tradition in literature with the journalistic tradition of social commentary. Her columns, ranging in subject matter from critiques of manners and fashion to analyses of the injustices suffered by married women, provide a kind of social history of her time. She makes fun of male pomposity, argues for intellectual equality, condemns excessive housework, and points out the double standards, all in a lively and colloquial style.

Fanny Fern was born in Portland, Maine, but her family moved to Boston soon after her birth. At the age of 26, she married and had three daughters before she was widowed. Unable to support herself and her children, she married again in 1849, but this marriage ended in divorce. She tried to support her family by taking work as a teacher and as a seamstress; she then began writing pieces for Boston papers. Her success was instantaneous, and after the publication of her collected pieces, Robert Bonner recruited her to write for the *New York Ledger*. In 1856, she married the biographer and journalist James Parton, who was eleven years her junior.

Fern's method often involved taking a text from a newspaper or other source and commenting on it. In the following piece, she quotes a short article concerning a "young Bloomer," that is, a follower of Amelia Bloomer, best known for designing the costume consisting of a short skirt over turkish trousers that came to be known as "bloomers." A number of women adopted this attire because it seemed better suited to their active life, but they abandoned it when it distracted from their message of equal rights for women.

"Mrs. Perry, a young Bloomer, has eloped from Monson, Massachusetts, with Levins Clough. When her husband found she was determined to go, he gave her one hundred dollars to start with."

A MODEL HUSBAND   From Fanny Fern, *Fern Leaves from Fanny's Port-Folio: Second Series* (Auburn, Buffalo: Miller, Orton & Mulligan, 1854) 116–17.

Magnanimous Perry! Had I been your spouse, I should have handed that "one hundred dollar bill" to Mr. Levins Clough, as a healing plaster for his disappointed affections—encircled your neck with my repentant arms, and returned to your home. Then, I'd mend every rip in your coat, gloves, vest, pants, and stockings, from that remorseful hour, till the millennial day. I'd hand you your cigar-case and slippers, put away your cane, hang up your coat and hat, trim your beard and whiskers, and wink at your sherry cobblers, whiskey punches, and mint juleps. I'd help you get a "ten strike" at ninepins. I'd give you a "night key," and be perfectly oblivious what time in the small hours you tumbled into the front entry. I'd pet all your stupid relatives, and help your country friends to "beat down" the city shopkeepers. I'd frown at all offers of "pin money." I'd let you "smoke" in my face till I was as brown as a herring, and my eyes looked as if they were bound with pink tape; and I'd invite that pretty widow Delilah Wilkins to dinner, and run out to do some shopping, and stay away till tea-time. Why! there's nothing I *wouldn't* do for you—you might have knocked me down with a feather, after such a piece of magnanimity. That "Levins Clough" could stand no more chance than a woodpecker tapping at an iceberg.

A LETTER FROM THE BATTLEFIELD
Sullivan Ballou

When the Ken Burns documentary on the Civil War aired on the Public Broadcasting System in the fall of 1991, part of the following letter was read on the first program of the series. The response was immediate and intense: Viewers wanted to hear the letter again, they wanted copies, and they wanted to know more about Ballou. Newspapers reprinted the letter in whole or in part to meet the public's needs, and some viewers, hungry for the "real thing," even wrote to Don Fehrenbacher, professor emeritus at Stanford University, who had originally sent the letter to Burns.

Major Sullivan Ballou, who had never served in battle, was a member of the 2nd Rhode Island unit. He wrote this letter to his wife, Sarah, on July 14, 1861. A week later, at the first Battle of Bull Run, July 21, 1861, he was killed.

Headquarters
Camp Clark
Washington D. C.

July 14th 1861

MY VERY DEAR WIFE,

The indications are very strong that we shall move in a few days perhaps tomorrow and lest I should not be able to write you again I feel impelled to write a few lines that may fall under your eye when I am no more. If it is necessary that I should fall on the battle field for my Country I am ready. I have no misgivings about or lack of

A LETTER FROM THE BATTLEFIELD From Sullivan Ballou, letter to Sarah Ballou, 14 July 1861, "Adin Ballou Papers," Illinois State Historical Library, Springfield, Illinois. Reprinted by permission. Punctuation and spelling regularized.

confidence in the course in which I am engaged, and my courage does not halt or falter. I know how American Civilization now leans upon the triumph of the Government and how great a debt we owe to those who went before us through the blood and suffering of the Revolution; and I am willing—perfectly willing—to lay down all my joys in this life to help maintain this Government and to pay that debt.

But my dear wife, when I know that with my own joys I lay down nearly all of yours, and replace them in this life with care and sorrow when after having eaten for long years the bitter fruit of orphanage myself, I must offer it as their only sustenance to my dear little children, is it weak or dishonourable that while the banner of purpose floats calmly and proudly in the breezes underneath my unbounded love for you my dear wife and children should struggle in fierce though useless contest with my love of country.

I cannot describe to you my feelings on this calm summer night when two thousand men are sleeping around me, many of them enjoying the last perhaps before that of Death. And I, suspicious that Death is creeping behind me with his fatal dart, am communing with God, my Country and thee. I have sought most closely and diligently and often in my breast for a wrong motive in thus hazarding the happiness of all that I love and I could not find one. A pure love of my Country and of the principles I have advocated before the people and the name of honour that I love more than I fear death have called upon me and I have obeyed. Sarah my love for you is deathless, it seems to bind me with mighty cables that nothing but Omnipotence can break. And yet my love of Country comes over me like a strong wind and bears me irresistibly with all those chains to the battle field. The memories of all the blissful moments I have enjoyed with you come crowding over me, and I feel most deeply grateful to God and you that I have enjoyed them so long. And how hard it is for me to give them up and turn to ashes the hopes of future years when, God willing, we might still have lived and loved together and seen our boys grow up to honourable manhood around us. I know I have but few claims upon Divine Providence but something whispers to me—perhaps it is the wafted prayer of my little Edgar—that I shall return to my loved ones unharmed. If I do not my dear Sarah never forget how much I loved you nor that when my last breath escapes me on the battlefield it will whisper your name. Forgive my many faults and the many pains I have caused you. How thoughtless how foolish I have sometimes been! How gladly would I wash out with my tears every little spot upon your happiness and struggle with all the misfortunes of the world to shield you and my children from harm, but I cannot. I must watch you from the spirit world and hover near you while you buffet the storms with your precious little freight—and wait with sad patience till we meet to part no more.

But Oh Sarah! if the dead can come back to this earth and flit unseen around those they love I shall be always with you in the brightest day and the darkest night amidst your happiest scenes and gloomiest hours <u>always</u> <u>always</u> and when the soft breeze fans your cheek it shall be my breath or the cool air your throbbing temple, it shall be my spirit passing by. Sarah do not mourn me dead. Think I am gone and wait for me for we shall meet again. As for my little boys they will grow up as I have done and never know a father's love and care.

Little Willie is too young to remember me long but my blue-eyed Edgar will keep my frolics with him among the dimmest memories of his childhood. Sarah, I have

unlimited confidences in your maternal care and your development of their characters. Tell my two mothers I call God's blessing upon them.

Oh! Sarah I wait for you <u>then</u> come to me and lead thither my children.

Sullivan

THE BRIDAL VEIL
Alice Cary

A lice Cary (1820–1871) was one of the most popular poets of the mid-nineteenth century.
Born in Ohio, she moved to New York to make her living by writing and was later joined
there by her sister, Phoebe, also a writer. The two established a literary salon that met at their
home regularly for fifteen years.

Cary, a strong supporter of abolition and of women's rights, was the first president of the
women's club now known as Sorosis. Her poems, novels, sketches, and short stories, which
were published in *Harper's,* the *Atlantic,* and *Putnam's* as well as in book form, reflected her
belief in the values of marriage and motherhood, but with some qualifications. The persona of
"The Bridal Veil," for instance, asks her husband to remember that she has "wings flattened
down and hid under my veil."

> We're married, they say, and you think you have won me,—
> Well, take this white veil from my head, and look on me:
> Here's matter to vex you, and matter to grieve you,
> Here's doubt to distrust you, and faith to believe you,—
> I am all as you see, common earth, common dew;
> Be wary, and mould me to roses, not rue!
>
> Ah! shake out the filmy thing, fold after fold,
> And see if you have me to keep and to hold,—
> Look close on my heart—see the worst of its sinning—
> It is not yours to-day for the yesterday's winning—
> The past is not mine—I am too proud to borrow—
> You must grow to new heights if I love you to-morrow.
>
> We're married! I'm plighted to hold up your praises,
> As the turf at your feet does its handful of daisies;
> That way lies my honor,—my pathway of pride,
> But, mark you, if greener grass grow either side,
> I shall know it, and keeping in body with you,
> Shall walk in my spirit with feet on the dew!
>
> We're married! Oh, pray that our love do not fail!
> I have wings flattened down and hid under my veil:
> They are subtle as light—you can never undo them,
> And swift in their flight—you can never pursue them,
> And spite of all clasping, and spite of all bands,
> I can slip like a shadow, a dream, from your hands.

THE BRIDAL VEIL   From Alice Cary, *Ballads, Lyrics, and Hymns* (Boston: Houghton Mifflin, 1865) 143–44.

Nay, call me not cruel, and fear not to take me,
I am yours for my lifetime, to be what you make me,—
To wear my white veil for a sign, or a cover,
As you shall be proven my lord, or my lover;
A cover for peace that is dead, or a token
Of bliss than can never be written or spoken.

HAPPY WOMEN
Louisa May Alcott

The stereotype of the single woman—usually called an old maid or a spinster—was that of a woman unable to attract a man for reasons of appearance, taste, or disposition. Often she became dependent on a relative, in whose home she filled the role of servant, caring for the children, nursing the sick, and performing other domestic tasks in exchange for room and board. Considered sexless, such women were often the object of pity and ridicule.

One of these spinsters, Louisa May Alcott (1832–1888), first found critical acceptance with *Hospital Sketches* (1863), an account of her time spent as a Civil War nurse, but she is probably best known as the author of *Little Women* (1868). In addition to her autobiographical, fictional, and poetic works, she wrote commentary on contemporary issues such as child labor, temperance, and suffrage. The following piece was published in the *New York Ledger*, the very popular paper which also published Fanny Fern's works.

One of the trials of woman-kind is the fear of being an old maid. To escape this dreadful doom, young girls rush into matrimony with a recklessness which astonishes the beholder; never pausing to remember that the loss of liberty, happiness, and self-respect is poorly repaid by the barren honor of being called "Mrs." instead of "Miss."

Fortunately, this foolish prejudice is fast disappearing, conquered by the success of a certain class belonging to the sisterhood. This class is composed of superior women who, from various causes, remain single, and devote themselves to some earnest work; espousing philanthropy, art, literature, music, medicine, or whatever task taste, necessity, or chance suggests, and remaining as faithful to and as happy in their choice as married women with husbands and homes. It being my good fortune to know several such, I venture to offer a little sketch of them to those of my young countrywomen who, from choice or necessity, stand alone, seeking to find the happiness which is the right of all.

Here is L., a rich man's daughter; pretty, accomplished, sensible, and good. She tried fashionable life and found that it did not satisfy her. No lover was happy enough to make a response in her heart, and at twenty-three she looked about her for something to occupy and interest her. She was attracted towards the study of medicine; became absorbed in it; went alone to Paris and London; studied faithfully; received her diploma, and, having practiced successfully for a time, was appointed the resident physician of a city hospital. Here, doing a truly womanly work, she finds no time for ennui, unhappiness, or the vague longing for something to fill heart and

HAPPY WOMEN   From Louisa May Alcott, "Happy Women," *New York Ledger* 11 Apr. 1868, rpt. in *Alternative Alcott,* ed. Elaine Showalter. (New Jersey: Rutgers UP, 1987) 203–06.

life, which leads so many women to take refuge in frivolous or dangerous amusements and pursuits. She never talks of her mission or her rights, but beautifully fulfils the one and quietly assumes the others. Few criticize or condemn her course, and none question her success. Respected and beloved by all who know her, she finds genuine satisfaction in her work, and is the busiest, happiest, most useful woman whom I know.

Next comes M., a brilliant, talented girl, full of energy, ambition, and noble aspirations. Poor, yet attractive, through natural gifts and graces, to her came the great temptation of such a girl's life—a rich lover; an excellent young man, but her inferior in all respects. She felt this, and so did he, but hoping that love would make them equals, he urged his suit.

"If I loved him," she said, "my way would be plain, and I should not hesitate a minute. But I do not; I've tried, and I am sure I *never* can feel toward him as I should. It is a great temptation, for I long to cultivate my talent to help my family, to see the world, and enjoy life, and all this may be done if I said 'Yes.' People tell me that I am foolish to reject this good fortune; that it is my duty to accept it; that I shall get on very well without love, and talk as if it were a business transaction. It is hard to say 'No'; but I *must,* for in marriage I want to look up, not down. I cannot make it seem right to take this offer, and I must let it go, for I dare not sell my liberty."

She made her choice, turned away from the pleasant future laid before her, and took up her load again. With her one talent in her hand she faced poverty, cheerfully teaching music, year after year; hoping always, complaining never, and finding herself a stronger, happier woman for that act: A richer woman also; for, though the husband was lost a true friend was gained—since the lover, with respect added to his love, said manfully, "She is right; God bless her!"

S. is poor, plain, ungifted, and ordinary in all things but one—a cheerful, helpful spirit, that loves its neighbor better than itself, and cannot rest till it has proved its sincerity. Few, so placed, would have lived forty hard, dull years without becoming either sharp and sour, or bitter and blue. But S. is as sweet and sunny as a child; and, to those who know her, the personification of content. The only talent she possesses is that of loving every helpless, suffering, forlorn and outcast creature whom she meets. Finding her round of home duties too small for her benevolence, she became one of the home missionaries, whose reports are never read, whose salaries are never paid of earth. Poverty-stricken homes, sick-beds, sinful souls, and sorrowing hearts attract her as irresistibly as pleasure attracts other women, and she faithfully ministers to such, unknown and unrewarded.

"I never had a lover, and I never can have you know. I'm *so* plain," she says, with a smile that is pathetic in its humility, its unconscious wistfulness.

She is mistaken here; for there are many to whom that plain face is beautiful, that helpful hand very dear. Her lovers are not of the romantic sort; but old women, little children, erring men, and forlorn girls give her an affection as endearing and sincere as any husband could have done. Few will know her worth here, but, in the long hereafter, I am sure S. will be blest with eternal beauty, happiness, and love.

A. is a woman of a strongly individual type, who in the course of an unusually varied experience has seen so much of what a wise man has called "the tragedy of modern married life," that she is afraid to try it. Knowing that for one of a peculiar nature like herself such an experiment would be doubly hazardous, she has obeyed instinct and become a chronic old maid. Filial and fraternal love must satisfy her, and grateful that such ties are possible, she lives for them and is content. Literature is a fond and faithful spouse, and the little family that has sprung up around her, though perhaps unlovely and uninteresting to others, is a profitable source of satisfaction to her maternal heart. After a somewhat tempestuous voyage, she is glad to find herself in a quiet haven whence she can look back upon her vanished youth and feel that though the blossom time of life is past, a little fruit remains to ripen in the early autumn coming on. Not lonely, for parents, brothers and sisters, friends and babies keep her heart full and warm; not idle, for necessity, stern, yet kindly teacher, has taught her the worth of work; not unhappy, for love and labor, like good angels, walk at either hand, and the divine Friend fills the world with strength and beauty for the soul and eyes that have learned to see it thankfully.

My sisters, don't be afraid of the words, "old maid," for it is in your power to make this a term of honor, not reproach. It is not necessary to be a sour, spiteful spinster, with nothing to do but brew tea, talk scandal and tend a pocket-handkerchief. No, the world is full of work, needing all the heads, hearts, and hands we can bring to do it. Never was there so splendid an opportunity for women to enjoy their liberty and prove that they deserve it by using it wisely. If love comes as it should come, accept it in God's name and be worthy of His best blessing. If it never comes, then in God's name reject the shadow of it, for that can never satisfy a hungry heart. Do not be ashamed to own the truth—do not be daunted by the fear of ridicule and loneliness, nor saddened by the loss of a woman's tenderest ties. Be true to yourselves; cherish whatever talent you possess, and in using it faithfully for the good of others you will most assuredly find happiness for yourself, and make of life no failure, but a beautiful success.

THE DREAM OF AN HOUR

Kate Chopin

Kate Chopin (1851–1904) was born in St. Louis and moved to New Orleans after her marriage to a Creole cotton broker. After her husband's death from swamp fever in 1883, Chopin returned to St. Louis with her six children and began to write. Her stories, which appeared in the leading popular magazines of the time, including *Harper's* and the *Atlantic Monthly*, were collected in *Bayou Folk* (1894) and *A Night in Acadie* (1897). Chopin also wrote three novels, the last of which, *The Awakening*, is probably the best known.

"The Dream of an Hour," which first appeared in *Vogue* magazine, is a brief but pointed story about the conflict between marriage and autonomy. Its surprise ending, a technique which was especially popular at the time, underscores the common tendency to interpret women's lives in patriarchal terms.

Knowing that Mrs. Mallard was afflicted with a heart trouble, great care was taken to break to her as gently as possible the news of her husband's death.

It was her sister Josephine who told her, in broken sentences; veiled hints that revealed in half concealing. Her husband's friend Richards was there, too, near her.

THE DREAM OF AN HOUR   From Kate Chopin, "The Dream of an Hour," *Vogue* Dec. 1894: 360.

It was he who had been in the newspaper office when intelligence of the railroad disaster was received, with Brently Mallard's name leading the list of "killed." He had only taken the time to assure himself of its truth by a second telegram, and had hastened to forestall any less careful, less tender friend in bearing the sad message.

She did not hear the story as many women have heard the same, with a paralyzed inability to accept its significance. She wept at once, with sudden, wild abandonment, in her sister's arms. When the storm of grief had spent itself she went away to her room alone. She would have no one follow her.

There stood, facing the open window, a comfortable, roomy armchair. Into this she sank, pressed down by a physical exhaustion that haunted her body and seemed to reach into her soul.

She could see in the open square before her house the tops of trees that were all aquiver with the new spring life. The delicious breath of rain was in the air. In the street below a peddler was crying his wares. The notes of a distant song which some one was singing reached her faintly, and countless sparrows were twittering in the eaves.

There were patches of blue sky showing here and there through the clouds that had met and piled one above the other in the west facing her window.

She sat with her head thrown back upon the cushion of the chair, quite motionless, except when a sob came up into her throat and shook her, as a child who has cried itself to sleep continues to sob in its dreams.

She was young, with a fair, calm face, whose lines bespoke repression and even a certain strength. But now there was a dull stare in her eyes, whose gaze was fixed away off yonder on one of those patches of blue sky. It was not a glance of reflection, but rather indicated a suspension of intelligent thought.

There was something coming to her and she was waiting for it, fearfully. What was it? She did not know; it was too subtle and elusive to name. But she felt it, creeping out of the sky, reaching toward her through the sounds, the scents, the color that filled the air.

Now her bosom rose and fell tumultuously. She was beginning to recognize this thing that was approaching to possess her, and she was striving to beat it back with her will—as powerless as her two white slender hands would have been.

When she abandoned herself a little whispered word escaped her slightly parted lips. She said it over and over under her breath: "free, free, free!" The vacant stare and the look of terror that had followed it went from her eyes. They stayed keen and bright. Her pulses beat fast, and the coursing blood warmed and relaxed every inch of her body.

She did not stop to ask if it were or were not a monstrous joy that held her. A clear and exalted perception enabled her to dismiss the suggestion as trivial.

She knew that she would weep again when she saw the kind, tender hands folded in death; the face that had never looked save with love upon her, fixed and gray and dead. But she saw beyond that bitter moment a long procession of years to come that would belong to her absolutely. And she opened and spread her arms out to them in welcome.

There would be no one to live for her during those coming years; she would live for herself. There would be no powerful will bending hers in that blind persistence with which men and women believe they have a right to impose a private will upon a fellow-creature. A kind intention or a cruel intention made the act seem no less a crime as she looked upon it in that brief moment of illumination.

And yet she had loved him—sometimes. Often she had not. What did it matter! What could love, the unsolved mystery, count for in face of this possession of self-assertion which she suddenly recognized as the strongest impulse of her being!

"Free! Body and soul free!" she kept whispering.

Josephine was kneeling before the closed door with her lips to the keyhole, imploring for admission. "Louise, open the door! I beg; open the door—you will make yourself ill. What are you doing, Louise? For heaven's sake open the door."

"Go away. I am not making myself ill." No; she was drinking in a very elixir of life through that open window.

Her fancy was running riot along those days ahead of her. Spring days, and summer days, and all sorts of days that would be her own. She breathed a quick prayer that life might be long. It was only yesterday she had thought with a shudder that life might be long.

She arose at length and opened the door to her sister's importunities. There was a feverish triumph in her eyes, and she carried herself unwittingly like a goddess of Victory. She clasped her sister's waist, and together they descended the stairs. Richards stood waiting for them at the bottom.

Some one was opening the front door with a latchkey. It was Brently Mallard who entered, a little travel-stained, composedly carrying his grip-sack and umbrella. He had been far from the scene of accident, and did not even know there had been one. He stood amazed at Josephine's piercing cry; at Richards' quick motion to screen him from the view of his wife.

But Richards was too late.

When the doctors came they said she had died of heart disease—of joy that kills.

HOW TO CHOOSE A WIFE

Alfred Henry Lewis

The following article was the first in a series which appeared in the *Illustrated Sunday Magazine*. The editors said the series was designed to balance the advice of women writers, most of them bachelor maids, "telling their humble sisters how to go about the difficult and somewhat dangerous task of choosing a husband."

Alfred Henry Lewis (d. 1914) was a popular writer at the turn of the century, Washington correspondent for the Chicago *Times*, and founder of *The Verdict*, a humorous New York weekly. He also wrote westerns and biographies.

There exists no doubt, I take it, as to the wisdom of wedlock. Is it not written among things holy, "Whoso findeth a wife, findeth a good thing"? Just as every man, to round out existence, should serve in one war, so should every man get married—once. Not that wars and wives have anything in common.

HOW TO CHOOSE A WIFE   From Alfred Henry Lewis, "How to Choose a Wife," *Illustrated Sunday Magazine of the Sunday Telegram* 3 Jan. 1909. Courtesy of the Worcester Historical Museum.

Aside from questions of instruction, and the wit-expanding effect of such experiment, there dwells self-safety not to say self-justice in marriage. Only married men succeed. The world's Washingtons, Jeffersons, Jacksons, Lincolns, Grants have one and all had wives. The bachelor, after thirty, is a suspect—like a fox in a barnyard. There was never but one President who was a bachelor, that was Buchanan; and we all know what nationally followed on the White House heels of Buchanan.

Yes, indeed, a man needs a wife for the same reason a statue needs a pedestal. She serves to keep him steady and morally perpendicular, and uplifts him so that he may be advantageously seen of men.

As the wharf is to the ship, so is the wife to her husband. Think of a ship with no place to start from, no place to return to and tie up! And yet that should be a picture of your bachelor—that Flying Dutchman of society. Wives are to husbands what seconds are to prize-fighters, and woe to him who finds himself in the ring of existence without one in his corner. A wife is her husband's best, and sometimes only, excuse for living. She is his endorser, without whom the world will refuse to take him at his face. She is the reason of all his virtues, two-thirds of his self-respect.

Having thus pleasantly and I should say sufficiently shown that a wife is a necessity, and has her place in nature with water, sun and air, the next thing is the business of choosing her. A nicer pencil might have said "art." But art is frivolous; business means the serious. I prefer therefore to call it "business"; for, if ever a man gets down to the practical affairs of life, it will be when he rides out to humanity in the herd, with a purpose of roping himself up a helpmeet.

There are certain prudent rules to be observed. No man, for one matter, should choose a wife unless the sun is up. Selecting a wife by candlelight is as full of risks as selecting silk by torchlight. And for your wife-picking, gas is no better than candles. What jeweler would buy diamonds after dark? Need I say more?

Proceeding then while the sun is shining, make sure that she is beautiful. Beauty, as a fact, in physiology, may be but skin deep; but its effects are not so superficial. I have said that you should be sure she is beautiful. Rather I should have phrased it: Be sure you think she is beautiful. There is a difference as well as a distinction. That great philosopher, the late Josh Billings, touched the profound core of what I would be at, in one of the issues of his almanac: Said he, "They do say love is blind, but I'm dinged if some fellows can't see more in their girls than I can."

Having—by consulting your own inner consciousness—settled that she is beautiful, carefully inquire out the measure of her riches. If she have more money than yourself, even if it be but a ten-dollar bill, go about on your heel and seek elsewhere. If she have enough to pay for her support, though her fortune should still sink below the level of your own, avoid her. And for these reasons. No woman can be so wholly pleased with a man as to make him, heart and soul, her husband, unless there be room in her destinies for her to need him, and rely upon him, and turn to him in those matters of bed and board and three meals a day, which together with the clothes on her back make up the bedplates of existence.

❧ ❧ ❧

Having considered her, whom you would make your soul's idol, for her beauty and her money-lack, look her over most heedfully with reference to her war-power. Our slant-skulled forbear, who went clothed of skins, ate his raw meat and saved his fire to pray to, was wont to keep the domestic peace with a club. Life was simpler then; albeit not so marvellously different from what it is today. Manners have changed; hearts haven't changed. Man nature, woman nature, husband nature, wife nature, one and all are now as they were in an age that beheld the cave bear, the saber-toothed tiger and the Irish elk. Look her over with reference to her power for war. Make sure that you can cope with her, and are stronger than is she.

No, you are not going to take a club to her. In our politer hour the mere thought of a club is odious. But all wars are not club wars. And while you and the lady in the case—so beautiful, so poor—are going to wed and live together and love each other until death doth you part, so also are you going to fight—a little.

She will begin it. Not because she hates you; not because she would hurt you; rather she will attack you simply to try you out. If you had a new staff, one upon which you must lean for the rest of your days, you would bear hard upon it, try its strength. So will a wife try the husband who must be her staff and her support.

And in that hour of domestic trial, see that you bear yourself doughtily and as a hero should. I lay down no program for your guidance; I may only tell you not to let her win. Mind you she doesn't want to win. Victory embarrasses, terrifies a woman. With the last word, what her instincts go groping for is a protector. To triumph would dissipate her dream. Concerning herself, she is sure of nothing except her own weakness. She lives proudly convinced that she cannot protect herself. What then must she feel, were she to find you—who should be as her sword and shield—her war-inferior? When that befalls you might better put out your hearth fire, destroy your habitation, and plow and sow its site with salt. Woman's love grows tallest, lives longest, when it looks up. It dies miserably if made to look down. And what is a husband conquered other than the dust beneath her little foot?

There, in its broader lines, I've covered this question of wife-choosing. There are minor details; but neither their importance nor my space encourages their present discussion. What, you would press me with queries! Her mentality? I am sure you may trust it to be as fine as your own. Money? It will in all chance be safer with her than with yourself. Her moral side? Prithee man, a word in thine ear! It is so sure to be a white improvement on your own that, between you and me, I'd say nothing about it.

THE WELL OF LONELINESS
Radclyffe Hall

When *The Well of Loneliness* was published in England in 1928, most readers and reviewers considered the novel about lesbianism to be obscene, and it was ultimately banned. Efforts to ban the book in the United States were less successful, and sales of over 20,000 copies made it a best-seller in 1929. Because of the furor caused by this, her first book, Hall (1856–1943) did not focus on lesbianism in any of her subsequent works.

Many American readers encountered lesbianism for the first time on the pages of *The Well of Loneliness*. The novel was often passed among young people secretly, and reading it became a kind of rite of passage. When Maya Angelou read it as a teenager, she questioned her own heterosexuality. Considered radical in the 1920s, Hall's analysis is considered outmoded today.

In the novel, Sir Philip, who had wanted a son, named his daughter Stephen. As she grew up, Stephen was allowed to dress up as Lord Nelson and to pursue activities that were considered "masculine." Sir Philip, sensing his daughter's difference, accepted her in a way that her mother, Anna, could not. In this excerpt, Martin, a friend of Stephen's, professes his love for her.

People gossiped a little because of the freedom allowed Martin and Stephen by her parents; but on the whole they gossiped quite kindly, with a great deal of smiling and nodding of heads. After all the girl was just like other girls—they almost ceased to resent her. Meanwhile Martin continued to stay on in Upton, held fast by the charm and the strangeness of Stephen—her very strangeness it was that allured him, yet all the while he must think of their friendship, not even admitting that strangeness. He deluded himself with these thoughts of friendship, but Sir Philip and Anna were not deluded. They looked at each other almost shyly at first, then Anna grew bold, and she said to her husband:

"Is it possible the child is falling in love with Martin? Of course he's in love with her. Oh, my dear, it would make me so awfully happy—" And her heart went out in affection to Stephen, as it had not done since the girl was a baby.

Her hopes would go flying ahead of events; she would start making plans for her daughter's future. Martin must give up his orchards and forests and buy Tenley Court that was now in the market; it had several large farms and some excellent pasture, quite enough to keep any man happy and busy. Then Anna would suddenly grow very thoughtful; Tenley Court was also possessed of fine nurseries, big, bright, sunny rooms facing south, with their bathroom, there were bars to the windows—it was all there and ready.

Sir Philip shook his head and warned Anna to go slowly, but he could not quite keep the great joy from his eyes, nor the hope from his heart. Had he been mistaken? Perhaps after all he had been mistaken—the hope thudded ceaselessly now in his heart.

🕊 🕊 🕊

Came a day when winter must give place to spring, when the daffodils marched across the whole country from Castle Morton Common to Ross and beyond, pitching camps by the side of the river. When the hornbeam made patches of green in the hedges, and the hawthorn broke out into small, budding bundles; when the old cedar tree on the lawn at Morton grew reddish pink tips to its elegant fingers; when the wild cherry trees on the sides of the hills were industriously putting forth both leaves and blossoms; when Martin looked into his heart and saw Stephen—saw her suddenly there as a woman.

Friendship! He marvelled now at his folly, at his blindness, his coldness of body and spirit. He had offered this girl the cold husks of his friendship, insulting her youth, her womanhood, her beauty—for he saw her now with the eyes of a lover. To a man such as he was, sensitive, restrained, love came as a blinding revelation. He knew little about women, and the little he did know was restricted to episodes that

THE WELL OF LONELINESS   From Radclyffe Hall, *The Well of Loneliness* (London: J. Cape, 1928) 96–101. Copyright © 1928 by Radclyffe Hall. Copyright renewed 1956 by Una Lady Troubridge. Reprinted by permission of Brandt & Brandt Literary Agents.

he thought best forgotten. On the whole he had led a fairly chaste life—less from scruple than because he was fastidious by nature. But now he was very deeply in love, and those years of restraint took their toll of poor Martin, so that he trembled before his own passion, amazed at its strength, not a little disconcerted. And being by habit a quiet, reserved creature, he must quite lose his head and become the reverse. So impatient was he that he rushed off to Morton very early one morning to look for Stephen, tracking her down in the end of the stables, where he found her talking to Williams and Raftery.

He said: "Never mind about Raftery, Stephen—let's go into the garden, I've got something to tell you." And she thought that he must have had bad news from home, because of his voice and his curious pallor.

She went with him and they walked on in silence for a while, then Martin stood still, and began to talk quickly; he was saying amazing, incredible things: "Stephen, my dear—I do utterly love you." He was holding out his arms, while she shrank back bewildered: "I love you, I'm deeply in love with you, Stephen—look at me, don't you understand me, beloved? I want you to marry me—you do love me, don't you?" And then, as though she had suddenly struck him, he flinched: "Good God! What's the matter, Stephen?"

She was staring at him in a kind of dumb horror, staring at his eyes that were clouded by desire, while gradually over her colourless face there was spreading an expression of the deepest repulsion—terror and repulsion he saw on her face, and something else too, a look as of outrage. He could not believe this thing that he saw, this insult to all that he felt to be sacred; for a moment he in his turn, must stare, then he came a step nearer, still unable to believe. But at that she wheeled round and fled from him wildly, fled back to the house that had always protected; without so much as a word she left him, nor did she once pause in her flight to look back. Yet even in this moment of headlong panic, the girl was conscious of something like amazement, amazement at herself, and she gasped as she ran: "It's Martin—Martin—" And again: "It's Martin!"

He stood perfectly still until the trees hid her. He felt stunned, incapable of understanding. All that he knew was that he must get away, away from Stephen, away from Morton, away from the thoughts that would follow after. In less than two hours he was motoring to London; in less than two weeks he was standing on the deck of the steamer that would carry him back to his forests that lay somewhere beyond the horizon.

꙰   ꙰   ꙰

No one questioned at Morton; they spoke very little. Even Anna forbore to question her daughter, checked by something that she saw in the girl's pale face.

But alone with her husband she gave way to her misgivings, to her deep disappointment: "It's heartbreaking, Philip. What's happened? They seemed so devoted to each other. Will you ask the child? Surely one of us ought to—"

Sir Philip said quietly: "I think Stephen will tell me." And with that Anna had perforce to be content.

Very silently Stephen now went about Morton, and her eyes looked bewildered and deeply unhappy. At night she would lie awake thinking of Martin, missing him, mourning him as though he were dead. But she could not accept this death without question, without feeling that she was in some way blameworthy. What was she, what manner of curious creature, to have been so repelled by a lover like Martin? Yet she had been repelled, and even her pity for the man could not wipe out that stronger feeling. She had driven him away because something within her was intolerant of that new aspect of Martin.

Oh, but she mourned his good, honest friendship; he had taken that from her, the thing she most needed—but perhaps after all it had never existed except as a cloak for this other emotion. And then, lying there in the thickening darkness, she would shrink from what might be waiting in the future, for all that had just happened might happen again—there were other men in the world beside Martin. Fool, never to have visualized this thing before, never to have faced the possibility of it; now she understood her resentment of men when their voices grew soft and insinuating. Yes, and now she knew to the full the meaning of fear, and Martin it was, who had taught her its meaning—her friend—the man she had utterly trusted had pulled the scales from her eyes and revealed it. Fear, stark fear, and the shame of such fear—that was the legacy left her by Martin. And yet he had made her so happy at first, she had felt so contented, so natural with him; but that was because they had been like two men, companions, sharing each other's interests. And at this thought her bitterness would all but flow over; it was cruel, it was cowardly of him to have deceived her, when all the time he had only been waiting for the chance to force this other thing on her.

But what was she? Her thoughts, slipping back to her childhood, would find many things in her past that perplexed her. She had never been quite like the other children, she had always been lonely and discontented, she had always been trying to be someone else—that was why she had dressed herself up as young Nelson. Remembering those days she would think of her father, and would wonder if now, as then, he could help her. Supposing she should ask him to explain about Martin? Her father was wise, and had infinite patience—yet somehow she instinctively dreaded to ask him. Alone—it was terrible to feel so much alone—to feel oneself different from other people. At one time she had rather enjoyed this distinction—she had rather enjoyed dressing up as a young Nelson. Yet had she enjoyed it? Or had it been done as some sort of inadequate, childish protest? But if so against what had she been protesting when she strutted about the house, masquerading? In those days she had wanted to be a boy—had that been the meaning of the pitiful young Nelson? And what about now? She had wanted Martin to treat her as a man, had expected it of him. . . . The questions to which she could find no answers would pile themselves up and up in the darkness; oppressing, stifling by sheer weight of numbers, until she would feel them getting her under; "I don't know—oh, God, I don't know!" she would mutter, tossing as though to fling off those questions.

Then one night towards dawn she could bear it no longer; her dread must give place to her need of consolation. She would ask her father to explain her to herself; she would tell him her deep desolation over Martin. She would say: "Is there anything strange about me, Father, that I should have felt as I did about Martin?" And then she would try to explain very calmly what it was she had felt, the intensity of it. She would try to make him understand her suspicion that this feeling of hers was a thing fundamental, much more than merely not being in love; much, much more than not wanting to marry Martin. She would tell him why she found herself so utterly bewildered; tell him how she had loved Martin's strong, young body, and his honest brown face, and his slow thoughtful eyes, and his careless walk—all these things she had loved. Then suddenly terror and deep repugnance because of that unforeseen change in Martin, the change that had turned the friend into the lover—in reality it had been no more than that, the friend had turned lover and had wanted from her what she could not give him, or indeed any man, because of that deep repugnance. Yet there should have been nothing repugnant about Martin, nor was she a child to have felt such terror. She had known certain facts about life for some time and they had not repelled her in other people—not until they had been brought home to herself had these facts both terrified and repelled her.

A TREE GROWS IN BROOKLYN
Betty Smith

Born in Brooklyn, Betty Smith (1896–1972) left school after the eighth grade and worked at various factory and clerical jobs. After moving to the Midwest, she attended the University of Michigan as a special student, won an Avery Hopwood Prize for drama, married, and had two daughters. She was primarily a playwright before she wrote her first novel, *A Tree Grows in Brooklyn*. Based on her own life and her mother's recollections, Smith's autobiographical work was an instant best-seller and was subsequently made into a film and a Broadway musical.

A Tree Grows in Brooklyn is the story of Francie Nolan's childhood and adolescence in the Brooklyn slums during the early part of the twentieth century. Although the sufferings and the joys of the Nolans are sentimentalized, the concrete details of their lives ring true. In the following excerpt, Francie is sixteen and working as a teletype operator when she meets Lee, a soldier on leave. Lee tells her he is engaged, but asks Francie to pretend she is his "best girl." He waits for her the next day after work, and they go dancing. When they leave the dance, Francie is faced with a choice between her values as a "good" girl and her own needs and desires.

They walked down the stairs slowly, the song following them. As they reached the street, they waited until the song died away.

. . . Pray each night for me,

Till we meet again.

"Let it be our song," he whispered, "and think of me every time you hear it."

As they walked, it started to rain and they had to run and find shelter in the doorway of a vacant store. They stood in the protected and dark doorway, held each other's hand and watched the rain falling.

"People always think that happiness is a faraway thing," thought Francie, "something complicated and hard to get. Yet, what little things can make it up; a place of shelter when it rains—a cup of strong hot coffee when you're blue; for a man, a cigarette for contentment; a book to read when you're alone—just to be with someone you love. Those things make happiness."

"I'm leaving early in the morning."

"Not for France?" Suddenly she was jolted out of her happiness.

"No, for home. My mother wants me for a day or two before . . ."

"Oh!"

"I love you, Francie."

"But you're engaged. That's the first thing you ever told me."

"Engaged," he said bitterly. "Everybody's engaged. Everybody in a small town is engaged or married or in trouble. There's nothing else to do in a small town.

"You go to school. You start walking home with a girl—maybe for no other reason than that she lives out your way. You grow up. She invites you to parties at her home. You go to other parties—people ask you to bring her along; you're expected to take her home. Soon no one else takes her out. Everybody thinks she's your girl and then . . . well, if you don't take her around, you feel like a heel. And then, because there's nothing else to do, you marry. And it works out all right if she's a decent girl (and most of the time she is) and you're a half-way decent fellow. No great passion but a kind of affectionate contentment. And then children come along and you give them the great love you kind of miss in each other. And the children gain in the long run.

"Yes, I'm engaged all right. But it isn't the same between her and me as it is between you and me."

"But you're going to marry her?"

He waited a long time before he answered.

"No."

She was happy again.

"Say it, Francie," he whispered. "Say it."

She said, "I love you, Lee."

"Francie . . ." there was urgency in his voice, "I may not come back from over there and I'm afraid . . . afraid. I might die . . . die, never having had anything . . . never . . . Francie, *can't* we be together for a little while?"

"We are together," said Francie innocently.

"I mean in a room . . . alone . . . Just till morning when I leave?"

"I . . . couldn't."

"Don't you *want* to?"

"Yes," she answered honestly.

"Then why. . . . "

"I'm only sixteen," she confessed bravely. "I've never been with . . . anybody. I wouldn't know how."

"That makes no difference."

"And I've never been away from home overnight. My mother would worry."

"You could tell her you spent the night with a girl friend."

"She knows I have no girl friend."

"You could think of some excuse . . . tomorrow."

"I wouldn't need to think of an excuse. I'd tell her the truth."

"You *would?*" he asked in astonishment.

"I love you. I wouldn't be ashamed . . . afterwards if I stayed with you. I'd be proud and happy and I wouldn't want to lie about it."

"I had no way of knowing, no way of knowing," he whispered as if to himself.

"*You* wouldn't want it to be something . . . sneaky, would you?"

"Francie, forgive me. I shouldn't have asked. I had no way of knowing."

"Knowing?" asked Francie, puzzled.

He put his arms around her and held her tightly. She saw that he was crying.

"Francie, I'm afraid . . . so afraid. I'm afraid that if I go away I'll lose you . . . never see you again. Tell me not to go home and I'll stay. We'll have tomorrow and the next day. We'll eat together and walk around or sit in a park or ride on top of a bus and just talk and be with each other. Tell me not to go."

"I guess you have to go. I guess that it's right that you see your mother once more before. . . . I don't know. But I guess it's right."

"Francie, will you marry me when the war's over—*if* I come back?"

"*When* you come back, I'll marry you."

"Will you, Francie? . . . please, will you?"

"Yes."

"Say it again."

"I'll marry you when you come back, Lee."

"And, Francie, we'll live in Brooklyn."

"We'll live wherever you want to live."

"We'll live in Brooklyn, then."

"Only if *you* want to, Lee."

"And will you write to me every day? *Every* day?"

"Every day," she promised.

"And will you write to me tonight when you get home and tell me how much you love me so that the letter will be waiting for me when I get home?" She promised. "Will you promise never to let anyone kiss you? Never to go out with anyone? To wait for me . . . no matter how long? And if I don't come back, never to *want* to marry anyone else?"

She promised.

And he asked for her whole life as simply as he'd ask for a date. And she promised away her whole life as simply as she'd offer a hand in greeting or farewell.

It stopped raining after a while and the stars came out. She wrote that night as she had promised—a long letter in which she poured out all her love and repeated the promises she had given.

She left a little earlier for work to have time to mail the letter from the Thirty-fourth Street post office. The clerk at the window assured her that it would reach its destination that afternoon. That was Wednesday.

She looked for but tried not to expect a letter Thursday night. There hadn't been time—unless he, too, wrote immediately after they had parted. But of course, he had to pack maybe—get up early to make his train. (It never occurred to her that *she* had managed to find time.) There was no letter Thursday night.

Friday, she had to work straight through—a sixteen hour shift—because the company was short-handed on account of an influenza epidemic. When she got home a little before two in the morning, there was a letter propped against the sugar bowl on the kitchen table. She ripped it open eagerly.

"Dear Miss Nolan:"

Her happiness died. It couldn't be from Lee because he'd write, "Dear Francie." She turned the page and looked at the signature. "Elizabeth Rhynor (Mrs.)" Oh! His mother. Or a sister-in-law. Maybe he was sick and couldn't write. Maybe there was an army rule that men about to go overseas couldn't write letters. He had asked someone to write for him. Of course. That was it. She started to read the letter.

> Lee told me all about you. I want to thank you for being so nice and friendly to him while he was in New York. He arrived home Wednesday afternoon but had to leave for camp the next week. He was home only a day and a half. We had a very quiet wedding, just the families and a few friends. . . .

Francie put the letter down. "I've been working sixteen hours in a row," she thought, "and I'm tired. I've read thousands of messages today and no words make sense right now. Anyhow, I got into bad reading habits at the Bureau—reading a column at a glance and seeing only one word in it. First I'll wash the sleep out of my eyes, have some coffee, and read the letter again. This time I'll read it right."

While the coffee heated, she splashed cold water on her face thinking that when she came to the part of the letter that said "wedding" she'd go on reading and the next words would be; "Lee was the best man. I married his brother you know."

Katie lying awake in her bed heard Francie moving about in the kitchen. She lay tense . . . waiting. And she wondered what it was she waited for.

Francie read the letter again.

> . . .wedding, just the families and a few friends. Lee asked me to write and explain why he hadn't answered your letter. Again thank you for entertaining him so nicely while he was in your city. Yours truly, Elizabeth Rhynor (Mrs.)

There was a postscript.

> I read the letter you sent Lee. It was mean of him to pretend to be in love with you and I told him so. He said to tell you he's dreadfully sorry. E. R.

Francie was trembling violently. Her teeth made little biting sounds. "Mama," she moaned. "*Mama!*"

Katie heard the story. "It's come at last," she thought, "the time when you can no longer stand between your children and heartache. When there wasn't enough food in the house you pretended that you weren't hungry so they could have more. In the cold of a winter's night you got up and put your blanket on their bed so they wouldn't be cold. You'd kill anyone who tried to harm them—I tried my best to kill that man in the hallway. Then one sunny day, they walk out in all innocence and they walk right into the grief that you'd give your life to spare them."

Francie gave her the letter. She read it slowly and as she read, she thought she knew how it was. Here was a man of twenty-two who evidently (to use one of Sissy's phrases) had been around. Here was a girl sixteen years old; six years younger than he. A girl—in spite of bright-red lipstick and grown-up clothes and a lot of knowledge picked up here and there—who was yet tremulously innocent; a girl who had come face to face with some of the evil of the world and most of its hardships, and yet had remained curiously untouched by the world. Yes, she could understand her appeal for him.

Well, what could she say? That he was no good or at best just a weak man who was easily susceptible to whoever he was with? No, she couldn't be so cruel as to say that. Besides the girl wouldn't believe her anyhow.

"Say something," demanded Francie. "Why don't you say something?"

"What can I say?"

"Say that I'm young—that I'll get over it. Go ahead and say it. Go ahead and lie."

"I know that's what people say—you'll get over it. I'd say it, too. But I know it's not true. Oh, you'll be happy again, never fear. But you won't forget. Everytime you fall in love it will be because something in the man reminds you of *him*."

"Mother. . . ."

Mother! Katie remembered. She had called her own mother "mama" until the day she had told her that she was going to marry Johnny. She had said, "Mother, I'm going to marry. . . ." She had never said "mama" after that. She had finished growing up when she stopped calling her mother "mama." Now Francie . . .

"Mother, he asked me to be with him for the night. Should I have gone?"

Katie's mind darted around looking for words.

"Don't make up a lie, Mother. Tell me the truth."

Katie couldn't find the right words.

"I promise you that I'll never go with a man without being married first—if I ever marry. And if I feel that I must—without being married, I'll tell you first. That's a solemn promise. So you can tell me the truth without worrying that I'll go wrong if I know it."

"There are two truths," said Katie finally.

"As a mother, I say it would have been a terrible thing for a girl to sleep with a stranger—a man she had known less than forty-eight hours. Horrible things might have happened to you. Your whole life might have been ruined. As your mother, I tell you the truth.

"But as a woman . . ." she hesitated. "I will tell you the truth as a woman. It would have been a very beautiful thing. Because there is only once that you love that way."

Francie thought, "I should have gone with him then. I'll never love anyone as much again. I wanted to go and I didn't go and now I don't want him that way anymore because *she* owns him now. But I wanted to and I didn't and now it's too late." She put her head down on the table and wept.

COMING OF AGE IN MISSISSIPPI

Anne Moody

Anne Moody was an activist in the Civil Rights struggles of the 1950s and 1960s. As a student at Tougaloo College, she worked with the National Association for the Advancement of Colored People (NAACP), the Congress of Racial Equality (CORE), and the Student Non-violent Coordinating Committee (SNCC) on various projects. She participated, for example, in an action to integrate the Woolworth lunch counter in Jackson, Mississippi.

When Moody's autobiography was published in 1969, it received high praise, especially for its powerful account of her gradual move toward militancy. But it is also a book about "coming of age" in other ways. The following excerpt recounts Moody's experience with her first boyfriend when she was 20 years old and a student at Natchez Junior College.

That second year at Natchez, I discovered that I had changed. The year before almost every boy on campus had tried to make it with me, especially the basketball boys, and I had turned them down one after the other. Now I found myself wondering whether I should have been so rude to them. When I saw girls and boys sneaking kisses out under the trees, I got curious. Sometimes I wished I had a boyfriend. I was twenty years old and I had never been kissed, not even a smack on the lips. I wanted to know how it felt.

There was a new basketball player on campus named Keemp, whom all the girls and boys were talking about. He was tall—six feet five—and slim. Besides being tall, he had a "cool" about him that most girls liked. So they all went around talking about how handsome he was. It was early October and we hadn't started practicing yet, so I didn't know whether he was a good player or not, but I certainly didn't think his looks were anything special. He looked just like my daddy without a mustache and I never thought Daddy was handsome. I used to see Keemp walking around on campus and wondered what was it that all the girls saw in him. Then too he made me wonder what all the women had seen in my daddy when he was young.

Keemp shot forty-some points during that game. He played better than I had ever seen him play. Just about every time he raised his arms, it was two points for us. When the game was over, the rest of the boys hugged him down to the floor, then picked him up and declared him "King of Basketball." As I watched him play and then saw how everyone loved him, it suddenly dawned upon me that he was a terrific person and that I was a fool to be thinking about quitting him.

When the boys let him go, he walked up to me smiling. Without saying a word, he put his arms around my shoulders and walked me to the bus. As he touched me, a warm current ran through my body.

As I sat on the bus beside Keemp that night, a feeling I had never known before came over me. He held my hands, and it seemed like every hormone in my body reacted. Neither one of us said a word. As the bus was coming to a stop, Keemp leaned over and gently placed his lips on mine. They were like a magnet slowly pulling my lips apart. Once my mouth was open his tongue explored areas that had never been touched by anything but a toothbrush. I completely forgot where I was until one of the boys sitting near us started banging on the basketball and yelling.

"Jesus! Y'aaaall! It finally happened! Keemp done did it!"

The bus had stopped. The lights were on and everybody was looking at us. Keemp wouldn't stop. He pretended that he didn't even hear the yelling, that we weren't on a bus surrounded by spectators. I tried to pull away but I was so weak I couldn't control myself, so I just gave in to his kisses.

Didn't anyone on the bus say one word or stir, not even Mrs. Evans. No one made a move to get off the bus until Keemp and I did. When Keemp finished kissing me, I saw that he had lipstick all over his mouth. My first reaction was to wipe it off real quick before anyone could see it. Keemp just smiled as I wiped it off. When I finished, he took me by the hand, pulled me up out of the seat, buried my head in his shoulder and we walked off the bus.

I was very embarrassed about the fact that my first kiss had been such a public thing. But I didn't regret the kiss at all. Once we were back on campus, Keemp and I greeted each other with a kiss every time we met.

We never did hide behind trees or posts to sneak kisses like the other students. When Mrs. Evans blinked the lights for the girls to come in, I'd give Keemp a smack on the lips right in front of her. Soon most of the other girls started smacking kisses on their boyfriends in front of Mrs. Evans too. Finally, one day Mrs. Evans called me in for a "conference" and accused me of leading the kissing game on campus.

During the first six months of our relationship I was happier than I had ever been. Keemp turned me on to so much that I made the first straight-A average that had been made at Natchez in many years. Studying was a cinch and everything else seemed so easy. But that spring when the basketball season was all over and the excitement of traveling was gone and boys and girls began swarming all over each other like bees, I slowly began to drift away from the whole scene. I had gotten tired of being part of "the club." There was something about the way couples were relaxing into relationships and making them everything that bothered me. I didn't want to get all wrapped up in Keemp the way some of the other girls did with their boyfriends. My relation with him had gradually become a brother–sister thing. He could tell I was moving away from him, so he got himself a girl in the city. I wasn't even jealous and I didn't say anything. I just didn't care. I knew I would be leaving him behind next year and figured he'd have somebody else. I pretended that I didn't know he had another girl and went on being friends with him. He was the best friend I had had since Lola, and I told him everything.

YOUR MARRIAGE

John F. DeYonker, D.O. and Rev. Thomas E. Tobin, C.SS.R.

Your Marriage is the program of premarital counseling that the Roman Catholic Church offered to couples in the Archdiocese of Detroit. This and similar manuals were used by thousands of men and women who turned to their priests, rabbis, and ministers for advice and instruction on marriage. "A Checklist for Husbands and Wives" summarizes the ideas which informed that instruction.

A CHECKLIST FOR HUSBANDS AND WIVES

Self-evaluation is always a useful means to encourage better performance.
At regular intervals it would be a good idea to read over this checklist.
Instead of scattering your efforts on many different points select one or two matters in which you will make determined efforts to improve. From time to time change the points for improvement.
To help communication and to better your marriage it might be a good idea to ask your partner to go over the list with you.

I. THE HUSBAND

AS A MAN DO I

Assume my role as leader, breadwinner, protector, teacher?

Follow high moral principles?

Recognize that marriage restricts the freedom I had as a single man?

Treat other women as I expect other men to treat my wife or daughter?

Fulfill the responsibilities of my job and strive to get ahead by study and hard work?

Keep myself neat and well-groomed so that my wife can be proud of me?

Make religion important in my life by learning more about it and practicing it better?

Improve myself intellectually by serious reading?

Better myself socially by becoming a good conversationalist?

Take an active part in community activities?

AS A HUSBAND DO I

Show my wife signs of affection and tell her very often that I love her?

Remember wedding anniversaries, birthdays, Mother's Day, Valentine's Day and special days of importance in my marriage?

Notice and make favorable comments on new dresses, hair-dos, and other personal things?

Inform my wife of the family's complete financial picture, salary, debts, insurance, etc.?

Show appreciation for her cooking, baking and housekeeping?

Give her the money she needs for the house as well as some money that she can use for herself?

Try to work out a budget with her?

Put some meaning into my kiss on leaving and returning home?

Make my wife and family happy and not afraid to see me come home?

Make sex an act of love?

Provide for her and the children in case of my death?

Treat her relatives and friends kindly and graciously?

Discuss frustrations and differences in an adult fashion with understanding, calmness and intelligence?

Consult her and take her into my confidence?

Have enough humility and love to seek professional help if our marriage needs it?

Tell or joke about our personal secrets and intimacies?

Readily forgive her human mistakes?

Make sarcastic remarks or act in a grouchy way?

Help her in household tasks? Feeding the baby? Changing diapers? Washing dishes?

Thoughtlessly tease too much?

Show leadership in religious practices, family prayers and devotions?

Act as a good host to her relatives and friends?

Gamble with money needed for the welfare of the family?

Drink excessively and cause unnecessary worry and trouble?

Misinterpret her attention to detail as nagging?

Date my wife by taking her out to dinner, shows, dances, etc.?

II. THE WIFE

AS A WOMAN DO I

Remember my dignity as a woman and the tremendous power of love that I have
to give?

Realize that I am guide, comforter, teacher, nurse, bookkeeper, judge, spiritual
director, mother confessor, cook, seamstress, housekeeper, buyer, banker and
entertainer?

Strive to develop my personality and live according to high principles?

Show respect to my husband especially in front of the children?

Take pride in my work and strive to do it well?

Fix my husband's breakfast? He likes it and it gives me a good start on the day.

Patiently wait until he does his chores? Do I spoil him by doing them myself?

Keep myself neat and well-groomed especially when he returns home from work?

Spiritually set a good example by avoiding vulgarity and cattiness, and by
promoting family prayer and reading?

Read good books and magazines, speak grammatically, make efforts to improve
myself, keep interested in current events and sports if my husband is interested?

AS A WIFE DO I

Recognize that my role is to complete rather than compete?

Give signs of affection and love to my husband and willingly accept his signs of
affection?

Show an interest in his work and the people with whom he works?

Act charitably and give subtle hints of approaching special days or anniversaries
and not wait for him to forget?

Make favorable comments on his appearance and try to improve it by proper
maintenance of his clothing and gifts of suitable clothing?

Try to save a little toward a nest egg for the future?

Kiss him when he leaves and returns from work?

Do little things for him to keep alive the fires of love?

Search for his virtues rather than his faults?

Belittle or frustrate his ambitions rather than give the necessary encouragement?

Respect his confidences and not reveal his faults and the intimacies of love?

Try to maintain a cheerful atmosphere in the home?

Stoop to using sex as a weapon to be given if he is a good boy and to be denied if
he is a bad boy?

Discuss frustrations and differences in an adult fashion?

Treat his relatives and friends courteously and respectfully?

Consult him in matters of importance about personal matters and points which
concern the children and come to a common decision?

Seek professional guidance if needed?

Avoid all types of open and subtle nagging?

Help him in his business or employment if necessary?

Thank him for many big and little things:
> his dependability as a good and steady provider
> help with household chores in time of sickness or a crowded schedule
> his interest in my welfare
> his willing acceptance of errands
> care of children so that I can have some free time
> a comfortable home with work-saving appliances
> tolerance of my whims
> phone calls when detained
> little kindnesses, courtesies, and signs of affection

See the spiritual value of even routine duties in marriage?

Try to economize and manage the household according to income?

Lie to cover up mistakes?

Understand that male thoughtlessness is not intentional? Insist on giving my husband detailed accounts of events in which he has no interest?

Leave him alone when he is tired or grouchy?

Have a snappy comeback to sting him whenever he says anything displeasing?

Show generosity in making sacrifices for him?

THE TOTAL WOMAN
Marabel Morgan

Marabel Morgan's *The Total Woman* (1973) was one of the best-selling nonfiction books of the mid-1970s. Presented as an aid to those whose marriages had lost their "sizzle," the book instructed women in the "secrets" of making their marriage "come alive": accept, admire, adapt (to), and appreciate your husband. Morgan also offered Total Woman classes, which enrolled tens of thousands. Each class ended in an "assignment," which the participants were to complete as soon as they got home and on which they reported the next day.

Marabel Morgan, a beauty queen who married right after she graduated from college, was a full-time wife, homemaker, and mother. After a few years, however, she found that although nothing was wrong with her marriage, the "sizzle" had gone out of it. Her book addressed the need for romance, for sexual fulfillment, and for a sense of self-worth among middle-class housewives like herself. The answers combined religious injunctions about wives being submissive to their husbands with techniques from "pop" psychology designed to improve communication. These, plus a no-holds-barred approach to sex in marriage, made her message a heady brew.

This book is not intended to be the ultimate authority on marriage. Far from it. I don't pretend to have an automatic, ready-to-wear answer for every marriage problem. I do believe it is possible, however, for almost any wife to have her husband absolutely adore her in just a few weeks' time. She can revive romance, reestablish communication, break down barriers, and put sizzle back into her marriage. It really is up to her. She has the power.

If, through reading and applying these principles, you become a Total Woman, with your husband more in love with you than ever before, my efforts in writing this book will have been rewarded.

ASSIGNMENT

MAN ALIVE

1. Accept your husband just as he is. Write out two lists—one of his faults and one of his virtues. Take a long, hard look at his faults and then throw the list away; don't ever dwell on them again. Only think about his virtues. Carry that list with you and refer to it when you are mad, sad, or glad.

2. Admire your husband every day. Refer to his virtue list if you need a place to start. Say something nice about his body today. Put his tattered ego back together with compliments.

3. Adapt to his way of life. Accept his friends, food, and life-style as your own. Ask him to write the six most important changes he'd like to see take place at your house. Read the list in private, react in private, and then set out to accomplish these changes with a smile. Be a "Yes, let's!" woman some time of every day.

4. Appreciate all he does for you. Sincerely tell him "Thank you" with your attitudes, actions, and words. Give him your undivided attention, and try not to make any telephone calls after he comes home, especially after 8:00 P. M.

SUPER SEX

Sex is an hour in bed at ten o'clock; super sex is the climax of an atmosphere that has been carefully set all day. Your attitude during your husband's first four waking minutes in the morning sets the tone for his entire day. The atmosphere for love in the evening can be set by you even before breakfast. Give him a kiss first thing tomorrow morning. Rub his back as he's waking up. Whisper in his ear. Slip into the bathroom to clear a few cobwebs before he wakes.

Remember, he can stand almost anything but boredom. The same nightgown month after month is not too exciting to any man. Treat him and yourself to some snazzy new ones. Have you ever looked so sexy in the morning that your husband called in late to the office? At least you can make him wish he could stay home.

One wife changes the sheets every few days while her husband is dressing for work. As she sprays the sheets with cologne, she purrs, "Honey, hurry home tonight." It gives him incentive for the whole day. If you expect great sex tonight, it should definitely start in the morning, with words. That's basic. Sex 201.

Edna St. Vincent Millay wrote, "'Tis not love's going hurts my days, but that it went in little ways." Marriage is but a basketful of those little things.

Tomorrow morning as your husband leaves for work, stand at the door and wave until he's out of sight. That's his last memory of you, in the open doorway. Make him want to hurry home.

In class recently, one cute girl I'll call Janet told how she had anxiously anticipated her husband's coming home one day. At four o'clock she called his office somewhat nervously and said, "Honey, I'm eagerly waiting for you to come home. I just crave your body."

Jack said, with great consternation, "Ummmmmmph."

"Is there someone there with you, darling?" she asked.

"Ummhum," came the same reply.

"Well, I'll see you soon, darling," she said.

"Ummhum," was his final utterance.

And they both hung up.

Five minutes later the phone rang. It was Jack. In unbelief he said, "Would you please repeat slowly what you said five minutes ago?"

The sequel to the story was almost as amusing. Janet called her girl friend, Barbara, to tell what had happened. Barbara couldn't wait to try it on her husband, Pete. She called his office number and when the male voice answered, she said, "Darling, I wanted to call to say that I just crave your body. Hurry home!"

The voice on the other end demanded, "Who is this?" Realizing that another man, not her husband, had answered the phone, Barbara quickly hung up, absolutely mortified.

That night when her husband came in the door, he said, "Wait until I tell you about Ron's phone call today. You'll never believe it!" (She never told him, by the way, who the anonymous caller had been.)

So when you call your husband's office, first be sure you've got the right man! Then keep it short, just long enough to let him know that you're ready and willing. It may be the greatest news he has heard all day.

LUNCHEON SPECIAL

If you pack your husband's lunch in the morning, try tucking in a surprise love note. Mail a beautiful card to his office (marked PERSONAL) that would brighten up his day. Or appear in person. I know of one woman who arrived at her husband's office at lunch hour with a picnic basket. Behind locked doors they spent the longest lunch hour the boss had taken in months. The secretaries are still talking about that one!

Arrange your day's activities so that you'll be totally and eagerly prepared as he walks in the door. A psychiatrist told me, "Lots of men would be less preoccupied with work—or other women—if their wives made coming home the most exciting part of the day."

I find that after a hard day at the office, most husbands don't usually arrange flowers and light the candles in the bedroom. At least mine doesn't, but he appreciates my efforts. And it's my privilege to do it.

Set an atmosphere of romance tonight. Set your table with cloth, flowers, and silver. Prepare his favorite dinner for him. Eat by candlelight; you'll light his candle!

Make up your mind to be available for him. Schedule your day so you won't start projects at nine o'clock. The number-one killer of love is fatigue, but you won't be exhausted if you're using your $25,000 plan. You'll have the energy to be a passionate lover.

Next, be sure the outside of your "house" is prepared. Bubble your troubles away at five o'clock. Of course, you'll be shaven, perfumed, and seductive in an utterly lovely outfit. Perhaps you're thinking, "Since I'm forty pounds overweight, I don't feel very seductive in my baby-doll pajamas." That's all right, he chose you because he loves you. Concentrate on your good points and he will, too. He won't be able to take his eyes off you. Best of all, he'll know how much you care.

Prepare now for making love tonight. This is part of our class assignment. In fact by the second week, the women are to be prepared for sexual intercourse every night for a week. When I gave the homework in one class, a woman muttered audibly, "What's she think I am, a sex maniac?"

Another gal told a Total Woman teacher, "I tried to follow the assignment this past week, but I couldn't keep up—I was only ready for sex six nights; Monday night I was just too tired." The teacher gave her a B–, but her husband gave her an A!

One Fort Lauderdale housewife told how she diligently prepared for love for seven straight nights, "whatever, whenever, and wherever," and it was her husband who couldn't take it. "I don't know what's happened to you, honey," he said with a weak grin, "but I love it!"

COMPANION, NOT COMPETITION

Sex can restore a bad mood or disagreement. One wife felt she had been wronged by her husband. Her pride took over and she refused to give in until he changed. The Bible advises, ". . . let not the sun go down upon your wrath." Watch that no bitterness or resentment takes root in you for it causes deep trouble.

Nip it in the bud. Don't let your grudge carry over to the next day. There is no place for resentment in a good marriage. Part of his problem may be his need for your sexual love. Talk it out and change your attitude. Often that's all it takes.

Love never makes demands. Love is unconditional acceptance of him and his feelings. He does not need competition at home; he's had that all day at work. He needs your companionship and compliments instead.

A mature couple does not demand perfection. They do not chase false goals, which can only end in disillusionment. They are willing to work together for each other's good, which produces a happy sexual adjustment.

Don't deprive your husband of intercourse when he acts like a bear. He may be tired when he comes home tonight. He needs to be pampered, loved, and restored. Fill up his tummy with food; soothe away his frustrations with sex. Lovemaking comforts a man. It can comfort you too.

In speaking to a men's service club recently, I told them some of the class assignments for super sex. The reason for the homework, I explained, was that sex comforts a man. The reaction of the men was completely unexpected. These sophisticated businessmen spontaneously shouted, pounded the tables, picked up their spoons, and clanged their water glasses!

Lovemaking is an art you can develop to any degree, according to *How to Be a Happily Married Mistress*. You can become a Rembrandt in your sexual art. Or, you can stay at the paint-by-numbers stage. One husband, by the way, felt his wife was more like Grandma Moses because she always wore a flannel granny gown. The benefits in your becoming a Rembrandt just cannot be overemphasized. You can begin now to be a budding artist. Tonight is your night for super sex. Prepare, anticipate, relax, and enjoy!

ASSIGNMENT

SEX 201

1. Be an atmosphere adjuster in the morning. Set the tone for love. Be pleasant to look at, be with, and talk to. Walk your husband to the car each morning and wave until he's out of sight.

2. Once this week call him at work an hour before quitting time, to say, "I wanted you to know that I just crave your body!" or some other appropriate tender term. Then take your bubble bath shortly before he comes home.

3. Thrill him at the front door in your costume. A frilly new nighty and heels will probably do the trick as a starter. Variety is the spice of sex.

4. Be prepared mentally and physically for intercourse every night this week. Be sure your attitude matches your costume. Be the seducer, rather than the seducee.

5. If you feel your situation involves a deeper problem, either psychological or physiological, seek professional help.

HERE COME THE BRIDES

John Krich

For people in countries ravaged by poverty, America is still the land of opportunity—and opportunists. As a result, poor women, especially poor Asian women, look toward marriage with American men as an opportunity to escape the sometimes grinding poverty of their homelands. And entrepreneurs are willing to provide the means by which these women can contact men seeking generally docile and subservient Asian wives. This marriage market is reminiscent of that of the nineteenth century when women needed to marry because they had no economic base of their own.

The following excerpts are from interviews that John Krich conducted with men and women who have availed themselves of this service. His article was published in *Mother Jones,* a magazine named for the labor leader, Mary Harris Jones (1830–1930), whose motto was "Pray for the dead and fight like hell for the living."

The condominiums come in mirror images, but not the occupants. On the front door of one stucco chalet hangs a Chinese character made of brass. Call it cross-cultural mistletoe for the couple living inside, another product of a growing American phenomenon. The husband turns out to be a small-town white kid come to the big city, prematurely middle-aged, middlebrow in his conspicuous collections of carvings and trophies, middle management, though never quite as managerial as he'd like, flashing a salesman's charm that readily gives way to anger. The wife is young, comely, and Asian: wearing house sandals but groomed for a party, a good listener whose skills have been severely taxed, uncomfortable with her new language but comforted by her new surroundings, covering her suspicion with drowsiness, a bit sunken along with the living room. As she offers tea and the homemade egg rolls called *lumpia*, nurses her newborn, and beams at the wedding album, it is hard to imagine that she was plucked from a row of snapshots in a mail-order catalog. Or that this marriage wasn't arranged in heaven, but in Hawaii—by an introduction service called Cherry Blossoms.

Then come the corrections in one another's version of events, made most gingerly; the nervous jokes about age difference; the curious blanks drawn when trying to remember the names of close in-laws; the references to unspecified conflicts and secret diaries where "he write that he travel looking for other girls to marry after me"; the questions that the wife pretends she can't grasp until she retreats into the "no comment" of a nap, causing the whispered confessions—which come whenever she "lets me out of her sight"—about how "it's been no picnic," about the bitching, the sulking, the misunderstandings.

And there's that troublesome word *love*, which is either actively disdained—in favor of talk about "trade-offs" or "liabilities and assets"—or flashed continually, like an expensive Javanese mask. Love is blind, as they say—especially in this context, where there's so much to be blind about. The longer they tell their story, the more this couple reveals the forces rending them apart, and the fears that made them cleave together. Cozy as it all seems, the world beyond keeps swirling through this condo. Settled on their white ottoman, they remain a man and woman in flight—like so many who have chosen the path of these postal courtships.

The men: *"The woman I yearn to spend my life with does not seem to reside in North America."*

The women: *"I believe the god will let us to be together one day. Is that a dream? I love only American music."*

That world is not only getting smaller; it's getting lonelier. Never has it been easier for nations to mingle, and never have expectations been greater for one culture to provide what the other lacks. Economic interdependencies give way to psychic ones: those with power seek those with beauty, those with money seek those with heart. It's not surprising then that the delivery of Asian brides to mostly white American grooms has, within the last five years, become a multimillion-dollar-a-year industry. Since there's a perceived shortage of U.S. homemakers willing to shoulder traditional matrimonial tasks, some entrepreneurs are going abroad—where the labor can be bought cheaper and the quality control kept more rigid. Imperialists of the heart, these men strike out for poorer lands in search of the raw materials necessary to the manufacture of their fantasies. If emotional fulfillment is as vital to U.S. national security as South African chrome, then it must be secured in regular shipments. Love itself has become the ultimate consumer good, and, as with so many others, an increasing number of shoppers are no longer buying American.

The catalogs: *"Congratulations! You have taken the first step towards discovering an eternal treasure! For many discerning men, there can be no other choice than a Lady of the Orient. These women possess wit, charm and grace unmatched anywhere in the world. [They] are faithful and devoted to their husbands. . . . When it comes to sex, they are not demonstrative; however, they are uninhibited [and] believe sex is healthy. She wakes up in the morning with a smile on her face and she* does *wake up in the morning! You have heard the phrase 'A Woman of the 80s.' We recommend a Woman for all time.* An Asian Woman!"

ɰ ɰ ɰ

Although no one has kept exact figures, it's a safe bet that 10,000 marriages have resulted from these air-mail relationships over the past 12 years. Most of the pen pal businesses are crude copies of the formula established by Cherry Blossoms, which, under the direction of Harvard Ph.D. and ex-hippie John Broussard, has become the highest-volume matchmaking shop. Begun at the whimsical request of a single male in 1974, Cherry Blossoms has now expanded to publishing three separate, bimonthly directories, running up to 48 pages, featuring Philippine "Island Blossoms," Asian women in general, and miscellaneous hopefuls from Peru to Yugoslavia. The services' fees run from $5 to $10 dollars for an introductory batch of a few sample addresses to $300 for all current and back issues—depending upon a variety of plans in which the subscriber may be offered "first crack" at a designated number of women. The clients also get their predilections listed in the services' register and their names placed in newspaper ads throughout the Far East.

Cherry Blossoms sends along a chatty newsletter describing women deemed less photogenic, offered at discount rates. This mimeographed sheet also alerts the men to "rotten apples": women who use their letters to solicit "samples of foreign currency" for their private collection or ask for donations for "typhoon relief."

ɰ ɰ ɰ

The men: *"American girls left me really disappointed. They look like tubs of lard stuffed into Levi's. They're pushy, spoiled rotten, and they talk like sailors. They're not cooperative, but combative—and they never appreciate what you do for them. In the morning, you wonder how many guys before me? Was it the football team? Maybe it's our fault, the fault of men for repressing them for so long. But they're not psychologically together. They just don't seem to know what they want."*

Haven't we heard this somewhere before? In a curious role reversal, these last of the supermachos offer the classic complaints women have long made about men: they're confused, immature, promiscuous; they're also opinionated and materialistic. They fear commitments and neglect personal satisfactions in favor of careers. They let themselves go to seed: one disgruntled husband even suggested that all women want is "to watch TV and booze it up." Worst of all, they tend to be smarter or more successful than the men, who are left exhausted by the jostling for position entailed by the recent redefining of sexual roles.

The men: *"It's not easy when everything is up for discussion. Why don't you do this? Why don't you do that? Even my mother gives me a hard time. She wants to know why I don't cook once in a while. Now I just smile and tell her, 'I'm retired from all that.' My wife smiles too."*

Few of these men are trailer park misfits or the sort of gents who paper their bedrooms in aluminum foil. In one of the many surveys that the introduction services trot out as proof of their mainstream appeal, the statistics indicate that those who seek Asian brides are above average in education, income, and status.

These same samplings tell us that the average age at marriage for the husbands is 52; for the wives, 32. The Asian bride trade is tailor-made for those men driven to sustain youth beyond its normal bounds. For divorced men and elderly widowers with more modest goals, it can simply be a quick means of re-acquiring a sock-sorter or a live-in nurse.

But the surveys cannot test the would-be husbands for insecurity. The more the men rail against the women's movement, the more they show themselves to be its unwanted offspring. They want a refuge from chaos: all of them speak of wanting someone "who'll be there every night," as one put it, "who won't cheat, and who I can trust to do right by me—even down to how she takes care of the dog." Responding to the lure of far-off places, these men seek the girl-next-door. Through no fault of their own, she's become the girl-next-continent.

🐦 🐦 🐦

The men: *"It's very safe. There are no messy endings. And it's slow enough that you really get to know someone—not like dating here, when suddenly you get in way over your head."*

Once they get to know someone, the men venture out to meet their pen pal —or pals. For some of them, their travels in search of Miss Right constitute their sole and fleeting opportunity to feel like swashbucklers. They recount their "shopping trips," as they call them, in a tone usually reserved for discoverers of the North Pole: "We didn't know each other. We're from two different cultures; and here, in the middle of Taipei, we were gonna meet up for a blind date, which was, when you think about it, unbelievable." Lo and behold, the sales clerks from Peoria cross the international date line to become the emperors of Quezon City! Their pen pals serve as a parade of willing tour guides, and the two-week vacation takes on the power of a hallucination. In such heady moments, they may forget that they came for a mate and instead use a variety of appetites—especially since, as one pointed out, "a lot of the girls, even if they're virgins, will spend the night with you if they think that will do the trick." Others concentrate dutifully on their chosen lady—presuming her charms match up to her penmanship—savoring a courtship whose Victorian pace is enforced by watchful relatives.

The men: *"I couldn't believe it once I got over there. The choices were mindboggling. All the girls called me 'Superman.' It was like I was a white god. You walk around here, you're just another schmuck. In Cebu City, the heads were turning. You'd think Robert Redford or Paul Newman hit town."*

The women: *"I tell him, if you make love to me, you must marry me. I thought him sincere because he travel to see my mother. Thirty hours to Mindanao. Even after he propose, he keeps looking. He go to Hong Kong, Malaysia, traveling around for long time to see pen pals there. He had other girlfriend in Philippines. I go up to his hotel room instead of waiting in the lobby. I find them together. Then the game was up."*

🐦 🐦 🐦

The men: *"I don't think the transition was too rough on her. She cried every day for two years."*

The women: *"I don't cry anymore. I used to write every day. Now I write only at Christmas. A neighbor teach me to play bingo. Now I have bingo; I don't miss my family so much."*

For the mail-order bride, commitment is the easy part. Once married and ensconced in the United States, the women find that persistent homesickness is only the first hurdle. The standard refugee traumas are bad enough, but these imported brides have to grapple in isolation with two equally challenging adjustments. They must learn the customs of a new country and a new husband all at once. Often, they become acquainted with the hindrances of the latter before they've been exposed to the opportunities of the former. If becoming an American is their main aim, they are at the complete mercy of their spouse for the three years until citizenship is granted—and the husband holds the power to deport her if she doesn't play by his rules. It is in this sense that every mail-order bride, no matter how willing, is a captive.

The women: *"That first year, I cannot go out by myself. I would get lost. I know how to drive. I got my license. I just don't know the area too well, and I'm afraid to talk to other people. . . . I rather stay in Taiwan. Speak my own language. I feel more useful there."*

The men: *"Most girls think they know what to expect, but they don't. Most of the guys lie and bullshit to them. They make them think this is the land of milk and honey. They assume that as soon as you get off the boat, there's a job waiting for you."*

A surprising number of these "traditionalist" couples want, or need, the women to seek employment. But lacking the language skills, or finding that their education counts for little, those who expect to work for a living quickly learn that those vaunted opportunities are not quite open at all.

And strangely enough, the common complaint that the husbands seem to voice is that they have gotten too much "loyal wife" for the money. These men who claim to abhor the assertiveness of their own countrywomen report that they can't communicate with their new partners until they've become a bit more like themselves. To a man, they speak of having to teach their wives to express their feelings, even anger. Americanization begins at home.

The women: *"It's true. I don't want to write check without his permission. I take a long time to learn to say it is not his money, but* our *money."*

The men: *"She won't go anywhere without me or do anything without me—not even go to sleep. She practically asks for permission to go to the toilet. She always says it's the Filipino way. And finally, sometimes, I have to just say, honey, this is not the god-damn Philippines. And this is my way."*

"My way" can be enforced with fists, although actual instances of wife battering among mail-order couples are difficult to trace. Many of the women are not aware of shelters and social services or are reluctant to use them for fear of deportation. For every rare one who does come forward, there are surely many more who must cope by themselves with some gradient of coercion. Challenged with evidence of abuse cases, the mail-order husbands like to cite the rumors they've heard of brides who take their American men for all the money they're worth, then disappear once they've got their citizenship papers. To the husband, one crime is no more justifiable than the other. In this bargain, the terror cuts both ways—and the keeper is often as fearful and watchful as the captive.

The men: *"My wife keeps saying she's going to walk out one of these days—I can't tell if she's kidding or not."*

The women: *"Here, I got more freedom. But mostly I don't look out window. My husband not like me talking. He's not bad man, just a nasty guy, with temper."*

Just as the situation breeds betrayal, sudden or gradual, so it provides incentives for success. It will take many years before we know whether these marriages prove any more durable than those of American marriages in general—although, statistically speaking, that wouldn't take much. Yet unlike their American counterparts, these newlyweds show an uncommon determination to bridge their differences. Few of the wives are going to casually give up on their effort: most have been schooled in making the best of it on the home front and do not accept divorce as an alternative. These women have cast too much aside—and the men have invested an equal amount in effort, cash, and the idealization of their quest.

The men: *"The first year was very tough. With the conflicts we had, if we hadn't already been married, we probably never would have gotten married."*

The women: *"Your mate is picked by God. You have only to be patient and get along."*

If Asian women seem more willing than their American sisters to make compromises, that is because some bring with them a different model of what marriage is supposed to provide. Where wedlock is seen primarily as a pragmatic partnership, it ceases to carry the burden as an emotional cure-all. This view of marriage, based in its most idealized form on mutual aid and on the slow unearthing of feeling, has certainly proven useful to the continuation of the species throughout the centuries—and it is one these 20th-century husbands strain to emulate.

The men: *"When I married her, I didn't love her. I admired her and I respected her, and I decided to take a chance. In the Asian tradition, one learns to love someone. And I feel it's growing every day. It's not the same thing as in the States. It comes slowly; it's healthier this way."*

The replacement of American homemakers with Asian stand-ins confirms the old axiom that "none are free until all are free." Still, taken as a whole, the phenomenon hardly represents a serious inroad into the gains made by women. These are gains that appear irreversible worldwide, and it will take a great deal more than a few thousand rather fragile "old-fashioned" marriages to reverse the tide. The march toward a workable equality of the sexes is not what's threatened by the growing attraction of white American males to Asian women and the ideal they are imagined to embody; the only thing threatened is the relatively new concept of marrying for passion and separating for lack of same. It is one more joust—this time from the male side—over our contemporary prescriptions for happiness.

The men: *"We believe in traditional roles—like the man washes the car, the woman sweeps. It's so easy to get along that way, where everything's clear."*

The women: *"It's not true that Asian men and American men different. Men are men everywhere—some help the women out, and some don't."*

Some American feminists and Asian-American organizations have condemned the mail-order trade as legalized prostitution and pen pal marriage as inherently abusive, but such rhetoric serves to obscure reality rather than transform it. If the Asian trade leads to a kind of slavery, then it is a volunteered servitude that is but a single link of chain apart from the unwritten contract that binds any man to any woman. Judging these brides by Western standards often means trying to convince the oppressed of just how unhappy they would feel if they could only see their true condition. Unfortunately, the path of human want is rarely politically correct, and history does not move by morally approved acts. Listening to the voices rising from these catalogs of need, what emerges is that those needs are not there to be labeled false or backward. They are there to be met.

The women: *"I am here in this stranger place, with no one can share my loneliness."* *"Do you think you can maybe like me, love me? Need someone for loving. Isn't a joke."*

There are bound to be more and more stories of intercultural courtship—where happy endings are unlikely, but surprise endings can do the same job. For often as not, the reprieve that's granted is that neither party ends up getting anything that resembles the order they've placed. "If it was really mail order," one husband joked, "I'd have made my wife a bit younger. And a lot richer!" Where a human heart is the cargo, the customer can never be sure of exactly what he's ordering or whether he ever gets it delivered intact. The no-fault bride turns out to know very well how to point a finger. The bullying husband ends up in an arm wrestle with his own stereotypes.

The men: *"Asian women are not the subservient types that the media make us believe."* *"They can be very strong willed. I'll tell you, my wife won't take no shit off nobody."*

The women: *"In America, it's not easy like I think. You can't pick money off the streets. It's hard work, enjoying my life."*

In the Posturepedic nuptial bed, over morning bowls of Raisin Bran, on proverbial weekend outings, it turns out that, most of the time, there's no Suzy Wong present, no Simon Legree. He is no John Wayne and she is no geisha. Instead of "inborn submissiveness," she demonstrates, with exposure to new possibilities, a pesky tendency toward human enlargement. Confronted with the silence that comes with slavish assent, reinforcing his solitude, he discovers rather enlightened cravings for a loud and living mate. Behind the triple locks of matrimony, the sprinkler systems and the electric eyes, they are not master and servant, but two people grappling with the long odds against durable understanding. Trapped in the most daunting circumstances, impelled by the most muddled intentions, all they can do is carry on the grim work of making the world one—with an ancient talisman hung outside for good luck.

WOMEN ARE NO GIVE-AWAYS
Abigail Van Buren

Abigail Van Buren (b. 1918) is the author of the nationally syndicated column "Dear Abby." She and her sister, Ann Landers, are probably the most widely read advice columnists of our time. In addition to her daily column, Van Buren has written for popular magazines, lectured extensively, and won numerous awards.

Although Van Buren advises readers on a wide range of topics from birth to death, she also belongs to the tradition of journalists who provided "advice to the lovelorn." Such newspaper features have reflected the society's changing mores, especially in the area of relationships between men and women. In her response to the following letter, Van Buren associates a traditional wedding practice with the historical view of women as property and indicates that change is in the wind.

Dear Abby: I am a 58-year-old woman. When I was a young girl, I attended a formal wedding and was greatly enraged when I heard the minister ask, "Who gives this woman . . . ?"

WOMEN ARE NO GIVE-AWAYS   From Abigail Van Buren, Dear Abby Column, *The* [Worcester, MA] *Evening Gazette* 12 Oct. 1983. Copyright © 1983. Reprinted by permission from Universal Press Syndicate.

The question still arouses my anger and I am amazed that more women are not insulted by this question—asked publicly yet!

Only the woman herself has the right to "give" herself to anyone, any time, for any reason.

I've finally begun to express defiantly my indignation when a bride-to-be tells me she is going to be "given away" by her father or stepfather. Of course, I am a "nut" to even suggest that a woman belongs to no one but herself and is not an inanimate object to be "given away."

Thanks for listening.—Margaret Jonas in San Francisco

Dear Margaret: The original marriage vows were written during biblical times when a woman was considered "chattel"—a piece of property owned by her father. He had the right to "give" her to her husband, who then regarded her as his property.

However, in recent years, many couples have requested that that portion of the marriage ceremony be omitted for the reason you cited.

1855 MARRIAGE CONTRACT
Lucy Stone and Henry B. Blackwell

Lucy Stone (1818–1893) was a leader of the women's rights movement of the nineteenth century. Because her family did not believe in education for females, she worked for several years to earn enough money to attend Oberlin College. When she graduated in 1847, she was the first woman from Massachusetts to earn a college degree.

Stone resolved "to call no man master" in 1838 when she read Sarah Grimké's essays. Like Grimké, Stone decided to forgo marriage in order to devote her life to speaking against slavery and for the rights of women; but the abolitionist Henry Blackwell pursued her and eventually won her hand. They were married in 1855 after both signed a contract that protested the injustice of laws concerning married women and that recognized marriage as "an equal and permanent partnership."

The protest was widely publicized. Thomas Wentworth Higginson, the minister who presided at the nuptials, and a friend of Emily Dickinson, sent a copy to the *Worcester Spy*, and it was later included in the *History of Woman Suffrage*, vol. I. Stone also retained her own name, for which she suffered great harassment; women who later did the same were called "Lucy Stoners."

It was my privilege to celebrate May day by officiating at a wedding in a farm-house among the hills of West Brookfield. The bridegroom was a man of tried worth, a leader in the Western Anti-Slavery Movement; and the bride was one whose fair name is known throughout the nation; one whose rare intellectual qualities are excelled by the private beauty of her heart and life.

I never perform the marriage ceremony without a renewed sense of the iniquity of our present system of laws in respect to marriage; a system by which "man and wife

1855 MARRIAGE CONTRACT   From Elizabeth Cady Stanton, et al, eds., *History of Woman Suffrage* 2nd ed., vol. 1 (Rochester: Charles Mann, 1889) 260–61.

are one, and that one is the husband." It was with my hearty concurrence, therefore, that the following protest was read and signed, as a part of the nuptial ceremony; and I send it to you, that others may be induced to do likewise.

Rev. Thomas Wentworth Higginson.

PROTEST

While acknowledging our mutual affection by publicly assuming the relationship of husband and wife, yet in justice to ourselves and a great principle, we deem it a duty to declare that this act on our part implies no sanction of, nor promise of voluntary obedience to such of the present laws of marriage, as refuse to recognize the wife as an independent, rational being, while they confer upon the husband an injurious and unnatural superiority, investing him with legal powers which no honorable man would exercise, and which no man should possess. We protest especially against the laws which give to the husband:

1. The custody of the wife's person.

2. The exclusive control and guardianship of their children.

3. The sole ownership of her personal, and use of her real estate, unless previously settled upon her, or placed in the hands of trustees, as in the case of minors, lunatics, and idiots.

4. The absolute right to the product of her industry.

5. Also against laws which give to the widower so much larger and more permanent an interest in the property of his deceased wife, than they give to the widow in that of the deceased husband.

6. Finally, against the whole system by which "the legal existence of the wife is suspended during marriage," so that in most States, she neither has a legal part in the choice of her residence, nor can she make a will, nor sue or be sued in her own name, nor inherit property.

We believe that personal independence and equal human rights can never be forfeited, except for crime; that marriage should be an equal and permanent partnership, and so recognized by law; that until it is so recognized, married partners should provide against the radical injustice of present laws, by every means in their power.

We believe that where domestic difficulties arise, no appeal should be made to legal tribunals under existing laws, but that all difficulties should be submitted to the equitable adjustment of arbitrators mutually chosen.

Thus reverencing law, we enter our protest against rules and customs which are unworthy of the name, since they violate justice, the essence of law.

(Signed),   *Henry B. Blackwell,*
                                          Lucy Stone.

Worcester Spy, 1855.

CAN A WOMAN BE LIBERATED AND MARRIED?
Caryl Rivers

Caryl Rivers (b. 1937) is a Professor of Journalism at Boston University and author of *Intimate Enemies* (1988), *Indecent Behavior* (1990), and *More Joy Than Rage: Crossing Generations with the New Feminism* (1992). She has written for a number of prestigious magazines and newspapers and was named Best Columnist for 1979 by the New England Women's Press Association.

In this account of her own and her husband's accommodations to the demands of marriage, parenthood, and two careers, Rivers attempts to answer the question posed in her title according to certain criteria. Her conclusion—"You can't have it all, all the time"—suggests the need for compromise, even in a family that can afford the cost of child care and other services, services which can reduce the need for compromise.

I can remember the exact moment when I was sure I was part of a "liberated" marriage. We were driving along a city street, my husband Alan at the wheel and the two kids, Steven, 8, and Alyssa, 5, in the back seat. Alyssa was clutching a grimy but beloved doll and tugging at the doll's equally grimy and shopworn dress. The overworked threads gave out and the sleeve pulled off. Alyssa looked at the sleeve and then, ignoring me, handed it to my husband and said, "Will you sew it for me, Daddy?"

He didn't sew the dress. He can't sew. I didn't sew the dress. I can't sew either. We gave it to his mother. She's the only one around who isn't all thumbs with a needle. But it was clear that my daughter's question indicated that her mind is—for the time being at least—free of a model of the universe in which the things men do and the things women do are separate spheres, solitary planets that orbit in their own paths, never touching. Since both my husband and I are writers, I suppose she assumes that what grown-ups do is sit in hot stuffy rooms and type a lot, now and then looking up to let out a string of cuss words. It may be the reason she says she would like to stay a kid for a long, long time.

I wonder sometimes if, by the time she grows up, society will be on its way to shattering the old sex-role stereotypes that have made so many men and women so miserable. I see young women today who were raised with one set of assumptions about woman's place and then confronted by the women's movement with a whole new life-style. Since I teach at the college level, I see a dogged professionalism growing among a great many women students. There is also a growing leeriness about any kind of permanent relationship with men. They prize their new-found freedom and are loath to give it up. The prospect of marriage and children seems terrifying—permanent bondage. I respect their seriousness and their need to achieve on their own. And yet, I wonder if some of them will end up like too many men, who sacrificed their emotional lives and wound up with a pension check, a gold watch and nobody who gives a damn.

Can a woman be both liberated and married? And a parent? Can a man? That is a question that is being asked often these days. I think the answer is yes, although one tends to hear more about the failures than the successes—the divorce rate, the runaway wives, the women in consciousness-raising groups who have their consciousnesses lifted right up and out of marriage. I know couples who are splitting up from too much change, too fast. Many of my contemporaries had a decade of very traditional marriages before the women's movement prompted them to try changing their lives. The life they had expected to be heaven when they were 20 turned out to be a source of frustration at 30. Now they are trying to change their way of life and are asking their husbands to adjust to women who are different—often exactly opposite—from the sweet young things they used to be. That sort of wrenching change is what tears marriages apart.

I also know couples who are trying to achieve a balance, as my husband and I are doing. It's easier for us because we started out with a set of expectations that weren't so far apart. He knew that I wanted to be a reporter as much as he wanted to be. We both knew we wanted children. I'm convinced that a liberated marriage, like ours, isn't just luck or a gift of Providence. It has a lot to do with what the bride and the bridegroom think they are at the outset and what they want to be.

I guess I would define a "liberated" marriage as one in which there is a rough parity of both the dirtwork and the glory—and, life being what it is, there is always more of the former. Everyone's solutions are different; ours is a sort of haphazard taking of turns. We have no formal contract about who will do what and when; we are not comfortable with rhetoric and don't really use the word "liberated" very much.

For a number of years, my husband worked full time and his income was the major one; my part-time income bought the extras. Recently I've been the one to work full time, with his income being supplemental. A rough breakdown of the work would probably go this way: Child care, about equal. He handles food shopping, most lunches, the car pool, trash, the dog and miscellaneous tidying. I am in charge of breakfast and dinner, vacuuming, the wash and the ponytail. We both wash dishes. All these chores shift when necessary, the way an outfield shifts over for left-handed hitters. My husband is totally unthreatened by being spotted with a dish towel in his hand. We have no household help, but we do have a baby sitter, a neighbor who comes over when the kids get home from school. She has four kids of her own. Things around the house are rarely dull.

We had always planned to have a family and neither of us has ever regretted that decision. The family unit is an emotional center of gravity in our lives. The kids, while they are a lot of work and a lot of worry, are also a constant source of delight—more than I had expected. They break me up constantly. My son, at the family Passover celebration, was asked the ritual question: "Why is this night different from all other nights?" He deadpanned, "Because on all other nights we eat spaghetti." My daughter announced the other day, out of the blue, "I wish my head was flat, like Frankenstein's, so I could carry things on it." In hindsight, my own upbringing was preparation for a liberated marriage.

I think, with some puzzlement now and then, of a line that Sylvia Plath wrote: "Every woman adores a fascist/the boot in the face, the brute." That rang false to me when I read it; only a masochist could adore a boot in the face. But then, I have known so many women schooled in masochism. I consider myself a feminist. I've written about women's issues, and I think I understand the twinges, the force, the maddening inconsistencies of the movement. One thing I have never really felt is the rage. I have been angry, resentful, just plain mad—but I have never owned the rage, particularly the sort that is unleashed against men. That kind of fury cannot, I suspect, be fired by proxy. It bears directly on something that has happened *to you*. The well of rage is personal, and why, I wondered, was it lacking in me? I grew up in the fifties, that queen of repressive decades, under the shadow of Anatomy Is Destiny.

Many women of my generation wore hobbles on their souls as crippling as the strips of cloth wrapped around the feet of Chinese girl babies to give them a "delicate" walk. Matina Horner, the psychologist who is now president of Radcliffe, discovered the hobbles in her studies of women's fear of success. For many women, particularly bright ones, to succeed in any intellectual task was also to fail as a woman. Those who broke free did not forget the feel of the hobbles. I never knew them. Many women look on men as despots, oppressors, owners of power, brutes. I cannot. I come from a line of liberated men.

There was a picture in my parents' house of my grandfather, my mother's father. I never knew him. He died before I was born. In his picture he seemed the very prototype of the Victorian paterfamilias, with his strong jaw and black full mustache. He raised his children to be hardy, self-reliant and ambitious—and one of them was a girl.

My mother was talking about him recently, and she said she had just realized how unusual it was that her father raised her like a boy. She was a tomboy, free to race and run and skin her knees. Chores were equally shared; she was not banished to the kitchen while her brothers did "men's work." Her father emphasized to her the need to be financially independent, and at one point offered to set her up in business. She chose to go to law school instead.

My mother met my father in law school. Those were the heady, vigorous years of the thirties, and the momentum of the suffrage movement had not yet waned. Women in the thirties breathed freer air than did my contemporaries. In the fifties, we were rebels without a cause; it was a dull toothache of a decade.

I had no strong sense, growing up, that my family was much different from others (although my mother practiced law until I was 5, when she went to join my father at a Navy base in Alabama). My father seemed nicer, funnier, than most fathers, but otherwise I did not perceive him as being that different. I did notice that he was more deeply involved in my life than other girls' fathers were involved in theirs. Those fathers seemed distant—loving, perhaps, but drifting like a cloud, miles above. The father of one of my friends always seemed to be sitting in a chair, smoking a cigar and reading a newspaper, cut off from our lives.

For my father, sports was the thread that bound our activities together. I was a baseball fanatic, and every year he and I went to Griffith Stadium to see Harry Truman or Dwight Eisenhower throw out the first ball.

When I started to play Catholic Youth Organization basketball in the seventh grade, I inherited a ready-made coach: my father. He had once played semipro basketball, and we had strategy sessions around the dining-room table. When the salt shakers would no longer suffice, the whole family would repair to the living room, where my father would assign positions to my mother, my brother and me, and we would run through a play. He taught me how to use my hips and elbows so the referee wouldn't see, and thanks to him, I was the only girl in the league who could execute a jump shot. (The jump shot was considered, I suppose, too strenuous or too unladylike for girls. This was tommyrot to my father, who knew that ladies didn't win ball games. You had to be aggressive if you wanted to be a good basketball player, he said.)

Basketball was serious business at our house. So what if it was only the C.Y.O. girls' team. It did not occur to me that whether or not we beat Blessed Sacrament was not of cosmic concern to everyone. I did notice that there were only a few fathers who went to the girls' games but a lot when the boys played. My father could not live out any fantasies through me. Clearly, I would never be a future Bob Cousy or Sammy Baugh. But our postgame session could not have been more serious if we had been talking about the Knicks or the Celtics instead of the St. Michael's varsity. My father never in any way gave me the impression that what I accomplished was less than it might have been because I was a girl. He was as proud as I of the little cluster of trophies resting on top of the TV set.

Later, when I abandoned basketball for tulle ballgowns with matching pumps and little dabs of perfume behind the ears, the trophies stayed on the TV. At first, I had wanted to pack them away, sure that my boyfriends would think me an Amazon with huge thighs, but my father argued that I had won them, and they ought to stay. He was right, of course. To pack away the trophies would have been betrayal of the rankest order—betrayal of my own past, my accomplishment.

Those were the days when women were supposed to be seen but not heard. In an article for The Ladies' Home Journal in 1954, Marlene Dietrich wrote that women should be like moons, floating about the male sun, shining in reflected glory. (The title of the article was "How to Be Loved.") I tried and inevitably flubbed. I was a lousy moon. I tried to lose prettily at tennis. I never lost that instinct for the jugular, developed in those C.Y.O. games. I won arguments with swains about admitting Red China to the U.N. I got good marks. Finally, I faced it. My mother and father had not produced a moon; they taught me to shine on my own.

Lacking a proper indoctrination in the national mores, I was a bit slow to sense all the nuances. I was truly puzzled by the male contempt for women that was so openly expressed around me. Men used the word for the female sexual organ as a term of utter scorn, and it was hatred, as much as lust, that dripped through the words of the guy who would mutter on a corner, "I'd like to—you, babe!" There was also a female contempt for men that was muted, indirect but had no less a sting.

I wonder how many men realize how deep and bitter runs the contempt of women. Barred so often from the arena, where the lights are hot and a man's performance is on display, women have the power of the people in the bleachers. They can criticize, ridicule and demand, safe in the knowledge that the stamina the arena demands will not be asked of them. Their weapon is not the Bronx cheer—that is too direct—but the well-timed laugh, the curl of a lip. If a man could listen in while his sex—or he himself—was being discussed by a group of "traditional, subservient" women, it would chill his blood. I have heard such discussions in which men were reduced to buffoons and incompetents by women who were supposed to love them—and hold them in awe. It is the power of the weak, never openly displayed because there is too much to lose.

I was astonished by all this, because contempt was something I had to learn about outside my own home. My mother and my father were equals in their house. If, as the years passed, their marriage was not the paradise that M.-G.-M. said marriage should be, it *was* rooted in the sort of loyalty and trust that can exist only between people of like weight and power. Never, in the entire time I was growing up, did I hear my father put my mother down. Never did I hear her mock him. I grew up believing that is how things were between men and women.

It may seem insignificant—or cute—to see ponytailed moppets out there playing shortstop in Little League. But consider. The women those girls will grow up to be will not be inclined to laugh at men when they fail, to mock them when their best turns out to be not good enough. They will have known what it feels like to take a third strike swinging or to bobble a grounder. Contempt will only vanish when women have a chance to play all the games now owned by men.

I always wanted to play—ever since I was a kid. I wanted to be where things were happening, not on the sidelines. When Alan and I were married, two years out of grad school, our careers had begun to progress at an even, steady rate. We worked on a small paper in New York State, then went on to jobs reporting politics and urban affairs, he in Baltimore and I in Washington. I must confess that I half-believed his work was more "serious" than mine because he was a man. I was happy, for a time, with the fact that I had been allowed into a man's game.

The real changes for us came with the birth of our first child. They had nothing to do with religion. Alan and I had agreed that the children would be raised in the Jewish religion and I would follow my own unorthodox brand of Catholicism. But with Steven's birth, we faced the problem of work roles. Now the responsibility for bringing home the bacon was Alan's. I was determined to continue my career by freelancing, but it was as if a large rock had been placed on the scale of our professional lives—on his side. I accepted the curtailments on my freedom. I did not get upset when he called at 11 and said he was going to have a drink with the other reporters. I know how one likes to talk shop after a hard day. But I had no one to talk shop with. If he called and said he had to miss dinner, I said, "Sure," because I knew about deadlines. But if I was working on a story, there was no one to call and say, "I won't be home," because the baby sitter had deadlines of her own. Sometimes I thought I was living vicariously through my husband's experiences. He was the one in the middle of things and I was on the periphery. I learned a new sensation—the "invisible woman" effect. There were times when we went to parties that people came up eagerly to speak to him and looked through me as if I didn't exist.

I became a hoarder of time. My work time was severely rationed. I would rarely ask Alan to give up something he had scheduled to baby-sit while I worked. In my mind I had assigned us places—he was first and I was way behind. I resented this, often. I resented the fact that he simply accepted this, as if it were the way of the world. He never said my work was not important. He was always careful to praise what I had done. But I had the feeling that his work was capital I important and mine was little i important.

When he designed a news show for public television and served as its anchorman and news editor, his working day ran from 9 A.M. to 9 P.M. or after. I was home alone night after night with the children. I kept active professionally but it was a great juggling act, calling the baby sitter, making sure Steven had clean underpants and that the meat for dinner was out of the freezer. My husband was exhausted when he came home at night. The 60-hour-plus week left him so frayed it took him half the weekend to get back to normal. I knew how important the idea of the show was to him.

At the same time I grew restive about the strain his work put on both of us, how it was beginning to isolate him from the family that was so important to both of us. He would remark, often, that he was missing seeing his daughter grow from an infant into a little girl. This was one of the major factors in his decision to leave television for a magazine job with more reasonable hours. If he had followed the traditional upwardly mobile success pattern, he would have gone on to "bigger" jobs that would have eaten up more and more of his time. Increasingly, I would have had to assume more and more of the burden of the household and the kids. I suspect that my resentment would have grown like a malevolent weed. He would have been too busy to see it growing. It could well have choked the life out of our relationship.

If the women's movement has had an impact on our personal balance, I guess it is because I felt more able to articulate my frustrations and he was able to understand that they were common to a great many women. He has been very considerate about trying to understand the things that were bugging me, to understand my need to be serious about my work, and I have tried not to get on a soapbox with movement speeches. We have the usual yelling matches now and then, but they are usually less intense than our disagreements over more cosmic issues, such as whether or not pouring the water from the dog's dish in the kitchen sink is a sanitary practice. I say the dog germs will gurgle down the sink and disappear and he sees rabies microbes dancing on the silverware.

I have to admit, too, that despite the limits on my freedom in the time I spent at home, the lack of economic pressure gave me the chance to experiment, to start off on roads that might lead nowhere. My first book, about growing up as a Catholic in America, was the result of one of those experiments. I would never have written it if I had been hiking after some politician on the trail of a headline.

I no longer feel that there is an inequality in our professional lives. Sure, I made sacrifices, but so has he. At different periods of our lives, we have both subsidized each other's work with time and money, and I have learned a simple truth that I should have known: You can't have it all, all of the time. Many of the men of my generation thought they could, so they tied themselves to the conveyor belt, thinking that women would manage their emotions. They wound up with a vacuum where part of their lives should have been. My husband and I don't want that to happen to us. So perhaps I will not climb every mountain and ford every stream (a cliché, but my daughter has played "The Sound of Music" to the point where the sight of whiskers on kittens makes me want to throw up) but I am damned sure I will get to a lot of them. My husband will climb back on the merry-go-round but he will know when to get off. There will be areas in which we can't compete with the people who work 16 hours a day, who eat, live and breathe only for work. So be it. As the children grow older, some of the old demands they make on us will dwindle, but the parents of teen-agers assure me that some dandy new ones will arise.

I hear some young people talking of the "division of child-care tasks" and it sounds very clean and scientific, something a computer could manage. It is not like that. As a reporter in urban America in the sixties and seventies, my husband got acclimated to the front lines. A black militant once tried to run him over, he patrolled the streets of New York with the Jewish Defense League, and he got hit with a tomato meant for Teddy Kennedy when the whites of Boston got upset over busing. He was accustomed to danger, tension, confusion and chaos—and then came the real test of his mettle: home.

This year, when he got a book contract, we pulled the big switch. He is now working at home, writing. Mornings he also takes care of Alyssa before she goes off to kindergarten. I work full time, teaching at Boston University. Here, in terms of a "division of child-care tasks," are a few highlights from an actual day in the life of a liberated man:

Somewhere between 6:30 and 7 we struggle out of bed and try to shuffle everybody in and out of one bathroom. Alan makes the bed and I wrestle with the ponytail. I cook bacon and he makes bologna sandwiches. He takes Steven, a third-grader, to school and I get Alyssa in the right coat and shoes for rain or shine. We hop in the car, because Alan will drive me to the university where I have a morning course. The traffic at the entrance to the Sumner Tunnel is its usual incredible snarl. Alyssa announces, brightly, "We are all going to play puppet hands!"

Alan moans, audibly. I groan. Puppet hands is a game she invented all by herself. In it, she turns her left hand into Cowey and her right hand into Horsey. The two of them converse in a screechy falsetto that would drive a saint to screaming heresy. But it doesn't stop there. My right hand is Frog and my left hand is Phyllis Frog. Alan's right hand is Fishy and his left hand is Elephant. Elephant is a morose sort, but Fishy has been too engaging for his own good. So Alyssa chants, in a sort of nagging chirp, "Fishy, where are you? Fishy? Fishy? Fiiiisssssshhhhyyyyyy!" until her father relents and Fishy speaks.

Through the tunnel, up Storrow Drive, Alyssa does puppet hands. My teeth are on edge. Alan drops me off at B.U. Alyssa waves good-by and I hear her saying, "Fishy, Fishy, want to hear me sing?" Alan's knuckles, where he grips the wheel, are turning white.

When he and Alyssa arrive home, Alan goes up to the attic-office to work. He has been at the typewriter for half an hour when peculiar sounds, accompanied by a peculiar smell, drift up the stairs. He goes down and discovers that the sounds are being made by Jane, the medium-sized family dog—loyal, dumb and cowardly—who is having an attack of diarrhea on the living-room rug. He drags Jane into the kitchen and starts to swab her off when Alyssa wanders in, wrinkles her nose and says, "I think I have to throw up." He hustles her out of the kitchen. Eventually, he gets back to work.

Next comes lunch time and the kindergarten car pool. After the noon car-pool run, there is a precious two and a half hours for work on the book. Then it is time to pick up Steven. Steven's cronies, Joey, Jonathan, Chris and Michael, ride along. Third-grade conversation—and particularly humor—is cheerfully and relentlessly anal. Punch lines involving excrement produce gales of laughter. Alan drives home, attempting to block out the punching, cackling and assorted animal sounds from the back seat.

Up in his office , he types vigorously for 12 minutes and eight seconds before he becomes aware of eyes boring into his back. It is Deanna, aged 3, our neighbor's daughter.

"Awan," she says. "Can I kiss Jane? Does Jane have jorms?" (Her version of germs.)

"You can kiss Jane. She hasn't got germs. Just don't kiss her on the mouth."

"Will I get a cold if I kiss Jane, Awan? Does Jane have jorms?"

"No jorms. I mean germs."

"Do you have jorms, Awan?"

"No."

"Does Alyssa have jorms?"

"No."

"Does Alyssa have jorms?"

"No. NOBODY HAS JORMS!"

Steven and Joey come charging in. There is a wounded pigeon on the lawn. Alan hollers at the kids not to touch the pigeon. Pigeons are filthy, plague-carrying birds. He calls the dog officer and waits on the lawn to make sure the pigeon doesn't hobble into the street and get run over, which would upset the children. The dog officer comes and takes the pigeon. Alan goes back to the typewriter. Nothing will come. The muse has vanished. The phone rings. It is I, his loving wife. "Are you having a nice day, dear?"

❦ ❦ ❦

My husband is, I think, one of a growing breed of free men who have not been stamped out of a mold like a chocolate bunny, who can dry a dish or wipe a runny nose without an attack of castration anxiety. I have known too many men struggling honestly with the new ambitions and hopes of women to think the liberated man is a rare species. But there are men—a great many, I suppose—who cannot function in anything but the old way, who must see women as satellites to sustain their own egos. I have known women married to such men: when the women began to grow in their own self-estimation, the marriages broke up.

I know other women who are sticking with marriages where there is a great deal of tension about sex roles and division of chores. They stay because they value the relationships and hope things will work out. Sometimes women are afraid to speak out. Other times they bark demands, forgetting that a marriage is not the U.A.W. bargaining table. Some marriages ought to fail, for the sanity of both parties. It is easy to say, in ringing tones, that a woman ought to up and leave any man who isn't liberated. But the formula that works for one person could be deadly for another.

I am optimistic, however, for the future of liberated marriage. I think it makes good sense. It is easier than the old model, because it allows both parties more options. I think it must be tough to be a man, looking ahead year after year after year to driving a cab or teaching high-school civics or selling insurance, with no prospects of climbing off the treadmill, even for a while. Is that really much better than the plight of the woman who looks ahead and sees an Everest of dirty dishes and unmade beds?

I have a feeling that the men and women of my daughter's generation will be dealing with their expectations earlier and in a more rational way than most of us did. My husband is always saying to Alyssa, "Girls can be doctors" or "Girls can be pilots" or "Girls can be anything they want." He will transmit to her the message my father (and my mother) beamed to me: You are a person of worth, of value, and it is your right to achieve and grow. My husband accorded me that right freely; I did not have to wrest it from him. If I am a free woman, and I believe I am, it is due in no small measure to the fact that I have lived with—and loved and been nurtured by—free men.

Part Five

Mothers

O f all the images of women, that of
woman as mother is the most
central and, perhaps, the most ambiva-
lent. During the earliest ages of human
history, the Great Goddess or Great
Mother was part of the myths of almost
all cultures. Representing the mystery of
life, of fecundity as well as decay, she
also appeared under the aegis of The
Terrible Mother. Although images of
mothers and motherhood vary from
culture to culture, they often contain
these dual elements of generation and
corruption. Their cultural relativity
derives from those economic, social, and
political forces that affect the balance
between these perceptions.

Such forces were at work in the
change from an agricultural to an industrialized economy which occurred during the early nineteenth century. In a
rural economy, most people worked at
home, where family responsibilities were
determined less strongly by gender.
When men went to work in urban centers, however, they expected to return at

*"THE RIGOR OF RAISING CHILDREN
OURSELVES MAKES CLEAR TO US OUR
MOTHERS' INCREDIBLE STRENGTH."*
—ANNA QUINDLEN

night to havens from the world of
commerce presided over by "angels in
the house." By the 1800s, the division

between public and private spheres, between male and female realms, had been drawn, and the "Mystique of Motherhood," which the emerging middle class fostered, became the expression of an ideal.

This ideal, shaped by the sentimentalization of women in general and of mothers in particular, was based on the belief that women possessed certain "feminine" qualities, that they were by nature warm, gentle, sensitive, nurturing, moral, self-sacrificing, patient, and enduring. Such worthy surrogates for absent fathers received certain rewards: their status was deemed sacred; they were considered the heart of the family's refuge; and they were allowed a certain amount of power over the activities of the household, especially those involving children.

Children, of course, were the primary responsibility of mothers. Serving as models, mothers instructed the young in moral perfection and thus shaped the character of the next generation. Nineteenth-century commentators, emphasizing this awesome responsibility, maintained that the health of the Republic itself depended on mothers. Although removed from public life, women ostensibly controlled, through their sons and daughters, the future of the public as well as the private sphere. The same could not be said, of course, about slave mothers and their children, who were separated from each other at the will of their owners. Slave narratives are filled with accounts of the suffering of slave mothers when their children were sold separately, without any consideration by the white slave traders and owners of the ideal of "sacred motherhood."

At the beginning of the nineteenth century, wives and children were considered the property of husbands and fathers; in cases of separation or divorce, fathers had first claim on their children and often took custody. As the economy shifted from rural to urban and children became less valuable as workers who contributed to the finances of the family, however, mothers were allowed custody, especially in cases involving young children.

At the same time, the ideal persisted. The "mother-women" whom Kate Chopin describes in *The Awakening* (1899) are the ideal's exemplars, but similar portraits, often sentimentalized, appeared frequently in the popular periodical literature. Religious leaders, taking their texts from the Old and New Testaments, praised the "valiant woman" and gratefully encouraged her active participation in their congregations. The authors of sentimental novels, many of them women, focused on the hearth and home; although their heroines were not usually mothers, they often had mothers or surrogates who reflected the ideal. In *Uncle Tom's Cabin,* Harriet Beecher Stowe imposed this ideal on the slave mother, Eliza, who risks life and limb for her child. Even Fanny Fern, who directed her pointed wit at male supremacy, wrote about mothers with great sentimentality and little humor.

Although unequally applied, the Mystique of Motherhood was most compelling during the nineteenth century, but it has persisted into the twentieth, especially in the popular advice literature designed for middle- and upperclass women. In their best-seller of 1947, *Modern Woman: The Lost Sex*, Ferdinand Lundberg and Marynia Farnham maintained that it is a woman's role as mother that validates her: "If a woman does not have children, she asks ingenuously"—and "ingenuously" is an important word here—"what is everything all about for her?" The acceptance and availability of birth control and abortion, of course, eventually made it possible for women not only to choose the number of children they wanted to have, but also to choose not to be mothers at all.

Whether we consider the nineteenth-century conception of the ideal mother or the modern version, it is clear that both describe a role that no human being can play without serious difficulty. The "true woman" may have believed that her *raison d'etre* was motherhood, but real mothers often asked: "Is this all there is?" Such questioning can be found in the private writing of women; in their literary works, where they speak through imagined characters; and in their public pronouncements.

Some women resisted the total selflessness that the ideal required, but they suffered the consequences. When Charlotte Perkins Gilman (1860–1935), one of the most influential thinkers of her time, gave up her daughter to be reared by the child's father and his second wife, she was accused of being "unnatural" and of giving up her child in order to obtain her freedom. Her own life was difficult at that time, and she wanted her daughter to grow up in a more stable environment. Similar concerns apparently prompted Jane Cannary Hickok, better known as Calamity Jane, to give up her daughter to be reared by friends. Jane's life was nomadic and adventurous, unfit, she thought, for a child. For some reason, criticism is harsher when daughters are involved, perhaps because of the special bond that mothers and daughters are said to share.

In Chopin's *The Awakening*, Edna Pontellier says to a friend: "I would give up the unessential; I would give my money, I would give my life for my children; but I wouldn't give myself." It is not surprising that hostile reviewers of the novel described Edna as an unfit mother. Mothers who behaved in this way were considered deviant, and they often suffered feelings of guilt and failure.

The heavy psychological toll of the Mystique of Motherhood was evident, not only in the "Mom" who sought some kind of power within the confines of the home, where guilt often became her means of social control, but in those women who subscribed to the ideal, tried to live up to it, and perceived themselves to be failures. Experts, of course, warned that the failure of mothers to measure up would have dire effects on their children. Indeed, Lundberg and Farnham connected the Holocaust to the behavior of Adolph Hitler's mother. It is only in the very recent past, in fact, that psychologists have begun to look beyond the behavior or attitudes of the mother for the causes of disturbance in children.

Despite the claim that anatomy is destiny, that destiny has been altered by the social and economic requirements of the time. The institution of motherhood is a social creation molded as much by economic and political forces as by biology, so it is subject to change. As a result, images of mothers during the last two centuries are often complex and even contradictory. In addition, the dominant American image was often modified, varied, reduced, or rejected by some ethnic and racial groups. Still, it is difficult to comprehend the enormity of the enterprise that socialized, trained, and educated millions of women—no matter what their skills and abilities, their talents and accomplishments, or their preferences—to fill this one role.

In *Women and Economics*, Gilman said that the role of mothers was "to bear and rear the majestic race to which they can never fully belong! To live vicariously forever, through their sons, the daughters being only another vicarious link. What a supreme and magnificent martyrdom." For many women, motherhood was martyrdom; but for many others, it was a demanding but happy experience which they lived with courage and strength, often against enormous physical and psychological odds.

THE SLAVE MOTHER

Frances Ellen Watkins Harper

Frances Ellen Watkins (1825–1911) was born in Baltimore of free parents. Self-educated, she worked as a seamstress before becoming an abolitionist lecturer and a writer. In 1860, she married Fenton Harper, but was widowed soon after the birth of their daughter. On her speaking tours, Harper often traveled alone, enduring extreme physical hardships and facing somewhat hostile crowds. After Emancipation, she continued to speak publicly, especially in opposition to lynching and in support of women's suffrage. By 1893, she was confident that "to-day we stand on the threshold of woman's era. . . . "

Harper's novel *Iola Leroy; or Shadows Uplifted* (1892) is the first novel by an African-American woman published in the United States. She also wrote ten volumes of poetry. Income from her writing, public readings, and literary lectures provided her with financial support during her later years.

Heard you that shriek? It rose
  So wildly on the air,
It seemed as if a burden'd heart
  Was breaking in despair.

Saw you those hands so sadly clasped—
  The bowed and feeble head—
The shuddering of that fragile form—
  That look of grief and dread?

Saw you the sad, imploring eye?
  Its every glance was pain,
As if a storm of agony
  Were sweeping through the brain.

She is a mother, pale with fear,
  Her boy clings to her side,
And in her kirtle vainly tries
  His trembling form to hide.

He is not hers, although she bore
  For him a mother's pains;
He is not hers, although her blood
  Is coursing through his veins!

He is not hers, for cruel hands
  May rudely tear apart
The only wreath of household love
  That binds her breaking heart.

THE SLAVE MOTHER   From Frances Ellen Watkins Harper, "The Slave Mother," *Poems on Miscellaneous Subjects* (Boston: Yerrington, 1854) 4–5.

His love has been a joyous light
  That o'er her pathway smiled,
A fountain gushing ever new,
  Amid life's desert wild.

His lightest word has been a tone
  Of music round her heart,
Their lives a streamlet blent in one—
  Oh, Father! must they part?

They tear him from her circling arms,
  Her last and fond embrace.
Oh! never more may her sad eyes
  Gaze on his mournful face.

No marvel, then, these bitter shrieks
  Disturb the listening air:
She is a mother, and her heart
  Is breaking in despair.

ONLY A MOTHER—NO TRIVIAL THING

Lucy Stone

When Lucy Stone became a mother in 1858, she had to interrupt her work as a speaker for abolition and the rights of women to care for her daughter. Although she missed being "on the road," Stone tried to live up to the ideal of wife and mother. However, in letters to her husband, who was often away, and to her sister-in-law and close friend, Antoinette Brown Blackwell (Nettie), she shared some of her ambivalence.

Although she had strongly supported the economic independence of wives, at the end of her life Lucy Stone told her daughter, Alice Stone Blackwell, that a wife should not take part in supporting the family: "She bears the children and her hands are full."

In her letter to Nettie, included here, Stone refers to Thomas Wentworth Higginson (1823–1911), the Unitarian minister who presided at her marriage and who later befriended Emily Dickinson. In the last letter, Nettie extends sympathy to Stone for her recent miscarriage.

Orange N.J., May 21, 1858

DEAREST HARRY,

It is a gloriously beautiful morning—the 21st of May and as the wretched boil I told you of in my last burst last night, I hope to get off to Father's next Wednesday. . . . I wish you could see our Sarah now. She is trying to creep—and *moves backward*, and around. She has the most radient little face, I ever saw and *is* a very promising child.

ONLY A MOTHER—NO TRIVIAL THING   From Lucy Stone, letter to Harry Blackwell, 21 May 1858; Lucy Stone, letter to Antoinette Brown Blackwell, 20 Feb 1859; Antoinette Brown Blackwell, letter to Lucy Stone, 29 Aug 1859. Blackwell Family Papers, Manuscript Division, Library of Congress.

I never feel her little cheek beside of mine,—never hear her quick coming breath—or her sweet baby voice, without the earnest purpose to gather to myself more symmetry of being—to sustain all my relations better—to be to her the example and so the guide she will need.

I *am* trying to be a good wife and mother. I have wanted to tell you how hard I am trying, but I *have* tried before and my miserable failures hitherto, make me silent now. But if I have conquered myself, or gained anything in all these weary weeks you will find it in my actions. I *hope* to be more to you, and better—when you come to me. I am glad too darling, that you feel the lack of dignity in the *running* to the station &c and that you will *try* to mend it. I will have the breakfast earlier, and we may, after all, be a model family yet. We will be patient with each other. I will try and have more time to read—and to go out with you, when I can, and not neglect Sarah.

Chicago Sunday, Feb. 20, 1859

DEAR NETTIE,

Today you are preaching for Mr. Higginson. It is the day you were to have been here. I felt a little chagrined at the result of our plan. Now if you will come I do think we can get you up some meetings that will pay you even better than $100, & your expenses.

Fred Douglass had a very large audience paying twenty-five cents, & you would draw as well as he did. I wish I felt the old impulse & power to lecture, both for the sake of cherished principles & to help Harry with the heavy burden he has to bear,—but I am afraid, & dare not trust Lucy Stone. I went to hear E.P. Whipple lecture on Joan d'Arc. It was very inspiring, & for the hour I felt as though all things were possible to me. But when I came home & looked in Alice's sleeping face & thought of the possible evil that might befall her if my guardian eye was turned away, I shrank like a snail into its shell, & saw that for these years I can be only a mother—no trivial thing either. I hope you gave a good sermon today.

Yours truly,

Lucy

Westport N.Y., Tuesday Aug. 29 '59

DEAR LUCY,

⚘ ⚘ ⚘

Dear Lucy we shall all be glad to see you again & so glad to have you in Orange or Bloomfield. I have missed you & wanted you back again often & often; but in these days I am not demonstrative over much & so have not said so; but now that the time approaches I very much rejoice. You must know that I have heard of the poor premature little baby & that I sympathize with you deeply. I have not spoken of it; but the temptation to do so has been great; but I did not know how you would feel about it & so was silent but at Saratoga Mrs. Hopper, Lucretia Motts daughter asked me if you had another child. I said no,—with a world of pain,—& she looked so surprised; said Mr. Somebody had seen you not long before; & they all were expecting we had heard something so evidently, that I did not know what to say, & so said nothing at all. Perhaps that is best, & yet I think every body who is so anxious to have Lucy speak again would feel better if they knew how impossible that has been & still must be for the present. I confess I should like to tell Susan. She does not blame you or feel hard towards you for not talking but she often says that *if* you are not *disabled* again she should be so glad to have you speak now & then, &c & in her heart I think cant quite understand . . . why you dont. Shall I still be silent on that point—I know how it has made your heart ache to lose so many new hopes. It is almost like losing something of ones own life, but Lucy dear when one had held a little living thing in ones arms for almost 4 months till its little face began to brighten with smiles when you looked in it that is sadder still. Sam was with me at intervals for two weeks. We had a grand time three days at lake George. I shall be at home by the end of the month perhaps before some few days. You will see the report of Eastern meetings in papers.

   I am too tired to write more. Write me at 78 South street & Sam will forward immediately.

Nettie

IMPRESSIONS OF AN INDIAN CHILDHOOD
Zitkala-Ša

Zitkala-Ša (1875–1938), or Gertrude Simmons Bonnin, was a nationally known writer and lecturer who founded the Council of American Indians in 1926. Born on the Pine Ridge Reservation in South Dakota, Zitkala-Ša (Red Bird) attended Earlham College and taught at the Carlisle Indian School in Pennsylvania. A talented violinist, she studied music at the Boston Conservatory and in Paris. After returning to the reservation in the early 1900s, she married Raymond T. Bonnin, a Sioux who worked for the U.S. Indian Service, and became an activist working for the rights of Native Americans.

   The popular images of Native-American women include those of the squaw, a large, silent, and inscrutable woman carrying a papoose; and the tender, shy, and submissive maiden. Most of the heroines, such as Pocahontas, the princess; and Kateri Tekakwitha, the saint, served white men. Zitkala-Ša's mother fits into none of these stereotypes. A single parent connected to an extended family, she remembers vividly the past suffering of her people and faces uneasy accommodations with the present for the future benefit of her children.

MY MOTHER

A wigwam of weather-stained canvas stood at the base of some irregularly ascending hills. A footpath wound its way gently down the sloping land till it reached the broad river bottom; creeping through the long swamp grasses that bent over it on either side, it came out on the edge of the Missouri.

IMPRESSIONS OF AN INDIAN CHILDHOOD   From Zitkala-Ša, "Impressions of an Indian Childhood," *Atlantic Monthly* Jan. 1900: 37–38, 41, 45–47. Copyright © 1900 by Zitkala-Ša, as first published in The Atlantic Monthly.

Here, morning, noon, and evening, my mother came to draw water from the muddy stream for our household use. Always, when my mother started for the river, I stopped my play to run along with her. She was only of medium height. Often she was sad and silent, at which times her full arched lips were compressed into hard and bitter lines, and shadows fell under her black eyes. Then I clung to her hand and begged to know what made the tears fall.

"Hush; my little daughter must never talk about my tears"; and smiling through them, she patted my head and said, "Now let me see how fast you can run to-day." Whereupon I tore away at my highest possible speed, with my long black hair blowing in the breeze.

I was a wild little girl of seven. Loosely clad in a slip of brown buckskin, and light-footed with a pair of soft moccasins on my feet, I was as free as the wind that blew my hair, and no less spirited than a bounding deer. These were my mother's pride,—my wild freedom and overflowing spirits. She taught me no fear save that of intruding myself upon others.

Having gone many paces ahead I stopped, panting for breath, and laughing with glee as my mother watched my every movement. I was not wholly conscious of myself, but was more keenly alive to the fire within. It was as if I were the activity, and my hands and feet were only experiments for my spirit to work upon.

Returning from the river, I tugged beside my mother, with my hand upon the bucket I believed I was carrying. One time, on such a return, I remember a bit of conversation we had. My grown-up cousin, Warca-Ziwin (Sunflower), who was then seventeen, always went to the river alone for water for her mother. Their wigwam was not far from ours; and I saw her daily going to and from the river. I admired my cousin greatly. So I said: "Mother, when I am tall as my cousin Warca-Ziwin, you shall not have to come for water. I will do it for you."

With a strange tremor in her voice which I could not understand, she answered, "If the paleface does not take away from us the river we drink."

"Mother, who is this bad paleface?" I asked.

"My little daughter, he is a sham,—a sickly sham! The bronzed Dakota is the only real man."

I looked up into my mother's face while she spoke; and seeing her bite her lips, I knew she was unhappy. This aroused revenge in my small soul. Stamping my foot on the earth, I cried aloud, "I hate the paleface that makes my mother cry!"

Setting the pail of water on the ground, my mother stooped, and stretching her left hand out on the level with my eyes, she placed her other arm about me; she pointed to the hill where my uncle and my only sister lay buried.

"There is what the paleface has done! Since then your father too has been buried in a hill nearer the rising sun. We were once very happy. But the paleface has stolen our lands and driven us hither. Having defrauded us of our land, the paleface forced us away.

"Well, it happened on the day we moved camp that your sister and uncle were both very sick. Many others were ailing, but there seemed to be no help. We traveled many days and nights; not in the grand happy way that we moved camp when I was a little girl, but we were driven, my child, driven like a herd of buffalo. With every step, your sister, who was not as large as you are now, shrieked with the painful jar until she was hoarse with crying. She grew more and more feverish. Her little hands and cheeks were burning hot. Her little lips were parched and dry, but she would not drink the water I gave her. Then I discovered that her throat was swollen and red. My poor child, how I cried with her because the Great Spirit had forgotten us!

"At last, when we reached this western country, on the first weary night your sister died. And soon your uncle died also, leaving a widow and an orphan daughter, your cousin Warca-Ziwin. Both your sister and uncle might have been happy with us to-day, had it not been for the heartless paleface."

My mother was silent the rest of the way to our wigwam. Though I saw no tears in her eyes, I knew that was because I was with her. She seldom wept before me.

❧ ❧ ❧

THE BIG RED APPLES

The first turning away from the easy, natural flow of my life occurred in an early spring. It was in my eighth year; in the month of March, I afterward learned. At this age I knew but one language, and that was my mother's native tongue.

From some of my playmates I heard that two paleface missionaries were in our village. They were from that class of white men who wore big hats and carried large hearts, they said. Running direct to my mother, I began to question her why these two strangers were among us. She told me, after I had teased much, that they had come to take away Indian boys and girls to the East. My mother did not seem to want me to talk about them. But in a day or two, I gleaned many wonderful stories from my playfellows concerning the strangers.

"Mother, my friend Judéwin is going home with the missionaries. She is going to a more beautiful country than ours; the palefaces told her so!" I said wistfully, wishing in my heart that I too might go.

Mother sat in a chair, and I was hanging on her knee. Within the last two seasons my big brother Dawée had returned from a three years' education in the East, and his coming back influenced my mother to take a farther step from her native way of living. First it was a change from the buffalo skin to the white man's canvas that covered our wigwam. Now she had given up her wigwam of slender poles, to live, a foreigner, in a home of clumsy logs.

"Yes, my child, several others besides Judéwin are going away with the palefaces. Your brother said the missionaries had inquired about his little sister," she said, watching my face very closely.

My heart thumped so hard against my breast, I wondered if she could hear it.

"Did he tell them to take me, mother?" I asked, fearing lest Dawée had forbidden the palefaces to see me, and that my hope of going to the Wonderland would be entirely blighted.

With a sad, slow smile, she answered: "There! I knew you were wishing to go, because Judéwin has filled your ears with the white men's lies. Don't believe a word they say! Their words are sweet, but, my child, their deeds are bitter. You will cry for me, but they will not even soothe you. Stay with me, my little one! Your brother Dawée says that going East, away from your mother, is too hard an experience for his baby sister."

Thus my mother discouraged my curiosity about the lands beyond our eastern horizon; for it was not yet an ambition for Letters that was stirring me. But on the following day the missionaries did come to our very house. I spied them coming up the footpath leading to our cottage. A third man was with them, but he was not my brother Dawée. It was another, a young interpreter, a paleface who had a smattering of the Indian language. I was ready to run out to meet them, but I did not dare to displease my mother. With great glee, I jumped up and down on our ground floor. I begged my mother to open the door, that they would be sure to come to us. Alas! They came, they saw, and they conquered!

Judéwin had told me of the great tree where grew red, red apples; and how we could reach out our hands and pick all the red apples we could eat. I had never seen apple trees. I had never tasted more than a dozen red apples in my life; and when I heard of the orchards of the East, I was eager to roam among them. The missionaries smiled into my eyes, and patted my head. I wondered how mother could say such hard words against them.

"Mother, ask them if little girls may have all the red apples they want, when they go East," I whispered aloud, in my excitement.

The interpreter heard me, and answered: "Yes, little girl, the nice red apples are for those who pick them; and you will have a ride on the iron horse if you go with these good people."

I had never seen a train, and he knew it.

"Mother, I'm going East! I like big red apples, and I want to ride on the iron horse! Mother, say yes!" I pleaded.

My mother said nothing. The missionaries waited in silence; and my eyes began to blur with tears, though I struggled to choke them back. The corners of my mouth twitched, and my mother saw me.

"I am not ready to give you any word," she said to them. "To-morrow I shall send you my answer by my son."

With this they left us. Alone with my mother, I yielded to my tears, and cried aloud, shaking my head so as not to hear what she was saying to me. This was the first time I had ever been so unwilling to give up my own desire that I refused to hearken to my mother's voice.

There was a solemn silence in our home that night. Before I went to bed I begged the Great Spirit to make my mother willing I should go with the missionaries.

The next morning came, and my mother called me to her side. "My daughter, do you still persist in wishing to leave your mother?" she asked.

"Oh, mother, it is not that I wish to leave you, but I want to see the wonderful Eastern land," I answered.

My dear old aunt came to our house that morning, and I heard her say, "Let her try it."

I hoped that, as usual, my aunt was pleading on my side. My brother Dawée came for mother's decision. I dropped my play, and crept close to my aunt.

"Yes, Dawée, my daughter, though she does not understand what it all means, is anxious to go. She will need an education when she is grown, for then there will be fewer real Dakotas, and many more palefaces. This tearing her away, so young, from her mother is necessary, if I would have her an educated woman. The palefaces, who owe us a large debt for stolen lands, have begun to pay a tardy justice in offering some education to our children. But I know my daughter must suffer keenly in this experiment. For her sake, I dread to tell you my reply to the missionaries. Go, tell them that they may take my little daughter, and that the Great Spirit shall not fail to reward them according to their hearts."

Wrapped in my heavy blanket, I walked with my mother to the carriage that was soon to take us to the iron horse. I was happy. I met my playmates, who were also wearing their best thick blankets. We showed one another our new beaded moccasins, and the width of the belts that girdled our new dresses. Soon we were being drawn rapidly away by the white man's horses. When I saw the lonely figure of my mother vanish in the distance, a sense of regret settled heavily upon me. I felt suddenly weak, as if I might fall limp to the ground. I was in the hands of strangers whom my mother did not fully trust. I no longer felt free to be myself, or to voice my own feelings. The tears trickled down my cheeks, and I buried my face in the folds of my blanket. Now the first step, parting me from my mother, was taken, and all my belated tears availed nothing.

Having driven thirty miles to the ferryboat, we crossed the Missouri in the evening. Then riding again a few miles eastward, we stopped before a massive brick building. I looked at it in amazement, and with a vague misgiving, for in our village I had never seen so large a house. Trembling with fear and distrust of the palefaces, my teeth chattering from the chilly ride, I crept noiselessly in my soft moccasins along the narrow hall, keeping very close to the bare wall. I was as frightened and bewildered as the captured young of a wild creature.

A WORD TO MOTHERS

Fanny Fern

Best known for her witty social commentary, Fanny Fern also wrote sentimental pieces, especially about mothers and children. After the death of her first husband and the divorce from her second, Fern became a single mother, responsible for the support of herself and her three daughters. Receiving little help from her relatives, some of whom were affluent, she lived in poverty until her writing earned her enough money to support her family. To the end of her life she was particularly sympathetic to the plight of poor mothers and their children.

"Dear mother," said a delicate little girl, "I have broken your China vase!"

"Well, you are a naughty, careless, troublesome little thing, always in some mischief. Go up stairs and stay in the closet till I send for you!"

And this was a Christian mother's answer to the tearful little culprit, who had struggled with, and conquered, the temptation to tell a falsehood to screen her fault! With a disappointed, disheartened look, the child obeyed; and, at that moment, was crushed in her little heart the sweet flower of truth, perhaps never again in after years to be revived to life. O, what were the loss of a thousand "vases," in comparison!

'Tis true, an angel might shrink from the responsibilities of a mother. It needs an angel's powers. The watch must never, for an instant, be let up; the scales of justice must always be nicely balanced; the hasty word, that the overtasked spirit sends to the lip, must die there ere it is uttered. The timid and sensitive child must have a

A WORD TO MOTHERS   From Fanny Fern, "A Word to Mothers," *Fern Leaves from Fanny's Port-Folio* (New York: Derby and Miller, 1853) 234–35.

word of encouragement in season; the forward and presuming, checked with gentle firmness; there must be no deception, no evasion, no trickery, for the keen eye of childhood to mark. And all this, when the exhausted frame sinks with ceaseless vigils, perhaps, and the thousand petty interruptions and unlooked-for annoyances of every hour, almost set at defiance any attempt at system. Still must that mother wear an unruffled brow, lest the smiling cherub on her knee catch the angry frown. Still must she "rule her own spirit," lest the boy, so apparently engrossed with his toys, repeat the next moment the impatient word his ear has caught. For all these duties, faithfully and conscientiously performed, a mother's reward is in secret and in silence. Even he, on whose earthly breast she leans, is too often unmindful of the noiseless struggle, until, too late, alas! he learns to value the delicate hand that has kept in unceasing flow the thousand springs of his domestic happiness!

But what if, in the task that devolves upon the mother, she utterly fail? What if she consider her duty performed when her child is fed, and warm, and clothed? What if the priceless soul be left to the chance-training of hirelings? What if she never teach those little lips to lisp "Our Father"? What if she launch her child upon life's stormy sea without rudder, or compass, or chart? God forbid that there should be many such mothers!

MOTHERHOOD TODAY AND YESTERDAY
Frank Crane, D.D.

Frank Crane, D.D. (1861–1928) was a popular pastor in Chicago (1896–1903) and in Worcester, Massachusetts (1904–1909) before he decided to become a journalist. He became an editorial writer for a syndicate of 100 newspapers as well as a prolific writer of popular books. The range of his interests is clearly indicated by the titles of some of his publications: *The Religion of Tomorrow* (1899), *Human Confessions* (1911), *War and World Government* (1915), *Adventures in Common Sense* (1916), *400 Four Minute Essays* (10 vols.) (1919), and *Why I Am a Christian* (1924).

Like so many other "experts," Dr. Crane tended to give advice to women as well as to men. The piece that follows was published in *The National Sunday Magazine Section* as "A Christmas Reflection" in 1915, but some of it sounds quite contemporary.

Mother! The subject reeks with platitudes. So does Love. So does Patriotism. So does God. For that matter so do all fundamental, vital subjects which, from age to age eternal, engage the thoughts and dreams of mankind.

The law holds, that any topic is of real and persistent interest to humanity in proportion to the amount of obvious, conventional and bromidic things said about it.

I dare therefore to take up this most hackneyed of themes and re-examine it. It is old, as water and air and sunshine and the Christmas spirit are old, but, like them, contains inexhaustible fountains of life-interest.

Let us plunge at once into the waters of sentiment. There is a poem which was in McGuffey's Fourth Reader, I think, that I studied in the little red school house of an Illinois town. I didn't appreciate it at the time. It implied a burden of experience of

---

MOTHERHOOD TODAY AND YESTERDAY   From Frank Crane, "Motherhood Today and Yesterday," *National Sunday Magazine Section* 2 Dec. 1915.

which a boy of eight or nine is incapable. But it has lain long in my memory, and with years has acquired a flavor of tenderness, as wine gets its bouquet by age. It was called "Rock me to Sleep, Mother." One verse ran:

> Come let your brown hair, just lighted with gold,
> Fall on your shoulders again as of old;
> Let it drop over my forehead tonight,
> Shading my faint eyes away from the light,
> For with its sunny-edged shadows once more
> Haply will throng the sweet visions of yore.
> Lovingly, softly its bright billows sweep—
> Rock me to sleep, mother; rock me to sleep!

This is doubtless not good poetry, judged by the standards of the university professor. It is not vers libre, nor Whitmanic, nor does there seem to be obscurity or soul-writhing or gripes in it enough to make it appeal to our present advanced state of culture. It is just a plain, undisguised drive at about the oldest emotion of mankind, the love for one's mother, and the surge of gentleness that rises when the recollection of her comes up from her form buried in the churchyard and the vision of her buried beneath the years.

But arising now in my memory it stirs the thought molecules significantly. Perhaps it will strike my brother-men likewise.

We dwell in cities. The women we meet are not as the women that we remember. They are society women, literary women, political women, shop girls, office girls, factory girls or stage girls, as our station and calling may lead us to encounter them.

The point is that very few of them nowadays are ordinary, old-fashioned mothers, and fewer and fewer of the girls are ambitious to become such.

I am in favor of woman's suffrage and the entire program of the emancipation of women from every arbitrary, custom-bound law, whether law in statute books or law of social convention, that restrains them from the same free self-expression that males enjoy. So don't misunderstand me.

But after we get past the first flush of our reform enthusiasm, which usually carries us farther than we intended, we shall have to back a bit to certain everlasting human verities. They move not, change not, but hold and govern humanity as the sun holds and governs the planets.

And one of the stablest of these immutable truths is the fixed relation of woman to man and to the child.

The typical woman is not unrelated. She is not the old maid nor the free companion of man's indulgence. She is the wife. That is nature. No voting can change it. By centuries of experiment humanity has settled it that monogamy is the only sex-relation that nearest satisfies the physical instincts and at the same time conserves and develops the spiritual life.

The typical woman is also the mother. The only known way of bringing children into existence is through the woman's body, and the best known way of moulding a child's soul is through the soul of the woman that bore him.

There is no getting away from these manifest facts, nor can any kind of life that does not recognize them be normal.

The query then presents itself: Do the women of today realize what their most signal influence upon the life of the world may be? Are they not losing sight of the tremendous and indispensable part they play in contributing to the success of their children?

In other words, does the average mother, especially in our large cities, rightly value and discharge her responsibility toward her children?

Further, does not the whole net sum of the permanency and efficiency of a nation depend upon its mothers?

And is a race of children brought up in community camps, tended by expert hirelings, drilled, trained and socialized out of all natural affection, to amount to much?

The man who wrote "Rock me to Sleep, Mother" was not a spoiled, pampered child. The mother of him doubtless spanked him when he needed it. But when he grew up he forgot the spanking, and remembered only the infinitude of caresses he received, the passionate, individual love of which he was the object, and the lessons and ideals of that mother who adored him as no other woman ever can.

So when we face the modern problems of woman and consider her struggles to free herself from a lot of nonsensical hereditary bondage, we must also face the question of whether in letting go she will let go too much.

It is not merely an issue of whether the old style of woman is to pass away; it is also to be pondered whether the old style of children is to pass away.

Is the time coming when men's hearts will not warm within them at such a bit of homely sentiment as "Rock me to Sleep, Mother?" Are we preparing future generations that shall think of mothers only as physical necessities and shall not look upon them as guardian angels, determining prophets of virtue, vicegerents of Deity?

When a man's mother dies it leaves a peculiar wound in him no other blow can inflict. He can get another wife. He can have many other woman-faces to cheer him. But when his mother goes he feels that the one unique woman-being of all this world or the next has dropped out of his life.

It is an old gushing spring of sentiment to be sure, but the world still quenches its thirst thereat. And from all new vistas and adventures the world turns again, as surely and as diurnally as the sun sets, to the Madonna vision—the Woman with the Child in her arms.

MOTHER-WORSHIP

Crystal Eastman

A powerful and radical thinker, writer, organizer, and speaker, Crystal Eastman (1881–1928) often acknowledged the support of her family and the special influence of her mother. After attending Vassar, Columbia University, and New York University Law School, Eastman became well known as an expert on industrial accidents and helped to get workmen's compensation laws passed in New York State. But it is especially her work for women's rights, for pay for housework, for suffrage, and for peace that led the historian Blanche Wiesen Cook to describe her as a "woman-identified woman."

According to Eastman, her parents were committed to a marriage of equals. Both Congregationalist ministers, they eventually became joint pastors of Park Church in Elmira, New York. The following article, which Eastman wrote anonymously for *The Nation* in 1927 as part of the series "These Modern Women," describes her strong and supportive family.

The story of my background is the story of my mother. She was a Middle-Western girl, youngest, cleverest, and prettiest of six daughters—children of an Irish gunsmith and a "Pennsylvania Dutch" woman of good family and splendid character. The gunsmith was a master of his trade but a heavy drinker, always ugly and often dangerous. My mother got away from home as soon as she could. After a year in a nearby coeducational college she taught school for a while and then married. The man she chose (for she was the sort of girl who has many chances) was a penniless but handsome and idealistic Yankee divinity student whom she met during that one college year. When he had secured his first parish, they were married.

For about eight years, during which there were four different parishes and four children were born, my mother was a popular, active, and helpful minister's wife. Then my father, who had always struggled against ill-health, suffered a complete nervous breakdown. He was forced to give up his church and his chosen profession. My mother had to support the family.

She began by teaching English literature in a girls' school. Before long she was giving Sunday-evening talks at the school. Then she began to fill outside engagements and finally she became a sort of supply-preacher to nearby country churches. About the year 1890, though she had had no theological education, she was ordained as a Congregational minister and called to be the pastor of a fairly large church in a well-to-do farming community. After three or four successful years, she and my father (who by this time had lost a good bit of money trying to be a farmer and a grocer but had begun to regain his health) were called as associate pastors to a big liberal church in a city of 40,000. It was my mother's reputation as a preacher that brought them this opportunity and she proved equal to the larger field. In time my father's health improved so that he could carry his share of the work, but my mother was always the celebrated member of the family.

I have a vivid memory of my mother when I was six years old. We are standing, my brother and I, in front of a run-down farmhouse on the edge of the town which had become our home. We have just said goodby to our mother and now we are watching her trip off down the hill to the school where she goes every day to teach. She turns to smile at us—such a beaming smile, such a bright face, such a pretty young mother. When the charming, much-loved figure begins to grow small in the distance, my brother, who is younger and more temperamental than I, begins to cry. He screams as loud as he can, until he is red in the face. But he cannot make her come back. And I, knowing she will be worried if she hears him, try to drag him away. By the time I was ten my mother had become a preacher.

Life was never ordinary where my mother was. She was always trying something new. She had an eager, active mind, and tremendous energy. She was preeminently an

MOTHER-WORSHIP   From Crystal Eastman, "Mother-Worship," *The Nation* 16 Mar. 1927: 283–84. This article is reprinted from The Nation magazine. Copyright The Nation Company Inc.

initiator. From the time I was thirteen we spent our summers like most middle-class, small-town American families, in a cottage beside a lake. And our life there, I suppose, would have been much like the life in thousands of other such summer communities, except for the presence of my mother. For one thing, she organized a system of cooperative housekeeping with three other families on the hillside, and it lasted for years. A cook was hired jointly, but the burden of keeping house, planning meals, buying meat and groceries from the carts that came along three times a week, getting vegetables and fruit from the garden, collecting the money, keeping track of guests, and paying the bills, shifted every week. At first it was only the mothers who took their turn at housekeeping. But as the children grew older they were included in the scheme, boys as well as girls. Toward the end we had all the fun of eating in a big jolly group and only one or two weeks of housekeeping responsibility during the whole summer.

We used to have Sunday night music and singing for the whole hillside at our cottage, with the grown-ups in the big room, and the children lying outside on the porch couches or off on the grass. We had "church" Sunday mornings, too, in our big room; after all we were the minister's family. But it was a very short informal "church" followed by a long swim, and any one who wanted to could preach. We took turns preaching as well as at keeping house, and we could choose the subjects of our own sermons.

Then one summer my mother started "symposiums." Once a week the mothers and older children and any fathers who happened to be around would gather on somebody's porch, listen to a paper, and then discuss it. I read a paper on "Woman" when I was fifteen, and I believe I was as wise in feminism then as I am now, if a little more solemn.

"The trouble with women," I said, "is that they have no impersonal interests. They must have work of their own, first because no one who has to depend on another person for his living is really grown up; and, second, because the only way to be happy is to have an absorbing interest in life which is not bound up with any particular person. Children can die or grow up, husbands can leave you. No woman who allows husband and children to absorb her whole time and interest is safe against disaster."

The proudest and happiest moment of my college days was when I met my mother in New York, as I did once a year, and went with her to a big banquet in connection with some ministers' convention she had come down to attend. She always spoke at the banquet, and she was always the best speaker. She was gay, sparkling, humorous, intimate, adorable. I would sit and love her with all my heart, and I could feel all the ministers loving her and rejoicing in her.

Almost always it is painful to sit in the audience while a near relative preaches, prays, or makes a speech. Husbands, wives, brothers, sisters, and children of the performers ought to be exempt from attending such public functions. My brothers and I always suffered when father preached, although, as preachers go, he was pretty good. At any rate he was beautiful to look at and had a large following of enthusiastic admirers. But when my mother preached we hated to miss it. There was never a moment of anxiety or concern; she had that secret of perfect platform ease which takes all strain out of the audience. Her voice was music; she spoke simply, without effort, almost without gestures, standing very still. And what she said seemed to come straight from her heart to yours. Her sermons grew out of her own moral and spiritual struggles. For she had a stormy, troubled soul, capable of black cruelty and then again the deepest generosities. She was humble, honest, striving, always beginning again to try to be good.

With all her other interests she was thoroughly domestic. We children loved her cooking as much as we loved her preaching. And she was all kinds of devoted mother, the kind that tucks you in at night and reads you a story, and the kind that drags you to the dentist to have your teeth straightened. But I must leave her now and try to fill out the picture. My father, too, played a large part in my life. He was a generous man, the kind of man that was a suffragist from the day he first heard of a woman who wanted to vote. One evening, after mother had been teaching for some time and had begun to know her power as a public speaker, she came to him as he lay on his invalid's couch.

"John," she cried, "I believe I could preach!"

"Mary!" he cried, jumping up in his excitement, "I *know* you could!"

This was in those early days when he had given up his own career as a minister, when he had cheerfully turned small farmer and had begun, on days when he was well enough, to peddle eggs and butter at the back doors of his former parishioners. From the moment he knew that my mother wanted to preach, he helped and encouraged her. Without his coaching and without his local prestige, it is doubtful if she could have been ordained. And my father stood by me in the same way, from the time when I wanted to cut off my hair and go barefoot to the time when I began to study law. When I insisted that the boys must make their beds if I had to make mine, he stood by me. When I said that if there was dishwashing to be done they should take their turn, he stood by me. And when I declared that there was no such thing in our family as boys' work and girls' work, and that I must be allowed to do my share of wood-chopping and outdoor chores, he took me seriously and let me try.

Once when I was twelve and very tall, a deputation of ladies from her church called on my mother and gently suggested that my skirts ought to be longer. My mother, who was not without consciousness of the neighbors' opinion, thought she must do something. But my father said, "No, let her wear them short. She likes to run, and she can't run so well in long skirts."

A few years later it was a question of bathing suits. In our summer community I was a ringleader in the rebellion against skirts and stockings for swimming. On one hot Sunday morning the other fathers waited on my father and asked him to use his influence with me. I don't know what he said to them but he never said a word to me. He was, I know, startled and embarrassed to see his only daughter in a man's bathing suit with bare brown legs for all the world to see. I think it shocked him to his dying day. But he himself had been a swimmer; he knew he would not want to swim in a skirt and stockings. Why then should I?

Beyond the immediate circle of my family there were other influences at work. My mother, among her other charms, had a genius for friendship. There were always clever, interesting, amusing women coming in and out of our house. I never thought of women as dull folk who sat and listened while the men talked. The little city where we lived was perhaps unusual. It was the home of six or seven distinguished persons, and not all of them were men.

In this environment I grew up confidently expecting to have a profession and earn my own living, and also confidently expecting to be married and have children.

It was fifty-fifty with me. I was just as passionately determined to have children as I was to have a career. And my mother was the triumphant answer to all doubts as to the success of this double role. From my earliest memory she had more than half supported the family and yet she was supremely a mother.

I have lived my life according to the plan. I have had the "career" and the children and, except for an occasional hiatus due to illness or some other circumstance over which I had no control, I have earned my own living. I have even made a certain name for myself. If I have not fulfilled the promise of my youth, either as a home-maker or as a professional woman, I have never wavered in my feminist faith. My mother has always been a beacon to me, and if today I sometimes feel a sense of failure it may be partly because I have always lived in the glow of her example. In their early struggle for survival against narrow-minded and prejudiced parents some of my contemporaries seem to have won more of the iron needed in the struggle of life than I got from my almost perfect parents.

MOM
Philip Wylie

Philip Wylie (1902–1971) was the son of a writer and a Presbyterian minister. After three years at Princeton, he became a staff writer for *The New Yorker*. A prolific author of novels, short stories, screen plays, and social commentaries, he is chiefly remembered today as the man who coined the term "Momism."

"Common Women" was the most controversial chapter in the most controversial book of 1942, *Generation of Vipers*. In iconoclastic style, Wylie swept the first of the mythical American triumvirate—motherhood, the flag, and apple pie—off her pedestal. A kind of pampered Cinderella, Mom seeks affluent Prince Charmings to provide her with luxury and leisure. As a mother, Mom overprotects her sons so that our society is itself "built to appease the rapacity of loving mothers." In this excerpt from "Common Women," Wylie gives us his image of Mom in all her glory.

Mom, however, is a great little guy. Pulling pants onto her by these words, let us look at mom.

She is a middle-aged puffin with an eye like a hawk that has just seen a rabbit twitch far below. She is about twenty-five pounds overweight, with no sprint, but sharp heels and a hard backhand which she does not regard as a foul but a womanly defense. In a thousand of her there is not sex appeal enough to budge a hermit ten paces off a rock ledge. She none the less spends several hundred dollars a year on permanents and transformations, pomades, cleansers, rouges, lipsticks, and the like—and fools nobody except herself. If a man kisses her with any earnestness, it is time for mom to feel for her pocketbook, and this occasionally does happen.

She smokes thirty cigarettes a day, chews gum, and consumes tons of bonbons and petits fours. The shortening in the latter, stripped from pigs, sheep and cattle,

---

shortens mom. She plays bridge with the stupid voracity of a hammerhead shark, which cannot see what it is trying to gobble but never stops snapping its jaws and roiling the waves with its tail. She drinks moderately, which is to say, two or three cocktails before dinner every night and a brandy and a couple of highballs afterward. She doesn't count the two cocktails she takes before lunch when she lunches out, which is every day she can. On Saturday nights, at the club or in the juke joint, she loses count of her drinks and is liable to get a little tiddly, which is to say, shot or blind. But it is her man who worries about where to acquire the money while she worries only about how to spend it, so he has the ulcers and colitis and she has the guts of a bear; she can get pretty stiff before she topples.

Her sports are all spectator sports.

She was graduated from high school or a "finishing" school or even a college in her distant past and made up for the unhappiness of compulsory education by sloughing all that she learned so completely that she could not pass the final examinations of a fifth grader. She reads the fiction in three women's magazines each month and occasionally skims through an article, which usually angers her so that she gets other moms to skim through it, and then they have a session on the subject over a canister of spiked coffee in order to damn the magazine, the editors, the author, and the silly girls who run about these days. She reads two or three motion-picture fan magazines also, and goes to the movies about two nights a week. If a picture does not coincide precisely with her attitude of the moment, she converses through all of it and so whiles away the time. She does not appear to be lecherous toward the moving photographs as men do, but that is because she is a realist and a little shy on imagination. However, if she gets to Hollywood and encounters the flesh-and-blood article known as a male star, she and her sister moms will run forward in a mob, wearing a joint expression that must make God rue his invention of bisexuality, and tear the man's clothes from his body, yea, verily, down to his B.V.D.'s.

Mom is organization-minded. Organizations, she has happily discovered, are intimidating to all men, not just to mere men. They frighten politicians to sniveling servility and they terrify pastors; they bother bank presidents and they pulverize school boards. Mom has many such organizations, the real purpose of which is to compel an abject compliance of her environs to her personal desires. With these associations and committees she has double parking ignored, for example. With them she drives out of the town and the state, if possible, all young harlots and all proprietors of places where "questionable" young women (though why they are called that—being of all women the least in question) could possibly foregather, not because she competes with such creatures but because she contrasts so unfavorably with them. With her clubs (a solid term!) she causes bus lines to run where they are convenient for her rather than for workers, plants flowers in sordid spots that would do better with sanitation, snaps independent men out of office and replaces them with clammy castrates, throws prodigious fairs and parties for charity and gives the proceeds, usually about eight dollars, to the janitor to buy the committee some beer for its headache on the morning after, and builds clubhouses for the entertainment of soldiers where she succeeds in persuading thousands of them that they are mom-sick and would rather talk to her than take Betty into the shrubs. All this, of course, is considered social service, charity, care of the poor, civic reform, patriotism, and self-sacrifice.

As an interesting sidelight, clubs afford mom an infinite opportunity for nosing into other people's business. Nosing is not a mere psychological ornament of her; it is a basic necessity. Only by nosing can she uncover all incipient revolutions against her dominion and so warn and assemble her co-cannibals.

Knowing nothing about medicine, art, science, religion, law, sanitation, civics, hygiene, psychology, morals, history, geography, poetry, literature, or any other topic except the all-consuming one of momism, she seldom has any especial interest in *what,* exactly, she is doing as a member of any of these endless organizations, so long as it is *something.*

MODERN WOMAN: THE LOST SEX

Ferdinand Lundberg and Marynia F. Farnham, M.D.

One of the most popular and influential advice books of this century was *Modern Woman: The Lost Sex* (1947) by journalist and financial expert Ferdinand Lundberg, and Dr. Marynia Farnham, a psychoanalyst. Influenced by Freudian theories, the authors argued that only by full involvement in domesticity and motherhood could women avoid marital difficulties, find personal and sexual happiness, and prevent emotional disturbance in their children. Published just after the end of World War II, the book was so popular that newsreels featured Dr. Farnham urging "Rosie the Riveter" to leave the work force and return to the home.

Journalists and authors echoed the assertion of these "experts" that modern woman had sacrificed her femininity on the altar of independence, a state unsuited to her nature. But, following the conventional wisdom that mothers alone are responsible for their childrens' behavior, Lundberg and Farnham held that even mothers who eschewed independence could cause neuroses in their children. The following passage is from a section entitled "The Slaughter of the Innocents," the title itself more than hinting at the authors' analysis of motherhood.

MOTHER AND CHILD

The spawning ground of most neurosis in Western civilization is the home. The basis for it is laid in childhood, although it emerges strongly later, usually from late adolescence until middle age, provoked by circumstances and conditions encountered in life. And as we have pointed out, the principal agent in laying the groundwork for it is the mother. Many women classified as housewives and mothers are just as disturbed as were the feminists, and for the same general reasons. There are mothers, for example, who, although not neurotic, feel dissatisfied with the life they are leading. The home offers them few energy outlets. The work they do in it does not bring them prestige. Others, neurotic by reason of their own childhood upbringing and the failure of life to provide them with satisfactory outlets, suffer from the same general affliction as the feminists—penis-envy. It is more repressed than it was in the feminists, but it is at work in the psychic depths.

The feminists, turning their backs on a feminine life, lived out, expressed, their penis-envy, and obtained great satisfaction thereby. The neurotically disturbed women who find themselves mothers and housewives, however, have *consciously* accepted the feminine way of life, are not aware that deep within them they suffer from the same general affliction as the feminists. For they were reared in homes greatly resembling those of the feminists, and they were subject to the same cultural influences. They could not escape.

Unlike the feminists, they have made sure of libidinal outlets in their lives. But they have increasingly foregone ego outlets, and have been unable at the same time to utilize their libidinal opportunities. Many of them, even though not neurotic, cannot help but feel passed by, inferior, put upon by society's denial of ego outlets for them. When they are neurotic they feel the lack even more. To a certain extent a woman can derive great ego satisfaction from playing a fully feminine role, but there are dangers in it both to herself and to her children. Too many women today are forced to derive their entire ego-support from their children, which they do at the expense of the children, to the danger of society. A child can never be an adult plaything and turn out well.

The mothers of neurotics and of persons with marked neurotic character traits, with very few exceptions break down into four broad categories, each susceptible of further breakdown until one reaches the great personal complexity of individuals. These categories, in each of which the mother carries out the pattern of her own upbringing and of the culture around her, are as follows:

1. The rejecting mother, who in various degrees from extreme to subtle, apes society around her and rejects the child. She ordinarily has no more than one, or at most two.

2. The oversolicitous or overprotective mother, who underneath closely resembles the rejecting mother but whose entire activity represents a conscious denial of her unconscious rejection.

3. The dominating mother, who is also very often a strict disciplinarian. This type obtains release for her misdirected ego-drives at the expense of the child. Denied other opportunities for self-realization, she makes her children her pawns, usually requires of them stellar performance in all their undertakings.

4. The over-affectionate mother, who makes up for her essentially libidinal disappointments through her children. Her damage is greatest with her sons, whom she often converts into "sissies"—that is, into passive-feminine or passive-homosexual males.

There is, on the other hand, the fully maternal mother, who fortunately accounts for perhaps 50 per cent or more of the births because she has more children than the other types. She does not reject her children, attempt to overprotect them out of her guilty anxiety, dominate them or convert them into lap dogs. She merely loves her children.

It is the first three types who produce the delinquents, the difficult behavior-problem children, some substantial percentage of criminals and persons who, although moving in socially approved channels, are a trouble to themselves, to close associates and often to society. Along with the over-affectionate mother, they also produce a large percentage of the confirmed alcoholics. Since somewhere around 40 to 50 per cent of the mothers are in the first three categories, the wide damage they do is obvious and warrants fuller discussion.

I STAND HERE IRONING
Tillie Olsen

Born in Omaha, Nebraska, in 1913, Tillie Olsen has lived most of her life in San Francisco, where she married Jack Olsen and reared four daughters. She began to write while leading what she calls "the triple life": mother and housewife; full- and part-time worker; and spare-time writer. Since then, she has won many awards for her work—from a Ford Foundation Grant to a Guggenheim Fellowship—and has been a writer-in-residence at some of the country's most prestigious colleges and universities.

Olsen's title story in her collection *Tell Me a Riddle* won the O. Henry Award for the best American short story of 1961. Her other works include *Yonnondio: From the Thirties* (1974), *Silences* (1978), and *Daughter to Mother* (1984). She is not a prolific writer: "The habits of a lifetime," she says in *Silences*, "when everything else had to come before writing are not easily broken, even when circumstances now often make it possible for writing to be first; habits of years—response to others, distractibility, responsibility for daily matters—stay with you, mark you, become you."

In some sense, it is the "habits of years" that have affected the relationship between mother and daughter in the following story. A mother's inner monologue about her eldest daughter, Emily, whose high school teacher has requested a meeting with her mother, the story examines the daughter's life and the mother's conscience.

I stand here ironing, and what you asked me moves tormented back and forth with the iron.

"I wish you would manage the time to come in and talk with me about your daughter. I'm sure you can help me understand her. She's a youngster who needs help and whom I'm deeply interested in helping."

"Who needs help." . . . Even if I came, what good would it do? You think because I am her mother I have a key, or that in some way you could use me as a key? She has lived for nineteen years. There is all that life that has happened outside of me, beyond me.

And when is there time to remember, to sift, to weigh, to estimate, to total? I will start and there will be an interruption and I will have to gather it all together again. Or I will become engulfed with all I did or did not do, with what should have been and what cannot be helped.

She was a beautiful baby. The first and only one of our five that was beautiful at birth. You do not guess how new and uneasy her tenancy in her now-loveliness. You did not know her all those years she was thought homely, or see her poring over her baby pictures, making me tell her over and over how beautiful she had been—and would be, I would tell her—and was now, to the seeing eye. But the seeing eyes were few or nonexistent. Including mine.

I nursed her. They feel that's important nowadays. I nursed all the children, but with her, with all the fierce rigidity of first motherhood, I did like the books then said. Though her cries battered me to trembling and my breasts ached with swollenness, I waited till the clock decreed.

Why do I put that first? I do not even know if it matters, or if it explains anything.

She was a beautiful baby. She blew shining bubbles of sound. She loved motion, loved light, loved color and music and textures. She would lie on the floor in her blue overalls patting the surface so hard in ecstasy her hands and feet would blur. She was a miracle to me, but when she was eight months old I had to leave her daytimes with the woman downstairs to whom she was no miracle at all, for I worked or looked for work and for Emily's father, who "could no longer endure" (he wrote in his good-bye note) "sharing want with us."

I was nineteen. It was the pre-relief, pre-WPA world of the depression. I would start running as soon as I got off the streetcar, running up the stairs, the place smelling sour, and awake or asleep to startle awake, when she saw me she would break into a clogged weeping that could not be comforted, a weeping I can hear yet.

After a while I found a job hashing at night so I could be with her days, and it was better. But it came to where I had to bring her to his family and leave her.

It took a long time to raise the money for her fare back. Then she got chicken pox and I had to wait longer. When she finally came, I hardly knew her, walking quick and nervous like her father, looking like her father, thin, and dressed in a shoddy red that yellowed her skin and glared at the pockmarks. All the baby loveliness gone.

She was two. Old enough for nursery school they said, and I did not know then what I know now—the fatigue of the long day, and the lacerations of group life in the kinds of nurseries that are only parking places for children.

Except that it would have made no difference if I had known. It was the only place there was. It was the only way we could be together, the only way I could hold a job.

And even without knowing, I knew. I knew the teacher that was evil because all these years it has curdled into my memory, the little boy hunched in the corner, her rasp, "why aren't you outside, because Alvin hits you? that's no reason, go out, scaredy." I knew Emily hated it even if she did not clutch and implore "don't go Mommy" like the other children, mornings.

She always had a reason why we should stay home. Momma, you look sick. Momma, I feel sick. Momma, the teachers aren't there today, they're sick. Momma, we can't go, there was a fire there last night. Momma, it's a holiday today, no school, they told me.

But never in direct protest, never rebellion. I think of our others in their three-, four-year-oldness—the explosions, the tempers, the denunciations, the demands—and I feel suddenly ill. I put the iron down. What in me demanded that goodness in her? And what was the cost, the cost to her of such goodness?

The old man living in the back once said in his gentle way: "You should smile at Emily more when you look at her." What *was* in my face when I looked at her? I loved her. There were all the acts of love.

It was only with the others I remembered what he said, and it was the face of joy, and not of care or tightness or worry I turned to them—too late for Emily. She does not smile easily, let alone almost always as her brothers and sisters do. Her face is closed and sombre, but when she wants, how fluid. You must have seen it in her pantomimes, you spoke of her rare gift for comedy on the stage that rouses a laughter out of the audience so dear they applaud and applaud and do not want to let her go.

Where does it come from, that comedy? There was none of it in her when she came back to me that second time, after I had had to send her away again. She had a new daddy now to learn to love, and I think perhaps it was a better time.

Except when we left her alone nights, telling ourselves she was old enough.

"Can't you go some other time, Mommy, like tomorrow?" she would ask. "Will it be just a little while you'll be gone? Do you promise?"

The time we came back, the front door open, the clock on the floor in the hall. She rigid awake. "It wasn't just a little while. I didn't cry. Three times I called you, just three times, and then I ran downstairs to open the door so you could come faster. The clock talked loud. I threw it away, it scared me what it talked."

She said the clock talked loud again that night I went to the hospital to have Susan. She was delirious with the fever that comes before red measles, but she was fully conscious all the week I was gone and the week after we were home when she could not come near the new baby or me.

She did not get well. She stayed skeleton thin, not wanting to eat, and night after night she had nightmares. She would call for me, and I would rouse from exhaustion to sleepily call back: "You're all right, darling, go to sleep, it's just a dream," and if she still called, in a sterner voice, "now go to sleep, Emily, there's nothing to hurt you." Twice, only twice, when I had to get up for Susan anyhow, I went in to sit with her.

Now when it is too late (as if she would let me hold and comfort her like I do the others) I get up and go to her at once at her moan or restless stirring. "Are you awake, Emily? Can I get you something?" And the answer is always the same: "No, I'm all right, go back to sleep, Mother."

They persuaded me at the clinic to send her away to a convalescent home in the country where "she can have the kind of food and care you can't manage for her, and you'll be free to concentrate on the new baby." They still send children to that place. I see pictures on the society page of sleek young women planning affairs to raise money for it, or dancing at the affairs, or decorating Easter eggs or filling Christmas stockings for the children.

They never have a picture of the children so I do not know if the girls still wear those gigantic red bows and the ravaged looks on the every other Sunday when parents can come to visit "unless otherwise notified"—as we were notified the first six weeks.

Oh it is a handsome place, green lawns and tall trees and fluted flower beds. High up on the balconies of each cottage the children stand, the girls in their red bows and white dresses, the boys in white suits and giant red ties. The parents stand below shrieking up to be heard and the children shriek down to be heard, and between them the invisible wall "Not To Be Contaminated by Parental Germs or Physical Affection."

There was a tiny girl who always stood hand in hand with Emily. Her parents never came. One visit she was gone. "They moved her to Rose Cottage" Emily shouted in explanation. "They don't like you to love anybody here."

She wrote once a week, the labored writing of a seven-year-old. "I am fine. How is the baby. If I write my leter nicly I will have a star. Love." There never was a star. We wrote every other day, letters she could never hold or keep but only hear read— once. "We simply do not have room for children to keep any personal possessions," they patiently explained when we pieced one Sunday's shrieking together to plead how much it would mean to Emily, who loved so to keep things, to be allowed to keep her letters and cards.

Each visit she looked frailer. "She isn't eating," they told us.

(They had runny eggs for breakfast or mush with lumps, Emily said later, I'd hold it in my mouth and not swallow. Nothing ever tasted good, just when they had chicken.)

It took us eight months to get her released home, and only the fact that she gained back so little of her seven lost pounds convinced the social worker.

I used to try to hold and love her after she came back, but her body would stay stiff, and after a while she'd push away. She ate little. Food sickened her, and I think much of life too. Oh she had physical lightness and brightness, twinkling by on skates, bouncing like a ball up and down up and down over the jump rope, skimming over the hill; but these were momentary.

She fretted about her appearance, thin and dark and foreign-looking at a time when every little girl was supposed to look or thought she should look a chubby blonde replica of Shirley Temple. The doorbell sometimes rang for her, but no one seemed to come and play in the house or be a best friend. Maybe because we moved so much.

There was a boy she loved painfully through two school semesters. Months later she told me how she had taken pennies from my purse to buy him candy. "Licorice was his favorite and I brought him some every day, but he still liked Jennifer better'n me. Why, Mommy?" The kind of question for which there is no answer.

School was a worry to her. She was not glib or quick in a world where glibness and quickness were easily confused with ability to learn. To her overworked and exasperated teachers she was an overconscientious "slow learner" who kept trying to catch up and was absent entirely too often.

I let her be absent, though sometimes the illness was imaginary. How different from my now-strictness about attendance with the others. I wasn't working. We had a new baby, I was home anyhow. Sometimes, after Susan grew old enough, I would keep her home from school, too, to have them all together.

Mostly Emily had asthma, and her breathing, harsh and labored, would fill the house with a curiously tranquil sound. I would bring the two old dresser mirrors and her boxes of collections to her bed. She would select beads and single earrings, bottle tops and shells, dried flowers and pebbles, old postcards and scraps, all sorts of oddments; then she and Susan would play Kingdom, setting up landscapes and furniture, peopling them with action.

Those were the only times of peaceful companionship between her and Susan. I have edged away from it, that poisonous feeling between them, that terrible balancing of hurts and needs I had to do between the two, and did so badly, those earlier years.

Oh there are conflicts between the others too, each one human, needing, demanding, hurting, taking—but only between Emily and Susan, no, Emily toward Susan that corroding resentment. It seems so obvious on the surface, yet it is not obvious. Susan, the second child, Susan, golden- and curly-haired and chubby, quick and articulate and assured, everything in appearance and manner Emily was not; Susan, not able to resist Emily's precious things, losing or sometimes clumsily breaking them; Susan telling jokes and riddles to company for applause while Emily sat silent (to say to me later: that was *my* riddle, Mother, I told it to Susan); Susan, who for all the five years' difference in age was just a year behind Emily in developing physically.

I am glad for that slow physical development that widened the difference between her and her contemporaries, though she suffered over it. She was too vulnerable for that terrible world of youthful competition, of preening and parading, of constant measuring of yourself against every other, of envy, "If I had that copper hair," "If I had that skin. . . ." She tormented herself enough about not looking like the others, there was enough of the unsureness, the having to be conscious of words before you speak, the constant caring—what are they thinking of me? without having it all magnified by the merciless physical drives.

Ronnie is calling. He is wet and I change him. It is rare there is such a cry now. That time of motherhood is almost behind me when the ear is not one's own but must always be racked and listening for the child cry, the child call. We sit for a while and I hold him, looking out over the city spread in charcoal with its soft aisles of light. "*Shoogily,*" he breathes and curls closer. I carry him back to bed, asleep. *Shoogily.* A funny word, a family word, inherited from Emily, invented by her to say: *comfort.*

In this and other ways she leaves her seal, I say aloud. And startle at my saying it. What do I mean? What did I start to gather together, to try and make coherent? I was at the terrible, growing years. War years. I do not remember them well. I was working, there were four smaller ones now, there was not time for her. She had to help be a mother, and housekeeper, and shopper. She had to set her seal. Mornings of crisis and near hysteria trying to get lunches packed, hair combed, coats and shoes found, everyone to school or Child Care on time, the baby ready for transportation. And always the paper scribbled on by a smaller one, the book looked at by Susan then mislaid, the homework not done. Running out to that huge school where she was one, she was lost, she was a drop; suffering over the unpreparedness, stammering and unsure in her classes.

There was so little time left at night after the kids were bedded down. She would struggle over books, always eating (it was in those years she developed her enormous appetite that is legendary in our family) and I would be ironing, or preparing food for the next day, or writing V-mail to Bill, or tending the baby. Sometimes, to make me laugh, or out of her despair, she would imitate happenings or types at school.

I think I said once: "Why don't you do something like this in the school amateur show?" One morning she phoned me at work, hardly understandable through the weeping: "Mother, I did it. I won, I won; they gave me first prize; they clapped and clapped and wouldn't let me go."

Now suddenly she was Somebody, and as imprisoned in her difference as she had been in anonymity.

She began to be asked to perform at other high schools, even in colleges, then at city and statewide affairs. The first one we went to, I only recognized her the first moment when thin, shy, she almost drowned herself into the curtains. Then: Was this Emily? The control, the command, the convulsing and deadly clowning, the spell, then the roaring, stamping audience, unwilling to let this rare and precious laughter out of their lives.

Afterwards: You ought to do something about her with a gift like that—but without money or knowing how, what does one do? We have left it all to her, and the gift has as often eddied inside, clogged and clotted, as been used and growing.

She is coming. She runs up the stairs two at a time with her light graceful step, and I know she is happy tonight. Whatever it was that occasioned your call did not happen today.

"Aren't you ever going to finish the ironing, Mother? Whistler painted his mother in a rocker. I'd have to paint mine standing over an ironing board." This is one of her communicative nights and she tells me everything and nothing as she fixes herself a plate of food out of the icebox.

She is so lovely. Why did you want me to come in at all? Why were you concerned? She will find her way.

She starts up the stairs to bed. "Don't get me up with the rest in the morning." "But I thought you were having midterms." "Oh, those," she comes back in, kisses me, and says quite lightly, "in a couple of years when we'll all be atom-dead they won't matter a bit."

She has said it before. She *believes* it. But because I have been dredging the past, and all that compounds a human being is so heavy and meaningful in me, I cannot endure it tonight.

I will never total it all. I will never come in to say: She was a child seldom smiled at. Her father left me before she was a year old. I had to work her first six years when there was work, or I sent her home and to his relatives. There were years she had care she hated. She was dark and thin and foreign-looking in a world where the prestige went to blondeness and curly hair and dimples, she was slow where glibness was prized. She was a child of anxious, not proud, love. We were poor and could not afford for her the soil of easy growth. I was a young mother, I was a distracted mother. There were the other children pushing up, demanding. Her younger sister seemed all that she was not. There were years she did not want me to touch her. She kept too much in herself, her life was such she had to keep too much in herself. My wisdom came too late. She has much to her and probably little will come of it. She is a child of her age, of depression, of war, of fear.

Let her be. So all that is in her will not bloom—but in how many does it? There is still enough left to live by. Only help her to know—help make it so there is cause for her to know—that she is more than this dress on the ironing board, helpless before the iron.

LESBIAN MOTHERS
Del Martin and Phyllis Lyon

Del Martin and Phyllis Lyon are coauthors of *Lesbian/Woman* and cofounders of a national lesbian organization, the Daughters of Bilitis. Their interest in lesbian mothers grew in part from Martin's experience as a mother and grandmother.

As Martin and Lyon state, "lesbian mother" may appear to be a contradiction in terms, since lesbian relationships are nonprocreative. But children from previous heterosexual relationships are often integrated into lesbian households. In their interviews with women who have established such households, the authors discovered a wide variation in experience. They also considered the reasons why some lesbian mothers are reluctant to enter into such arrangements. The common denominator in both cases is often fear: Some fear the reactions of their children; others fear the loss of custody; many fear both. At the root of these fears, Martin and Lyon point out, is the homophobia of our society.

 Until recently American society has regarded the phrase *lesbian mother* as a contradiction in terms. Because lesbian relationships are between two women and are therefore nonprocreative, it was automatically assumed that there was no such thing as a lesbian mother.

Researchers who have done studies on female homosexuality have directed their attention primarily to sexual behavior. While they have noted that most lesbians have had some heterosexual experience before engaging in lesbian relationships, they have failed to recognize that a significant number of these women do have children.

Lesbians, like other women in our society, have been raised with the expectation of becoming wives and mothers. Those who sought "professional help" were assured that their lesbian feelings would disappear when they met the right man, got married, and had children. But this doesn't happen.

As a result, there are many lesbian mothers trying in various ways to cope with a hostile society which recognizes and seeks to protect only traditional, and often outmoded, concepts of family and parenthood. Lesbian women have in the past been deprived of their children or forced to live a deception. Only now, with a new consciousness and new honesty, are lesbian mothers beginning to emerge as individuals—strong in their concepts of motherhood and determined to fight for their children.

For Sandra and Madeleine, moving their six children, all under the age of eight, into a five-bedroom, three-bathroom house was a joyful experience. "We have a viable and exciting family unit which runs smoothly, each one being taught to love and care for the other. We pooled our financial resources; one of us works and the other takes care of the house and kids. Everything was working out well until our ex-husbands took us to court to try to get the children away from us."

By order of a Seattle court—which rejected the testimony of a psychiatrist and social worker that the children appear adjusted and healthy—the two women have been forced to separate. The judge did not order that the homosexual relationship end, only that it would be in the "best interests" of the children that they not be living under one roof. Considering the high rate of divorce, it is not unusual for homes to have no male models for children, the judge admitted. "But it is unusual to have homes with two mothers as models." He also said he realized separate residences could prove to be a financial burden, but his "prime interest is the welfare of the children."

In a similar decision last year in San Jose, California, the judge awarded custody of three children to their mother Cam, an admitted lesbian. Though it was the first

LESBIAN MOTHERS   From Del Martin and Phyllis Lyon, "Lesbian Mothers," *Ms.* Oct. 1973: 78–80. Originally published in Ms. magazine. Copyright by and reprinted with permission of the authors.

time an admitted or proved lesbian won a child custody contest, the court restricted Cam's relationship with her lover, also a mother. The two women are to see each other only when Cam's children are in school or visiting their father. Joan Bradford ("Found Women," *Ms.*, January, 1973), the attorney for the plaintiff, is appealing the decision on the grounds of the Constitutional right of freedom of association.

Not long ago a Southern California judge awarded two small children, a girl and a boy, to the mother despite inferences about her lesbian tendencies, because "children need their mothers in their earlier years." However, the son is to be turned over to the father at age five. Apparently, there is no similar concern about the daughter.

Lesbian mothers who want to be honest with their children must also be realistic. Children who know the truth often have to be trusted not to tell it to their fathers or friends. Jean, a divorced mother of two—a daughter, eleven, and a son, eight—has instructed her children not to tell their father of her new relationship. She has been criticized for placing too heavy a burden on their young shoulders. Yet an inadvertent remark while visiting with their father, or to a neighbor or relative, could mean permanent separation. In terms of the children themselves, Jean has no qualms. "I have no fear about whether my children will grow up gay or straight. I want to teach them about relationships rather than roles."

Though a 1967 decision of the California appellate court prohibits denying a mother child custody merely because she is a lesbian, Jean, a San Franciscan, is aware that the courts, while ruling in "the best interests of the children," routinely interpret that to be a heterosexual environment. Despite favorable psychiatric testimony regarding the "fitness" of a lesbian as a parent, judges are still inclined to award custody to the father in such cases. These decisions are not based upon the qualifications of the mother, but rather on the assumption that her children will more than likely become homosexuals. Yet, of the thousands of lesbian women we have met over the years, all were products of a heterosexual union, all were raised in a heterosexual environment, all were taught a totally heterosexual value system, and all were assumed to be heterosexual. It happens very rarely, according to Dr. Harvey E. Kaye, a New York psychiatrist who observed numerous homosexual family situations, that such a parent turns her child away from heterosexuality.

Lesbian mothers believe that the problems they face in raising their children would not be much different from those encountered by heterosexual divorcées if it weren't for society's crippling *homophobia*—the fear that gay parents will, wittingly or unwittingly, bring up gay children. Since 10 percent of the population may be homosexual, lesbian mothers estimate that 90 percent of their children will turn out to be heterosexual no matter what the environment—just as they themselves turned out to be lesbian in spite of growing up in heterosexual environments.

Knowing this and being acutely aware of the damage that can be done by pigeonholing children into ill-fitting roles, Jean is simply concerned that her children grow up to be free human beings. "I want them to feel good about themselves, whoever they are and whatever 'other people' may think.

"In the meantime, I'm not trying to hide the pain of our present reality from my children. We all love each other very much. If we want to stay together, we need to protect our family unit together. So far, the kids have been able to deal with it."

Jean's situation is shared by many other women—women who in most cases did not discover, or face up to, their lesbian feelings until after marriage and motherhood; women who then sought divorces without divulging the lesbian identity that would endanger their custody of their children; women who live alone with their children but who may have a personal relationship with another woman outside the home; women who have preferred the constancy of establishing the lesbian lover as an integral part of the family unit, a stepparent, as it were.

Aside from the constant threat of exposure that could result in their losing their children, these women also worry about having male friends with whom their daughters and sons can identify; about when and if they should tell their children of their own lesbian identity; and about the reactions of their children should they bring a lesbian lover into the household. Those who are open about their lesbianism, at least with their friends and children, have joined groups such as San Francisco's Lesbian Mothers Union. Here they can socialize and rap about problems they encounter as lesbian heads-of-household. They also form babysitting co-ops and hold picnics so that their children can mingle and make friends with other youngsters with similar lifestyles.

The question asked most often of lesbian mothers is, "What do you do about the absence of a father image for your sons?" Many lesbians, especially those who are feminists, resent this question because it implies their daughters are not as important. Furthermore, there usually is a biological father who has visiting privileges and whose visits can in some cases disrupt the household, presenting a negative male image rather than a positive one.

For example, when Shirley's exhusband comes to see his two-year-old son on weekends, she must hide any evidence of the woman she lives with. "We scurry around and take things down from the bulletin board and hide the extra toothbrush," she explains indignantly. "Ann even has to get out of the house till he's gone." This gives the child a feeling that his father would be hurt or angered by honesty.

The absence of a father image does not concern many lesbian mothers. In fact, having sons grow up to be like their fathers is frequently considered undesirable. Lesbian mothers are eager to raise sons to relate to women as people, as equals. What really worries these mothers is the influence of their sons' peers, of television, and of the schools which still perpetuate stereotypes.

"We can't control that," Jerry, who has a young son, explains, "but we try. Some of our gay male friends have become sensitive to the problem and have been helpful with my son, Paul. Also we see to it that we have a wide range of friends coming into our home—both women and men, gay and straight."

"My fourteen-year-old son doesn't have to be *macho* to know that he is a man," a Chicana mother says. "He doesn't have to role-play in order to prove his manhood. He knows he is male and is having no trouble with his identity. What he doesn't understand is what all the fuss is about, why his friends have to pretend to be something they are not."

A lesbian mother, who doesn't relate to men "at all," claims, "My sons don't need a male image. They need a human image. The best thing I can do is make them aware." Other lesbian mothers may not be willing to forgo all relationships with men, yet they agree that nonsexist male models are hard to come by.

Because of their feminist consciousness, many lesbian mothers are confident of giving their daughters a positive self-image. Some, however, are subject to the same societal pressures that affect heterosexual mothers. Laura, for instance, admitted that she had worried about her daughter developing a proper female identification. "A couple of years ago, when Linda was six, she wanted Hot-Wheels for Christmas, and it threw me in to a fit," Laura remembers. "Meg and I sat and discussed it for hours." Linda did not get the toy cars. Laura realizes now, however, that she had given in to those societal pressures that dictate dolls and surrogate household appliances for little girls, and cars and chemistry sets for little boys.

Before the days of Gay Liberation and the Women's Movement, most lesbian mothers were apt to try to conceal their lesbianism from their children. One we know went to the extreme of cutting herself off completely from any contact with the gay community or from any possibility of an adult love relationship. Instead she devoted her energies solely to the job of "mothering." Now, young women prefer to be open and honest with their children, to be free enough to display affection in front of them, as heterosexual couples do. "The important thing," according to Barbara, "is that there is love and security in the home and that my child grows up with the idea of *two people* loving each other."

But it's one thing inside the home, quite another on the outside. Barbara described the time she put her arm around Carole as they were walking down the street, and her nine-year-old son, Jim, stopped her. "Don't do that. I understand, but other people don't."

Sarah and Diane, in their late thirties, merged their families three years ago, which made them responsible for nine children. "Neither of us cares what the girls turn out to be—whatever makes them happy," Sarah says. "If they become lesbians, it's the unfair shake they'd get from society that will bother us. Truthfully, we don't feel they will ever find as beautiful a relationship with a man as they would with a woman. Perhaps we are biased by our own experience. But despite all our efforts to the contrary, we still see the 'typical male' qualities developing in our own sons."

"We didn't have any more problems bringing these kids together than a straight couple would with his, hers, and ours," Diane added. "It's difficult to tell whether they accept or reject our relationship. My eighteen-year-old boy definitely rejects it, and Sarah's nineteen-year-old daughter, who is married, accepts it. The rest would be just guesses. Two sons have been difficult, but we aren't sure if it's because of 'us' or just resentment over the divorce. The sixteen-year-old boy shows definite signs of homosexuality."

Bringing teenage sons into a new family constellation with two women heading the household presents more difficulties than when younger children are involved. Gerri, confused by the responses of her fourteen-year-old son, says, "He genuinely likes Mary and her ten-year-old daughter as people—that's evident. But he is upset to the point of threatening violence and running away (though I don't think he is likely to do either), about living in an all female household where his *machismo* is not honored. I know this is a transition time in his life. Our new family arrangement makes it especially difficult for him. But I don't know how to make him feel good as a human being, a male person, a family member, when he sees male chauvinism as the only example all around him as the way *good* men are. My choice of a woman as the most fulfilling partner must be threatening to him, too, I guess. But he can't articulate any of this very well."

Many lesbian mothers remain captive in unsatisfactory heterosexual marriages because they fear exposure or cannot overcome a traditional need for the male.

Others are being blackmailed into giving up their children for the same reasons. As awareness and support grow, more and more lesbian mothers are coming out into the open to declare that their relationships are viable and valid, and that they are just as capable of raising children as are heterosexuals. Many women no longer flinch at taking their cause to the courts. Increasingly, psychologists and sociologists are backing them up, and some courts are acknowledging that mothering abilities exist because of the individual, not because of sex orientation.

After interviewing many of these women, we feel there was only one logical conclusion to make. What is important in deciding custody cases is the relationship between parent and child, not the parent's sexual orientation. If parents stopped worrying about artificial sex roles, and concentrated on teaching their children how to develop healthy human relationships, perhaps we might put an end to the Battle of the Sexes—woman against man, heterosexual against homosexual.

EVERYDAY USE

Alice Walker

Alice Walker was born in Eatonton, Georgia, in 1944, attended Spelman College, and then Sarah Lawrence. After graduation, during the 1960s, she worked on voter registration in Jackson, Mississippi. Her published works include five books of poetry, a children's biography of Langston Hughes, an edition of the selected works of Zora Neale Hurston, and five novels. In 1982, *The Color Purple* won both the National Book Award and the Pulitzer Prize for fiction and was subsequently made into a film. Her latest novel, *Possessing the Secret of Joy,* deals with the practice of female genital mutilation.

Walker's work illuminates the lives of ordinary people and underscores the importance of family connections. "In the black family," she says, "love, cohesion, support, and concern are crucial since the racist society constantly acts to destroy the black individual, the black family unit, the black child. In America black people have only themselves and each other."

"Everyday Use," which was included in *Best Short Stories of 1973*, is about a mother who must decide which of her daughters will have the family quilts: Dee, who wants the quilts to hang on her wall as evidence of her "heritage"; or Maggie, who would put the quilts to "everyday use." The mother's decision reflects her own values, as well as her sensitivity to both daughters, even though she must deny one.

I will wait for her in the yard that Maggie and I made so clean and wavy yesterday afternoon. A yard like this is more comfortable than most people know. It is not just a yard. It is like an extended living room. When the hard clay is swept clean as a floor and the fine sand around the edges lined with tiny, irregular grooves, anyone can come and sit and look up into the elm tree and wait for the breezes that never come inside the house.

Maggie will be nervous until after her sister goes: she will stand hopelessly in corners, homely and ashamed of the burn scars down her arms and legs, eying her sister with a mixture of envy and awe. She thinks her sister has held life always in the palm of one hand, that "no" is a word the world never learned to say to her.

EVERYDAY USE   From Alice Walker, *In Love & Trouble: Stories of Black Women* (New York: Harcourt, 1973) 47–59. Copyright © 1973 by Alice Walker. Reprinted by permission of Harcourt Brace & Company.

You've no doubt seen those TV shows where the child who has "made it" is confronted, as a surprise, by his own mother and father, tottering in weakly from backstage. (A pleasant surprise, of course: what would they do if parent and child came on the show only to curse out and insult each other?) On TV mother and child embrace and smile into each other's faces. Sometimes the mother and father weep, the child wraps them in his arms and leans across the table to tell how he would not have made it without their help. I have seen these programs.

Sometimes I dream a dream in which Dee and I are suddenly brought together on a TV program of this sort. Out of a dark and soft-seated limousine I am ushered into a bright room filled with many people. There I meet a smiling, gray, sporty man like Johnny Carson who shakes my hand and tells me what a fine girl I have. Then we are on the stage and Dee is embracing me with tears in her eyes. She pins on my dress a large orchid, even though she has told me once that she thinks orchids are tacky flowers.

In real life I am a large big-boned woman with rough, man-working hands. In the winter I wear flannel nightgowns to bed and overalls during the day. I can kill and clean a hog as mercilessly as a man. My fat keeps me hot in zero weather. I can work outside all day, breaking ice to get water for washing; I can eat pork liver cooked over the open fire minutes after it comes steaming from the hog. One winter I knocked a bull calf straight in the brain between the eyes with a sledgehammer and had the meat hung up to chill before nightfall. But of course all this does not show on television. I am the way my daughter would want me to be; a hundred pounds lighter, my skin like an uncooked barley pancake. My hair glistens in the hot bright lights. Johnny Carson has much to do to keep up with my quick and witty tongue.

But that is a mistake. I know even before I wake up. Who ever knew a Johnson with a quick tongue? Who can even imagine me looking a strange white man in the eye? It seems to me I have talked to them always with one foot raised in flight, with my head turned in whichever way is farthest from them. Dee, though. She would always look anyone in the eye. Hesitation was no part of her nature.

"How do I look, Mama?" Maggie says, showing just enough of her thin body enveloped in pink skirt and red blouse for me to know she's there almost hidden by the door.

"Come out into the yard," I say.

Have you ever seen a lame animal, perhaps a dog run over by some careless person rich enough to own a car, sidle up to someone who is ignorant enough to be kind to him? That is the way my Maggie walks. She has been like this, chin on chest, eyes on ground, feet in shuffle, ever since the fire that burned the other house to the ground.

Dee is lighter than Maggie, with nicer hair and a fuller figure. She's a woman now, though sometimes I forget. How long ago was it that the other house burned? Ten, twelve years? Sometimes I can still hear the flames and feel Maggie's arms sticking to me, her hair smoking and her dress falling off her in little black papery flakes. Her eyes seemed stretched open, blazed open by the flames reflected in them. And Dee. I see her standing off under the sweetgum tree she used to dig gum out of; a look of concentration on her face as she watched the last dingy gray board of the house fall in toward the red-hot brick chimney. Why don't you do a dance around the ashes? I'd wanted to ask her. She had hated the house that much.

I used to think she hated Maggie too. But that was before we raised the money, the church and me, to send her to Augusta to school. She used to read to us without pity; forcing words, lies, other folks' habits, whole lives upon us two, sitting trapped and ignorant underneath her voice. She washed us in a river of make-believe, burned us with a lot of knowledge we didn't necessarily need to know. Pressed us to her with the serious way she read, to shove us away, like dimwits, at just the moment we seemed about to understand.

Dee wanted nice things. A yellow organdy dress to wear to her graduation from high school; black pumps to match a green suit she'd made from an old suit somebody gave me. She was determined to stare down any disaster in her efforts. Her eyelids would not flicker for minutes at a time. Often I fought off the temptation to shake her. At sixteen she had a style of her own: and knew what style was.

I never had an education myself. After second grade the school was closed down. Don't ask my why: in 1927 colored asked fewer questions than they do now. Sometimes Maggie reads to me. She stumbles along good-naturedly but can't see well. She knows she is not bright. Like good looks and money, quickness passed her by. She will marry John Thomas (who has mossy teeth in an earnest face), and then I'll be free to sit here and I guess just sing church songs to myself. Although I never was a good singer. Never could carry a tune. I was always better at a man's job. I used to love to milk till I was hooked in the side in '49. Cows are soothing and slow and don't bother you, unless you try to milk them the wrong way.

I have deliberately turned my back on the house. It is three rooms, just like the one that burned, except the roof is tin; they don't make shingle roofs anymore. There are no real windows, just some holes cut in the sides, like the portholes in a ship, but not round and not square, with rawhide holding the shutters up on the outside. This house is in a pasture too, like the other one. No doubt when Dee sees it she will want to tear it down. She wrote me once that no matter where we "choose" to live, she will manage to come see us. But she will never bring her friends. Maggie and I thought about this and Maggie asked me, "Mama, when did Dee ever *have* any friends?"

She had a few. Furtive boys in pink shirts hanging about on washday after school. Nervous girls who never laughed. Impressed with her, they worshiped the well-turned phrase, the cute shape, the scalding humor that erupted like bubbles in lye. She read to them.

When she was courting Jimmy T she didn't have much time to pay to us, but turned all her fault-finding power on him. He *flew* to marry a cheap city girl from a family of ignorant, flashy people. She hardly had time to recompose herself.

When she comes I will meet . . . but there they are!

Maggie attempts to make a dash for the house, in her shuffling way, but I stay her with my hand. "Come back here," I say. And she stops and tries to dig a well in the sand with her toe.

It is hard to see them clearly through the strong sun. But even the first glimpse of leg out of the car tells me it is Dee. Her feet were always neat looking, as if God himself had shaped them with a certain style. From the other side of the car comes a short, stocky man. Hair is all over his head a foot long and hanging from his chin like a kinky mule tail. I hear Maggie suck in her breath. "Uhnnnh," is what it sounds like. Like when you see the wriggling end of a snake just in front of your foot on a road. "Uhnnnh."

Dee, next. A dress down to the ground, in this hot weather. A dress so loud it hurts my eyes. There are yellows and oranges enough to throw back the light of the sun. I feel my whole face warming from the heat waves it throws out. Earrings gold too, and hanging down to her shoulders. Bracelets dangling and making noises when she moves her arm up to shake the folds of the dress out of her armpits. The dress is loose and flows, and as she walks closer, I like it. I hear Maggie go "Uhnnnh" again. It is her sister's hair. It stands straight up like the wool on a sheep. It is black as night and around the edges are two long pigtails that rope about like small lizards disappearing behind her ears.

"Wa-su-zo-Tean-o!" she says, coming on in that gliding way the dress makes her move. The short stocky fellow with the hair to his navel is all grinning and he follows up with, "Asalamalakim, my mother and sister!" He moves to hug Maggie but she falls back, right up against the back of my chair. I feel her trembling there, and when I look up I see the perspiration falling off her skin.

"Don't get up," says Dee. Since I am stout it takes something of a push. You can see me trying to move a second or two before I make it. She turns, showing white heels through her sandals, and goes back to the car. Out she peeks next with a Polaroid. She stoops down quickly and snaps off picture after picture of me sitting there in front of the house with Maggie cowering behind me. She never takes a shot without making sure the house is included. When a cow comes nibbling around the edge of the yard she snaps it and me and Maggie *and* the house. Then she puts the Polaroid on the back seat of the car, and comes up and kisses me on the forehead.

Meanwhile Asalamalakim is going through motions with Maggie's hand. Maggie's hand is as limp as a fish, and probably as cold, despite the sweat, and she keeps trying to pull it back. It looks like Asalamalakim wants to shake hands but wants to do it fancy. Or maybe he don't know how people shake hands. Anyhow, he soon gives up on Maggie.

"Well," I say. "Dee."

"No, Mama," she says. "Not 'Dee,' Wangero Leewanika Kemanjo!"

"What happened to 'Dee'?" I wanted to know.

"She's dead," Wangero said. "I couldn't bear it any longer, being named after the people who oppress me."

"You know well as me you was named after your aunt Dicie," I said. Dicie is my sister. She named Dee. We called her "Big Dee" after Dee was born.

"But who was *she* named after?" asked Wangero.

"I guess after Grandma Dee," I said.

"And who was she named after?" asked Wangero.

"Her mother," I said, and saw Wangero was getting tired. "That's about as far back as I can trace it," I said. Though, in fact, I probably could have carried it back beyond the Civil War through the branches.

"Well," said Asalamalakim, "there you are."

"Uhnnnh," I heard Maggie say.

"There I was not," I said, "before 'Dicie' cropped up in our family, so why should I try to trace it that far back?"

He just stood there grinning, looking down on me like somebody inspecting a Model A car. Every once in a while he and Wangero sent eye signals over my head.

"How do you pronounce this name?" I asked.

"You don't have to call me by it if you don't want to," said Wangero.

"Why shouldn't I?" I asked. "If that's what you want us to call you, we'll call you."

"I know it might sound awkward at first," said Wangero.

"I'll get used to it," I said. "Ream it out again."

Well, soon we got the name out of the way. Asalamalakim had a name twice as long and three times as hard. After I tripped over it two or three times he told me to just call him Hakim-a-barber. I wanted to ask him was he a barber, but I didn't really think he was, so I didn't ask.

"You must belong to those beef-cattle peoples down the road," I said. They said "Asalamalakim" when they met you too, but they didn't shake hands. Always too busy: feeding the cattle, fixing the fences, putting up salt-lick shelters, throwing down hay. When the white folks poisoned some of the herd, the men stayed up all night with rifles in their hands. I walked a mile and a half just to see the sight.

Hakim-a-barber said, "I accept some of their doctrines, but farming and raising cattle is not my style." They didn't tell me, and I didn't ask, whether Wangero (Dee) had really gone and married him.

We sat down to eat and right away he said he didn't eat collards and pork was unclean. Wangero, though, went on through the chitlins and corn bread, the greens and everything else. She talked a blue streak over the sweet potatoes. Everything delighted her. Even the fact that we still used the benches her daddy made for the table when we couldn't afford to buy chairs.

"Oh, Mama!" she cried. Then turned to Hakim-a-barber. "I never knew how lovely these benches are. You can feel the rump prints," she said, running her hands underneath her and along the bench. Then she gave a sigh and her hand closed over Grandma Dee's butter dish. "That's it!" she cried. "I knew there was something I wanted to ask you if I could have." She jumped from the table and went over to the corner where the churn stood, the milk in it clabber by now. She looked at the churn and looked at it.

"This churn top is what I need," she said. "Didn't Uncle Buddy whittle it out of a tree you all used to have?"

"Yes," I said.

"Uh huh," she said happily. "And I want the dasher too."

"Uncle Buddy whittle that too?" asked the barber.

Dee (Wangero) looked up at me.

"Aunt Dee's first husband whittled the dash," said Maggie so low you almost couldn't hear her. "His name was Henry, but they called him Stash."

"Maggie's brain is like an elephant's," Wangero said, laughing. "I can use the churn top as a centerpiece for the alcove table," she said, sliding a plate over the churn, "and I'll think of something artistic to do with the dasher."

When she finished wrapping the dasher the handle stuck out. I took it for a moment in my hands. You didn't even have to look close to see where hands pushing the dasher up and down to make butter had left a kind of sink in the wood. In fact, there were a lot of small sinks; you could see where thumbs and fingers had sunk into the wood. It was beautiful light yellow wood, from a tree that grew in the yard where Big Dee and Stash had lived.

After dinner Dee (Wangero) went to the trunk at the foot of my bed and started rifling through it. Maggie hung back in the kitchen over the dishpan. Out came Wangero with two quilts. They had been pieced by Grandma Dee, and then Big Dee and me had hung them on the quilt frames on the front porch and quilted them. One was in the Lone Star pattern. The other was Walk Around the Mountain. In both of them were scraps of dresses Grandma Dee had worn fifty and more years ago. Bits and pieces of Grandpa Jarrell's paisley shirts. And one teeny faded blue piece, about the size of a penny matchbox, that was from Great Grandpa Ezra's uniform that he wore in the Civil War.

"Mama," Wangero said sweet as a bird. "Can I have these old quilts?"

I heard something fall in the kitchen, and a minute later the kitchen door slammed.

"Why don't you take one or two of the others?" I asked. "These old things was just done by me and Big Dee from some tops your grandma pieced before she died."

"No," said Wangero. "I don't want those. They are stitched around the borders by machine."

"That'll make them last better," I said.

"That's not the point," said Wangero. "These are all pieces of dresses Grandma used to wear. She did all this stitching by hand. Imagine!" She held the quilts securely in her arms, stroking them.

"Some of the pieces, like those lavender ones, come from old clothes her mother handed down to her," I said, moving up to touch the quilts. Dee (Wangero) moved back just enough so that I couldn't reach the quilts. They already belonged to her.

"Imagine!" she breathed again, clutching them closely to her bosom.

"The truth is," I said, "I promised to give them quilts to Maggie, for when she marries John Thomas."

She gasped, like a bee had stung her.

"Maggie can't appreciate these quilts!" she said. "She'd probably be backward enough to put them to everyday use."

"I reckon she would," I said. "God knows I been saving 'em for long enough with nobody using 'em. I hope she will!" I didn't want to bring up how I had offered Dee (Wangero) a quilt when she went away to college. Then she had told me they were old-fashioned, out of style.

"But they're *priceless!*" she was saying now, furiously; for she has a temper. "Maggie would put them on the bed and in five years they'd be in rags. Less than that!"

"She can always make some more," I said. "Maggie knows how to quilt."

Dee (Wangero) looked at me with hatred. "You just will not understand. The point is these quilts, *these* quilts!"

"Well," I said, stumped, "what would *you* do with them?"

"Hang them," she said. As if that was the only thing you *could* do with quilts.

Maggie, by now, was standing in the door. I could almost hear the sound her feet made as they scraped over each other.

"She can have them, Mama," she said, like somebody used to never winning anything, or of having anything reserved for her. "I can 'member Grandma Dee without the quilts."

I looked at her hard. She had filled her bottom lip with checkerberry snuff, and it gave her face a kind of dopey, hangdog look. It was Grandma Dee and Big Dee who taught her how to quilt herself. She stood there with her scarred hands hidden in the folds of her skirt. She looked at her sister with something like fear, but she wasn't mad at her. This was Maggie's portion. This was the way she knew God to work.

When I looked at her like that something hit me in the top of my head and ran down to the soles of my feet. Just like when I'm in church and the spirit of God touches me and I get happy and shout. I did something I never had done before: hugged Maggie to me, then dragged her on into the room, snatched the quilts out of Miss Wangero's hands and dumped them into Maggie's lap. Maggie just sat there on my bed with her mouth open.

"Take one or two of the others," I said to Dee.

But she turned without a word and went out to Hakim-a-barber.

"You just don't understand," she said, as Maggie and I came out to the car.

"What don't I understand?" I wanted to know.

"Your heritage," she said. And then she turned to Maggie, kissed her, and said, "You ought to try to make something of yourself too, Maggie. It's really a new day for us. But from the way you and Mama still live you'd never know it."

She put on some sunglasses that hid everything above the tip of her nose and her chin.

Maggie smiled; maybe at the sunglasses. But a real smile, not scared. After we watched the car dust settle I asked Maggie to bring me a dip of snuff. And then the two of us sat there just enjoying, until it was time to go in the house and go to bed.

 ————————————————————————————

MY DAUGHTER AND ME: DÉJÀ VU OVER AND OVER AGAIN

Jane Adams

The following article appeared in *Lear's* magazine, a publication directed primarily at an audience of mature women. When she was young, Frances Loeb Lear (b.1927), the founder of the magazine, had worked as an assistant buyer at Bloomingdale's and as a buyer at Lord & Taylor; later, she owned her own business. After her divorce from Norman Lear in her late 50s, however, she started *Lear's,* a slick and chic magazine designed to illustrate the strength and beauty of older women. *Lear's* ceased publication after the March 1994 issue.

Jane Adams, the author of this piece, is the author of three novels and six works of nonfiction, including *Wake Up, Sleeping Beauty: How to Live Happily Ever After* (1990). In her article for *Lear's,* she examines her relationships with her mother and with her daughter.

God forgive me, I never wanted a daughter. I saw myself as the mother of sons, lusty strapping fellows, all bashfulness and bonhomie. Barbara Stanwyck in *The Big Valley* was my role model, as were the unsung heroines of the Ponderosa, who, before departing for heaven, taught the Cartwright boys respect, perseverance, and good table manners.

"Girls know so many more ways to break your heart," I used to say. "With boys all you have to worry about are fast cars and shameless hussies."

A lot I knew. I raised a son as well as a daughter, and he made me cry more than she did. But early in her adolescence—that awful year before she got her period—she nearly drove me round the bend. In the middle of an attack of raging, surging hormones (mine as well as hers) I wailed, "It's not fair! I was 13 once, and I hated it then! Why do I have to go through it again?" It was a rhetorical, not entirely logical question, the kind that usually preceded her storming out of my presence, slamming the door.

But not this time. This time she knew I was a lot more upset than she was—just as crazy, maybe crazier. She knew my clenched, white-knuckled hands wanted to strangle her; she knew she had gone almost, if not quite, too far.

"When you were my age," she asked, "did you ever promise yourself that when you had a daughter you'd be a better mom than yours was? Well, unless you're willing to be 13 again, you never will be."

Suddenly I was surrounded by mirrors, like the ones in department store dressing rooms that exaggerate every flaw. The images reflected back at me were multiple and unforgiving. Close up, each was distinct, individual. My mother, my daughter, myself.

At the moment of truth I usually focus on the middle distance (particularly when trying on bathing suits), and in the middle distance we are all one. But I could not escape the painful images confronting me: I was 13 now, and I hated my mother. I was my mother, and I wanted to kill that 13-year-old girl. I was myself, hating my daughter, terrified at what I had become, the mother from hell I'd sworn I'd never be.

There is no other human being who can cause you so much pain—or so much joy—as a daughter. She embodies all your pasts—physical, historical, spiritual, emotional—and links you to the future. You cannot hide from her as you can from a son, or indeed from any man, because from the day she is born she can read your mind as no man ever will. This beautiful creature you grew in your body is so exactly like yourself: Not even the intimacy of sexual communion can match the mirror imaging, the intensity, of the symbiotic bond between mother and daughter.

If you understand and accept your daughter, you understand and accept yourself; if you do not, you destroy the chance to build a relationship that offers renewal and richness for a lifetime. The dreams you have for a daughter are the same dreams you had for yourself, those deferred as well as those fulfilled. And since your emotional investment in her is, by nature, greater than in any other person, its ultimate dividends are greater too.

But mother and daughter are engaged in an ongoing psychodrama that makes it difficult to remember such things. And unless you remember your history you are doomed to repeat it. The words that come out of your mouth are your mother's words, and you don't believe you're really saying them. When your daughter is suffering some private grief or public humiliation, you tell her she'll laugh about it someday. When she sleeps on her hair wrong, you won't let her stay home from school. Despite your best intentions you find yourself repeating every clichéd inanity, even and especially the well-known Bubbe's Curse: "Someday when you have a daughter of your own, she'll eat your heart out the way you do mine." As baseball's Yogi Berra said, in a slightly different context, "It's déjà vu all over again."

Some of us never grow out of adolescence—our daughters' or our own—without incurring emotional damage. We retreat to our corners and nurse our wounds; scar tissue forms, and we come to terms with it—or we don't. Every time somebody's mother dies, we tell ourselves we have to clear up unfinished business with our own while we can, before she takes our anger, guilt, selfish thoughts, and unmet expectations to her grave. And then we don't, and we mourn the missed opportunity or go on shadowboxing with the destroyer, judge, and critic who haunts our waking dreams: the mother we never vanquished, the mother we never can.

I had thought the problems I'd had with my own mother were the result of a generation gap, one I reasoned would never separate my daughter, Jenny, and me. She and I seemed contemporaneous in a way my mother and I never were. My mother was a wife nearly all her life, and she considered all her other roles, pursuits, and interests secondary. Jenny is single, and now so am I; we both nourish careers and consciousness with equal devotion. My mother loved and lived with only one man; my daughter and I have lived through different times, socially and sexually. Our politics, values, and lifestyles are remarkably similar, despite the 26 years between us.

I used to believe that I would be able to avoid making the mistakes with my daughter that my mother made with me. In fact, I hung my hopes on it. Once Jenny was through singing the puberty blues I paraded my wonderful relationship with her in front of my mother in a game of one-upmanship. Even when our relationship wasn't that great, I said, "Gotcha!" Even when I had to pretend that the ring in Jenny's nose was beautiful, that it was fine with me that she was dropping out of school, that I was happy when she took up with a boy who was definitely trouble waiting to happen. And the more I pretended, the more my mother shook her head in dismay.

It took me a long time to face up to the truth that my daughter and I are not peers, not contemporaries, and we never have been, although it sometimes feels that way. Economically, socially, sexually, and vocationally, the world in which Jenny grew up is as different from my world as mine was from my mother's. My daughter and I are both the New Woman, but she is newer than I am, and that makes all the difference.

Perhaps because I raised her alone, I couldn't protect her from reality the way my parents protected me. I tried not to make rules without giving a reason, and I rarely ended an argument with the dreaded words "because I said so." I didn't make the same mistakes my mother made with me; I made other ones. And now, when as an adult Jenny is making decisions that will determine the course of her life—decisions about career, marriage, children—I am galled to discover that it is just as hard to let her make them by herself, particularly when they seem to be wrong decisions, as it must have been for my mother.

The fact is, just as my mother's reality differed from mine, so does Jenny's, even though we're both artists and she loves the Grateful Dead too. The generation gap is real, and only by each standing on our own opposite side of it, acknowledging the distance between us, can we bridge it.

"You'll have a lot of friends, but you only have one mother," my own mother used to warn, and I would laugh—but she was right. Certainly Jenny and I are friends, but that's a corollary to our connection: Would I take the liberties with a friend, no matter how close, that I so often and easily take with her? Even with a husband or lover, would I be so soluble, so unrespecting of boundaries, so unable to distinguish self from other?

Throughout life our histories follow us into all of our relationships, but in no other is that history so vital, so profound, as in the relationship we have with our daughters. We may re-create our history, we may revise it, but, no matter what our choices, we are always reacting to it. We remother ourselves through our daughters, in good ways and bad. And in doing so, we respond to our own unmet childhood needs and expectations, to a separateness never acknowledged, to an inclusion never accomplished.

And somewhere during the postparenting years, if we're lucky, we get the chance to mend or amend the delicate connection that adolescence—nature's own psychosis—may have frayed, or even ripped apart. This calls for a midcourse correction: attention to our daughters' needs, not our own; tolerance for their uniqueness. Our daughters may have our eyes, our smile, our sense of humor, but they have their own way of thinking, doing, feeling—different from ours, perhaps, but no less valid or deserving of respect.

In my mother's hospital room, in the last hours before her death, my daughter whispered to me, "Go home, Mom, and get some sleep." I wanted to but could not: Weren't there debts to be settled, attention to be paid? "I'll be here for Bubbe if she wakes up," Jenny said. But wasn't deathwatch a daughter's duty, a mother's due? Or was there, perhaps, an example to be set?

"When it's your turn, I'll be here too," she whispered, and once again we were one—my mother, my daughter, myself. But this time I was not afraid.

SEPARATING MOM FROM THE CONCEPT CALLED MOTHER

Anna Quindlen

Anna Quindlen (b. 1953) worked as a reporter for the *New York Post* after her graduation from Barnard College in 1974. In the early 1980s, she began writing for the *New York Times* and won many awards. In 1992 she became the third woman in history to win the Pulitzer Prize for commentary. *Living Out Loud* (1988), a collection of over sixty of Quindlen's columns, was published to favorable reviews, and her novel, *Object Lessons* (1991), was also well received.

Quindlen has been able to integrate her professional and domestic life, especially in the past few years when she has written a twice-weekly column for the *Times* from her home. She and her husband, Gerald Krovatin, have three children. "Anybody who tries to convince me that foreign policy is more important than child rearing," says Quindlen, "is doomed to failure."

 For several years after my mother's death, I felt about Mother's Day the way I suppose recently divorced people feel about Valentine's Day. It seemed to be an organized effort by the immediate world to spit in my eye, and I gladly would have set fire to every card in every card rack in every card shop in town. In time, the rage abated, and what remained in its place was an emotionless

SEPARATING MOM FROM THE CONCEPT CALLED MOTHER   From Anna Quindlen, "Life in the 80s: Separating Mom from the Concept Called Mother," *The New York Times* 6 May 1987. Copyright © 1987 by The New York Times Company. Reprinted by permission.

distance. Mother's Day became much like Passover, a holiday that people like me did not celebrate.

Secretly, I suspected that I would be reconciled to it someday, when I had children, when I was a mother. This conclusion seemed logical and sensible and was completely wrong. Mother's Day is still fraught with strong emotion now, if only because each year I feel like a fraud. It is undeniable that I have given birth to two children; I remember both occasions quite vividly. But the orchid corsage, the baby-pink card with the big M in curly script, the burnt toast on a tray in bed—they belong to someone else, some other kind of person, some sort of moral authority. They belong to Mother, and each of us knows quite well who that person is, and always will be.

That person is a concept. I suppose that is where it all goes wrong. I know few people who have managed to separate the two. My friends speak about their mothers, about their manipulations and criticisms and pointed remarks, and when I meet these same women I can recognize very little of them in the child's description. They usually seem intelligent, thoughtful, kind. But I am not in a position to judge. To me they are simply people, not some lifelong foil, a yardstick by which to measure myself, to publicly find mother wanting, to privately find the fault within.

And yet I know the feeling. Although she was long dead when I had my children, my mother and I were then somehow equals, peers, alike in my mind. That was the most disconcerting feeling of my life. I was part of a generation of women so different from their mothers as to sometimes be a palpable insult, daughters who were perhaps as likely to model themselves on the male parent as the female one.

For all of my life my mother had been the other: I was aggressive, she was passive. (Perhaps simply reserved?) I was intellectual, she was not. (Perhaps not given the opportunity?) I was gregarious, she was shy. (Perhaps simply more selective in her attachments?) At a family gathering recently, several people I have not seen since I was a girl approached and said they knew who I was because I looked exactly like my mother. I was chilled to the bone. How dare they? How dare they consign me to her shoes? How dare they allow me to fill them?

But in some sense I have slipped into them simply by having children of my own. Nearly every day some echo of my mother's mothering wafts by me, like the aroma of soup simmering on some stove down the street. Even as we swear we will not do some of the horrible things they did, not pull the thumb like a cork from our children's mouths, not demand that they clean their plates, our mothers' words come full-blown out of our mouths, usually in anger: "If you do that it will be the last thing you do." "You've got another think coming." "Over my dead body." "Because I said so, that's why." Even as we enumerate their shortcomings, the rigor of raising children ourselves makes clear to us our mothers' incredible strength. We fear both. If they are not strong, who will protect us? If they are not imperfect, how can we equal them?

Perhaps those conflicting emotions help us reconcile ourselves to our mothers, make us able to apprehend the shadow of a human being, just raising other human beings the best she can, beneath the terrible weight of the concept.

In the beginning it is difficult. I have envied my friends who have had their mothers to help them with new babies, then felt the envy evaporate at the distress and doubt my friends sometimes felt about who was really the mother here. "No girl becomes a woman until she has lost her mother," someone once told me. And there was the proof: women reduced to children again in a way I never could be.

Yet it is having children that can smooth the relationship, too. Mother and daughter are now equals. That is hard to imagine, even harder to accept, for among other things, it means realizing that your own mother felt this way, too—unsure of herself, weak in the knees, terrified about what in the world to do with you. It means accepting that she was tired, inept, sometimes stupid, that she, too, sat in the dark at 2 A.M. with a child shrieking across the hall and no clue to the child's trouble.

Most of this has little to do with the specific women involved. In my case that is certainly true. This firestorm is not about one sweet, gentle mother, perhaps tough and demanding inside, and one tough, demanding daughter, now sweet and gentle with her own children. It has to do with Mother with a capital M: someone we are afraid to be and afraid that we can never be. It has to do with a torch being passed, with finding it hot to hold, with looking up at the person who has given it to you and accepting that without it, she is no Valkyrie, just a woman muddling through, much like me, much like you.

Part Six

Workers

In the 1970s, a perfume manufacturer adopted Peggy Lee's popular 1963 song, "I'm a Woman," for a television commercial. In it, a dressed-for-success, briefcase-carrying superwoman brags to her man that because she's a woman she "can bring home the bacon" and "fry it up in the pan." But, lest she sound too threatening, she reassures him—in the sexiest of voices—that she can do it all, "and never let [him] forget [he's] a man!" Quite simply, this advertisement summarized the popular image of the day's working woman: assertive enough to be an executive, but seductive enough to wear perfume; independent enough to bring home the bacon, but domestic enough to cook it up in the pan. She managed it all—career, home, and family. But the truth of the matter is that the work lives of real women rarely match the popular images of them tendered by the media. Cooking dinner? Just stir it up in the pan! The image of housework conveyed in the ad belies the labor involved. And the woman's status in the

"SHE'S MAKING HISTORY, WORKING FOR VICTORY,
ROSIE, THE RIVETER."
—WORLD WAR II SONG,
"ROSIE THE RIVETER"

paid labor force notwithstanding, she still does most of the cooking, along with the rest of the housework.

In spite of all the "labor-saving" devices invented for the home during the present century, women spend about as much time on household tasks as did their colonial and nineteenth-century foresisters because new duties have evolved to replace outmoded ones. Most women today, for example, do not have to carry water from wells for their children's baths, but their foresisters did not feel obliged to bathe their children as frequently as modern standards require. And today, although the laundry no longer has to be boiled, clothes are washed more often than they were just a few generations ago.

Before the 1970s, television commercials rarely featured women doing out-of-the-home work. This helped foster the popular myth that women had only recently entered the paid labor force. Women were, in fact, among the first wage-earners in this country. Moreover, poor and working-class women, immigrant women, and women of color have always worked outside the home in greater numbers than their middle-class or white counterparts. What has changed is the proportion of women in paid employment. From 1850 to 1900 women's participation increased from 10 to 20 percent, to 30 percent by 1950, and to almost 60 percent by 1990. By the year 2000, 80 percent of women are expected to be in the workplace.

These figures, however, do not include the unpaid labor done by women. The slave women of the South worked in the fields just as the men did. Other women, especially among the poor and working class, stretched the family budget by growing food for their families, taking boarders into their homes, or doing laundry or mending for more affluent families. Despite the labor involved, housework is not counted in the Gross National Product. Yet estimates of the annual costs of replacing a full-time wife and mother range as high as $80,000.

Like the popular images of working women promoted in soap operas and romantic novels, the perfume commercial suggests that women have glamorous, exciting, high-paying careers. But as Mary Harris "Mother" Jones, the famous labor organizer, chided over seventy years ago, "women don't have careers . . . they have jobs." For most women, Mother Jones' remark remains true.

Historical factors help explain some of the reasons for this. Early in this century the tragic fire at the Triangle Shirtwaist Company in New York City called attention to the exploitation of women workers. More than one hundred sweatshop workers died when they were unable to evacuate their sixth-floor factory—the exits had been locked from the outside to prevent them from taking unauthorized breaks. Reformers like Frances Perkins, who later became Secretary of Labor in Franklin Roosevelt's administration and was the first woman to hold cabinet rank, and Florence Kelley, founder of the National Consumer's League, led a crusade to improve the working conditions of women and children. As a result, in state after state, new laws restricted the number of hours and shifts women could work, established a minimum wage for them (but not for men), and specified the maximum amount of weight they could lift. Although designed to improve the situation of working women, this legislation had the effect over time of helping to segregate them in the labor force by keeping them out of many jobs. It thus contributed to the wage differential between male and female workers. This type of "protective" legislation was not overturned until 1964 when Title VII of the Civil Rights Act banned discrimination by gender.

Sex segregation and discrimination nonetheless remain common features of the workplace. Eight out of ten working women today do not work in professional, technical, or managerial positions. In addition, women tend to be clustered in a smaller number of occupations than are men. Nearly 40 percent are in clerical jobs. The percentage of women in the trades, or skilled blue-collar work, is extremely small. Furthermore, many of the women in professional, technical, or managerial occupations are in such traditionally "feminine" fields as nursing or elementary school teaching.

The myth that women work only for extra "pin money" is another problem which has plagued women workers. Many managers and male workers assume that women do not use their wages to support families, or for other economic necessities, but rather only to buy "extras." The implication that women are secondary earners with no pressing financial needs functions to keep their wages low. However, women continue to protest this stereotype, and unions such as Nine to Five and Women Office Workers, as well as some older and larger unions, have begun organizing drives. Women's union activity is not new. Historically, women played an active role in the labor movement, even though some unions barred them from membership; they were among the first to strike in the nineteenth century. Women such as Sarah Bagley, Mother Jones, and Elizabeth Gurley Flynn were well-known labor organizers. Some women went to jail for their efforts; some even lost their lives. They, and the countless women they represented, inspired union songs celebrating women workers

such as the popular "Bread and Roses." Yet in the 1940 "Union Maid," Woody Guthrie's heroine still advised: "You girls who want to be free / Just take a tip from me! / Get you a man who's a union man / And join the Ladies' Auxiliary."

Women face not only condescension but also sexual harassment on the job. This problem gained a great deal of attention after the testimony of Professor Anita Hill before the Senate Judiciary Committee's hearings for President George Bush's nominee to the United States Supreme Court, Judge Clarence Thomas. Hill's testimony inspired many women to speak out and to bring charges against those harassing them. Employers and workers alike began to take the problem much more seriously.

Women in professional positions confront other problems in the workplace as well. If the woman in the perfume commercial lands a professional job, she may find herself moving down the "mommy track." Much ado has been made in the popular media about women professionals willing to take this mommy track— give up higher pay for extra time with their families—but many women see it as a way for corporations to discriminate. Furthermore, despite women's movement into the middle ranks of management, many still bump their heads against the "glass ceiling" as the top ranks of most occupations remain virtually closed to women.

Sooner or later, fast track or mommy track, the woman in the commercial's real-life counterpart will burn the bacon. She will find her juggling act—job, family, housework—exhausting. Findings from studies demonstrate that women still bear the brunt of housework and child care even as they move into the labor force. Making matters worse is the fact that the United States continues to fall short of other nations in availability of child care or parental leave policies. The Family Leave Act of 1993 provides only minimum relief, and exceptions apply. Until we eliminate the assumption that child care and domestic duties are women's responsibility, speaking of working women strictly in terms of paid employment will continue to be misleading.

LETTERS OF A WOMAN HOMESTEADER
Elinore Rupert Stewart

The letter reprinted below comes from a series of letters published in *The Atlantic Monthly* in 1913 and 1914. The editors described them as "genuine letters, written without thought of publication, simply to tell a friendly story." The writer of the letters, they noted, was a young widow who moved to Denver, where she supported herself and her two-year-old daughter, Jerrine, by working as a "house-cleaner and laundress." Later, "seeking to better herself," she took a position as a housekeeper for Stewart, a "well-to-do" cattle rancher. Her letters, written to a former employer, began in 1909, shortly after her arrival at the Stewart ranch in Wyoming, and ended in 1913, by which time she and Stewart had wed.

In the letter below, Rupert recounts a summer of work and a day of "play" that might sap even the hardiest of people.

Burnt Fork, Wyo., Sept. 11

DEAR MRS. CONEY—

This has been for me the busiest, happiest summer I can remember. I have worked very hard but it has been work that I really enjoy. Help of any kind is very hard to get here, and Mr. Stewart had been too confident of getting men, so that haying caught him with too few men to put up the hay. He had no man to run the mower and he could n't run both the mower and the stacker, so you can fancy what a place he was in.

I don't know that I ever told you, but my parents died within a year of each other and left six of us to shift for ourselves. Our people offered to take one here and there among them until we should all have a place, but we refused to be raised on the halves and so arranged to stay at Grandmother's and keep together. Well, we had no money to hire men to do our work so had to learn to do it ourselves. Consequently I learned to do many things which girls more fortunately situated don't even know have to be done. Among the things I learned to do was the way to run a mowing machine. It cost me many bitter tears because I got sunburned, and my hands were hard, rough, and stained with machine oil, and I used to wonder how any Prince Charming could overlook all that in any girl he came to. For all I had ever read of the Prince had to do with his "reverently kissing her lily-white hand," or doing some other fool trick with a hand as white as a snowflake. Well, when my Prince showed up he did n't lose much time in letting me know that "Barkis was willing," and I wrapped my hands in my old checked apron and took him up before he could catch his breath. Then there was no more mowing, and I almost forgot that I knew how until Mr. Stewart got into such a panic. If he put a man to mow, it kept them all idle at the stacker, and he just could n't get enough men. I was afraid to tell him I could mow for fear he would forbid me to do so. But one morning, when he was chasing a last hope of help, I went down to the barn, took out the horses and

---

went to mowing. I had enough cut before he got back to show him I knew how, and as he came back man-less he was delighted as well as surprised. I was glad because I really like to mow, and besides that, I am adding feathers to my cap in a surprising way. When you see me again you will think I am wearing a feather duster, but it is only that I have been said to have almost as much sense as a "mon," and that is an honor I never aspired to, even in my wildest dreams.

I have done most of my cooking at night, have milked seven cows every day, and have done all the hay-cutting, so you see I have been working. But I have found time to put up thirty pints of jelly and the same amount of jam for myself. I used wild fruits, gooseberries, currants, raspberries and cherries. I have almost two gallons of the cherry butter, and I think it is delicious. I wish I could get some of it to you, I am sure you would like it.

We began haying July 5 and finished September 8. After working so hard and so steadily I decided on a day off, so yesterday I saddled the pony, took a few things I needed, and Jerrine and I fared forth. Baby can ride behind quite well. We got away by sun-up and a glorious day we had. We followed a stream higher up into the mountains and the air was so keen and clear at first, we had on our coats. There was a tang of sage and of pine in the air, and our horse was midside deep in rabbit-brush, a shrub just covered with flowers that look and smell like goldenrod. The blue distance promised many alluring adventures, so we went along singing and simply gulping in Summer. Occasionally a bunch of sage chickens would fly up out of the sage-brush, or a jack-rabbit would leap out. Once we saw a bunch of antelope gallop over a hill, but we were out just to be out, and game did n't tempt us. I started, though, to have just as good a time as possible, so I had a fish-hook in my knapsack.

Presently, about noon, we came to a little dell where the grass was as soft and as green as a lawn. The creek kept right up against the hills on one side and there were groves of quaking asp and cotton-woods that made shade, and service-bushes and birches that shut off the ugly hills on the other side. We dismounted and prepared to noon. We caught a few grasshoppers and I cut a birch pole for a rod. The trout are so beautiful now, their sides are so silvery, with dashes of old rose and orange, their speckles are so black, while their backs look as if they had been sprinkled with gold-dust. They bite so well that it does n't require any especial skill or tackle to catch plenty for a meal in a few minutes.

In a little while I went back to where I had left my pony browsing, with eight beauties. We made a fire first, then I dressed my trout while it was burning down to a nice bed of coals. I had brought a frying pan and a bottle of lard, salt, and buttered bread. We gathered a few service-berries, our trout were soon browned, and with water, clear, and as cold as ice, we had a feast. The quaking aspens are beginning to turn yellow, but no leaves have fallen. Their shadows dimpled and twinkled over the grass like happy children. The sound of the dashing, roaring water kept inviting me to cast for trout, but I did n't want to carry them so far, so we rested until the sun was getting low and then started for home, with the song of the locusts in our ears warning us that the melancholy days are almost here. We would come up over the top of a hill into the glory of a beautiful sunset with its gorgeous colors, then down into the little valley already purpling with mysterious twilight. So on, until, just at dark, we rode into our corral and a mighty tired, sleepy little girl was powerfully glad to get home.

After I had mailed my other letter I was afraid that you would think me plumb bold about the little Bo-Peep, and was a heap sorrier than you can think. If you only knew the hardships these poor men endure. They go two together and sometimes it is months before they see another soul, and rarely ever a woman. I would n't act so free in town, but these men see people so seldom that they are awkward and embarrassed. I like to put them at ease, and it is to be done only by being kind of hail-fellow-well-met with them. So far not one has ever misunderstood me and I have been treated with every courtesy and kindness, so I am powerfully glad you understand. They really enjoy doing these little things like fixing our dinner, and if my poor company can add to any one's pleasure I am too glad.

Sincerely yours,

Elinore Rupert

Mr. Stewart is going to put up my house for me in pay for extra work. I am ashamed of my long letters to you, but I am such a murderer of language that I have to use it all to tell anything.

Please don't entirely forget me. Your letters mean so much to me and I will try to answer more promptly.

I GO TO WORK

Florence Kelley

In 1892 when Florence Kelley went to work, women had to invent new career opportunities for themselves. In this essay, Kelley recounts her pioneering, and often dangerous, work as a special agent of the Illinois Bureau of Labor Statistics to investigate sweatshop labor in Chicago; as a supervisor of U.S. Commissioner of Labor Carroll D. Wright's national study of urban slum conditions (1892); as the first chief of factory inspection in Illinois (appointed in 1893); as supervisor of *Hull House Maps and Papers* (1895); and as investigator of health, working, and living conditions in the tenements of Chicago.

Kelley served as executive secretary of the new National Consumers' League from 1899 until her death in 1932. She also worked in a host of Progressive Era campaigns. Kelley's autobiographical sketch below begins with her arrival at the door of the recently founded Hull House Settlement in Chicago "[o]n a snowy morning between Christmas 1891 and New Year's 1892. . . ."

My first activity, begun that week, was conducting for a few months a small experimental employment office for working girls and women. It was a tiny space in a corner of the building then adjoining Hull-House, occupied as a morgue and undertaking establishment by an Irish-American mentioned with respect in the neighborhood because he was rumored to have various cripples and two deaths to his credit.

It soon turned out that both employers and applicants for domestic work were too few in the Hull-House region to afford a basis for a self-supporting employment office. Yet finding work for people of every conceivable qualification, from high

---

I GO TO WORK   From Florence Kelley, "I Go to Work," *Survey Graphic* 1 June 1927: 271–74, 301.

federal and state offices to rat-catching, forms a continuing chapter in the history of the House. But this has never been commercial.

In my first year at Hull-House, Carroll D. Wright, U. S. commissioner of commerce and labor, in charge of a federal study of the slums of great cities, entrusted me with the Chicago part of the enquiry. With a group of schedule men under my guidance, we canvassed a square mile extending from Hull-House on the west to State Street on the east, and several long blocks south. In this area we encountered people of eighteen nationalities.

Hull-House was, we soon discovered, surrounded in every direction by home-work carried on under the sweating system. From the age of eighteen months few children able to sit in high chairs at tables were safe from being required to pull basting threads. In the Hull-House kindergarten children used with pleasure blunt, coarse needles for sewing bright silk into perforated outlines of horses, dogs, cats, parrots, and less known creatures on cards. They did this in the intervals between singing, modeling and playing active games. At home they used equally coarse sharp needles for sewing buttons on garments. The contrast was a hideously painful one to witness, especially when the children fell asleep at their work in their homes.

Out of this enquiry, amplified by Hull-House residents and other volunteers, grew the volume published under the title Hull-House Maps and Papers. One map showed the distribution of the polyglot peoples. Another exhibited their incomes (taken by permission from the federal schedules) indicated in colors, ranging from gold which meant twenty dollars or more total a week for a family, to black which was five dollars or less total family income. There was precious little gold and a superabundance of black on that income map!

The discoveries as to home work under the sweating system thus recorded and charted in 1892 (that first year of my residence) led to the appointment at the opening of the legislature of 1893, of a legislative commission of enquiry into employment of women and children in manufacture, for which Mary Kenney and I volunteered as guides. Because we knew our neighborhood, we could and did show the commissioners sights that few legislators had then beheld; among them unparalleled congestion in frame cottages which looked decent enough, though drab and uninviting, under their thick coats of soft coal soot. One member of the Commission would never enter any sweatshop, but stood in the street while the others went in, explaining that he had young children and feared to carry them some infection.

This Commission had been invented as a sop to labor and a sinecure, a protracted junket to Chicago, for a number of rural legislators. Our overwhelming hospitality and devotion to the thoroughness and success of their investigation, by personally conducted visits to sweatshops, though irksome in the extreme to the law-givers, ended in a report so compendious, so readable, so surprising that they presented it with pride to the legislature. We had offered it to them under the modest title, Memorandum for Legislative Commission of 1893. They renamed it. The subject was a new one in Chicago. For the press the sweating system was that winter a sensation. No one was yet blasé.

With backing from labor, from Hull-House, from the Henry Demarest Lloyds and their numberless friends, the Commission and the report carried almost without opposition a bill applying to manufacture, and prescribing a maximum working day not to exceed eight hours for women, girls and children, together with child labor safeguards based on laws then existing in New York and Ohio, and quite advanced. There was a drastic requirement in the interest of the public health that tenement houses be searched for garments in process of manufacture, and goods found exposed in homes to contagious diseases be destroyed on the spot. Owners of goods produced under the sweating system were required to furnish to the inspectors on demand complete lists of names and addresses of both contractors and home workers.

The bill created a state factory inspection department on which was conferred power, with regard to tenement-made goods found on infected premises, unique in this country in 1893. Illinois changed, at a single stride, from no legislation restricting working hours in manufacture for men, women or children, by day, by night, or by the week, to a maximum eight-hours day for girls and for women of all ages, in all branches of manufacture.

When the new law took effect, and its usefulness depended upon the personnel prescribed in the text to enforce it, Governor Altgeld offered the position of chief inspector to Mr. Lloyd, who declined it and recommended me. I was accordingly made chief state inspector of factories, the first and so far as I know, the only woman to serve in that office in any state.

There had been suspiciously little opposition in the press or the legislature while our drastic bill was pending. It had passed both houses, and was signed by Governor Altgeld fairly early in the spring. Indeed the enactment of this measure, destined to be a milestone in the national history of our industry and our jurisprudence, was almost unnoticed.

My appointment dated from July 12, 1893. The appropriation for a staff of twelve persons was $12,000 a year, to cover salaries, traveling expenses, printing, court costs, and rent of an office in Chicago. The salary scale was, for the Chief $1,500 a year; for the first assistant, also a woman, Alzina P. Stevens $1,000; and for each of the ten deputies of whom six were men $720. Needless to say this had been voted by a legislature predominantly rural.

It was Governor Altgeld's definite intent to enforce to the uttermost limit this initial labor law throughout his term of office. He was a sombre figure; the relentless hardship of his experience as boy and youth had left him embittered against Fate, and against certain personal enemies, but infinitely tender towards the sufferings of childhood, old age and poverty. He was an able, experienced lawyer, and his sense of justice had been outraged by the conduct of the trial of the Anarchists. Indeed, no one yet knows who threw the fatal bomb in the Haymarket riots. The men who were hanged were charged with conspiracy to do a deed of which no one has ever known the actual doer. All the evidence against them was circumstantial, and in this respect the trial is, so far as I know, still unique in the history of American jurisprudence, the only trial closely resembling it in any considerable degree being that of the Molly Maguires in the mining regions of Pennsylvania in the early seventies of the Nineteenth Century. To Governor Altgeld's mind the whole Illinois retributive procedure presented itself as terrorism.

To the personnel of the newly created department for safeguarding women and children who must earn their living in manufacture, Governor Altgeld showed convincingly a passionate desire to use every power conferred for the benefit of the most inexperienced and defenseless elements in industry in Illinois.

My first effort to apply the penalty for employing children below the age of sixteen years without the prescribed working paper, led me to the office of the district attorney for Cook County. This was a brisk young politician with no interest whatever in the new law and less in the fate of the persons for whose benefit it existed. The evidence in the case I laid before him was complete. An eleven-years-old boy, illegally engaged to gild cheap picture frames by means of a poisonous fluid, had lost the use of his right arm, which was paralyzed. There was no compensation law and no prohibition of work in hazardous occupations. There was only a penalty of twenty dollars for employing a child without the required certificate. The young official looked at me with impudent surprise and said in a tone of astonishment:

"Are you calculating on *my* taking the case?"

I said: "I thought you were the district attorney."

"Well," he said, "suppose I am. You bring me this evidence this week against some little two-by-six cheap picture-frame maker, and how do I know you won't bring me a suit against Marshall Field next week? Don't count on me. I'm overloaded. I wouldn't reach this case inside of two years, taking it in its order."

That day I registered as a student in the Law School of Northwestern University for the approaching fall term, and received in June, 1894, a degree from that University whose graduates were automatically empowered to practice before the Supreme Court of Illinois. Credit was given for my reading law with Father in Washington in 1882, my studies in Zurich, and one year in the senior class in Chicago. The lectures were given in the evening and did not interfere with my administrative work.

In Chicago, in the winter and spring and summer of 1893, all available public spirit and creative energy were centered upon the World's Fair. The name was not an exaggeration. World-wide publicity had brought together works of all the arts in such profusion, and of such superior quality as have never since been assembled on this continent.

Two less famous occurrences of 1893 in Chicago were the financial and industrial panic with protracted unemployment and wretched suffering, and the epidemic of smallpox which followed a neglected case on the Midway of the Exposition. These horrors carried over throughout the year 1894, and with the latter I was excitingly identified.

At the close of the Fair, the hideous fact could no longer be concealed that smallpox had been gradually spreading from the Midway to the homes of some garment workers on the West Side. It was mandatory upon us to seek, as soon as we learned this, all clothing in process of manufacture in such places and, if exposure to the presence of the infection was clearly provable, to destroy the goods on the premises. We could never learn with any approach to accuracy how nearly all of the exposed goods we ultimately found.

Daily reports to the Board of Health with requests for immediate vaccination of the exposed dwellers in tenements placarded with the yellow smallpox card, produced no results. Milkmen came and went as usual. The families of patients, vaccinated and unvaccinated alike, visited the corner grocery and went their way to the factories. Among the immigrants who were the bulk of the garment-making home workers, the only really safe ones were those who had had smallpox in the old country, or who had been vaccinated at Ellis Island as a preliminary to admission to this country. Babies born after landing had little chance of surviving, for the vaccination ordinance was as little enforced as any other law. Many infants and little children we found concealed on closet shelves, wrapped in bundles, sometimes to keep them from being vaccinated, sometimes to keep them—with the disease so fully developed that concealment was unthinkable—from being sent to the sorely dreaded hospital. Not until Gov. Altgeld announced he was about to call a conference of the governors of Indiana, Wisconsin, Iowa, Missouri and Kentucky, with a view to instituting an embargo upon all shipments of products of the needle trades from Chicago, did the owners of the goods believe that the new law must be obeyed. They then instituted in good earnest a campaign of vaccination in their factories, their contract shops, and the tenements to which these latter sent out goods. So strong was the feeling against vaccination in the tenements that one promising young surgeon working with the vaccination squad was disabled for life for his profession, his elbow being shattered by a shot from an excited tailor.

The non-transmissibility of smallpox germs in woolen fabrics seems never to have been definitely proved. Without reference to the epidemic the occasional appearance of isolated cases on lonely farms in the Northwest, throughout 1924, could not be explained, especially when it coincided as it frequently did, with the previous receipt of woolen garments from the Chicago mail-order houses.

The Illinois Association of Manufactures, established in 1893, seems not to have been in working order until after the new law took effect in July, or to have been too feeble to make any timely opposition. No sooner, however, had we begun to enforce the statute against violators in the tenement houses, by urging their employers to cut off supplies of work during the period of the epidemic, warning them that goods found in the presence of infection would be summarily destroyed, than many workers showed us letters from the Manufacturers' Association promising protection if they were molested by inspectors who were, the letters said, operating under a new law clearly unconstitutional.

From that day the Illinois labor law has never been without strenuous opposition, sometimes open, sometimes concealed, from that active body. When a labor measure for women or minors has been strengthened on paper, or a valuable new one enacted, the quality of the administering officials has been reduced, if this could be achieved.

This reactionary but undeniably permanent power of the Illinois Manufacturers' Association was formerly chargeable to a grievous error of the exceedingly powerful trade unions, viz: their neglect of, and contempt for, statutory safeguards compared with negotiations of the organized workers through their unions. Since 1920, however, this responsibility is shared by the rank and file of women voters who fail to line up effectively behind the most important labor measures. Together voting women and organized voting labor could always win.

STENOGRAPHY IN NEW YORK CITY
G.E.D.

When the letter below was written, stenography and other secretarial positions had only recently opened to women. We know little about the author of this letter except that she, like hundreds of other women, responded to a call in 1908 from *Harper's Bazar* requesting letters "written by those girl readers who have gone through the experience of coming to the city and either succeeding or failing there, during the last ten years." In her letter, G.E.D. writes of sexual harassment but had no name for it, since the term *sexual harassment* was not coined until the 1970s.

 Five years ago my father and my mother died within one month of each other, leaving me, at nineteen years of age, wholly dependent upon my own exertions. I had graduated from the high school at seventeen, taken a post-graduate course the year after, won a scholarship for college, where I had spent one year, when I was called home, not to return again.

After paying the expenses of my parents' illness and the funeral expenses, I counted as my sole worldly possession one hundred dollars. With this I determined to make my worldly career. A friend of mine advised me to become a stenographer as the surest and swiftest way of making a living. I took fifty dollars and learned stenography, and during the three months I spent in mastering it, I worked every spare moment I had, doing embroidery and other odd "jobs" which my friends or acquaintances happened to have and, knowing my circumstances, kindly let me do for them. This gave me sufficient spare money to pay my board and lodging, while I did my laundry work myself, thus leaving intact my remaining fifty dollars, which I wished to guard jealously to assist me until I could secure a much-needed position in some city.

After my three months of study and hard work I completed my course.

I left my native town in the Mohawk Valley one cold, blistering day in March for New York. The fear and trembling which filled my heart on that eventful day would be impossible to describe. When I arrived at the Grand Central Station I was met by some school acquaintances, who assured me that I would have no trouble in getting a position in a week or two at the longest. Their buoyant hopes helped to revive my spirits, and I felt quite like a new being as they took me to their boarding-place on West Twenty-fourth Street.

After a night's rest, I felt more like doing something. There is something about the noises, the teeming life, of New York which always puts new life into me, something of the fighting spirit; a feeling, as it were, that the fittest will survive.

I purchased several papers, and plodded faithfully through their multitude of "ads." I took the addresses of some I intended to call upon, and wrote several letters to those who gave no address. The first office I visited was a lawyer's. He wanted a stenographer, and would pay six dollars a week. I asked him if he thought a young lady could live in New York on that, and clothe herself. He said he expected young women had friends who helped them out. I was too indignant to speak for a moment, but when I got my breath I politely informed him that I was not that kind of a young woman, and bade him good afternoon. I went no farther that day; to be quite frank, I went back to my boarding-place and had a good cry, wondering if all men were like that. The next day I started out again, though in rather a dejected mood. The first "ad" I answered the second day was that of a doctor who desired a stenographer at once, good wages paid. It sounded rather well, I thought, and I felt that this time I would meet a gentleman. The doctor was very kind and seemed to like my appearance and references; as to salary, he offered me fifteen dollars a week, with a speedy prospect of more. As I was leaving his office, feeling that at last I was launched safely upon the road to a good living, he said, casually, "I have an auto, and as my wife doesn't care for that sort of thing, I shall expect you to accompany me frequently on pleasure trips." That settled the doctor; I never appeared. After that experience I was ill for two weeks, a result of my hard work, suffering, and discouragement.

One day as I sat rather hopelessly gazing out of my window, I received a gentleman's card, with a request that I call at once at a large wholesale dry-goods house in the lower part of the city in reference to my application sent in two weeks before. I hastened to call, and was greeted by a kindly, grayhaired old gentleman of the old school, the kind who respects all womankind because his mother was a woman. He looked my letters of reference over carefully, and hired me at once. The wages were not high—only nine dollars to start; but it seemed to me that nine dollars from such a man was worth twenty or a hundred from some others. I worked at this place for two years, and I endeavored faithfully to give two dollars' worth of work for every dollar I received, and I think I succeeded. That my desire to please was not unnoticed by the firm was proved by the fact that my salary was steadily increased until, when I left, a year ago, I was getting twenty-two dollars a week.

G.E.D.

HOW I FOUND AMERICA
Anzia Yezierska

The selection below is from Anzia Yezierska's popular novel, *Hungry Hearts* (1920). The narrator, like many other Jewish immigrant women from Eastern Europe, came to America in search of economic security and freedom of political and religious expression. Many landed in the sweatshops of New York City, where the "No Irish Need Apply" signs of the 1860s had been replaced by "No Jews" for most other types of employment. The myth that the streets of America were paved with gold was sharply displaced for these immigrants by the misery of the working and living conditions awaiting them.

My eyes were shutting themselves with sleep. Blindly, I felt for the buttons on my dress, and buttoning I sank back in sleep again—the deadweight sleep of utter exhaustion.

"Heart of mine!" my mother's voice moaned above me. "Father is already gone an hour. You know how they'll squeeze from you a nickel for every minute you're late. Quick only!"

I seized my bread and herring and tumbled down the stairs and out into the street. I ate running, blindly pressing through the hurrying throngs of workers—my haste and fear choking each mouthful.

HOW I FOUND AMERICA   From Anzia Yezierska, *Hungry Hearts* (Cambridge: Houghton Mifflin, 1920) 265–73.

I felt a strangling in my throat as I neared the sweatshop prison; all my nerves screwed together into iron hardness to endure the day's torture.

For an instant I hesitated as I faced the grated window of the old dilapidated building—dirt and decay cried out from every crumbling brick.

In the maw of the shop, raging around me the roar and the clatter, the clatter and the roar, the merciless grind of the pounding machines. Half maddened, half deadened, I struggled to think, to feel, to remember—what am I—who am I—why was I here?

I struggled in vain—bewildered and lost in a whirlpool of noise.

"America—America—where was America?" it cried in my heart.

The factory whistle—the slowing-down of the machines—the shout of release hailing the noon hour.

I woke as from a tense nightmare—a weary waking to pain.

In the dark chaos of my brain reason began to dawn. In my stifled heart feelings began to pulse. The wound of my wasted life began to throb and ache. My childhood choked with drudgery—must my youth too die—unlived?

The odor of herring and garlic—the ravenous munching of food—laughter and loud, vulgar jokes. Was it only I who was so wretched? I looked at those around me. Were they happy or only insensible to their slavery? How could they laugh and joke? Why were they not torn with rebellion against this galling grind—the crushing, deadening movements of the body, where only hands live and hearts and brains must die?

A touch on my shoulder. I looked up. It was Yetta Solomon from the machine next to mine.

"Here's your tea."

I stared at her, half hearing.

"Ain't you going to eat nothing?"

"Oi weh! Yetta! I can't stand it!" The cry broke from me. "I did n't come to America to turn into a machine. I came to America to make from myself a person. Does America want only my hands—only the strength of my body—not my heart—not my feelings—my thoughts?"

"Our heads ain't smart enough," said Yetta, practically. "We ain't been to school like the American-born."

"What for did I come to America but to go to school—to learn—to think—to make something beautiful from my life. . . ."

"Sh-sh! Sh-sh! The boss—the boss!" came the warning whisper.

A sudden hush fell over the shop as the boss entered. He raised his hand.

Breathless silence.

The hard, red face with pig's eyes held us under its sickening spell. Again I saw the Cossack and heard him thunder the ukaz.

Prepared for disaster, the girls paled as they cast at each other sidelong, frightened glances.

"Hands," he addressed us, fingering the gold watch-chain that spread across his fat belly, "it's slack in the other trades and I can get plenty girls begging themselves to work for half what you're getting—only I ain't a skinner. I always give my hands a show to earn their bread. From now on, I'll give you fifty cents a dozen shirts instead of seventy-five, but I'll give you night-work, so you need n't lose nothing." And he was gone.

The stillness of death filled the shop. Each one felt the heart of the other bleed with her own helplessness.

A sudden sound broke the silence. A woman sobbed chokingly. It was Balah Rifkin, a widow with three children.

"Oi weh!" She tore at her scrawny neck. "The blood-sucker—the thief! How will I give them to eat—my babies—my babies—my hungry little lambs!"

"Why do we let him choke us?"

"Twenty-five cents less on a dozen—how will we be able to live?"

"He tears the last skin from our bones!"

"Why did n't nobody speak up to him?"

"Tell him he could n't crush us down to worse than we had in Russia?"

"Can we help ourselves? Our life lies in his hands."

Something in me forced me forward. Rage at the bitter greed tore me. Our desperate helplessness drove me to strength.

"I'll go to the boss!" I cried, my nerves quivering with fierce excitement. "I'll tell him Balah Rifkin has three hungry mouths to feed."

Pale, hungry faces thrust themselves toward me, thin, knotted hands reached out, starved bodies pressed close about me.

"Long years on you!" cried Balah Rifkin, drying her eyes with a corner of her shawl.

"Tell him about my old father and me, his only bread-giver," came from Bessie Sopolsky, a gaunt-faced girl with a hacking cough.

"And I got no father or mother and four of them younger than me hanging on my neck." Jennie Feist's beautiful young face was already scarred with the gray worries of age.

America, as the oppressed of all lands have dreamed America to be, and America *as it is,* flashed before me—a banner of fire! Behind me I felt masses pressing—thousands of immigrants—thousands upon thousands crushed by injustice, lifted me as on wings.

I entered the boss's office without a shadow of fear. I was not I—the wrongs of my people burned through me till I felt the very flesh of my body a living flame of rebellion.

I faced the boss.

"We can't stand it!" I cried. "Even as it is we're hungry. Fifty cents a dozen would starve us. Can you, a Jew, tear the bread from another Jew's mouth?"

"You, fresh mouth, you! Who are you to learn me my business?"

"Were n't you yourself once a machine slave—your life in the hands of your boss?"

"You—loaferin—money for nothing you want! The minute they begin to talk English they get flies in their nose. . . . A black year on you—trouble-maker! I'll have no smart heads in my shop! Such freshness! Out you get . . . out from my shop!"

Stunned and hopeless, the wings of my courage broken, I groped my way back to them—back to the eager, waiting faces—back to the crushed hearts aching with mine.

As I opened the door they read our defeat in my face.

"Girls!" I held out my hands. "He's fired me."

My voice died in the silence. Not a girl stirred. Their heads only bent closer over their machines.

"Here, you! Get yourself out of here!" The boss thundered at me. "Bessie Sopolsky and you, Balah Rifkin, take out her machine into the hall. . . . I want no big-mouthed Americanerins in my shop."

Bessie Sopolsky and Balah Rifkin, their eyes black with tragedy, carried out my machine.

Not a hand was held out to me, not a face met mine. I felt them shrink from me as I passed them on my way out.

In the street I found I was crying. The new hope that had flowed in me so strong bled out of my veins. A moment before, our togetherness had made me believe us so strong—and now I saw each alone—crushed—broken. What were they all but crawling worms, servile grubbers for bread?

I wept not so much because the girls had deserted me, but because I saw for the first time how mean, how vile, were the creatures with whom I had to work. How the fear for bread had dehumanized their last shred of humanity! I felt I had not been working among human beings, but in a jungle of savages who had to eat one another alive in order to survive.

And then, in the very bitterness of my resentment, the hardness broke in me. I saw the girls through their own eyes as if I were inside of them. What else could they have done! Was not an immediate crust of bread for Balah Rifkin's children more urgent than truth—more vital than honor?

Could it be that they ever had dreamed of America as I had dreamed? Had their faith in America wholly died in them? Could my faith be killed as theirs had been?

Gasping from running, Yetta Solomon flung her arms around me.

"You golden heart! I sneaked myself out from the shop—only to tell you I'll come to see you to-night. I'd give the blood from under my nails for you—only I got to run back—I got to hold my job—my mother—"

I hardly saw or heard her—my senses stunned with my defeat. I walked on in a blind daze—feeling that any moment I would drop in the middle of the street from sheer exhaustion.

Every hope I had clung to—every human stay—every reality was torn from under me. I sank into bottomless blackness. I had only one wish left—to die.

Was it then only a dream—a mirage of the hungry-hearted people in the desert lands of oppression—this age-old faith in America—the beloved, the prayed-for "golden country"?

Had the starved villagers of Sukovoly lifted above their sorrows a mere rainbow vision that led them—where—where? To the stifling submission of the sweatshop or the desperation of the streets!

"O God! What is there beyond this hell?" my soul cried to me. "Why can't I make a quick end to myself?"

A thousand voices within me and about me answered:

"My faith is dead, but in my blood their faith still clamors and aches for fulfillment—*dead generations whose faith though beaten back still presses on—a resistless, deathless force!*

"In this America that crushes and kills me, their spirit drives me on—to struggle—to suffer—but never to submit."

In my desperate darkness their lost lives loomed—a living flame of light. Again I saw the mob of dusty villagers crowding around my father as he read the letter from America—their eager faces thrust out—their eyes blazing with the same hope, the same age-old faith that drove me on—

THE TRAFFIC IN WOMEN
Emma Goldman

Emma Goldman was an ardent feminist and anarchist who spoke out in favor of free love and birth control at a time when they were rarely discussed in public and never without consequence. Goldman spent time in jail for circulating birth control information. Throughout her life, the plight of poor and working-class women remained a central focus of her feminism.

Born in Russia, Goldman lived in a Jewish ghetto until she emigrated to the United States in her teens. After arriving, she was quickly radicalized by the exploitation she endured and observed.

Goldman's anarchism was central to her feminism. To her, anarchism represented true freedom for all individuals. She believed that people would act in mutually beneficial ways were it not for the oppression of social institutions. She viewed institutional arrangements, including marriage, as inherently restrictive to human freedom. Like other feminists of her day, she saw a clear link between the economic oppression of women as wives and as prostitutes, pointing out the similarity between women who sell their bodies as prostitutes and those who sell theirs as wives. The essay below first appeared in *Anarchism and Other Essays* (1911).

Our reformers have suddenly made a great discovery—the white slave traffic. The papers are full of these "unheard-of conditions," and lawmakers are already planning a new set of laws to check the horror.

It is significant that whenever the public mind is to be diverted from a great social wrong, a crusade is inaugurated against indecency, gambling, saloons, etc. And what is the result of such crusades? Gambling is increasing, saloons are doing a lively business through back entrances, prostitution is at its height, and the system of pimps and cadets is but aggravated.

How is it that an institution, known almost to every child, should have been discovered so suddenly? How is it that this evil, known to all sociologists, should now be made such an important issue?

To assume that the recent investigation of the white slave traffic (and, by the way, a very superficial investigation) has discovered anything new, is, to say the least, very foolish. Prostitution has been, and is, a widespread evil, yet mankind goes on its business, perfectly indifferent to the sufferings and distress of the victims of prostitution. As indifferent, indeed, as mankind has remained to our industrial system, or to economic prostitution.

Only when human sorrows are turned into a toy with glaring colors will baby people become interested—for a while at least. The people are a very fickle baby

THE TRAFFIC IN WOMEN   From Emma Goldman, *Anarchism and Other Essays* (New York: Mother Earth, 1911) 183–200.

that must have new toys every day. The "righteous" cry against the white slave traffic is such a toy. It serves to amuse the people for a little while, and it will help to create a few more fat political jobs—parasites who stalk about the world as inspectors, investigators, detectives, and so forth.

What is really the cause of the trade in women? Not merely white women, but yellow and black women as well. Exploitation, of course; the merciless Moloch of capitalism that fattens on underpaid labor, thus driving thousands of women and girls into prostitution. With Mrs. Warren these girls feel, "Why waste your life working for a few shillings a week in a scullery, eighteen hours a day?"

Naturally our reformers say nothing about this cause. They know it well enough, but it doesn't pay to say anything about it. It is much more profitable to play the Pharisee, to pretend an outraged morality, than to go to the bottom of things.

≈ ≈ ≈

Nowhere is woman treated according to the merit of her work, but rather as a sex. It is therefore almost inevitable that she should pay for her right to exist, to keep a position in whatever line, with sex favors. Thus it is merely a question of degree whether she sells herself to one man, in or out of marriage, or to many men. Whether our reformers admit it or not, the economic and social inferiority of woman is responsible for prostitution.

Just at present our good people are shocked by the disclosures that in New York City alone one out of every ten women works in a factory, that the average wage received by women is six dollars per week for forty-eight to sixty hours of work, and that the majority of female wage workers face many months of idleness which leaves the average wage about $280 a year. In view of these economic horrors, is it to be wondered at that prostitution and the white slave trade have become such dominant factors?

≈ ≈ ≈

Dr. Alfred Blaschko, in *Prostitution in the Nineteenth Century,* is even more emphatic in characterizing economic conditions as one of the most vital factors of prostitution.

"Although prostitution has existed in all ages, it was left to the nineteenth century to develop it into a gigantic social institution. The development of industry with vast masses of people in the competitive market, the growth and congestion of large cities, the insecurity and uncertainty of employment, has given prostitution an impetus never dreamed of at any period in human history."

And again Havelock Ellis, while not so absolute in dealing with the economic cause, is nevertheless compelled to admit that it is indirectly and directly the main cause. Thus he finds that a large percentage of prostitutes is recruited from the servant class, although the latter have less care and greater security. On the other hand, Mr. Ellis does not deny that the daily routine, the drudgery, the monotony of the servant girl's lot, and especially the fact that she may never partake of the companionship and joy of a home, is no mean factor in forcing her to seek recreation and forgetfulness in the gaiety and glimmer of prostitution. In other words, the servant girl, being treated as a drudge, never having the right to herself, and worn out by the caprices of her mistress, can find an outlet, like the factory or shopgirl, only in prostitution.

The most amusing side of the question now before the public is the indignation of our "good, respectable people," especially the various Christian gentlemen, who are always to be found in the front ranks of every crusade. Is it that they are absolutely ignorant of the history of religion, and especially of the Christian religion? Or is it that they hope to blind the present generation to the part played in the past by the Church in relation to prostitution? Whatever their reason, they should be the last to cry out against the unfortunate victims of today, since it is known to every intelligent student that prostitution is of religious origin, maintained and fostered for many centuries, not as a shame, but as a virtue, hailed as such by the Gods themselves.

❦ ❦ ❦

In modern times the Church . . . does not openly demand tribute from prostitutes. She finds it much more profitable to go in for real estate, like Trinity Church, for instance, to rent out death traps at an exorbitant price to those who live off and by prostitution.

Much as I should like to, my space will not admit speaking of prostitution in Egypt, Greece, Rome, and during the Middle Ages. The conditions in the latter period are particularly interesting, inasmuch as prostitution was organized into guilds, presided over by a brothel queen. These guilds employed strikes as a medium of improving their condition and keeping a standard price. Certainly that is more practical a method than the one used by the modern wage-slave in society.

It would be one-sided and extremely superficial to maintain that the economic factor is the only cause of prostitution. There are others no less important and vital. That, too, our reformers know, but dare discuss even less than the institution that saps the very life out of both men and women. I refer to the sex question, the very mention of which causes most people moral spasms.

It is a conceded fact that woman is being reared as a sex commodity, and yet she is kept in absolute ignorance of the meaning and importance of sex. Everything dealing with that subject is suppressed, and persons who attempt to bring light into this terrible darkness are persecuted and thrown into prison. Yet it is nevertheless true that so long as a girl is not to know how to take care of herself, not to know the function of the most important part of her life, we need not be surprised if she becomes an easy prey to prostitution, or to any other form of a relationship which degrades her to the position of an object for mere sex gratification.

It is due to this ignorance that the entire life and nature of the girl is thwarted and crippled. We have long ago taken it as a self-evident fact that the boy may follow the call of the wild; that is to say, that the boy may, as soon as his sex nature asserts itself, satisfy that nature; but our moralists are scandalized at the very thought that the nature of a girl should assert itself. To the moralist prostitution does not consist so much in the fact that the woman sells her body, but rather that she sells it out of wedlock. That this is no mere statement is proved by the fact that marriage for monetary considerations is perfectly legitimate, sanctified by law and public opinion, while any other union is condemned and repudiated. Yet a prostitute, if properly defined, means nothing else than "any person for whom sexual relationships are subordinated to gain."*

* Guyot, *La Prostitution*

"Those women are prostitutes who sell their bodies for the exercise of the sexual act and make of this a profession."*

In fact, Banger goes further; he maintains that the act of prostitution is "intrinsically equal to that of a man or woman who contracts a marriage for economic reasons."

Of course, marriage is the goal of every girl, but as thousands of girls cannot marry, our stupid social customs condemn them either to a life of celibacy or prostitution. Human nature asserts itself regardless of all laws, nor is there any plausible reason why nature should adapt itself to a perverted conception of morality.

Society considers sex experiences of a man as attributes of his general development, while similar experiences in the life of a woman are looked upon as a terrible calamity, a loss of honor and of all that is good and noble in a human being. This double standard of morality has played no little part in the creation and perpetuation of prostitution. It involves the keeping of the young in absolute ignorance on sex matters, which alleged "innocence," together with an overwrought and stifled sex nature, helps to bring about a state of affairs that our Puritans are so anxious to avoid or prevent.

Not that the gratification of sex must needs lead to prostitution; it is the cruel, heartless, criminal persecution of those who dare divert from the beaten track, which is responsible for it.

Girls, mere children, work in crowded, overheated rooms ten to twelve hours daily at a machine, which tends to keep them in a constant over-excited sex state. Many of these girls have no home or comforts of any kind; therefore the street or some place of cheap amusement is the only means of forgetting their daily routine. This naturally brings them into close proximity with the other sex. It is hard to say which of the two factors brings the girl's over-sexed condition to a climax, but it is certainly the most natural thing that a climax should result. That is the first step toward prostitution. Nor is the girl to be held responsible for it. On the contrary, it is altogether the fault of society, the fault of our lack of understanding, of our lack of appreciation of life in the making; especially is it the criminal fault of our moralists, who condemn a girl for all eternity, because she has gone from the "path of virtue"; that is, because her first sex experience has taken place without the sanction of the Church.

The girl feels herself a complete outcast, with the doors of home and society closed in her face. Her entire training and tradition is such that the girl herself feels depraved and fallen, and therefore has no ground to stand upon, or any hold that will lift her up, instead of dragging her down. Thus society creates the victims that it afterwards vainly attempts to get rid of. The meanest, most depraved and decrepit man still considers himself too good to take as his wife the woman whose grace he was quite willing to buy, even though he might thereby save her from a life of horror. Nor can she turn to her own sister for help. In her stupidity the latter deems herself too pure and chaste, not realizing that her own position is in many respects even more deplorable than her sister's of the street.

"The wife who married for money, compared with the prostitute," says Havelock Ellis, "is the true scab. She is paid less, gives much more in return in labor and care, and is absolutely bound to her master. The prostitute never signs away the right over

---

*Banger, *Criminalité et Condition Economique*

her own person, she retains her freedom and personal rights, nor is she always compelled to submit to man's embrace."

Nor does the better-than-thou woman realize the apologist claim of Lecky that "though she may be the supreme type of vice, she is also the most efficient guardian of virtue. But for her, happy homes would be polluted, unnatural and harmful practice would abound."

Moralists are ever ready to sacrifice one-half of the human race for the sake of some miserable institution which they can not outgrow. As a matter of fact, prostitution is no more a safeguard for the purity of the home than rigid laws are a safeguard against prostitution. Fully fifty per cent. of married men are patrons of brothels. It is through this virtuous element that the married women—nay, even the children—are infected with venereal diseases. Yet society has not a word of condemnation for the man, while no law is too monstrous to be set in motion against the helpless victim. She is not only preyed upon by those who use her, but she is also absolutely at the mercy of every policeman and miserable detective on the beat, the officials at the station house, the authorities in every prison.

❧ ❧ ❧

Those who sit in a glass house do wrong to throw stones about them; besides, the American glass house is rather thin, it will break easily, and the interior is anything but a gainly sight.

❧ ❧ ❧

An educated public opinion, freed from the legal and moral hounding of the prostitute, can alone help to ameliorate present conditions. Wilful shutting of eyes and ignoring of the evil as a social factor of modern life, can but aggravate matters. We must rise above our foolish notions of "better than thou," and learn to recognize in the prostitute a product of social conditions. Such a realization will sweep away the attitude of hypocrisy, and insure a greater understanding and more humane treatment. As to a thorough eradication of prostitution, nothing can accomplish that save a complete transvaluation of all accepted values—especially the moral ones—coupled with the abolition of industrial slavery.

THE LIFE AND TIMES OF ROSIE THE RIVETER
Connie Field

One of the strongest images of the twentieth-century American working woman is that of "Rosie the Riveter." Celebrated in song and depicted by Norman Rockwell, "Rosie" represented women who left the confines of their traditional place, the home, to help out in the factories during World War II and then to go back home when the men returned from the trenches. But the lives of real women workers differed substantially from the propaganda, as is abundantly clear from the words of the five women whom Connie Field interviewed in the 1980s for her documentary film, *The Life and Times of Rosie the Riveter.* The film, which aired on PBS's "The American Experience" in 1988, juxtaposes newsreels, War Department films, and other media with the narratives of the five workers: Lola Weixel, Brooklyn; Margaret Wright, Los Angeles; Wanita Allen, Detroit; Gladys Belcher, Richmond, California; and Lyn Childs, San

Francisco. Reproduced below are the words to the song, "Rosie the Riveter" and excerpts from the interviews. None of the other material from the documentary appears here except for the announcement of the bombing of Pearl Harbor. In the interviews, we hear about the lives of the participants just prior to World War II, during the war, and in the years following.

SONG

While other girls attend their favorite cocktail bars,
Sipping dry martinis, munching caviar,
There's a girl who's really putting them to shame
Rosie is her name.
All the day long, whether rain or shine,
She's a part of the assembly line.
She's making history, working for victory,
Rosie, the Riveter.
Keeps a sharp lookout for sabotage,
Sitting up there on the fuselage
That little frail can do more than a male can do,
Rosie, the Riveter.
Rosie's got a boyfriend, Charlie,
Charlie, he's a Marine.
Rosie is protecting Charlie,
Working overtime on the riveting machine.
When they gave her a production E
She was as proud as a girl could be,
There's something new about, red, white and blue about,
Rosie, the Riveter.
Everyone stops to admire the scene.
Rosie at work on the B-19.
She's never twittery, nervous or jittery,
Rosie, Rosie, the Riveter.
What if she's smeared full of oil and grease,
Doing her bit for the old lend lease,
She keeps the gang around, they love to hang around,
Rosie, Rosie, Rosie, the Riveter.

Lola Weixel

The very first job I ever had was in a novelty factory. They made party goods. Party hats, noisemakers, these things that kids blow that has a feather at the end, rolls up. I forget what they call them. I was still in high school. Times were very bad. And I was very struck by the bright colors and tinselly things that we were working with, and the sadness on the faces of the people who were doing it. It was so boring. It was so, just, you know, one sort of, one movement all the time. Paste, staple. Put it down. Staple. Do it, staple. Do it, staple. A hundred forty-four and you've made a dime.

THE LIFE AND TIMES OF ROSIE THE RIVETER   From *The Life and Times of Rosie the Riveter,* dir. Connie Field, Direct Cinema, 1988. Courtesy of Direct Cinema Limited, Santa Monica, CA.

Margaret Wright

We lived in, oh, my goodness, I guess you would call it slums. We couldn't afford electricity because of the Depression. We used oil lamps, kerosene oil lamps. I did work at what we call private family, like for a dollar a day. We were called kitchen mechanics, and we got Thursday off, and every other Sunday, maybe, if we were very good.

Gladys Belcher

We raised corn, cane, and we'd top the cane, and strip it, and run it through a molasses mill. We made molasses, and we made everything we ate, came off of that farm. But my husband died. My mother-in-law, the farm belonged to her, and she sold it. And I hitched up my team and my wagon, and made a covered wagon, and drove from ninety miles northeast of St. Louis to Springfield. My mother lived at Springfield. I thought, oh, lord, what'll I do now?

Wanita Allen

Well, I was working in a job, doing housework, but it was sort of a different kind of housework. You're treated more like one of the family, and I, I really liked it there. And they had two children. But one day, she called me and told me to come listen to the radio.

🦅 🦅 🦅

NEWSREEL

Reporter

We interrupt this program to bring you a special news bulletin. The Japanese have attacked Pearl Harbor, Hawaii, by air, President Roosevelt has just announced.

🦅 🦅 🦅

Margaret Wright

When factory work opened up, it was like a godsend, because, there, you was earning pretty good money and my Social Security number, I remember it from heart, almost from the first day. . . . I thought that was so terrific that I had a Social Security card, and I carried it around in my purse. They sent me right out, as soon as I got my Social Security card, to a factory.

Lola Weixel

We were going to get in on the ground floor, and be welders forever and ever. And the work on gliders, too, was really very much what I wanted, because if there was, it was almost an art, as well as a skill. It was a very, very beautiful kind of work.

Lyn Childs

They said, come on, we can go and get in the shipyards. And so when I tried to get into the shipyards, they told me I had to go to school, and then I found out about Samuel Gompers, and I went to Samuel Gompers, and took the training for a shipfitter.

Lola Weixel

Men had been telling us all along the line that oh, it takes six years to become a welder. You've got to be an apprentice, you've got to be this. They had been sold a bill of goods in their lives, you see. It wasn't true at all. It just worked out for bosses to do that. Actually, it could be learned, and learned well, if it was taught well, in a short period of time.

Margaret Wright

And it wasn't any time before we got the knack of it, because for one thing, women's hands weren't as big and clumsy as men. We had to grind our own tools. So therefore it was easier for us to know when to stop grinding, how to take the machine loose. We had—I don't know—more of a subtle touch with it. Really, we did better than the men.

Lola Weixel

The men, you know, sometimes they treated us pretty badly, because to, to a man, when a woman walked in, it meant that a man went to war. And even though the population was very much in favor of the war, on an individual basis, who the hell wants to go to war.

Wanita Allen

I knew I was a riveter, because with all this training, and I really said, this is really going to be nice. But when they sent me in there, they sent me to the foundry. Three-fourths of the women that they sent in there were blacks, so they sent just enough white women to say that we do have white women here. I expected to see something like I saw in that training center. I expected to see everything all set up to go to start riveting. I said, well, this training is just wasted, then.

Lyn Childs

We went to Moore's Shipyard, to be signed in because they'd called and said they needed four fitters. And when we got there, the superintendent took the three white persons that was with me, and left me sitting outside and came back in about forty-five minutes and said, no, we don't have any openings. It was clear they didn't want a black woman in an elite trade of shipfitting. God, I was so mad, and I got out, and I said, "Is there anything else open?" and they said yes, they had welders and burner jobs open, and the superintendent says, "Well, you have to go back to school to learn to burn." And I said, "No, I don't. You just give me a test and see if I can burn." I got myself down like I'd seen the burners do, and getting ready to start to cut, and he says, "Never mind," he says, "you'll do. I'll send you in as a first-stage burner." And I said, "Okay," and he says, "You'll be making a dollar five cents an hour." If I had gone in as a shipfitter's helper, I would have only been making 85, so I was delighted. Here I was, making more money in five minutes than all the rest of them were making when they went in as helpers. So, that's how I got into the shipyard. And, I became the only woman ever to make shell burner at Moore's Shipyard.

Gladys Belcher

I have worked from the double bottoms clear up to the crow's nest. There's only about three feet you have to set down in there to work in the double bottoms, and you can't work in there very long, because it gets pretty well filled up with smoke. And then you have to get out. I welded on the deck, the big slabs of iron that lay on the deck, I welded those together. Welding on the deck is really fun. I enjoyed every bit of it.

Wanita Allen

Oh, it was good to work with people. It's, it's something about the camaraderie that you really need on a job. If the job was hard, and everybody's working hard, you don't mind. It's just that sharing, and all doing it together.

Lola Weixel

Lunch hour would find us spread out on the sidewalk, women welders with our little outfits, and usually a quart of milk in one hand and a salami sandwich in the other. Workers from other shops on the streets would look at us, and we'd say we were welders, and we were interlopers, and we had a happy attitude toward our work, that they, of course, really did not have, because they were at the middle and at the end of their stories, and we felt we were at the beginning.

Margaret Wright

When I worked at Lockheed or any of the factories, I worked an eight-hour shift. If they asked me to work overtime, I got paid for overtime. So it was, it was a big difference there. It was more like I had more control over what was going on. And there was another difference, too. Instead of working alone all the time, like you do in domestic work, because you're in the kitchen or wherever you're at, by yourself, I was always with a bunch of other women.

❧ ❧ ❧

Lola Weixel

I needed to do, to take care of my laundry. I needed to do, to help with the housework when I got home. I was living with my husband's mother at the time, and various other relatives. We were all sort of together for the war. And things had to be done, and there was never any understanding, or any respect really given to women for their life outside of the workplace. And I admit, I, myself, never even gave much thought to women workers who had children, how they were managing.

Lyn Childs

When I came to San Francisco to work, and went to work in the shipyards, I had a little child that I had to leave behind. I had to leave her with my mother because up here, I didn't think I would have any place for her to stay. And I was going into a new community, and a new town, and I didn't want to bring my child with me. And I left her with my mother, and that was one of the most awful things that I think I ever did to anybody, because even today, that child hurts because she felt, because I promised her that, give me one year away, and I'll come back and get you. And that one year stretched into two years, and finally into three years, and ended up almost five years before I could go back and get her. And that's one of the things that's very bad. If there had been any kind of conditions under which I could have brought her with me, I certainly would have brought her.

Wanita Allen

I don't know. I never heard of any, you know, where I could take my children anyway. There mostly were private ones, and they were way out. I'm sure they must have had them. I had to put my daughter in boarding school. The other one was with her dad. I'd always had her with me, and to have to send her away—but I, you know, ran into so many brick walls, you know, keeping her in private homes and everything. If it wasn't one thing that was happening it was something else.

Margaret Wright

My kid was little, and so I worked at night. And so I would get home in the morning. I didn't have a washing machine, so I washed by hand, hung the clothes on the line. Then I would have to clean the house, bathe the baby. Then I would have to go shopping.

Lola Weixel

There were lots of dishes every night, pots. My mother-in-law was not young. I would certainly not see her do the dishes. Now, my brother-in-law, who was also, he was a, he worked at the Brooklyn Navy Yard, and I guess I just accepted it. After dinner he would lie down on the couch and listen to jazz records. And I felt the need to pitch in in the kitchen.

Wanita Allen

It just got too much. And I tried so hard to, to make them see that ten hours was just too much for me. I didn't mind doing eight, and an occasional nine, but ten was just too much. I just couldn't do it. And I wrote grievance after grievance, which, you just never get anywhere with it.

Lyn Childs

I was working down in the hold of a ship. There was about six Filipino men, and over these men was a nineteen-year-old officer of the ship. And this big white guy went over and started to kick this poor Filipino. And none of the white men that was working down there in the hold with me had said one word to this guy, and I had sat there, and I was getting madder and madder and madder by the minute. I sprang to my feet, and I turned on my torch, and I had a flame about six or seven feet out in front of me. And I walked up to him and I said—do you want me to say the real language?—I said to him, "You so-and-so, if you go, lift one more foot, I'll cut your guts out." That was my exact words, I was so mad with him. And then he starts to tell me that he had been trained in boot camp, that any national group who was dark-skinned was beneath all white people. When he started crying, I began to feel sorry for him, because he was crying, he was really crying, he was real frightened. And I was frightened. I didn't know what I was doing, you know. But in the end, I turned my torch off. And I sat down on the steps with him. About that time, the intercom on board the ship started to announce, Lyn Childs, report to Colonel Hickman immediately. So, I said, I guess this is it, so I went up to Colonel Hickman's office. And behind me came all of these men. They were all lined up behind—and I said, "Where are you guys going?" They said, "we're going with you." He says, "I just wanted to see Lyn Childs." And they said, "Well, you see all of us, because we're all, we're all down there, and we all didn't have guts enough to do what she did, and we're with her." So he said, "Come into this office," and he came out and had one of the guards take me inside the office, and he closed the door real fast to keep them out, and he says, "What kind of Communist activity are you carrying on down in the hold?" And I said, "Communist, what is that?" He says, "You know what I'm talking about. You're a com—" and I said, "Well if Communists object to the kind of treatment that man was putting on those Filipinos, and would come to their rescue," I said, "then I am the biggest Communist you ever saw in your life." I said, "That is great. I'm a commie." He said, "Don't say that so loud!" And I said, "Well, you asked me, was I a Communist, and you're saying I am, and I said I am—" He said, "Shhh! Hush!" He said, "Don't say that so loud." He says, "I think you ought to get out of here and go back to work." And I said, "Well, you called me, why did you call me?" He said, "Well, never mind what I called you for. Go back to work."

I had been always one of these individuals who felt that I could handle my own problems my own way, and do things myself. I didn't ever ask anybody to do anything to help me out in any way. Well, what, what was the results of going with all those people, going behind me, taught me one thing. That when a bunch of people come with you, that could make a colonel say, "Hush! Get out of here, go back to work."

When we finished one of those beautiful ships, and I remember them—two of them went down the way without me. One of them, I rode down with it. It was an inspiring, thrilling thing. Here is something you have done, you've worked on, and once it went down into the water and withstood the test of staying afloat, I don't know how to describe it, it's a thrill, your whole body is thrilled from it. Because you've done something that's worthwhile.

Lola Weixel

One night, close to Christmas, we were really cold, in spite of working with the torches, because the wind was blowing through the broken windows. We had, we'd put, stuff rags in, into the holes, but it was no good. My co-worker, who was a black man from the South, and I were doing our usual trip around the bomb case, welding the sides, and this particular night, I think I was feeling a little low altogether, the war was taking a long, long time, and the men were away, not for a year or two, but for the duration, which might mean forever, and it was beginning to wear on me. And my partner, as he passed by, he raised up his goggles, and he really smiled into my face, and he said to me in Yiddish, "Arbeit macht das leiben ziess." And I looked at him, and it was, it was the sweetest thing he could have said to me at that moment. Work makes life sweet.

꙰ ꙰ ꙰

Wanita Allen

We were glad the war was over, we really were. 'Cause even though you didn't have anybody over there, you're working with everybody else that had somebody over there, and they're so glad, 'cause, you know, their husbands and brothers are coming home. And so naturally, you just get in the spirit of it with them. You know, everybody's celebrating.

Lola Weixel

My husband was home, he had been sent home a week before, and it was simply, it was simply marvelous—for a lot of people—and not so marvelous for others, who had lost loved ones. But the feeling of the day was happy. And of course, at that point, we felt that even the losses had been for a very, very good cause. We had to look at it that way.

Lyn Childs

The women were laid off first, and then the less senior black men were laid off next, and then last but not—as time went on, finally, many of the white workers were laid off. But, originally the first ones laid off was women.

Gladys Belcher

I knew that the job would terminate when the war was over, and that's why I went, I'd work my shift, go on down to the welding school, and I took it all. You see, just to be a welder, you don't have to take it all, but I took it all, the acetylene, and oh, there's about three or four different kinds of welding. And I went to school after work for four hours, so that when I got out of there, I could get a job of welding, because I really enjoyed it, and I really liked it.

Lola Weixel

We believed that the, the economy was going to burgeon, it would be splendid, we would rebuild the cities, we would do all these things, because, before the war, we didn't have all these skilled people. But now, we had—the war would be over, it would be time to do all the good and beautiful things for America, because fascism was destroyed.

Gladys Belcher

They was an ad in the paper, and I heard, too, that they were needing welders at Mare Island. So I took my card and all my credentials and everything, and I went out there, and I laid my papers on the desk, and he looked at 'em, and he said, "It's all right." He said, "If you was a man, we'd hire you, but we can't hire you, you're a woman."

Lyn Childs

The biggest thing I felt was the fact that now I had just to go back to the field of searching for another job to make a living. With no income, no nothing coming in, and you're walking the street, going from place to place, looking for a job.

Lola Weixel

They had sold us a bill of goods, they had trained us. We did what we had really been set out to do, and everything else was something that we had wished to do. There were no plans, wherever these plans are made, to keep us. And this was very clear to me by then. So, I just took my next step, because I was a working person. Not only a welder, I was a working person, someone who had to keep working.

Gladys Belcher

You have a lot of responsibility, especially a widow woman, a lone woman. My children had to be taken care of, and I'd bought a little home, it had to be paid for. I had to get a job somewhere, somehow. I knew that. So that's what I was thinking about, when I left there. I got a job in a restaurant working in the kitchen. Hot, hard work. Heavy lifting. It was a lot harder than working in the shipyard. And, a lot less pay. I worked there seventeen years in that big kitchen, seventeen years to the day.

Margaret Wright

I had a daughter I had to feed, so after I couldn't get these other jobs, well then, I had to fall back on the only other thing I knew, and that was doing domestic work, and it was a very defeating thing for me. Very.

Lyn Childs

I got a job in Cosgrave's Department Store, working as a stock girl. They had black people working in the stores, but they all worked behind the scenes, in the toilets as maids, in the stockrooms as, hanging up stock and keeping the stock in order, pressing and things like that—no, they didn't even have pressers.

Wanita Allen

So I went to the airport, and got a job out there, in the, right back in the cafeteria. I could always get these jobs, but I, even though I didn't want them. Anytime there's a restaurant job, or a dishwashing job or cooking job, I always felt like blacks could always get those, 'cause they save those jobs for us.

Lola Weixel

I did mimeographing, and then they took in a new machine called dexographing, and that was sort of interesting, they taught me darkroom work. I liked welding better, because it was a special thing. As I said, I always, at the end of the day, I always felt I accomplished something. It was good. There was a product, there was something to be seen. If it could have been—it would have been the same way, it would have been better, if it had not been for the war. All I really wanted was, one day, to make a very beautiful ornamental gate. That was something I wanted to do. I still think about it when I pass a beautiful gate. I say, was that so much to want?

❧ ❧ ❧

Lola Weixel

Oh yes, yes. Everybody was having babies. After the war, my God! It was like a deluge of babies. When I went to have my first baby, there wasn't even room. People were having their, were doing labor in the halls. I mean, it was really, it was unbelievable. Oh yes. Everybody, everybody and her sister was having a baby.

Margaret Wright

The articles in the magazines changed, they started telling you how to cook things that took a long time, you know, during the war they was telling you how to cook dishes that you cook quick and get on to work. Now, they were telling you how to cook dishes that took a full day. There were more articles in there about raising your children, and the psychological development of your children. They never mentioned that, you know, any psychological development, before the war. The movies changed to romantic, kind of macho wars, the man was back home, and the woman was submissive and the man was macho. Before, both of them was macho. The nurse was dying with the soldier in the field. Now, it was a whole different, a whole different tack, and a whole different kind of propaganda, to let women know what they should be doing.

Lola Weixel

I believe, and I know that lots of the women who went to training with me, and who worked with me, believed that we were the new woman. We believed it. I think to America at large, while they may have known what our contribution was to the production of this country, we were largely a joke. A big joke. A shapely girl with a hot sign on her pants, a girl who was quivering for her man to come home and go back to the kitchen. That's exactly the picture that was given. And, I think that they prepare women psychologically for whatever role the society feels at that particular point they want her to play. After losing so many men, America wanted babies. And, we wanted babies. That was okay. But we gave up everything for that. We gave up everything. We were really a smart looking group of ladies, and we all loved one another, and I hope for that feeling in this country again, but not for a war.

AMERICAN WOMAN'S DILEMMA
Frances Levison

The selection below appeared in 1947 in *Life,* one of the most popular pictorial magazines of this century. After World War II the social emphasis shifted from woman as paid worker to woman as wife and mother. Powerful economic inducements lay behind efforts to convince women that their place was in the home, having and raising children, not in the paid labor force. When the men returned to their jobs, women were fired from the more lucrative and stable industrial jobs. The increasing emphasis on consumption of household durable goods helped create a hothouse for the growth of the "feminine mystique." Although this ideology focused primarily on white, middle-class women, its repercussions affected the lives of all women in the United States, regardless of race or color.

 Mrs. John McWeeney of Rye, N.Y., has a big, good-looking husband who works in a nut and bolt company and three children, Shawn, a grave little 4-year-old; John, called "Rusty," almost 2, and baby Mark, 4 months old. She lives in a bright new seven-room house that has a safe backyard for Shawn and Rusty to play in and a number of modern machines to help her with her household chores. She uses a diaper service and she can afford a cleaning woman once a week who does the heavy laundry.

AMERICAN WOMAN'S DILEMMA   From Frances Levison, "American Woman's Dilemma," *Life* 16 June 1947: 101. Copyright © 1947 Time, Inc. Frances Levison, Life Magazine. Reprinted with permission of the author.

But even under these better than average circumstances Marjorie McWeeney's hours are long and her work demanding. She must keep an eye on her children during their 70 waking hours a week and also watch over them when they are supposed to be in bed but may actually be popping down the stairs to ask for water or an extra goodnight kiss.

[T]he household tasks that Marjorie must accomplish every week [are numerous]. She has a crib and four beds to make up each day, totaling 35 complete bed-makings a week. She has hundreds of knives, forks and utensils to wash, food to buy and prepare for a healthy family of five and a whole house to dust and sweep. Every day of the week Marjorie must stick to the minimum schedule of chores listed in the time column.

Actually Marjorie's chores are much lighter than they would have been a few generations ago. She cleans with machinery propelled by electricity, she uses food prepared in canneries, she buys clothes factory-made to fit every member of the family. But her jobs, though relieved of old-time drudgery, have none of the creative satisfactions of home baking, home preserving, home dressmaking. And, because her family unit is small with no aunts or cousins in the household, all the time she saves from housework must go into supervision of her children. Unless she makes special arrangements with a baby-sitter, she has no relief from child care.

Many women in Marjorie's position feel that this is a life of drudgery, that it is not good for Marjorie, a graduate of a junior college, to stay with small children long, continuous hours. Marjorie herself has no desire to work outside. Because as an individual she likes the job that she does, she has no problem right now. Like most busy young housewives, however, she gives little thought to the future—to satisfactory ways of spending the important years after her children have grown up and left home.

Her Work

6:30	Nurse baby
7:15	Dress Shawn, Rusty
7:30	Fix breakfast
7:45	Breakfast for all
8:00	Husband John to work
	Wash dishes
	Clean downstairs
	Call grocer's
9:00	Shawn, Rusty in yard
	Bathe baby
	Make beds
	Clean upstairs
10:30	Nurse baby
11:00	Fix lunch
11:30	Lunch for Shawn, Rusty
12:00	John home
	Lunch with John
1:00	John to work
	Naps for Shawn, Rusty
	Wash dishes
	Nap for Marjorie

2:30	Nurse baby
2:45	Rouse Shawn, Rusty
3:00	Shawn, Rusty play
	Gardening outdoors
	Or
	Mending indoors
5:00	Fruit juice for baby
	Fix supper
5:30	Supper for Shawn, Rusty
6:00	John home
	Baths for Shawn, Rusty
6:30	Shawn, Rusty in bed
	Nurse baby
7:00	Dress for dinner
7:15	Cocktail with John
7:30	Fix dinner
8:00	Dinner with John
9:00	Wash dishes
10:30	Nurse baby
10:45	Take Shawn, Rusty
	to bathroom
11:00	Bed

FULL-TIME CAREER

Many young girls go right on working at fulltime jobs after they get married because they find offices and factories more satisfying than housework and child care. This is a good plan but only if they are very successful and earn enough money to provide their children with secure and well-run homes.

[Some women] have exceptional careers. One runs her own public relations firm, the other is a top-ranking lawyer. Together with their husbands they have family incomes which run well into five figures. Their households are staffed with expertly trained help, so that they can enjoy their non-working hours in leisurely comfort with their children.

But for Mrs. Joseph Gloss, a factory employee, things are not so simple. She and her husband do not make enough money to hire a servant and have had to board out their 4-year-old son during the week. Recently a sister came to stay and look after the child, but if she leaves, the mother will again have to resign herself to seeing her boy only on weekends.

IDLENESS

MILLIONS OF WOMEN FIND TOO MUCH LEISURE
CAN BE HEAVY BURDEN

The Bureau of Labor Statistics lists 20 million women, nearly half of all adult female Americans, as essentially idle. They do not have children under 18, they are not members of the labor force, they do not work on farms, nor are they aged or infirm. With not nearly enough to do, many of them are bored stiff.

The fact that time hangs heavily on their hands is not entirely their fault. Many are over 40 and belong to a generation which frowned on work for any but poverty-stricken women. Their husbands have worked hard to give them an easeful life. Now that they have it, it is a burden. This is because an untrained woman has difficulty finding satisfying tasks to fill her days. Social work, which once busied many women, is now largely handled by professionals. As a result, many of these "idle" women fall back on numbing rounds of club meetings and card-playing. They read too much low-grade fiction and escape too readily into dream realms of movies and soap operas.

It is this group that has become the butt of the cartoonists and of critical social commentators. Marynia Farnham and Ferdinand Lundberg, in their best-seller, *Modern Woman: The Lost Sex,* complain, "Some unknown percentage of the women classified as housewives are functionally little more than wastrels seething into afternoon movies, tea shops, cocktail lounges, expensive shopping centers."

In this desert of wasted time, a few women, particularly young ones, nevertheless, are discovering that there are more satisfying and useful ways of spending their days.

PART-TIME CAREER

One solution for a bored housewife or an idle woman is the part-time career. It is usually possible for a housewife, once her children are off to school, to find a few hours a week to begin a program of absorbing work. As her children grow independent, she can give more and more time to her outside interests.

Young women who can afford to work without pay can make useful, satisfying careers out of civic and charitable work if they take time to develop professional skills like Mrs. Johnson. Part-time jobs are harder to find and not all are as glamorous as that of a television announcer. . . . But the other women . . . have all found jobs they like.

In some communities play clubs for children and group sitter plans are giving housewives time to spend away from home. Multiple laundries, "washeterias," where women can do their washing pleasantly and quickly by machine, are helping too. Once she has arranged for free hours, it is up to each woman to fill this time with really satisfying efforts. She will find it much easier to make a beginning at this while still in her 20s and 30s.

If she finds none of the jobs . . . suited to her individual needs, she might read books for a publisher, do research projects for an author, write scripts for local radio broadcasts. She might prefer to bake cakes at home for community sale. She might open a bookshop, run a circulating library of art prints for the town museum, design Christmas cards, sell real estate, open a school for women's handwork, become a laboratory assistant in a hospital or work on a town slum-clearance project with other women. She might discover that certain businesses in her locale such as department stores are giving their regular staff two-day weekends and need part-time help to fill in the extra days.

When she finds really satisfying work to do she will discover that she is more interesting to her friends, to her husband and to herself. . . .

DOLORES HUERTA: A WOMAN OF THE BOYCOTT
Barbara Baer and Glenna Matthew

In 1974, the United Farm Workers' agreement with California growers expired. As they were trying to win second contracts, the UFW discovered that the Teamsters, another union, had already signed with the growers. As a result, the UFW had to fight both the growers and the Teamsters to get their contracts back. It was not until 1977 that the two unions signed a pact ending their dispute.

The selection below begins as the United Farm Workers are about to embark on a national boycott of grapes. In it, Dolores Huerta, vice president of the United Farm Workers, speaks about the challenges and rewards for women in the union.

Los Altos, Calif.

Dolores Huerta, vice president of the United Farm Workers, was standing on a flat-bed truck beside Cesar Chavez. She didn't show her eight-and-a-half months' pregnancy, but she looked very tired from the days and nights of organizing cross-country travel plans for the hundreds of people who were now waiting in the parking lot alongside the union headquarters at Delano, Calif. She leaned down and talked with children, her own and others. Small children held smaller ones, fathers carried babies on their shoulders.

The parking lot was filled with cars, trucks and busses, decorated with banners and signs. People sang strike songs and Chavez spoke to them about the boycott. Dolores listened intently, nodding, brushing her straight black hair away from her face from time to time and smiling softly at the children. A priest blessed the cars and busses whose destinations read like a history of the great American migrations—in reverse: "*Hasta la Victoria*—Miami!"; "*Viva la Huelga*—Cleveland!"; "*Hasta la Boycott*—Pittsburgh!"

᠀ ᠀ ᠀

We had come to Delano specifically to meet Dolores Huerta. As we waited for the caravan to leave, she told us to look well at the other women. These women were "nonmaterialistic." They packed up their families and pledged them to stay out on the boycott until the union got its grape and lettuce contracts back. If the woman of a family refuses, Dolores said, the family either breaks up or is lost to the union. Families are the most important part of the UFW because a family can stick it out in a strange place, on $5 a week per person, the wage everyone in the union is paid (plus expenses). Often the leaders would be women because women were strong in the home and becoming stronger in the union. The women decided the fate of the union, Dolores told us.

᠀ ᠀ ᠀

DOLORES HUERTA: A WOMAN OF THE BOYCOTT   From Barbara Baer and Glenna Matthew, "The Women of the Boycott," *The Nation* 23 Feb. 1974: 232–38. Copyright © 1974, The Nation Company, Inc.

Dolores was the first person Chavez called upon to work with him organizing farm workers into a union. That was more than a dozen years ago. She became the UFW's first vice president, its chief negotiator, lobbyist, boycott strategist and public spokeswoman. And in partnership, Dolores and Chavez formulated the UFW's non-violent and democratic philosophy.

In 1955, Fred Ross brought Dolores Huerta to a meeting of the Community Service Organization in Stockton, and she has been in political action ever since. Ross, working in San Jose with Saul Alinsky, had taken Cesar Chavez to his first CSO meeting there. Both Dolores and Chavez say they owe their present lives to Fred Ross, and they keep drawing the thin, spare man, now 60, away from his book about the union and back into UFW struggles.

When Dolores began organizing, she already had six children and was pregnant with a seventh. Nearly twenty years later, there are ten children, and Dolores is still so slim and graceful that we find it hard to imagine her in her youth, the age of her daughter. She has not saved herself for anything, has let life draw and strain her to a fine intensity. It hasn't made her tense, harsh or dry. She shouts a lot and laughs with people. She tells us she has a sharp tongue but it seems to us she has an elusiveness of keeping her own counsel, mixed with complete directness and willingness to spend hours talking. Her long black hair is drawn back from high cheek bones, her skin is tanned reddish from the sun on the picket line, and in her deep brown eyes is a constant humor that relieves her serious manner.

Contradictions in her life must have taken, and continue to take, a toll: her many children, Catholic faith and a divorce, her high-strung nerves and the delicate health we know she disregards. It must be that her work, the amount she has accomplished and the spirit she instills in others, have healed the breaks. We talked to Dolores Huerta for several hours in the union offices when the last cars had left Delano.

"I had a lot of doubts to begin with, but I had to act in spite of my conflict between my family and my commitment. My biggest problem was not to feel guilty about it. I don't any more, but then, everybody used to lay these guilt trips on me, about what a bad mother I was, neglecting my children. My own relatives were the hardest, especially when my kids were small; you know, they were stair steps—I had six and one on the way when I started—and I was driving around Stockton with all these little babies in the car, the different diaper changes for each one. It's always hard, not just because you're a woman but because it's hard to really make that commitment. It's in your own head. I'm sure my own life was better because of my involvement. I was able to go through a lot of very serious personal problems and survive them because I had something else to think about. Otherwise, I might have gotten engulfed in my personal difficulties and, I think, I probably would have gone under.

"If I hadn't met Fred Ross then, I don't know if I ever would have been organizing. People don't realize their own worth and I wouldn't have realized what I could do unless someone had shown faith in me. At that time we were organizing against racial discrimination—the way Chicanos were treated by police, courts, politicians. I had taken the *status quo* for granted, but Fred said it could change. So I started working.

"The way I first got away from feeling guilty about neglecting my family was a religious cop-out, I guess. I had serious doubts whether I was doing the right thing, giving kids a lousy supper to go to a council meeting. So I would pray and say, if what I was doing wasn't bearing fruit, then it would be a sign I shouldn't be doing it.

When good things came out of my work, when it bore fruit, I took that as a sign I should continue and that the sacrifices my family and I were making were justified.

"Of course, I had no way of knowing what the effects on my kids would be. Now, ten years later, I can look back and say it's O.K. because my kids turned out fine, even though at times they had to fend for themselves, other people took care of them, and so on. I have a kind of proof: my ex-husband took one of my kids, Fidel, during the first strike. We didn't have any food or money, there was no way I could support him. He was eating all right, like all the strikers' kids, but on donations. So my ex-husband took the boy until he was 11. I got him back just last year. He had a lot of nice clothes and short hair, but he was on the verge of a nervous breakdown. When my ex-husband tried to take another boy, the judge ruled against him. You could see the difference when you compared the two kids—one was skinny and in raggedy clothes and with long hair, but real well, happy. Fidel is coming back now to the way he used to be, and he's got long hair too.

"We haven't had a stable place to live—I haven't been anywhere for more than two months, except in New York on the boycott—since 1970. But taking my kids all over the states made them lose their fear of people, of new situations. Most of us have to be mobile. But the kids are in school, they go to school and work on the boycott. Even the ten-year-olds are out on the boycott in the cities.

"My kids are totally politicized mentally and the whole idea of working without materialistic gain has made a great difference in the way they think. When one of our supporters came to take my daughter to buy new clothes in New York, she was really embarrassed. We never buy new clothes, you know, we get everything out of the donations. She said, 'Mama, the lady wanted to buy me a lot of new things, but I told her they didn't fit me.' You know, she came home with a couple of little things to please the lady, but she didn't want to be avaricious. Her values are people and not things. It has to be that way—that's why everyone who works full-time for the union gets $5 a week, plus gas money and whatever food and housing they need to live on, live on at the minimum they can."

How has it happened, we asked, that in the very culture from which the word *"machismo"* derives, the women have more visible, vocal and real power of decision than women elsewhere? Dolores told us that the union had made a conscious effort to involve women, given them every chance for leadership, but that the men did not always want it.

"I really believe what the feminists stand for. There is an undercurrent of discrimination against women in our own organization, even though Cesar goes out of his way to see that women have leadership positions. Cesar always felt strongly about women in the movement. This time, no married man went out on the boycott unless he took his wife. We find day care in the cities so the women can be on the picket line with the men. It's a great chance for participation. Of course we take it for granted now that women will *want* to be as involved as men. But in the beginning, at the first meetings, there were only men. And a certain discrimination still exists. Cesar—and other men—treat us differently. Cesar's stricter with the women, he demands more of us. But the more I think of it, the more I'm convinced that the women have gotten stronger because he expects so much of us. You could even say it's gotten lopsided . . . women are stronger than the men.

"Women in the union are great on the picket line. More staying power, and we're nonviolent. One of the reasons our union *is* nonviolent is that we want our women and children involved, and we stay nonviolent because of the women and children.

"One time the Teamsters were trying to provoke a fight to get our pickets arrested. Forty, fifty police were waiting with paddy wagons. We had about 300 people. The Teamsters attacked the line with 2 × 4 boards. I was in charge of the line. We made the men go to the back and placed the women out in front. The Teamsters beat our arms but they couldn't provoke the riot they wanted, and we didn't give in. The police stood there, watched us get beaten; the D.A. wouldn't even let us sign a *complaint.* But we had gained a lot of respect from our men. Excluding women, protecting them, keeping women at home, that's the middle-class way. Poor people's movements have always had whole families on the line, ready to move at a moment's notice, with more courage because that's all we had. It's a class not an ethnic thing."

We knew that the women of the UFW found themselves in a unique situation. Unlike the sex-determined employment of the urban poor, the jobs of farm worker women and men had always been the same. They *had* to work, but it wasn't housework or even factory work, separating them from men. Women had picked, pruned and packed in fields, cannery and shed side by side with men. But would the women decide to let the men organize the union? Dolores Huerta had spoken for herself alone; the resolution of conflicts between family and political, union action, would come to each UFW woman in her own terms.

꿈 꿈 꿈

Dolores herself had told us that she didn't hesitate to argue. "You know, Cesar has fired me fifteen times, and I must have quit about ten. Then, we'll call each other up and get back to work. There have been times when I should have fought harder. When he tells me now, 'you're getting really impossible, arguing all the time,' I say, 'you haven't seen anything yet. I'm going to get worse.' Because from now on I'm going to fight really, really hard when I believe something. There have been times I haven't. I can be wrong, too, but at least it will be on the record how I felt."

꿈 꿈 꿈

There is a religious fervor about the union, which has made its members call it La Causa. Perhaps the closeness of the Catholic Church to the movement is one more reason women have been able to identify with its goals. The UFW women have brought their personal strength and their faith to the union; the union in turn has reinforced and completed their lives by giving them a direct form of action and an ideal.

Dolores, very religious herself, told us that women were most important to the union because a woman determined the fate of a whole family. If a *wife* was for the union, Dolores said, then the husband would be, too. If she was not, if she was afraid or too attached to her home and possessions, then the family usually stayed out of the union, or it broke up. There had been a number of broken marriages that had cost the union the strength of a united family.

꿈 꿈 꿈

Women have paid different prices for making the union part of their lives. The 100 women who spent weeks in Fresno jails last summer (for violating anti-picket injunctions) ranged from minors to great-grandmothers. There were field workers and nuns, lay religious women and union officials. For some of the Chicano women, it was a reminder of previous jailings when no nuns had been present and the guards had beaten "the Mexicans." For others, it was the first time, and almost a vacation from their daily lives. Workhardened baked hands became almost soft. All the women shared their experiences—the farm workers told city women like Dorothy Day, editor of the *Catholic Worker,* about their struggle, and learned from her about women's movements in the cities and in the Church.

🐝 🐝 🐝

"My mother was one of those women who do a lot. She was divorced, so I never really understood what it meant for a woman to take a back seat to a man. My brothers would say, 'Mama spoiled you,' because she pushed me to the front. When I was first involved in organizing, my mom would watch the kids for me, but then she got involved herself and she couldn't baby-sit any more. She won the first prize in Stockton for registering voters and increasing membership.

"To tell the truth, I was prejudiced against women for a long time and I didn't realize it. I always liked to be with men because I thought they were more interesting and the women only talked of kids. But I was afraid of women, too. It was in the union that I lost my fear of being around women. Or put it this way, I learned to respect women. Cesar's wife, Helen Chavez, helped me more than anyone else. She was really committed to home. Actually, Cesar's toughest organizing jobs were on Helen, his wife, and Richard, his brother. They wanted to lead their own lives. Helen kept saying she wouldn't do anything, and she's so strong and stubborn you couldn't convince her to change her mind. She took care of the food and the kids, and while Cesar was organizing she was supporting them, too, working in the fields. Cesar, keeping his *machismo* intact in those days, would make her come home and cook dinner.

"We wanted her to learn the credit union bookkeeping. We yelled at her one night into the kitchen, 'You're going to be the assistant bookkeeper.' She yelled back, 'No, I won't either,' but we voted her the job. Boy was she mad! But you should see her books. We've been investigated a hundred times and they never find a mistake."

🐝 🐝 🐝

"When Cesar put me in charge of negotiations in our first contract, I had never seen a contract before. I talked to labor people, I got copies of contracts and studied them for a week and a half, so I knew something when I came to the workers. Cesar almost fell over because I had my first contract all written and all the workers had voted on the proposals. He thought we ought to have an attorney, but really it was better to put the contracts in a simple language. I did all the negotiations myself for about five years. Women should remember this: be resourceful, you can do anything, whether you have experience or not. Cesar always says that the first education of people is how to be people and then the other things fall into place.

"I think women are particularly good negotiators because we have a lot of patience, and no big ego trips to overcome. Women are more tenacious and that helps a great deal. It unnerves the growers to negotiate with us. Cesar always wanted to have an *all-woman* negotiating team. Growers can't swear back at us or at each other. And then we bring in the ethical questions, like how our kids live. How can the growers really argue against what should be done for human beings just to save money?"

🌾 🌾 🌾

We asked Dolores whether she had ever been scared, or lacked confidence in her ability to organize people.

"Of course. I've been afraid about everything until I did it. I started out every time not knowing what I was to do and scared to death. When Cesar first sent me to New York on the boycott it was the first time we'd done anything like that. There were no ground rules. I thought, 11 million people in New York, and I have to persuade them to stop buying grapes. Well, I didn't do it alone. When you need people, they come to you. You find a way . . . it gets easier all the time."

I'M NOBODY'S GIRL: NEW YORK'S NEW INDENTURED SERVANTS

Maria Laurino

When we think of indentured servitude, we usually think of a practice in colonial America, when, in exchange for the price of passage to the colonies and room and board, the émigré agreed to serve a master for a set period of time. In this 1986 article, Laurino attributes the term, "indentured servitude," to some contemporary women: domestic laborers. The article predates the 1993 controversy surrounding presidential nominees who had not paid social security taxes for the illegal immigrants they hired as domestic laborers.

"At seven o'clock I get up. I begin with the laundry. I vacuum the bedrooms and make the beds. There are five bedrooms, three bathrooms. Every day I wash the bathrooms and the kitchen floor. She gives me the list to do the shopping. Then I do the ironing. Every Friday I polish the silver. Every two weeks I wash all the walls. She puts her fingers to the woodwork to check if it's clean. She tells me to get on my hands and knees to scrub the carpet. In the summertime I take care of her grandchild. Always people come over for dinner and I clean up after them. Sometimes it's 3 A.M. before I get to sleep."

Michelle, a 29-year-old Haitian woman, recalls her first job as a live-in domestic in New York, where she earned roughly $1.70 an hour for over 88 hours of labor a week. She has a soft, round face and cherubic smile, and talks steadily, rarely revealing any anger. The gaze of her deep brown eyes is distant; emotionally, she's removed

---

I'M NOBODY'S GIRL: NEW YORK'S NEW INDENTURED SERVANTS   From Maria Laurino, "I'm Nobody's Girl: New York's New Indentured Servants," *The Village Voice* 31. 41 (1986). Reprinted by permission of the author and The Village Voice.

from the story she tells. Michelle came here in 1982, and through a friend found a job cleaning the apartment of a wealthy, middle-aged couple on West End Avenue. She worked from Monday to Saturday morning, over 16 hours each weekday for $150 a week plus room and board. She was seldom given a lunch hour and was questioned every time she took something from the refrigerator. Because the house was kosher, she was told not to bring in Haitian food.

The endless hours of domestic work took their toll—during her year-and-a-half stay Michelle lost 22 pounds and much of her tightly curled dark hair. Often her days off were spent in bed. "When I was in the kitchen, if the woman needed a tea-spoon of sugar in her coffee I would have to stop whatever I was doing, run over and place it in her cup. Can you imagine that?"

Unlike many women who leave Haiti and become domestic workers in the states, Michelle came from a wealthy family. As a child she went to private schools and had servants in her own home. In New York, Michelle spent many nights crying alone in her room adjacent to the kitchen, a space just large enough for a bureau and bed. She had wanted to leave Haiti, but never envisioned such a life.

Eventually Michelle found out about a Haitian women's program and begged its director to help get her another job. Until last year—she recently married a Haitian who's an American citizen, enabling her to get working papers—she cleaned for a family who treated her "like a human being" and encouraged her to go back to school. Yet she still worked over 12 hours a day, Monday through Saturday morning, and was paid $150 a week.

Michelle is among the new breed of domestic and child-care workers in this city—immigrants, mostly illegal, from Haiti, the English-speaking Caribbean, and Latin America. In the past 20 years, as many black American women have been able to move out of domestic work into better-paying clerical jobs, illegal aliens have filled their shoes. And with more and more white middle-class women needing child care—in 1960, 19 per cent of married women with children worked; today the figure is 54 per cent—the business of employing illegal aliens is booming.

Domestic work, traditionally a low-status, low-paying woman's job, is one of the only options for the illegal immigrant. Her working conditions depend on whether she can get a permanent resident visa—the coveted green card. Without it, even college-educated immigrants are shut out from all but the least-desired jobs—sweat-shops are the other possibility.

The seduction of the live-in domestic route is employer sponsorship for a green card. To the immigrant, it seems a worthy gamble: a few years work as a domestic may lead to citizenship. The sponsoring employer needs to prove it's a necessity to have a live-in domestic or that there aren't enough Americans to fill the job.

❧ ❧ ❧

Mary Ann Thomas, head of a Haitian women's program for the American Friends Service Committee, says that 40 per cent of the approximately 125 calls she receives from domestics each month are cases of "pure exploitation." Sexual harassment is so common that many women ask to work for elderly couples. Helene, for example, was a live-in domestic for a woman—call her Mrs. R., as Helene had to do—who demanded a daily massage with a clean house. Formerly a teacher in Haiti, Helene would have to sit on her employer each day, rubbing her body, massaging her breasts. When Helene protested, Mrs. R. accused her of pursuing Mr. R. Three weeks later she had to look for another job.

The domestic worker who complains, inviting the wrath of her employer, not only risks losing her job, but could be deported. Some families actually confiscate the woman's passport to ensure her loyalty.

❧ ❧ ❧

These immigrants, seeking refuge from the political and economic turmoil of their homelands, have become New York's newest indentured servants.

On a Monday morning the Pavillion maid agency is packed. Over a dozen women patiently wait for a brief interview. Hispanic women wearing dresses that look home-made speak to each other in their native tongue; most of the Caribbean women sit alone. As the room fills, the receptionist brings out more small, white plastic chairs that seem better fit for a playroom than an office. She quickly returns to her desk, grabbing the unstoppable phone. "We try to sell the girls," she says, looking up from her half-glasses.

The going rates are $150 a week plus room and board for an inexperienced woman from the English-speaking Caribbean. Haitians come cheaper. Their starting salary ranges from $100 to $125 a week, but most agencies won't work with them because of the language barrier—the women speak Creole—and Americans' fear of AIDS. A Hispanic woman who doesn't know English is likely to start at $200 a week, since she's white. (Federal guidelines say that live-in domestics should be paid $200 a week in addition to room and board.)

Most of the Caribbean women are reluctant to talk about their lives, and worry that a reporter may be an immigration officer. Jennifer, a domestic worker in Jamaica, came here to make more money. She was working for $160 a week, but the family no longer needs her and she's out of a job. Another woman, Marie, says she's cleaning houses to make enough money to enroll in a computer training program. She'll say no more and gets up to be interviewed. Jennifer, young and timid, seems interested in talking but is afraid to answer questions. She describes her housekeeping chores. "Is my story not good enough?" she quietly asks. Sylvie, a shy, young woman from St. Vincent, has been working as a live-in maid for an Upper East Side family, but is looking for another job. She cleans, cooks, does the laundry, and takes care of a 13-month-old child for $160 a week. Sylvie sends part of her salary to her family in St. Vincent. Her husband is in New York, but she only gets to see him on weekends. "I never do housekeeping in St. Vincent, but it's what you have to do when you come here," she reluctantly explains.

"About 75 per cent of our job orders are sleep-in," says Keith Greenhouse, proudly leafing through the pile of applications on his desk. Greenhouse, who with his two brothers runs this agency started by their father 26 years ago, tells me that Pavillion has one major competitor—Miss Dixie—and serves the metropolitan area, including Long Island, Westchester, and Connecticut. The agency boasts rich and famous clients like the Rockefellers, the Nixons, Leona Helmsley, and *Penthouse*'s Bob Guccione. (Big names don't necessarily mean big bucks. A live-in domestic working in the home of a famous designer-jeans manufacturer says she earns $175 a week and hasn't received a raise since 1982.) And one thing Greenhouse has learned in years of running a maid service: "There's almost as many bad employers as good ones."

The agency acts as an intermediary between "the girls" (who are never called women) and the employers. Greenhouse tries to dispel standard myths: "Sometimes they don't want to hire a Jamaican girl because they hear Jamaicans have bad attitudes." He also coaches applicants, telling them, for example, not to ask how many hours a week the job entails. "If they ask that question on an interview, they know nothing about housekeeping. There are no set hours. A live-in domestic must be very, very flexible."

🌿 🌿 🌿

Housework and child care in our patriarchal society mean unpaid women's work. No specialized skills are required; this work is what all women were raised to do. Such a devaluation of labor provides employers with a generations-old rationale for paying low wages. And since no one has ever calculated just how long it takes to care for a child or make a home inviting, domestics say it's common for employers to demand far more than is physically possible during an eight-hour shift.

Litikia, a Paraguayan domestic who has worked here for 14 years, complains, "Women never want to pay enough money." The morning we spoke she was particularly upset; she talked rapidly in broken English, trying to veil her wounded pride. Litikia had just been fired from one of her jobs without any notice or explanation. She says that her employer demanded too much in one day, and when she asked for overtime—on top of her $7.50-an-hour wage—the woman simply refused.

"First thing I do is go to the bedroom," she says, describing in careful detail her daily chores. "I change the linen. If I find nightgowns and pajamas I wash and iron and put them away. Then I wash the carpet in the bathroom. I clean and dust and wash the mirror. All the time that mirror is dirty. There are three bathrooms. I clean them all. And two other bedrooms for the girls. There's the dining room, living room, and kitchen. I wash all the floors, dust, and polish the silver. It's hard to do your job. All this in one day and it's still not enough. She always wants more, more, more. . . ."

Domestics often portray women employers as villains, while describing men as amiable, disinterested bystanders. Yet while the woman may be the putative employer, the man is most likely the primary breadwinner, with a good deal of control over financial decisions. Litikia's employer answers to a husband who may not want to pay more for the woman who takes on his wife's household role. This society considers a domestic not a service for both spouses, but a replacement for the wife. Therefore, employers usually determine her salary by figuring out what percentage of the wife's income she will cost. (How many times have you heard the complaint that child care uses up so much of the woman's salary it doesn't pay for her to work?) If they looked at the entire family's income, they could set a fairer wage.

There's also a whole class of women returning to the work force who can't afford to pay a lot of money for domestic help. Middle- and working-class families that need child care have few options. Publicly funded day-care centers are so scarce that 95 per cent of those eligible are denied access. For families with incomes too high for subsidized care, there are only 21 licensed, independent centers throughout New York City. Without a national child-care policy providing adequate public subsidies, and until men are willing to share housework and childrearing equally, the working mother finds help or gives up her job.

The double shift—or *doble journada,* as Latin American feminists call it—is the predicament of the working woman who must perform one paid job in the workplace and another, unpaid, in the home. Paradoxically, the poorly paid domestic worker, by cleaning her house and caring for her child, helps "liberate" the white middle-class woman who enters the male workplace. The domestic will most likely leave her own children with relatives back in the islands while she earns enough money to support them.

The intimate yet depersonalized relationship between women employers and domestics complicates the working arrangement. The professional atmosphere of the office melts in the privacy of one's home. While the domestic is responsible for maintaining outward appearances, ensuring that the home looks respectable, she may also play the analyst, learning to handle the employer's bad day at the office. She knows the personal details of the employer's life, yet will most likely address her as Miss or Mrs.—and in return, she'll be called by her first name. She develops a close relationship with the children she helps raise, and accepts an abrupt termination of that bond. Of course there isn't any monetary compensation for this dimension of her work, and no matter how much "of the family" she's considered, she is in the end an outsider, who may wear a white uniform, who most likely eats alone.

Some employers try to establish a purely functional, professional relationship. One woman, a psychologist, says that she is uncomfortable with the idea of servants and is happy to be at work in her office while the domestic cleans her house: "I think if she were serving me, bringing me food, I'd feel like I was exploiting her. But I don't think housework is a terrible thing to do. I don't think office work is any more glorious."

Sponsoring someone for a green card, however, usually leads to a more personal relationship. The same woman had previously hired an illegal alien who, she says, became "irresponsible" after getting a green card. When the domestic left the woman was dissatisfied. "I wasn't protecting her, or paying her Social Security, so I knew that she had to take care of her needs. But in the end, I felt taken advantage of."

While some families develop strong personal ties to the domestic, their feelings may be independent of the worker's needs. One woman recalled trying to leave a live-in job once she had gotten a green card. The employer would break down crying, begging her to stay, telling her it was unfair to leave after all they had done for her. When the employer discovered a set of suitcases and realized her serious intentions, she was thrown out of the house that night.

The working arrangement can benefit both parties, depending on the employer's generosity. Some families urge domestics to continue their schooling or introduce them to a culture very different from their own. Still, it's an unequal power relationship—the domestic doesn't get what is hers by right, but what the employer chooses to give. Other employers prefer the built-in subservience of a woman without a green card: "They are very dependable because you know they can't leave. . . . The only problem is when our family goes away on trips she can't come along," one woman said.

The feminist movement has never adequately addressed this displacement of a woman's "second shift" down the class ladder. To some extent, the feminist carries a double burden. Our society holds her to a higher moral standard—than her husband, for example—if she decides to pursue her own professional interests.

Advocates for domestic workers hold the feminist accountable for oppressing the woman who takes on "her" domestic role, just as the workers themselves blame the woman, not the male breadwinner, for their poor salaries. In the 1960s black women argued that feminists were predominantly intellectuals, out-of-touch with what it meant to be discriminated against by both gender and race. Today, the politically active immigrant is making the same charge: "Feminist women are fighting for their type of freedom, like running for political office. They don't see what's going on with the lower-class worker," says Myriam Dorismé, head of a Haitian center in Brooklyn.

❦ ❦ ❦

The feminist movement is concerned with correcting inequities in traditionally low-paying female jobs; the comparable worth battle is the best example of this commitment. Yet, so far, better pay for housework hasn't been included in the pay equity struggle. On the surface, there are obvious political reasons: this battle is easier to wage in the workplace than in the home, and many pay equity cases are decided at the bargaining table. But excluding housework from the comparable worth discussion suggests that the nature of this labor isn't "serious" enough to evaluate. Also, bringing up class conflict among women makes middle-class feminists uncomfortable. And many women still share the cultural assumption that work they've performed through the centuries for nothing isn't worth a decent wage. (Wages for Housework, a 1970s left-feminist movement, did address the devaluation of housework, arguing that the state should pay housewives a salary. But the campaign's strategy was murky, with no real discussion of how this government intervention would be achieved.)

Efforts to unionize household workers have also been fruitless. While the National Committee on Household Employment gained some momentum in New York a few years back, today it's dormant. The dwindling labor movement, whose troubles are intensified by the erosion of their industrial base, needs to organize new groups of workers to survive. Yet the political and economic climate isn't conducive to such expansion, and trade unionists have largely resisted it. Organizing domestics is extremely difficult, since women work in individual households and are often unaware of basic rights. The unique cultural, political, and economic background of each immigrant group further complicates any efforts to unify. Ironically, domestic workers in South Africa, who face the same problems of no minimum wage, benefits, or written contracts—albeit under much harsher circumstances—have rallied together and unionized.

Despite these difficulties, unionization—to establish decent wages, sick leave, paid vacation, and medical benefits—is one of the best possibilities for improving the domestic worker's lot. Politically active women helped organize a domestic workers' union in Canada a few years back, and feminists should study their successful methods. Since unions need to reach out to reestablish themselves as a powerful political force, perhaps there's hope for such a feminist-labor coalition.

❦ ❦ ❦

Illegal domestics are often wary of outsiders and refuse to discuss their work or employers. The women are very proud and explain that this is what's available for someone without a green card. While sweatshop workers are at least ensured set hours and minimum wage, some women prefer domestic work, explaining that the degree of exploitation in individual homes is easier to handle. In cultures where women are not breadwinners, it's "safer" to be a domestic. Work that's an extension of the household role is less likely to threaten husbands who are also seeking employment.

"Migrants, particularly women, internalize low self-esteem," says Mary Garcia Castro, coeditor of *Enough Is Enough,* a forthcoming book on domestic service. "Many women choose domestic work because they can hide. As a domestic worker they don't need to speak English, the mistress will show them what to do."

         ❧   ❧   ❧

"I AM NOT A MAID. I AM A HOUSEHOLD TECHNICIAN. I AM NOT YOUR GIRL. I AM A GROWN WOMAN. IF I WERE YOUR GIRL YOU WOULD NOT LEAVE ME WITH YOUR CHILD OR YOUR MOTHER. I'M NOBODY'S GIRL."

A classroom full of women repeated this chant, learning basic survival skills about domestic service in New York. Haitian community groups have recently formed household training programs, teaching women that it's unacceptable to work 12 hours at a flat rate. Live-ins are told they're not responsible for any household chores on their day off; an employer can't ask the domestic leaving for the day to stay a few extra hours to help prepare a dinner party. To relieve anxiety, women performed role reversals in one class, with the maid becoming the employer.

There's a feeling of tenacity and strength among domestic workers who come to community centers looking for support and escape from their isolation. Their attitude is often optimistic, their goals well defined. Some younger, college-educated domestics are simply refusing employer sponsorship for green cards, preferring instead to find men who will "marry" them temporarily. The women know that immigration is cracking down on this practice, but they still feel it's worth the risk to avoid complete subservience to their employers. In one section of Brooklyn, West Indian workers shun the title "domestic," and are choosing only the higher status child-care positions. This growing pride among new immigrant groups could lead to more concrete activism. As Latin America's organized domestics are putting it, "Let's not beg for favors, just demand our rights."

A PINK-COLLAR WORKER'S BLUES

Karen Kenyon

Secretaries are often chosen for their youthfulness, sexual attractiveness, and compliance as much as for their clerical skills. Regardless of their age or professionalism, secretaries are still referred to as "girls." They are called by their first names while being expected to address male bosses by their formal titles. Many secretaries are expected to be office wives—listening sympathetically to others, cheering them up, making coffee, cleaning off desks, and running personal errands for them.

This short essay, written in 1982 for *Newsweek*'s "My Turn," a column open for editorials on issues of current interest, addresses some of the dilemmas faced by women working in the pink-collar ghetto.

More and more women every day are going out to work. A myth has grown around them: the myth of the "new woman." It celebrates the woman executive. It defines her look (a suit), and her drink (Dewar's or perhaps a fine white wine). It puts her "in charge." But it neglects to say whom she is in charge of—probably some other women.

The world still needs helpers, secretaries and waitresses, and the sad truth is that mostly women fill these serving roles. Today more women hold clerical jobs than ever before (4 million in 1950 and 20 million in 1981). Wherever we look, we see the image of the successful woman executive but, in fact, most women are going out to become secretaries. The current totals: 3 million women in management and 20 million clerical employees. So for the majority of working women—the so-called "pink-collar workers"—liberation from home is no liberation at all.

Recently I took a job as a part-time secretary in a department office of a university. I thought the financial security would be nice (writers never have this) and I needed the sense of community a job can bring. I found there is indeed a sense of community among secretaries. It is, in fact, essential to their emotional survival.

HUMAN BEINGS: I felt a bit like the author of "Black Like Me," a Caucasian who had his skin darkened by dye and went into the South, where he experienced what it was like to be black. Here I was, "a person," disguised as "a secretary." This move from being a newly published author to being a secretary made it very clear to me that the same people who are regarded as creative human beings in one role will be demeaned and ignored in another.

I was asked one day to make some Xerox invitations to a party, then told I could keep one (not exactly a cordial invitation, I thought). The next day I was asked, "Are you coming to the party?" I brightened and said, "Well, maybe I will." I was then told, "Well, then, would you pick up the pizza and we'll reimburse you."

A friend of mine who is an "administrative assistant" told me about a campus party she attended. She was engaged in a lively, interesting conversation with a faculty wife. The wife then asked my friend, "Are you teaching here?" When my friend replied, "Well, no, actually I'm a secretary," the other woman's jaw dropped. She then said, "Don't worry. Nobody will ever guess."

I heard secretaries making "grateful" remarks like, "They really treat us like human beings here." To be grateful for bottom-line treatment was, I felt, a sorry comment.

We think we have freed our slaves, but we have not. We just call them by a different name. Every time people reach a certain status in life they seem to take pride in the fact that they now have a secretary.

It is a fact that it has to be written very carefully into a job description just what a secretary's duties are, or she will be told to clean off the desk, pick up cleaning and the like. Women in these jobs are often seen as surrogate wives, mothers and servants—even to other women.

Many times, when a secretary makes creative contributions she is not given her due. The work is changed slightly by the person in charge, who takes the credit. Most secretaries live in an area between being too assertive and being too passive.

A PINK-COLLAR WORKER'S BLUES   From Karen Kenyon, "A Pink-Collar Worker's Blues," *Newsweek* 4 Oct. 1982: 15. Copyright © 1982 by Karen Kenyon. Originally published in Newsweek. Reprinted by permission of Multimedia Product Development, Inc.

Often a secretary feels she has to think twice before stepping in and correcting the grammar, even when she knows her "superior" can't frame a good sentence.

ENVY: When after three months I announced to my co-workers that I was quitting, I was met with kind goodbyes. In some I caught a glimpse of perhaps a gentle envy, not filled with vindictiveness at all, but tinged with some remorse. "I'm just a little jealous that someone is getting out of prison," admitted one woman. "I wish I'd done that years ago," said another.

Their faces remain in my heart. They stand for all the people locked into jobs because they need the money, because they don't know where else to go, afraid there's no place else, because they don't have the confidence or feel they have the chance to do anything else.

I was lucky. I escaped before lethargy or repressed anger or extreme eagerness to please took over. Before I was drawn over the line, seduced by the daily rewards of talk over coffee, exchanged recipes, the photos of family members thumbtacked to the wall near the desk, the occasional lunches to mark birthdays and departures.

I am free now, but so many others are trapped in their carpeted, respectable prisons. The new-woman myth notwithstanding, the true tale of the woman on her own most often ends that way.

As I see it, the slave mentality is alive and well. It manicures its nails. It walks in little pumps on tiny cat feet. It's there every time a secretary says, "Yes, I'll do that. I don't mind" or finds ashtrays for the people who come to talk to someone else. The secretary has often forgotten her own dream. She is too busy helping others to realize theirs.

WORLDLY LESSONS

Lynda Edwards

Bob Jones University received national attention in 1983 over its traditional social policies. A four-year, private, Christian fundamentalist college founded in 1927, the university has an enrollment of approximately 5,000 students. It is located about 150 miles northeast of Atlanta, Georgia. In this selection, Lynda Edwards describes the curriculum designed to prepare women students for careers.

 Bob Jones University, nestled here in the South Carolina hill country, is all butter-yellow buildings bordered by purple magnolia blossoms and a fountain sparkling with pink and blue-lighted spumes; the paint-box colors belie a serious house on serious earth. In a classroom where 20 female students sat recently, Bibles and notebooks stacked neatly before them, facing half a dozen headless dress forms draped in deft knockoffs of Todd Oldham and Donna Karan, Prof. Diane Hay of the home economics department was teaching one of her popular "safe beauty classes."

Like all B.J.U. classes, this one begins with prayer. Mrs. Hay—61, tall, slender and elegant—invoked God to help the girls absorb the lecture and guide them to ideal careers. Then she held up the image consultants' bible: "Dress for Success" by John T. Malloy. "I know you're familiar with this book," she said, "but what I want to talk about today is God's dress-for-success program."

She opened her Bible to I Corinthians 6:19: " . . . Ye are not your own. For ye are bought with a price; therefore glorify God in your body, and in your spirit, which are God's." The girls bowed their heads to take notes, then looked up.

"Ye are bought with a price," Mrs. Hay repeated softly. "Your beauty, the talent and luck that will pave your way, have been paid for by your Lord. He must be your guide in the outside world." It was so quiet you could hear bees buzzing outside. "In the workplace," she went on, "it is wrong for any girl to wear a garment that arouses in any man desires that cannot be righteously fulfilled outside of marriage. The Bible also warns us not to be so masculine that we threaten men. If your talk is spiritual, but your look is cold, hard, carnal and calculating, the outside is what's believed."

Mrs. Hay rested a hand on a dress form clad in a chic cream wraparound blouse, slim brown skirt and leopard print belt. "I want you to look like you belong in the 1990s—*your* time—not the 1950s," she said smiling. "Style is your armor. Fashion says take off, forget your feelings, get used to this. Style comforts you, gives you confidence. Then, beauty serves you."

Like the feminist author Camille Paglia, fundamentalists (those who interpret the Bible literally, as opposed to evangelicals, who interpret it individually) have always believed that feminine beauty wields a nearly occult power, wreaking havoc if unharnessed, having a redemptive effect if properly cast. In 1986, Beverly LaHaye, president of Concerned Women of America, a group of female religious advocates drawn from both the fundamentalist and evangelical movements, wrote of the "supernaturalism" inherent in a woman's beauty, and its potential for good or evil in the workplace.

Such a belief made women's presence at work problematic. So for decades, fundamentalist women were directed to find safe harbors working in the home or in low-wage jobs at Christian hospitals or schools, said Paul Hetrick, the public affairs director of the Family Research Council, a Washington research organization that calls itself a "conservative pro-family advocate." The council is lobbying to alter the tax code to favor married couples with children, and mothers without paying jobs.

But since the late 1980s, fundamentalist women, like many other conservative American women, have had to adapt to the new economic realities and enter the workplace. In "Children at Risk," his 1990 book on family values, Gary Bauer, the president of the Family Research Council, extols working mothers who "believe in responsible living, the traditional standards of right and wrong, and in the God of our fathers." And last November, the child psychologist Dr. James Dobson, on his popular radio program, "Focus on Family," implored churches to show "respect, compassion and justice" to fundamentalist career women. Such women, Mr. Bauer and Dr. Dobson assert, are engaged in the "ministry of business."

At Bob Jones, besides professional skills, women learn to navigate a money-fueled culture that, when deconstructed, seems as ritualistically complex and socially treacherous as Edith Wharton's belle époque. Through Bible-based lessons, female students learn how faith should inform their dress, deportment, conversational skills, etiquette and business ethics. If the lessons hold, they forge a lifelong spiritual cordon sanitaire around the fundamentalist as she encounters the snares of the secular office.

B.J.U., which has about 5,000 students, was founded in 1927 to combat liberalism, according to its recruiting brochure, and is influential enough to have snagged Presidents Ronald Reagan and George Bush as speakers. Although it is not accredited, it attracted recruiters from 40 corporations last year, including Dun & Bradstreet, Arthur Andersen and KPMG Peat Marwick. A CNN recruiter asked the career services director, Dave Williams, whether fundamentalists proselytize fellow workers. "I told him the stereotype of church ladies pushing leaflets in a parking lot is out of date," Mr. Williams said. "The best on-the-job witness we can give is being the company's best employee."

Other fundamentalist Bible colleges do not trivialize the Bob Jones charm and beauty courses; in fact, schools like Liberty College, founded by the Rev. Jerry Falwell, have less elaborate versions. They are viewed as a smart way to tackle a public relations problem. When consumers hear I.B.M. they think of computers; say fundamentalism, and even some fundamentalists concede that people think of Jimmys— Swaggart and Bakker—and bad women with big hair.

In her book, "Beauty and the Best," Beneth Jones, the wife of the university's president, Bob Jones 3d, rebuts the myth that equates the fashions of the wholesome 50s with holiness: "The hold-on-to-the-death attitude of Christian women with bouffant hair is a case in point. All that backcombing and high-piling was so hopelessly outmoded by the blow-dry era that those who clung to it made spectacles of themselves."

Mrs. Hay was discussing legs. The students wore floral prints and pastel silks that swept their ankles; B.J.U. requires that skirts cover the knee whether a woman is standing or sitting.

"A man's eye travels from the floor up," Mrs. Hay said. "A Christian woman wants to do everything she can to draw his eye to her face because that is where her character is revealed. Accessories can guide his eye." She held silvery earrings up for the class to see. "An honest, brave, lovely face does more for your career that any dress can."

For most of the students, these classes, which are introduced to freshmen as an interdisciplinary orientation program, provide the first glimpse of the secular business world. "Most of our girls have college-educated parents earning low incomes— or nothing, if they're missionaries," said Bobbie Yearick, a drama professor. And, she theorized, upper-income managers, male and female, suspect working-class prettiness as being somehow insubordinate. She tells her students: "You're being scrutinized all the time. Be aware of what your face and voice are expressing at all times."

Since Proverbs 15:13 advises believers that "a merry heart maketh a cheerful countenance," and because even the grimmest of corporate cultures demand some measure of jollity and faux camaraderie, a happy face is a high priority. Mrs. Hay and Mrs. Yearick cited the perky countenance of Mary Hart on "Entertainment Tonight" as scripturally ideal.

"A woman must be sure her eyes inspire friendliness, not familiarity, in male co-workers," Mrs. Yearick said. No half-lowered lids or fluid gazes. "The voice should be bright, firm and free of all inflection. Men will claim to read anything in a tone."

But most female students at B.J.U. say they don't worry about inciting uncontrollable lust. What they do worry about is being mistaken for what fundamentalist preachers call "she-men": power-mad, humorless, Joan Crawford-y boss women who emasculate male, and backstab female, subordinates. Erin Rodman, a red-haired education major who looks like a runway model, began working at 14 on a bean farm, then was a waitress at a pizza parlor to help pay family bills. "I was always very aloof, very professional to avoid harassment," she said. "But a man who wants to harass you will."

Mrs. Hay recounted this tale of one fraught encounter: A student was at her part-time job when a male co-worker made a pass at her. She told him to leave her alone and walked toward the door. He yanked her blouse collar and shouted, "Why do you advertise if you don't deliver?" She came to Mrs. Hay in tears. "We thought her dress might have caused him to misjudge a good book by a flashy cover," Mrs. Hay said, adding the skirt was "a little too short" and the blouse "a little too unbuttoned."

"We spent six months reforming her style," she said.

Later, Dave McQuaid, director of media relations at Bob Jones, having heard that Mrs. Hay had recounted the story, said: "Journalists rap us as saying women bring harassment on themselves when we don't think that. Understand that Mrs. Hay's expertise is esthetics."

Miss Rodham wants a career in public school administration. "Most of us going on to work in the real world worry about having to wear a tough shell," she said. "It's the emphasis on femininity, especially Mrs. Jones's lessons, that's most useful to us."

Mrs. Jones teaches on a stage before 500 freshmen in a sea-foam-green room ordinarily used for chamber music recitals. The stage, backed by an emerald scrim, is scattered with a few strangely numinous props—a podium, a chair, a coat rack, wooden steps. Mrs. Jones was once a B.J.U. drama major. On stage, she acts out what her book calls "Special Challenges to Grace: Putting On or Removing a Coat; Exiting a Car; Sitting on Table-Attached Picnic Benches." The basics, too: walking and sitting in a chair.

For table-etiquette lessons, the students study diagrams, mapping the way from salad knife to shellfish fork. "I remind that in the real world, even if their business lunch is at McDonald's, they're representing not just their company but their faith," she said.

Students practice being an envoy for both at the university's "management house," a three-bedroom ranch house on campus built of lavender brick. It was originally intended to be a place for future homemakers to hone cooking and house-keeping skills. Now, it's also a laboratory for making parties and conversations. Students attend on-campus operatic and philharmonic productions to learn how to recognize arias, movements and au courant wear. Their aim is to be able to move among the cultural elite.

Four girls live at the house in four-week stints, during which a faculty member rates their progress as they plan and cook 56 meals, including a formal seven-course dinner. Faculty members are guests, simulating the roles of boss and boss's spouse. Students are graded on being hosts (giving the house tour, correctly matching dinner partners), culinary skills, presentation and conversation.

"I was shy and got an unfavorable critique for allowing long conversation pauses at the parties when I was hostess," said a business major and international banking aspirant who would not give her name because she had several job interviews lined up. "I also performed badly on icebreakers."

The faculty adviser gave her some pointers: Observe body language. Practice discussing stories in U.S. News & World Report, Fortune, the local paper and The New York Times. Quote The Times for the definitive secular view of the world. Ask the shyest person an open-ended question every 20 minutes. Keep any purpose to your social chat unstated, thus preserving the lightness of chance.

"I was so depressed I thought I'd never get it," the student said. "I thought maybe the Lord was pointing me to a job where I'd just deal with numbers."

The adviser made her the host of the formal dinner. She prayed for an hour before dawn. That evening, lulls occurred only when everyone was eating, wallflowers bloomed, and each guest exhibited his or her store of interesting shop talk. Two guests gave her business cards. "It was a sign," she said. "I'm not to be shy anymore."

In the business school, the hallways are dotted with Bible verses in calligraphy: "Servants, be obedient to them that are your masters . . . not with the eyeservice as men-pleasers but doing the will of God from the heart," reads one; there are verses about quenching eternal thirst above the water fountains. All the classroom doors were open; a teacher could be heard drilling students on oil and soybean futures.

Alan Carper, 37, spent over a decade in the corporate world before coming here to teach B.J.U.'s senior management classes. One lesson focuses on the fundamentalist manager's dual responsibility to an H.I.V.-positive employee—defend his privacy and protect him from ostracism by colleagues—based on Christ's ministry to the sick. Another focuses on the Bible's exegesis of sexual harassment.

"And the bottom line is, no one asks for it," he said. "It's not a sexual crime. A harasser's aggression and rage would come out in other ways if the woman didn't exist. It's a crime of power. A female supervisor could harass a male subordinate, as in the story of Joseph and Potiphar's wife."

He follows the politically correct route of all American business schools till he hits a deadman's curve: whistleblowing. "If a Christian employee witnesses harassment of a co-worker, he or she must come to the co-worker's aid and corroborate her testimony," he said. "The Bible says not to give false witness, even if lying wins you favor with the powers that be." If a corporation sides with the harasser, the fundamentalist may have to resign. "We believe God will open up a path to an ethical corporation to replace the one that is lost," he explained.

It seems a hard fate for a young professional woman, especially after B.J.U. has invested so much time and energy in grooming her for the workplace. "But we don't want our career women to have their egos depend on some corporation," Mrs. Yearick said. "Fundamentalism is our path. The only real power is the power to walk away.

"It's like soldiers: all you have for protection are the things you can carry. For a young woman, that is her faith, her grace and a lovely face."

THE DEBATE OVER LA DIFFÉRENCE
Barbara Presley Noble

The debates of the 1980s and 1990s on the glass ceiling and the mommy track have been accompanied by debates over differences between female and male leadership styles. The question of whether women as a group have a leadership style distinct from that of men has become grist for the talk show, magazine, and newspaper mills. In the article below, Noble presents both sides of the debate.

A woman who makes it to the top of a company is likely to act more like the men who reach the same heights than like women farther down the corporate food chain. That, at least, was the widespread belief when, in 1990, the Harvard Business Review published an article that begged to differ.

"The Ways Women Lead," by Judy B. Rosener, reported that women were doing very well, thank you, and they were doing it by "behaving like women."

Her study of 456 successful female executives revealed, she wrote, that men and women use very different leadership styles. Men prefer a "command and control" style in dealing with subordinates—relying on orders, appeals to self-interest, rational decision-making and rewards. Women prefer to work "interactively," sharing power and information, motivating by appeals to organizational goals and promoting empowerment.

Ms. Rosener's article and a book—"The Female Advantage," by Sally Helgesen—helped inspire dozens of other works that elaborate on the "difference" point of view. Women, the theory goes, are intuitive, anti-hierarchical, process-oriented, tolerant of ambiguity and not invested in power; they think in webs of many factors, not in straight lines. Men, by contrast, are logical, hierarchical, goal-oriented, intolerant of ambiguity and interested in power for power's sake.

In part because there may be some tiny and slippery kernel of truth to these gender paradigms, in part because they appeal to some firmly held if dubious beliefs, advocates of the "female advantage" and "difference" theories reign along with gurus of quality and customer service as the people corporations want to hear from today.

But many researchers on the subject say the theories appear to be grounded more in anecdote and interpretation than in well-constructed studies and hard data. These researchers argue that there is little substantial evidence that men and women are fundamentally different, even if it might seem so because of the different expectations placed upon them and the divergent courses their lives take.

"I just don't see any good evidence for the 'difference' perspective," said Myra Strober, a labor economist at Stanford University. "It glorifies existing stereotypes" of female behavior.

These researchers argue that managers who talk about recruiting women to create a nurturing, anti-hierarchical ambience at work may foster resentment among women and men who don't fit the models and among employees who think one group is being favored over another. What is more, they warn, it would be hard to make a case for legal protections for women in the workplace if they are indeed superior.

❧ ❧ ❧

Managers may interpret the recognition of differences as permission to indulge in stereotypes. People act as they do "for all kinds of reasons, including gender, race, birth order, geography," said Stephen Paskoff, president of Employment Learning Innovations in Atlanta, which provides training for companies on workplace legal issues. "Programs that focus on differences can be very divisive and potentially illegal. They trivialize the reality that we are complex. The proper way of looking at it is that people manage differently because people are different."

Ms. Rosener declines to be drawn into a nasty face-off with other academics, and points to the differences in motivation between herself and her critics. "They are lifelong academics," the 64-year-old author said. "I got tenure when I was 52, my Ph.D. when I was 50. I'm interested in generating ideas and insights. I don't think professional managers go and look at academic studies and look at methodology. They're looking for ideas that help them do their jobs better."

"I would rather have managers act on a belief that women have positive qualities than on a belief that we're no different," she said. She noted with irritation that now that the characteristics attributed to women are regarded as positive, it is no longer kosher to talk about them. "Now everyone wants to say they have nothing to do with gender," she said.

Ms. Rosener would like to see the corporate world transformed in women's image. Carol Scott, a management professor at U.C.L.A., thinks a lot of people—women and men—also want change, but she would like to push the discussion beyond male-female differences.

"We have to get off the notion that there are men and women in corporations," Ms. Scott said. "In fact, there are many different groups. We have a thing about who we work with, a notion that we must have a comfort level. We have to get comfortable with a wider range of people."

❧ ❧ ❧

Ms. Rosener, whatever the technical merits of her study and the potential dangers of its implications, clearly cracked open a window. Her most important contribution, she said, is that she has made a lot of women who felt uncomfortable feel O.K. She knows because she continues to get letters from them.

She was invited to speak later this year to the spouses, mostly wives, of a powerful cabal of young chief executives—high achievers not particularly sensitive to women's issues. The wives didn't want a fashion show this year, they wanted to know why a glass ceiling is impeding women's progress in corporations. The current president agreed to let her speak, Ms. Rosener said, when she revealed that she was once one of the organization's wives.

She will explain the glass ceiling and may engage in a little subversion by encouraging the wives to suggest that their husbands get themselves some training in the topic.

Part Seven

Sisters

*"TRY TO BE WORTHY OF YOUR FORESISTERS, LEARN FROM YOUR HISTORY, LOOK FOR
INSPIRATION TO YOUR ANCESTRESSES."*

—*ADRIENNE RICH*

Custom prescribes that women's associations with one another take a backseat to their relationships with men. So commonly understood is this norm that numerous advertisements use it as part of their story line. In one telephone commercial playing upon this convention, two young women are together when one gets a call. "He's back," she tells the other, cupping her hand over the receiver. "I'm not very good at writing either," she helps him apologize for not keeping in touch. "Saturday night?" She repeats his inquiry, looking at her friend who raises her hands in mock surrender.

So the message is clear: women's plans with one another can be preempted by a man without so much as a whimper of protest from the rejected friend. "Enter male date, lover, or partner and exit female friend" remains the unwritten rule governing women's friendships. The maxim teaches women not to feel guilty about breaking an engagement with a woman friend to go out with a man—any man—and not to show anger, hurt, or disappointment when you are the jilted friend. To show such emotions breaches the tacit understanding.

Women without men have been viewed variously as incomplete, lonely, frustrated, sick, or monstrous. A woman who chooses the convent, people whisper, must have done so because she could not get a man, was jilted by one, or is suffering from unrequited love. Widows, especially those who lose husbands early in life, almost always are described as lonely and are expected to remarry after a short time. Friends and neighbors pitied nineteenth-century spinsters for not having husbands and children, and Farnham and Lundberg, in their 1947 best-seller, *Modern Woman: The Lost Sex,* described single career women as sexually perverse.

Even though we live in an era when more women are free to choose to live alone, or with other women, pressures still arise to give them pause about such choices. Literature presenting lesbian themes, perspectives, and experiences describes the value of being woman-identified, but for many, coming out continues to be a difficult decision. Lesbians are often vilified as man-haters and singled out as targets by hate groups. Lesbians also face myriad challenges regarding such basic rights as loving one another, living together, and bearing and raising children. But laws and conventions are changing, and more lesbian couples and families now live openly and happily in communities throughout the country.

The popular view is that because of their rivalry, women cannot and should not ally with each other. Self-appointed advice givers warn against trusting a woman for she will stab you in the back, connive against you, lie to you, gossip about you, and surely steal your man. A legion of characters from novels, stories, films, advertisements, and soap operas act out these stereotypes *ad nauseam,* and to complicate matters, some women do fulfill these expectations. Biological sisters have not been spared from the presumption that they compete for men also. From Irving Berlin's famous pair in *White Christmas*—"Lord help the mister who comes between me and my sister/ And Lord help the sister who comes between me and my man"—to the older sister in the recent commercial for hair coloring who boasts about looking younger than her sister, female siblings are shown in contention.

But in spite of popular images depicting women as unable to maintain lasting relationships and associations, female friendships play a crucial role in the lives of women. Carroll Smith-Rosenberg, in her highly acclaimed essay on upper-class nineteenth-century white women, found evidence of large, intergenerational networks of supportive female friends and relatives. Working-class and poor women have long maintained informal networks, taking turns babysitting, swapping children's clothing, listening to one another, and sometimes sharing food and shelter. African-American women have written about "othermothers," women who were there for children whose mothers could not be. Other informal female networks come to mind as well. Suburban coffee klatches arose from the loneliness of young wives who moved to the suburbs in unprecedented numbers after World War II. Isolation was a problem for women earlier on the prairie; but there, too, women came together to help one another, as Susan Glaspell's popular play *Trifles* illustrates. And friendships, strong and true, remain the staple of books and stories written for a voracious preadolescent female readership.

Conventional critics fail to acknowledge the long history of female friendships and associations. Women have used their friendships as buffers between themselves and the male-dominated world. In 1838, Sarah Grimké signed her *Letters on the Equality of the Sexes and the Condition of Women,* "Thine in the bonds of womanhood." Correspondence between nineteenth-century feminists illustrates the sustenance these women gave one another in the face of skeptical and hostile responses from family, acquaintances, and the public at large.

In the late nineteenth century and early twentieth century, large numbers of women came together in religious, social, and civic associations for purposes of social reform. The Consumers League, formed in 1890, worked hard to improve working conditions for women and for passage of child labor laws. The Settlement House movement, in which young women, and some young men, moved into slum neighborhoods to share the lives of the poor, and to experiment with new approaches to old social problems, was in full swing. Although many of the women participating in these activities were white, middle-class, and Protestant, women from other social classes and ethnic groups organized for change and to support one another as well. The National Association of Colored Women's Clubs held its first conference in 1895. Working-class women helped to found the Women's Trade Union League in 1903, and in 1912, Jewish women established Hadassah, the Women's Zionist Organization.

"Consciousness-raising" and other female-centered support groups that developed during the 1970s offered women asylum from an unaccepting world. Women also came together at this time to accomplish important social changes, much as their nineteenth-century and early twentieth-century sisters had done.

Even though women's experiences with one another stand in opposition to the stereotypes, negative images of sorority die hard. Today, a movement is afoot which celebrates the sisterhood of women. And perhaps films such as *A League of Their Own, Fried Green Tomatoes,* and *Strangers in Good Company* herald a new era when the popular media will both appreciate and honor the diverse manifestations of women's relationships with one another.

LETTERS OF EMILY DICKINSON (1845, 1848, AND 1854)

Emily Dickinson

The letters below, a small sample of the hundreds poet Emily Dickinson (1830–1886) wrote during her life, were penned during her fifteenth, eighteenth, and twenty-fourth years and addressed to her friend Abiah Root.

Emily met Abiah in 1843 while attending Amherst Academy in Massachusetts. Later Abiah transferred to a school closer to her home, and Emily left the academy to attend Mt. Holyoke Female Seminary in South Hadley. Although only three letters are reproduced below, many passed between the two before Abiah's marriage in 1854. And even though Emily Dickinson is hardly a typical young woman of her day, or any other, we can garner from her letters to Abiah much that is representative of experiences of young women of her social class and time.

As Dickinson's network of intimates narrowed over time, she became closer to her mother, sister, and sister-in-law. Living in virtual seclusion, she wrote over seventeen hundred poems which she arranged in tidy bundles and placed in her dresser drawer. Of these, only seven were published before she died at the age of fifty-five.

7 May 1845

TO ABIAH ROOT

DEAR ABIAH,

It seems almost an age since I have seen you, and it is indeed an age for friends to be separated. I was delighted to receive a paper from you, and I also was much pleased with the news it contained, especially that you are taking lessons on the "piny," as you always call it. But remember not to get on ahead of me. Father intends to have a piano very soon. How happy I shall be when I have one of my own! Old Father Time has wrought many changes here since your last short visit. Miss S. T. and Miss N. M. have both taken the marriage vows upon themselves. Dr. Hitchcock has moved into his new house, and Mr. Tyler across the way from our house has moved into President Hitchcock's old house. Mr. C. is going to move into Mr. T.'s former house, but the worst thing old Time has done here is he has walked so fast as to overtake Harriet Merrill and carry her to Hartford on last week Saturday. I was so vexed with him for it that I ran after him and made out to get near enough to him to put some salt on his tail, when he fled and left me to run home alone. . . . Viny went to Boston this morning with father, to be gone a fortnight, and I am left alone in all my glory. I suppose she has got there before this time, and is probably staring with mouth and eyes wide open at the wonders of the city. I have been to walk to-night, and got some very choice wild flowers. I wish you had some of them. Viny and I both go to school this term. We have a very fine school. There are 63 scholars. I have four studies. They are Mental Philosophy, Geology, Latin, and Botany. How large they sound, don't they? I don't believe you have such big studies. . . . My plants look finely now. I am going to send you a little geranium leaf in this letter, which you must press for me. Have you made you an herbarium yet? I hope you will if you have not, it would be such a treasure to you; 'most all the girls are making one. If you do, perhaps I can make some additions to it from flowers growing around here. How do you enjoy your school this term? Are the teachers as pleasant as our old schoolteachers? I expect you have a great many prim, starched up young ladies there, who, I doubt not, are perfect models of propriety and good behavior. If they are, don't let your free spirit be chained by them. I don't know as there [are] any in school of this stamp. But there 'most always are a few, whom the teachers look up to and regard as their satellites. I am growing handsome very fast indeed! I expect I shall be the belle of Amherst when I reach my 17th year. I don't doubt that I shall have perfect crowds of admirers at that age. Then how I shall delight to make them await my bidding, and with what delight shall I witness their suspense while I make my final decision. But away with my nonsense. I have written one composition this term, and I need not assure you it was exceedingly edifying to myself as well as everybody else. Don't you want to see it? I really wish you could have a chance. We are obliged to write compositions once in a fortnight, and select a piece to read from some interesting book the week that we don't write compositions.

We really have some most charming young women in school this term. I sha'n't call them anything but women, for women they are in every sense of the word. I must, however, describe one, and while I describe her I wish Imagination, who is ever present with you, to make a little picture of this self-same young lady in your mind, and by her aid see if you cannot conceive how she looks. Well, to begin. . . . Then just imagine her as she is, and a huge string of gold beads encircling her neck, and don't she present a lively picture; and then she is so bustling, she is always whizzing about, and whenever I come in contact with her I really think I am in a hornet's nest. I can't help thinking every time I see this singular piece of humanity of Shakespeare's description of a tempest in a teapot. But I must not laugh at her, for I verily believe she has a good heart, and that is the principal thing now-a-days. Don't you hope I shall become wiser in the company of such virtuosos? It would certainly be desirable. Have you noticed how beautifully the trees look now? They seem to be completely covered with fragrant blossoms. . . . I had so many things to do for Viny, as she was going away, that very much against my wishes I deferred writing you until now, but forgive and forget, dear A., and I will promise to do better in future. Do write me soon, and let it be a long, long letter; and when you can't get time to write, send a paper, so as to let me know you think of me still, though we are separated by hill and stream. All the girls send much love to you. Don't forget to let me receive a letter from you soon. I can say no more now as my paper is all filled up.

Your affectionate friend,

Emily E. Dickinson

South Hadley, 16 May 1848

TO ABIAH ROOT

MY DEAR ABIAH,

You must forgive me, indeed you must, that I have so long delayed to write you, and I doubt not you will when I give you all my reasons for so doing. You know it is customary for the first page to be occupied with apologies, and I must not depart from the beaten track for one of my own imagining. . . . I had not been very well all winter, but had not written home about it, lest the folks should take me home. During the week following examinations, a friend from Amherst came over and spent a week with me, and when that friend returned home, father and mother were duly notified of the state of my health. Have you so treacherous a friend?

Now knowing that I was to be reported at home, you can imagine my amazement and consternation when Saturday of the same week Austin arrived in full sail, with orders from head-quarters to bring me home at all events. At first I had recourse to words, and a desperate battle with those weapons was waged for a few moments, between my *Sophomore* brother and myself. Finding words of no avail, I next resorted to tears. But woman's tears are of little avail, and I am sure mine flowed in vain. As you can imagine, Austin was victorious, and poor, defeated I was led off in triumph. You must not imbibe the idea from what I have said that I do not love home—far from it. But I could not bear to leave teachers and companions before the close of the term and go home to be dosed and receive the physician daily, and take warm drinks and be condoled with on the state of health in general by all the old ladies in town.

Haven't I given a ludicrous account of going home sick from a boarding-school? Father is quite a hand to give medicine, especially if it is not desirable to the patient, and I was dosed for about a month after my return home, without any mercy, till at last out of mere pity my cough went away, and I had quite a season of peace. Thus I remained at home until the close of the term, comforting my parents by my presence, and instilling many a lesson of wisdom into the budding intellect of my only sister. I had almost forgotten to tell you that I went on with my studies at home, and kept up with my class. Last Thursday our vacation closed, and on Friday morn, midst the weeping of friends, crowing of roosters, and singing of birds, I again took my departure from home. Five days have now passed since we returned to Holyoke, and they have passed very slowly. Thoughts of home and friends "come crowding thick and fast, like lightnings from the mountain cloud," and it seems very desolate.

Father has decided not to send me to Holyoke another year, so this is my *last term*. Can it be possible that I have been here almost a year? It startles me when I really think of the advantages I have had, and I fear I have not improved them as I ought. But many an hour has fled with its report to heaven, and what has been the tale of me? . . . How glad I am that spring has come, and how it calms my mind when wearied with study to walk out in the green fields and beside the pleasant streams in which South Hadley is rich! There are not many wild flowers near, for the girls have driven them to a distance, and we are obliged to walk quite a distance to find them, but they repay us by their sweet smiles and fragrance.

The older I grow, the more do I love spring and spring flowers. It is so with you? While at home there were several pleasure parties of which I was a member, and in our rambles we found many and beautiful children of spring, which I will mention and see if you have found them,—the trailing arbutus, adder's tongue, yellow violets, liver-leaf, blood-root, and many other smaller flowers.

What are you reading now? I have little time to read when I am here, but while at home I had a feast in the reading line, I can assure you. Two or three of them I will mention: *Evangeline, The Princess, The Maiden Aunt, The Epicurean,* and *The Twins and Heart* by Tupper, complete the list. Am I not a pedant for telling you what I have been reading? Have you forgotten your visit at Amherst last summer, and what delightful times we had? I have not, and I hope you will come and make another and a longer, when I get home from Holyoke. Father wishes to have me at home a year, and then he will probably send me away again, where I know not . . . .

Ever your own affectionate

Emily E. Dickinson

P. S. My studies for this series are Astronomy and Rhetoric, which take me through to the Senior studies. What are you studying now, if you are in school, and do you attend to music? I practise only one hour a day this term.

about 25 July 1854

TO ABIAH ROOT

MY DEAR CHILD,

Thank you for that sweet note, which came so long ago, and thank you for asking me to come and visit you, and thank you for loving me, long ago, and today, and too for all the sweetness, and all the gentleness, and all the tenderness with which you remember me—your quaint, old fashioned friend.

I wanted very much to write you sooner, and I tried frequently, but till now in vain, and as I write tonight, it is with haste, and fear lest something still detain me. You know my dear Abiah, that the summer has been warm, that we have not a girl, that at this pleasant season, we have much company—that this irresolute body refuses to serve sometimes, and the indignant tenant can only hold it's peace—all this you know, for I have often told you, and yet I say it again, if mayhap it persuade you that I do love you indeed, and have not done neglectfully. Then Susie, our dear friend, has been very ill for several weeks, and every hour possible I have taken away to her, which has made even smaller my "inch or two, of time." Susie is better now, but has been suffering much within the last few weeks, from a Nervous Fever, which has taken her strength very fast. She has had an excellent Nurse, a faithful Physician, and her sister has been unwearied in her watchfulness, and last of all, *God* has been loving and kind, so to reward them all, poor Susie just begins to trudge around a little—went as far as her garden, Saturday, and picked a few flowers, so when I called to see her, Lo a bright bouquet, sitting upon the mantel, and Susie in the easy-chair, quite faint from the effort of arranging them—I make my story long, but I knew you loved Susie—Abiah, and I thought her mishaps, quite as well as her brighter fortunes, would interest you.

I think it was in June, that your note reached here, and I did snatch a moment to call upon your friend. Yet I went in the dusk, and it was Saturday evening, so even then, Abiah, you see how cares pursued me—I found her very lovely in what she said to me, and I fancied in her face so, although the gentle dusk would draw her curtain close, and I did'nt see her clearly. We talked the most of you—a theme we surely loved, or we had not discussed it in preference to all. I would love to meet her again—and love to see her longer.

Please give my love to her, for your sake. You asked me to come and see you—I must speak of that. I thank you Abiah, but I don't go from home, unless emergency leads me by the hand, and then I do it obstinately, and draw back if I can. Should I ever leave home, which is improbable, I will with much delight, accept your invitation; till then, my dear Abiah, my warmest thanks are your's, but don't expect me. I'm so old fashioned, Darling, that all your friends would stare. I should have to bring my work bag, and my big spectacles, and I half forgot my grandchildren, my pin-cushion, and Puss—Why think of it seriously, Abiah—*do* you think it my *duty* to leave? Will you write me again? Mother and Vinnie send their love, and here's a kiss from me—

Good Night, from Emily—

TRIFLES: A PLAY IN ONE ACT
Susan Glaspell

Susan Glaspell (1876–1948) was born in Davenport, Iowa, attended Drake University, and pursued graduate studies at the University of Chicago. Returning to her hometown, she worked as a reporter but gave up journalism in 1901 to pursue a career as a full-time writer. Her short stories appeared in popular magazines such as *Harper's Bazar* and the *Ladies' Home Journal* and appealed to a wide female readership. Glaspell married George Cram Cook in 1913 and moved to Cape Cod, where Cook established the Provincetown Players. Glaspell wrote plays for the group and in 1916 appeared in the role of Mrs. Hale in *Trifles* at the Wharf Theater. Her last play, *Alison's House* (1930), based on the life of Emily Dickinson, won the 1931 Pulitzer Prize for drama.

Glaspell's *Trifles*—one of the most frequently performed one-act plays—and the short-story version, "A Jury of Her Peers," are based on a trial she covered as a reporter. In *Trifles,* Glaspell captures the extreme isolation and loneliness of women living on the prairie.

SCENE:

The kitchen in the now abandoned farmhouse of JOHN WRIGHT, *a gloomy kitchen, and left without having been put in order—unwashed pans under the sink, a loaf of bread outside the bread-box, a dish-towel on the table—other signs of incompleted work. At the rear the outer door opens and the* SHERIFF *comes in followed by the* COUNTY ATTORNEY *and* HALE. *The* SHERIFF *and* HALE *are men in middle life, the* COUNTY ATTORNEY *is a young man; all are much bundled up and go at once to the stove. They are followed by the two women—the* SHERIFF'S *wife first; she is a slight wiry woman, a thin nervous face.* MRS. HALE *is larger and would ordinarily be called more comfortable looking, but she is disturbed now and looks fearfully about as she enters. The women have come in slowly, and stand close together near the door.*

COUNTY ATTORNEY

[*Rubbing his hands.*] This feels good. Come up to the fire, ladies.

TRIFLES: A PLAY IN ONE ACT   From Susan Glaspell, *Plays* (New York: Dodd, Mead, 1920) 1–30. *Trifles* copyright © 1951 by Walter H. Baker Company. Reprinted by permission of Baker's Plays.

MRS. PETERS

[*After taking a step forward.*] I'm not—cold.

SHERIFF

[*Unbuttoning his overcoat and stepping away from the stove as if to mark the beginning of official business.*] Now, Mr. Hale, before we move things about, you explain to Mr. Henderson just what you saw when you came here yesterday morning.

COUNTY ATTORNEY

By the way, has anything been moved? Are things just as you left them yesterday?

SHERIFF

[*Looking about.*] It's just the same. When it dropped below zero last night I thought I'd better send Frank out this morning to make a fire for us—no use getting pneumonia with a big case on, but I told him not to touch anything except the stove—and you know Frank.

COUNTY ATTORNEY

Somebody should have been left here yesterday.

SHERIFF

Oh—yesterday. When I had to send Frank to Morris Center for that man who went crazy—I want you to know I had my hands full yesterday. I knew you could get back from Omaha by today and as long as I went over everything here myself—

COUNTY ATTORNEY

Well, Mr. Hale, tell just what happened when you came here yesterday morning.

HALE

Harry and I had started to town with a load of potatoes. We came along the road from my place and as I got here I said, "I'm going to see if I can't get John Wright to go in with me on a party telephone." I spoke to Wright about it once before and he put me off, saying folks talked too much anyway, and all he asked was peace and quiet—I guess you know about how much he talked himself; but I thought maybe if I went to the house and talked about it before his wife, though I said to Harry that I didn't know as what his wife wanted made much difference to John—

COUNTY ATTORNEY

Let's talk about that later, Mr. Hale. I do want to talk about that, but tell now just what happened when you got to the house.

HALE

I didn't hear or see anything; I knocked at the door, and still it was all quiet inside. I knew they must be up, it was past eight o'clock. So I knocked again, and I thought I heard somebody say, "Come in." I wasn't sure, I'm not sure yet, but I opened the door—this door [*Indicating the door by which the two women are still standing.*] and there in that rocker—[*Pointing to it.*] sat Mrs. Wright.

[*They all look at the rocker.*]

COUNTY ATTORNEY

What—was she doing?

HALE

She was rockin' back and forth. She had her apron in her hand and was kind of—pleating it.

COUNTY ATTORNEY

And how did she—look?

HALE

Well, she looked queer.

COUNTY ATTORNEY

How do you mean—queer?

HALE

Well, as if she didn't know what she was going to do next. And kind of done up.

COUNTY ATTORNEY

How did she seem to feel about your coming?

HALE

Why, I don't think she minded—one way or other. She didn't pay much attention. I said, "How do, Mrs. Wright, it's cold, ain't it?" And she said, "Is it?"—and went on kind of pleating at her apron. Well, I was surprised; she didn't ask me to come up to the stove, or to set down, but just sat there, not even looking at me, so I said, "I want to see John." And then she—laughed. I guess you would call it a laugh. I thought of Harry and the team outside, so I said a little sharp: "Can't I see John?" "No," she says, kind o' dull like. "Ain't he home?" says I. "Yes," says she, "he's home." "Then why can't I see him?" I asked her, out of patience. "'Cause he's dead," says she. *"Dead?"* says I. She just nodded her head, not getting a bit excited, but rockin' back and forth. "Why—where is he?" says I, not knowing what to say. She just pointed upstairs—like that [*Himself pointing to the room above.*]. I got up, with the idea of going up there. I walked from there to here—then I says, "Why, what did he die of?" "He died of a rope around his neck," says she, and just went on pleatin' at her apron. Well, I went out and called Harry. I thought I might—need help. We went upstairs and there he was lyin'—

COUNTY ATTORNEY

I think I'd rather have you go into that upstairs, where you can point it all out. Just go on now with the rest of the story.

HALE

Well, my first thought was to get that rope off. It looked . . . [*Stops, his face twitches.*] . . . but Harry, he went up to him, and he said, "No, he's dead all right, and we'd better not touch anything." So we went back down stairs. She was still sitting that same way. "Has anybody been notified?" I asked. "No," says she, unconcerned. "Who did this, Mrs. Wright?" said Harry. He said it business-like—and she stopped pleatin' of her apron. "I don't know," she says. "You don't *know?*" says Harry. "No," says she. "Weren't you sleepin' in the bed with him?" says Harry. "Yes," says she, "but I was on the inside." "Somebody slipped a rope round his neck and strangled him and you didn't wake up?" says Harry. "I didn't wake up," she said after him. We must 'a looked as if we didn't see how that could be, for after a minute she said, "I sleep sound." Harry was going to ask her more questions but I said maybe we ought to let her tell her story first to the coroner, or the sheriff, so Harry went fast as he could to Rivers' place, where there's a telephone.

COUNTY ATTORNEY

And what did Mrs. Wright do when she knew that you had gone for the coroner?

HALE

She moved from that chair to this one over here [*Pointing to a small chair in the corner.*] and just sat there with her hands held together and looking down. I got a feeling that I ought to make some conversation, so I said I had come in to see if John wanted to put in a telephone, and at that she started to laugh, and then she stopped and looked at me—scared. [*The* COUNTY ATTORNEY, *who has had his notebook out, makes a note.*] I dunno, maybe it wasn't scared. I wouldn't like to say it was. Soon Harry got back, and then Dr. Lloyd came, and you, Mr. Peters, and so I guess that's all I know that you don't.

COUNTY ATTORNEY

[*Looking around.*] I guess we'll go upstairs first—and then out to the barn and around there. [*To the* SHERIFF.] You're convinced that there was nothing important here—nothing that would point to any motive.

SHERIFF

Nothing here but kitchen things.
[*The* COUNTY ATTORNEY, *after again looking around the kitchen, opens the door of a cupboard closet. He gets up on a chair and looks on a shelf. Pulls his hand away, sticky.*]

COUNTY ATTORNEY

Here's a nice mess.
[*The women draw nearer.*]

MRS. PETERS

[*To the other woman.*] Oh, her fruit; it did freeze. [*To the* LAWYER.] She worried about that when it turned so cold. She said the fire'd go out and her jars would break.

SHERIFF

Well, can you beat the women! Held for murder and worryin' about her preserves.

COUNTY ATTORNEY

I guess before we're through she may have something more serious than preserves to worry about.

HALE

Well, women are used to worrying over trifles.
[*The two women move a little closer together.*]

COUNTY ATTORNEY

[*With the gallantry of a young politician.*] And yet, for all their worries, what would we do without the ladies? [*The women do not unbend. He goes to the sink, takes a dipperful of water from the pail and pouring it into a basin, washes his hands. Starts to wipe them on the roller-towel, turns it for a cleaner place.*] Dirty towels! [*Kicks his foot against the pans under the sink.*] Not much of a housekeeper, would you say, ladies?

MRS. HALE

[*Stiffly.*] There's a great deal of work to be done on a farm.

COUNTY ATTORNEY

To be sure. And yet [*With a little bow to her.*] I know there are some Dickson county farmhouses which do not have such roller towels.
[*He gives it a pull to expose its full length again.*]

MRS. HALE

Those towels get dirty awful quick. Men's hands aren't always as clean as they might be.

COUNTY ATTORNEY

Ah, loyal to your sex, I see. But you and Mrs. Wright were neighbors. I suppose you were friends, too.

MRS. HALE

[*Shaking her head.*] I've not seen much of her of late years. I've not been in this house—it's more than a year.

COUNTY ATTORNEY

And why was that? You didn't like her?

MRS. HALE

I liked her all well enough. Farmers' wives have their hands full, Mr. Henderson. And then—

COUNTY ATTORNEY

Yes—?

MRS. HALE

[*Looking about.*] It never seemed a very cheerful place.

COUNTY ATTORNEY

No—it's not cheerful. I shouldn't say she had the homemaking instinct.

MRS. HALE

Well, I don't know as Wright had, either.

COUNTY ATTORNEY

You mean that they didn't get on very well?

MRS. HALE

No, I don't mean anything. But I don't think a place'd be any cheerfuller for John Wright's being in it.

COUNTY ATTORNEY

I'd like to talk more of that a little later. I want to get the lay of things upstairs now.
    [*He goes to the left, where three steps lead to a stair door.*]

SHERIFF

I suppose anything Mrs. Peters does'll be all right. She was to take in some clothes for her, you know, and a few little things. We left in such a hurry yesterday.

COUNTY ATTORNEY

Yes, but I would like to see what you take, Mrs. Peters, and keep an eye out for anything that might be of use to us.

MRS. PETERS

Yes, Mr. Henderson.
    [*The women listen to the men's steps on the stairs, then look about the kitchen.*]

MRS. HALE

I'd hate to have men coming into my kitchen, snooping around and criticizing.
    [*She arranges the pans under the sink which the* LAWYER *had shoved out of place.*]

MRS. PETERS

Of course it's no more than their duty.

MRS. HALE

Duty's all right, but I guess that deputy sheriff that came out to make the fire might have got a little of this on. [*Gives the roller towel a pull.*] Wish I'd thought of that sooner. Seems mean to talk about her for not having things slicked up when she had to come away in such a hurry.

MRS. PETERS

    [*Who has gone to a small table in the left rear corner of the room, and lifted one end of a towel that covers a pan.*] She had bread set.
    [*Stands still.*]

MRS. HALE

    [*Eyes fixed on a loaf of bread beside the breadbox, which is on a low shelf at the other side of the room. Moves slowly toward it.*] She was going to put this in there. [*Picks up loaf, then abruptly drops it. In a manner of returning to familiar things.*] It's a shame about her fruit. I wonder if it's all gone. [*Gets up on the chair and looks.*] I think there's some here that's all right, Mrs. Peters. Yes—here; [*Holding it toward the window.*] this is cherries, too. [*Looking again.*] I declare I believe that's the only one. [*Gets down, bottle in her hand. Goes to the sink and wipes it off on the outside.*] She'll feel awful bad after all her hard work in the hot weather. I remember the afternoon I put up my cherries last summer.

[*She puts the bottle on the big kitchen table, center of the room. With a sigh, is about to sit down in the rocking-chair. Before she is seated realizes what chair it is; with a slow look at it, steps back. The chair which she has touched rocks back and forth.*]

MRS. PETERS

Well, I must get those things from the front room closet. [*She goes to the door at the right, but after looking into the other room, steps back.*] You coming with me, Mrs. Hale? You could help me carry them.

[*They go in the other room; reappear, MRS. PETERS carrying a dress and skirt, MRS. HALE following with a pair of shoes.*]

MRS. PETERS

My, it's cold in there.

[*She puts the clothes on the big table, and hurries to the stove.*]

MRS. HALE

[*Examining the skirt.*] Wright was close. I think maybe that's why she kept so much to herself. She didn't even belong to the Ladies Aid. I suppose she felt she couldn't do her part, and then you don't enjoy things when you feel shabby. She used to wear pretty clothes and be lively, when she was Minnie Foster, one of the town girls singing in the choir. But that—oh, that was thirty years ago. This all you was to take in?

MRS. PETERS

She said she wanted an apron. Funny thing to want, for there isn't much to get you dirty in jail, goodness knows. But I suppose just to make her feel more natural. She said they was in the top drawer in this cupboard. Yes here. And then her little shawl that always hung behind the door. [*Opens stair door and looks.*] Yes, here it is.

[*Quickly shuts door leading upstairs.*]

MRS. HALE

[*Abruptly moving toward her.*] Mrs. Peters?

MRS. PETERS

Yes, Mrs. Hale?

MRS. HALE

Do you think she did it?

MRS. PETERS

[*In a frightened voice.*] Oh, I don't know.

MRS. HALE

Well, I don't think she did. Asking for an apron and her little shawl. Worrying about her fruit.

MRS. PETERS

[*Starts to speak, glances up, where footsteps are heard in the room above. In a low voice.*] Mr. Peters says it looks bad for her. Mr. Henderson is awful sarcastic in a speech and he'll make fun of her sayin' she didn't wake up.

MRS. HALE

Well, I guess John Wright didn't wake up when they was slipping that rope under his neck.

MRS. PETERS

No, it's strange. It must have been done awful crafty and still. They say it was such a—funny way to kill a man, rigging it all up like that.

MRS. HALE

That's just what Mr. Hale said. There was a gun in the house. He says that's what he can't understand.

MRS. PETERS

Mr. Henderson said coming out that what was needed for the case was a motive; something to show anger, or—sudden feeling.

MRS. HALE

[*Who is standing by the table.*] Well, I don't see any signs of anger around here. [*She puts her hand on the dish towel which lies on the table, stands looking down at table, one half of which is clean, the other half messy.*] It's wiped to here. [*Makes a move as if to finish work, then turns and looks at loaf of bread outside the breadbox. Drops towel. In that voice of coming back to familiar things.*] Wonder how they are finding things upstairs. I hope she had it a little more red-up up there. You know, it seems kind of *sneaking*. Locking her up in town and then coming out here and trying to get her own house to turn against her!

MRS. PETERS

But Mrs. Hale, the law is the law.

MRS. HALE

I s'pose 'tis. [*Unbuttoning her coat.*] Better loosen up your things, Mrs. Peters. You won't feel them when you go out.
    [MRS. PETERS *takes off her fur tippet, goes to hang it on hook at back of room, stands looking at the under part of the small corner table.*]

MRS. PETERS

She was piecing a quilt.
    [*She brings the large sewing basket and they look at the bright pieces.*]

MRS. HALE

It's log cabin pattern. Pretty, isn't it? I wonder if she was goin' to quilt it or just knot it?

[*Footsteps have been heard coming down the stairs. The* SHERIFF *enters followed by* HALE *and the* COUNTY ATTORNEY.]

SHERIFF

They wonder if she was going to quilt it or just knot it!

[*The men laugh, the women look abashed.*]

COUNTY ATTORNEY

[*Rubbing his hands over the stove.*] Frank's fire didn't do much up there, did it? Well, let's go out to the barn and get that cleared up.

[*The men go outside.*]

MRS. HALE

[*Resentfully.*] I don't know as there's anything so strange, our takin' up our time with little things while we're waiting for them to get the evidence. [*She sits down at the big table smoothing out a block with decision.*] I don't see as it's anything to laugh about.

MRS. PETERS

[*Apologetically.*] Of course they've got awful important things on their minds. [*Pulls up a chair and joins* MRS. HALE *at the table.*]

MRS. HALE

[*Examining another block.*] Mrs. Peters, look at this one. Here, this is the one she was working on, and look at the sewing! All the rest of it has been so nice and even. And look at this! It's all over the place! Why, it looks as if she didn't know what she was about!

[*After she has said this they look at each other, then start to glance back at the door. After an instant* MRS. HALE *has pulled at a knot and ripped the sewing.*]

MRS. PETERS

Oh, what are you doing, Mrs. Hale?

MRS. HALE

[*Mildly.*] Just pulling out a stitch or two that's not sewed very good. [*Threading a needle.*] Bad sewing always made me fidgety.

MRS. PETERS

[*Nervously.*] I don't think we ought to touch things.

MRS. HALE

I'll just finish up this end. [*Suddenly stopping and leaning forward.*] Mrs. Peters?

MRS. PETERS

Yes, Mrs. Hale?

MRS. HALE

What do you suppose she was so nervous about?

MRS. PETERS

Oh—I don't know. I don't know as she was nervous. I sometimes sew awful queer when I'm just tired. [MRS. HALE *starts to say something, looks at* MRS. PETERS, *then goes on sewing.*] Well I must get these things wrapped up. They may be through sooner than we think. [*Putting apron and other things together.*] I wonder where I can find a piece of paper, and string.

MRS. HALE

In that cupboard, maybe.

MRS. PETERS

[*Looking in cupboard.*] Why, here's a bird-cage. [*Holds it up.*] Did she have a bird, Mrs. Hale?

MRS. HALE

Why, I don't know whether she did or not—I've not been here for so long. There was a man around last year selling canaries cheap, but I don't know as she took one; maybe she did. She used to sing real pretty herself.

MRS. PETERS

[*Glancing around.*] Seems funny to think of a bird here. But she must have had one, or why would she have a cage? I wonder what happened to it.

MRS. HALE

I s'pose maybe the cat got it.

MRS. PETERS

No, she didn't have a cat. She's got that feeling some people have about cats—being afraid of them. My cat got in her room and she was real upset and asked me to take it out.

MRS. HALE

My sister Bessie was like that. Queer, ain't it?

MRS. PETERS

[*Examining the cage.*] Why, look at this door. It's broke. One hinge is pulled apart.

MRS. HALE

[*Looking too.*] Looks as if someone must have been rough with it.

MRS. PETERS

Why, yes.
  [*She brings the cage forward and puts it on the table.*]

MRS. HALE

I wish if they're going to find any evidence they'd be about it. I don't like this place.

MRS. PETERS

But I'm awful glad you came with me, Mrs. Hale. It would be lonesome for me sitting here alone.

MRS. HALE

It would, wouldn't it? [*Dropping her sewing.*] But I tell you what I do wish, Mrs. Peters. I wish I had come over sometimes when *she* was here. I—[*Looking around the room.*]—wish I had.

MRS. PETERS

But of course you were awful busy, Mrs. Hale—your house and your children.

MRS. HALE

I could've come. I stayed away because it weren't cheerful—and that's why I ought to have come. I—I've never liked this place. Maybe because it's down in a hollow and you don't see the road. I dunno what it is, but it's a lonesome place and always was. I wish I had come over to see Minnie Foster sometimes. I can see now—
  [*Shakes her head.*]

MRS. PETERS

Well, you mustn't reproach yourself, Mrs. Hale. Somehow we just don't see how it is with other folks until—something comes up.

MRS. HALE

Not having children makes less work—but it makes a quiet house, and Wright out to work all day, and no company when he did come in. Did you know John Wright, Mrs. Peters?

MRS. PETERS

Not to know him; I've seen him in town. They say he was a good man.

MRS. HALE

Yes—good; he didn't drink, and kept his word as well as most, I guess, and paid his debts. But he was a hard man, Mrs. Peters. Just to pass the time of day with him—[*Shivers.*] Like a raw wind that gets to the bone. [*Pauses, her eye falling on the cage.*] I should think she would 'a wanted a bird. But what do you suppose went with it?

MRS. PETERS

I don't know, unless it got sick and died.
  [*She reaches over and swings the broken door, swings it again, both women watch it.*]

MRS. HALE

You weren't raised round here, were you? [MRS. PETERS *shakes her head.*] You didn't know—her?

MRS. PETERS

Not till they brought her yesterday.

MRS. HALE

She—come to think of it, she was kind of like a bird herself—real sweet and pretty, but kind of timid and—fluttery. How—she—did—change. [*Silence; then as if struck by a happy thought and relieved to get back to every day things.*] Tell you what, Mrs. Peters, why don't you take the quilt in with you? It might take up her mind.

MRS. PETERS

Why, I think that's a real nice idea, Mrs. Hale. There couldn't possibly be any objection to it, could there? Now, just what would I take? I wonder if her patches are in here—and her things.
    [*They look in the sewing basket.*]

MRS. HALE

Here's some red. I expect this has got sewing things in it. [*Brings out a fancy box.*] What a pretty box. Looks like something somebody would give you. Maybe her scissors are in here. [*Opens box. Suddenly puts her hand to her nose.*] Why—[MRS. PETERS *bends nearer, then turns her face away.*] There's something wrapped up in this piece of silk.

MRS. PETERS

Why, this isn't her scissors.

MRS. HALE

    [*Lifting the silk.*] Oh, Mrs. Peters—its—
    [MRS. PETERS *bends closer.*]

MRS. PETERS

It's the bird.

MRS. HALE

    [*Jumping up.*] But, Mrs. Peters—look at it! Its neck! Look at its neck! It's all—other side *to.*

MRS. PETERS

Somebody—wrung—its—neck.
    [*Their eyes meet. A look of growing comprehension, of horror. Steps are heard outside.* MRS. HALE *slips box under quilt pieces, and sinks into her chair. Enter* SHERIFF *and* COUNTY ATTORNEY. MRS. PETERS *rises.*]

COUNTY ATTORNEY

[*As one turning from serious things to little pleasantries.*] Well, ladies have you decided whether she was going to quilt it or knot it?

MRS. PETERS

We think she was going to—knot it.

COUNTY ATTORNEY

Well, that's interesting, I'm sure. [*Seeing the birdcage.*] Has the bird flown?

MRS. HALE

[*Putting more quilt pieces over the box.*] We think the—cat got it.

COUNTY ATTORNEY

[*Preoccupied.*] Is there a cat?
[MRS. HALE *glances in a quick covert way at* MRS. PETERS.]

MRS. PETERS

Well, not *now*. They're superstitious, you know. They leave.

COUNTY ATTORNEY

[*To* SHERIFF PETERS, *continuing an interrupted conversation.*] No sign at all of anyone having come from the outside. Their own rope. Now let's go up again and go over it piece by piece. [*They start upstairs.*] It would have to have been someone who knew just the—
[MRS. PETERS *sits down. The two women sit there not looking at one another, but as if peering into something and at the same time holding back. When they talk now it is in the manner of feeling their way over strange ground, as if afraid of what they are saying, but as if they can not help saying it.*]

MRS. HALE

She liked the bird. She was going to bury it in that pretty box.

MRS. PETERS

[*In a whisper.*] When I was a girl—my kitten—there was a boy took a hatchet, and before my eyes—and before I could get there—[*Covers her face an instant.*] If they hadn't held me back I would have—[*Catches herself, looks upstairs where steps are heard, falters weakly.*]—hurt him.

MRS. HALE

[*With a slow look around her.*] I wonder how it would seem never to have had any children around. [*Pause.*] No, Wright wouldn't like the bird—a thing that sang. She used to sing. He killed that, too.

MRS. PETERS

[*Moving uneasily.*] We don't know who killed the bird.

MRS. HALE

I knew John Wright.

MRS. PETERS

It was an awful thing was done in this house that night, Mrs. Hale. Killing a man while he slept, slipping a rope around his neck that choked the life out of him.

MRS. HALE

His neck. Choked the life out of him.
[*Her hand goes out and rests on the bird-cage.*]

MRS. PETERS

[*With rising voice.*] We don't know who killed him. We don't *know.*

MRS. HALE

[*Her own feeling not interrupted.*] If there'd been years and years of nothing, then a bird to sing to you, it would be awful—still, after the bird was still.

MRS. PETERS

[*Something within her speaking.*] I know what stillness is. When we homesteaded in Dakota, and my first baby died—after he was two years old, and me with no other then—

MRS. HALE

[*Moving.*] How soon do you suppose they'll be through, looking for the evidence?

MRS. PETERS

I know what stillness is. [*Pulling herself back.*] The law has got to punish crime, Mrs. Hale.

MRS. HALE

[*Not as if answering that.*] I wish you'd seen Minnie Foster when she wore a white dress with blue ribbons and stood up there in the choir and sang. [*A look around the room.*] Oh, I *wish* I'd come over here once in a while! That was a crime! That was a crime! Who's going to punish that?

MRS. PETERS

[*Looking upstairs.*] We mustn't—take on.

MRS. HALE

I might have known she needed help! I know how things can be—for women. I tell you, it's queer, Mrs. Peters. We live close together and we live far apart. We all go through the same things—it's all just a different kind of the same thing. [*Brushes her eyes, noticing the bottle of fruit, reaches out for it.*] If I was you I wouldn't tell her her fruit was gone. Tell her it *ain't.* Tell her it's all right. Take this in to prove it to her. She—she may never know whether it was broke or not.

MRS. PETERS

[*Takes the bottle, looks around for something to wrap it in; takes petticoat from the clothes brought from the other room, very nervously begins winding this around the bottle. In a false voice.*] My, it's a good thing the men couldn't hear us. Wouldn't they just laugh! Getting all stirred up over a little thing like a—dead canary. As if that could have anything to do with—with—wouldn't they *laugh!*
[*The men are heard coming down stairs.*]

MRS. HALE

[*Under her breath.*] Maybe they would—maybe they wouldn't.

COUNTY ATTORNEY

No, Peters, it's all perfectly clear except a reason for doing it. But you know juries when it comes to women. If there was some definite thing. Something to show—something to make a story about—a thing that would connect up with this strange way of doing it—
[*The women's eyes meet for an instant. Enter* HALE *from outer door.*]

HALE

Well, I've got the team around. Pretty cold out there.

COUNTY ATTORNEY

I'm going to stay here a while by myself. [*To the* SHERIFF.] You can send Frank out for me, can't you? I want to go over everything. I'm not satisfied that we can't do better.

SHERIFF

Do you want to see what Mrs. Peters is going to take in?
[*The* LAWYER *goes to the table, picks up the apron, laughs.*]

COUNTY ATTORNEY

Oh, I guess they're not very dangerous things the ladies have picked out. [*Moves a few things about, disturbing the quilt pieces which cover the box. Steps back.*] No, Mrs. Peters doesn't need supervising. For that matter, a sheriff's wife is married to the law. Ever think of it that way, Mrs. Peters?

MRS. PETERS

Not—just that way.

SHERIFF

[*Chuckling.*] Married to the law. [*Moves toward the other room.*] I just want you to come in here a minute, George. We ought to take a look at these windows.

COUNTY ATTORNEY

[*Scoffingly.*] Oh, windows!

SHERIFF

We'll be right out, Mr. Hale. [HALE *goes outside. The* SHERIFF *follows the* COUNTY ATTORNEY *into the other room. Then* MRS. HALE *rises, hands tight together, looking intensely at* MRS. PETERS, *whose eyes make a slow turn, finally meeting* MRS. HALE'S. *A moment* MRS. HALE *holds her, then her own eyes point the way to where the box is concealed. Suddenly* MRS. PETERS *throws back quilt pieces and tries to put the box in the bag she is wearing. It is too big. She opens box, starts to take bird out, cannot touch it, goes to pieces, stands there helpless. Sound of knob turning in the other room.* MRS. HALE *snatches the box and puts it in the pocket of her big coat. Enter* COUNTY ATTORNEY *and* SHERIFF.]

COUNTY ATTORNEY

[*Facetiously.*] Well, Henry, at least we found out that she was not going to quilt it. She was going to—what is it you call it, ladies?

MRS. HALE

[*Her hand against her pocket.*] We call it—knot it, Mr. Henderson.

[*Curtain.*]

LETTER TO FANNY QUINCY HOWE
Maimie Pinzer

Born in 1885 to Polish-Russian immigrant parents, Maimie Pinzer lived comfortably in Philadelphia until she was thirteen, when the murder of her father plunged the family into poverty. Forced by her mother to quit school and keep house, an embittered Maimie took a job as a salesgirl in a downtown department store to earn spending money. After she stayed away from home with a man for several days, her mother denounced her as a prostitute, had her arrested, thrown into jail, and sent to the Magdalen Home for wayward girls. Maimie and her mother remained estranged, in spite of attempts at reconciliation.

In 1910, Maimie met social worker Herbert Welsh, who encouraged her reform. To help Maimie, he arranged for her to correspond with Boston philanthropist Fanny Quincy Howe. After a futile search for respectable employment that would support her adequately, Maimie considered returning to her former life. But with financial aid from Welsh, she completed stenography school.

Moving to Montreal in 1914, Maimie started a letter-writing and duplicating firm, but business faltered because of the war. It was at that time that Maimie began giving help to young prostitutes. In 1915, when the following letter was written, she opened the Montreal Mission, a halfway house, but financial problems and police harassment forced its closing in 1917. She married Ira Benjamin that year, and they returned to the United States in 1918. We know nothing about Maimie's life after 1922, when her last letter to Howe was written.

May, 1915

Will you just forget that I wrote the last two or three pages of the letter you received the other day?

I feel they were written under conditions that made me overdraw the conditions. I've no doubt they made me appear a martyr—and occasionally I am not above playing that role, even though there is only a tiny excuse for it.

LETTER TO FANNY QUINCY HOWE   From Maimie Pinzer, "To Fanny Quincy Howe," May 1915, *The Maimie Papers,* ed. Ruth Rosen, Sue Davidson (Old Westbury: Feminist P, 1977) 271–78. Published by the Feminist Press at The City University of New York. All rights reserved.

It is true my mother was most exasperating on that day, but I think my description of the annoyance was a bit overdrawn. You know the old adage about it taking "two to make a quarrel"—it still holds good. Unconsciously, I did make this quarrel. And had my mother, during a great stress of mind, written to a sympathetic friend, her views of the situation—I've no doubt, I should appear to be the terrible one.

I don't really know what "riled" her—only that I am sure I am as much to blame as she. She left that night. I was not able to go to the depot to see her off, as my head and eye ached. I cried myself into this condition. She was seen off by Mr. B. and five girls—Gabrielle, Stella, Alice, Lou and Margaret.

She told Mr. Benjamin (who knew of the "rift in the lute," but not of the conditions) that I lost sight of the fact that her "boys" were very dear to her—hence, our quarrel. But to save my life, I don't know how this applies. For I've no recollection of their names being mentioned in anything unusual, until my brother wrote a very trying letter—insulting, inasmuch as he knew that I, or some friend of mine, must read it to her. Even when the letter came, I said nothing. But I confess I cried a great deal, for I was hurt—because I always counted on this brother's love, and hoped sometime to go to see him. That he lived in comparative ease and luxury, I never commented upon, nor asked him for any assistance. I always thought that he must know my condition. And he knows, too, that I have been trying to live clean; and as he did not send me at any time a penny or a gift, no matter how slight, I thought probably he did not credit the fact that I had been living the life where one receives nothing except that which they earn—and gave it no more thought.

Enough of this. I hope they all have plenty—and I will hope some day to have them all feel downright sorry for their neglect. For I am a sister—and they throw away daily what I suffer for lack of.

My mother left, having made peace with me, for which I was duly grateful—for it would have been a pity to have her go in anger, when she stopped here through two months of continual harmony.

I wish to write you a little about Stella—for I recall I left off directly in the part where I expected to tell you of her.

This girl is no different than thousands of girls, except in appearance—she is "different" in that she is far more beautiful than most girls.

She is a type, and I know the type well.

When I act in anything for her, I see a composite picture of Stellas, Maimies, etc.—their number is legion. I know so well her every thought and action. And even better than she does, I know her hopes. You will hardly be able to grasp this, not ever having lived thru it, but my recollections of the same thing when I was seventeen are very fresh, and very readily brought to mind.

Stella and her type are innately refined. Perhaps not in the sense that some might call refined, but that word suffices to explain that she is the opposite of "bourgeois." That her parents and environments are sordid is an accepted fact; and that [they] have refused to drop into the same rut and have had an idea to outgrow the conditions they were born into, makes them "different." And this difference is frowned upon, and only bad can be seen in it.

If she and the rest of her type were ugly in face or form, they would have no trouble, no matter how different their views. But there's the rub. Stella, being pretty, is the subject of petty jealousies. When the mother is a natural one and has the love of

God in her heart, she takes pride in her daughter's pretty face and pretty ways. But Stella's mother and my mother, and many mothers of this type, prefer their children to run along in the same groove that they've made, and any indication of anything else is sensed as immoral, and done to lure men.

I can recall one incident in my life that will furnish proof that this is so.

When I was sixteen, I was home for a week or two—and a man who delivered crackers to our store spoke to me at the door, then went in; and I heard him say to my mother, "Who is that girl?" and, my mother telling him, he went off on a long string of compliments. I could hear them, and see their faces in a reflection from the showcase mirror. Among other things, I heard him say, "Are they her own teeth?" And my mother answered she *thought* so. All the time, the expression on my mother's face never changed; and the expression was plainly that she experienced great agony of mind when I was discussed. I was young, and though I had always been conscious that I had wonderfully regular teeth and that they were generally thought false because their formation was so perfectly even—still, this man's compliments seemed to stay with me.

I had a little money—for I was posing then, in the nude, for the art classes—and that evening I asked a drug clerk, showing him my teeth, what I should buy to preserve them. For everyone, directly after admiring them, would say, "You should take every precaution to preserve them"—and yet I did nothing except rub them with a rough towel to make them shine.

He advised Listerine and toothbrush and prepared chalk. I bought the outfit and, taking it home, placed it on my table, after having used it. The next day when I returned, I knew something had happened by Mother's threatening face and by the scared attitude of my brother and sis.

Nothing daunted, I went upstairs to clean up—for at that time Mr. Benjamin was my "beau," and I was home so as to see him. He lived directly across the road. I found my Listerine, chalk and powder gone! I called downstairs and learned that Mom had them. I came downstairs, and when I asked her for them, she turned on me and before my brother and sister. She attacked me after this fashion: "You have no shame to bring those kind of things in to a decent home! Your poor sister— everyone will damn her along with you. You disgraceful hussy—to put such things on a table!" etc. All this in Yiddish.

I wasn't surprised, because this wasn't anything unusual. Anything I introduced was frowned upon. But I couldn't understand the "disgraceful" part of it until when I met Mr. Benjamin . . . and he knew of it too; for my mother always liked to parade her troubles in order to win sympathy, and she had confided the whole affair to Mr. Benjamin's father.

It developed that she went to a drugstore conducted by a Hebrew and asked what these things were for—the Listerine and the white lumps. The man no doubt told her it was used to keep the mouth in condition, the Listerine being a wash prepared to keep the mouth free from disease. That was enough. Of course, I only surmised this explanation—for how could a druggist say otherwise? She had it (and told Bernard Benjamin) that I was doing unnatural things with my mouth and that the druggist told her the solution was used only to prevent disease from such practices—and that explained why I didn't become pregnant. And I had to live in that neighborhood and know for certain everyone who would listen had been told this.

Now then: this one circumstance is repeated daily by thousands of mothers whose daughters, naturally, living in a new age and learning the newer things, want them, and are continually hounded because they want to live different. I could write everlastingly of experiences such as I wrote in the above, one surprising you more than the other. But they wouldn't surprise Stella—or her type, whatever her name— for they are living thru the same thing with variations.

And somehow—Stella is Maimie. Do you get the idea?

I am afraid I am not able enough to describe how I mean this. But I know every heartache and longing "Maimie" had. And instead of running true to form—which is, that being older and not desiring the same pleasures, one must condemn them in a younger person—I foresee what will make this girl's lot easier and relieve that terrible pressure that everyone condemns her—and love her instead.

Do you know, it is a bit selfish? For I never think of her as Stella, but as Maimie at seventeen—and any kindness shown her is really shown to the Maimie of about ten years ago.

Last night, we were returning home at a little before tea time. Stella said, looking in the window of a very fine shop, "Gee! I could eat one of those cucumbers." I said, "I like them too, but they are too expensive yet," and we walked on. As we passed other grocer shops, I could see her eyes hunting down the cucumbers, but she said no more. As we neared St. Lawrence Main (where there are tiny shops and things are cheaper), I said, "Stella, you run along the Main and buy a cucumber, while I go in and get tea ready." I figured in my mind how to make up for this extravagance. (The cucumber was 15 cents—and we could get a half-dozen eggs for that.) I got tea ready, and though Stella should have been back in five minutes, there was no Stella. I was very hungry. I walked to the door several times, but no Stella in sight. Then I telephoned to nearby grocers, asking if the "red-haired girl" [was there] (or, rather, as I really said, "*Est La tete rouge elle la?*") [sic], but no one had seen Stella. Finally, when three-fourths of an hour had elapsed, I decided to eat alone, for I was certain she had run into her mother or drunken father and was obliged to go home with them. I ate with a heavy heart—for Stella had on a new suit that Mr. Welsh sent her and a hat newly retrimmed (it was my last summer's one), and I knew her mother would tear it off her back. She has had the suit a month or more, but does not wear it home, as her mother would say she had only gotten it one way, and perhaps destroy it. Imagine my surprise, then, when the bell rang and in walked Stella . . . frisky, and she danced around for several seconds before she saw the displeasure on my face. She immediately became serious, and got her broth off the stove and brought it out and began eating it. But it seemed every mouthful was choking her. Still, I said nothing—only about our food and the necessity that she eat bread with her broth (she has broth twice a day but I live on vegetables, cereals, eggs, etc.).

Had I soundly berated her and demanded to know where she had been, I would have done as her mother and Maimie's mother would do—and I wanted to do as Helen Howe's mother would do. For I know girls of seventeen years can't have perfect understanding of things. When she finished her tea, the tears were falling, though she made no sound. I cleared the table while she washed and dried the few dishes. After that, I got a book that we are reading. It is a little girl's book, but I read it for Stella's sake, and I like it myself. It is called *Little Women*—you surely know it.

As I settled down to read it, she walked over and put her head in my lap while she sat on the floor. And she cried steadily while I patted her head. (Such wonderful hair as she has—I believe I will enclose a lock to show you the colour and texture, which is like wire.) As she got quieter, I began reading, and she stayed on the floor. Still I didn't ask her where she had been.

We undressed and retired. And after I put the light out, she asked me if she might tell me. It was that she had met a chap, and he was going to meet a girl whom Stella knew from her church. And she wanted the girl to see her suit, and she didn't think it would take so long—etc., etc. Now, what an unusual thing! Doesn't this happen almost every day with young girls—and what of it? But Stella's mother (or mine, for that matter) would beat her and tirade for hours.

I will guarantee that this girl will never do that particular thing again—though tomorrow she may do something equally exasperating.

I hope I have been able to make you understand about Stella. I never permit myself to feel anything toward her but the love "Maimie" never got any in her youth, except from men, for short periods—and she was always hungry for a woman's love. And when, as I wrote you, Mr. Welsh shows her more attention than he does to me—I confess, I feel hurt; but she never knows it (nor does he). And I never permit jealousy to hurt Stella thru the other girls—for this was the bane of "Maimie's" existence in her youth.

I don't recall whether I wrote you before of her parents, home, etc. . . . . Her mother is a sober, industrious woman, but a horrible shrew. This she isn't altogether to blame for, as her husband (Stella's father) is a common drunk, having helped to support their six children only in fits and starts. The mother was before her marriage a domestic, and since then has done "day work." The father is a street laborer. Their home is typical; but poverty has made it even more squalid than the usual home of this sort of people.

From such a place this Stella came—and it is hardly to be believed. She is absolutely beautiful. Just now, due to the ravages of the disease, of which (I believe) I wrote you, she is painfully thin. Last night, I bathed and massaged her, and the thought came to me . . . that to describe the physical condition of this girl, I couldn't say anything better than that she looks when naked as do the pictures of people depicting famine in India, or some such place. This isn't a bit overdrawn. But this will be changed, now that we have the disease in check.

When Stella was eight years old, she was already with men. Now, the phenomenal part of it all is, that she could meet people who have had experience with girls of her sort, and they would never detect that she was anything but a nice girl out of a home where there is harmony and contentment.

I can recall distinctly that I was ever on the alert as a girl to learn the things that distinguished "nice" people from the other kind. I don't know just why I thought this desirable, inasmuch as I didn't show any desire to live as "nice" people did. But I can recall hundreds of times when I would meet a man, son of "nice" people; and he, thinking to come down to the level of a girl of my sort, would either express himself coarsely or in language that would not be considered good English by "nice" people; and I would take great pleasure in correcting him, thinking to show that it wasn't necessary to come down—I would come up. In this way, I learned much. Often it wasn't their speech, sometimes their mannerisms at or away from the table.

But I knew all this because I wanted to know, and nothing ever escaped me. If I was with a man in a restaurant and I knew he was of plebeian people, I never troubled to study him, but kept my eyes glued on someone at a nearby table whose appearance stamped them as of "nice" people; and if I saw once that people of this sort did not bite bread but broke it, I never bit bread again in my life—etc. I had no trouble to learn, because I wanted to so much. But with Stella it is all different. She isn't as keen witted as I was; and she never has a "purpose" for anything—and I was full of them. She isn't observing. Apparently when she did associate promiscuously with men, they were of various sorts. And while she knew some . . . sons of nice people—I refused to know any other kind. Yet in spite of all this, she has the earmarks of a lady bred and born. When it is necessary for her to act on her initiative, she will instinctively do what a lady would do. Isn't this surprising, for a girl from a home of that sort, who has had no experience in any other home until she came here?

As for cleanliness—though perhaps I had to teach her a few things, she is wonderfully cleanly in her habits. All this appeals to me. I am anxious to see what she will be, if I am permitted to do for her as I should have been done by as a child.

Last month I advertised for work, offering my services as a worker in a home for my keep. The night the ad appeared, Stella perused the paper indifferently, but noticed this ad. She asked if I meant the place for myself. And when I said I did, I noticed she was very white, and her eyes a bit staring. All of a sudden she keeled over into a dead faint, without another word. I was alone. (Mother had gone to see Alice, who didn't stay here then and who was ill.) I tried simple means to revive her. But as I became frightened, I started to shriek, and my front neighbor came in and then brought a doctor from two doors above. The doctor said, after reviving her, she had a shock, and her heart isn't very strong.

When Mother came, I had Stella in bed and resting, though she wasn't asleep and her eyes still staring. . . . I got into bed and soothed her. She put her mouth to my ear and repeated, over and over, "Maimie don't go away"—but softly, so that Mother couldn't hear. I assured her I wouldn't. And I won't—now that you and Miss Huntington have made it possible for me to stay.

Will you let me know whether you think I am right—or rather, whether it is foolish of me to live over Maimie's youth in Stella?

IN THE LAUNDRY ROOM

Alice Childress

*L*ike *One of the Family . . . Conversations from a Domestic's Life* (1956/1986) is Alice Childress' account of sixty-two conversations between Mildred, an African-American day worker, and her friend Marge. The topics of Mildred's conversations—monologues, really—cover a variety of subjects, from the relationship between domestic service workers and their employers to African-American history and nationalism.

Alice Childress (b. 1920), novelist, poet, actor, director, and playwright, has written several award-winning novels and plays. She was the recipient of the first Paul Robeson Award from the Black Filmmakers Hall of Fame. Before becoming a successful artist, however, she did domestic work for a short time to make ends meet. In the selection below, Childress takes up the issue of race, class, and sisterhood.

Marge . . . Sometimes it seems like the devil and all his imps are tryin' to wear your soul case out. . . . Sit down, Marge, and act like you got nothin' to do. . . . No, don't make no coffee, just sit. . . .

Today was laundry day and I took Mrs. M . . .'s clothes down to the basement to put them in the automatic machine. In a little while another houseworker comes down—a white woman. She dumps her clothes on the bench and since my bundle is already in the washer I go over to sit down on the bench and happen to brush against her dirty clothes. . . . Well sir! She gives me a kinda sickly grin and snatched her clothes away quick. . . .

Now, you know, Marge, that it was nothin' but the devil in her makin' her snatch that bundle away 'cause she thought I might give her folks gallopin' pellagra or somethin'. Well, honey, you know what the devil in me wanted to do! . . . You are right! . . . My hand was just itchin' to pop her in the mouth, but I remembered how my niece Jean has been tellin' me that *poppin'* people is not the way to solve problems. . . . So I calmed myself and said, "Sister, why did you snatch those things and look so flustered?" She turned red and says, "I was just makin' room for you." Still keepin' calm, I says, "You are a liar." . . . And then she hung her head.

"Sister," I said, "you are a houseworker and I am a houseworker—now will you favor me by answering some questions?" She nodded her head. . . . The first thing I asked her was how much she made for a week's work and, believe it or not, Marge, she earns less than I do and *that ain't easy.* . . . Then I asked her, "Does the woman you work for ask you in a *friendly* way to do extra things that ain't in the bargain and then later on get *demandin'* about it?" . . . She nods, yes. . . . "Tell me, young woman," I went on, "does she cram eight hours of work into five and call it *part time?*" . . . She nods yes again. . . .

Then, Marge, I added, "I am not your enemy, so don't get mad with me just because you ain't free! . . . Then she speaks up fast, 'I am free!' . . . All right," I said. "How about me goin' over to your house tonight for supper?" . . . "Oh," she says, "I room with people and I don't think they . . ." I cut her off. . . . "If you're free," I said, "you can pick your own friends without fear."

Wait a minute, Marge, let me tell it now. . . . "How come," I asked her, "the folks I work for are willin' to have me put my hands all over their chopped meat patties and yet ask me to hang my coat in the kitchen closet instead of in the hall with theirs?" . . . By this time, Marge, she looked pure bewildered. . . . "Oh," she said, "it's all so mixed up I don't understand!"

"Well, it'll all get clearer as we go along," I said. . . . "Now when you got to plunge your hands in all them dirty clothes in order to put them in the machine . . . how come you can't see that it's a whole lot safer and makes more sense to put your hand in mine and be friends?" Well, Marge, she took my hand and said, "I want to be friends!"

I was so glad I hadn't popped her, Marge. The good Lord only knows how hard it is to do things the right way and make peace. . . . All right now, let's have the coffee, Marge.

꙰ ── ꙰

MAUREEN PEAL
Toni Morrison

Toni Morrison was awarded the 1993 Nobel Prize for Literature, the first African-American woman to receive this honor. Her novels include *Jazz, Beloved,* for which she won the Pulitzer Prize in 1987, *Tar Baby, Song of Solomon, Sula,* and *The Bluest Eye*—from which the selection below is reprinted. She is also the author and editor of works of non-fiction.

The Bluest Eye (1970/1993), Toni Morrison's first novel, tells the tragic story of Pecola Breedlove, a black girl obsessed with Shirley Temple, who wishes she had blue eyes so that people would love her. The story is narrated by Claudia MacTeer, one of Pecola's classmates. Through narrator's eyes, we see the way ideal images of beauty and other standards of the dominant white culture impose themselves on African-American girls. Maureen Peal, a new schoolmate of Claudia and her sister Freida's, embodies many attributes deemed desirable on the basis of these standards. We witness their imposition on the girls and the community as well as the narrator's eventual ability to see them for what they are.

In the Afterword of the 1993 edition, Morrison wrote, "With very few exceptions, the initial publication of *The Bluest Eye* was like Pecola's life: dismissed, trivialized, misread. And it has taken twenty-five years to gain for her the respectful publication this edition is."

My daddy's face is a study. Winter moves into it and presides there. His eyes become a cliff of snow threatening to avalanche; his eyebrows bend like black limbs of leafless trees. His skin takes on the pale, cheerless yellow of winter sun; for a jaw he has the edges of a snowbound field dotted with stubble; his high forehead is the frozen sweep of the Erie, hiding currents of gelid thoughts that eddy in darkness. Wolf killer turned hawk fighter, he worked night and day to keep one from the door and the other from under the windowsills. A Vulcan guarding the flames, he gives us instructions about which doors to keep closed or opened for proper distribution of heat, lays kindling by, discusses qualities of coal, and teaches us how to rake, feed, and bank the fire. And he will not unrazor his lips until spring.

Winter tightened our heads with a band of cold and melted our eyes. We put pepper in the feet of our stockings, Vaseline on our faces, and stared through dark icebox mornings at four stewed prunes, slippery lumps of oatmeal, and cocoa with a roof of skin.

But mostly we waited for spring, when there could be gardens.

By the time this winter had stiffened itself into a hateful knot that nothing could loosen, something did loosen it, or rather someone. A someone who splintered the knot into silver threads that tangled us, netted us, made us long for the dull chafe of the previous boredom.

This disrupter of seasons was a new girl in school named Maureen Peal. A high-yellow dream child with long brown hair braided into two lynch ropes that hung down her back. She was rich, at least by our standards, as rich as the richest of the white girls, swaddled in comfort and care. The quality of her clothes threatened to derange Frieda and me. Patent-leather shoes with buckles, a cheaper version of which we got only at Easter and which had disintegrated by the end of May. Fluffy sweaters the color of lemon drops tucked into skirts with pleats so orderly they

MAUREEN PEAL   From Toni Morrison, *The Bluest Eye* (New York: Washington Square P, 1972) 52–72. Copyright © 1970 by Toni Morrison. Reprinted by permission of International Creative Management, Inc.

astounded us. Brightly colored knee socks with white borders, a brown velvet coat trimmed in white rabbit fur, and a matching muff. There was a hint of spring in her sloe green eyes, something summery in her complexion, and a rich autumn ripeness in her walk.

She enchanted the entire school. When teachers called on her, they smiled encouragingly. Black boys didn't trip her in the halls; white boys didn't stone her, white girls didn't suck their teeth when she was assigned to be their work partners; black girls stepped aside when she wanted to use the sink in the girls' toilet, and their eyes genuflected under sliding lids. She never had to search for anybody to eat with in the cafeteria—they flocked to the table of her choice, where she opened fastidious lunches, shaming our jelly-stained bread with egg-salad sandwiches cut into four dainty squares, pink-frosted cupcakes, stocks of celery and carrots, proud, dark apples. She even bought and liked white milk.

Frieda and I were bemused, irritated, and fascinated by her. We looked hard for flaws to restore our equilibrium, but had to be content at first with uglying up her name, changing Maureen Peal to Meringue Pie. Later a minor epiphany was ours when we discovered that she had a dog tooth—a charming one to be sure—but a dog tooth nonetheless. And when we found out that she had been born with six fingers on each hand and that there was a little bump where each extra one had been removed, we smiled. They were small triumphs, but we took what we could get— snickering behind her back and calling her Six-finger-dog-tooth-meringue-pie. But we had to do it alone, for none of the other girls would cooperate with our hostility. They adored her.

When she was assigned a locker next to mine, I could indulge my jealousy four times a day. My sister and I both suspected that we were secretly prepared to be her friend, if she would let us, but I knew it would be a dangerous friendship, for when my eye traced the white border patterns of those Kelly-green knee socks, and felt the pull and slack of my brown stockings, I wanted to kick her. And when I thought of the unearned haughtiness in her eyes, I plotted accidental slammings of locker doors on her hand.

As locker friends, however, we got to know each other a little, and I was even able to hold a sensible conversation with her without visualizing her fall off a cliff, or giggling my way into what I thought was a clever insult.

One day, while I waited at the locker for Frieda, she joined me.

"Hi."

"Hi."

"Waiting for your sister?"

"Uh-huh."

"Which way do you go home?"

"Down Twenty-first Street to Broadway."

"Why don't you go down Twenty-second Street?"

"'Cause I live on Twenty-first Street."

"Oh. I can walk that way, I guess. Partly, anyway."

"Free country."

Frieda came toward us, her brown stockings straining at the knees because she had tucked the toe under to hide a hole in the foot.

"Maureen's gonna walk part way with us."

Frieda and I exchanged glances, her eyes begging my restraint, mine promising nothing.

It was a false spring day, which, like Maureen, had pierced the shell of a deadening winter. There were puddles, mud, and an inviting warmth that deluded us. The kind of day on which we draped our coats over our heads, left our galoshes in school, and came down with croup the following day. We always responded to the slightest change in weather, the most minute shifts in time of day. Long before seeds were stirring, Frieda and I were scruffing and poking at the earth, swallowing air, drinking rain. . . .

As we emerged from the school with Maureen, we began to moult immediately. We put our head scarves in our coat pockets, and our coats on our heads. I was wondering how to maneuver Maureen's fur muff into a gutter when a commotion in the playground distracted us. A group of boys was circling and holding at bay a victim, Pecola Breedlove.

Bay Boy, Woodrow Cain, Buddy Wilson, Junie Bug—like a necklace of semiprecious stones they surrounded her. Heady with the smell of their own musk, thrilled by the easy power of a majority, they gaily harassed her.

"Black e mo. Black e mo. Yadaddsleepsnekked. Black e moe black e moe ya dadd sleeps nekked. Black e mo . . ."

They had extemporized a verse made up of two insults about matters over which the victim had no control: the color of her skin and speculations on the sleeping habits of an adult, wildly fitting in its incoherence. That they themselves were black, or that their own father had similarly relaxed habits was irrelevant. It was their contempt for their own blackness that gave the first insult its teeth. They seemed to have taken all of their smoothly cultivated ignorance, their exquisitely learned self-hatred, their elaborately designed hopelessness and sucked it all up into a fiery cone of scorn that had burned for ages in the hollows of their minds—cooled—and spilled over lips of outrage, consuming whatever was in its path. They danced a macabre ballet around the victim, whom, for their own sake, they were prepared to sacrifice to the flaming pit.

Black e mo Black e mo Ya daddy sleeps nekked.
Stch ta ta stch ta ta
stach ta ta ta ta ta

Pecola edged around the circle crying. She had dropped her notebook, and covered her eyes with her hands.

We watched, afraid they might notice us and turn their energies our way. Then Frieda, with set lips and Mama's eyes, snatched her coat from her head and threw it on the ground. She ran toward them and brought her books down on Woodrow Cain's head. The circle broke.

Woodrow Cain grabbed his head.

"Hey, girl!"

"You cut that out, you hear?" I had never heard Frieda's voice so loud and clear.

Maybe because Frieda was taller than he was, maybe because he saw her eyes, maybe because he had lost interest in the game, or maybe because he had a crush on Frieda, in any case Woodrow looked frightened just long enough to give her more courage.

"Leave her 'lone, or I'm gone tell everybody what you did!"

Woodrow did not answer; he just walled his eyes.

Bay Boy piped up, "Go on, gal! Ain't nobody bothering you."

"You shut up, Bullet Head." I had found my tongue.

"Who you calling Bullet Head?"

"I'm calling you Bullet Head, Bullet Head."

Frieda took Pecola's hand. "Come on."

"You want a fat lip?" Bay Boy drew back his fist at me.

"Yeah. Gimme one of yours."

"You gone get one."

Maureen appeared at my elbow, and the boys seemed reluctant to continue under her springtime eyes so wide with interest. They buckled in confusion, not willing to beat up three girls under her watchful gaze. So they listened to a budding male instinct that told them to pretend we were unworthy of their attention.

"Come on, man."

"Yeah. Come on. We ain't got time to fool with them."

Grumbling a few disinterested epithets, they moved away.

I picked up Pecola's notebook and Frieda's coat, and the four of us left the playground.

"Old Bullet Head, he's always picking on girls."

Frieda agreed with me. "Miss Forrester said he was incorrigival."

"Really?" I didn't know what that meant, but it had enough of a doom sound in it to be true of Bay Boy.

While Frieda and I clucked on about the near fight, Maureen, suddenly animated, put her velvet-sleeved arm through Pecola's and began to behave as though they were the closest of friends.

"I just moved here. My name is Maureen Peal. What's yours?"

"Pecola."

"Pecola? Wasn't that the name of the girl in *Imitation of Life?*"

"I don't know. What is that?"

"The picture show, you know. Where this mulatto girl hates her mother cause she is black and ugly but then cries at the funeral. It was real sad. Everybody cries in it. Claudette Colbert too."

"Oh." Pecola's voice was no more than a sigh.

"Anyway, her name was Pecola too. She was so pretty. When it comes back, I'm going to see it again. My mother has seen it four times."

Frieda and I walked behind them, surprised at Maureen's friendliness to Pecola, but pleased. Maybe she wasn't so bad, after all. Frieda had put her coat back on her head, and the two of us, so draped, trotted along enjoying the warm breeze and Frieda's heroics.

"You're in my gym class, aren't you?" Maureen asked Pecola.

"Yes."

"Miss Erkmeister's legs sure are bow. I bet she thinks they're cute. How come she gets to wear real shorts, and we have to wear those old bloomers? I want to die every time I put them on."

Pecola smiled but did not look at Maureen.

"Hey." Maureen stopped short. "There's an Isaley's. Want some ice cream? I have money."

She unzipped a hidden pocket in her muff and pulled out a multifolded dollar bill. I forgave her those knee socks.

"My uncle sued Isaley's," Maureen said to the three of us. "He sued the Isaley's in Akron. They said he was disorderly and that that was why they wouldn't serve him, but a friend of his, a policeman, came in and beared the witness, so the suit went through."

"What's a suit?"

"It's when you can beat them up if you want to and won't anybody do nothing. Our family does it all the time. We believe in suits."

At the entrance to Isaley's Maureen turned to Frieda and me, asking, "You all going to buy some ice cream?"

We looked at each other. "No," Frieda said.

Maureen disappeared into the store with Pecola.

Frieda looked placidly down the street; I opened my mouth, but quickly closed it. It was extremely important that the world not know that I fully expected Maureen to buy us some ice cream, that for the past 120 seconds I had been selecting the flavor, that I had begun to like Maureen, and that neither of us had a penny.

We supposed Maureen was being nice to Pecola because of the boys, and were embarrassed to be caught—even by each other—thinking that she would treat us, or that we deserved it as much as Pecola did.

The girls came out. Pecola with two dips of orange-pineapple, Maureen with black raspberry.

"You should have got some," she said. "They had all kinds. Don't eat down to the tip of the cone," she advised Pecola.

"Why?"

"Because there's a fly in there."

"How you know?"

"Oh, not really. A girl told me she found one in the bottom of hers once, and ever since then she throws that part away."

"Oh."

We passed the Dreamland Theater, and Betty Grable smiled down at us.

"Don't you just love her?" Maureen asked.

"Uh-huh," said Pecola.

I differed. "Hedy Lamarr is better."

Maureen agreed. "Ooooo yes. My mother told me that a girl named Audrey, she went to the beauty parlor where we lived before, and asked the lady to fix her hair like Hedy Lamarr's, and the lady said, 'Yeah, when you grow some hair like Hedy Lamarr's.'" She laughed long and sweet.

"Sounds crazy," said Frieda.

"She sure is. Do you know she doesn't even menstrate yet, and she's sixteen. Do you, yet?"

"Yes." Pecola glanced at us.

"So do I." Maureen made no attempt to disguise her pride. "Two months ago I started. My girl friend in Toledo, where we lived before, said when she started she was scared to death. Thought she had killed herself."

"Do you know what it's for?" Pecola asked the question as though hoping to provide the answer herself.

"For babies." Maureen raised two pencil-stroke eyebrows at the obviousness of the question. "Babies need blood when they are inside you, and if you are having a baby, then you don't menstrate. But when you're not having a baby, then you don't have to save the blood, so it comes out."

"How do babies get the blood?" asked Pecola.

"Through the like-line. You know. Where your belly button is. That is where the like-line grows from and pumps the blood to the baby."

"Well, if the belly buttons are to grow like-lines to give the baby blood, and only girls have babies, how come boys have belly buttons?"

Maureen hesitated. "I don't know," she admitted. "But boys have all sorts of things they don't need." Her tinkling laughter was somehow stronger than our nervous ones. She curled her tongue around the edge of the cone, scooping up a dollop of purple that made my eyes water. We were waiting for a stop light to change. Maureen kept scooping the ice cream from around the cone's edge with her tongue; she didn't bite the edge as I would have done. Her tongue circled the cone. Pecola had finished hers; Maureen evidently liked her things to last. While I was thinking about her ice cream, she must have been thinking about her last remark, for she said to Pecola, "Did you ever see a naked man?"

Pecola blinked, then looked away. "No. Where would I see a naked man?"

"I don't know. I just asked."

"I wouldn't even look at him, even if I did see him. That's dirty. Who wants to see a naked man?" Pecola was agitated. "Nobody's father would be naked in front of his own daughter. Not unless he was dirty too."

"I didn't say 'father.' I just said 'a naked man.'"

"Well . . ."

"How come you said 'father'?" Maureen wanted to know.

"Who else would she see, dog tooth?" I was glad to have a chance to show anger. Not only because of the ice cream, but because we had seen our own father naked and didn't care to be reminded of it and feel the shame brought on by the absence of shame. He had been walking down the hall from the bathroom into his bedroom and passed the open door of our room. We had lain there wide-eyed. He stopped and looked in, trying to see in the dark room whether we were really asleep—or was it his imagination that opened eyes were looking at him? Apparently he convinced himself that we were sleeping. He moved away, confident that his little girls would not lie open-eyed like that, staring, staring. When he had moved on, the dark took only him away, not his nakedness. That stayed in the room with us. Friendly-like.

"I'm not talking to you," said Maureen. "Besides, I don't care if she sees her father naked. She can look at him all day if she wants to. Who cares?"

"You do," said Frieda. "That's all you talk about."

"It is not."

"It is so. Boys, babies, and somebody's naked daddy. You must be boy-crazy."

"You better be quiet."

"Who's gonna make me?" Frieda put her hand on her hip and jutted her face toward Maureen.

"You all ready made. Mammy made."

"You stop talking about my mama."

"Well, you stop talking about my daddy."

"Who said anything about your old daddy?"

"You did."

"Well, you started it."

"I wasn't even talking to you. I was talking to Pecola."

"Yeah. About seeing her naked daddy."

"So what if she did see him?"

Pecola shouted, "I never saw my daddy naked. Never."

"You did too," Maureen snapped. "Bay Boy said so."

"I did not."

"You did."

"I did not."

"Did. Your own daddy, too!"

Pecola tucked her head in—a funny, sad, helpless movement. A kind of hunching of the shoulders, pulling in of the neck, as though she wanted to cover her ears.

"You stop talking about her daddy," I said.

"What do I care about her old black daddy?" asked Maureen.

"Black? Who you calling black?"

"You!"

"You think you so cute!" I swung at her and missed, hitting Pecola in the face. Furious at my clumsiness, I threw my notebook at her, but it caught her in the small of her velvet back, for she had turned and was flying across the street against traffic.

Safe on the other side, she screamed at us, "I *am* cute! And you ugly! Black and ugly black e mos. I *am* cute!"

She ran down the street, the green knee socks making her legs look like wild dandelion stems that had somehow lost their heads. The weight of her remark stunned us, and it was a second or two before Frieda and I collected ourselves enough to shout, "Six-finger-dog-tooth-meringue-pie!" We chanted this most powerful of our arsenal of insults as long as we could see green stems and rabbit fur.

Grown people frowned at the three girls on the curbside, two with their coats draped over their heads, the collars framing the eyebrows like nuns' habits, black garters showing where they bit the tops of brown stockings that barely covered the knees, angry faces knotted like dark cauliflowers.

Pecola stood a little apart from us, her eyes hinged in the direction in which Maureen had fled. She seemed to fold into herself, like a pleated wing. Her pain antagonized me. I wanted to open her up, crisp her edges, ram a stick down that hunched and curving spine, force her to stand erect and spit the misery out on the streets. But she held it in where it could lap up into her eyes.

Frieda snatched her coat from her head. "Come on, Claudia. 'Bye, Pecola."

We walked quickly at first, and then slower, pausing every now and then to fasten garters, tie shoelaces, scratch, or examine old scars. We were sinking under the wisdom, accuracy, and relevance of Maureen's last words. If she was cute—and if anything could be believed, she *was*—then we were not. And what did that mean? We were lesser. Nicer, brighter, but still lesser. Dolls we could destroy, but we could not destroy the honey voices of parents and aunts, the obedience in the eyes of our peers, the slippery light in the eyes of our teachers when they encountered the Maureen Peals of the world. What was the secret? What did we lack? Why was it important? And so what? Guileless and without vanity, we were still in love with ourselves then. We felt comfortable in our skins, enjoyed the news that our senses released to us, admired our dirt, cultivated our scars, and could not comprehend this unworthiness. Jealousy we understood and thought natural—a desire to have what somebody else had; but envy was a strange, new feeling for us. And all the time we knew that Maureen Peal was not the Enemy and not worthy of such intense hatred. The *Thing* to fear was the *Thing* that made *her* beautiful, and not us.

FRIENDSHIP, FEMINISM AND BETRAYAL
Susan Lee

What happens to an intimate friendship between two women after one of them marries? In many cases, the friendship suffers because, as the saying goes, "Three's a crowd." But Susan Lee's essay reflects the rethinking many women have been doing about the nature of their friendships. In the essay below, she ponders the difficulties women face as they struggle to develop models of female friendships that defy conventional expectations, but which, as her essay illustrates, also present their own set of complications.

Home for Christmas my first year in college, I spoke to my best friend from high school. Elizabeth and I stayed on the phone for 45 minutes, but we had nothing very much to say to each other. After the conversation, I was upset. I remember wanting to tell my mother, who asked what the matter was, about the weirdness of discovering that this woman and I, who had talked every school day for five years no longer had anything in common. All I could do was cry.

Except for a brief, awkward visit to my house a month later when my father died, a church wedding where Elizabeth married a man I'd gone out with in seventh grade, and two short stopovers in southern New Jersey, I don't remember ever seeing or speaking to her again.

We used to spend hours talking about our relationships with boys. We never discussed our relationship with each other. Except for the few minutes with my mother who told me she thought Elizabeth and I never had anything in common, and my once making a distinction between acquaintances and friends, I'd never spoken about what I considered a real friendship.

Many people have expressed agreement with Cicero that "friendship can only exist between good men." I'm not one of them. As a 30-year-old woman who has had friends since grade school, I have been very concerned with those friendships. Yet only in the last few years have such relationships been acknowledged as being as important as they've always been.

It was always commonplace for girls in my high school to spend a great deal of time together. It was also commonplace for a girl to spend Saturdays with another girl listening to Johnny Mathis albums, trying on clothes to find something that fit right, or babysitting and then having the evening that was planned together usurped by some boy calling up for a date. When this happened to me, I felt betrayed. I

FRIENDSHIP, FEMINISM AND BETRAYAL   From Susan Lee, "Friendship, Feminism and Betrayal," *The Village Voice* 9 June 1975: 11–12. Reprinted by permission of the author and The Village Voice.

never said anything. It didn't occur to me that this wasn't the natural order of things. I didn't know anyone who complained, nor do I remember anyone who ever turned down a boy because she'd already made plans with a girl.

One woman I know said that if as a teenager she had told her parents she'd prefer being with a girl than a boy, they would have sent her to a doctor.

Even now, this past summer, when I was home for a few weeks because my mother was sick, my mother only asked questions about the men who called. One night when I was coming into the city, she discovered I was going to see a woman instead of the man who had just called.

All she said was, "Oh?" Within that one word was more archness than I'd ever heard placed in such a small space.

A male friend of mine suggested that, as kids, if a girl could turn down another girl, for a boy, maybe the girls weren't friends. What he didn't understand is how power works, how it matters who gets to set the dates, how important one telephone call can be, and how helpless someone can feel waiting for it.

But girls didn't deny each other because we weren't friends. We could only do it because we were and because boys weren't, and because they got to make the call and we didn't.

Still, a friend of mine recently remembered that she once was leaving a girl to go out on a date. Her girlfriend's mother, who was very hurt for her daughter, stopped her and said that when she was young, girls knew the value of friendship.

Now, each of us knows what this woman meant. We might express it in terms of a heightened woman's consciousness. We might talk of it in terms of respect for each of our relationships. My friend didn't. She went out on her date. She knew what was flexible in her life and what wasn't. The given of having friends then was that we understood the same rules. The same given remains except that some of the rules are changing.

૬ ૬ ૬

The Greeks and Romans featured "friendship" in their society. From what I can tell, such friendship was a code word for male homosexual relationships.

The Old Testament emphasizes loyalty to family. Friendship, as we understand it, was hardly known. The New Testament uses the word "friend" slightly more but is as little interested in the relationships outside the family or group of coreligionists as the Old Testament.

While members of African tribes have exchanged names and had friendship ceremonies for generations, friendships have not been considered very important in Western cultures until fairly recently.

It would be difficult to date the advent of magnanimity, trust, and accord first manifesting itself as friendship among westerners. Studying friendship in the Plymouth Bay Colony, one historian decided that friendship, as we know it, did not exist. Far more central was devotion to a religious ideal. If you were in concord with that, you remained in relationship with your neighbors. If not, the relationship would be severed. Very possibly, regardless of your history, you were expelled.

American literature is full of male buddies who are supposedly friends; although they may hardly speak to each other, they would only be too glad to die for each other. I'm not sure if this palship is friendship.

Hardly any fiction deals with friendship between women. Doris Lessing's "The Golden Notebook" uses a relationship between two women as the backdrop for examining one of their lives in depth. Fay Weldon's recent "Female Friends" deals more directly with the subject. The women, unfortunately, are victims who continually slash at each other and whose friendship somehow remains as eternal as the sea.

Many studies have been done about interpersonal relationships. These however, usually deal with dating heterosexual couples. Most, like Erich Fromm in his book about different kinds of love, ignore friendship. The closest Fromm could come was brotherly love. The few that mention friendship concentrate on the architecture of friendship and on the network of who is friendly with whom. The conclusions usually have to do with the proximity of a physical, mental, or emotional sort. One study, for example, reveals that boys of the same height tend to be friends.

Friendship has become so institutionalized in our culture that a recent book combined the notion that everyone should have a good friend with the alienated sense that each person should be her or his own best friend.

My guess is that as the family breaks down, friendships will grow in importance. In my own life, as I have relied less and less on the idea of marriage for myself, the more I've come to see the friendships that I've had for years and years as the ongoing relationships in my life.

College was a relatively easy place to find people I liked. Condescending as it might have sounded to me then, we each had our futures ahead of us. It seemed possible to get on with a large number of people. Still, most of my college friends and acquaintances disappeared from my life almost as soon as I left the campus. Like Elizabeth and I, we had little more in common than living near each other.

I used to think affection was enough for friendship, but I no longer believe that. Affection can be sufficient for lovers in a way it isn't for friends. But then, people "fall in" love. Someone is a lover after a few days. A friendship, where love develops, often takes years.

A friend is someone I can be myself with; with a lover, I'm all too often someone else, someone I'd rather be. With a friend, I'm a person; with a lover, I'm a person [*sic*].

I can only be myself when there is a shared community of interests between the other person and me. I began to realize how important this was when I got to graduate school in San Francisco and met other people who cared intimately about the same work I did. No longer was someone's impending wedding date the ongoing center of a conversation.

I found people who perceived what went on outside of them and how they acted in the world in many of the same ways I did. I was not as aware of the need for loyalty to friends as I am now. If I fall under the illusion that I was particularly unusual in the way that I treated other women, I remind myself of the green rocking chair in my San Francisco living room. I gave this chair up to any man who came into my house and kept it for myself if another woman was there.

One relationship developed into something more than shared after classroom time. Both Linda and I were dedicated to writing fiction and to working out our lives so that we'd be able to write. And, however different Linda and I were, I was conscious that our friendship had a loyalty and a respect for each other that other friendly relationships did not have.

We spent hours discussing our lives, our work, our dailyness. Where a lover and I take endless time concerning ourselves with ourselves and our specific relationship, Linda and I were spectators at the landscapes of each other's lives. We were more like adjacent lands sharing common borders than the same property itself. It seemed to me that not only did I have my life, but I had hers as well, to see the working out of our goal to become the best writers we possibly could.

A friend like Linda is a reflection of what I value, in a way a lover is not necessarily. I like to be friends with what is best in me and with what I'm interested in. While I, and several of my friends, too often excuse our choice of lovers as irrational or necessary acts, we take the responsibility for whom we've chosen as friends.

Still, I'm far more conscious of lovers than I am of friends. Though this is changing, I usually think about friends when something is wrong between us. When I'm in love, I'm almost always aware of my lover.

When I was in California and Linda didn't call or was late for an appointment, I assumed there was a good reason. When a lover messes up, I'm quick to think it's our relationship. Friends don't take things as personally as lovers do. There's less expectation and more politeness with friends, who are taken far more for granted than lovers. Yet the reality in my life is that friends are more constant. Lovers come and go except for those who become my friends and stay near me.

Even understanding this, it didn't occur to me to stay in California because of my friends. Linda, abiding by the same implicit rules I did, never mentioned my remaining to me; I don't know if she thought of it. Another friend confronted me; he asked how I could leave the people I freely acknowledged loving more than anyone else. It was enough for me that I was bored and dissatisfied in San Francisco and wanted to come back to New York.

The following year, I returned to the West Coast for Linda's wedding to another writer. Our relationship had deepened into the assumption that we were each other's friend. Although I had fears about the marriage which Linda was all too aware of, I didn't think of not going to give support. I hoped that if any woman could manage writing and a marriage, Linda would.

I tried seeing her for several weeks yearly in Italy or France where she lived. What I didn't admit to myself after one visit to Praiano was how the three of us were developing. I was writing; Thomas, Linda's husband, was writing; only Linda wasn't.

A year and a half later in Paris, I couldn't help seeing what I hadn't wanted to see in Italy. Thomas wrote constantly, and Linda talked about writing. When he worked, we had to whisper. One night when Linda went into her study to work, Thomas interrupted her. I expected her to tell him to leave her alone as she so assiduously left him. Instead, he talked her out of doing anything but spending time with him and me. She acceded to him as she did in much else of what he wanted. She had become a wife.

My visit to Paris was disastrous. Whenever I tried talking about what I found appalling, Linda turned the discussion to my love relationships of the previous year which had not been ones she would have liked to have had. My anger at what I construed as her growing passivity remained unarticulated and high.

I came home and didn't answer a cheery letter ignoring the realities of my stay. A few months later, I wrote a very disturbed explanatory response and did not hear from Linda again.

I knew she'd stopped speaking to her childhood best friend because the woman had once flirted with Thomas. I was aware she'd given me up because of what she thought was an opposite reaction to the man she chose to live with and to the way she led her life.

Six months later, I was speaking to an editor in the publishing house which had signed Thomas's novel and found out Linda and Thomas were in New York for a few weeks.

Sorting out my resentment at having lost my closest friendship, I called them. Linda answering, we talked awkwardly and arranged dinner for that night. I thought the two of us might be able to resolve our difficulties. Perhaps I had been wrong. Deep friendship is hard to come by, and I was prepared to do what I could to salvage this one.

When Linda arrived at the restaurant, she said Thomas would be there with some of his friends within half an hour. I was dumbfounded. She and I were to have had dinner alone.

By the next day, I was furious. Living outside English-speaking countries, Linda might have missed the American women's movement. Still, she taught a college course on women in Paris. She couldn't be as unaware of turning into a passive, dependent person as she seemed to be. If she and I weren't going to be friends, I at least wanted to make clear what bothered me.

But she didn't want to hear it. As far as she was concerned, I was hostile. Finally, she agreed to meet.

There we were at the Buffalo Road House: I, with a tennis racket, T-shirt, and dungarees; she, with the latest long Parisian swirl skirt. We were surrounded by four booths of male couples who all stopped talking as we began.

I gathered they all thought we were the lovers Thomas had believed we were years before. I wanted to turn around and say, "No, no. This is worse. We were friends, and now we're not going to be."

We drank wine and were each very upset. Surprising me, she told me that I had betrayed her. She, who long before defined a friend as someone who knew you and loved you anyway, said I didn't trust her. On my side, I was sure she was the one who betrayed our original friendship. She was the one who'd given up her life for someone else's needs.

I argued, somewhat disingenuously, that I was never hostile to her but to her role as wife. I remember thinking that we were never as close as I had thought.

Linda said, "If Thomas ever was as nasty about you as you've been about him, I would have divorced him a long time ago."

I thought this was not only untrue but gratuitous. Thomas, whose novel includes such lines as, "He stuck his throbbing cock into her Hawaiian cunt," could afford to be magnanimous. There was little reason for him to complain. I could talk all I wanted of the need for women to struggle. While he and his friends discussed how liberated they were, he knew Linda's allegiance and investment were more and more in him and his future and less so in her own.

Then she said that since she and I had stopped corresponding, she's started a novel about the friendship between two women and had gotten more than 100 pages into it.

She and I haven't spoken since. I've hoped she would finish that novel. Not only do I want her to write, I want to read about a friendship through her eyes, and I want something to come out of our relationship.

But I'm being disingenuous again. While acting as an external conscience to a friend might sound touching and be theoretically correct, the reshaping of people, luckily for friendship, is traditionally—and usually without success—left to lovers. Linda knew what I was upset about. At one point when I was in Paris talking to Thomas about each of our projects, Linda burst out, "Don't you both see? *I'm* the one in trouble." Thomas denied what I perceived was true. Linda didn't need me to be tiresome or belligerent about it. Even more, she didn't need someone who she sensed didn't trust her enough to overcome it.

While I now know I can no longer be friendly with someone who acts like a "wife," I think Linda was right about my betraying her. I acted like one of the Plymouth Bay colonists. In effect, I said that specific beliefs and actions meant more than our history together.

Still, I'm angry. I know very well that other people's supposedly durable friendships turn out unexpectedly fragile and break fairly easily. Yet, however necessary my betrayal was, this woman and I had made a commitment to each other, the alternative was not to have gone on being friends. We were too on edge with each other to do that. All we could have done was to fade away from each other without having had the courage to talk about our differences at all.

When I was young, I thought my friends *had* to act as they did. As a result, I overlooked many decisions that I fundamentally disagreed with. Now, due to the women's movement, I assume each of my friends takes responsibility for her life. Because I no longer consider us powerless, I no longer can forgive acting as if we were.

While a heightened women's consciousness has resulted in our openly valuing friendships more highly than we did before, this same consciousness had caused me, and other women, to demand more of these relationships. The validity of each of our lives has become an issue that might have been passed by before and now can no longer be.

Often, these new pressures are too great for many of these friendships to bear. I know there are no models to go by to put them back together. I know we have to develop new models of not only keeping friendships but having them at all.

Yet to venture that friendships often break apart because of social and political dislocations doesn't alleviate my wanting friendships that last or my being hurt that this relationship with Linda, which I had assumed would be one of these, no longer exists.

Looking back on what happened between us, I can understand the pressures on her to choose as she did. I can wish her well. I can understand my own development which made me make demands that others might find unreasonable. I can do a lot of things, but what I feel—not by Linda so much as by historical circumstance—is cheated.

IN AMERIKA THEY CALL US DYKES
The Boston Gay Collective

The selection below is reprinted from the first commercial edition of *Our Bodies, Ourselves* (1972), a compendium of medical, sexual, and political information originally developed in the 1970s for a course about women's bodies by the Boston Women's Health Collective.

The book has undergone a number of major revisions, and today *The New Our Bodies, Ourselves* (1992) is featured in bookstores and libraries in the United States and   other countries.

Hailed as a "best book for young adults" by the American Library Association, *Our Bodies, Ourselves* continues to enjoy brisk sales. Royalties from the book help support the non-profit organization's distribution of other health-related material.

SARAH.   I'm twenty-five, and I "came out" when I slept with a friend a year ago. We have been lovers ever since. But it took me about six months to actively assert my gay identity and feel bound to figuring out what gay politics was or could be. I understood my reluctance to being labeled "lesbian" after listening to a couple of gay women at a gay bar react violently to the word. They saw themselves as human beings, not as labels. But, I thought, that's just not the way people deal with each other in this society. They give you labels whether you take them or not. They reminded me too much of myself ten or fifteen years ago when I responded similarly to being called a Jew.

From the sixth grade on, I was the only Jew in my school. Everyone informed me of that; and it was no compliment coming from their mouths. I thought of myself as smart, capable, good at science and math. I was going to be another Marie Curie. But I was also intimidated by other peoples' judgments; I had to figure out how to fit in. "No, we don't bury our dead standing up," I would say. I really wanted to have friends, and I did get close to girls and boys. But I was always on the fence; they might always turn around and say "You're a Jew." This explains a lot of my reluctance to identify myself as gay and say "I'm a lesbian."

I thought I could have what people would call a gay relationship with my friend and not have to get into gay women's liberation or see myself as a lesbian. I had the choice not to do that. I knew by calling myself a lesbian I was asking for disapproval, distance, and perhaps violence, from most people. And since I had gone through it once, why ask for it again? So for a long time I did not identify. Then I realized that while ideally no one wants to be labeled, I do live in a society where people react to each other that way, and I don't have any control over that. I can't deny how people relate to me. Yes, I'm Jewish and I'm a lesbian.

I'm one of those women who "came out" with the women's movement. Women's Liberation made me think about my past, about when I was a kid and liked to play football and baseball. To me the accusation "You throw like a girl" was a terrible put-down—I didn't want to be lumped in with the "girl" category. I realized when thinking about my family that my parents had similar expectations for me and my brother—except that it was impressed on me to be nice, considerate, concerned for others in ways my brother was rarely pressed to show.

I thought about how, in junior high, the boys looked at the girls as developing bodies. They would yell, "Pearl Harbor, surprise attack!" as they grabbed our breasts and forced us down on the ground to get the "big feel." I know it scared me then, but how could I deal with my anger and fear when what was so important

IN AMERIKA THEY CALL US DYKES   From The Boston Women's Health Collective, *Our Bodies, Ourselves* (New York: Simon & Schuster, 1971) 57–59. Copyright © 1971, 1973, 1976 by the Boston Women's Health Collective, Inc. Reprinted by permission of Simon & Schuster, Inc.

among girls was to be accepted by the boys? And having a boyfriend was often a protection from those other boys.

In ninth grade, a group of girls got close. We used to hug and kiss each other a lot and have slumber parties. Most of us had boyfriends, but we seemed very important to each other. Once in a while someone would say, "What are you, a homo?" and we'd laugh. It didn't mean anything and it didn't change our behavior in any way.

That's the only reference to homosexuality before college that I can remember. In college I got hit with Freud and latent homosexual tendencies. What did this mean for me, who had always been more emotionally attached to women than to men? In freshman year my roommate and I became very close and dependent on each other, but neither of us could handle the intensity; that happened to me a lot with female friends. In psychotherapy I asked (indirectly of course) if I had "those tendencies." After about fifteen minutes the therapist figured out the question and asked, "Are you wondering if you're a lesbian?" Me: "Not really—ahh, I'm just wondering what you think about those tendencies." "You've given no indications of that," he said. Phew! was my reaction, not knowing what those "indications" were! (That's a story of how expertise has power over people's lives.) So I didn't worry about being a lesbian, but continued to build close friendships with women; and the problems those emotional attachments brought weren't lessened.

After college I felt the sadness of women friends going in different directions without the question of sharing our lives, like there would be with boyfriends. I went with a guy for three years, but he was never more important to me than two of my female friends. That was to my liking, not his. He wanted to get married, but since marriage wasn't part of any world I could imagine for myself, he married another woman two months after we split up. Sometimes my friendships with women were threatened by their jealous boyfriends. With these feelings, I could no longer ignore the women's movement. I read something another woman had written about her—and my—experiences. Fantastic! I wasn't alone. I began thinking that men didn't understand friendship; that they were sexual prowlers wanting all the attention focused on them; whereas my relationships with women seemed natural, exciting, and intense.

Working with Women's Liberation in Boston meant being with women all the time. A group of us who weren't really close but were friends would hang out together, circle-danced at a bar, played basketball. Diana was one of them. She and I found we could tune into each other's survival tactics: her piercing, allusive quips weren't offensive to me. What a relief. We could accept each other without many hurt feelings, we shared a lot of interests and criticisms of the women's movement. Eventually we slept together. That was over a year ago.

DIANA.   When I was a kid, I was always a tomboy. In seventh grade the situation changed—I went to a private school where I didn't know anyone and all my friends were girls. I never got to know any of the boys and couldn't see why anyone would want to—they were picking on younger kids, harassing women teachers, and so on. It seemed as though you couldn't get to know them as friends, but only flirt with them. I didn't want to flirt, so I didn't go to parties everyone else was going to. I knew of course that when boys and girls grew up they were supposed to mysteriously start being attracted to each other. I thought that would happen to me, too, later. But the kids in my class just seemed to be playing at being grown up.

In junior high I started identifying more strongly as a girl. Boys were becoming more and more of an alien group. I still hated stockings and frills, but I certainly didn't want to be a boy anymore.

We had dancing classes in junior high. One night between dances a cold breeze started blowing through the open window. I reached over and touched Margaret's knee and asked her if she was getting cold too. She shrank back in mock horror and said, "What's the matter, Diana, are you a lesbian?" Everyone nearby started snickering. I didn't know what a lesbian was, but I knew I didn't want to be one. Later I found out; there was a lot of joking and taunting among girls in my class about lesbianism, which they viewed as sick and disgusting.

I went to an all-girls boarding school for high school. I was happy to be in an all-girls school, because I thought of boys as people you couldn't act naturally with, people who would make the classroom atmosphere tense and uptight. I began to worry consciously about being a lesbian. I knew that wherever I went, women attracted my attention, never men. If I rode on a bus or subway I would watch the faces of all the women. My emotional attachments were all to women and I had crushes on women friends. But I thought that if my attachments weren't sexual I was okay. I tried imagining sex with one of the seniors and was repelled by the thought. That was a relief. I said to myself that I was attracted to girls' *faces,* not their bodies. I told myself, "I just think Kitty's body is beautiful from an *esthetic* point of view, not a sexual one."

I was a tactophobe—a word we invented to mean someone who was afraid of touching people. I was afraid that if I touched other girls I would like it and keep on touching them. So I became repulsed at the idea, to save myself from perversion.

I went to college, and as I began sleeping with boys I began to lose some of my fear of being a lesbian. I enjoyed sex with boys at first, though I didn't much enjoy being with them otherwise, and was always trying to think up reasons not to see my boyfriend. I thought men were boring, and I still felt I had to act very artificially with them.

I began to go on a campaign to become more boy-oriented. I tried consciously to watch more men and fewer women in the subway. I wanted to feel turned on to men, not because it would be enjoyable, but because I was afraid I would not be a complete woman otherwise.

One summer I went to Latin America. There the women are much more physical with each other, walking arm in arm, dancing close together, and touching each other more. I liked this freedom and thought that it showed how culture-bound our definitions of homosexuality are. I got close to one woman, a nurse named Edna. Before I left I spent a day at her house. We were sitting on her bed and she started sucking my finger. I was totally turned on. As I left I thought, Oh no, there's no denying it anymore. I'm a lesbian. Bisexuality did not occur to me as a possibility, although I knew the term. I thought if I was turned on to women, I must accept the fact of being a total queer.

I got into the women's movement, and felt an enormous relief that I would no longer have to play roles with men and act feminine and sweet, dress in skirts and heels, and do all the things I'd done on dates. Then I began to feel hatred for men for having forced me into these roles. During this time I would buy women's papers as soon as they came out and look immediately for articles by gay women. I began to hang out with gay women, who turned out to be regular people, not the stereotypes

I had imagined. On a gut level I was beginning to realize that gayness was not a sickness. One night I went out for a long walk, and when I got home I had decided I was a lesbian. For me it was not a decision to become a lesbian. It was a question of accepting and becoming comfortable with feelings that I had always had.

I don't know if I would ever have "come out" if it hadn't been for the women's movement. The women's movement first led me to question the "naturalness" of the male–female roles that I had always largely accepted. Because I thought that role-playing heterosexuality was "the way it's supposed to be," whenever I rebelled against these roles I was afraid that this meant I was not a complete woman, that there was something wrong with me—not enough sex hormones, no doubt. The women's movement helped me to reject these roles, and with them every reason for struggling to be heterosexual. I realized femaleness was something I was born with, it was not something others could reward me with when I acted "feminine," or take away from me as a punishment. . . .

A CENTURY OF BEING SISTERS
Sarah Booth Conroy

Dr. Elizabeth "Bessie" Delany, a dentist, is 102 and Sarah "Sadie" Delany, an educator, is 104. They are the authors of *Having Our Say: The Delany Sisters' First 100 Years* (1993), a best-selling autobiography which they wrote with Amy Hill Hearth. Sarah Booth Conroy, who interviewed them at their home overlooking Manhattan, says, "If you listen hard enough to them, you could see the history of your people and your country become real."

Indeed, these two sisters, who chose never to marry despite many a proposal, "saw Jim Crow laws come and go," had careers, and who remain independent, have brought to life for us a history long overdue and sorely needed. In doing so, they have challenged stereotypes of race and age.

 Dr. Delany and Miss Delany like to be addressed with respect. In their day, the well-brought-up used titles for all adults, especially anyone older or more august. People of color rightly resented being exceptions to the rule, called by their first names as though they were children or "no-account." The sisters' father foiled that insult by never speaking of his wife outside the family except as Mrs. Delany. And she returned the compliment. Dr. Delany said, "Most people never learned their first names."

Miss Delany graduated from Pratt Institute and then Columbia University. She was the first colored (her word) woman to teach domestic science in white New York schools. Dr. Delany earned her dentistry degree at Columbia to become the second Negro (her word) woman to practice in New York.

To Dr. Delany the word "black" is to be taken literally, as in the color. (If the 10 Delany children stood together, they would make a rainbow of colors, a heritage from their African, American Indian and Anglo-Saxon ancestors.) They also don't like being referred to as African American. "I prefer to think of myself as an American, that's all!" said Dr. Delany with a firm nod affirming her dislike of categorizing citizens.

Both Delanys, who've enjoyed good health for most of their lives, agree that one of the reasons they've lived so long is "staying away from doctors."

Dr. Delany likes to tell the story about the time a doctor insisted on giving her sister a senility test. She not only passed with a high grade, but the following year, when he insisted on doing it again, she recited all his questions from the year before as well as the correct answers.

Though their stories have just now been written down by Amy Hearth, the sisters have always been outspoken—Dr. Delany more than her sister. "People learned not to mess with me from the Day One. If Sadie is molasses, then I am vinegar! Sadie is sugar and I'm the spice."

Miss Delany, reputed to be more diplomatic than her sister, has her own distinctly Southern methods of getting her way. Another teacher once said that Miss Delany, when told to do something, would smile sweetly—and do as she liked.

They both taught school in the South to earn money to go to college, worked summers for a time in a factory. For the last 75 years or so, they've lived together in New York. They were much courted—though under strict chaperonage—as young women. They still keep that unmistakable air of women secure in their beauty. They like to joke that they've lived so long "because we never had husbands to worry us to death!"

The sisters are as close to being immortal as one could hope to be. Why, they've been around to see Halley's comet twice—1910 and 1986—though, "it wasn't as good the second time," said Dr. Delany.

Having attained the position of oracles, they are quite happy to make pronouncements on anything that has transpired in the past 100 years or so. The sisters are not satisfied with the progress of civil rights. They think the Vietnam War turned voters' attention away from discrimination.

"We approve of Mrs. Clinton," they say, almost in unison. "We sent her our book, but we haven't heard if she's read it."

Dr. Delany said about the only thing she hasn't done that she'd like to do is to go to the White House and meet Hillary Rodham Clinton. They approve of her as they did of the Jimmy Carters and the Lyndon Johnsons—and, they add, the Trumans. Eleanor Roosevelt was their favorite First Lady.

They met her through their brother Hubert Delany. He was justice of the Domestic Relations Court in Manhattan in the 1940s. (Earlier, he was Marian Anderson's attorney when Mrs. Roosevelt's support made it possible for her to sing at the Lincoln Memorial. That was after the Daughters of the American Revolution wouldn't let her sing in their Constitution Hall.)

As the sisters told the story about Eleanor Roosevelt's manners: "When we came into the room, there she was. She jumped up like a jack rabbit to greet Mama, taking her hand. It was pretty wonderful to see the former First Lady of the United States jump up, so repectful-like, to greet Mama, an old colored lady."

Now it's the sisters' time to be famous. You'd better believe they are enjoying it. "We are having a ball! I wake up in the middle of the night just to enjoy the excitement. It's nice to be alive and know so much," said Dr. Delany.

The Delanys don't receive just anybody. For one thing, they have no phone, nor do they open the door to strangers.

"We have to rely on the mail or Bessie's intuition," said Miss Delany. "I ask her every morning, 'Is anyone coming today?' And she's always right. She said Amy was coming Sunday. And I told her, "Why, Amy never comes on Sunday.' But she did and Bessie said, 'I told you.'"

Dr. Delany admits to having second sight. "Though my mother tried to keep me from using it," she said. "I think she worried for fear it was the Devil telling me things. I suspect she had the sight too."

"Lots of time I just know. I'm never surprised." Not even at age. "I expect to live as long as Moses—120 years."

She also knew the book would be a success. And it is. They've received mail from all over since they became famous. Kodansha International has printed 100,000 copies in this country and another large printing in Japan. It's a Book-of-the-Month Club selection. On CBS's "Sunday Morning," they did a bit of yoga and then counseled host Charles Kuralt on his weight. They've also been on the Oprah Winfrey show, CNN and Black Entertainment Television.

The Delany parlor is commodious, with chairs and settees intended for people who sit properly and don't slump. "We don't have a rocking chair in the house," said Miss Delany, as though anyone would dare think they were ever idle.

The sisters fussed because the adjoining solarium, where the plants usually bloom, is set up with a hospital bed for Miss Delany's recovery from a broken hip. "We just knew we had to get her out of hospital," said Dr. Delany, or "she never would get well."

"I can hardly wait to get back to my yoga exercises," said Miss Delany. They do their calisthenics while watching a television show. Miss Delany claims it as her idea: "When mother came to live with us, I could see she was getting stiff, so we started the exercises—we learned we were doing yoga later. It did us a lot of good." Their mother lived to be 95. Dr. Delany didn't take up yoga until she was 80.

The sisters proudly show pictures of themselves doing their routine, discreetly posed in exercise *dresses*. Their other precautions: boiling their water and eating seven vegetables a day.

The "maiden ladies," as they call themselves, are not only nimble in body, but agile in mind. They read newspapers every day, watch "The MacNeil/Lehrer News-Hour" every night. They are spirited, in full possession of faculties that started out better than most.

Dr. Delany is irked because at 98, she had to give up climbing a ladder and trimming the trees to create a vista of Manhattan. Their duplex is surrounded by great stone pillars supporting a fence. They first came to the house 36 years ago, among the first of their color to move to Mount Vernon.

A cleaning woman who's more than 80 comes on Saturdays. Nearby relatives grocery-shop for them and relay telephone messages. Dr. Delany gave up driving in her late eighties.

Part Eight

Visions

"IF WE MUST CONSIDER HER AS A CITIZEN, AS A MEMBER OF A GREAT NATION, SHE MUST HAVE THE SAME RIGHTS AS ALL OTHER MEMBERS."

—ELIZABETH CADY STANTON

A woman is nobody. A wife is everything. A pretty girl is equal to ten thousand men, and a mother is, next to God, all powerful. . . . The ladies of Philadelphia, therefore, under the influence of the most serious "sober second thoughts," are resolved to maintain their rights as Wives, Belles, Virgins, and Mothers, and not as Women.

[Philadelphia] *Public Ledger and Daily Transcript* (c. 1848)

This *Ledger* editorial was written in response to the "Declaration of Sentiments" adopted by the delegates to the Seneca Falls convention in 1848 (reprinted in Part Two). Millions of words would follow as American women struggled for equality. But nowhere would the basic opposition to feminism be stated as baldly or as clearly: "A woman is nobody"; her life had meaning only in relation to men; only as belle and virgin, wife and mother did she matter. This is the precise set of ideas against which feminists, from the very outset of the women's movement, have fought. They have discovered that for a woman to become a person in her own right is a formidable task. The editorial provides an important clue as to why this is so, namely, the power of images to reduce women to the sum of the roles they play. So, as women look forward, seeking to imagine a nonsexist world, they also necessarily look back at the travails and triumphs of their foremothers in combating these images. A visionary must also be something of a historian.

As women consider their struggles to reshape American culture, they see, echoed so faithfully by the *Ledger*'s editor, the ruling assumption that a woman is a cipher, a *tabula rasa.* On this blank surface men write whatever they wish.

They write "belle," and women find themselves staring into mirrors trying to decide if they are really pretty. Or they write "mother," and women find themselves living not for themselves but for their offspring. Here indeed is the heart of the matter: Should women live their lives for themselves or should they continue to live largely for others? Since the whole of their lives is at stake in this question, political struggles—be they for the vote or for victims' rights in rape cases—are only the beginning of women's crusade to gain control of their lives.

Beginnings, however, are of vital import; political struggles matter very much, which is why the first selection in this section is Sojourner Truth's celebrated address of 1853 on the need for women's rights. On the other hand, one of the lessons of the suffrage movement is that access to the formal levers of power is no guarantee that women will actually exercise that power. One need only look at the male monopoly on high political office, just now beginning to crack—a full three generations after women won the vote—to see how intransigent the male establishment truly is.

A key tactic used to keep women in their traditional "place," and away from the corridors of power, is the cultural message that women can find fulfillment only as belles, wives, and mothers. Men do not need to choose between fatherhood and a public career; however, in sermons, magazine articles, movie scripts, advertising copy, song lyrics, and newspaper editorials, women are told that they must choose between family and career. The belief that you can do both is dismissed as the "myth" that you can be "superwoman."

So long as that message is heard on all sides, only the exceptionally brave or gifted will resist. Changing the message—and it has begun to change—

depends upon women gaining a measure of control over the command posts of culture. One of the most important of these is the pulpit, and several of the documents included here address the roles of women in religion. Other important command posts include the university lecture hall, the editorial offices of magazines and newspapers, and the programming offices of studios. Here are found the people who create the images that tell us what it means to be a good mother (or belle or wife). As women gain access to these positions, cultural messages change. At the heart of this section are two commencement addresses given at Smith College, a generation apart. The first, delivered in 1955 by Adlai E. Stevenson, the Democratic candidate for president in 1952 and 1956, echoed the *Ledger* editorial of the previous century: Women's purpose lay in making their husbands and children better citizens. A generation later, poet and feminist theorist Adrienne Rich, posed the same question—what is the purpose of a Smith education?—but arrived at an altogether different answer.

Charlotte Perkins Gilman confronted the central question of her time and ours: What must change if women are to have lives of their own? Opponents of the suffrage amendment, like foes of the equal rights amendment sixty years later, attempting to predict the changes that would occur if women became their own persons, prophesied the decline of marriage and the family. Feminists often replied that the opposite would be true. The vote, National American Suffrage Association president Carrie Chapman Catt repeatedly claimed, would not change the family or marriage at all. Charlotte Perkins Gilman, Elizabeth Cady Stanton, and latter-day radicals like Shulamith Firestone hold that these bedrock institutions are precisely what need changing most. In some ways Stanton's is the most radical voice of all for if, unlike Gilman and Firestone, she did not imagine ways of socializing child care or abolishing monogamy, she did explore "The Solitude of Self" that necessarily accompanies being one's own person.

Today's feminists are no closer to unanimity than were those of Gilman's and Catt's day. Nor have old arguments about women's true nature been put to rest. Wendy Kaminer claims that recent trends within the movement inadvertently reinvigorate old stereotypes of feminine fragility. Such criticisms are heard more and more frequently, especially from those who identify themselves as believers in feminism. Clearly, one of the basic challenges feminism faces is accommodating divergent points of view while still seeking a consensus on fundamental issues.

Many feminists today seek to move beyond mere toleration on matters of sexual orientation to a call for feminism to embrace difference. In "Where Is the Love?" June Jordan concludes that every formulation of the meaning of liberation, every feminist vision, must enable each of us to affirm *all* the aspects of our lives. This means feminism must enable us to love ourselves and each other.

ADDRESS ON WOMAN'S RIGHTS
Sojourner Truth

This speech was delivered at the 1853 Woman's Rights Convention held in New York City. The woman's rights movement had, even within the five years since the first convention at Seneca Falls, attracted a host of critics. Large numbers of men attended the 1853 meetings to jeer and harass the speakers. Their antics brought Sojourner Truth, a noted advocate of the abolition of slavery, to the podium. A former slave, Truth drew parallels between the positions of women and African Americans based upon her own experience. And she did so with a deeply held religious conviction.

Sojourner Truth, a tall colored woman, well known in antislavery circles, and called the Lybian Sybil, made her appearance on the platform. This was the signal for a fresh outburst from the mob; for at every session every man of them was promptly in his place, at twenty-five cents a head. And this was the one redeeming feature of this mob—it paid all expenses, and left a surplus in the treasury. Sojourner combined in herself, as an individual, the two most hated elements of humanity. She was black, and she was a woman, and all the insults that could be cast upon color and sex were together hurled at her; but there she stood, calm and dignified, a grand, wise woman, who could neither read nor write, and yet with deep insight could penetrate the very soul of the universe about her. As soon as the terrible turmoil was in a measure quelled

SHE SAID: Is it not good for me to come and draw forth a spirit, to see what kind of spirit people are of? I see that some of you have got the spirit of a goose, and some have got the spirit of a snake. I feel at home here. I come to you, citizens of New York, as I suppose you ought to be. I am a citizen of the State of New York; I was born in it, and I was a slave in the State of New York; and now I am a good citizen of this State. I was born here, and I can tell you I feel at home here. I've been lookin' round and watchin' things, and I know a little mite 'bout Woman's Rights, too. I come forth to speak 'bout Woman's Rights, and want to throw in my little mite, to keep the scales a-movin'. I know that it feels a kind o' hissin' and ticklin' like to see a colored woman get up and tell you about things, and Woman's Rights. We have all been thrown down so low that nobody thought we'd ever get up again; but we have been long enough trodden now; we will come up again, and now I am here.

I was a-thinkin', when I see women contendin' for their rights, I was a-thinkin' what a difference there is now, and what there was in old times. I have only a few minutes to speak; but in the old times the kings of the earth would hear a woman. There was a king in the Scriptures; and then it was the kings of the earth would kill a woman if she come into their presence; but Queen Esther come forth, for she was oppressed, and felt there was a great wrong, and she said I will die or I will bring my complaint before the king. Should the king of the United States be greater, or more crueler, or more harder? But the king, he raised up his sceptre and said: "Thy

---

ADDRESS ON WOMAN'S RIGHTS   From Susan B. Anthony, Elizabeth Cady Stanton, and Matilda Joslyn Gage, eds., *History of Woman Suffrage*, vol. 1 (New York: Fowler & Wells, 1881) 193–94.

request shall be granted unto thee—to the half of my kingdom will I grant it to thee!" Then he said he would hang Haman on the gallows he had made up high. But that is not what women come forward to contend. The women want their rights as Esther. She only wanted to explain her rights. And he was so liberal that he said, "the half of my kingdom shall be granted to thee," and he did not wait for her to ask, he was so liberal with her.

Now, women do not ask half of a kingdom, but their rights, and they don't get 'em. When she comes to demand 'em don't you hear how sons hiss their mothers like snakes, because they ask for their rights; and can they ask for anything less? The king ordered Haman to be hung on the gallows which he prepared to hang others; but I do not want any man to be killed, but I am sorry to see them so short-minded. But we'll have our rights; see if we don't; and you can't stop us from them; see if you can. You may hiss as much as you like, but it is comin'. Women don't get half as much rights as they ought to; we want more, and we will have it. Jesus says: "What I say to one, I say to all—watch!" I'm a-watchin'. God says: "Honor your father and your mother." Sons and daughters ought to behave themselves before their mothers, but they do not. I can see them a-laughin', and pointin' at their mothers up here on the stage. They hiss when an aged woman comes forth. If they'd been brought up proper they'd have known better than hissing like snakes and geese. I'm 'round watchin' these things, and I wanted to come up and say these few things to you, and I'm glad of the hearin' you gave me. I wanted to tell you a mite about Woman's Rights, and so I came out and said so. I am sittin' among you to watch; and every once and awhile I will come out and tell you what time of night it is.

THE SOLITUDE OF SELF
Elizabeth Cady Stanton

Elizabeth Cady Stanton, the founding president of the National American Woman Suffrage Association, delivered this address on the morning of January 17, 1892, at a hearing before the Judiciary Committee of the U.S. House of Representatives. That evening she again delivered the address before the annual convention of the N.A.W.S.A., her last appearance at these gatherings. She took the occasion to step down from the presidency in favor of her long-time friend and colleague Susan B. Anthony. "The Solitude of Self" is a sort of valedictory address, a meditation on what Stanton, after more than forty years of activism, was convinced was the "strongest reason" for women having equal rights. Anthony and Isa Husted Harper, editors of volume four of *The History of Woman Suffrage,* wrote of the occasion: "The mental and physical vigor of Mrs. Stanton was much commented upon as in a rich and resonant voice she read the speech . . . entitled The Solitude of Self . . . [which] is considered by many to be her masterpiece."

The point I wish plainly to bring before you on this occasion is the individuality of each human soul; our Protestant idea, the right of individual conscience and judgment; our republican idea, individual citizenship. In discussing the rights of woman,

---

THE SOLITUDE OF SELF   From Elizabeth Cady Stanton, "The Solitude of Self," *The Woman's Column* Jan. 1892: 2–3.

we are to consider, first, what belongs to her as an individual, in a world of her own, the arbiter of her own destiny, an imaginary Robinson Crusoe, with her woman, Friday, on a solitary island. Her rights under such circumstances are to use all her faculties for her own safety and happiness.

Secondly, if we consider her as a citizen, as a member of a great nation, she must have the same rights as all others members, according to the fundamental principles of our Government.

Thirdly, viewed as a woman, an equal factor in civilization, her rights and duties are still the same—individual happiness and development.

Fourthly, it is only the incidental relations of life, such as mother, wife, sister, daughter, which may involve some special duties and training. . . .

The strongest reason for giving woman all the opportunities for higher education, for the full development of her faculties, her forces of mind and body; for giving her the most enlarged freedom of thought and action; a complete emancipation from all forms of bondage, of custom, dependence, superstition; from all the crippling influences of fear—is the solitude and personal responsibility of her own individual life. The strongest reason why we ask for woman a voice in the government under which she lives; in the religion she is asked to believe; equality in social life, where she is the chief factor; a place in the trades and professions, where she may earn her bread, is because of her birth-right to self-sovereignty; because, as an individual, she must rely on herself. No matter how much women prefer to lean, to be protected and supported, nor how much men desire to have them do so, they must make the voyage of life alone, and for safety in an emergency, they must know something of the laws of navigation. To guide our own craft, we must be captain, pilot, engineer; with chart and compass to stand at the wheel; to watch the winds and waves, and know when to take in the sail, and to read the signs in the firmament over all. It matters not whether the solitary voyager is man or woman; nature, having endowed them equally, leaves them to their own skill and judgment in the hour of danger, and, if not equal to the occasion, alike they perish.

To appreciate the importance of fitting every human soul for independent action, think for a moment of the immeasurable solitude of self. We come into the world alone, unlike all who have gone before us, we leave it alone, under circumstances peculiar to ourselves. No mortal ever has been, no mortal ever will be like the soul just launched on the sea of life. There can never again be just such a combination of prenatal influences; never again just such environments as make up the infancy, youth and manhood of this one. Nature never repeats herself, and the possibilities of one human soul will never be found in another. No one has ever found two blades of ribbon grass alike, and no one will ever find two human beings alike. Seeing, then, what must be the infinite diversity in human character, we can in a measure appreciate the loss to a nation when any large class of the people is uneducated and unrepresented in the government.

We ask for the complete development of every individual, first, for his own benefit and happiness. In fitting out an army, we give each soldier his own knapsack, arms, powder, his blanket, cup, knife, fork and spoon. We provide alike for all their individual necessities; then each man bears his own burden.

❧ ❧ ❧

In youth our most bitter disappointments, our brightest hopes and ambitions, are known only to ourselves. Even our friendship and love we never fully share with another; there is something of every passion, in every situation, we conceal. Even so in our triumphs and our defeats. . . .

We ask no sympathy from others in the anxiety and agony of a broken friendship or shattered love. When death sunders our nearest ties, alone we sit in the shadow of our affliction. Alike amid the greatest triumphs and darkest tragedies of life, we walk alone. On the divine heights of human attainment, eulogized and worshipped as a hero or saint, we stand alone. In ignorance, poverty and vice, as a pauper or criminal, alone we starve or steal; alone we suffer the sneers and rebuffs of our fellows; alone we are hunted and hounded through dark courts and alleys, in by-ways and high-ways; alone we stand in the judgment seat; alone in the prison cell we lament our crimes and misfortunes; alone we expiate them on the gallows. In hours like these we realize the awful solitude of individual life, its pains, its penalties, its responsibilities; hours in which the youngest and most helpless are thrown on their own resources for guidance and consolation. Seeing, then, that life must ever be a march and a battle, that each soldier must be equipped for his own protection, it is the height of cruelty to rob the individual of a single natural right.

To throw obstacles in the way of a complete education is like putting out the eyes; to deny the rights of property is like cutting off the hands. To refuse political equality is to rob the ostracized of all self-respect; of credit in the market place; of recompense in the world of work, of a voice in choosing those who make and administer the law, a choice in the jury before whom they are tried, and in the judge who decides their punishment. [Think of] . . . woman's position! Robbed of her natural rights, handicapped by law and custom at every turn, yet compelled to fight her own battles, and in the emergencies of life to fall back on herself for protection. . . .

The young wife and mother, at the head of some establishment, with a kind husband to shield her from the adverse winds of life, with wealth, fortune and position, has a certain harbor of safety, secure against the ordinary ills of life. But to manage a household, have a desirable influence in society, keep her friends and the affections of her husband, train her children and servants well, she must have rare common sense, wisdom, diplomacy, and a knowledge of human nature. To do all this, she needs the cardinal virtues and the strong points of character that the most successful statesman possesses. An uneducated woman trained to dependence, with no resources in herself, must make a failure of any position in life. But society says women do not need a knowledge of the world, the liberal training that experience in public life must give, all the advantages of collegiate education; but when for the lack of all this, the woman's happiness is wrecked, alone she bears her humiliation; and the solitude of the weak and the ignorant is indeed pitiable. In the wild chase for the prizes of life, they are ground to powder.

In age, when the pleasures of youth are passed, children grown up, married and gone, the hurry and bustle of life in a measure over, when the hands are weary of active service, when the old arm chair and the fireside are the chosen resorts, then men and women alike must fall back on their own resources. If they cannot find companionship in books, if they have no interest in the vital questions of the hour, no interest in watching the consummation of reforms with which they might have been identified, they soon pass into their dotage. The more fully the faculties of the mind are developed and kept in use, the longer the period of vigor and active inter-est in all around us continues. If, from a life-long participation in public affairs, a woman feels responsible for the laws regulating our system of education, the discipline of our jails and prisons, the sanitary condition of our private homes, pub-lic buildings and thoroughfares, an interest in commerce, finance, our foreign rela-tions, in any or all these questions, her solitude will at least be respectable, and she will not be driven to gossip or scandal for entertainment.

The chief reason for opening to every soul the doors to the whole round of human duties and pleasures is the individual development thus attained, the resources thus provided under all circumstances to mitigate the solitude that at times must come to everyone.

. . . Inasmuch, then, as woman shares equally the joys and sorrows of time and eternity, is it not the height of presumption in man to propose to represent her at the ballot box and the throne of grace, to do her voting in the state, her praying in the church, and to assume the position of high priest at the family altar?

Nothing strengthens the judgment and quickens the conscience like individual responsibility. Nothing adds such dignity to character as the recognition of one's self-sovereignty; the right to an equal place, everywhere conceded—a place earned by personal merit, not an artificial attainment by inheritance, wealth, family and posi-tion. Conceding, then, that the responsibilities of life rest equally on man and woman, that their destiny is the same, they need the same preparation for time and eternity. The talk of sheltering woman from the fierce storms of life is the sheerest mockery, for they beat on her from every point of the compass, just as they do on man, and with more fatal results, for he has been trained to protect himself, to resist, and to conquer. Such are the facts in human experience, the responsibilities of individual sovereignty. Rich and poor, intelligent and ignorant, wise and foolish, virtuous and vicious, man and woman; it is ever the same, each soul must depend wholly on itself.

Whatever the theories may be of woman's dependence on man, in the supreme moments of her life, he cannot bear her burdens. Alone she goes to the gates of death to give life to every man that is born into the world; no one can share her fears, no one can mitigate her pangs; and if her sorrow is greater than she can bear, alone she passes beyond the gates into the vast unknown.

From the mountain-tops of Judea long ago, a heavenly voice bade his disciples, "Bear ye one another's burdens"; but humanity has not yet risen to that point of self-sacrifice; and if ever so willing, how few the burdens are that one soul can bear for another! . . .

So it ever must be in the conflicting scenes of life, in the long, weary march, each one walks alone. We may have many friends, love, kindness, sympathy and charity, to smooth our pathway in everyday life, but in the tragedies and triumphs of human experience, each mortal stands alone.

But when all artificial trammels are removed, and women are recognized as indi-viduals, responsible for their own environments, thoroughly educated for all posi-tions in life they may be called to fill; with all the resources in themselves that liberal thought and broad culture can give; guided by their own conscience and judgment, trained to self-protection, by a healthy development of the muscular system, and skill in the use of weapons and defence; and stimulated to self-support by a knowledge of the business world and the pleasure that pecuniary independence must ever give; when women are trained in this way, they will in a measure be fitted for those hours of solitude that come alike to all, whether prepared or otherwise. As in our extremity we must depend on ourselves, the dictates of wisdom point to complete individual development.

𝔞 𝔞 𝔞

We see reason sufficient in the outer conditions of human beings for individual liberty and development, but when we consider the self-dependence of every human soul, we see the need of courage, judgment and the exercise of every faculty of mind and body, strengthened and developed by use, in woman as well as man.

Whatever may be said of man's protecting power in ordinary conditions, amid all the terrible disasters by land and sea, in the supreme moments of danger, alone woman must ever meet the horrors of the situation. The Angel of Death even makes no royal pathway for her. Man's love and sympathy enter only into the sunshine of our lives. In that solemn solitude of self, that links us with the immeasurable and the eternal, each soul lives alone forever. A recent writer says: "I remember once, in crossing the Atlantic, to have gone upon the deck of the ship at midnight, when a dense black cloud enveloped the sky, and the great deep was roaring madly under the lashes of demoniac winds. My feeling was not of danger or fear (which is a base surrender of the immortal soul) but of utter desolation and loneliness; a little speck of life shut in by a tremendous darkness. . . . "

And yet, there is a solitude which each and every one of us has always carried with him, more inaccessible than the ice-cold mountains, more profound than the midnight sea; the solitude of self. Our inner being which we call ourself, no eye nor touch of man or angel has ever pierced. It is more hidden than the caves of the gnome; the sacred adytum of the oracle; the hidden chamber of Eleusinian mystery, for to it only omniscience is permitted to enter.

Such is individual life. Who, I ask you, can take, dare take on himself the rights, the duties, the responsibilities of another human soul?

A UNIQUE HISTORY
Charlotte Perkins Gilman

In order to believe in the possibility of change one has to be able to imagine a different world. Hence, feminists have long speculated on what a truly egalitarian social order might be like. One of the most entertaining, as well as incisive, of these visions is Charlotte Perkins Gilman's *Herland,* a utopian novel about a society without men. The story opens as three young adventurers, all male, hear rumors about a land where there are only women. Despite their inability to believe that such a country could really exist, they set out to find it, and find it they do. Herland's prosperous and efficient appearance serves only to strengthen their conviction that there *must* be men around somewhere. The three are captured and examined concerning the outside world by the women of Herland who, in return, explain to the skeptical men how their country came to consist only of women.

Gilman firmly believed that gender stereotyping warped both men and women. She devoted much of her energy to identifying human, as opposed to male or female, characteristics. As a consequence, *Herland* is less about how women might get along without men than it is about how human beings might form a society without oppression.

And this is what happened, according to their records:

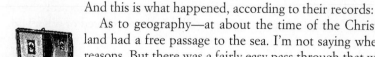

As to geography—at about the time of the Christian era this land had a free passage to the sea. I'm not saying where, for good reasons. But there was a fairly easy pass through that wall of mountains behind us, and there is no doubt in my mind that these people were of Aryan stock, and were once in contact with the best civilization of the old world. They were "white," but somewhat darker than our northern races because of their constant exposure to sun and air.

The country was far larger then, including much land beyond the pass, and a strip of coast. They had ships, commerce, an army, a king—for at that time they were what they so calmly called us—a bi-sexual race.

What happened to them first was merely a succession of historic misfortunes such as have befallen other nations often enough. They were decimated by war, driven up from their coastline till finally the reduced population, with many of the men killed in battle, occupied this hinterland, and defended it for years, in the mountain passes. Where it was open to any possible attack from below they strengthened the natural defenses so that it became unscalably secure, as we found it.

They were a polygamous people, and a slave-holding people, like all of their time; and during the generation or two of this struggle to defend their mountain home they built the fortresses, such as the one we were held in, and other of their oldest buildings, some still in use. Nothing but earthquakes could destroy such architecture—huge solid blocks, holding by their own weight. They must have had efficient workmen and enough of them in those days.

They made a brave fight for existence, but no nation can stand up against what the steamship companies call "an act of God." While the whole fighting force was doing its best to defend their mountain pathway, there occurred a volcanic outburst, with some local tremors, and the result was the complete filling up of the pass—their only outlet. Instead of a passage, a new ridge, sheer and high, stood between them and the sea; they were walled in, and beneath that wall lay their whole little army. Very few men were left alive, save the slaves; and these now seized their opportunity, rose in revolt, killed their remaining masters even to the youngest boy, killed the old women too, and the mothers, intending to take possession of the country with the remaining young women and girls.

But this succession of misfortunes was too much for those infuriated virgins. There were many of them, and but few of these would-be masters, so the young women, instead of submitting, rose in sheer desperation and slew their brutal conquerors.

This sounds like Titus Andronicus, I know, but that is their account. I suppose they were about crazy—can you blame them?

There was literally no one left on this beautiful high garden land but a bunch of hysterical girls and some older slave women.

That was about two thousand years ago.

A UNIQUE HISTORY   From Charlotte Perkins Gilman, *Herland* (New York: Pantheon Books, 1979). Originally published in *The Forerunner,* 1915: 54–61.

At first there was a period of sheer despair. The mountains towered between them and their old enemies, but also between them and escape. There was no way up or down or out—they simply had to stay there. Some were for suicide, but not the majority. They must have been a plucky lot, as a whole, and they decided to live—as long as they did live. Of course they had hope, as youth must, that something would happen to change their fate.

So they set to work, to bury the dead, to plow and sow, to care for one another.

Speaking of burying the dead, I will set down while I think of it, that they had adopted cremation in about the thirteenth century, for the same reason that they had left off raising cattle—they could not spare the room. They were much surprised to learn that we were still burying—asked our reasons for it, and were much dissatisfied with what we gave. We told them of the belief in the resurrection of the body, and they asked if our God was not as well able to resurrect from ashes as from long corruption. We told them of how people thought it repugnant to have their loved ones burn, and they asked if it was less repugnant to have them decay. They were inconveniently reasonable, those women.

Well—that original bunch of girls set to work to clean up the place and make their living as best they could. Some of the remaining slave women rendered invaluable service, teaching such trades as they knew. They had such records as were then kept, all the tools and implements of the time, and a most fertile land to work in.

There were a handful of the younger matrons who had escaped slaughter, and a few babies were born after the cataclysm—but only two boys, and they both died.

For five or ten years they worked together, growing stronger and wiser and more and more mutually attached, and then the miracle happened—one of these young women bore a child. Of course they all thought there must be a man somewhere, but none was found. Then they decided it must be a direct gift from the gods, and placed the proud mother in the Temple of Maaia—their Goddess of Motherhood— under strict watch. And there, as years passed, this wonder-woman bore child after child, five of them—all girls.

I did my best, keenly interested as I have always been in sociology and social psychology, to reconstruct in my mind the real position of these ancient women. There were some five or six hundred of them, and they were harem-bred; yet for the few preceding generations they had been reared in the atmosphere of such heroic struggle that the stock must have been toughened somewhat. Left alone in the terrific orphanhood, they had clung together, supporting one another and their little sisters, and developing unknown powers in the stress of new necessity. To this pain-hardened and work-strengthened group, who had lost not only the love and care of parents, but the hope of ever having children of their own, there now dawned the new hope.

Here at last was Motherhood, and though it was not for all of them personally, it might—if the power was inherited—found here a new race.

It may be imagined how those five Daughters of Maaia, Children of the Temple, Mothers of the Future—they had all the titles that love and hope and reverence could give—were reared. The whole little nation of women surrounded them with loving service, and waited, between a boundless hope and an equally boundless despair, to see if they, too, would be mothers.

And they were! As fast as they reached the age of twenty-five they began bearing. Each of them, like her mother, bore five daughters. Presently there were twenty-five New Women, Mothers in their own right, and the whole spirit of the country changed from mourning and mere courageous resignation to proud joy. The older women, those who remembered men, died off; the youngest of all the first lot of course died too, after a while, and by that time there were left one hundred and fifty-five parthenogenetic women, founding a new race.

They inherited all that the devoted care of that declining band of original ones could leave them. Their little country was quite safe. Their farms and gardens were all in full production. Such industries as they had were in careful order. The records of their past were all preserved, and for years the older women had spent their time in the best teaching they were capable of, that they might leave to the little group of sisters and mothers all they possessed of skill and knowledge.

There you have the start of Herland! One family, all descended from one mother! She lived to a hundred years old; lived to see her hundred and twenty-five great-granddaughters born; lived as Queen-Priestess-Mother of them all; and died with a nobler pride and a fuller joy than perhaps any human soul has ever known—she alone had founded a new race!

The first five daughters had grown up in an atmosphere of holy calm, of awed watchful waiting, of breathless prayer. To them the longed-for motherhood was not only a personal joy, but a nation's hope. Their twenty-five daughters in turn, with a stronger hope, a richer, wider outlook, with the devoted love and care of all the surviving population, grew up as a holy sisterhood, their whole ardent youth looking forward to their great office. And at last they were left alone; the white-haired First Mother was gone, and this one family, five sisters, twenty-five first cousins, and a hundred and twenty-five second cousins, began a new race.

Here you have human beings, unquestionably, but what we were slow in understanding was how these ultra-women, inheriting only from women, had eliminated not only certain masculine characteristics, which of course we did not look for, but so much of what we had always thought essentially feminine.

The tradition of men as guardians and protectors had quite died out. These stalwart virgins had no men to fear and therefore no need of protection. As to wild beasts—there were none in their sheltered land.

The power of mother-love, that maternal instinct we so highly laud, was theirs of course, raised to its highest power; and a sister-love which, even while recognizing the actual relationship, we found it hard to credit.

Terry, incredulous, even contemptuous, when we were alone, refused to believe the story. "A lot of traditions as old as Herodotus—and about as trustworthy!" he said. "It's likely women—just a pack of women—would have hung together like that! We all know women can't organize—that they scrap like anything—are frightfully jealous."

"But these New Ladies didn't have anyone to be jealous of, remember," drawled Jeff.

"That's a likely story," Terry sneered.

"Why don't you invent a likelier one?" I asked him. "Here *are* the women—nothing but women, and you yourself admit there's no trace of a man in the country." This was after we had been about a good deal.

"I'll admit that," he growled. "And it's a big miss, too. There's not only no fun without 'em—no real sport—no competition; but these women aren't *womanly.* You know they aren't."

That kind of talk always set Jeff going; and I gradually grew to side with him. "Then you don't call a breed of women whose one concern is motherhood—womanly?" he asked.

"Indeed I don't," snapped Terry. "What does a man care for motherhood—when he hasn't a ghost of a chance at fatherhood? And besides—what's the good of talking sentiment when we are just men together? What a man wants of women is a good deal more than all this 'motherhood'!"

As to Terry's criticism, it was true. These women, whose essential distinction of motherhood was the dominant note of their whole culture, were strikingly deficient in what we call "femininity." This led me very promptly to the conviction that those "feminine charms" we are so fond of are not feminine at all, but mere reflected masculinity—developed to please us because they had to please us, and in no way essential to the real fulfillment of their great process.

To return to the history:

They began at once to plan and build for their children, all the strength and intelligence of the whole of them devoted to that one thing. Each girl, of course, was reared in full knowledge of her Crowning Office, and they had, even then, very high ideas of the molding powers of the mother, as well as those of education.

Such high ideals as they had! Beauty, Health, Strength, Intellect, Goodness—for these they prayed and worked.

They had no enemies; they themselves were all sisters and friends. The land was fair before them, and a great future began to form itself in their minds.

The religion they had to begin with was much like that of old Greece—a number of gods and goddesses; but they lost all interest in deities of war and plunder, and gradually centered on their Mother Goddess altogether. Then, as they grew more intelligent, this had turned into a sort of Maternal Pantheism.

Here was Mother Earth, bearing fruit. All that they ate was fruit of motherhood, from seed or egg or their product. By motherhood they were born and by motherhood they lived—life was, to them, just the long cycle of motherhood.

But very early they recognized the need of improvement as well as of mere repetition, and devoted their combined intelligence to that problem—how to make the best kind of people. First this was merely the hope of bearing better ones, and then they recognized that however the children differed at birth, the real growth lay later—through education.

Then things began to hum.

As I learned more and more to appreciate what these women had accomplished, the less proud I was of what we, with all our manhood, had done.

You see, they had had no wars. They had had no kings, and no priests and no aristocracies. They were sisters, and as they grew, they grew together—not by competition, but by united action.

We tried to put in a good word for competition, and they were keenly interested. Indeed, we soon found from their earnest questions of us that they were prepared to believe our world must be better than theirs. They were not sure; they wanted to know; but there was no such arrogance about them as might have been expected.

We rather spread ourselves, telling of the advantages of competition: how it developed fine qualities; that without it there would be "no stimulus to industry." Terry was very strong on that point.

"No stimulus to industry," they repeated, with that puzzled look we had learned to know so well. *"Stimulus? To Industry?* But don't you *like* to work?"

"No man would work unless he had to," Terry declared.

"Oh, no *man!* You mean that is one of your sex distinctions?"

"No, indeed!" he said hastily. "No one, I mean, man or woman, would work without incentive. Competition is the—the motor power, you see."

"It is not with us," they explained gently, "so it is hard for us to understand. Do you mean, for instance, that with you no mother would work for her children without the stimulus of competition?"

No, he admitted that he did not mean that. Mothers, he supposed, would of course work for their children in the home; but the world's work was different—that had to be done by men, and required the competitive element.

All our teachers were eagerly interested.

"We want so much to know—you have the whole world to tell us of, and we have only our little land! And there are two of you—the two sexes—to love and help one another. It must be a rich and wonderful world. Tell us—what is the work of the world, that men do—which we have not here?"

"Oh, everything," Terry said grandly. "The men do everything, with us." He squared his broad shoulders and lifted his chest. "We do not allow our women to work. Women are loved—idolized—honored—kept in the home to care for the children."

"What is 'the home'?" asked Somel a little wistfully.

But Zava begged: "Tell me first, do *no* women work, really?"

"Why, yes," Terry admitted. "Some have to, of the poorer sort."

"About how many—in your country?"

"About seven or eight million," said Jeff, as mischievous as ever.

IS THE CIVILIZED WORLD
BECOMING WOMANIZED?

Rene Mansfield

A few years before Charlotte Perkins Gilman published *Herland* in installments in *The Forerunner,* Rene Mansfield wrote "Is the Civilized World Growing Womanized?" for *The Woman Beautiful. The Woman Beautiful* was, according to editor Idah McGlone Gibson, the "mouthpiece" of "the cult of beauty." Beauty, McGlone Gibson proclaimed, existed "in art, in nature, in the home, in business life"; it was physical and also psychological. Not very surprisingly, beauty was, to judge from the articles the magazine published, mostly a matter of fashion, makeup, and diet.

What is surprising is that such a magazine would publish "Is the Civilized World Becoming Womanized?" with its flat assertion that the "conveniences of civilization are largely a result of man's adoption of the means of protection and ways of comfort originally provided for the 'fair sex'" and its claim that the day is soon coming when women will be men's equals if not their superiors.

There is an old saying that "woman was first a beast of burden, then a domestic animal, then a slave, then a servant, and last of all a minor." Is our age making the history that will force the next century to add—"then man's equal, and now his ruler?" Certain it is that an army of women safeguarded with the vigor of new freedom are assaulting daily, with intelligence and determination, the bulwark of man's hitherto exclusive domain. They are pushing aside with firm, tenacious hands the gate-keepers armed with tradition and public opinion; they are thronging into commerce, law, art, and politics; they are invading man's "land of plenty" and seizing the top-most commercial, literary, and professional plums.

Of the three hundred and three gainful occupations scheduled in the last census in the United States, women were found to be employed in all but eight. It is estimated that one out of every sixteen of the total population of women and children works for a living. In France, where the convent has tried to preserve tradition intact these many years, it was discovered not long ago, to the Frenchman's amazement, that thirty per cent of the applicants for admission to the Ecole des Beaux Arts were women. In Russia, twenty-five thousand women are employed on the Russian state railways alone. In Denmark, Norway, and Finland hundreds sail the seas as pilots and state officials. Our own Great Lakes carry steamships and yachts piloted by women who have qualified for the government certificate.

Woman's name is legion in the annals of high finance, in banking, in industry, in the courts, on the stage, in the studio, in the production of literary and dramatic art, and at the polls.

All over the world this arm is wresting slow but certain victory from the powers that be. Will the next century see woman with a firm foot upon the neck of man vanquished economically, artistically, professionally, and politically? He has always pretended to place his neck under her yielding foot gallantly and sentimentally, but if he feels it held there with no sentimentality at all, what is likely to happen to his pride? Will our great-grand-children see a complete reversal of the old order which made the male the stronger sex and the female the weaker?

Dr. Emil Reich, the Hungarian historian, in a lecture in London some time ago, declared that such a condition now prevails in this country. "In America," he said, "woman commands; man does not count. The last man who came to America was Christopher Columbus." The Doctor meant, of course, that women had assumed a sort of tyranny over men simply as a result of their selfish egotism, not because of any special qualifications for power. But may it not hold true absolutely as well as theoretically in the next century?

If the young woman of today is not the intellectual equal of the young man, this lack is compensated by her great volition and determination to succeed—qualities which thinkers everywhere observe are becoming conspicuous by their absence from the characters of the present generation of young men. Educators point to the tenacity of purpose of girl students, to their superiority of concentration and memory and their quick intuition.

IS THE CIVILIZED WORLD BECOMING WOMANIZED?   From Rene Mansfield, "Is the Civilized World Becoming Womanized?" *The Woman Beautiful* July 1909: 23.

Scientists point to the fact that woman is undoubtedly in the lead in physical evolution. She represents more nearly than man the human type to which the race is approximating; that is to say, she resembles more nearly the infant type, and as man advances in civilization he approaches more nearly the feminine type. The small-boned, large-headed, delicate-faced man of the highest civilization is nearer to the typical woman than is the savage.

Perhaps Goethe, the poet scientist, hinted a deeper interpretation when he ended his Faust with

> All of mere transient date
> As symbol showeth;
> Here the inadequate
> To fullness groweth;
> Here the ineffable
> Wrought is in love;
> The ever womanly
> Draws us above.

In fact, along lines of industrialism, where man is particularly prone to claim the rights of inventor and pioneer, he simply has followed in the footsteps of woman, adopting the primitive ways and means—improving, enlarging, cooperating, and finally monopolizing them. The military age is past and the industrial arts devised by woman are in the ascendancy. She has accepted the proverbial fate of all inventors with apparent docility for many hundreds of years. Will the next century see her a victor in the smokeless (though no powderless) battle that she is now waging for her pristine rights of author and originator?

While the primitive man did naught but "fish and hunt and sit about," she, so they tell us, was creating all the industries of the present day. Perhaps the neighborhood where the savage and his wife and the little savages chose to locate did not provide caves to boom the locality, or perhaps every cave at all desirable was occupied. While the man went off to hunt, the primitive woman became the primeval architect and constructed a rude shelter of grasses or skins for her little ones. When the hunter returned and cast before her a great deer, it was she who converted the dead animal into food and clothing for the family. She straightway became the first cutler by striking off a sharp flake of flint for a knife. Then, as she deftly removed the skin she became a butcher of some skill. Curriers and tanners may trace their trade from this primitive woman who rolled up the hide, dressed it, smoked it, curried it, and broke it with crude stone implements.

Tailors and dressmakers may well adopt for their patron saint the savage woman who, with scissors of flint, needle of bone and thread of sinew, fashioned clothing for her family. From the leather which she prepared by a special process of her own she made the moccasins. She dressed dolls for her little ones with scraps of fur, feathers, and trimmings of colored shells or seeds. Perhaps she constructed an elaborate head-dress for herself which would bear comparison in point of riotous color and eccentricity with the modern creation of the millinery art. She adorned the walls of her hut or wigwam with examples of pictorial art, produced with a sharp stick and a bundle of hairs. If very fastidious, she made a mat for the floor from grasses about her.

Woman was not only "first a beast of burden"—she was the first beast of burden. With a great basket strapped across her forehead she went into the fields and returned with a load of roots and seeds and acorns. These she crushed into a mortar or rolled them on a stone slab, and at once she assumed the role of the original miller. When she dropped seeds into the ground, pulled up weeds that choked useful plants, or dug roots from the ground, she became the first gardener and farmer as well as nurseryman. When she brewed and stewed certain herbs or roots to give to the injured hunter or to the little savages in spring time, she entered the ranks of the professionals and was beyond doubt the very first M.D. She was the mother of all spinners and weavers, upholsterers and sail makers. She was the inventor of every form and use of pottery, and became the first decorative artist in the world when she added to her textures bits of yellow, red, or green.

Now, with the advance of civilization and the passing of the military era, man set about laying the foundation of the industrial age. He seized upon the crude inventions of the primitive woman, and with the skill of undivided effort he improved upon them all. Today the carrying strap the savage woman wore over her forehead is the railway train; her simple hand-mill, the roller mill; her crude scraper for softening hides, great tanneries and shoe factories; her bit of clay and pebble, the potter's wheel; her digging stick, the plow.

Man has even usurped her domestic domain. He elevates cooking to an art and calls himself chef. He elevates dressmaking to an art and calls himself Worth or Paquin. He puts up preserves and calls himself Heinz. And not only does he follow woman's lead, it would seem, in the things that make for progress and for money, but in all the refinements and niceties of civilization must he acknowledge himself the imitator. St. Clement opined that it was not fit for the tender foot of woman to go unshod, so she donned footgear; then man also began to wear it, and now he clothes his feet with greater precaution than the tenderest woman. The conveniences of civilization are largely a result of man's adoption of the means of protection and ways of comfort originally provided for the "fair sex."

So it would seem that while woman has been evolving from the beast of burden to the equal, she has been the silent power behind all progress; and it may be that she is moving slowly, unconsciously, perhaps, toward a power that will make her the super-woman.

A PURPOSE FOR MODERN WOMAN
Adlai Stevenson

Adlai Stevenson was the keeper of the flame of New Deal liberalism during the Eisenhower years. A former governor of Illinois, he was the Democratic presidential nominee in both 1952 and 1956. He was still the first choice of the party's most liberal wing, led by former first lady Eleanor Roosevelt, in 1960 when the Democrats instead turned to John Kennedy. Stevenson served as U.S. Ambassador to the United Nations during the Kennedy administration. The speech reprinted here was given by Stevenson at Smith, one of the leading women's colleges. His topic was what "modern" women should do with their education and their lives.

What is striking about Stevenson's address is his assumption that the Smith graduating class of 1955 shared his view that their "primary task" was "making homes" and raising children. One can measure something of the impact of the contemporary women's movement by comparing Stevenson's Smith College commencement address with another given almost a quarter of a century later by poet Adrienne Rich.

I think there is much you can do about our crisis in the humble role of housewife.

The peoples of the West are still struggling with the problems of a free society and just now are in dire trouble. For to create a free society is at all times a precarious and audacious experiment. Its bedrock is the concept of man as an end in himself. But violent pressures are constantly battering away at this concept, reducing man once again to subordinate status, limiting his range of choice, abrogating his responsibility and returning him to his primitive status of anonymity in the social group. I think you can be more helpful in identifying, isolating and combatting these pressures, this virus, than you perhaps realize.

Let me put it this way: individualism has promoted technological advance, technology promoted increased specialization, and specialization promoted an ever closer economic interdependence between specialties.

As the old order disintegrated into this confederation of narrow specialties, each pulling in the direction of its particular interest, the individual person tended to become absorbed literally by his particular function in society. Having sacrificed wholeness of mind and breadth of outlook to the demands of their specialties, individuals no longer responded to social stimuli as total human beings; rather they reacted in partial ways as members of an economic class or industry or profession whose concern was with some limited self-interest.

Thus this typical Western man, or typical Western husband, operates well in the realm of means, as the Romans did before him. But outside his specialty, in the realm of ends, he is apt to operate poorly or not at all. And this neglect of the cultivation of more mature values can only mean that his life, and the life of the society he determines, will lack valid purpose, however busy and even profitable it may be.

And here's where you come in: to restore valid, meaningful purpose to life in your home; to beware of instinctive group reaction to the forces which play upon you and yours, to watch for and arrest the constant gravitational pulls to which we are all exposed—your workaday husband especially—in our specialized, fragmented society, that tend to widen the breach between reason and emotion, between means and ends.

And let me also remind you that you will live, most of you, in an environment in which "facts," the data of the senses, are glorified, and values—judgments—are assigned inferior status as mere "matters of opinion." It is an environment in which art is often regarded as an adornment of civilization rather than a vital element of it, while philosophy is not only neglected but deemed faintly disreputable because "it never gets you anywhere." Even religion, you will find, commands a lot of earnest allegiance that is more verbal than real, more formal than felt.

You may be hitched to one of these creatures we call "Western man" and I think part of your job is to keep him Western, to keep him truly purposeful, to keep him whole. In short—while I have had very little experience as a wife or mother—I think one of the biggest jobs for many of you will be to frustrate the crushing and

A PURPOSE FOR MODERN WOMAN   From Adlai Stevenson, "A Purpose for Modern Woman," commencement address, Northampton MA, Smith College, 1955. *Woman's Home Companion* Sept. 1955: 29–31.

corrupting effects of specialization, to integrate means and ends, to develop that balanced tension of mind and spirit which can be properly called "integrity."

This assignment for you, as wives and mothers, has great advantages. In the first place, it is home work—you can do it in the living-room with a baby in your lap or in the kitchen with a can opener in your hand. If you're really clever, maybe you can even practice your saving arts on that unsuspecting man while he's watching television!

And, secondly, it is important work worthy of you, whoever you are, or your education, whatever it is, because we will defeat totalitarian, authoritarian ideas only by better ideas; we will frustrate the evils of vocational specialization only by the virtues of intellectual generalization. Since Western rationalism and Eastern spiritualism met in Athens and that mighty creative fire broke out, collectivism in various forms has collided with individualism time and again. This twentieth-century collision, this "crisis" we are forever talking about, will be won at last not on the battlefield but in the head and heart.

So you see, I have some rather large notions about you and what you have to do to rescue us wretched slaves of specialization and group thinking from further shrinkage and contraction of mind and spirit. But you will have to be alert or you may get caught yourself—even in the kitchen or the nursery—by the steady pressures with which you will be surrounded.

And now that I have dared to suggest what you should do about your husbands and friends, I am, recklessly, going to even make some suggestions about your children as well.

In the last 50 years, so much of our thinking has been in terms of institutional reform—reform of the economic system, social security, the use and misuse of government, international co-operation, et cetera. All this thinking has been necessary and salutary but somewhere along the line, the men and women whose personalities and potentialities will largely determine the spirit of such institutions have been lost to sight. Worse than that, we have even evolved theories that the paramount aim of education and character formation is to produce citizens who are "well adjusted" to their institutional environment, citizens who can fit painlessly into the social pattern.

While I am not in favor of maladjustment, I view this cultivation of neutrality, this breeding of mental neuters, this hostility to eccentricity and controversy, with grave misgiving. One looks back with dismay at the possibility of a Shakespeare perfectly adjusted to bourgeois life in Stratford, a Wesley contentedly administering a county parish, George Washington going to London to receive a barony from George III, or Abraham Lincoln prospering in Springfield with nary a concern for the preservation of the crumbling union.

In this decisive century it seems to me that we need not just "well-adjusted," "well-balanced" personalities, not just better groupers and conformers (to casually coin a couple of words) but more idiosyncratic, unpredictable characters (that rugged frontier word "ornery" occurs to me); people who take open eyes and open minds out with them into the society which they will share and help to transform. In short, we need all kinds of people, not just one standard variety.

But before any of you gallant girls swear any mighty oaths about fighting the shriveling corruptions and conformations of mind and spirit, before you adopt any rebellious resolutions for the future, make no mistake about it: it is much easier to get yourself and yours adjusted and to accept the conditioning which so many social pressures will bring to bear upon you. After all, tribal conformity and archaic dictatorship could not have lasted so long if they did not accord comfortably with basic human needs and desires. The modern dictators are reviving a very ancient and encrusted way of life. Hitler discovered this. The Fascists knew it. The Communists are busy brainwashing, all over Asia. And what they are washing out is precisely independence of judgment and the moral courage with which to back such judgments. And there are, alas, some leaders in our country who certainly have a brainwashing glint in their eye when they meet with an unfamiliar idea.

Women, especially educated women, have a unique opportunity to influence us, man and boy, and to play a direct part in the unfolding drama of our free society. But I am told that nowadays the young wife or mother is short of time for such subtle arts, that things are not what they used to be; that once immersed in the very pressing and particular problems of domesticity, many women feel frustrated and far apart from the great issues and stirring debates for which their education has given them understanding and relish. Once they read Baudelaire. Now it is the Consumers' Guide. Once they wrote poetry. Now it's the laundry list. Once they discussed art and philosophy until late in the night. Now they are so tired they fall asleep as soon as the dishes are finished. There is, often, a sense of contraction, of closing horizons and lost opportunities. They had hoped to play their part in the crisis of the age. But what they do is wash the diapers. (Or do they any longer?)

Now I hope I have not painted too depressing a view of your future, for the fact is that Western marriage and motherhood are yet another instance of the emergence of individual freedom in our Western society. Their basis is the recognition in women as well as men of the primacy of personality and individuality. I have just returned from sub-Sahara Africa where the illiteracy of the African mother is a formidable obstacle to the education and advancement of her child and where polygamy and female labor are still the dominant system.

The point is that whether we talk of Africa, Islam or Asia, women "never had it so good" as you do. And in spite of the difficulties of domesticity, you have a way to participate actively in the crisis in addition to keeping yourself and those about you straight on the difference between means and ends, mind and spirit, reason and emotion—not to mention keeping your man straight on the differences between Botticelli and Chianti.

In brief, if one of the chief needs in these restless times is for a new quality of mind and heart, who is nearer to the care of this need, the cultivation of this quality, than parents, especially mothers, who educate and form the new generation?

So, add to all of your concerns for Western man, your very special responsibility for Western children. In a family based upon mutual respect, tolerance and understanding affection, the new generation of children—the citizens of tomorrow—stand their best chance of growing up to recognize the fundamental principle of free society—the uniqueness and value and wholeness of each individual human being. For this recognition requires discipline and training. The first instinct of all our untutored egos is to smash and grab, to treat the boy next door as a means, not an end, when you pinch his air rifle, or deny the uniqueness of your small sister's personality when you punch her in the stomach and snatch her lollipop.

Perhaps this is merely to say that the basis of any tolerable society—from the small society of the family up to the great society of the state—depends upon its members learning to love. By that I do not mean sentimentality or possessive emotion. I mean the steady recognition of others' uniqueness and a sustained intention to seek their good. In this, freedom and charity go hand in hand, and they both have to be learned. Where better than in the home? And by whom better than the parents, especially the mother?

In short, far from the vocation of marriage and motherhood leading you away from the great issues of our day, it brings you back to their very center and places upon you an infinitely deeper and more intimate responsibility than that borne by the majority of those who hit the headlines and make the news and live in such a turmoil of great issues that they end by being totally unable to distinguish which issues are really great.

In modern America the home is not the boundary of a woman's life. There are outside activities aplenty. But even more important is the fact, surely, that what you have learned and can learn will fit you for the primary task of making homes and whole human beings in whom the rational values of freedom, tolerance, charity and free inquiry can take root.

I hope you'll not be content to wring your hands, feed your family and just echo all the group, the tribal ritual refrains. I hope you'll keep everlastingly at the job of seeing life steady and seeing it whole. And you can help others—husbands, children, friends—to do so too. You may, indeed you must, help to integrate a world that has been falling into bloody pieces. History's pendulum has swung dangerously far away from the individual and you may, indeed you must, help to restore it to the vital center of its arc.

Long ago at the origins of our way of life it was written of a valiant woman in the Book of Proverbs: "Strength and beauty are her clothing; and she shall laugh in the latter day. She hath opened her mouth to wisdom and the law of clemency is on her tongue; she hath looked well to the paths of her house and hath not eaten her bread idle. Her children rose up and called her blessed; her husband, and he praised her."

I could wish you no better vocation than that. I could wish a free society no better hope for the future. And I could wish you no greater riches and rewards.

COMMENCEMENT ADDRESS
AT SMITH COLLEGE, 1979
Adrienne Rich

On the surface, the graduates to whom Adrienne Rich delivered this address in 1979 were very much like those who listened to Adlai Stevenson in 1955. "Smithies" of both eras were women of privilege, even though, by 1979, more were women of color and fewer came from affluent backgrounds. However, as Rich noted, all had received an elite education. Even so, they were also "outsiders," she maintained, because they were women in what was still a man's world.

Rich is a distinguished poet, essayist, and feminist theorist. Among her other works is *Of Woman Born: Motherhood As Experience and Institution* (1976).

I have been very much moved that you, the class of 1979, chose me for your commencement speaker. It is important to me to be here, in part because Smith is one of the original colleges for women, but also because she has chosen to continue identifying herself as a women's college. We are at a point in history where this fact has enormous potential, even if that potential is as yet unrealized. The possibilities for the future education of women that haunt these buildings and grounds are enormous, when we think of what an independent women's college might be: a college dedicated both to teaching women what women need to know, and, by the same token, to changing the landscape of knowledge itself. The germ of those possibilities lies symbolically in The Sophia Smith Collection, an archive much in need of expansion and increase, but which by its very existence makes the statement that women's lives and work are valued here, and that our foresisters, buried and diminished in male-centered scholarship, are a living presence, necessary and precious to us.

Suppose we were to ask ourselves, simply: What does a woman need to know, to become a self-conscious, self-defining human being? Doesn't she need a knowledge of her own history; of her much-politicized female body; of the creative genius of women of the past—the skills and crafts and techniques and visions possessed by women in other times and cultures, and how they have been rendered anonymous, censored, interrupted, devalued? Doesn't she, as one of that majority who are still denied equal rights as citizens, enslaved as sexual prey, unpaid or underpaid as workers, withheld from her own power—doesn't she need an analysis of her condition, a knowledge of the women thinkers of the past who have reflected on it, a knowledge too of women's world-wide individual rebellions and organized movements against economic and social injustice, and how these have been fragmented and silenced? Doesn't she need to know how seemingly natural states of being, like heterosexuality, like motherhood, have been enforced and institutionalized to deprive her of power? Without such education, women have lived and continued to live in ignorance of our collective context, vulnerable to the projections of men's fantasies about us as they appear in art, in literature, in the sciences, in the media, in the so-called humanistic studies. I suggest that not anatomy, but enforced ignorance, has been a crucial key to our powerlessness.

There is—and I say this with sorrow—there is no women's college today which is providing young women with the education they need for survival as whole persons in a world which denies women wholeness—that knowledge which, in the words of Coleridge, "returns again as power." The existence of Women's Studies courses offers at least some kind of lifeline: but even Women's Studies can amount simply to compensatory history; too often they fail to challenge the intellectual and political structures that must be challenged if women as a group are ever to come into collective, non-exclusionary freedom. The belief that established science and scholarship—which have so relentlessly excluded women from their making—are "objective" and "value free" and that feminist studies are "unscholarly," "biased," and "ideological" dies hard. Yet the fact is that all science, and all scholarship, and all art, are ideological; there is no neutrality in culture. And the ideology of the education you have just

COMMENCEMENT ADDRESS AT SMITH COLLEGE, 1979   From Adrienne Rich, *Blood, Bread, and Poetry: Selected Prose 1979–1985* (New York: W. W. Norton, 1986) 1–10. Copyright © 1979, 1986 by Adrienne Rich. Reprinted by permission of the author and W. W. Norton & Company, Inc.

spent four years acquiring in a women's college, has been largely, if not entirely, the ideology of white male supremacy, a construct of male subjectivity. The silences, the empty spaces, the language itself, with its excision of the female, the methods of discourse, tell us as much as the content, once we learn to watch for what is left out, to listen for the unspoken, to study the patterns of established science and scholarship with an outsider's eye. One of the dangers of a privileged education for women is that we may lose the eye of the outsider, and come to believe that those patterns hold for humanity, for the universal, and that they include us.

And so I want to talk today about privilege, and about tokenism, and about power. Everything I can say to you on this subject comes hard-won, from the lips of a woman privileged by class and skin-color, a father's favorite daughter, educated at Radcliffe, then casually referred to as the Harvard "Annex." Much of the first four decades of my life was spent in a continuous tension between the world the Fathers taught me to see, and had rewarded me for seeing, and the flashes of insight that came through the eye of the outsider. Gradually those flashes of insight, which at times could seem like brushes with madness, began to demand that I struggle to connect them with each other, to insist that I take them seriously. It was only when I could finally affirm the outsider's eye as the source of a legitimate and coherent vision, that I began to be able to do the work I truly wanted to do, live the kind of life I truly wanted to live, instead of carrying out the assignments I had been given as a privileged woman and a token.

For women, all privilege is relative. Some of you were not born with class or skin-color privilege; but you all have the privilege of education, even if it is an education which has largely denied you knowledge of yourselves as women. You have, to begin with, the privilege of literacy; and it is well for us to remember that, in an age of increasing illiteracy, sixty per cent of the world's illiterates are women. Between 1960 and 1970, according to a UNESCO report, the number of illiterate men in the world rose by 8 million; while the number of illiterate women rose by 40 million. And the number of illiterate women is increasing. Beyond literacy, you have the privilege of training and tools which can allow you to go beyond the content of your education and re-educate yourselves—to debrief yourselves, we might call it, of the false messages of your education in this culture, the messages telling you that women have not really cared about power or learning or creative opportunities, because of a psychobiological need to serve men and produce children; that only a few atypical women have been exceptions to this rule; the messages telling you that woman's experience is neither normative, nor central, to human experience. You have the training and the tools to do independent research, to evaluate data, to criticize, and to express in language and visual forms what you discover. This is a privilege, yes; but only if you do not give up in exchange for it the deep knowledge of the unprivileged, the knowledge that, as a woman, you have historically been viewed and still are viewed as existing, not in your own right, but in the service of men. And only if you refuse to give up your capacity to think like a woman; even though in the graduate schools and professions to which many of you will be going, you will be praised and rewarded for "thinking like a man."

The word "power" is highly charged for women. It has been so long associated, for us, with the use of force, with rape, with the stockpiling of weapons, with the ruthless accrual of wealth and the hoarding of resources, with the power that acts only in its own interest, despising and exploiting the powerless—including women and children. The effects of this kind of power are all around us; even literally in the water we drink and the air we breathe, in the form of carcinogens and radioactive wastes. But for a long time now, feminists have been talking about redefining power; about that meaning of power which returns to the root: *posse, potere, pouvoir*—to be able, to have the potential, to possess and use one's energy of creation: *transforming power.* An early objection to feminism—in both the 19th and 20th centuries—was that it would make women behave like men—ruthlessly, exploitatively, oppressively. In fact, radical feminism looks to a transformation of human relationships and structures in which power, instead of a thing to be hoarded by a few, would be released to and from within the many, shared in the form of knowledge, expertise, decision-making, access to tools, as well as in the basic forms of food and shelter and health care and literacy. Feminists—and many non-feminists—are, and rightly so, still concerned with what power would mean in such a society, and with the relative differences in power among women as a group here and now. Which brings me to a third meaning of power where women are concerned: the false power which masculine society offers to a few women, on condition that they use it to maintain things as they are, and that they essentially "think like men." This is the meaning of female tokenism: that power withheld from the vast majority of women is offered to a few, so that it may appear that any truly qualified woman can gain access to leadership, recognition and reward; hence, that justice based on merit actually prevails. The token woman is encouraged to see herself as different from most other women; as exceptionally talented and deserving; and to separate herself from the wider female condition; and she is perceived by "ordinary" women as separate also: perhaps even as stronger than themselves.

Because you are, within the limits of all women's ultimate outsiderhood, a privileged group of women, it is extremely important for your future sanity that you understand the way tokenism functions. Its most immediate contradiction is that, while it seems to offer the individual token woman a means to realize her creativity, to influence the course of events, it also, by exacting of her certain kinds of behavior and style, acts to blur her outsider's eye, which could be her real source of power and vision. Losing her outsider's vision, she loses the insight which both binds her to other women and affirms her in herself. Tokenism essentially demands that the token deny her identification with women as a group, especially with women less privileged than she: if she is a lesbian, that she deny her relationships with individual women; that she perpetuate rules and structures and criteria and methodologies which have functioned to exclude women, that she renounce or leave undeveloped the critical perspective of her female consciousness. Women unlike herself—poor women, women of color, waitresses, secretaries, housewives in the supermarket, prostitutes, old women—become invisible to her; they may represent too acutely what she has escaped or wished to flee.

Jill Conway tells me that ever-increasing numbers of you are going on from Smith to medical and law schools. The news, on the face of it, is good: that, thanks to the feminist struggle of the past decade, more doors into these two powerful professions are open to women. I would like to believe that any profession would be better for having more women practicing it, and that any woman practicing law or medicine would use her knowledge and skill to work to transform the realm of health care and the interpretations of the law, to make them responsive to the needs of all those—women, people of color, children, the aged, the dispossessed—for whom they function today as repressive controls. I would like to believe this, but it will not happen *even* if fifty per cent of the members of these professions are women, unless those women refuse to be made into token insiders, unless they zealously preserve the outsider's view and the outsider's consciousness.

For no woman is really an insider in the institutions fathered by masculine consciousness. When we allow ourselves to believe we are, we lose touch with parts of ourselves defined as unacceptable by that consciousness; with the vital toughness and visionary strength of the angry grandmothers, the shamanesses, the fierce market-women of the Ibo, the marriage-resisting women silk-workers of pre-revolutionary China, the millions of widows, midwives and women healers tortured and burned as witches for three centuries in Europe, the Beguines of the 12th century, who formed independent women's orders outside the domination of the Church, the women of the Paris Commune who marched on Versailles, the uneducated housewives of the Women's Cooperative Guild in England who memorized poetry over the washtub and organized against their oppression as mothers, the women thinkers discredited as "strident," "shrill," "crazy," or "deviant," whose courage to be heretical, to speak their truths, we so badly need to draw upon in our own lives. I believe that every woman's soul is haunted by the spirits of earlier women who fought for their unmet needs and those of their children and their tribes and their peoples, who refused to accept the prescriptions of a male church and state, who took risks and resisted as women today—like Inez Garcia, Yvonne Wanrow, Joan Little, Cassandra Peten—are fighting their rapists and batterers. Those spirits dwell in us, trying to speak to us; but we can choose to be deaf; and tokenism, the myth of the "special" woman, the unmothered Athena sprung from her father's brow, can deafen us to their voices.

In this decade now ending, as more women are entering the professions (though still suffering sexual harassment in the workplace, though still, if they have children, carrying two full-time jobs, though still vastly outnumbered by men in upper-level and decision-making jobs), we need most profoundly to remember that early insight of the feminist movement as it evolved in the late sixties: *that no woman is liberated until we all are liberated.* The media flood us with messages to the contrary: telling us that we live in an era when "alternate life-styles" are freely accepted, when "marriage contracts" and "the new intimacy" are revolutionizing heterosexual relationships: that shared parenting and the "new fatherhood" will change the world. And we live in a society leeched upon by the "personal growth" and "human potential" industry, by the delusion that individual self-fulfillment can be found in thirteen weeks or a weekend, that the alienation and injustice experienced by women, by Black and Third World people, by the poor, in a world ruled by white males, in a society which fails to meet the most basic needs, and which is slowly poisoning itself, can be mitigated or solved by Transcendental Meditation. Perhaps the most succinct expression of this message I have seen is the appearance of a magazine for women called "SELF." The insistence of the feminist movement, that each woman's selfhood is precious, that the feminine ethic of self-denial and self-sacrifice must give way to a true woman-identification, which would affirm our connectedness with all women, is perverted into a commercially profitable and politically debilitating narcissism. It is important for each of you, toward whom many of these messages are especially directed, that you discriminate clearly between "liberated life-style" and feminist struggle, and that you make a conscious choice.

It's a cliché of Commencement speeches that the speaker ends with a peroration telling the new graduates that however badly past generations have behaved, their generation must save the world. I would rather say to you, women of the Class of 1979: try to be worthy of your foresisters, learn from your history, look for inspiration to your ancestresses. If this history has been poorly taught to you, if you do not know it, then use your educational privilege to learn it. Learn how some women of privilege have compromised the greater liberation of women, how others have risked their privileges to further it; learn how brilliant and successful women have failed to create a more just and caring society, precisely because they have tried to do so on terms that the powerful men around them would accept and tolerate. Learn to be worthy of the women of every class, culture, and historical age who did otherwise, who spoke boldly when women were jeered and physically harassed for speaking in public: who—like Anne Hutchinson, Mary Wollstonecraft, the Grimké sisters, Abbey Kelley, Ida B. Wells Barnett, Susan B. Anthony, Lillian Smith, Fannie Lou Hamer—broke taboos: who resisted slavery—their own and other people's. To become a token woman—whether you win the Nobel Prize or merely get tenure at the cost of denying your sisters—is to become something less than a man indeed, since men are loyal at least to their own world-view, their laws of brotherhood and male self-interest. I am not suggesting that you imitate male loyalties; with the philosopher Mary Daly, I believe that the bonding of women must be utterly different, and for an utterly different end: not the misering of resources and power, but the release, in each other, of the yet unexplored resources and transformative power of women, so long despised, confined, and wasted. Get all the knowledge and skill you can, in whatever professions you enter; but remember that most of your education must be self-education, in learning the things women need to know, and in calling up the voices we need to hear within ourselves.

I am going to end by reading a short poem of mine; it is called "Power":*

POWER

Living in the earth-deposits of our history

Today a backhoe divulged out of a crumbling flank of earth
one bottle   amber   perfect   a hundred-year-old
cure for fever   or melancholy   a tonic
for living on this earth   in the winters of this climate
Today I was reading about Marie Curie:
she must have known she suffered   from radiation sickness
her body bombarded for years   by the element
she had purified
It seems she denied to the end
the source of the cataracts on her eyes
the cracked and suppurating skin   of her finger-ends
till she could no longer hold   a test-tube or a pencil

---

*Adrienne Rich, "Power," rpt. from *The Dream of a Common Language, Poems 1974–1977* (New York: W. W. Norton, 1978). Copyright © 1978 by W. W. Norton Company, Inc.

She died   a famous woman   denying
her wounds
denying
her wounds   came   from the same source as her power

Adrienne Rich

WHAT IT WOULD BE LIKE IF WOMEN WIN
Gloria Steinem

Gloria Steinem, the founder and first editor of *Ms.* magazine, as well as a best-selling author, has long been sought out by the establishment media as a spokesperson for the women's movement. In this 1970 *Time* essay she outlined some of the major changes she thought American society would have to undergo were the feminist cause to triumph. *Time* regarded her suggestions as fantasies, and Steinem herself referred to them as "utopian." Even so, it is the essential moderation of Steinem's views that led *Time* to commission the essay in the first place, and it is clear that one of her major goals was to reassure *Time* readers that women could win without men having to lose.

Read in conjunction with Shulamith Firestone's more radical "Alternatives" the essay suggests the range and diversity of feminist thought as the contemporary women's movement gathered momentum in the late 1960s and early 1970s.

Any change is fearful, especially one affecting both politics and sex roles, so let me begin these utopian speculations with a fact. To break the ice.

Women don't want to exchange places with men. Male chauvinists, science-fiction writers and comedians may favor that idea for its shock value, but psychologists say it is a fantasy based on ruling-class ego and guilt. Men assume that women want to imitate them, which is just what white people assumed about blacks. An assumption so strong that it may convince the second-class group of the need to imitate, but for both women and blacks that stage has passed. Guilt produces the question: What if they could treat us as we have treated them?

That is not our goal. But we do want to change the economic system to one more based on merit. In Women's Lib Utopia, there will be free access to good jobs—and decent pay for the bad ones women have been performing all along, including housework. Increased skilled labor might lead to a four-hour workday, and higher wages would encourage further mechanization of repetitive jobs now kept alive by cheap labor.

With women as half the country's elected representatives, and a woman President once in a while, the country's *machismo* problems would be greatly reduced. The old-fashioned idea that manhood depends on violence and victory is, after all, an important part of our troubles in the streets, and in Viet Nam. I'm not saying that women leaders would eliminate violence. We are not more moral than men; we are only uncorrupted by power so far. When we do acquire power, we might turn out to have an equal impulse toward aggression. Even now, Margaret Mead believes that women fight less often but more fiercely than men, because women are not taught the rules of the war game and fight only when cornered. But for the next 50 years or so, women in politics will be very valuable by tempering the idea of manhood into something less aggressive and better suited to this crowded, post-atomic planet. Consumer protection and children's rights, for instance, might get more legislative attention.

Men will have to give up ruling-class privileges, but in return they will no longer be the only ones to support the family, get drafted, bear the strain of power and responsibility. Freud to the contrary, anatomy is not destiny, at least not for more than nine months at a time. In Israel, women are drafted, and some have gone to war. In England, more men type and run switchboards. In India and Israel, a woman rules. In Sweden, both parents take care of the children. In this country, come Utopia, men and women won't reverse roles; they will be free to choose according to individual talents and preferences.

⌘ ⌘ ⌘

If role reform sounds sexually unsettling, think how it will change the sexual hypocrisy we have now. No more sex arranged on the barter system, with women pretending interest, and men never sure whether they are loved for themselves or for the security few women can get any other way. (Married or not, for sexual reasons or social ones, most women still find it second nature to Uncle-Tom.) No more men who are encouraged to spend a lifetime living with inferiors; with housekeepers, or dependent creatures who are still children. No more domineering wives, emasculating women, and "Jewish mothers," all of whom are simply human beings with all their normal ambition and drive confined to the home. No more unequal partnerships that eventually doom love and sex.

In order to produce that kind of confidence and individuality, child rearing will train according to talent. Little girls will no longer be surrounded by air-tight, self-fulfilling prophecies of natural passivity, lack of ambition and objectivity, inability to exercise power, and dexterity (so long as special aptitude for jobs requiring patience and dexterity is confined to poorly paid jobs; brain surgery is for males).

Schools and universities will help to break down traditional sex roles, even when parents will not. Half the teachers will be men, a rarity now at preschool and elementary levels; girls will not necessarily serve cookies or boys hoist up the flag. Athletic teams will be picked only by strength and skill. Sexually segregated courses like auto mechanics and home economics will be taken by boys and girls together. New courses in sexual politics will explore female subjugation as the model for political oppression, and women's history will be an academic staple, along with black history, at least until the white-male-oriented textbooks are integrated and rewritten.

⌘ ⌘ ⌘

As for the American child's classic problem—too much mother, too little father—that would be cured by an equalization of parental responsibility. Free nurseries, school lunches, family cafeterias built into every housing complex, service companies that will do household cleaning chores in a regular, businesslike way, and more responsibility by the entire community for the children: all these will make it possible for both mother and father to work, and to have equal leisure time with the children at home. For parents of very young children, however, a special job category, created by Government and unions, would allow such parents a shorter work day.

The revolution would not take away the option of being a housewife. A woman who prefers to be her husband's housekeeper and/or hostess would receive a percentage of his pay determined by the domestic relations courts. If divorced, she might be eligible for a pension fund, and for a job-training allowance. Or a divorce could be treated the same way that the dissolution of a business partnership is now.

If these proposals seem farfetched, consider Sweden, where most of them are already in effect. Sweden is not yet a working Women's Lib model; most of the role-reform programs began less than a decade ago, and are just beginning to take hold. But that country is so far ahead of us in recognizing the problem that Swedish statements on sex and equality sound like bulletins from the moon.

Our marriage laws, for instance, are so reactionary that Women's Lib groups want couples to take a compulsory written exam on the law, as for a driver's license, before going through with the wedding. A man has alimony and wifely debts to worry about, but a woman may lose so many of her civil rights that in the U. S. now, in important legal ways, she becomes a child again. In some states, she cannot sign credit agreements, use her maiden name, incorporate a business, or establish a legal residence of her own. Being a wife, according to most social and legal definitions, is still a 19th century thing.

Assuming, however, that these blatantly sexist laws are abolished or reformed, that job discrimination is forbidden, that parents share financial responsibility for each other and the children, and that sexual relationships become partnerships of equal adults (some pretty big assumptions), then marriage will probably go right on. Men and women are, after all, physically complementary. When society stops encouraging men to be exploiters and women to be parasites, they may turn out to be more complementary in emotion as well. Women's Lib is not trying to destroy the American family. A look at the statistics on divorce—plus the way in which old people are farmed out with strangers and young people flee the home—shows the destruction that has already been done. Liberated women are just trying to point out the disaster, and build compassionate and practical alternatives from the ruins.

❧ ❧ ❧

What will exist is a variety of alternative life-styles. Since the population explosion dictates that childbearing be kept to a minimum, parents-and-children will be only one of many "families": couples, age groups, working groups, mixed communes, blood-related clans, class groups, creative groups. Single women will have the right to stay single without ridicule, without the attitudes now betrayed by "spinster" and "bachelor." Lesbians or homosexuals will no longer be denied legally binding marriages, complete with mutual-support agreements and inheritance rights. Paradoxically, the number of homosexuals may get smaller. With fewer overpossessive mothers and fewer fathers who hold up an impossibly cruel or perfectionist idea of manhood, boys will be less likely to be denied or reject their identity as males.

❧ ❧ ❧

If Women's Lib wins, perhaps we all do.

ALTERNATIVES
Shulamith Firestone

Gloria Steinem's 1970 "utopian speculations" may now seem mild, but Shulamith Firestone's ideas, published that same year, still retain their ability to shock. This is due, in no small measure, to her willingness to contemplate the end of marriage and the family, two institutions that Steinem argued might actually be strengthened if women were liberated from their second-class status. A member of what was then called the "new left," Firestone was a self-proclaimed "revolutionary," but, like Charlotte Perkins Gilman, she joined conservative critics of feminism in linking women's liberation to the overthrow of the traditional family.

The classic trap for any revolutionary is always, "What's your alternative?" But even if you *could* provide the interrogator with a blueprint, this does not mean he would use it: in most cases he is not sincere in wanting to know. In fact this is a common offensive, a technique to deflect revolutionary anger and turn it against itself. Moreover, the oppressed have no job to convince all people. All *they* need know is that the present system is destroying them.

But though any specific direction must arise organically out of the revolutionary action itself, still I feel tempted here to make some "dangerously utopian" concrete proposals—both in sympathy for my own pre-radical days when the Not-Responsible-For-Blueprint Line perplexed me, and also because I am aware of the political dangers in the peculiar failure of imagination concerning alternatives to the family. There are, as we have seen, several good reasons for this failure. First, there are no precedents in history for feminist revolution—there have been women revolutionaries, certainly, but they have been used by male revolutionaries, who seldom gave even lip service to equality for women, let alone to a radical feminist restructuring of society. Moreover, we haven't even a literary image of this future society; there is not even a *utopian* feminist literature in existence. Thirdly, the nature of the family unit is such that it penetrates the individual more deeply than any other social organization we have: it literally gets him "where he lives." I have shown how the family shapes his psyche to its structure—until ultimately, he imagines it absolute, talk of anything else striking him as perverted. Finally, most alternatives suggest a loss of even the little emotional warmth provided by the family, throwing him into a panic. The model that I shall now draw up is subject to the limitations of any plan laid out on paper by a solitary individual. Keep in mind that these are not meant as final answers, that in fact the reader could probably draw up another plan that would satisfy as well or better the four structural imperatives laid out above. The following proposals, then, will be sketchy, meant to stimulate thinking in fresh areas rather than to dictate the action.

※ ※ ※

What is the alternative to 1984 if we could have our demands acted on in time?

ALTERNATIVES   From Shulamith Firestone, *The Dialectic of Sex: The Case for Feminist Revolution* (New York: Morrow, 1970) 226–34. Copyright © 1970 by Shulamith Firestone. Bantam edition, 1971.

The most important characteristic to be maintained in any revolution is *flexibility.* I will propose, then, a program of multiple options to exist simultaneously, interweaving with each other, some transitional, others far in the future. An individual may choose one "life style" for one decade, and prefer another at another period.

1) *Single Professions.* A single life organized around the demands of a chosen profession, satisfying the individual's social and emotional needs through its own particular occupational structure, might be an appealing solution for many individuals, especially in the transitional period.

Single professions have practically vanished, despite the fact that the encouragement of reproduction is no longer a valid social concern. The old single roles, such as the celibate religious life, court roles—jester, musician, page, knight, and loyal squire—cowboys, sailors, firemen, cross-country truck drivers, detectives, pilots had a prestige all their own: there was no stigma attached to being professionally single. Unfortunately, these roles seldom were open to women. Most single female roles (such as spinster aunt, nun, or courtesan) were still defined by their sexual nature.

Many social scientists are now proposing as a solution to the population problem the encouragement of "deviant life styles" that by definition imply nonfertility. Richard Meier suggests that glamorous single professions previously assigned only to men should now be opened to women as well, for example, "astronaut." He notes that where these occupations exist for women, e.g., stewardess, they are based on the sex appeal of a young woman, and thus can be only limited way stations on the way to a better job or marriage. And, he adds, "so many limitations are imposed [on women's work outside the home] . . . that one suspects the existence of a culture-wide conspiracy which makes the occupational role sufficiently unpleasant that 90 percent or more would choose homemaking as a superior alternative." With the extension of whatever single roles still exist in our culture to include women, the creation of more such roles, and a program of incentives to make these professions rewarding, we could, painlessly, reduce the number of people interested in parenthood at all.

2) *"Living Together."* Practiced at first only in Bohemian or intellectual circles and now increasingly in the population at large—especially by metropolitan youth— "living together" is becoming a common social practice. "Living together" is the loose social form in which two or more partners, of whatever sex, enter a nonlegal sex/companionate arrangement the duration of which varies with the internal dynamics of the relationship. Their contract is only with each other; society has no interest, since neither reproduction nor production—dependencies of one party on the other—is involved. This flexible non-form could be expanded to become the standard unit in which most people would live for most of their lives.

At first, in the transitional period, sexual relationships would probably be monogamous (single standard, female-style, this time around), even if the couple chose to live with others. We might even see the continuation of strictly nonsexual group living arrangements ("roommates"). However, after several generations of nonfamily living, our psychosexual structures may become altered so radically that the monogamous couple, or the "aim-inhibited" relationship, would become obsolescent. We can only guess what might replace it—perhaps true "group marriages," transexual group marriages which also involved older children? We don't know.

The two options we have suggested so far—single professions and "living together"—already exist, but only outside the mainstream of our society, or for brief periods in the life of the normal individual. We want to *broaden* these options to include many more people for longer periods of their lives, to transfer here instead all the cultural incentives now supporting marriage—making these alternatives, finally, as common and acceptable as marriage is today.

But what about children? Doesn't everyone want children sometime in their lives? There is no denying that people now feel a genuine desire to have children. But we don't know how much of this is the product of an authentic liking for children, and how much is a displacement of other needs. We have seen that parental satisfaction is obtainable only through crippling the child: The attempted extension of ego through one's children—in the case of the man, the "immortalizing" of name, property, class, and ethnic identification, and in the case of the woman, motherhood as the justification of her existence, the resulting attempt to live through the child, child-as-project—in the end damages or destroys either the child or the parent, or both when neither wins, as the case may be. Perhaps when we strip parenthood of these other functions, we will find a real instinct for parenthood even on the part of men, a simple physical desire to associate with the young. But then we have lost nothing, for a basic demand of our alternative system is some form of intimate interaction with children. If a parenthood instinct does in fact exist, it will be allowed to operate even more freely, having shed the practical burdens of parenthood that now make it such an anguished hell.

But what, on the other hand, if we find that there is no parenthood instinct after all? Perhaps all this time society has persuaded the individual to have children only by imposing on parenthood ego concerns that had no proper outlet. This may have been unavoidable in the past—but perhaps it's now time to start more directly satisfying those ego needs. As long as natural reproduction is still necessary, we can devise less destructive cultural inducements. But it is likely that, once the ego investments in parenthood are removed, artificial reproduction will be developed and widely accepted.

3) *Households.* I shall now outline a system that I believe will satisfy any remaining needs for children after ego concerns are no longer part of our motivations. Suppose a person or a couple at some point in their lives desire to live around children in a family-size unit. While we will no longer have reproduction as the life goal of the normal individual—we have seen how single and group nonreproductive life styles could be enlarged to become satisfactory for many people for their whole lifetimes and for others, for good portions of their lifetime—certain people may still prefer community-style group living permanently, and other people may want to experience it at some time in their lives, especially during early childhood.

Thus at any given time a proportion of the population will want to live in reproductive social structures. Correspondingly, the society in general will still need reproduction, though reduced, if only to create a new generation.

The proportion of the population will be automatically a select group with a predictably higher rate of stability, because they will have had a freedom of choice now generally unavailable. Today those who do not marry and have children by a certain age are penalized: they find themselves alone, excluded, and miserable, on the margins of a society in which everyone else is compartmentalized into lifetime generational families, chauvinism and exclusiveness their chief characteristic. (Only in Manhattan is single living even tolerable, and that can be debated.) Most people are still forced into marriage by family pressure, the "shotgun," economic considerations, and other reasons that have nothing to do with choice of life style. In our new reproductive unit, however, with the limited contract (see below), childrearing so diffused as to be practically eliminated, economic considerations non-existent, and all participating members having entered only on the basis of personal preference, "unstable" reproductive social structures will have disappeared.

This unit I shall call a *household* rather than an extended family. The distinction is important: The word *family* implies biological reproduction and some degree of division of labor by sex, and thus the traditional dependencies and resulting power relations, extended over generations; though the size of the family—in this case, the larger numbers of the "extended" family—may affect the strength of this hierarchy, it does not change its structural definition. "Household," however, connotes only a large grouping of people living together for an unspecified time, and with no specified set of interpersonal relations. How would a "household" operate?

LIMITED CONTRACT.   If the household replaced marriage perhaps we would at first legalize it in the same way—if this is necessary at all. A group of ten or so consenting adults of varying ages* could apply for a license as a group in much the same way as a young couple today applies for a marriage license, perhaps even undergoing some form of ritual ceremony, and then might proceed in the same way to set up house. The household license would, however, apply only for a given period, perhaps seven to ten years, or whatever was decided on as the minimal time in which children needed a stable structure in which to grow up—but probably a much shorter period than we now imagine. If at the end of this period the group decided to stay together, it could always get a renewal. However, no single individual would be contracted to stay after this period, and perhaps some members of the unit might transfer out, or new members come in. Or, the unit could disband altogether.

There are many advantages to short-term households, stable compositional units lasting for only about a decade: the end of family chauvinism, built up over generations, of prejudices passed down from one generation to the next, the inclusion of people of all ages in the child rearing process, the integration of many age groups into one social unit, the breadth of personality that comes from exposure to many rather than to (the idiosyncrasies of) a few, and so on.

CHILDREN.   A regulated percentage of each household—say one-third—would be children. But whether, at first, genetic children created by couples within the household, or at some future time—after a few generations of household living had severed the special connection of adults with "their" children—children were produced artificially, or adopted, would not matter: (minimal) responsibility for the early physical dependence of children would be evenly diffused among all members of the household.

---

* An added advantage of the household is that it allows older people past their fertile years to share fully in parenthood when they so desire.

But though it would still be structurally sound, we must be aware that as long as we use natural childbirth methods, the "household" could never be a totally liberating social form. A mother who undergoes a nine-month pregnancy is likely to feel that the product of all that pain and discomfort "belongs" to her ("To think of what I went through to have you!"). But we want to destroy this possessiveness along with its cultural reinforcements so that no one child will be *a priori* favored over another, so that children will be loved for their own sake.

But what if there is an instinct for pregnancy? I doubt it. Once we have sloughed off cultural superstructures, we may uncover a sex instinct, the normal consequences of which *lead* to pregnancy. And perhaps there is also an instinct to care for the young once they arrive. But an instinct for pregnancy itself would be superfluous— could nature anticipate man's mastery of reproduction? And what if, once the false motivations for pregnancy had been shed, women no longer wanted to "have" children at all? Might this not be a disaster, given that artificial reproduction is not yet perfected? But women have no special reproductive *obligation* to the species. If they are no longer willing, then artificial methods will have to be developed hurriedly, or, at the very least, satisfactory compensations—other than destructive ego investments—would have to be supplied to make it worth their while.

Adults and older children would take care of babies for as long as they needed it, but since there would be many adults and older children sharing the responsibility— as in the extended family—no one person would ever be involuntarily stuck with it.

Adult/child relationships would develop just as do the best relationships today: some adults might prefer certain children over others, just as some children might prefer certain adults over others—these might become lifelong attachments in which the individuals concerned mutually agreed to stay together, perhaps to form some kind of non-reproductive unit. Thus all relationships would be based on love alone, uncorrupted by objective dependencies and the resulting class inequalities. Enduring relationships between people of widely divergent ages would become common.

LEGAL RIGHTS AND TRANSFERS.   With the weakening and severance of the blood ties, the power hierarchy of the family would break down. The legal structure—as long as it is still necessary—would reflect this democracy at the roots of our society. Women would be identical under the law with men. Children would no longer be "minors," under the patronage of "parents"—they would have full rights. Remaining physical inequalities could be legally compensated for: for example, if a child were beaten, perhaps he could report it to a special simplified "household" court where he would be granted instant legal redress.

Another special right of children would be the right of immediate transfer: if the child for any reason did not like the household into which he had been born so arbitrarily, he would be helped to transfer out. An adult on the other hand—one who had lived one span in a household (seven to ten years)—might have to present his case to the court, which would then decide, as do divorce courts today, whether he had adequate grounds for breaking his contract. A certain number of transfers within the seven-year period might be necessary for the smooth functioning of the household, and would not be injurious to its stability as a unit so long as a core remained. (In fact, new people now and then might be a refreshing change.) However, the unit, for its own best economy, might have to place a ceiling on the number of transfers in or out, to avoid depletion, excessive growth, and/or friction.

LESBIANS AND WOMEN'S LIBERATION: "IN ANY TERMS SHE SHALL CHOOSE"

Vivian Gornick

Women's rights advocates, from the days of Elizabeth Cady Stanton and Susan B. Anthony, have had to contend with vituperative attacks not only upon their ideas but also upon their personal lives. From the first this has included accusations of lesbianism. The accusation is still heard, but today's feminists no longer simply deny it as slander. Lesbian feminists have been outspoken in claiming the right to full participation in the women's movement, and, after no little struggle, have largely succeeded in obtaining their goal. Some lesbians have argued, in addition, that only a truly "woman-centered woman" can be a real feminist. Mainstream organizations like NOW have rejected that position, but do see gay liberation as a fundamental component of women's liberation.

Vivian Gornick's essay, written as feminists first began to debate the role of lesbians in the movement, proved very influential, perhaps because she placed the controversy within the context of a larger vision of what feminism ought to be. Gornick, a frequent contributor to the *Village Voice* and other publications, is co-editor of *Woman in Sexist Society: Studies in Power and Powerlessness* (1971) and author of *The Romance of American Communism* (1977).

A month ago I spent a weekend in the company of a prominent feminist, a dedicated and intelligent woman who, in the course of the time we passed together, spoke out passionately against the open recognition of lesbianism in the movement, claiming—along with *Time* magazine—that the women's movement would destroy its credibility out there in "middle America" if it should publicly support lesbians as a legitimate element in feminism and in the movement. I found this position appalling, and I feel now that it raises an issue that must be argued more specifically than I had recently thought. For just as it seemed transparently certain to that feminist that open recognition of lesbianism in the women's movement would imperil the life of the movement, so it seems equally clear to me that denial of lesbianism in the women's movement will insure the death of the movement.

Hundreds of women in the feminist movement are lesbians. Many of them have worked in the women's movement from its earliest days of organized activity. They were in NOW three and four years ago, working steadily along with heterosexual women for the redress of grievances that affected them all; they are scattered today across the entire political board of women's organizations. They probably have more to gain from feminism than any other single category of women, both in the most superficial sense and in the more profound one. Certainly, they have more to *teach* feminists about feminism than has any other single category of human being—man or woman. And yet, until only this past year, lesbians have lived the same crypto-life in the movement that they live outside it. Sitting next to a heterosexual feminist who might rise in distress at a meeting to say, "Oh, let's not do *that*. They'll think we're a bunch of lesbians," the lesbian in the next seat could not rise and say, "But I *am* a lesbian," because her admission would have forced to the surface a wealth of fears only half understood, which would then quickly have been converted into panic and denunciation. It was an old, old story to the lesbians, one for which they could have written the script, and one which feminists should feel eternal shame for having played a part in.

It is the very essence of the lesbian's life that she leads an underground existence; that she cannot openly state the nature of her emotional-sexual attachments without thereafter enduring the mark of Cain; that in innumerable places and under all varieties of circumstances she experiences every manner of insult and injury to the soul that can be inflicted by the insensitive and the unperceiving; that in every real sense she is one of the invisible of the earth. It is this element almost alone, separated out from the multiple elements of her defining experience, that determines the character of the lesbian's life and often the shape of her soul. To live with the daily knowledge that what you are is so awful to the society around you that it cannot be revealed is to live with an extraordinary millstone slung from one's neck, one that weighs down the body and strangles the voice.

Imagine, then, the feeling of those lesbians who joined the feminist movement only to find themselves once more unable to be themselves. Here they were, women doubly cast out of society, both as women and as homosexuals, joined together in the feminist struggle for selfhood, being victimized by other women. For there's no mistaking it: the heterosexual feminist who disconnected herself, politically and spiritually, from the homosexual feminist sitting next to her (and did so most especially when she was saying, "Look, I don't care what *anybody* does in her private life, but there's no public place in the movement for that sort of thing") was disavowing that homosexual feminist, and thus victimizing her. The irony of it all was that in actuality the heterosexual feminist was victimizing herself even more, for that disavowal strikes at the bottommost roots of feminism, attacking the movement in its most vital parts, threatening its ideological life at the source.

Feminism, classically, has grown out of woman's conviction that she is "invisible" upon the earth; that the life she leads, the defining characteristics that are attributed to her, the destiny that is declared her natural one are not so much the truth of her real being and existence as they are a reflection of culture's willful *need* that she be as she is described. The feminist movement is a rebellious *no* to all that; it is a declaration of independence against false description of the self; it is a protest dedicated to the renunciation of that falsity and the courageous pursuit of honest self-discovery. The whole *point* of the feminist movement is that each and every woman shall recognize that the burden and the glory of her feminism lie with defining herself honestly *in any terms she shall choose.*

Sexual self-definition is primary to the feminist movement. After all, the movement's entire life is predicated on the idea that woman's experience has been stunted by society's falsifying views of the nature of her sexuality. Feminists are now saying to male civilization, "Your definition of my sexuality is false, and living inside that falsehood has now become intolerable to me. I may not know what I *am,* but I surely know what I am *not,* and it is offensive to my soul to continue to act what I am not." Thus, in essence, the feminist's course is really charted on the path of discovery of the sexual self. What *is* the actual nature of a woman's sexuality? What *are* its requirements? To what genuine extent does it exert pressure on her to fulfill herself through sexual love? To what extent will that miracle of force and energy—if diverted elsewhere—blossom into an altogether other and transformed kind of human being? Who knows? No one has the answers. We are only just beginning to formulate the questions.

Seen in this perspective, homosexuality in women represents only a variant of the fundamental search for the sexual self-understanding that is primary in the struggle to alter radically the position of women in this culture. In a word: some feminists are homosexual, and others are heterosexual; the point is not that it is wrong and frightening to be one or right and relieving to be the other; the point is that *whatever* a woman's sexual persuasion, it is compelling, and she must be allowed to follow her inclinations openly and honestly without fear of castigation in order to discover the genuine self at the center of her sexuality.

That, for me, is the true politics of the feminist movement. It is woman recognizing that she is a fully developed human being with the responsibility to discover and live with her own self, which means creating an emotional environment in which that self can not only act but be prepared to take the consequences for those acts as well. The determination of what the self is, or should be, is a matter of individual choice that must be honored by the movement, and acknowledged as a legitimate reference to the movement's ultimate aims.

What is most astonishing in all this is that the open flare-up last year between homosexual and heterosexual feminists is living proof of this deepest influence of the feminist movement on the need to be oneself. After enduring in silence for a number of years the movement's virtual denial of their existence, NOW's lesbians suddenly emerged a year ago as the Radicalesbians, demanding acknowledgment, and forming a consciousness-raising group of their own, thereby taking the movement at its word and using feminism's most valuable technique for support and definition as well. Most heterosexual feminists were initially startled by the lesbians' outburst, but many immediately grasped that the deepest principles of feminism were involved here and offered ready alliance. The lesbians were demonstrating for all those who had eyes to see that much of the movement's rhetoric had never been tested, that the issue of sexual liberation was an amazingly complex one, that at last the question of sexual fear was being turned on themselves. Many feminists did not see these things, however, and many, to this day, continue to see the open acknowledgment of lesbianism in the movement as irrelevant, or a threat to the movement's survival.

The claim that the question of lesbianism is irrelevant to the movement—that the struggle for recognition as a lesbian belongs properly to gay liberation and not to the women's movement—seems to me openly fallacious. The point is not that lesbians in the movement are homosexual; the point is that they are *feminists*: self-proclaimed, fully participating feminists who are being told, in a movement predicated on the notion that women are the victims of sexism, that the dominating principle of their sexuality is to be kept under wraps because the women out there in "middle America" simply wouldn't understand. This is the kind of emotional response masquerading as political analysis that panders to all our emotional and sexual fears. It encourages us to remain afraid of ourselves and to inflict injustice on each other in the name of our fears. And is that not what sexism is all about? If our emotional and sexual fears are not at the bottom of the condition that has brought us to feminism, what on earth is? Would we then not all profit immeasurably from the emotional daring involved in facing down the fear of lesbianism in the movement, and recognizing *it* for the true irrelevancy in the feminist struggle to reclaim our lives?

What I find more distressing than the charge of irrelevancy, however, is the aggressive talk from feminists that admission of lesbianism in the women's movement is a threat to the growth of the movement. From *Time* magazine I can take it, but from feminists it goes unbearably against the grain. If anything is a threat to the movement, it is the fear of taking just action in the name of political expediency. If anything will destroy this movement, it is losing sight of the fact that what feminism is genuinely all about is calling the shots as we see them. To be possessed of a bit of emotional truth, and then to go publicly against that truth because it is politically "wiser" to do so, is to totally misperceive the *real* politics of feminism—which has not to do with altering legislation or building a political party or taking over the government or uselessly increasing ranks. The real politics of feminism has to do with filling the social atmosphere with increased feminist consciousness and letting acculturation do its job. Nothing—absolutely nothing—is "wiser" than that, *Time* magazine and Kansas City housewives notwithstanding.

Really, the whole thing is so bewildering. Three years ago the women's movement was a renegade movement, willing to speak truths nobody wanted to hear. Suddenly, on this issue, it is being told it must speak *only* those truths middle-class America is willing to hear. And this is absurd, for in reality all the apprehension is groundless. When Ti-Grace first said, "Love is an institution of oppression," everybody panicked. Now, a year and a half later, the most respectable ladies in the movement don't bat an eyelash when the guilty phrase is invoked, and *Time* magazine nods knowingly. Clearly, then, if we stick to our guns, the rightness of our perceptions will obtain, and in two years' time lesbianism in the movement will be a fact of boring respectability in Omaha.

And that is all it should ever be. In radical circles in the movement there is now a rather alarming swing left toward the suddenly fashionable superiority of lesbianism, and the half-assed notion that the only "true" relationships for a feminist are with other women. One hears the silliness of the intellectual decision to become a lesbian because it's good for you, and worse, one hears a belligerent arrogance in some lesbians that amounts to angry revenge. One morning on Nanette Rainone's WBAI "Womankind" program I heard a lesbian assert that a woman couldn't really be considered a feminist unless she "related" to women in every way. Now that is power politics—nothing more, nothing less—and it is up to the straining honesty in both homosexual and heterosexual feminists to keep the central issue uncluttered and free of hysteria.

And the central issue is the question of self-definition for all women. What must be learned from the acceptance of lesbianism in the movement is that radically different truths inform different lives, and that as long as those truths are not antisocial they must—each and every one of them—be respected. If feminism is to have any historical significance, it certainly will be because it has taken an important place in this latest convulsion of the humanist movement to remind civilization that human lives become painful and useless when they cease to feel the truth of their own experience.

In the end, the feminist movement is of necessity the work of a radical feminist sensibility, and the fear of open recognition of lesbianism is the work of a liberal feminist sensibility. The falseness of the liberal's position is that while she apparently sorrows over the pain of the world, she offers only distant sympathy, when what is needed is partisan courage. By offering sympathy instead of courage, she increases rather than reduces the pain of this world.

WOMEN AND SPIRITUALITY:
TWO CONTEMPORARY VIEWS

Gender-based distinctions affect every aspect of our lives. None perhaps are more impor-tant, certainly none are more clearly or insistently drawn, than those found in religious matters. The Roman Catholic Church, like many other religious organizations, reserves its high-est ministerial roles for men: Only men can be priests, and only priests can be bishops. For cen-turies female Catholic clergy, called sisters or nuns, accepted their role as handmaidens. But, the wave of change associated with the Second Vatican Council of the early 1960s—changes that included the abandonment of the Latin Mass and a much-increased say in church affairs for the laity—caused many nuns to question the traditional restrictions placed upon them. Sis-ter M. Theresa Kane, R.S.M., sought to speak for those Catholic women who felt torn between their devotion to the Church and their conviction that its treatment of them was unfair.

Starhawk, a self-proclaimed witch, seeks to speak for those women whose quarrel with the Judeo-Christian tradition runs deeper than a dissatisfaction with the ministerial roles open to women. Their goal, in the words of theologian Mary Daly is to move "beyond God the Father." For some, this means recovering an earlier "goddess-based" religious tradition and linking it with a reverence for the earth founded upon the ecology movement. For others, it means developing a nongendered spirituality within or without the Judeo-Christian tradition.

Starhawk is the best-selling author of *The Spiral Dance: A Rebirth of the Ancient Religion of the Great Goddess* (1979), *The Fifth Sacred Thing* (1993), a utopian novel, and other works.

STATEMENT TO POPE JOHN PAUL II
Sister M. Theresa Kane, R.S.M.

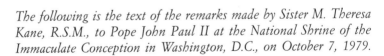

The following is the text of the remarks made by Sister M. Theresa Kane, R.S.M., to Pope John Paul II at the National Shrine of the Immaculate Conception in Washington, D.C., on October 7, 1979.

In the name of the women religious gathered in this shrine dedicated to Mary, I greet you, Your Holiness Pope John Paul the Second. It is an honor, a privilege and an awesome responsibility to express in a few moments the sentiments of women present at this shrine dedicated to Mary, the Patroness of the United States and the Mother of all humankind. It is appropriate that a woman's voice be heard in this shrine and I call upon Mary to direct what is in my heart and on my lips during these moments of greeting.

I welcome you sincerely; I extend greetings of profound respect, esteem and affec-tion from women religious throughout this country. With the sentiments experienced

STATEMENT TO POPE JOHN PAUL II   From M. Theresa Kane, "Statement to Pope John Paul II: Be Mindful of the Intense Suffering and Pain," *Redbook* April 1980: 151. Copyright © 1980 by The Hearst Corporation.

by Elizabeth when visited by Mary, our hearts too leap with joy as we welcome you—you who have been called the Pope of the People. As I welcome you today, I am mindful of the countless number of women religious who have dedicated their lives to the Church in this country in the past. The lives of many valiant women who were catalysts of growth for the United States Church continue to serve as heroines of inspiration to us as we too struggle to be women of courage and hope during these times.

Women religious in the United States entered into the renewal efforts in an obedient response to the call of Vatican II. We have experienced both joy and suffering in our efforts. As a result of such renewal women religious approach the next decade with a renewed identity and a deep sense of our responsibilities to, with and in the Church.

Your Holiness, the women of this country have been inspired by your spirit of courage. We thank you for exemplifying such courage in speaking to us so directly about our responsibilities to the poor and the oppressed throughout the world. We who live in the United States, one of the wealthiest nations of the earth, need to become ever more conscious of the suffering that is present among so many of our brothers and sisters, recognizing that systemic injustices are serious moral and social issues that need to be confronted courageously. We pledge ourselves in solidarity with you in your efforts to respond to the cry of the poor.

As I share this privileged moment with you, Your Holiness, I urge you to be mindful of the intense suffering and pain that is part of the life of many women in these United States. I call upon you to listen with compassion and to hear the call of women, who comprise half of humankind. As women we have heard the powerful messages of our Church addressing the dignity and reverence for all persons. As women we have pondered upon these words. Our contemplation leads us to state that the Church, in its struggle to be faithful to its call for reverence and dignity for all persons, must respond by providing the possibility of women as persons being included in all ministries of our Church. I urge you, Your Holiness, to be open to and respond to the voices coming from the women of this country who are desirous of serving in and through the Church as fully participating members.

Finally I assure you, Pope John Paul, of the prayers, support and fidelity of the women religious in this country as you continue to challenge us to be of holiness for the sake of the Kingdom. With these few words from the joyous, hope-filled prayer, the Magnificat, we call upon Mary to be your continued source of inspiration, courage and hope: "May your whole being proclaim and magnify the Lord; may your spirit always rejoice in God your savior; the Lord who is mighty has done great things for you; holy is God's name."

POWER, AUTHORITY, AND MYSTERY:
ECOFEMINISM AND EARTH-BASED SPIRITUALITY
Starhawk

Earth-based spirituality is rooted in three basic concepts that I call immanence, interconnection, and community. The first—immanence—names our primary understanding that the Earth is alive, part of a living cosmos. What that means is that spirit, sacred, Goddess, God—whatever you want to call it—is not found outside the world somewhere—it's in the world: it *is* the world, and it is us. Our goal is not to get off the wheel of birth nor to be saved from something. Our deepest experiences are experiences of connection with the Earth and with the world.

When you understand the universe as a living being, then the split between religion and science disappears because religion no longer becomes a set of dogmas and beliefs we have to accept even though they don't make any sense, and science is no longer restricted to a type of analysis that picks the world apart. Science becomes our way of looking more deeply into this living being that we're all in, understanding it more deeply and clearly. This itself has a poetic dimension. I want to explore what it means when we really accept that this Earth is alive and that we are part of her being. Right now we are at a point where that living being is nearly terminally diseased. We need to reverse that, to turn that around. We really need to find a way to reclaim our power so that we can reverse the destruction of the Earth.

When we understand that the Earth itself embodies spirit and that the cosmos is alive, then we also understand that everything is interconnected. Just as in our bodies: what happens to a finger affects what happens to a toe. The brain doesn't work without the heart. In the same way, what happens in South Africa affects us here: what we do to the Amazon rain forest affects the air that we breathe here. All these things are interconnected, and interconnection is the second principle of Earth-based spirituality.

Finally, when we understand these interconnections, we know that we are all part of a living community, the Earth. The kind of spirituality and the kind of politics we're called upon to practice are rooted in community. Again, the goal is not individual salvation or enlightenment, or even individual self-improvement, though these may be things and *are* things that happen along the way. The goal is the creation of a community that becomes a place in which we can be empowered and in which we can be connected to the Earth and take action together to heal the Earth.

Each of these principles—immanence, interconnection, and community—calls us to do something. That call, that challenge, is the difference between a spirituality that is practiced versus an intellectual philosophy. The idea that the Earth is alive is becoming an acceptable intellectual philosophy. Scientists have conferences on the Gaia hypothesis without acknowledging that this is exactly what people in tribal cultures, what Witches, shamans, and psychics, have been saying for thousands of years. But there's a difference between accepting it as a scientific philosophy and really living it. Living with the knowledge that the cosmos is alive causes us to do something. It challenges us. Earth-based spirituality makes certain demands. That is, when we start to understand that the Earth is alive, she calls us to act to preserve her life. When we understand that everything is interconnected, we are called to a politics and set of actions that come from compassion, from the ability to literally feel *with* all living beings on the Earth. That feeling is the ground upon which we can build community and come together and take action and find direction.

Earth-based spirituality calls us to live with integrity. Once we know that we're all part of this living body, this world becomes the terrain where we live out spiritual growth and development. It doesn't happen anywhere else, and the way we do it is by enacting what we believe, by taking responsibility for what we do.

These values are not limited to any particular tradition. They can be found in many, many different spiritual traditions and within many different political groups. For me, they come out of my tradition, which is the Pagan tradition, the Wiccan tradition, the old pre-Christian Goddess religion of Europe. We have a certain perspective that I believe can be valuable politically and that is, in some way, linked to what I see ecofeminism and the Green movement attempting. It's not that I think everyone has to be a Witch to be an ecofeminist, or that all Greens should be Witches—pluralism is vitally important in all our movements. It's that I do feel that Pagan values and perspectives can make important contributions to ecofeminist analysis and organizing.

❦   ❦   ❦

What Witches and Pagans do is practice magic. I like the definition of magic that says, "Magic is the art of changing consciousness at will." I also think that's a very good definition of political change—changing consciousness on a mass scale in this country. And one of the things we learn when we practice magic is that the results don't necessarily happen immediately. They unfold over time, and they always unfold in surprising ways, which is why we talk about our spiritual tradition in terms of mystery rather than answers and dogma and certainty. We talk about what it is we don't know and can only wonder about and be amazed at.

There is a certain way that magic works: it is, in a sense, a technology. When we want to do something, to change consciousness, for example, we first need an image of the change we want to create. We need a vision.

The same is true for political work. If we want to change consciousness in this nation, we first need to have a vision in our minds of what we want to change it into. We need to have an image, and we need to create that image and make it strong. And we need to direct energy and, in some way, ground it in reality.

The vision we want to create must also reflect a different model of power, one rooted in our understanding of the Earth as alive. We live in a system where power is *power-over,* that is, domination and control; it is a system in which a person or group of people has the right to tell other people what to do, to make their decisions, to set standards they have to live up to. The system may be overtly coercive, like a prison, or it may be benign on the surface, but it is still a system of power. And we internalize the system of domination. It lives inside us, like an entity, as if we were possessed by it.

Ecofeminism challenges all relations of domination. Its goal is not just to change who wields power, but to transform the structure of power itself. When the spirit is immanent, when each of us is the Goddess, is God, we have an inalienable right to be here and to be alive. We have a value that can't be taken away from us, that doesn't have to be earned, that doesn't have to be acquired. That kind of value is central to the change we want to create. That's the spell we want to cast.

❦   ❦   ❦

. . . Transforming consciousness so that we can preserve and sustain the Earth is a long-term project. We need the communities we create around that task to be sustainable. There are going to be times when we're active and it's exciting and we're obsessed by action, and there are going to be times when we pull back and nurture ourselves and heal and take care of ourselves. There are times when each of us gives a lot to a group, and times when each should get something back from the group, times when the giving and taking in a group balance out. Nobody should be stuck always having to be the leader, the organizer, or the one who pulls it all together. These tasks should rotate. And nobody should get stuck being the nurturer, the one everyone complains to, the mediator, the one who smooths everything over.

It is true that sometimes doing political work involves making sacrifices, and it may involve suffering. It's also true that around the world, people are suffering tremendously right now because of the policies of this country, the historical decisions and choices this country has made. We have to oppose and change these policies, and to do that we have to be willing to take risks. But sometimes in the nonviolence movement there's a kind of idealization of suffering. And I don't think that serves us. It comes out of the fantasy that people will see us suffering for our cause, be impressed by our nobility and sincerity, and be attracted to join and suffer with us.

Gandhi was a great man, but his ideas don't always fit for a lot of us, particularly for women. Gandhi said we have to accept the suffering and take it in. Women have been doing that for thousands and thousands of years, and it hasn't stopped anything much—except a lot of women's lives. In some ways, it's also not ecological. Rather than absorb the violence, what we need to do is to find some way to stop it and then transform it, to take that energy and turn it into creative change. Not to take it on ourselves.

The actual unsung truth about a lot of organizing is that it feels really good, and that's why people do it, again and again and again. It feels good because when we're actually organizing and taking action to stop the destruction of the Earth, we're doing an act of healing and we are free. There are few times when we are free in this culture and this is one of them. We need to speak about the joy and wildness and sense of liberation that comes when we step beyond the bounds of the authorities to resist control and create change.

Finally, I think that the spell we need to cast, the model we need to create, has to be open to mystery, to the understanding that we don't know everything about what's going on and we don't know exactly what to do about it. The mystery can be expressed in many ways. For one person it might be expressed through ritual, through celebration, chanting, and meditation; in some groups it might be expressed through humor, through making fun of what everybody else is doing. In some groups it might be expressed both ways. We can't define how a group or individual is going to experience it, but we can attempt to structure things so that we don't have dogmas and party lines, so we remain open to many possibilities of the sacred.

These are some ideas of how we build communities and what kinds of communities we might want to create.

☙ ☙ ☙

Along with seeing issues as interconnected, we need to all be able to envision new kinds of organizing. We need to envision a movement where our first priority is to form community, small groups centered around both personal support and action, and to make that what people see as their ongoing, long-term commitment. We don't have to commit ourselves to some big, overall organization. We can commit ourselves to eight other people with whom we can say, "We can form a community to do political and spiritual work and find support over a long period of time." Then our communities can network and form organizations around issues and around tasks as needed, and can dissolve the larger organizations and networks when they're not needed.

FEMINISM'S IDENTITY CRISIS
Wendy Kaminer

In the more than three decades since Betty Friedan's *The Feminine Mystique* helped give birth to the contemporary women's movement, feminism has achieved some major victories and suffered some major setbacks. Whether feminism can build upon its successes, or whether the movement is in danger of inadvertently strengthening the hand of some of its most determined opponents, is the question raised in Wendy Kaminer's "Feminism's Identity Crisis." Kaminer, a frequent contributor to *The Atlantic Monthly* and other magazines, is one of many critics, proclaiming themselves to be feminists, who argue that recent developments in feminist thinking signal a dangerous recrudescence of ideas about woman's nature that historically have been used to keep women in their "place."

THE WAGES OF EQUALITY

Ambivalence about equality sometimes seems to plague the feminist movement almost as much today as it did ten years ago, when it defeated the Equal Rights Amendment. Worth noting is that in the legal arena feminism has met with less success than the civil-rights movement. The power of the civil-rights movement in the 1960s was the power to demonstrate the gap between American ideals of racial equality and the American reality for African-Americans. We've never had the same professed belief in sexual equality: federal equal-employment law has always treated racial discrimination more severely than sex discrimination, and so has the Supreme Court. The Court has not extended to women the same constitutional protection it has extended to racial minorities, because a majority of justices have never rejected the notion that some degree of sex discrimination is only natural.

The widespread belief in equality demonstrated by polls is a belief in equality up to a point—the point where women are drafted and men change diapers. After thirty years of the contemporary women's movement, equal-rights feminism is still considered essentially abnormal.

🦋 🦋 🦋

In the 1980s this debate about sex and law became a cottage industry for feminist academics, especially post-modernists who could take both sides in the debate, in celebration of paradox and multiculturalism. On one side, essentialism—a belief in natural, immutable sex differences—is anathema to postmodernists, for whom sexuality itself, along with gender, is a "social construct." Sensitivity to race- and class-based differences among women also militates against a belief in a monolithic feminine culture: from a postmodern perspective, there is no such category as "woman." Taken to its logical conclusion, this emphasis on the fragmentation of the body politic makes postmodern feminism an oxymoron: feminism and virtually all our laws against sex discrimination reflect the presumption that women do in fact constitute a political category. On the other side, to the extent that postmodernism includes multiculturalism, it endorses tribalism, or identity politics, which for some feminists entails a strong belief in "women's ways." Thus the theoretical rejection of essentialism is matched by an attitudinal embrace of it.

Outside academia, debates about sex and justice are sometimes equally confused and confusing, given the political and ideological challenges of affirmative-action programs and the conflicting demands on women with both career aspirations and commitments to family life. Feminists often have to weigh the short-term benefits of protecting wage-earning mothers (by mommy-tracking, for example) against the long-term costs of a dual labor market. Sometimes ideological clarity is lost in complicated strategy debates. Sometimes ideological conflicts are put aside when feminists share a transcendent social goal, such as suffrage or reproductive choice. And sometimes one ideological strain of feminism dominates another. In the 1970s equal-rights feminism was ascendant. The 1980s saw a revival of protectionism.

Equal-rights feminism couldn't last. It was profoundly disruptive for women as well as men. By questioning long-cherished notions about sex, it posed unsettling questions about selfhood. It challenged men and women to shape their own identities without resort to stereotypes. It posed particular existential challenges to women who were accustomed to knowing themselves through the web of familial relations. As Elizabeth Cady Stanton observed more than a hundred years ago, equal-rights feminism challenges women to acknowledge that they are isolated individuals as well. Stressing that like "every human soul" women "must make the voyage of life alone," Stanton, the mother of seven and a political organizer who spent most of her life in crowds, exhorted women to recognize the "solitude of self."

This emphasis on individual autonomy didn't just scare many women; it struck them as selfish—as it might be if it were unaccompanied by an ongoing commitment to family and community. Twenty years ago feminists made the mistake of denigrating homemaking and volunteer work. It's hard to imagine how else they might have made their case. Still, the feminist attack on volunteering was simplistic and ill-informed. Feminists might have paid attention to the historical experiences of middle-class African-American women combining paid work, volunteering, and family life. They might have paid attention to the critical role played by the volunteer tradition in the nineteenth-century feminist movement. Women's sense of their maternal responsibilities at home and in the wider world was at the core of their shared social conscience, which feminists ignored at their peril.

❧ ❧ ❧

Given the absence of social and institutional support—family leave and day care—it's not surprising that women would turn for sustenance to traditional notions of sex difference. The belief that they were naturally better suited to child care than men would relieve them of considerable anger toward their husbands. As Victorian women invoked maternal virtue to justify their participation in the public sphere, so contemporary American women have used it to console themselves for the undue burdens they continue to bear in the private one.

Notions of immutable sex differences explained a range of social inequities—the plight of displaced homemakers, the persistence of sexual violence, the problems of women working double shifts within and outside the home. The general failure of hard-won legal rights to ensure social justice (which plagued civil-rights activists as well as feminists) might have been considered a failure of government—to enforce civil-rights laws and make them matter or to provide social services. It might have been considered a failure of community—our collective failure to care for one another. Instead it was roundly condemned as a failure of feminism, because it provided convenient proof of what many men and women have always believed—that biology is destiny after all. Equal-rights feminism fell out of favor, even among feminists, because it made people terribly uncomfortable and because legal rights were not accompanied by a fair division of familial and communal responsibilities.

Vying for power today are poststructural feminists (dominant in academia in recent years), political feminists (office-holders and lobbyists), different-voice feminists, separatist feminists (a small minority), pacifist feminists, lesbian feminists, careerist feminists, liberal feminists (who tend also to be political feminists), anti-porn feminists, eco-feminists, and womanists. These are not, of course, mutually exclusive categories, and this is hardly an exhaustive list. New Age feminists and goddess worshippers widen the array of alternative truths. And the newest category of feminism, personal-development feminism, led nominally by Gloria Steinem, puts a popular feminist spin on deadeningly familiar messages about recovering from addiction and abuse, liberating one's inner child, and restoring one's self-esteem.

The marriage of feminism and the phenomenally popular recovery movement is arguably the most disturbing (and potentially influential) development in the feminist movement today. It's based partly on a shared concern about child abuse, nominally a left-wing analogue to right-wing anxiety about the family. There's an emerging alliance of anti-pornography and anti-violence feminists with therapists who diagnose and treat child abuse, including "ritual abuse" and "Satanism" (often said to be linked to pornography). Feminism is at risk of being implicated in the unsavory business of hypnotizing suspected victims of abuse to help them "retrieve" their buried childhood memories. Gloria Steinem has blithely praised the important work of therapists in this field without even a nod to the potential for, well, abuse when unhappy, suggestible people who are angry at their parents are exposed to suggestive hypnotic techniques designed to uncover their histories of victimization.

But the involvement of some feminists in the memory-retrieval industry is only one manifestation of a broader ideological threat posed to feminism by the recovery movement. Recovery, with its absurdly broad definitions of addiction and abuse, encourages people to feel fragile and helpless. Parental insensitivity is classed as child abuse, along with parental violence, because all suffering is said to be equal (meaning entirely subjective); but that's appropriate only if all people are so terribly weak that a cross word inevitably has the destructive force of a blow. Put very simply, women need a feminist movement that makes them feel strong.

Enlisting people in a struggle for liberation without exaggerating the ways in which they're oppressed is a challenge for any civil-rights movement. It's a particularly daunting one for feminists, who are still arguing among themselves about whether women are oppressed more by nature or by culture. For some feminists, strengthening women is a matter of alerting them to their natural vulnerabilities.

There has always been a strain of feminism that presents women as frail and naturally victimized. As it was a hundred years ago, feminist victimism is today most clearly expressed in sexuality debates—about pornography, prostitution, rape, and sexual harassment. Today sexual violence is a unifying focal point for women who do and women who do not call themselves feminists: 84 percent of women surveyed by *Redbook* considered "fighting violence against women" to be "very important." (Eighty-two percent rated workplace equality and 54 percent rated abortion rights as very important.) Given this pervasive, overriding concern about violence and our persistent failure to address it effectively, victimism is likely to become an important organizing tool for feminism in the 1990s.

Feminist discussions of sexual offenses often share with the recovery movement the notion that, again, there are no objective measures of suffering: all suffering is said to be equal, in the apparent belief that all women are weak. Wage-earning women testify to being "disabled" by sexist remarks in the workplace. College women testify to the trauma of being fondled by their dates. The term "date rape," like the term "addiction," no longer has much literal, objective meaning. It tends to be used figuratively, as a metaphor signifying that all heterosexual encounters are inherently abusive of women. The belief that in a male-dominated culture that has "normalized" rape, "yes" can never really mean "yes" has been popularized by the anti-pornography feminists Andrea Dworkin and Catharine MacKinnon. (Dworkin devoted an entire book to the contention that intercourse is essentially a euphemism for rape.) But only five years ago Dworkin and MacKinnon were leaders of a feminist fringe. Today, owing partly to the excesses of multiculturalism and the exaltation of victimization, they're leaders in the feminist mainstream.

Why is feminism helping to make women feel so vulnerable? Why do some young women on Ivy League campuses, among the most privileged people on the globe, feel oppressed? Why does feminist victimology seem so much more pervasive among middle- and upper-class whites than among lower-income women, and girls, of color? Questions like these need to be aired by feminists. But in some feminist circles it is heresy to suggest that there are degrees of suffering and oppression, which need to be kept in perspective. It is heresy to suggest that being raped by your date may not be as traumatic or terrifying as being raped by a stranger who breaks into your bedroom in the middle of the night. It is heresy to suggest that a woman who has to listen to her colleagues tell stupid sexist jokes has a lesser grievance than a woman who is physically accosted by her supervisor. It is heresy, in general, to question the testimony of self-proclaimed victims of date rape or harassment, as it is heresy in a twelve-step group to question claims of abuse. All claims of suffering are sacred and presumed to be absolutely true. It is a primary article of faith among many feminists that women don't lie about rape, ever; they lack the dishonesty gene. Some may call this feminism, but it looks more like femininity to me.

Blind faith in women's pervasive victimization also looks a little like religion. "Contemporary feminism is a new kind of religion," Camille Paglia complains, overstating her case with panache. But if her metaphor begs to be qualified, it offers a nugget of truth. Feminists choose among competing denominations with varying degrees of passion, and belief; what is gospel to one feminist is a working hypothesis to another. Still, like every other ideology and "ism"—from feudalism to capitalism to communism to Freudianism—feminism is for some a revelation. Insights into the dynamics of sexual violence are turned into a metaphysic. Like people in recovery who see addiction lurking in all our desires, innumerable feminists see men's oppression of women in all our personal and social relations. Sometimes the pristine earnestness of this theology is unrelenting. Feminism lacks a sense of black humor.

Of course, the emerging orthodoxy about victimization does not infect all or even most feminist sexuality debates. Of course, many feminists harbor heretical thoughts about lesser forms of sexual misconduct. But few want to be vilified for trivializing sexual violence and collaborating in the abuse of women.

THE ENEMY WITHIN

. . . It's not surprising that we haven't achieved equality; we haven't even defined it. Nearly thirty years after the onset of the modern feminist movement, we still have no consensus on what nature dictates to men and women and demands of law. Does equality mean extending special employment rights to pregnant women, or limiting the Sixth Amendment rights of men standing trial for rape, or suspending the First Amendment rights of men who read pornography? Nearly thirty years after the passage of landmark federal civil-rights laws, we still have no consensus on the relationship of individual rights to social justice. But, feminists might wonder, why did rights fall out of favor with progressives just as women were in danger of acquiring them?

The most effective backlash against feminism almost always comes from within, as women either despair of achieving equality or retreat from its demands. The confident political resurgence of women today will have to withstand a resurgent belief in women's vulnerabilities. Listening to the sexuality debates, I worry that women feel so wounded. Looking at feminism, I wonder at the public face of femininity.

WHERE IS THE LOVE?
June Jordan

Poet June Jordan delivered "Where Is the Love" to the 1978 National Black Writers Conference at Howard University as part of a forum on "Feminism and the Black Woman Writer." "The session was going to be hot," Jordan recalled, because some in the African-American intellectual community equated feminism with lesbianism, and "the taboo on feminism, within the Black intellectual community, had long been exceeded in its orthodox severity only by the taboo on the subject of the lesbian." As moderator and opening speaker, Jordan "wanted to see if it was possible to say things that people believe they don't want to hear, without having to kick ass and without looking the fool for holding out your hand." Her prescription for how it might be possible to speak unwelcome truths—and to gain a hearing for them—concludes this volume.

As I think about anyone or any thing—whether history or litera- ture or my father or political organizations or a poem or a film— as I seek to evaluate the potentiality, the life-supportive commitment/possibilities of anyone or any thing, the decisive question is, always, *Where is the love?* The energies that flow from hatred, from negative and hateful habits and attitudes and dogma do not promise something good, something I would choose to cherish, to honor with my own life. It is always the love, whether we look to the spirit of Fannie Lou Hamer, or to the spirit of Agostinho Neto, it is always the love that will carry action into positive new places, that will carry your own nights and days beyond demoralization and away from suicide.

I am a feminist, and what that means to me is much the same as the meaning of the fact that I am Black: it means that I must undertake to love myself and to respect myself as though my very life depends upon self-love and self-respect. It means that I must everlastingly seek to cleanse myself of the hatred and the contempt that sur- rounds and permeates my identity, as a woman, and as a Black human being, in this particular world of ours. It means that the achievement of self-love and self-respect will require inordinate, hourly vigilance, and that I am entering my soul into a strug- gle that will most certainly transform the experience of all the peoples of the earth, as no other movement can, in fact, hope to claim: because the movement into self- love, self-respect, and self-determination is the movement now galvanizing the true, the unarguable majority of human beings everywhere. This movement explicitly demands the testing of the viability of a moral idea: that the health, the legitimacy of any status quo, any governing force, must be measured according to the experiences of those who are, comparatively, powerless. Virtue is not to be discovered in the con- duct of the strong vis-à-vis the powerful, but rather it is to be found in our behavior and policies affecting those who are different, those who are weaker, or smaller than we. How do the strong, the powerful, treat children? How do we treat the aged among us? How do the strong and the powerful treat so-called minority members of the body politic? How do the powerful regard women? How do they treat us?

Easily you can see that, according to this criterion, the overwhelming reality of power and government and tradition is evil, is diseased, is illegitimate, and deserves nothing from us—no loyalty, no accommodation, no patience, no understanding— except a clear-minded resolve to utterly change this total situation and, thereby, to change our own destiny.

As a Black woman, as a Black feminist, I exist, simultaneously, as part of the pow- erless and as part of the majority peoples of the world in two ways: I am powerless as compared to any man because women, per se, are kept powerless by men/by the powerful; I am powerless as compared to anyone white because Black and Third World peoples are kept powerless by whites/by the powerful. I am the majority because women constitute the majority gender. I am the majority because Black and Third World peoples constitute the majority of life on this planet.

And it is here, in this extreme, inviolable coincidence of my status as a Black fem- inist, my status as someone twice stigmatized, my status as a Black woman who is

WHERE IS THE LOVE   From June Jordan, "Where Is the Love?" *Essence* Sept. 1978: 62ff. Reprinted by permission of the author.

twice kin to the despised majority of all the human life that there is, it is here, in that extremity, that I stand in a struggle against suicide. And it is here, in this extremity, that I ask, of myself, and of any one who would call me sister, *Where is the love?*

The love devolving from my quest for self-love and self-respect and self-determination must be, as I see it, something you can verify in the ways that I present myself to others, and in the ways that I approach people different from myself. How do I reach out to the people I would like to call my sisters and my brothers and my children and my lovers and my friends? If I am a Black feminist serious in the undertaking of self-love, then it seems to me that the legitimate, the morally defensible character of that self-love should be such that I gain and gain and gain in the socio-psychic strength needed so that I may, without fear, be able and willing to love and respect women, for example, who are not like me: women who are not feminists, women who are not professionals, women who are not as old or as young as I am, women who have neither job nor income, women who are not Black.

And it seems to me that the socio-psychic strength that should follow from a morally defensible Black feminism will mean that I become able and willing, without fear, to love and respect all men who are willing and able, without fear, to love and respect me. In short, if the acquirement of my self-determination is part of a world-wide, an inevitable, and a righteous movement, then I should become willing and able to embrace more and more of the whole world, without fear, and also without self-sacrifice.

This means that, as a Black feminist, I cannot be expected to respect what somebody else calls self-love if that concept of self-love requires my suicide to any degree. And this will hold true whether that somebody else is male, female, Black, or white. My Black feminism means that you cannot expect me to respect what somebody else identifies as Good of The People, if that so-called Good (often translated into *manhood* or *family* or *nationalism*) requires the deferral or the diminution of my self-fulfillment. We *are* the people. And, as Black women, we are most of the people, any people, you care to talk about. And, therefore, nothing that is Good for The People is good unless it is good for me, as I determine myself.

When I speak of Black feminism, then, I am speaking from an exacerbated consciousness of the truth that we, Black women, huddle together, miserably, on the very lowest levels of the economic pyramid. We, Black women, subsist among the most tenuous and least likely economic conditions for survival.

When I speak of Black feminism, then, I am not speaking of sexuality. I am not speaking of heterosexuality or lesbianism or homosexuality or bisexuality; whatever sexuality anyone elects for his or her pursuit is not my business, nor the business of the state. And, furthermore, I cannot be persuaded that one kind of sexuality, as against another, will necessarily provide for the greater happiness of the two people involved. I am not talking about sexuality. I am talking about love, about a steady-state deep caring and respect for every other human being, a love that can only derive from a secure and positive self-love.

As a Black woman/feminist, I must look about me, with trembling, and with shocked anger, at the endless waste, the endless suffocation of my sisters: the bitter sufferings of hundreds of thousands of women who are the sole parents, the mothers of hundreds of thousands of children, the desolation and the futility of women trapped by demeaning, lowest-paying occupations, the unemployed, the bullied, the beaten, the battered, the ridiculed, the slandered, the trivialized, the raped, and the sterilized, the lost millions and multimillions of beautiful, creative, and momentous lives turned to ashes on the pyre of gender identity. I must look about me and, as a Black feminist, I must ask myself: *Where is the love?* How is my own lifework serving to end these tyrannies, these corrosions of sacred possibility?

As a Black feminist poet and writer I must look behind me with trembling, and with shocked anger, at the fate of Black women writers until now. From the terrible graves of a traditional conspiracy against my sisters in art, I must exhume the works of women writers and poets such as Georgia Douglas Johnson (who?).

In the early flush of the Harlem Renaissance, Georgia Johnson accomplished an astonishing, illustrious life experience. Married to Henry Lincoln Johnson, U.S. Recorder of Deeds in Washington, D.C., the poet, in her own right, became no less than Commissioner of Conciliation for the U.S. Department of Labor (*who was that again? Who?*). And she, this poet, furthermore enjoyed the intense, promotional attention of Dean Kelley Miller, here at Howard, and W.E.B. Du Bois, and William Stanley Braithwaite, and Alain Locke. And she published three volumes of her own poetry and I found her work in Countee Cullen's anthology, *Caroling Dusk,* where, Countee Cullen reports, she, Georgia Douglas Johnson, thrived as a kind of Gwendolyn Brooks, holding regular Saturday night get-togethers with the young Black writers of the day.

And what did this poet of such acclaim, achievement, connection, and generosity, what did this poet have to say in her poetry, and who among us has ever heard of Georgia Douglas Johnson? And is there anybody in this room who can tell me the name of two or three other women poets from the Harlem Renaissance? And why did she die, and why does the work of all women die with no river carrying forward the record of such grace? How is it the case that whether we have written novels or poetry or whether we have raised our children or cleaned and cooked and washed and ironed, it is all dismissed as "women's work"; it is all, finally, despised as nothing important, and there is no trace, no echo of our days upon the earth?

Why is it not surprising that a Black woman as remarkably capable and gifted and proven as Georgia Douglas Johnson should be the poet of these pathetic, beggarly lines:

> I'm folding up my little dreams
> within my heart tonight
> And praying I may soon forget
> the torture of their sight
> *"My Little Dreams"*

How long, how long will we let the dreams of women serve merely to torture and not to ignite, to enflame, and to ennoble the promise of the years of every lifetime? And here is Georgia Douglas Johnson's poem "The Heart of a Woman":

> The heart of a woman goes forth with the dawn,
> As a lovebird, softwinging, so restlessly on,
> Afar o'er life's turrets and vales does it roam
> In the wake of those echoes the heart calls home.

The heart of a woman falls back with the night
And enters some alien cage in its plight,
And tries to forget it has dreamed of the stars,
While it breaks, breaks, breaks on the sheltering bars.

And it is against such sorrow, and it is against such suicide, and it is against such deliberated strangulation of the possible lives of women, of my sisters, and of powerless peoples—men and children—everywhere, that I work and live, now, as a feminist trusting that I will learn to love myself well enough to love you (whoever you are), well enough so that you will love me well enough so that we will know exactly where is the love: that it is here, between us, and growing stronger and growing stronger.